Social Work in Canada

Steven Hick
Carleton University

Jackie Stokes
Thompson Rivers University

Social Work in Canada

An introduction
Fourth edition

THOMPSON

Information on how to obtain copies of this book is available at:

Website: www.thompsonbooks.com
E-mail: publisher@thompsonbooks.com
Phone: 416-766-2763 / Fax:416-766-0398

Library and Archives Canada Cataloguing in Publication

Hick, Steven F., author

Social work in Canada : an introduction / Steven Hick and Jackie Stokes. — Fourth edition

Includes bibliographical references and index.

ISBN 978-1-55077-256-2 (paperback)

1. Social service—Canada—Textbooks. I. Stokes, Jackie, author II. Title.

HV105.H525 2016 361.30971 C2016-900098-2

Managing Editor: Jane McNulty
Senior Editor: Kelly Stern
Copy Editor (Stories): Sara Goodchild
Proofreaders: Camilla Blakeley, Sara Goodchild, Rob Williams
Indexer: Patricia Furdek
Design: Gary Blakeley, Blakeley Words+Pictures
Technical Illustration: Vince Satira

Canada

We acknowledge the support of the Government of Canada.
Printed in Canada.
3 4 5 21 20 19

Brief Contents

Contents

Author Team

Lead Authors

Steven Hick, Ph.D., Carleton University (retired)

Steven was an award-winning professor of social work and is the author of the companion text, *Social Welfare in Canada*. He has practised at home and abroad as a human rights worker, social services worker, and social policy analyst. He is the co-founder of War Child Canada. Steven currently teaches insight meditation and mindfulness-based interventions.

Jackie Stokes, Ed.D., Assistant Professor, School of Social Work and Human Service, Thompson Rivers University

Jackie has an M.S.W. from the University of Northern British Columbia and an Ed.D. from Simon Fraser University. She has practised social work in northern British Columbia for more than 20 years, primarily in the areas of substance use and child protection.

Contributing Authors

Tod Augusta-Scott, M.S.W., R.S.W. ("Wade's Story")

Tod is known internationally for his work with domestic violence, narrative therapy, and restorative justice. He has spent more than 20 years as the coordinator of Bridges—a domestic violence counselling, research, and training institute in Nova Scotia. He has taught at Dalhousie University School of Social Work. Tod received the Distinguished Service Award from the Canadian Association of Social Workers in 2013.

Kevin Barnes-Ceeney, Ph.D., Assistant Professor, Henry C. Lee College of Criminal Justice and Forensic Science, University of New Haven ("Kevin's Story")

Kevin's research interests include the implementation of risk assessment and case management services. Trained as a probation officer in Wales, he has worked in Kazakhstan, the United States, Jamaica, and Rwanda.

Cindy Blackstock, Ph.D.

A member of the Gitxsan First Nation, Cindy works with children and adults to address the systemic disadvantage that First Nations children experience .

Kaila de Boer, B.S.W., R.S.W. ("Mark's Story")

Kaila is the Director of Mental Wellness and Healing with the Nunatsiavut Government's Department of Health and Social Development. She is also a graduate student at the School of Social Work at McGill University.

David Este, Ph.D., Professor, Faculty of Social Work, University of Calgary

David's interests include mental health, non-profit management, multicultural social work practice, and qualitative research.

Elizabeth Fast, Ph.D., Assistant Professor, Department of Applied Human Sciences, Concordia University

Elizabeth is Métis, originally from St. François-Xavier, Manitoba. Her research interests include cultural identities, urban Indigenous youth, and transforming child welfare practices.

Roy Hanes, Ph.D., Associate Professor, School of Social Work, Carleton University

Roy has taught a social work and persons with disabilities course since 1993. He is a member of the Council of Canadians with Disabilities and a founding member of both the Persons with Disabilities Caucus of the Canadian Association for Social Work Education and the Canadian Disability Studies Association.

Barb Juett, M.S.W., R.S.W. ("The Shadbous' Story"; "The Raynors' Story")

Barb's interests include helping parents work through their feelings of grief and loss related to parenting a child with special needs. She is an active member of the Complex Care Advisory Committee and teaches an online course at Algonquin College in the Autism and Behavioural Science Program.

Patti LaBoucane-Benson, Ph.D. (Human Ecology)

Patti's doctoral work focused on Aboriginal Family Resilience. She has worked for Native Counselling Services of Alberta (NCSA) for 21 years and is currently the Director of Research, Training and Communication. She also leads the development, facilitator training, and implementation of a healing program curriculum for NCSA.

Daniel W.L. Lai, Ph.D., Chair Professor of Social Work and Gerontology; Head, Department of Applied Social Sciences, Director, Institute of Active Ageing, The Hong Kong Polytechnic University; former Professor of Social Work, University of Calgary

Daniel's interests include population ageing, immigration, social policy, mental health, health, health care, research, evaluation, post-secondary education, social work, non-profit management, statistical data analysis, quantitative research, and qualitative research.

Sandra Loucks Campbell, M.S.W., Ph.D., former adjunct Assistant Professor, University of Waterloo

Sandra's abiding passion throughout her career was her interest in improving the lives of older persons. She served as Chair of the Ontario Association of Social Workers' Issues of Aging Committee from 1995 to 2015. She also chaired a team of seven authors in the creation of the OASW's *Elder Abuse Handbook for Service Providers*.

The Faculty of Social Work at the University of Waterloo presented Sandra with the 2010 Graduate Honour Award for outstanding work in the field of social work.

Dennis McDermott, B.S.W., R.S.W. ("Theresa and Sarah's Story")

Dennis has worked in the areas of mental health, substance use, and homelessness. He is an ally to and has worked extensively with First Nations programs and families in Toronto.

H. Monty Montgomery, Ph.D., Assistant Professor, University of Regina, Saskatoon

Harpell Montgomery (Monty) is of Mi'kmaq ancestry from the Eastern Shore area of Nova Scotia. His major fields of professional interest are First Nations child welfare program development and practice, information technology/management for social work practitioners, and online distance learning with Aboriginal adult learners.

Sharicka Reid, B.A. (Honours)

Sharicka has worked with mental health consumers at the Canadian Mental Health Association and has experience supporting individuals with dual diagnosis and concurrent disorders. She heads up the office of the Family Association for Mental Health Everywhere in Brampton, Ontario.

Christa Sato, M.S.W. student, Faculty of Social Work, University of Calgary; Calgary Project Site Coordinator, Strength in Unity

Christa is pursuing her M.S.W. in International and Community Development. Her thesis research focuses on processes that have enabled second-generation Filipino males in Calgary to complete university studies.

Raven Sinclair (Kahkakiw), Ph.D., Associate Professor, Faculty of Social Work, University of Regina, Saskatoon

Raven is a member of the Nehiyawak (Cree) Nation. Her academic and research interests include Indigenous knowledge and research methodologies, Aboriginal child welfare and adoption, colonial and decolonization theories, and mental health and wellness.

Kathleen C. Sitter, Ph.D., Assistant Professor, School of Social Work, Memorial University

Kathleen's research interests include participatory research, social media and social work, visual methodologies, and critical disability studies.

Stewart J. Smith, M.S.W, R.S.W., part-time Professor of Social Work, King's University College; Counsellor, Daya Counselling Centre

Stewart is employed as a therapist in a community agency that provides counselling services. He also has a private practice and works part-time as an instructor at King's University College's School of Social Work. In September 2015, he began studies in the Ph.D. program in social work at Wilfrid Laurier University in Kitchener, Ontario.

Sarah Todd, Ed.D., M.S.W., B.A./B.S.W., Associate Professor, School of Social Work, Carleton University

Sarah is currently involved in two research projects supporting grassroots youth organizations in carrying out research and evaluation. Her other research interests include community work, social work education, gender, and sexuality.

Adje van de Sande, M.S.W., Ph.D., Associate Professor, School of Social Work, Carleton University

Adje teaches Research Methods and Statistics at the undergraduate and graduate levels with a focus on community-based participatory research. His research interests focus on poverty reduction and research ethics.

Preface

This book fills a need for an introductory-level text written from a truly Canadian perspective. Unlike many other texts, which tend to emphasize techniques, this book emphasizes the importance of being clear about one's values and world view before beginning to practise social work. Accordingly, the book does not pretend to provide an easy, step-by-step recipe that can be applied to every problem. Throughout the text, there is an emphasis on the need for students to think deeply about issues—particularly controversial ones—before arriving at a suitable approach to a problem and a subsequent course of action.

Acknowledgements

This book began in discussions with Allan Moscovitch at Carleton University and would not have been possible without Keith Thompson's commitment to the work. The primary intention was to give a voice to people who are directly involved in the field. Special thanks to the authors of previous editions whose work provided a foundation for this new edition: Gordon Bruyere for his contribution on the history of Indigenous peoples; Shirley Judge and Judy E. MacDonald for their contributions on social work with women; Bernice Moreau for advice on the history of Black Canadians; and Sarah Todd and Martha Wiebe, the original authors of much of the material on group and community practice.

We extend thanks as well to Mark Creedon, former Executive Director of Catholic Family Services Peel-Dufferin; Lin Fang of the University of Toronto; Ben Carniol of Ryerson University; Vanda Sinha of McGill University; Rachel Levine-Katz of Citizen Advocacy; and Christine Cooper, Executive Director of the Family Association for Mental Health Everywhere (FAME) for their invaluable advice, assistance, and referrals. Thanks also to Izra Fitch for permission to reproduce her artwork on page 187, which won the 2010 Mathieu Da Costa Challenge.

Two new features of this edition—Stories from the Field and Social Worker Profiles—owe their existence to the generosity of many caring individuals situated all across Canada. We thank those clients and practitioners who agreed to share their stories with us as a means of modelling "social work in action" for the readers of this book. In all stories but three, names and identities have been changed to respect privacy and confidentiality. Thank you to Selishia and to Marla Szobota for sharing their stories with us in Chapters 5 and 8 respectively, and thanks as well to Marva J. Ferguson for her help with "June's Story" in Chapter 8.

We also thank the 14 social work practitioners profiled in this book, who took time out of their busy schedules to reflect on and describe in illuminating detail the nature of the work they do—and why they do it.

We extend deep appreciation as well to the many instructors and students who have used the book in their courses, thereby encouraging us to pursue this new edition. Suggestions for improvement are always welcome and will be considered for incorporation in future editions.

We wish to pay a special tribute to contributing author Dr. Sandra Loucks Campbell, who completed her final tasks related to this project shortly before her death on March 25, 2016. Sandra brought a wealth of experience and tremendous dedication to the creation of original material for Chapters 6 and 11, for which we are forever grateful.

A Note About the Evolving Language of Social Work

Language expresses our identity; it reflects who we are and who we aspire to be. Language also reveals our social location, that is, our age, gender, educational level, the region of the country we live in, ethnic background, and socio-economic status. The language that social workers use reflects the knowledge and values of the profession. This language is much more than a "politically correct" way of speaking; it represents ideals and principles related to respect for individual dignity, recognition of diversity, and the pursuit of social justice.

Much attention has been given to language throughout this book. Language referring to government ministries, legislation, agencies, services, and organizations is contextual, and it is important to accommodate regional realities that are often in flux.

It is important, and respectful, to use terminology that correlates with the choices and preferences of the individuals or groups with whom we are working. Also, the terminology used by a member of a community could be offensive if used by someone outside the community.

Although we cannot provide a definitive list of social work terminology, we have developed some principles that may eventually prove helpful in your own social work practice:

People first. Social workers respect the holistic nature of individuals; clearly, no one can be defined solely by one quality. Rather than using terms such as "disabled," "homeless," or "stutterer," social workers tend to say "a person with a disability", "people who are homeless," or "a person with a stutter."

Stigma reduction. It is important to ensure that our language does not marginalize, discriminate against, or disempower people in any way. In the field of mental health and substance use, much work has been done to decrease negative stereotyping. Terms such as "crazy" and "addict" show a lack of understanding about the nature of mental health and substance use. Instead, we tend to use phrases such as "individuals who may have a mental health problem"; "individuals with a lived experience of mental illness"; or "a person who uses substances or has a substance use disorder."

Indigenous peoples. Many diverse and autonomous groups comprise the original inhabitants of Canada. The *Canadian Constitution Act, 1982* recognizes three groups of Aboriginal peoples: Indians, Métis, and Inuit. As a general rule, it is important to use terminology that a group itself recognizes and that is consistent with their socio-political relationships. Terminology related to collective groups is continually evolving. This evolution can be seen in changes to the name of our federal ministry from Indian and Northern Affairs Canada (INAC), to Aboriginal Affairs and Northern Development Canada (AANDC), and, more recently, to Indigenous and Northern Affairs Canada (INAC). At the time of the writing of this book, common wisdom suggested that "Indigenous" was preferable to "Aboriginal" as a collective term. However, several terms for our country's original inhabitants have been used in various chapters. This is not to suggest interchangeability, but rather to recognize regional and provincial/territorial differences and specific cultural contexts.

LGBTQ+. The social work profession recognizes that sexual and gender identities are fluid. It would be impossible to develop a glossary of the terms that people might use to describe the spectrum of sexual and gender diversity. We have chosen to use "LGBTQ+" as a collective term for individuals who identify as lesbian, gay, bisexual, transsexual, intersex, queer, asexual, non-gendered, and other identities.

New to this edition

An invitation to join the profession

Social workers help to make a positive difference in people's lives and communities. But what exactly does social work entail and what do social workers do?

This expanded and updated edition is designed to help beginning students appreciate the indispensable role that social workers play in Canadian society. It seeks to give students a sense of the enormous impact they can have if they choose social work as a career path. It explores new topics such as Indigenous social work, mental health and recovery, and distinctive aspects of social work in the province of Québec.

In Focus features

The field of social work is unique, and its scope is wide. Social work theory encompasses psychology, sociology, community development, and socio-political change. Social workers view problems from a multi-factorial perspective. They draw on knowledge from a variety of sources and make it uniquely their own.

The special features included throughout this book provide an opportunity for beginning students to reflect on the many complex issues that have a bearing on everyday life—topics such as income inequality, mental health, child welfare, gender and race relations, immigration, climate change, and many, many more.

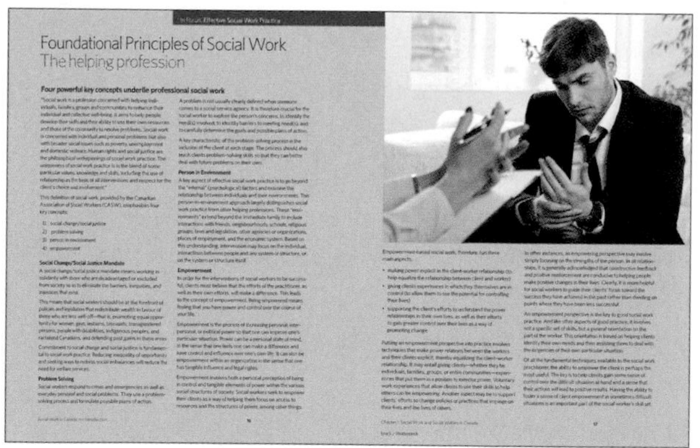

Social work practice

Social work is an exciting and innovative field of study and practice. Standardized best practices and core competencies are crucial in social work, yet new ideas and new techniques continually emerge in the search for effective interventions and lasting solutions.

Each chapter includes one or more two-page overviews that summarize the principles underlying effective social work practice.

These overviews can serve as study aids as well as guides to best practices in the field.

Family Group Conferences

Darlene's Story...
Facing grief and addiction

Stories from the field

Social workers share a particular interest in the needs and strengths of those who are vulnerable, oppressed, and/or living in poverty. The 34 stories throughout this volume narrate the real-world experiences of practitioners and their clients as they confront obstacles together.

Background information for each story contextualizes social work interventions that promote the well-being of individuals, families, communities, and society. After reading each story, students answer reflection questions to deepen their understanding of social work principles and methods.

Dennis McDermott

Chapter 1 Review

Social worker profiles

What better way for students to assess whether this is the profession for them than to read first-person accounts from social work practitioners themselves?

At the end of each substantive chapter is a profile of a social worker involved in front-line, direct service work with clients in a wide variety of settings.

These practising professionals reveal what they love about the work they do, what they do, and the challenges they have encountered along the way. Beginning students can judge for themselves whether or not social work is an interesting career path for them to pursue.

Go digital—Online 24/7

This textbook is available for the first time as a complete digital resource for students!

Accessible through your favourite modern web browser—online, anytime, and for the full duration of your course—this is the perfect complement to the print book itself. And, since we've optimized the design and layout to handle most common screen sizes on the market today, learning and studying while on-the-go has never been easier. We invite you to give it a try!

Visit www.thompsonbooks.com for more information.

Social Work and Social Welfare in Canada

"Social workers are all laying the foundation of the civilization of the future."
Eglantyne Jebb (1876–1928), founder of Save the Children

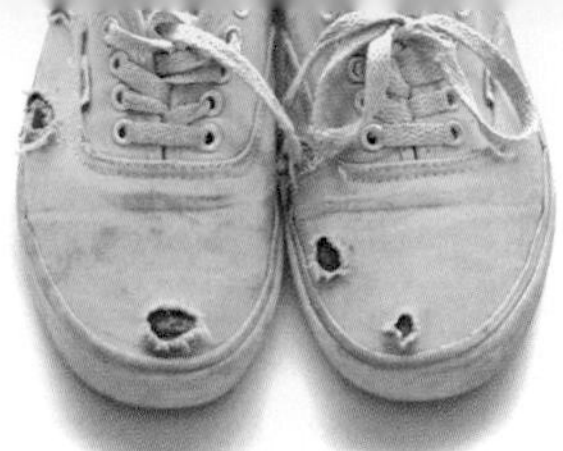

An Introduction

1

Canadians generally are not aware of the crucial role social workers play.

ne hundred years ago, private charity was one of the only recourses for persons in distress (and even then, it was only available to a small part of the population). Today, however, public (government-run or government-funded) social programs and services are widespread and affect nearly every Canadian at some point in his or her life. Nevertheless, while social services are commonplace, Canadians generally are not very aware of the history of social work in this country or of the crucial role social workers play in our lives. This book is an effort to redress that imbalance. We hope that it will help you become familiar with the key concepts and issues in social work practice in Canada today.

In this chapter, you will learn how to...

- explain the Canadian social welfare system and the types of problems it is meant to address
- describe the differences between "private" and "public" welfare services and between the two approaches to social welfare provision
- list various "universal" and "selective" income security programs in Canada
- use the concepts of "casework" and of "direct" and "indirect" social work to describe in broad terms what social workers do
- identify several roles that social workers may play and several qualities they should develop
- explain the difference between a social worker and a social service worker
- describe the educational paths and employment opportunities available to social workers in Canada
- understand the importance of knowing Canada's colonial history when working with Indigenous peoples
- discuss the ethical dilemmas that social workers may encounter and some guidelines that may help navigate such situations
- describe "self-care" and its importance to the well-being of social workers

Key Concepts

- Welfare state
- Social services
- Income security
- Social policies / Social programs
- Public welfare / Private welfare
- Residual view / Institutional view
- Universal prorgrams / Selective programs
- Direct social work/ Indirect social work
- Caseworker
- Social worker
- Social service worker
- Self-care

Focusing Question

In what ways are social workers a part of Canadians' lives today?

Canada's "Social Safety Net"

The term "**welfare state**" is fequently used to describe a system of government whereby the state actively undertakes to protect the health and well-being of its citizens, especially those in financial need. The key elements of a welfare state are: (1) the use of the powers invested in government to provide essential social services to citizens, and (2) the use of grants, taxes, pensions, and other programs to provide basic income security. It is within this complex web of income security programs and social services that social workers practise their craft. The welfare state is, as it has loosely been described, a "social safety net." It "catches" individuals and families in need and is designed to help them get back on their feet.

The kinds of difficulties that individuals and their families may face are three-fold: economic, personal, and family-related.

- **Economic survival.** Retirement, unemployment, decreasing income, and rising prices are examples of contingencies that affect *economic survival.*
- **The integrity of the person.** Disability, illness, violence, homelessness, substance use, racism, discrimination, warfare, and death are examples of contingencies that affect *the integrity of the person.*
- **Survival of the family.** Separation, divorce, the care of aging family members, and additional children are contingencies that threaten the very *survival of the family.*

In countries where the social safety net is weak or non-existent, there is little or no protection of this kind and individuals are left to fend for themselves. The Canadian social safety net gives citizens a greater sense of security and, many would argue, a greater sense of belonging.

Social Services and Income Security

The services provided by professional social workers are part of a range of activities that fall more generally under the term "social welfare." Social welfare, in this wider sense, includes not only the **social services** proper (such as child protection, women's shelters, and counselling) but also a range of **income security** provisions that provide monetary or other material benefits to supplement income or maintain minimum income levels (such as Employment Insurance, Social Assistance, Old Age Security, and Workers' Compensation).

The distinction between the social services and income security is an important one, but one that is often hard to maintain in real life. The distinction is often a source of confusion for beginning social workers because frequently, difficulties come in pairs or in even more complex combinations. For example, a man who becomes ill or has an accident may also lose his job and, as a result, his home. A woman who is subjected to violence may be forced to leave her home and may need help obtaining child support as well as personal income support. A man with a substance use disorder may lose his job and be at risk of ending up homeless, incarcerated, or in the mental health system. Thus, social services are often needed to deal with problems that have their roots in economic insecurity and vice versa.

This book deals with the social services and the everyday practice of social work. It does not cover in any depth the complex income security programs in Canada that provide monetary assistance to individuals and families. However, because a basic understanding of the income security system is necessary for effective social work practice, it is a good idea to gain an overview of this vast field. A companion volume, *Social Welfare in Canada: Understanding Income Security,* more fully examines the income security field.

Welfare state
A system of government in which the state plays an active role in the protection and advancement of the social and economic well-being of its citizens, based on the principles of equality of opportunity and the redistribution of wealth. Countries that generally follow this model —Britain, Canada, Germany, France, the Netherlands, and the Nordic countries, for example—are often referred to as "welfare states."

Social services
Non-monetary personal or community services, such as daycare, housing, crisis intervention, and support groups, provided by the state and non-profit organizations

Income security
Income support in the form of social insurance, social assistance, and income supplementation that can be unconditional or based on an income or needs test; it can also be provided through the tax system

The federal government has created various social programs designed to boost employment rates, especially among youth. Some programs provide tax credits to employers who hire and train apprentices in certain trades, such as construction. On February 12, 2016 Prime Minister Justin Trudeau marked his 100th day in office by announcing a major boost to the Canada Summer Jobs Program, which helps students find work during the summer. The federal government spent $106 million on the program in 2015 to help create more than 34,000 summer jobs. New funding of up to $113 million each year for the next three years will allow the program to offer nearly 70,000 summer jobs to students from 2016 until 2018. The program aims to provide much-needed work experience for students while supporting small businesses and organizations that provide important community services.

Heated Debates

The basic goal of the Canadian social welfare system is not to replace individual initiative but rather to help people through difficult times until they can rebuild their lives. Few would dispute that when people desperately need help, the state, if not fellow citizens, should lend a helping hand. Yet the role of the state in providing welfare services is controversial. Some people reject the idea that the state should play any part at all, even in relation to helping our most vulnerable citizens. Others see a modest role for government—but only when all else fails. Still others want to see the state play a larger, more active role in redressing inequalities and creating social harmony by working to improve the lives of all citizens. Debates over the proper role of social welfare are far-reaching and can be heated; a cool head is a useful asset, especially to a new social worker.

Social services are provided to citizens through social policies developed by various levels of government and are delivered by means of specific social policies and programs.

- **Social policies.** These are the overall rules and regulations, laws, and other administrative directives that set the framework for state social welfare activity. For example, universal medicare is a social policy to which the Government of Canada is committed.
- **Social programs.** These are specific initiatives that follow from and implement social welfare policies. Continuing with the medicare example, there are special incentives or programs to encourage newly accredited physicians to move to outlying areas, thus ensuring greater equality of access to medical services (in line with the commitment to universal medicare for Canadians).

Despite the services and systems in place to help those in need in Canada, some people still "fall through the cracks" because of program cutbacks, stricter eligibility criteria, or increased unemployment.

The Delivery of Social Programs and Services

The network of social welfare laws, policies, and programs currently in place around the country is vast. This complex system provides an underlying buffer against contingencies that can arise, often unexpectedly, and cause great hardship for individuals and their families. It is through such programs that the Canadian state creates opportunities for individuals experiencing difficulties in their lives and helps them get back on their feet.

On both the income security and the social services sides, there are different classes of welfare services. One important distinction is between public and private welfare programs.

Public Welfare Services

Because Canada is a federal state, **public welfare** is provided, in different forms, through the three levels of government: the federal or national government, the provincial and territorial governments, and the regional and municipal governments. Typically, agencies are created and charged with overseeing and delivering income security and social services to citizens on behalf of the government.

As well, there are "public" non-government agencies that provide services. These include advisory and appeal boards, which are the creations of government (federal, provincial, or municipal), consisting of members who are appointed from the public by government. They are either completely independent or quasi-independent of the government's own agencies.

Private Welfare Services

There is also what can be referred to as **private welfare**, or programs funded by voluntary charitable contributions from individuals and private organizations, by fees people pay for the services they receive, or by funds spent by corporations to provide social welfare services to their employees.

Here, a distinction can be drawn between two types of private delivery organizations: private non-profit and private for-profit.

- **Non-profit organizations** are mandated to provide a service or an activity, but not to create a profit. In Canada, these organizations are often registered, and rules and regulations govern their operation. Many are incorporated as non-profit corporations. Often, they receive funds from one or more levels of government. Indeed, governments seem to be moving more toward this delivery model. By moving services into non-unionized smaller agencies, labour costs and liability are lowered.
- **For-profit organizations** are prevalent in certain income security areas (for example, pensions and insurance) and social service areas (for example, nursing homes, psychotherapy, home care, and child care). They essentially provide services for a fee and generate a profit for the owner offering the service. With government cutbacks in recent years, more and more services are being provided by for-profit or commercial agencies.

Non-profit and for-profit service providers, along with public government and non-government agencies, form the backbone of the social welfare system in Canada today. Sometimes it is an uneasy alliance. Advocates of private, for-profit welfare maintain that a for-profit system allows more choice (for example, private pension and insurance plans). Opponents point out, however, that the private system favours those most able to afford it, fosters social inequality, and undermines the public system.

A Global Definition

After a four-year consultation, the International Federation of Social Workers (IFSW) framed a new definition of social work practice in 2014:

"Social work is a practice-based profession and an academic discipline that promotes social change and development, social cohesion, and the empowerment and liberation of people. Principles of social justice, human rights, collective responsibility, and respect for diversities are central to social work. Underpinned by theories of social work, social sciences, humanities and Indigenous knowledge, social work engages people and structures to address life challenges and enhance wellbeing."

Approaches to Social Welfare Provision

In general, the idea that governments should provide income security and social supports to citizens if they are genuinely in need is not highly disputed in Canada (although it certainly is in the United States). Nevertheless, major disputes arise in determining exactly which groups are genuinely in need and to what extent they may need state assistance. Canadian governments have moved back and forth between two broad approaches to social welfare. These are sometimes referred to as the "residual view" and the "institutional view."

- **The residual view.** In this view, social welfare is a limited response to human need, implemented only when all else fails. It is based on the premise that there are two "natural" ways through which an individual's needs are met: the family and the market economy. The state should only step in when these normal supports fail. Social welfare should be targeted to those most in need, and typically, benefits are at a low level (so as to discourage abuse).
- **The institutional view.** In this view, social welfare exists to ensure that everyone has a reasonable standard of living and health. In a complex industrial society such as ours, the argument goes, access to income supports and social services promotes a sense of civic solidarity and helps to even out inequalities that may be no fault of the individual concerned.

Until the Great Depression of the 1930s and its aftermath, social welfare programs in Canada were essentially residualist in nature. Welfare was only for those demonstrably in need. In the period after World War II, the idea that welfare services were necessary to any civilized society became more widespread. Since the turn of the century, if not earlier, policymakers have reverted to a more restricted notion, making cutbacks in welfare spending across the board.

Many Canadian communities have agencies that provide geared-to-income housing for families and individuals, including older Canadians.

"Universal" and "Selective" Programs and Services

When designing social welfare programs, a key distinction is whether they are universal or selective.

- **Universal programs.** These programs are available to everyone in a specific category (such as people aged 65 and over, people with disabilities, or children) on the same terms and as a right of citizenship. The idea is that all persons are equally eligible to receive program benefits, regardless of income or financial situation.
- **Selective programs.** These programs target those who are found to be in need or eligible, based on a means (or income) test or a needs test. A means test determines eligibility based on the income of the prospective recipient. The benefit is reduced according to income level, and there is always a level at which no benefit is granted. A needs test determines eligibility based on the income and the need of the prospective recipient. Eligibility criteria are used to define need, which is then compared to the prospective recipient's life situation.

Old Age Security (OAS)
Benefits for older Canadians have been in place for nearly 100 years. Currently, Canadians 65 or older may be eligible for an Old Age Security pension if they have lived in the country for a specified number of years.

In the post-World War II era, universal programs were seen as a way to build national solidarity. More recently, they have been viewed as too expensive and have all but disappeared. The foremost objection to universal programs is their cost. Giving a benefit to everyone, regardless of income, means that even the wealthy get a benefit. Universal programs are less expensive to administer, however, as they do not require the scrutiny of every person's situation to determine eligibility.

Selective programs are often viewed as more efficient and less costly, as benefits are only provided to those most in need. However, identifying eligible recipients using means or needs tests can be administratively complex and costly and take money out of the system that could be directed toward benefits. In some cases, the higher administrative costs are being partially avoided by using the tax system as a method of determining eligibility and dispensing benefits. Increasingly, social policy experts are seeing that some selective programs are necessary for tackling poverty and inequality.

While some programs include aspects of universality, there are no income security programs remaining that can be exactly defined as universal. Health care and education are examples of universal service programs, but they are not income security programs. In the past, a number of universal income security programs were available to Canadians. Family Allowance, which was available from 1944 to 1993, is the most commonly cited example. All families with a child under the age of 18 were entitled to a financial benefit. Because of the progressive tax system, wealthier people paid much of the costs back through taxation, but it was nevertheless an acknowledgement of citizenship entitlement and of the importance and cost of raising children. In 1993, the Family Allowance was redesigned to become a targeted program, the Canada Child Tax Benefit (CCTB), only available to low- and middle-income families.

The Universal Child Care Benefit (UCCB) was introduced by the Conservative government in 2006 as a taxable benefit. In 2015, the Conservative government enhanced the UCCB to include a new benefit for children aged 6 through 17 and payments for children under the age of 6 were increased. Following up on an election campaign promise, early in 2016 the new Liberal government announced the Canada Child Benefit program, which pays up to $6,400 per child under age 6 and up to $5,400 per child aged 6 through 17. However, under the new program, the child benefits begin to phase out starting at $30,000 in net family income.

Selective Entitlements

All of Canada's other income security programs offer selective entitlements. Most have complex selection criteria based on income, work history, or the willingness to find a job. Employment Insurance (EI), for example, is based on an insurance principle with eligibility tied to employment and income levels. Everyone within the broad category of "employee" pays into the program, so in this sense it is comprehensive, but a strict set of criteria determines who is eligible to receive benefits. The level of benefits depends on one's earnings and contributions. With more demands being placed on the system, the debate over the amount and duration of EI payments is likely to heat up.

Other programs are based on how much money one has and whether it meets one's needs. To be eligible for social assistance, one must prove that one's income and assets fall below a certain level. In provinces with workfare, such as Ontario and Alberta, applicants must also comply with an employment or training placement.

Subsidized housing is another example of selective programming. Through the Canada Mortgage and Housing Corporation, the federal government helps to improve access to affordable housing programs across the country. Most are administered by the provinces and territories.

Sister Elizabeth Kelliher (1923–2013) spent decades of her life advocating for social housing for residents of the downtown east side of Vancouver, British Columbia.

What Do Social Workers Do?

Those who choose social work as their profession are typically motivated by humanitarian and egalitarian values, and by a desire to understand how society works and to make it better for everyone. Whatever the combination of factors that leads a person into the profession, social work demands more than just the desire to "do good." The practitioner needs to have the analytical and hands-on skills, as well as the maturity and personal stability, that will allow her or him to bring about effective change.

Social workers provide support and guidance for people confronted with unforeseen events, such as accidents or illness, or with crises, such as sudden unemployment or homelessness.

In 2005, the Canadian Association of Social Workers (CASW) formulated a new *Code of Ethics,* replacing the 1994 code, and added a separate document entitled *Guidelines for Ethical Practice*. The *Code*'s preamble defines social work practice as follows:

> The social work profession is dedicated to the welfare and self-realization of all people; the development and disciplined use of scientific and professional knowledge; the development of resources and skills to meet individual, group, national, and international changing needs and aspirations; and the achievement of social justice for all. The profession has a particular interest in the needs and empowerment of people who are vulnerable, oppressed, and/or living in poverty. Social workers are committed to human rights as enshrined in Canadian law, as well as in international conventions on human rights created or supported by the United Nations.

Over the past few years, the number of social workers has risen sharply. This rise is primarily attributable to the much greater range and intensity of social service needs, such as unstable family structures, family violence, child poverty, the aging of the population and the switch to home care, stress, substance use, dropping out of school, behavioural problems, and traumatic events. The fact that a growing proportion of these needs are handled by members of other occupations has only slightly slowed employment growth in this occupation. We will most likely see this trend continue over the next few years.

Direct and Indirect Social Work

It is common to distinguish between two types of social work.

- **Direct social work** involves working face-to-face with people as individuals to provide services such as counselling, group work, and community development. This is typically done through a public (or publicly-funded) social service agency or institution, such as a hospital or child welfare agency.
- **Indirect social work** involves working with organizations that formulate, analyze, develop, and evaluate social policies and programs. It typically means working with social service agencies, research groups, and other groups whose purpose is to advocate for those in need.

The different kinds of practice can also be described as being either micro, mezzo, or macro social work.

- **Micro social work** refers to direct practice with individuals and families.
- **Mezzo social work** is social work with groups and communities.
- **Macro social work** involves working with organizations or communities to improve or change laws or policies in general society.

Whether involved directly with citizens or indirectly through research, social workers are above all committed to serving people who are vulnerable or in need. They are there when circumstances are challenging or go wrong, or when people need help.

Casework and Beyond

The traditional notion of the social worker is that of a **caseworker**—a practitioner doing one-on-one counselling with individuals or families, usually working as part of a social service agency. Casework is what social workers are so highly respected for in the public eye. It is what social workers do "on the ground," every day; they become intimately involved, one-on-one, with many diverse populations, including the homeless, older adults, women, children and youth, LGBTQ+ persons, and persons with disabilities. They work in many different employment settings—in child welfare and family service agencies, schools, mental health clinics and hospitals, child guidance centres, industrial and labour organizations, and criminal justice settings. They bring a broad range of background knowledge and experience to help individuals and families in need.

Casework, then, involves doing rigorous and indispensible practical work with individuals and families, often in extremely difficult circumstances. Underlying this work is a body of theoretical knowledge and "best practices" that social work practitioners can call upon to help determine the best course of action. Because they have a deeper grasp of complex social issues and social problems, more often than not social workers also find themselves involved in advocacy, policy research, and even social movements.

Social workers in the field of corrections are increasingly in demand, due in part to a shift in focus to the mental and physical health care needs of persons who are in conflict with the law.

Foundational Principles of Social Work
The helping profession

Four powerful key concepts underlie professional social work

"Social work is a profession concerned with helping individuals, families, groups and communities to enhance their individual and collective well-being. It aims to help people develop their skills and their ability to use their own resources and those of the community to resolve problems. Social work is concerned with individual and personal problems but also with broader social issues such as poverty, unemployment and domestic violence. Human rights and social justice are the philosophical underpinnings of social work practice. The uniqueness of social work practice is in the blend of some particular values, knowledge and skills, including the use of relationship as the basis of all interventions and respect for the client's choice and involvement."

This definition of social work, provided by the Canadian Association of Social Workers (CASW), emphasizes four key concepts:

1) social change/social justice
2) problem solving
3) person in environment
4) empowerment

Social Change/Social Justice Mandate

A social change/social justice mandate means working in solidarity with those who are disadvantaged or excluded from society so as to eliminate the barriers, inequities, and injustices that exist.

This means that social workers should be at the forefront of policies and legislation that redistribute wealth in favour of those who are less well-off—that is, promoting equal opportunity for women, gays, lesbians, bisexuals, transgendered persons, people with disabilities, Indigenous peoples, and racialized Canadians, and defending past gains in these areas.

Commitment to social change and social justice is fundamental to social work practice. Reducing inequality of opportunity and seeking ways to redress social imbalances will reduce the need for welfare services.

Problem Solving

Social workers respond to crises and emergencies as well as everyday personal and social problems. They use a problem-solving process and formulate possible plans of action.

A problem is not usually clearly defined when someone comes to a social service agency. It is therefore crucial for the social worker to explore the person's concerns, to identify the need(s) involved, to identify barriers to meeting need(s), and to carefully determine the goals and possible plans of action.

A key characteristic of the problem-solving process is the inclusion of the client at each stage. The process should also teach clients problem-solving skills so that they can better deal with future problems on their own.

Person in Environment

A key aspect of effective social work practice is to go beyond the "internal" (psychological) factors and examine the relationship between individuals and their environments. This person-in-environment approach largely distinguishes social work practice from other helping professions. These "environments" extend beyond the immediate family to include interactions with friends, neighbourhoods, schools, religious groups, laws and legislation, other agencies or organizations, places of employment, and the economic system. Based on this understanding, intervention may focus on the individual, interactions between people and any system or structure, or on the system or structure itself.

Empowerment

In order for the interventions of social workers to be successful, clients must believe that the efforts of the practitioner, as well as their own efforts, will make a difference. This leads to the concept of empowerment. Being empowered means feeling that you have power and control over the course of your life.

Empowerment is the process of increasing personal, interpersonal, or political power so that one can improve one's particular situation. Power can be a personal state of mind, in the sense that one feels one can make a difference and have control and influence over one's own life. It can also be empowerment within an organization in the sense that one has tangible influence and legal rights.

Empowerment involves both a personal perception of being in control and tangible elements of power within the various social structures of society. Social workers seek to empower their clients as a way of helping them focus on access to resources and the structures of power, among other things.

Empowerment-based social work, therefore, has three main aspects:

- making power explicit in the client-worker relationship (to help equalize the relationship between client and worker)
- giving clients experiences in which they themselves are in control (to allow them to see the potential for controlling their lives)
- supporting the client's efforts to understand the power relationships in their own lives, as well as their efforts to gain greater control over their lives as a way of promoting change

Putting an empowerment perspective into practice involves techniques that make power relations between the workers and their clients explicit, thereby equalizing the client-worker relationship. It may entail giving clients—whether they be individuals, families, groups, or entire communities—experiences that put them in a position to exercise power. Voluntary work experiences that allow clients to use their skills to help others can be empowering. Another aspect may be to support clients' efforts to change policies or practices that impinge on their lives and the lives of others.

In other instances, an empowering perspective may involve simply focusing on the strengths of the person. In all relationships, it is generally acknowledged that constructive feedback and positive reinforcement are conducive to helping people make positive changes in their lives. Clearly, it is more helpful for social workers to guide their clients' focus toward the success they have achieved in the past rather than dwelling on points where they have been less successful.

An empowerment perspective is the key to good social work practice. And like other aspects of good practice, it involves not a specific set of skills, but a general orientation on the part of the worker. This orientation is based on helping clients identify their own needs and then assisting them to deal with the exigencies of their own particular situation.

Of all the fundamental techniques available to the social work practitioner, the ability to empower the client is perhaps the most useful. The key is to help clients gain some sense of control over the difficult situation at hand and a sense that their actions will lead to positive results. Having the ability to foster a sense of client empowerment in sometimes difficult situations is an important part of the social worker's skill set.

The Role of the Social Worker

The social work profession is a personally taxing one. It requires a unique range of aptitudes and skills. Social workers and social service workers are called upon to uphold the highest standards of care and professionalism in relation to their clients and the highest professional and ethical standards in their relations with their colleagues.

A social work practitioner may need to assume a number of different roles, depending on the nature of their job and the approach to practice that they use. Obviously, the role that is selected and applied is the one that will be the most effective with a particular client in the particular circumstances.

Below are just some of the many roles that the social worker or social service worker needs to assume in the course of their work in helping clients get back on their feet:

- **Strategist.** The role of strategist involves the worker in helping people organize to help themselves; for example, helping a community identify problems, explore and select strategies, and organize and mobilize to address the problems.
- **Broker.** A broker links individuals and groups who need help; for example, linking a woman who is abused by her partner to a shelter for battered women.
- **Advocate.** In the role of advocate, the worker provides leadership in advocating on behalf of a person or in challenging an institution's decision not to provide services.
- **Initiator.** The initiator calls attention to problems or the problems a particular policy or program may cause and follows up with colleagues or with an interdisciplinary team.
- **Mediator.** The role of mediator involves participating as a neutral player in disputes between parties to help them reconcile differences or achieve mutually beneficial agreements.
- **Negotiator.** As a negotiator, the social worker is allied with one side in a dispute and tries to achieve agreement by bargaining on his or her client's behalf.
- **Activist.** The activist seeks to change institutions and structures in society, helping to organize people to shift power and resources to oppressed or disadvantaged groups.
- **Educator.** As an educator, the social worker provides information and resources and raises awareness of problems and solutions.
- **Coordinator.** The social worker is frequently a coordinator, bringing all the pieces together in an organized manner to accomplish a task.
- **Researcher.** As a researcher, the social worker gathers information for inclusion in databases and stays abreast of new findings in her or his field.
- **Facilitator.** The group facilitator may lead a group activity as part of group therapy, a self-help group, or any other type of group.
- **Spokesperson.** The social worker may be engaged as a public speaker at schools, at conferences or workshops, at events staged by service organizations, at meetings with police, or at gatherings within related agencies.

In whatever context social workers find themselves, they conduct themselves in a professional manner, using the knowledge and skills they have at their disposal and taking into account the specific needs of the client and the range of interventions currently available.

Qualities of a Good Social Worker

Social workers must

- have concern and compassion for others,
- be able to listen and understand someone's problems,
- propose short- and long-term solutions and communicate these clearly to their clients,
- demonstrate respect for others and a capacity to analyze the client's situation without being judgemental, and
- be prepared to defend the rights of their clients.

Social Workers and Social Service Workers

A social work practitioner may be either a social worker or a social service worker. While there is not a clear separation between the two bodies of knowledge associated with a social worker and a social service worker, these categories are not interchangeable.

"Diagnostic services" are the purview of social workers (or in some provinces clinical social workers), whereas "diagnosis" has been excluded from the scope of practice for social service work. This means the **social worker** can make a series of judgements as to the nature of a situation and formulate the actions to be taken, or not taken, actions for which the social worker can be held accountable. The **social service worker**, on the other hand, may follow a suggested course of action based on a diagnosis, but he or she will not be the person who has arrived at such a judgement. The rationale for this is that the certification process is different for the social worker and the social service worker. The shorter time frame for the completion of a social service work program generally limits the depth and breadth of the interpersonal and social theory taught to social service workers.

For example, the Ontario College of Social Workers and Social Service Workers specifies the scope of practice of the profession of *social work* as "the assessment, diagnosis, treatment, and evaluation of individual, interpersonal, and societal problems through the use of social work knowledge, skills, interventions, and strategies, to assist individuals, dyads, families, groups, organizations, and communities to achieve optimum psychosocial and social functioning." When the College specifies the scope of practice for *social service work*, the words "diagnosis" and "psychosocial" are omitted.

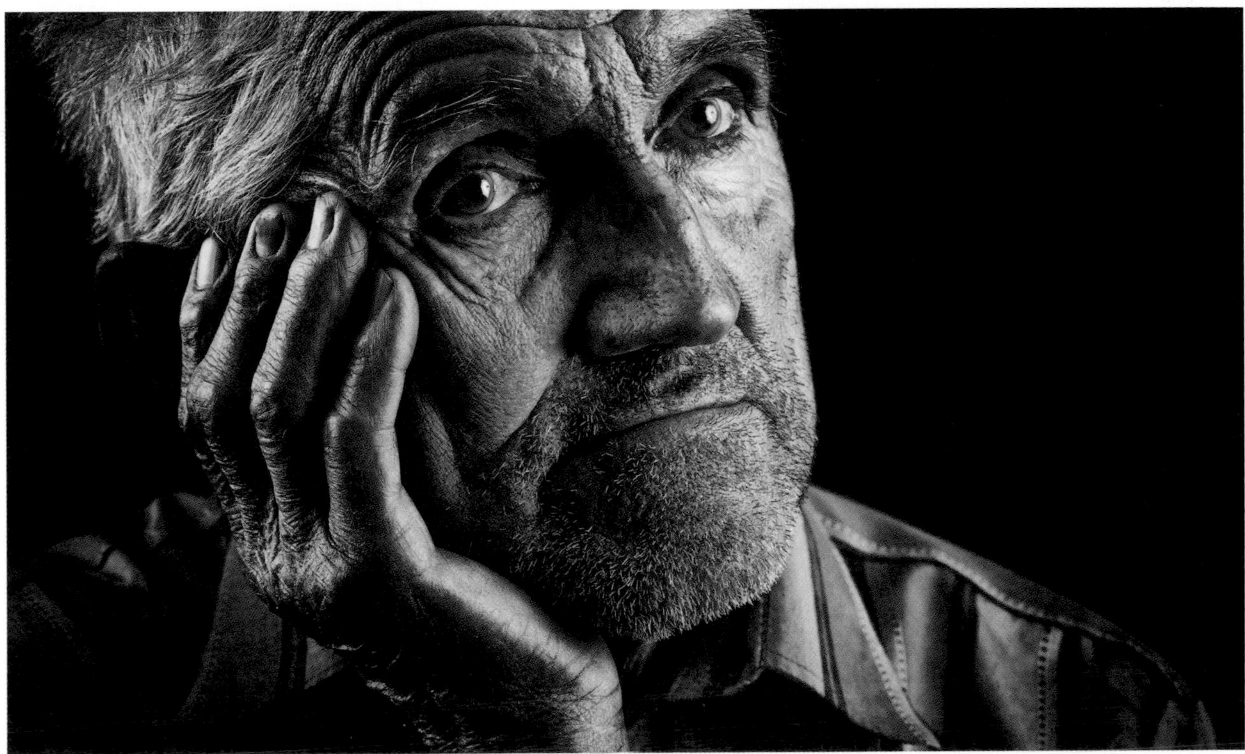

Social work professionals engage with a wide variety of people of different genders, cultures, religions, and economic backgrounds. They may work directly with individuals and families or with groups and communities to bring about social change.

The Education and Employment of Social Workers

Whatever type of work is pursued, some post-secondary education is required in order to practise in the field of social work. In general, a university-trained person is referred to as a "social worker," whereas a community college-trained individual is called a "social service worker." In some provinces and in everyday contexts, this distinction is often ignored, although obviously university-trained individuals will have more years of training behind them.

The first trained Canadian social workers graduated from the University of Toronto's Department of Social Services in 1914. Until the early 1970s, social work schools in Canada were accredited by the American Council of Social Work Education. There are now thirty-five universities offering social work degrees and forty-six community colleges offering diplomas, which are accredited by the Canadian Association of Social Work Educators (CASWE). A Bachelor of Social Work (B.S.W.) degree normally requires four years of university study. At least one additional year of graduate study is required for the Master of Social Work (M.S.W.) degree. A Diploma in Social Service Work from a community college requires at least two years of training. Those holding a non-social work undergraduate degree normally must complete two years of study for a Master of Social Work degree. There are currently twenty-nine M.S.W. programs offered in Canada.

Post-graduate study leading to a doctoral degree in social work is normally pursued by those who wish to teach at a university or those involved in high-level research, social policy, or large-scale administration. Eleven Canadian universities offer Ph.D.s in social work: Memorial University of Newfoundland, McGill University, University of Ottawa, University of Toronto, York University, McMaster University, Wilfrid Laurier University, University of Windsor, University of Manitoba, University of Calgary, and University of British Columbia.

Employment Opportunities in Social Work

The career opportunities for qualified social workers today are quite diverse, ranging from various public institutions to private practice and occurring within many different fields of experience.

- **Health and social services.** Job settings in this area include family and child welfare agencies, hospitals and other health care facilities, group homes and hostels, substance use treatment facilities, and Social Assistance offices.
- **Government services.** A large number of social workers work directly for some level of government, although this setting is declining as more and more services are devolved to community agencies. These services include statutory services such as child welfare or probation (in some jurisdictions), planning and administration of programs, correctional facilities, and the justice system.
- **Communities.** Community organizers work out of community health centres, resource centres, and other grassroots organizations to provide counselling and support to local communities.
- **Research.** The federal, provincial/territorial, and local governments frequently call upon social workers to conduct surveys and carry out research that affects social work practice in various settings.
- **Self-employment.** A small but growing number of social workers are self-employed, operating out of private offices and offering services directly to the public for per-session fees, or contracting out their services to large organizations.

Employment Statistics for Social Workers*

Employment by Gender

Males	15.5% (51.9%)
Females	84.5% (48.1%)

Employment by Age

15-24	2.5% (13.3%)
25-44	64.5% (42.7%)
45-64	32.1% (41.1%)
65+	0.9% (2.8%)

Employment Status

Full time	84.4% (81.2%)
Part time	15.6% (18.8%)

Average annual Income

Annual	$52,000 ($50,300)

Generally starts at about $30,000 a year and can increase to about $90,000 for more senior professionals in supervisory positions.

*Figures in parentheses reflect statistics for the entire Canadian labour force.

Source: Statistics Canada. (2011). *National Household Survey (NHS)*. Ottawa: Statistics Canada.

Unionization and Salaries in Social Work
Toward a just compensation

Today, many Canadian social workers are members of public sector unions. Indeed, the social work profession was part of the wider unionization of the public sector during the 1960s and 1970s, when, for the first time, public sector employees were permitted to join a union.

There was some debate over whether social workers should unionize, since social workers had their own professional associations and trade unions were traditionally associated with industrial workers. This matter was resolved by a division of labour. The associations represent social workers on issues pertaining to the development of the profession, education of members, and in social issues and social policy. The unions represent them in the areas of pay and working conditions. The associations and the unions in effect complement each other and both have mandates to act for those they represent.

According to 2008 Service Canada data, 69 percent of social workers belong to unions, compared with 32 percent for all occupations. Forty-five percent of community and social service workers are unionized. The largest unions representing social workers are the Canadian Union of Public Employees (CUPE) and the Public Service Alliance of Canada (PSAC). CUPE members are represented by provincial level divisions and sectors. For example, CUPE Ontario is broken down into five sectors: municipal, health care, school boards, university and social services. Social workers in children's aid societies, community living, children's care centres, municipal social services, community agencies (such as women's shelters), and municipal and charitable homes for the aged are all unionized.

Social workers have benefited from unions in ways similar to other workers. Unions have helped to raise salaries, improve working conditions, and enhance job security. Pressure from female social workers and from the broader women's movement has encouraged the unions to address important issues such as equal pay, child care, maternity leave, pensions, and sexual harassment.

Unions in social work agencies have also played another important role that is less well recognized. Labour unions have, throughout history, advocated for improved social programs, income security, and social services. Programs such as Employment Insurance and medicare would not exist today without pressure from the labour sector. As these programs come under increasing pressure from funding cuts, the unions are again playing a key role in opposing cutbacks.

Salaries of Social Workers

Historically, social workers were among the lowest-paid service workers. Over the past ten years, the profession has enhanced its prominence through the establishment of provincial regulatory bodies called colleges. They regulate practice and control the qualifications necessary to enter the profession. This has brought credibility and growth to the profession.

Over the past decade, the number of social workers has risen sharply. This can be attributed to expansion in the range of services undertaken by social workers and the intensity of needs. According to 2015 Service Canada data, the average annual employment growth rate was 2.5 percent for social work, compared to 0.8 percent for all other occupations. This trend is expected to continue.

According to 2015 Service Canada data, 84.5 percent of social workers are women (compared to 48.1 percent for all others), and 84.4 percent work full time (compared to 81.2 percent for all others). The proportion of women in the profession has grown. According to census data, women held approximately 80 percent of social work jobs in 2006, a slightly higher proportion than in 1991 (73 percent). This proportion should continue to grow slightly over the next few years, since women make up between 80 and 90 percent of bachelor's and master's degree graduates. Social workers no longer languish near the bottom of the income scale, with the annual average income topping $52,000, compared with $50,300 for all other occupations.

Québec Distinction

A distinction must be drawn between social workers as defined by the National Occupational Classification (NOC) and those who are members of the *Ordre des travailleurs sociaux et des thérapeutes conjugaux et familiaux du Québec.* The NOC numbers include many social workers who are not members of the Québec *Ordre.*

This situation should change in the coming years, however, owing to the passage in 2009 of Bill 21 on the modernization of professional practices in mental health and human relations. This legislation limits previously unregulated practices to designated professionals only. Thus, a large number of human relations officers and community organizers who did not belong to the *Ordre* can be expected to join it in the near future. As well, the number of members of the *Ordre* increased by over 30 percent in 2012–2013, due largely to Bill 21.

Indigenous Social Work Education
Decolonial pedagogy for future generations

By Raven Sinclair

A decolonial pedagogy will ensure that we not only talk the talk of social justice, but that we lace up our metaphorical moccasins and walk the talk as well

In 2004, I wrote an article titled "Aboriginal Social Work Education in Canada: Decolonizing pedagogy for the seventh generation," and in this updated revision I include two key changes. First, I changed the term "Aboriginal" to "Indigenous." This is a significant shift as it reflects the evolution of Indigenous social work in the last decade. The original term "Aboriginal" is the constitutionally recognized term for Indigenous peoples in Canada. Using the term "Indigenous" in some ways represents a reclaiming of Indigenous identity because it is a self-identified and applied term. Its dictionary meaning is "native to," which is appropriate in relation to First Peoples in North America and elsewhere. The term is also non-specific. It can serve to remind us that there are over 600 Indigenous communities speaking over 60 Indigenous languages in Canada. Thus, when we reflect upon Indigenous peoples and issues, we must ask, "To which nation are we referring?"

Second, I changed "Decolonizing" to "Decolonial" pedagogy. "Decolonial" refers to the critical analysis and practical options that arise from critiquing and separating from the "colonial matrix of power." Walter Mignolo (2011) explains this matrix as the colonial "racial and patriarchal foundation of knowledge" upon which Western social, political, and economic structures are based. Decolonial thinking and doing in social work require us to critique colonialism in Canada. This means analyzing the social, political, and economic incentives behind, for example, the slaughter of the buffalo, the killing of Inuit sled dogs, and the residential school system. Decolonial "doing" requires us to take action. Indigenous social work is a decolonial approach because it is based on critical analysis of colonial history and its consequences. Its intention is to foster effective practice to alleviate the harms caused by colonialism and to confront its contemporary manifestions (known as "neocolonialism"). These include ongoing systemic inequities, oppression, discrimination, and racism.

But decolonial pedagogy goes further. It asserts traditional knowledge and tribal wisdom—which existed long before Western social work—as the theoretical, philosophical, and practice bases for social work education. Examples of decolonial pedagogy include Kathy Absolon's article "Navigating the Landscape of Practice: Dbaagmowin of a Helper" (2009); Cindy Baskin's book *Strong Helpers' Teachings: The Value of Indigenous Knowledges in the Helping Professions* (2012); Jacquie Green's narrative about the significance of Oolichan fishing for the Haisla in her chapter "*Gyawaglaab* (Helping One Another): Approaches to best practice through teachings of Ooolichan fishing" (2009); and Renee Linklater's book *Decolonizing Trauma Work: Indigenous Stories and Strategies*. These works, among many others, demonstrate how Indigenous knowledge and wisdom can inform and shape social work theory and practice. Indigenous social work has come a long way in a short period of time!

The Origins of Indigenous Social Work Education

Indigenous social work emerged from the Indigenous social movement of the 1970s that was sparked by the social revolution of the 1960s. In Canada, this movement saw the implementation of the Bill of Rights and the Indigenous franchise. Indigenous social work evolved in response to our Elders' call for social work that was sociologically relevant to Indigenous peoples. Recognizing that Western-trained social workers might be unable to meet the needs of the Indigenous population, several Indigenous social work programs were initiated in the early 1970s. One of the first was the First Nations University of Canada (formerly the Saskatchewan Indian Federated College) School of Indian Social Work, established in 1974. Currently, there are several Indigenous undergraduate social work programs, as well as three Indigenous M.S.W. programs. In addition, many Canadian universities offer Indigenous specializations.

In 2015, the student caucus of the Canadian Association for Social Work Education (CASWE) moved that all schools of social work in Canada include mandatory Indigenous social work classes at the B.S.W. and M.S.W. levels. The motion was passed unanimously by representatives of all accredited social work schools in Canada.

Since 1974, Indigenous social work has evolved: it draws upon generalist theory and practice while paying particular attention to colonial history and its traumatic outcomes. Social work education's theoretical foundation is tribal knowledge and wisdom. Indigenous social work aims to train both Indigenous and non-Indigenous social workers so that they understand colonial history, its intergenerational and contemporary effects on Indigenous peoples, and how to best practise social work with Indigenous peoples.

Contemporary generalist cross-cultural approaches and anti-oppressive social work education are valuable in and of themselves. However, Indigenous peoples require social work praxis (theory and practice) that go deeper. Generalist social work does not focus sufficiently on Indigenous issues. Also, the social work profession and social work education have not been free from colonial influence. In the words of Brazilian activist and educator Paulo Freire (2001), "the social worker, as much as the educator, is not a neutral agent, either in practice or in action." Indeed, many early social work practices were complicit with government colonial actions and those who protested were silenced (Moran, 1992).

When Indigenous peoples began to protest the residential schools system and the schools began to close due to disrepair in the late 1950s, the child welfare system suddenly emerged. It led, almost overnight, to the over-representation of Indigenous children in the child welfare system that we see today. Social work was responsible for child welfare apprehensions of Indigenous children who were transracially adopted or institutionalized in long-term foster care. We refer to this period as the "Sixties Scoop" (Johnston, 1983), and Dr. Lauri Gilchrist has termed the post-1990 ongoing over-representation the "Millennium Scoop."

The numbers of Indigenous children being adopted out via the foster care system are still high. Because of policy and legal mechanisms, we are in a period that I refer to as the "Foster Care Scoop." Indigenous peoples have long decried child removal as genocidal—the deliberate destruction of Indigenous culture.

The social work profession is beginning to account for its role in colonialism and to contribute to a decolonial pedagogy. This involves going beyond theoretical understandings of inequity and recognizing that Indigenous systems of knowledge and action can guide mainstream social work education and practice. However, we must first be willing to accept that other epistemologies, or world views, exist. Karen Martin (2003) describes epistemology as "ways of knowing, doing, and being" in the world. These ways of knowing, being, and doing reflect a nation's philosophies and ethics. These in turn shape how families, communities, and institutions operate. By extension, world views also inform how we operate in the helping fields.

Raven Sinclair (shown at left during a mentoring session with students) is an Associate Professor in the Faculty of Social Work at the University of Regina in Saskatoon.

Indigenous Ethics

Indigenous epistemology includes two key principles: the ethic of relationality and the ethic of reciprocity. You may have heard of the Indigenous concept of "All My Relations." This term refers to the ethic of relationality. Thomas King (1990) describes this ethic as the recognition of our commonality as humans, and our connectedness to all life forms, including the Earth. (See the quotation below.) This ethic imposes upon us the responsibility to treat each other and the world in the way we would treat our closest relative.

The second principle is the ethic of reciprocity. This ethic refers to the concept of balance through giving and receiving. We see this ethic play out in ceremonies, acts of gift giving, and tobacco offering. The act of offering tobacco or gifts is done in any context in which a request is made or in which there is an anticipation of receiving. The aim is to maintain balance in the physical world and, more importantly, in the metaphysical and spiritual realms. The purpose of striving for balance is to maintain spiritual, mental, emotional, and physical wellness and harmony.

Our Collective Social Work Journey Forward

Indigenous social work offers a decolonial pedagogy that contributes to the theoretical and practice knowledge of social work. It is meant for everyone. However, our social locations as Indigenous or non-Indigenous educators and practitioners will determine how we take up the insights and integrate them into our practices. Regardless of who we are, a decolonial pedagogy is a moral call and a contemporary cultural imperative. It asks us to be critical of inequity and injustice, to learn from tribal wisdom, and to take action to relieve suffering. A decolonial pedagogy will ensure that we not only talk the talk of social justice, but that we lace up our metaphorical moccasins and walk the talk as well.

"'All My Relations' is first a reminder of who we are and of our relationship with both our family and our relatives. It also reminds us of the extended relationship we share with all human beings. But the relationships that Native people see go further, the web of kinship extending to the animals, to the birds, to the fish, to the plants, to all the animate and inanimate forms that can be seen or imagined. More than that, 'All My Relations' is an encouragement for us to accept the responsibilities we have within this universal family by living our lives in a harmonious and moral manner" (King, 1990: 1).

Balancing Ethical Responsibilities in Social Work

The Canadian Association of Social Workers (CASW) Code of Ethics (2005) and the companion document *Guidelines for Ethical Practice* provide guidance on ethical practice in social work. The Code of Ethics outlines six key values: (1) respect for the inherent dignity and worth of persons; (2) pursuit of social justice; (3) service to humanity; (4) integrity of professional practice; (5) confidentiality in professional practice; and (6) competence in professional practice. To clarify the interpretation and application of these values, the *Guidelines* outline in further detail the ethical responsibilities related to clients, colleagues, the profession, and society, plus ethical conduct in the workplace, in private practice, and in research settings.

Social workers must occasionally balance urgent and practical intervention measures with ethical or "political" considerations. In many cases the code of ethics and agency policy align. However, sometimes social workers confront situations in which the policy and regulations of the agency conflict with what they, as experienced social workers, see as being in the best interests of their client. As well, the standards and ethics of the profession may be inconsistent with the established procedures and practices of a particular agency. Balancing one's beliefs, professional standards, and agency rules can be difficult. In this context, the social worker's place of employment can be either a source of empowerment or a source of strain.

Ethical Decision Making Related to Social Work

Ethical dilemmas often arise, for example, in income support and child welfare cases. Based on their assessment, social workers often refer clients to particular services for which they qualify. However, part of the mandate of social welfare organizations is to spend public money wisely. Therefore, social workers must ensure that the client is genuinely in need and eligible for assistance, while representing the client's interests as fairly as possible. Striking a balance is often easier said than done. Similarly, in child welfare cases (where a child welfare worker is expected to act in the best interests of the child), the social worker may be criticized for leaving a child in a home or for taking the child away from a family prematurely. Such dilemmas are aggravated when large caseloads or tight budgets make it difficult for social workers to provide services in ways that are consistent with their professional and personal beliefs.

Social workers confront ethical issues on a daily basis. For example, a client may present a gift to show their appreciation. Or, they may disclose something that is questionable under the law. A social worker may be legally obliged to pursue a course of action (e.g., with respect to privacy and access to information). Here is a five-step process for ethical decision making:

(1) Identify the key ethical issues in the situation.

(2) Identify the relevant ethical guidelines within your province's or territory's social work code of ethics or any employer-based ethical guidelines.

(3) Identify which ethical principles are of major importance in this particular situation and which are not. This is the rational and straightforward part of the process.

(4) Acknowledge and examine your own emotions and values. This is where virtue-based ethical decision making may be helpful.

(5) Outline an action plan that is appropriate for the situation at hand.

Ethical decision making becomes easier when social workers consult with colleagues, supervisors, or professional associations for assistance and support in working through the dilemma.

Virtue-Based Ethics

Virtue-based ethics takes the stance that social workers are motivated to be virtuous and caring because they believe it is the right thing to do. In accordance with this approach, the following five questions may help in ethical decision making:

- What are my feelings and intuition telling me to do?
- How can my values inform my decision? Will they hinder or help?
- How will other people be affected by my decision?
- How would I feel if this decision was made public?
- What decision would best define who I am as a person?

Emerging Digital Platforms in Social Work
Risks and benefits of online spaces

By Kathleen C. Sitter

New media can blur the boundaries between the personal and the public

The last two decades have seen an immense expansion in the number of young professionals using social media to stay informed and connected. Social workers are increasingly using electronic technology in their practice. At the practitioner level, email and Internet-mediated direct practice is ubiquitous, and sources of information for evidence-based practice are easily accessed online. At the agency level, software programs are used for service planning and delivery and for case management reporting (NASW, 2005). Technology has changed the ways in which social workers respond to the demands of practice in virtually every area of the profession.

Social media sites provide many benefits to the service user and the global community. Benefits include sharing information and resources with a wider audience at a low cost, community building, research promotion, and imparting ideas and expertise on issues that impact health and well-being (CASW, 2014). However, there are also risks and challenges that require social workers to assess both their personal and professional use of digital technology with a critical eye.

Technology and Learning

Today, instructors' efforts to prepare students to engage in social work practice include the appropriate use of social media within their work contexts. Young professionals learn how online encounters and communication might influence and shape future face-to-face encounters.

The incorporation of the ethical use of social media is an evolving topic in social work education. One example is provided by Dr. Tarsem Singh Cooner at the University of Birmingham in the United Kingdom, who incorporates an enquiry-based blended learning design into the university's social work curriculum. Students explore issues such as online safety; projecting and maintaining a professional online image; maintaining personal and professional boundaries; using social networks to develop and share effective professional practice; and working for the benefit of future service users. Cooner has also developed a mobile phone/tablet app to help social workers explore how to navigate the ethical issues inherent in using social media in social work.

Other examples of integrating digital literacy skills in the classroom include creating collaborative digital stories to explore social justice, oppression, and diversity (Walsh, Shier, Sitter, and Sieppert, 2010). Still other examples include developing blended advocacy strategies that combine online applications such as Facebook posts and Vine with face-to-face engagements (Sitter, 2015). (Vine is a short-form video-sharing service that allows users to share looping video clips lasting six seconds. American microblogging website Twitter acquired Vine in October 2012, just before its official launch. By the end of 2015, Vine had 200 million active users.)

Social Media in University Settings

The term "participatory media" refers to visual, mobile, and social media applications and platforms in which the audience plays an active role in collecting, reporting, analyzing, and disseminating content. Participatory media are increasingly being used in classrooms, practice settings, and schools of social work, resulting in the increased development of social media policies in university settings. All social work students should ensure familiarity with and an understanding of their university's technology policies.

As students move toward professional practice, beginning in the classroom and continuing in their practicums, it is important for them to think critically about professional-personal boundaries, self-disclosure, dual and multiple relationships, privacy, and conflict of interest (Johns, 2012). Social work students, faculty members, and social workers are individuals with private lives. However, off-duty conduct matters and may have a bearing on social workers' professional lives and, in some cases, on how fit they are to graduate or to practise. As social media are intricately integrated into our daily lives, social work students and professionals may possess a false sense of online security and privacy. Early in their career, professionals may not recognize the potentially unintended audience or the permanency of the information they share (Fang et al., 2014).

Multiple examples of the impact of personal behaviour on career potential have been portrayed in the media (e.g., Dalhousie University dentistry students who participated in posting misogynistic Facebook entries) and at universities (e.g., students violating another student's privacy by making a video of a presentation without consent, or students posting information about practicum placements on Facebook). Public figures and politicians have been exposed on the basis of photographs taken of them or speeches they made many years ago, for which they are held accountable in the present.

The Ethical Use of Digital Technology in Social Work

Online self-help support groups have been available since the early 1980s, and today online counselling services, chat counselling, video counselling, and cyber therapy using 3-D avatars are readily available. Social workers have a responsibility to use technology proficiently and to assess the advantages and disadvantages of practising technology-based social work. Ethical practice aimed at protecting vulnerable clients and upholding the values of the profession is required for electronic and online communication, just as it is required for face-to-face interactions (ACSW, 2013). Key ethical issues that arise when using any electronic technology are client privacy and confidentiality, informed consent, conflict of interest, boundaries, consultation and client referral, termination and interruption of services, documentation, and research evidence (Reamer, 2013). Increasingly, provincial Colleges of Social Workers are developing standards of practice to govern the ethical use of technology.

The Personal Is Public

Fang, Mishna, Zhang, Van Wert, and Bogo (2014) coined the term "the personal is public," referring to the lack of separation between our online and offline selves. "Personal" posts may be neither private nor secure. Anyone can pull up a post, and bystanders can click the "Like" button or other emoticon or comment on the post, thus inadvertently creating an increasingly public forum for the initial post. As Fang et al. (2014) illustrate in their case examples, a student might make a derogatory comment about another student, a social work colleague, or an instructor, which the targeted person can view when "mutual friends" participate in the post string, and the situation can escalate. Just as worrisome are those observers who silently endorse the post regardless of hateful or oppressive comments. These bystanders are witnesses to bullying behaviour, similar to that of children in a schoolyard.

Implications for Social Work Practice

Opportunities abound to act as leaders in the emerging use of digital and social media literacies in practice contexts. While participatory media do not afford a magical solution in confronting problems in our work, it is a tool that can serve to amplify clients' voices, mobilize support, and foster connections that transfer knowledge both online and offline.

Digital technology requires thoughtful consideration of its strengths and limitations. We need to move beyond our fear of the unknown and look at the potential of technology to support the individuals, groups, and communities we work alongside.

Factors Affecting Practitioner Well-Being

Individuals are attracted to social work for many different reasons. Some are motivated by altruism—a desire to do good for others—often associated with personal experiences (positive or negative). Others are guided by professional or political motivations. Some wish to work in a field where they can advocate for the rights of marginalized individuals and groups.

Unfortunately, the increasing emphasis on managerialism (or what might be called "the social control" aspect of social work) means that many social work practitioners experience a mismatch between initial good intentions and real-life experience. Stevens et al. (2012) proposed that this "mismatch that may be one factor leading to the high stress and burnout levels found in social workers" (p. 33). Carey (2008) found that although employment opportunities remained good for social workers, "morale among the majority of employees was poor" (p. 90). He stated that "there was also a feeling among staff that social work was becoming devalued as a profession, and respondents identified a stronger sense of job insecurity and loss of autonomy (particularly when working with other professionals)" (p. 90).

A study of 175 social workers employed by the Children's Aid Society of Toronto in 2004 revealed that 82.7 percent of workers reported that they had been exposed to at least one critical incident at work (including the death of a client, threats, or assault). Seventy percent reported experiencing stress as a result of a critical incident.

A Potentially Rewarding Career

Other studies have found higher levels of job satisfaction. Rural and remote northern practice in Canada has long been a starting point for many social work professionals. Although they may be recruited to the North for job opportunities, many (although not all) decide to stay because of job satisfaction.

Graham and colleagues (2012) note that challenges of social practice in the North include isolation, personal-professional conflicts, or practice training that conflicts with Indigenous ways of knowing. In his study of 91 social workers in the Northwest Territories and northwestern Ontario, he found general satisfaction with their work and professional roles. Interestingly, working in child welfare (typically associated with high stress levels in southern, urban centres) was found to be a predictor of satisfaction with work and profession in the north. The authors suggested that "community size creates a context which might determine or impact key socio-cultural and socio-political interactions within the social environment, which then in turn impacts practitioner well-being."

It is sometimes argued that social workers must try to "desensitize" themselves when they work in the child welfare field. Of course, in practice this is nearly impossible. To do their jobs effectively, social workers must be sensitive to the needs and feelings of the children and families with whom they are involved. This level of commitment and engagement may be the key to their success in this difficult area of practice.

One way to offset stress and enhance job satisfaction is to engage in professional development activities among colleagues, especially those from different regions of the country. The feeling of being part of a large and diverse community of gifted professionals, which comes from attending conferences, workshops, and webinars where ideas are exchanged and effective practice strategies are shared, can be energizing. The ongoing learning and friendships that emerge from collegial interactions can help sustain one's dedication to the job.

Signs and Symptoms of Stress

Signs and symptoms of stress or trauma among child welfare workers include:

- intrusion symptoms, such as recurrent dreams and repetitive thoughts;
- avoidance symptoms, including social isolation and avoidance of high-stress situations; and
- arousal symptoms, such as anxiety and irritability.

Source: Lambert, L. and Regehr, C. (2005). ***Stress, Trauma, and Support in Child Welfare Practice.*** Research Institute for Evidence-Based Social Work. Children's Aid Society of Toronto. University of Toronto.

Self-Care

Social work is a noble profession to be sure, but a disconcerting phenomenon in this field has received considerable attention—the extent of worker burnout among dedicated social workers. As "burnout" can happen to anyone in a stressful occupation, it may be more accurate in the social work context to refer to such a phenomenon as "vicarious trauma" or "compassion fatigue."

The term "compassion fatigue" refers to the anxiety resulting from dealing with emotionally difficult cases under increased workplace pressure and increased workloads. This type of stress occurs among social workers and others who are faced with increasing responsibility and less and less control over how the work is to be completed.

Self-care is an important and integral part of the profession of social work. There are multiple ways to practice self-care; however, the ABC mnemonic is an easy way to remember the steps necessary toward effective self-care practices:

- **Awareness.** This involves knowing yourself, your needs, and your limits. Knowing your coping mechanisms (both healthy and unhealthy) and your triggers will assist you in applying coping techniques and identifying your triggers in your practice.
- **Balance and boundaries.** This involves finding a balance between work, play, rest, and home activities, and enjoying set times each day during which you detach yourself from work.
- **Consultation and connection.** When you are in doubt about a troubling issue or case, consult with colleagues, supervisors, and/or other supports available to you.

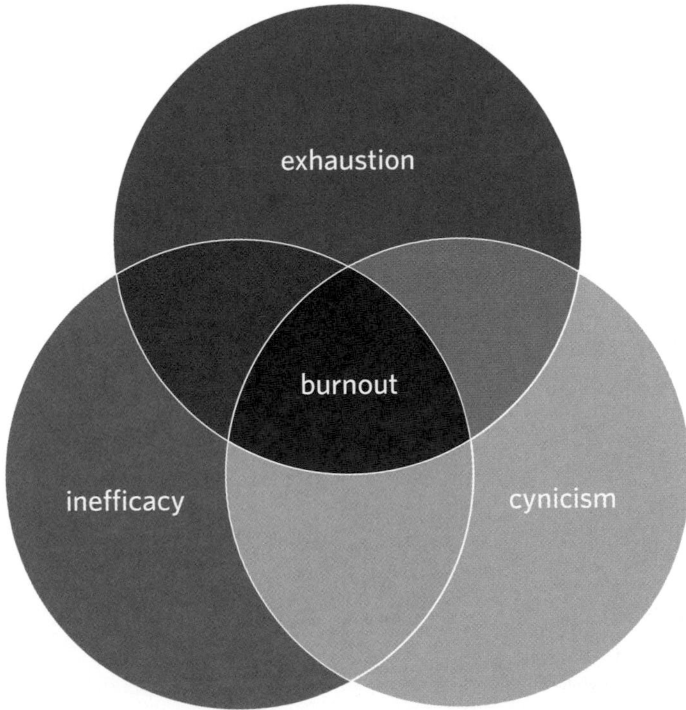

Figure 1.1 Professional burnout resulting from exhaustion, feelings of inefficacy, and negativity can be offset by developing awareness of one's strengths, limitations, and the need for balance and boundaries.

Dennis McDermott

Dennis McDermott is a Registered Social Worker who is employed by the Family Association for Mental Health Everywhere (FAME) in downtown Toronto.

The values and insights imparted by an inspiring mentor during Dennis McDermott's university studies helped him attain his goal of working in the community health sector.

Although I had decided to enter a social work program after I completed high school, it was not until the third year of my undergraduate program that I decided I wanted to be a full-fledged practising social worker.

Because I come from a family of health-care providers, volunteerism and community involvement have always been important to me. I initially entered the social work bachelor's degree program to learn more about social justice and how I might advocate for change to systems of social oppression. Previously, I had worked at group homes, shelters, and recreation centres to expand my understanding. However, I sometimes felt disheartened at the steepness of the hills that are often faced by people: poverty, ableism, racism, gender discrimination, and many others.

Valuable Lessons

In my final year of university, I was mentored by a wonderful and highly experienced supervisor during a job placement. He instilled in me the values that I cherish today. He taught his students that we should work to be good people first and foremost and that this would carry over into our practice. He taught us that sometimes the only choices we have are the hard ones, but that we still have to choose. Finally, he taught us that we should give the same amount of care, compassion, and consideration to each client, realizing that although we may not reach everyone, we will at the very least reach someone.

I was fortunate to earn money while studying. Through summer jobs working with children, people with disabilities, and residents of homeless shelters, I accumulated a solid experience base from which to transition into the workaday world. I sought out different positions in both clinical and community settings in various fields, ranging from disabilities to mental health and substance use. Many of these jobs were short-term contracts, such as relief or maternity leave positions. But they assisted me in eventually achieving my goal of working full-time in the community health sector.

I currently work as a Family Support Worker (FSW) for the Family Association for Mental Health Everywhere (FAME). I have been with FAME for just under two years. I provide education, counselling, and advocacy for families caring for a loved one with a mental health challenge. Much of what I do involves community outreach, workshops, and liaising with other community organizations for the benefit of families. The FSW position requires a well-rounded education and an up-to-date knowledge base in terms of therapies, laws, and programs for the benefit of our clientele. I searched for quite a while to find a position like the one I now hold, and after years of pursuing my goal, I am happy to be doing the work that I do.

There are multiple oppressive factors that challenge the families with whom I work. In a large urban centre, many families and their loved ones experience a high degree of poverty, homelessness, and substance use disorder. A large population of individuals requiring care, in the midst of such complex issues, poses many challenges for myself and service providers throughout the city. It is important to try to balance my own needs with the amount of time, care, and focus that I give to each client, so I can provide effective service.

The most important part of building trust and a strong rapport with my clients is to maintain a practice of open discourse. Many of the clients I have met over the years have felt a distressing lack of control over their own circumstances. Acting in ways that imply that we as practitioners are in charge of our clients' life decisions and ultimate stability can be disempowering for them. Therefore, establishing openness and equality in my relationships with clients creates a sense of trust, so that, despite everything, they know I support them fully as they discover how to regain control over their own lives.

Chapter 1 Review

Review Questions

1. What are the main components of the social welfare system in Canada?
2. Define and compare the following terms: (1) social policies and social programs, and (2) public welfare and private welfare.
3. Define the different types of social work practice.
4. Distinguish between the residual and the institutional approaches to social welfare provision.
5. Explain the four key concepts underlying the Canadian Association of Social Workers' definition of social work practice.
6. What is meant by a "decolonial pedagogy" in social work education?
7. What are the six key values outlined in the Canadian Association of Social Workers' Code of Ethics?
8. Name some factors related to practitioner well-being.

Exploring Social Work

1. This chapter describes different views of the role of social welfare in our society (residual, institutional, structural). Which "position" do you feel least comfortable with? Discuss your ideas with another student and write a statement explaining why this approach is inadequate.
2. In 2005 the CASW formulated a new Code of Ethics and Guidelines for Ethical Practice. The 1994 code contained the philosophical statement that social work is founded on humanitarian and equalitarian ideals. Do you think the new code provides a vision of an ideal society for social work to pursue? Explain your answer.
3. Select one digital technology related to social work practice that you find promising in terms of advancing a social cause or causes, and explain how you think it enhances advocacy.
4. Empowerment is often mentioned within the context of social work practice. Write a two-page paper on the concept of empowerment and how a social worker might apply an empowerment perspective when working with individuals and families.

Websites

Caledon Institute of Social Policy
www.caledoninst.org
Established in 1992, the Caledon Institute of Social Policy is a private, non-profit organization. The Institute does not depend on government funding and is not affiliated with any political party. Its goal is to "inform and influence opinion and to foster public discussion on poverty and social policy." Caledon's high-quality research and analysis covers a broad range of social policy areas.

Canadian Council on Social Development (CCSD)
www.ccsd.ca
CCSD is an independent, not-for-profit organization that partners and collaborates with all sectors (not-for-profit, philanthropic, government, business) and communities to advance solutions to today's toughest social challenges. CCSD is one of Canada's most authoritative voices promoting better social and economic security for all Canadians. The CCSD's main activity is research focusing on concerns such as income security, employment, poverty, child welfare, and pensions.

Canadian Centre for Policy Alternatives (CCPA)
www.policyalternatives.ca
The Canadian Centre for Policy Alternatives is an independent, non-partisan research institute concerned with issues of social, economic, and environmental justice. Founded in 1980, the CCPA is one of Canada's leading progressive voices in public policy debates. It has a national office in Ottawa and provincial offices in British Columbia, Saskatchewan, Manitoba, Ontario, and Nova Scotia.

Toward a History of Social Work in Canada

"What is my life if I am no longer useful to others?"

Johann Wolfgang von Goethe (1749–1832)

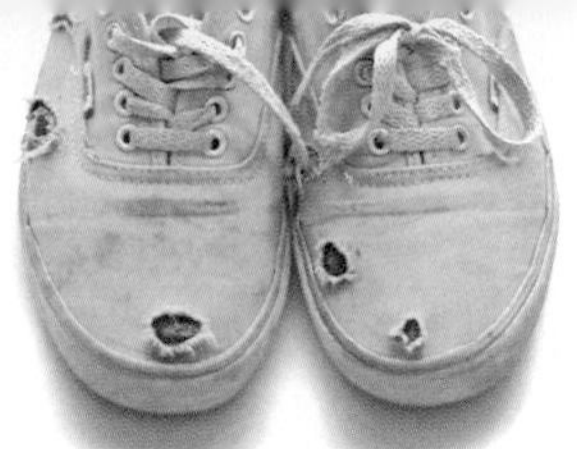

Jackie Stokes

The Emergence of a Profession

2

The expectation was the state would ensure the well-being of its citizens.

he systematic giving of relief to those in need coincides, more or less, with the upheaval caused by the Industrial Revolution and, in particular, with the consolidation of the wage-labour system (capitalism). Broadly speaking, poverty relief in the nineteenth century came in the form of either the poorhouse or the workhouse. In the twentieth century, it shifted to the provision of food and other necessities, and later to direct financial support.

Following World War II, social welfare expanded in the industrialized societies of the west, and so did the social work profession itself. The expectation was that the state would ensure the economic and social security of its citizens. During the last quarter of the last century, however, there was a shift toward more selective coverage, accompanied by funding cutbacks by successive federal and provincial governments. The result was greater stress for clients and larger caseloads for social workers.

Today is a challenging but exciting time to be a social worker: there is a pressing need to campaign for restored funding for social services so that all human necessities can be met. At the same time, innovative practice models that work for clients are required. Social workers are valued now more than ever before; it is a good time to enter the profession.

In this chapter, you will learn how to...

- distinguish the various eras in the history of social work
- identify many of the key individuals, organizations, and initiatives involved in the history of the profession
- understand some recurring themes and debates within the profession and their relevance to social work practice today
- understand the distinctive history and evolution of social service provision and social work practice in Québec
- understand the unique role of Canadian social work in relation to Indigenous peoples, both in the past and the present, as we move toward reconciliation
- make sense of social service policy and practice, and of the challenges faced by both clients and social workers today

Key Concepts

- Deserving poor/ Undeserving poor
- Charity Organisation Society (COS)
- Settlement house movement
- Social minimum
- Scientific philanthropy
- Casework
- Social Gospel movement
- The Great Depression
- Diagnostic approach/ Functional approach

Focusing Question

It has been said that those who don't learn from history are destined to repeat it. What are some essential lessons we can learn from the history of social work in Canada?

The Nineteenth Century: The Era of Moral Reform

In the nineteenth century, public assistance in English Canada largely followed England's example. In the face of the massive social disruption that had been caused by rapid industrialization, early English legislation required local parishes to provide relief to poor people if they were elderly, ill, or disabled.

The parishes were organized by the Church of England. Each had a local council that was responsible for assisting the poor, or providing "poor relief." The *Poor Law of 1601* and its reform in 1832 carefully distinguished between two types of relief: one for the elderly and sick, who could receive relief in almshouses or poorhouses, and one for the able-bodied poor, who were made to labour in workhouses in exchange for relief. The purpose of the latter type of aid was to make the seeking of such public assistance shameful and demeaning.

The Deserving and Undeserving Poor

Following a request for assistance, a charity visitor would be designated to interview the applicant in his or her home. The visitors were volunteers, generally men and women from the upper classes or people from the ranks of the emerging professional and business classes. While the work required experience and skill, proposals to hire full-time, paid visitors met with resistance from people in positions of power.

A visitor's first task was to classify the applicant as either "deserving" or "undeserving" poor.

- **Deserving poor.** People designated as deserving poor were seen as being of good moral character and only temporarily out of luck through no fault of their own. The deserving poor did not ask directly for help, and were clean and tidy.
- **Undeserving poor.** The undeserving poor were those individuals deemed to be lazy or morally degenerate.

Once an applicant was judged to be deserving, he or she had to appear before a committee of trustees, who made the final decision to grant aid. The board granted aid in only about half of the cases determined to be circumstances of destitution.

In Canada in the early nineteenth century, relief was provided primarily by private philanthropic societies. Organizations such as the Society for Improving the Condition of the Poor of St. John's (1808), the Society for Promoting Education and Industry among the Indians and Destitute Settlers in Canada (1827), the Kingston Benevolent Society (1821), the Halifax Poor Man's Friend Society (1820), and the Montréal Ladies' Benevolent Society (1832) were preoccupied with the termination of begging and the value of labour. Relief, rarely provided as cash but rather in the form of food or other necessities, was usually given in return for work. These same organizations, however, resisted the introduction of more scientific methods of charity that were advocated from the 1830s onwards (Rooke and Schnell, 1983: 46–56). (The topic of "scientific philanthropy" will be discussed later in this chapter.)

The relief provided by the volunteers of numerous charities and church parishes was soon deemed disorganized and inefficient, as there was very little regulation or coordination. Toronto alone had 43 different charity organizations by 1894. Over time, these agencies developed training programs for their volunteers, which formed the basis for the University of Toronto's Social Services Program, established in 1914.

In the nineteenth century, even children were forced to work in factories and on farms for relief from poverty. For many families, it was more important for a child to bring home a wage than to get an education. Dangerous working conditions and long hours meant that children worked as hard as adults, but no laws existed to protect them.

Children were less expensive to employ than adults, and they were easier to discipline. In rural areas, children as young as five worked in "agricultural gangs." In 1821, approximately 49 percent of Britain's workforce was under the age of 20. The *Factory Act* of 1833 made it illegal for textile factories to employ children under 9 years of age.

Government regulations eventually limited the number of hours in a day children worked in factories, but employers were not necessarily liable for accidents until 1937.

Poor Laws have existed in England since 1349. The Black Death (bubonic plague) had killed a large percentage of the population (illustrated above), and labour was in short supply. The first Poor Law forced all able-bodied persons to work.

The Charity Organisation Society

In 1869, proponents of better organization for charitable assistance in England formed the London-based **Charity Organisation Society (COS)** to coordinate the efforts of the various charities. The COS brought order to the chaos created by the activities of 640 charitable institutions. The voluntary work conducted under the auspices of the COS was possibly the most widespread attempt to help the poor. Workers in this organization were expected to cooperate with other charities and with the agents of the Poor Law.

The COS believed that indiscriminate material relief would cause pauperism: it could lure a person from thrift and hard work into a life of dependency and reliance on handouts. The COS believed that the charity visitors could serve as models of the value of hard work and thrift.

However, these visitors encountered many difficulties and soon sought out specific training and "scientific methods" to cope with them. As these visitors became more familiar with standardized techniques of providing assistance, they began practising what came to be called social "casework" (Copp, 1974: 108–120).

The popularity of the COS stemmed partly from the relief it accorded to local taxpayers; money could be saved if private charities used unpaid volunteers and members of religious orders (Blyth, 1972: 21). The COS was renamed the Family Welfare Association in 1946 and still operates in Britain today as Family Action, a registered family-support charity.

The Protestant Charity Organization Society arrived in Montréal in 1901, following an earlier effort to organize a charity in Toronto. It was primarily directed by businessmen and upper-class women who believed that poverty was the fault of the individual.

The Settlement House Movement

The aspect of social work concerned with community work has its roots in the **settlement house movement**. The term derived from the notion of "settling in," whereby relief workers would take up residence in the very neighbourhoods they were helping. The purpose of settlement houses was to bring the youth of the educated middle class and the charitable gentry to live among urban residents—a kind of mission to the poor. Canon Barnett, the founder of the movement in England, explained that the idea was "to bridge the gap that industrialism had created between rich and poor, to reduce the mutual suspicion and ignorance of one class for the other, and to do something more than give charity.... They would make their settlement an outpost of education and culture" (Davis, 1967: 6).The first settlement house was established in the east end of London in 1884. It was named Toynbee Hall, after Arnold Toynbee, an Oxford University historian who had settled in the same neighbourhood and had died in 1883.

From the 1880s through to the 1930s, the settlement house movement was a major factor in the emergence of social work. Jane Addams was the most prominent American to transport the idea of social settlements to the United States, founding Hull House in Chicago in 1889. William Lyon Mackenzie King, later to become prime minister of Canada, worked at Hull House in the 1890s, learning about the charitable work of Addams and others (Addams, 1961: viii; Ferns and Ostry, 1976: 37). Evangelia, the first settlement house in Toronto, was founded in 1902 by Libby Carson and Mary Bell with the support of the Toronto YWCA. Carson had founded several other settlement houses, including Christadora House in New York in 1897.

Toynbee Hall in Whitechapel was founded in 1884 as part of the settlement house movement in London, England. The house is pictured here as it was in 1902.

Several other settlement houses were established in Canada during this period. In Winnipeg, J.S. Woodsworth (who later became the first leader of the Co-operative Commonwealth Federation, the forerunner of the present-day New Democratic Party) directed the All People's Mission, which was founded in 1907. In Montréal, the University Settlement House was established in 1909; and in Toronto, the University Settlement was founded in 1910, the Central Neighbourhood House in 1911, and the St. Christopher House in 1912. Most large Canadian cities had at least one settlement house by World War I. The first schools of social work in Canada were connected to, or often were started by, settlement workers (Davis, 1967: 3–25).

Jane Addams (1860-1935)
Jane Addams was a founder of the U.S. settlement house movement and is considered one of the early influences on professional social work.

The Dawning of Public Welfare

Social work occurs within a socio-political environment, and, therefore, understanding the historical context ensures an appreciation of the roots and progression of social work practice. The shifts and tensions within social welfare and social work practice in Canada have been influenced by historical developments in the United States and the United Kingdom.

A renowned (now retired) social work professor at the University of British Columbia, Dennis T. Guest, provides a complete history of social welfare in Canada in his book, *The Emergence of Social Security in Canada* (3rd edition, 1997). This in-depth study offers shrewd insights into the nuts and bolts of social policy development in Canada. Relying heavily on Guest's work, this chapter provides an overview of some critical junctures in the socio-political environment and the eventual consequences for Canadian social work practice.

Canada has its own unique history, in part reflecting the ideology of socialism, which combines the liberal ideology of maximizing individual freedom and liberty with the feudal or conservative values concerned with the group aspects of human life (Guest, 1997: 18). The ideological spectrum, as it is presented in Canadian history, is markedly different from that in the United States. The Canadian ideological spectrum "emphasizes the notion of equality of condition through cooperative, collective actions, displacing the liberal emphasis on equality of opportunity with its connotation of competitive struggle" (Guest, 1997: 18). The rest of this chapter explores major historical influences on the evolution of social work throughout the twentieth century and the early part of the twenty-first century.

World War I (1914-1918), in particular, produced profound changes in the social and economic structure of Canada. The federal government began to assume a role in moulding social and economic resources, by imposing, for example, a federal income tax on personal income. "The government became the sole support of hundreds of disabled soldiers, their wives and children, and the widows and orphans of the men killed in battle" (Guest, 1997: 49).

Increased attention to the plight of one-parent families, alongside lobbying by women's organizations, led to the provision of Mothers' Pensions. Initially residual in nature, this program eventually became a mother's allowance program in all provinces. Programs such as this one foreshadowed public welfare programs, given their centralized administrative structures, specially trained staff, and funding supplied by provincial treasuries. These programs replaced the previous capricious discretionary power of local poor-relief administration (Guest, 1997: 64).

The first five decades of the twentieth century, however, continued to be influenced by values related to individualism; according to this ideology, poverty was seen as a result of personal failing or character weakness. Some may argue that remnants of that ideology persist today.

At the Turn of the Twentieth Century: The Era of Social Reform

As the twentieth century approached, urbanization and industrialization accelerated. Canadian political figure J.S. Woodsworth summed up this phenomenon: "Canada is leaving the country for the city." Social reformers became increasingly appalled by the exploitation of children and the risks to safety in work sites that were often more like detention centres.

Public discourse began to focus on the relationship between government and its citizens, and public opinion underwent marked transformations. "The doctrines of laissez-faire and of individualism were being challenged by notions of social justice, by a concern for the well-being of the group and of the wider interests of the community as a whole" (Guest, 1997: 26).

In the late nineteenth century, those involved in the charity movement gradually came to realize that what was needed was a more socially oriented approach, rather than one based on a moral world view.

The Emergence of the Notion of a Social Minimum

Gradually, the notion of a **social minimum** began to emerge. This viewpoint maintains that a political community should seek to ensure that its members can all enjoy at least a minimally decent standard of living. At the turn of the twentieth century, social reform became a multi-faceted public issue. Free public education and public libraries were established in larger Canadian cities and towns, and government entered into the field of public health, initially to combat outbreaks of cholera, smallpox, and typhoid. Work conditions were regulated.

In 1897, one of the first social survey research studies was carried out by H.B. Ames in Montréal. Published under the title *The City Below the Hill*, the study illuminated the conditions of the poorest residents of Montréal. Other studies by social reformers, such as J.J. Kelso in Toronto and J.S. Woodsworth in Winnipeg, contributed to an understanding of poverty and what could be done to alleviate it. These studies led to an emerging urban reform movement.

Scientific philanthropy was a movement first undertaken in England in the 1860s by members of the Protestant social and economic elite in an effort to curtail urban poverty and begging. The notion of scientific philanthropy departed from moral judgements of deservedness and was rooted instead in the ideals of social reform and progress that were becoming popular at the time. A person in need was now seen as having an objective problem, and the role of the relief worker was to help him or her deal with the problem. Gathering factual information would lead to an understanding of the causes of the person's problem, and in turn, to a solution. The theory underlying scientific philanthropy was that "the scientific spirit pointed toward self-correction and consensus" (Leiby, 1978: 91).

Scientific philanthropy
An approach to social work that rejected moral judgements and encouraged a "scientific" assessment of human behaviour and ways of finding solutions

The gradual shift from private charity work toward more social scientific methods occurred more or less at the same time in Britain, the United States, and Canada. Between 1877 and 1920, scientific charity spread rapidly to most northeastern and midwestern large- and medium-sized cities in the United States, and from there, to Canada.

In addition to the social survey research studies mentioned above, the federal government launched scientific inquiries into the factors underlying social ills and disparities. Royal Commissions, such as the Dominion Commission on the Relations of Labour and Capital (1889), the Ontario Royal Commission on the Prisons (1890), and the Dominion Board of Inquiry into the Cost of Living (1915), also contributed to increased awareness of the social causes of poverty and inequity and a growing interest in social service and social work.

Eventually, the shift to scientific philanthropy provided the foundation for the birth of social work as a profession.

The Rise of Trained Social Workers

Modern **casework**—the use of systematic methods of investigation, assessment, and decision making in social work practice—was strongly influenced by Mary Richmond (1861-1928), who worked for the Charity Organisation Societies of Baltimore and Philadelphia. Richmond argued that the casework technique could approach a "scientific understanding of social dynamics and human behaviour" (Pitsula, 1979: 39). Her 1917 text, *Social Diagnosis*, was used in the training of relief workers, and its contents reflect "the strong influence played by medicine in Miss Richmond's conception of social casework" (Coll, 1973: 85-86). In *Social Diagnosis*, Richmond describes the social work process as follows:

1) Collection of social data on family history, and data pertaining to the problem at hand;

2) Critical examination of the material, leading to diagnosis; and

3) Development of a case plan with the involvement of the client.

Casework
Social work that is directly concerned with the problems, needs, and adjustments of individual cases, especially those involving a study of a person's family history and personal circumstances.
A social worker out in the field helping and interacting with families and children is an example of casework.

In her analysis of social work, Richmond used the term "diagnosis" deliberately, borrowing the term from medicine. Her thinking became the basis of what would become known as the "medical model" of social work.

The Social Service Commission in Toronto first introduced the practice of professional casework in Canada. The Commission was appointed by the city in 1911, and employed staff who were paid for their work. It requested that the House of Industry in Toronto hire paid staff to operate their relief program. The distribution of relief was coordinated according to modern social work principles, as described in the Commission's 1916 annual report:

> Distress is relieved with care and sympathy, but the emphasis is not placed on mere relief giving. With each family helped, the work includes co-operation with other agencies, diagnosis of need, decision as to remedy, application of remedy, subsequent care, and tabulation of results. This is not haphazard "tinkering" with human beings but a real effort to render constructive and progressive service (Social Service Commission, 1916).

In 1914, the University of Toronto established a Department of Social Services for the scientific study of society. This was the first program in Canada to undertake the task of training social workers. In 1918, McGill University opened Canada's second English-language social work training program, the School of Social Study and Training.

The Shift from Moral to Social Reform

After World War I (1914-1918), the emergent social work profession was called upon to assist with the resettlement of war veterans and with others who were not poor but who needed assistance. In 1918, Charlotte Whitton was chosen to assist the Reverend J.G. Shearer at the Social Service Council of Canada, and she thus began a period of 25 years of intense involvement in social work and in the development of the social services. By 1921, the Social Service Council had become the Social Welfare Division of the Department of Public Health, illustrating the shift from the premise of moral to social reform.

In fact, social work gradually became a secular and scientific alternative to moral and religious endeavours to help disadvantaged members of society. As this replacement occurred during the early part of the twentieth century, however, religious faith continued to be central to the practice of a great deal of social work, as the next section describes.

During World War I, government agencies devoted to social welfare expanded, leading to increased professionalism in the public sector. The War provided opportunities for social workers to apply casework skills in the treatment of soldiers with "shell shock" (now known as "post-traumatic stress disorder").

J. S. Woodsworth (1874–1942)
James Shaver Woodsworth observed the failure of industrial capitalism to meet the needs of working people in Canada and Britain. When Woodsworth was elected to Parliament in the federal election of 1921 as the member for Winnipeg North Centre, his first resolution focused on unemployment insurance.

Social Gospel, Social Work, and Social Action

During this era of social reform, Canadian social work was strongly influenced by the **Social Gospel movement**. In the latter part of the nineteenth century, campaigns for a more socially oriented church, one that would apply Christian ethics to social problems, began to appear within the major Protestant churches. Anglican, Methodist, Presbyterian, and Congregationalist church members pushed for a "social gospel" concerned with justice and social action. Their interests included social inequality, poverty, alcoholism, crime, racial tensions, slums, the environment, child labour, labour rights, education, and the impending danger of war. Black denominations, especially the African Methodist Episcopal church (AME) and the African Methodist Episcopal Zion church (AMEZ), actively supported the movement, as well.

The Social Gospel wings of these churches started many of the settlement houses in Canada, offering services such as daycare, education, and health care to needy people in poor neighborhoods. The YMCA, which had been created mid-century to help rural youth adjust to the city without losing their religion, had by the 1890s become a powerful instrument of the Social Gospel movement.

In 1907, the main Protestant churches established the Moral and Social Reform League. The League became the Social Service Council of Canada in 1914, with the Reverend J.G. Shearer serving as its first director. The Council remained the main social service advocacy organization in Canada for the next 20 years. Several leading members of Canada's trade union movement were active in the Council. After 1925, however, it declined in significance and was replaced by the Canadian Association of Social Workers in 1927.

The Social Gospel movement had especially strong supporters in Canada's prairie provinces. J.S. Woodsworth was born in Ontario in 1874 and was raised in Manitoba. He became interested in social welfare work while studying at Oxford University in England. He returned to Canada, took a position as a Methodist minister in Winnipeg, and began working with the city's poor immigrants. He helped develop the efforts of social workers there, which then spread to other parts of Canada. Woodsworth founded and served as secretary of the Social Welfare League in 1913. As part of the settlement house movement, he created the All People's Mission, which provided a variety of direct social services. He campaigned for compulsory education, juvenile courts, and the construction of playgrounds. In the 1930s, Woodsworth and Alberta MP William Irvine founded the Co-operative Commonwealth Federation (CCF), later the New Democratic Party, on Social Gospel principles. The CCF, led by Tommy Douglas (himself a Baptist minister), took power in Saskatchewan in 1944 and introduced universal medicare, family allowance, and old-age pensions.

Social Gospel reformers such as Woodsworth were greatly influenced by (and greatly influenced) the Canadian labour movement, particularly with regard to worker control of enterprises and workers' direct participation in decision making.

In the churches, this spirit manifested itself as the social gospel, implying the achievement of justice in this world rather than in the next. For these reformers, service to other human beings was considered a form of service to God. Many Canadian historians, such as Ramsey Cook (1985), view social work as the secular replacement of the social gospel movement.

Social Work and the Great Depression of the 1930s

The Great Depression of the 1930s left an indelible mark on Canadian society and on the emerging social work profession. This was an extremely difficult time of mass unemployment, widespread hardship, and seriously reduced living standards. In 1933, for example, nearly one quarter of the labour force was unemployed. For many Canadians, the Depression shattered forever the idea that market forces should be left unregulated. Most people came to view unemployment as a socio-economic problem requiring a national response, rather than as a personal problem to be solved by charity. During this period, attitudes changed greatly, as did Canadian political life. The late 1920s and the 1930s saw intense class conflict, as well as trade union development and militancy.

This period saw remarkable growth in the number of social workers. The 1941 census recorded 1,805 social workers in Canada, which represented a 65 percent increase from 1931. During this decade, expanding social service agencies administered relief to a large percentage of the population. "During the harsh social conditions of the winter of 1931," note social historians Therese Jennissen and Colleen Lundy, "social workers were overburdened with people in need" (Jennissen and Lundy, 2006).

The Great Depression played a significant role in the shaping of Canada's welfare state and in the expansion of the social work profession. It ultimately led to the establishment of government-funded social programs and a growing need for trained social workers to run these programs. Today, social workers are employed in a variety of fields, serving many diverse populations, and the profession continues to pursue its mission of achieving social justice and ensuring the welfare of all Canadians.

Social Gospel movement
A movement that began in the 1880s among the Anglican, Methodist, Presbyterian, and Congregationalist churches; its advocates favoured a more socially oriented church that would work to improve living and labour conditions, as well as basic social justice

The Great Depression
A worldwide economic downturn that originated in the United States in 1929 and lasted until the late 1930s or early 1940s

In 1935, more than 1,000 men from British Columbia travelled by train toward Ottawa. They were protesting the federal government's decision to establish temporary "unemployment relief camps" instead of creating a program of reasonable work and wages.

The History of Social Work in Québec
An overview from colonial days to today

By Adje van de Sande

From Church domination to secular bureaucratization

From the early part of the seventeenth century to the 1960s, health and social services for the large francophone majority of Québec were operated and often controlled by the Catholic Church. Services for the much smaller anglophone minority were offered by Protestant, Jewish, or lay organizations. Most schools in Québec were either staffed by religious orders or had a significant presence of these orders.

All of this changed in the 1960s when Québec entered a period known as the Quiet Revolution.

This period was marked by a radical transformation of Québec society as the state took control of health and social services. Nevertheless, to understand the history of social work in Québec, one needs to look first at the role played by the Catholic Church.

Canada's First Social Worker?

The first services provided to French settlers were developed by someone who has been called Canada's first social worker (Yelaja, 1985). Marguerite Bourgeoys (1620–1700) was a native of Troyes, France. In 1640, she joined an organization of women tasked with educating poor girls, whose families could not afford to send them to live with and be educated by the cloistered nuns at the monastery. The director of this group of teachers was the sister of the Sieur de Maisonneuve, who had founded Ville-Marie (now Montréal) in 1642.

Because she was a layperson and not a cloistered nun, Marguerite was chosen to accompany de Maisonneuve back to Montréal. She arrived in New France in 1653 with a personal mission to educate children and, in 1658, she opened a girls' school in an abandoned stable.

In addition to teaching, Marguerite provided support to *les filles du roi*, or "the daughters of the king," orphaned girls who had been sent from France to marry French settlers. She also founded a community of non-cloistered women (the Congregation of Notre Dame of Montréal), and opened a girls' boarding school in Montréal, a school for Indigenous youth, and a school to teach home economics to young women.

Marguerite devoted her life to promoting education and social support to French settlers and earned the title of the patron saint of Québec educators. After a long illness, she died in Montréal in 1700. She was beatified in 1950 and canonized in 1982 (Stanké, 1987).

Pre-Confederation Health and Social Services

Before Confederation, Québec's population was concentrated in the rural areas along the shores of the St. Lawrence River. An informal support system in rural villages was well established. In times of need, people were expected to turn first to their families, followed by their parish, and, in extreme cases, to the state. During this period, the population did not see a need for a profession such as social work. However, this did not mean that rural families were not in need of help in one form or another. Fecteau (1989) points out that famine and epidemics, for example, were a normal part of people's lives.

During these early years, Québec modelled its programs for needy citizens after those in France, which included three types of institutions:

- the Hôtels-Dieu, which took care of sick people who had no families;
- the Hôtels-généraux, which looked after poor homeless people; and
- *les bureaux des pauvres*, which were established in Québec City, Montréal, and Trois Rivières. These "offices of the poor" were supervised by a priest who organized periodic collections and then distributed the funds to the needy (Ives, Denov, and Sussman, 2015).

Another charitable organization imported from France was the St. Vincent de Paul Societies. These societies were first established in Québec City in 1846 and spread throughout the province, providing support to poor people, elderly individuals, migrants, and orphans (Ives et al., 2015).

The role of the Catholic Church in Québec during this early period, however, is still a matter of debate. Some historians remain convinced that the Church was responsible for all programs and services, but Mayer (2002) cautions that, while it did have an influential role and provided most of the direct services, it did not have complete autonomy. Many of the activities of the Church in providing assistance were controlled by the state through a variety of laws.

Fecteau (1989) also argues that the Catholic Church played a less important role than is commonly believed. According to Fecteau, the lower clergy would have filled the role of informants about the level of poverty but would not normally have provided direct support, such as financial assistance or food. Nevertheless, the fact remains that the Church played an important role in the practice and the evolution of social work (van de Sande, Beauvolsk, and Renault, 2011).

From Confederation to the Depression

Canada after Confederation was characterized by rapid industrialization. As was the case elsewhere in Canada, the urban population in Québec saw rapid growth, particularly in Montréal. This growth was based on two factors: immigration and internal migration. The rural villages were abandoned for work

opportunities in factories located in the large urban centres. Working conditions were very difficult. The workers, including children, put in long hours at very low wages and without protection against disease or work-related accidents.

It was not until the early 1930s, during the Great Depression, that social work as a profession appeared in French Canada. The working conditions of the lower class had already attracted the attention of the affluent class, mostly women, who worked as volunteers and provided assistance to poor families. These women, who were the forerunners of professional social workers, based their charitable activities on the belief that the poor were in their situation because of moral and spiritual weakness (van de Sande et al., 2011).

In 1934, through the efforts of l'Abbé Charles-Édouard Bourgeois, the first social work agency opened its doors in Trois Rivières, Québec. It was operated by the Catholic Diocese of the region of Trois Rivières and became a model for agencies across the province (Ives et al., 2015).

The Birth of a Profession

The needs of poor and destitute people during the Depression were so great, however, that they overwhelmed the capacity of these early social workers. It became apparent that paid professionals with special training were needed. The only professional training available at that time was at the Montréal School of Social Work at McGill University, an English institution. Because of the belief that the School of Social Work at McGill was based on a Protestant philanthropic and neutral perspective, a francophone Québecer wishing to study there needed special permission from the Archbishop (Groulx, 1983).

The first person to take the initiative to develop a francophone school of social work was Sister Marie Gérin-Lajoie. Having been influenced by Mary Richmond and the Charity Organisation Society, as well as by Jane Addams and the settlement house movement, Sister Marie Gérin-Lajoie was the first French-Canadian woman to receive a university degree. She went on to study social work at Columbia University in New York City. In 1922 she founded the Institut Notre-Dame-du-Bon-Conseil for women interested in Catholic social work practice. The Institute conferred its first social work diploma in 1934 (Mayer, 2002).

In large part because Gérin-Lajoie was a woman and did not have the support of the clergy, the Institute was not well accepted by the Québec establishment. It was left to l'Abbé Lucien Desmarais to open the first school of social work in 1940. This school was annexed to the University of Montréal in 1942. A year later, Laval University opened its school of social work. During this period, social work schools and agencies were heavily influenced by Catholic values, and the main intervention approach was "casework," which was primarily based on a Freudian theoretical orientation (Mayer, 2002).

The "Hands-Off" Approach of Maurice Duplessis

The 1940s and 1950s in Québec were designated as *la grande noirceur,* "the great darkness" (Mayer, 2002: 212). Québec was under the control of the National Union government of Maurice Duplessis (shown here), premier from 1944 to 1959.

While the federal government in Ottawa used the report published in 1943 by Leonard Marsh as a model for the development of the Canadian version of the welfare state, the Québec government chose to go in the opposite direction, favouring a "laissez-faire" approach to the economy and to social security (Vaillancourt, 1988). Supported by the alliance between the Québec establishment and the Catholic Church, the Duplessis government believed that the responsibility for the poor rested with municipalities and parishes, and not with the provincial government (Mayer, 2002).

The Revolutionary 1960s

As stated earlier, everything changed during the 1960s, when Québec experienced its Quiet Revolution. The state took back control of health and social services, and the Catholic Church lost much of its influence. The professionalization of social work was strengthened by the creation of *la Corporation des travailleurs sociaux professionnels du Québec* in 1958. The organization was legally incorporated in 1960 (van de Sande et al., 2011) and is now known as *l'Ordre des travailleurs sociaux et des thérapeutes conjugaux et familiaux du Québec*.

The *Castonguay-Nepveu Report*, published in 1971, provided a blueprint for the complete reorganization of health and social services. During this period, three other events contributed to the professionalization of social work: 1) the creation of the Ministry of Social Affairs in 1970, 2) the adoption of the act respecting health and social services (Bill 65) in 1971, and 3) the establishment of the new public health system and social services of Québec in 1972 (Mayer, 2002).

Recent Decades of Cutbacks

The 1960s and 1970s were characterized by an interventionist policy on the part of Québec in the field of health and social services, but the decades since then have seen a complete reorganization of the "welfare state" and major cutbacks in services. Successive recessions (for example, the oil crisis of 1973 and the economic crisis of 1981) and inflation combined with stagnation convinced governments in Ottawa and Québec that poverty and unemployment are influenced by global economic factors and that government intervention alone will not solve these problems.

The government's priority was to make the economies of Canada and Québec more competitive in the face of a growing deficit. This was done through budget cuts to social programs, cuts to unemployment insurance benefits and social assistance, and tax cuts. The federal government in Ottawa significantly reduced its contributions to provincial programs, including health, education, and housing, forcing the provinces to transfer financial responsibility for programs such as child care and housing to municipalities or individuals.

These "neo-liberal" measures did result in reduced government deficits and a more competitive economy, but also caused considerable increases in poverty and unemployment levels (van de Sande et al., 2011).

The economic and social policies of Québec and Canada during this period significantly impacted the practice of social work. While the literature reflected an exploration of alternative approaches based on Marxist and feminist principles, the daily practices in state-regulated agencies, such as those for the protection of children and young offenders, were characterized by more bureaucratic control. In Québec, the Rochon Commission was very critical of the functioning of health and social services. Several measures were proposed to make these programs operate more efficiently (Mayer, 2002). Meanwhile, community organizations saw their budgets cut or redirected. Inevitably, many began to take short-term, task-oriented approaches to counselling (van de Sande et al., 2011).

Since 2000, previous reforms have continued, fostering the emergence of new service arrangements. In 2001, the Clair Commission published its report on the functioning of the health and social services and made recommendations for better "governance" of the network, with increased pressure to privatize health services (Mayer, 2002). The great reform of 2004 was another important turning point, which saw the creation of health and social service centres and transformed the relationship between social and medical professions. This new streamlining took place across the province and resulted in a merger of institutions. Health and social service programs were grouped by region or sub-region and administered by one body (Rondeau and Commelin, 2005). The impact of these reforms on the profession of social work in Québec has not been entirely positive. According to Carignan (2014), the Québec government has made a concerted effort to bureaucratize and de-professionalize social work, resulting in a loss of its professional autonomy. Carignan adds that social workers in Québec are now faced with having their practice regulated by a set of very specific competencies.

Social work and social services in Québec have evolved dramatically since colonial days, when they were dominated by the Catholic Church. The 1960s and 1970s brought the Quiet Revolution, an era of state intervention which saw the Church's influence decline. This was followed by a reduction of state-sponsored programs, a bureaucratization of the social work profession, and an off-loading of services to the private sector. Clearly, social work in Québec has gone through tremendous change. It will continue to evolve, and despite its challenges, it has earned recognition as an essential part of the health and social services system in Québec.

The Mid-Twentieth Century: The Era of Applied Social Science

During World War II (1939-1945), the Canadian federal and provincial governments began to realize that social services were not a luxury, but a vital part of a smoothly functioning economy. These services were required to assist the many returning war veterans and their families. The war ended a period of massive unemployment, sped up industrialization and urbanization, doubled the number of women in the labour force, and increased, and legitimized, government intervention in the economy.

In the post-World War II period, a time of rapid economic growth and mass consumption, career opportunities for social workers began to open up. As a more scientific view of human services emerged, the education of social workers gradually shifted from agency-based, volunteer training to a university-based, professional formal education. Originally based on the concept of charity, social work had evolved from a set of rules to guide volunteers helping the poor into a philosophy that embodied many of the principles of modern casework and techniques that could be transmitted by education and training (Woodroofe, 1962: 54). Social work in Canada had gained professional prominence in 1927 when the Canadian Association of Social Workers (CASW) was established. In 1947, the first professional social work degree (Master of Social Work) was offered by the University of Toronto. In 1966, the university awarded the first Bachelor of Social Work degree (Armitage, 1970).

The Aftermath of World War II

Following World War II, the federal Liberal government legislated a series of social welfare measures that were, in retrospect, seemingly intended to forestall the election of more CCF party members to the House of Commons. The CCF had achieved considerable popularity during the war with a social reform platform. The Liberals were also concerned with the possibility of a recession, which could cause considerable social unrest. The federal government therefore introduced the Family Allowance, which put more funds into the hands of families, helping to spur more economic growth. In 1951, through a constitutional amendment, the federal government introduced a federally financed and administered universal Old Age Pension. Several years later, they introduced benefit programs for persons with disabilities. (See Chapter 13 for more information about this topic.)

Many of these programs led to the expansion of employment in the administration of new services and programs, precipitating a fundamental change in the nature of Canadian social work and the emergence of a profession. Social work opportunities were now shifting from mainly private, volunteer agencies to government departments or government-financed agencies.

The ideas of Austrian neurologist and psychoanalyst Sigmund Freud (1856-1939) had an impact on how social workers practised their profession during this period. Debate occurred between the adherents of the Freudian or diagnostic approach and the newer functional approach. In the **diagnostic approach**, emphasis was placed on understanding the psychic condition of the individual by reference to causal events in his or her early life. This approach required a skilled worker who could diagnose the problem and carry out a plan for treatment.

The **functional approach** was based more on the belief in the potential of clients to determine their own direction in life with the assistance of a skilled social worker. The role of the worker was to establish a sound, structured relationship with the client and thereby to facilitate a process of personal change (Goldstein, 1973: 38–39).

New Models of Social Work Practice Emerge

In the 1960s, the social work profession renewed its interest in poverty as a result of anti-poverty measures instituted by the federal government. Community organizing initiatives sprang up in major cities across the country. In Ontario, a second generation of more radical social workers unionized, forming the Federation of Children's Aid Staff in the early 1970s. Several years later, this group of unions joined the Canadian Union of Public Employees (CUPE), which today represents a large number of social workers who are employed by municipalities across the country.

A range of new models of social work practice also appeared in the 1960s and 1970s, such as the generic or integrated approach, the problem-solving approach, the behaviour modification approach, and the structural approach. The latter was based, in part, on a critique of approaches to individual and family social work that tended to seek explanations for and solutions to problems within the individual alone and not within the institutions or structures of society. (See Chapter 4.)

Diagnostic approach
Emphasizes an understanding of an individual's problem by reference to causal events in his or her early life

Functional approach
Based on the belief in the potential of individuals to determine their own future directions in life

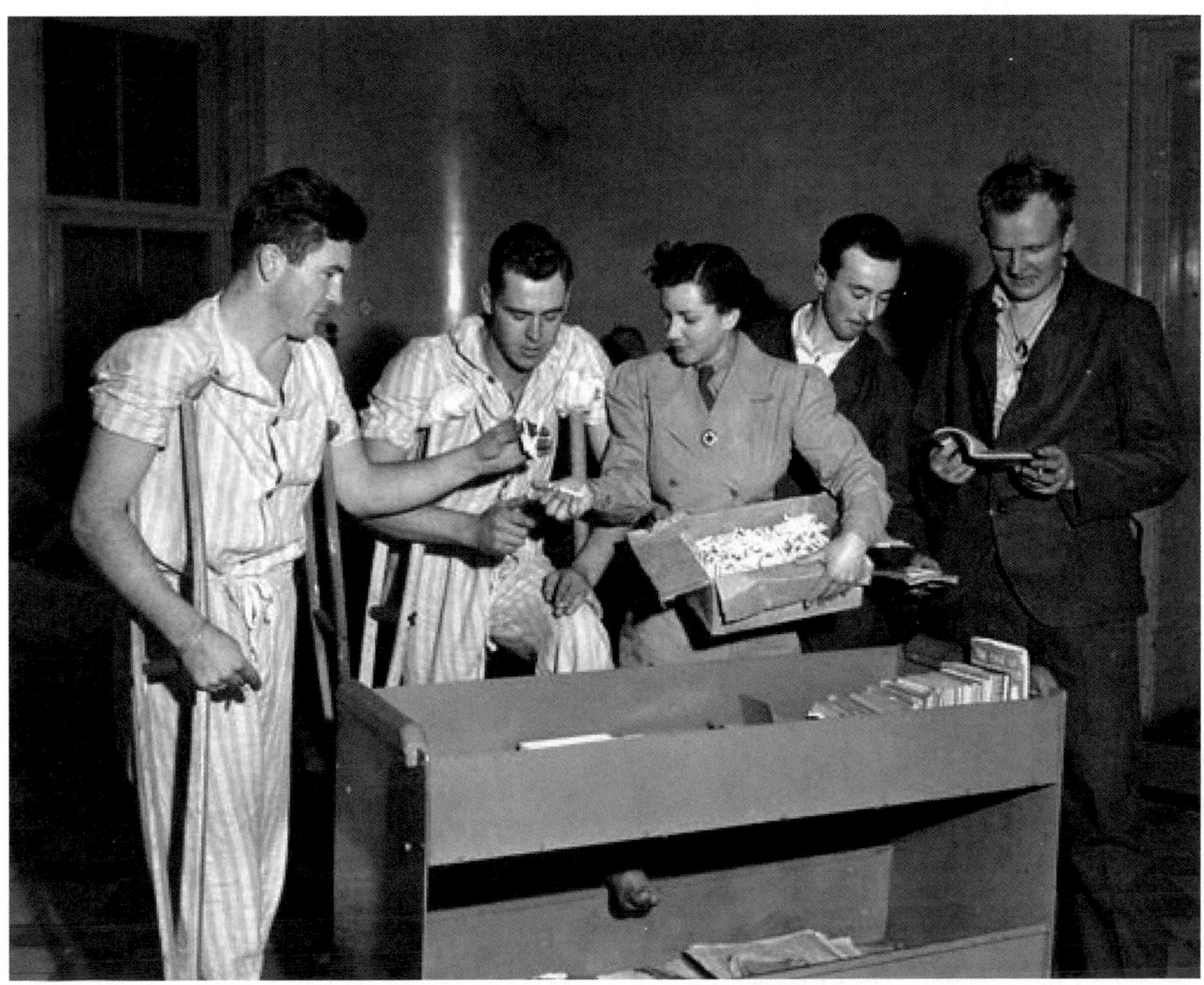

Social worker Mary Wright hands out Red Cross supplies to wounded soldiers in 1944. Helping to organize and distribute charitable aid has long been an important activity for Canadian social workers.

The Expansion of Social Services and Social Work

Despite the economic expansion of the post-war years, demands on private organizations for relief grew. The few church and private charities could not keep up. Pressure was put on the federal government by these organizations and by the Canadian Welfare Council, which presented the case for a national program of support for those who were unemployed but not eligible for other assistance.

The 1956 *Unemployment Insurance Act* provided federal assistance to the provinces for the so-called unemployed but employable person who did not have access to other income security programs or employment income. A condition of this assistance was that the province could not impose a residency requirement on an applicant.

This federal legislation marked the beginning of modernization of relief administration, which led to the passage of the Canada Assistance Plan in 1966. By offering to share 50 percent of the provincial costs of welfare and social services, the federal government effected key changes in Social Assistance, transforming it into a publicly financed and administered program. This was accompanied by a rapid expansion of social services in child welfare, child care, and other services for people in need.

The period from 1963 to 1973 saw the expansion of income security and social service programs. By the end of this period, Canada had become a welfare state with a public system of health and hospital care and expanded or new income security programs for children, the unemployed, single parents, and persons with disabilities.

Public or publicly financed social services, including child welfare and child care, were also expanded, many of which were extended for the first time to meet the needs of the Indigenous population, including those on reserves. Social workers were required to administer these new programs and deliver the expanded services. The number of persons who identified themselves as social workers in the census rose from 3,495 in 1951 to 30,535 in 1971; most of that increase occurred in the decade following 1961.

Increasing Demand for Social Work Programs

This increased demand for trained social work staff led to increased enrolment in college and university social work programs. The Canadian Association of Schools of Social Work (CASSW) was established in 1967 to oversee professional university-based education programs in Canada. Currently, there are 34 universities and 46 colleges providing social work and social service education. Social workers now earn wages that are comparable to nurses and teachers, with hospitals and child welfare agencies currently employing the largest numbers of social workers.

At its inception, casework was the predominant form of social work practice, but by the mid-twentieth century both group work and community work were added to approaches to social work. Additionally, some universities have recognized social administration and social policy as important areas of practice. By the 1970s, there was a proliferation of approaches that included both diagnostic and functional approaches, as well as the generalist, the problem-solving, and the structural approaches—all testifying to the importance of the field of social work to the Canadian society and economy. (Chapter 3 will explore the characteristics of these approaches in greater detail.)

Regulating the Social Work Profession

Today, each Canadian province and territory has legislation governing the practice of social work. The primary purpose of regulatory legislation is to protect the public through the oversight of social work practice. Provincial/territorial legislation governs who can use the title of social worker, requires a public register of regulated social workers, and outlines a process for investigating complaints. In most Canadian jurisdictions, the social work profession's regulatory body is separate from its advocacy association.

The British Columbia *Social Workers Act* (2008) serves to control the titles "Registered Social Worker" (R.S.W.) and "Social Worker," allowing exemptions for certain situations. The *Act* established the British Columbia College of Social Workers, which maintains a continuing competence program to promote high standards of practice. It also stipulates the requirements for full registration as a social worker, including the successful completion of an exam.

Similarly, in Manitoba, *The Social Work Profession Act* (2009), proclaimed into law in 2014, oversees professional designations to protect the public interest and promote public confidence in the profession of social work. The Manitoba College of Social Workers also recently introduced a continuing competence program, with the first reporting cycle to begin in 2017.

The Ontario College of Social Workers and Social Service Workers protects the interest of the public by regulating social work practice through the *Social Work and Social Service Work Act* (1998). This *Act* also stipulates a mandatory continuing competence program. Hearings of the College's Discipline Committee are posted and open to the public.

The Occasional Evil of Angels
Learning from the experiences of Aboriginal peoples and social work[1]

By Cindy Blackstock

"There is a need to affirm and support traditional ways of helping that have sustained Aboriginal communities for generations"

This paper explores how the propensity of social workers to make a direct and unmitigated connection between good intentions, rational thought, and good outcomes forms a white-noise barrier that substantially interferes with our ability to see negative outcomes resulting directly or indirectly from our works. The paper begins by outlining the harm experienced by Aboriginal children, before exploring how two fundamental philosophies that pervade social service practice impact Aboriginal children: 1) an assumption of pious motivation and effect, and 2) a desire to improve others. Finally, the paper explores why binding reconciliation and child welfare are a necessary first step toward developing social work services that better support Aboriginal children and families.

Social workers have significant impacts on the lives of children and families every day—especially children experiencing maltreatment. The beliefs that we know what good is, are good, and can instill good in others, are so ingrained in the social work fabric that there is little meaningful conversation about our potential to do harm. Even when confronted by graphic evidence of harm arising from social work actions, our historical response has often been to protect ourselves from seeing what we perhaps fear the most—we, the good guys, doing the harm.

This piece begins by reflecting on social work policies and practices with Aboriginal children that have been termed "poor practice" by many, and "cultural genocide" by some (Balfour, 2004), before urging the social work profession to actively engage in a meaningful process of reconciliation with Aboriginal peoples.

What's the Harm?

Herwitz (2003) argues that the first step in reconciliation is to understand the harm by hearing it in a way that cannot be rationalized or abided. This is a fundamental first step for social work. We must learn from our professional past in order to avoid replicating past mistakes with Aboriginal peoples and other groups. Elder Wilma Guss (2004) suggests that those who did the harm do not have the right to define it or define the solutions to redress it. The definition of harm and the solutions to the harm are the first property of those who experienced it. This piece argues that a lack of knowledge and critical reflection on social work's role in colonialism erodes our ability to work effectively with Aboriginal peoples and engage in reconciliation.

Aboriginal peoples have lived on the lands now known as Canada for thousands of years (Muckle, 1999). These diverse and complex societies embrace different linguistic, cultural, political, and spiritual systems reflecting their distinct ecological settings. Despite their diversity, Aboriginal peoples share a common belief in the interdependence of all living, spiritual, and physical forms; a preference for communal rights; and a high regard for knowledge handed down in a sacred trust from one generation to another (Auger, 2001). These beliefs influenced all ways of knowing and being, including systems for caring and educating children and youth (Auger, 2001; Sinclair, Bala, Lilles, and Blackstock, 2004). No society was ever without its challenges, and each community had laws and responses to help children who were receiving inadequate care. These responses included placement of the child with other community members, conflict resolution, and redistribution of community resources to ensure parents could care for their children (Blackstock, 2003). Unlike in today's social work practice, placement outside of the home never resulted in the complete severance of a parent's responsibility for the child. Parental roles were simply redefined so that the parent could safely and properly support their child to the degree they were able (Auger, 2001). To my knowledge, no Aboriginal language in Canada has a word for child removal or apprehension as defined in contemporary child welfare law.

Aboriginal concepts and systems of care sustained generations of Aboriginal children until the British and French arrived on the eastern shores of what is now North America in the late 1400s and early 1500s. At the time, both colonial powers were

Assembly of First Nations National Chief Perry Bellegarde and Cindy Blackstock, First Nations Child and Family Caring Society Executive Director, address the Canadian Human Rights Tribunal ruling regarding discrimination against First Nations children in care. The ruling calls for the redesign of the child welfare system and its funding mode to ensure First Nations are given culturally appropriate services.

The FNCFCS and the AFN filed a complaint against Ottawa with the Canadian Human Rights Commission in February 2007. Cindy Blackstock told reporters the January 2016 ruling was a "complete victory" for children, but questions why the fight was ever necessary.

feudal monarchies interested in expanding their respective empires, with limited compromise or respect for the "savages" who lived on the new lands (Canada, 1996). Although the earliest contact was described as mutually beneficial, as Europeans traded survival information and trade access for goods, it changed when European motivations shifted to settlement and resource extraction. Colonial powers initiated efforts to eradicate the Indians[2] through the intentional introduction of diseases such as smallpox and tuberculosis, removal of Indians from their traditional lands, imposition of restrictions of Indian movements, reckless harvesting of natural resources, and, upon Confederation, the regulation of Indians and lands reserved for Indians through the federal government's *Indian Act* (Canada, 1996).

Deaths from disease, starvation, and willful murder related to colonization resulted in the complete eradication of some Indian communities, such as the Beothuck of Newfoundland, and an overall 80 percent (approx. 400,000) reduction in the Indian population from the time of contact until 1871 (Canada, 1996). This loss of life was most significantly experienced by Aboriginal children who, along with being the most vulnerable to death by disease, also experienced the profound grief associated with losing so many members of their family and community.

This harm was compounded by Canada's introduction of compulsory attendance at residential schools designed to assimilate Indian children and thereby eliminate what senior government officials termed "the Indian problem."[3] These schools, run by Christian churches and funded by the federal government, operated from the time of Confederation until 1996, when the last one closed in Saskatchewan (Department of Indian and Northern Affairs Canada, 2003). The *Indian Act* authorized Indian Agents to remove every Indian child between 5 and 15 years old from their parents' care and place them in often distant residential schools. The schools themselves were poorly constructed, using the cheapest possible material and workmanship, and thus were prolific incubators for the spread of tuberculosis and smallpox. In fact, Duncan Campbell Scott, Superintendent of Indian Affairs for the first three decades of the twentieth century, estimated that up to 50 percent of Indian children died in the schools from disease or maltreatment (Milloy, 1999). The federal government was advised of the problem by Dr. P.H. Bryce, Indian Affairs Medical Officer, as early as 1907, but its efforts to rectify the situation were inadequate and lacked any sustained effort. In fact, the lack of government action motivated Bryce to publish his findings in magazines and newspapers, hoping that the public would become enraged and force the government into positive action. Sadly, despite Bryce's best efforts, the reports were met with silence and had little effect on government policy and practice (Milloy, 1999). This inaction prompted Queens Council S.H. Blake to note that "in that the government fails to obviate the preventable causes of death, it brings itself in unpleasant nearness to manslaughter" (Milloy, 1999: 77).

There was child maltreatment as well. Throughout the history of residential schools, dating back as early as 1896, Indian Agents and others advised the federal government of life-threatening incidents of physical abuse, emotional abuse, neglect, and servitude (Canada, 1996; Milloy, 1999). Even after several deaths due to child maltreatment were reported, the federal government and the churches failed to implement measures necessary to protect Indian children (Milloy, 1999). Residential schools began closing in the mid 1940s, with the last federally-run school finally closing its doors in 1996.

There is very little evidence that the voluntary sector, including human rights groups, did anything significant to disrupt residential schools or the colonial policies of government overall (Blackstock, 2009). Even though children's aid societies had been operating in Ontario since the early 1900s (Sealander, 2003)—and thus logically must have been aware of Bryce's frequent public statements about the preventable deaths of children in the schools—there is no record of a children's aid society ever intervening. Even as reports of abuse and neglect at the schools increased across the country, I know of no records suggesting that children's aid organizations took note of the reports or did anything meaningful to intervene. A joint submission to the Senate and House of Commons in 1946 by the Canadian Association of Social Workers (CASW) and the Canadian Welfare Council (CWC) indicates that social workers were well aware of the residential schools (Special Joint Committee of the Senate and House of Commons, 1946). The CASW and CWC joint submission suggested that Aboriginal peoples should be assimilated into Canadian society, and although shortcomings with the residential schools were acknowledged, the CASW and CWC noted that "[W]e feel they [residential schools] have a place in a well-rounded system of Indian education, particularly insofar as they meet special needs."[4] Even if one argued that the CASW and CWC did not, for some reason, know about the prolific and preventable deaths from tuberculosis and other factors at the time of their testimony, this was clearly outlined in other parts of the report where their own evidence is reproduced, and yet there is no evidence that the CASW or CWC took up any meaningful campaigns to address the problems.

To be fair, the CASW and CWC did successfully advocate with the federal government to ensure that child welfare services were provided to Indian children on reserves.[5] However, this advocacy was not accompanied by a persistent campaign to close the residential schools themselves. In fact, social workers were active participants in the placement of Aboriginal children in residential schools as late as the 1960s (Caldwell, 1967; Canada, 1996).

The professional oversight bodies did not effectively monitor the quality of child welfare services that mainstream social workers began providing on reserves. This lack of invigilation, accompanied by a systemic ignorance of the impacts of colonization, often resulted in the mass removal of Aboriginal children and their placement in non-Aboriginal homes—often permanently (Caldwell, 1967). This pattern of mass removals became known as the "60s scoop." It was not unusual for so many children to be removed that a bus would be hired by child welfare workers to transport them out of the reserve (Union of B.C. Indian Chiefs, 2002).

Upon completing his investigation into the impacts of the 60s scoop practice on Aboriginal communities in Manitoba, Judge Edwin Kimmelman said that these mass removals amounted to "cultural genocide" (Balfour, 2004). Some provinces and territories responded to Kimmelman's concerns by setting temporary moratoriums on the adoption of Aboriginal children by non-Aboriginal parents, but little was done to redress the poverty, social exclusion, and impacts of colonization that had resulted in these children being removed from their families in the first place.

In the early 1980s, the federal government began to respond to First Nations demands to operate their own child welfare programs so they could stem the tide of children leaving the community. These programs, known as First Nations child and family service agencies, operate pursuant to provincial legislation and are funded by the federal government (MacDonald and Ladd, 2000). Although the agencies have made substantial gains in ensuring that services are culturally based and that children are given the best chance to stay in their community, they express concern regarding inequitable funding and the imposition of provincial legislation and standards that have substantially failed Aboriginal children (Blackstock, 2003). A national policy review conducted in 2000 confirmed First Nations concerns that the current funding structure from the federal government does not provide sufficient resources for children to stay safely in their home—although there is no funding cap on resources for children removed from their home (MacDonald and Ladd, 2000). A more recent and detailed analysis found that the funding inequality is in the order of $109 million per annum (Auditor General of Canada, 2008; Loxley et al., 2005). This means that at-home child maltreatment prevention services, which are broadly available to other Canadian children, are not provided to First Nations children on reserve, resulting in an astronomical over-representation of Status Indian[6] children in care (Blackstock, 2009). Child in care data from three provinces indicates that 0.67 percent of non-Aboriginal children were in care as of May 2005, as compared to 10.23 percent of Status Indian children. Overall, Status Indian children were 15 times more likely to be placed in child welfare care than non-Aboriginal children (Blackstock, Prakash, Loxley, and Wien, 2005).

As *Maclean's* magazine (2004) noted, "the numbers of Status Indians taken into care has jumped by 71.5 percent between 1995 and 2001—something experts put down to the general level of poverty and relative underfunding of First Nations child welfare agencies—the situation can only fuel racial inequality and discord. In a verdict shared by adoption advocates across the country, ACC [Adoption Council of Canada] chair Sandra Scarth calls the overall situation 'appalling'" (Ferguson, 2004).

By 2007, the federal government had done little to redress the drastic funding shortfalls, prompting the Assembly of First Nations and the First Nations Child and Family Caring Society of Canada to file a complaint with the Canadian Human Rights Commission, alleging that the federal government's conscious underfunding of child welfare amounted to racial discrimination within the meaning of the *Canadian Human Rights Act*. The federal government did not actively dispute the central claim that child welfare funding is inequitable and yet pursued a plethora of technical objections in an apparent effort to derail or delay the hearing of this important case on its merits (Blackstock, 2009). The case went to trial before the Canadian Human Rights Tribunal in 2013 and concluded in the fall of 2014. The Tribunal released its landmark ruling in January of 2016, substantiating the discrimination complaint and ordering the federal government to cease its discriminatory practices (First Nations Child and Family Caring Society of Canada et al. v. Attorney General of Canada, 2016 CHRT 2). Although this case was broadly covered in the Canadian press and the engagement of social workers is growing, support from non-Aboriginal social work organizations was not proportional to the gravity of the injustice at issue in this case.

Responding to the Harm: The Search for Social Work

One would think that responding to the needs of First Nations children and families would be a national priority for social work—the reality is that it is not. Whilst social work authorities, academics, and professional bodies acknowledge the over-representation of Aboriginal children in care, they typically devote very limited financial resources or sustained effort to redress it. For example, in 2004 a provincial child welfare authority allocated only 20 percent of its family support budget to Aboriginal families, despite the fact that Aboriginal children comprised over 80 percent of all children in care (Flette, 2005). Another province only placed 2.5 percent of Aboriginal children in care with culturally matched homes, despite a statutory obligation to do so (British Columbia Children's Commission, 1998). Additionally, although several non-Aboriginal social work regional and national umbrella organizations identify Aboriginal children as an organizational priority, an examination of programs, budgets, and outcomes rarely reflects any significant or sustained focus that is proportionate to the scope of the problem. From a research perspective, investment in national Aboriginal child welfare research is modest, representing approximately $350,000 in 2004, whereas keeping Status Indian children on-reserve in care cost the federal government over $300 million. By 2009, the reality was even more bleak, with a national investment of approximately $100,000, whilst the child welfare expenditures for First Nations children on-reserve had grown to well over $400 million due to rising rates. There are, of course, promising exceptions where social workers and social work organizations have meaningfully worked with First Nations to redress the over-representation of children in care, but these continue to be the exception. These positive examples need to be recognized and supported—but they should spur us on to further progressive action and not reinforce a professional slumber.

Despite the indications that social work requires a courageous invigilation of its impacts on Aboriginal families, mainstream social work largely considers itself to have taken the steps necessary to insulate itself from its egregious actions of the past. We talk about the residential school and 60s scoop eras as if they were safely packed away. But is this true? Have we as social workers really learned from our past mistakes?

The following sections explore how professional notions of improvement, professional piety, mandates and borders, and distorted knowledge and culturally appropriate services may have contributed to social work's unfortunate history with Aboriginal peoples in Canada. This list is not exhaustive and is meant to inspire broad-based conversation to promote professional learning.

Both Sides of Improvement

The notion of improving other people is endemic to social work. It is a source of both moral nobility and trepidation. It implies an ability to accurately define another's deficit and to locate its importance in his or her life, and assumes the efficacy of external motivations and sensibilities to change. As interventions with Aboriginal children by non-Aboriginal helping professionals testify, there is a delicate balance between the freedom and dignity of individuals and societies at one end and cultural arrogance and oppression on the other.

Research suggests that social workers should avoid drumming up solutions to "Aboriginal issues" by themselves and instead invest in a relationship where the right of Aboriginal peoples to make the best decisions affecting them is affirmed and supported. The wisdom of this approach is documented by Chandler and Lalonde (1998), who found that although First Nations children in British Columbia have one of the highest suicide rates in the world, more than 90 percent of the suicides occurred in 10 percent of the province's First Nations communities. In fact, some First Nations reported a zero percent suicide rate over the 13 years prior to the study. Chandler and Lalonde (1998) wanted to know what differences existed between communities that could account for such a wide variation in suicide rates. Findings indicate that First Nations communities with a low suicide rate or no suicide rate exercised high levels of community-based decision making, as represented by First Nations service delivery in child welfare, health, education, and fire and police services. High levels of female participation in First Nations governments and advancement toward self-government were also factors. The work of Cornell and Kalt (1992) complements Chandler and Lalonde's findings. They found that communities with sustained socio-economic development also had highly developed community decision-making authorities. They argue that effective capacity building must be preceded by affirmation of Aboriginal decision making. This finding challenges the assumption that Aboriginal peoples must build capacity to have decision making capacity passed to them.

As Chandler and Lalonde (1998) observe, many Aboriginal communities have systems in place to prevent youth suicide, and these systems are so effective that their youth suicide rates are substantially lower than in non-Aboriginal communities. What is needed is to ensure that other Aboriginal communities have access to the information and resources needed to implement their own solutions.

This does not mean that non-Aboriginal social service providers get to walk away. As many Elders have said, "We did not get here alone, and we are not leaving alone." It does mean shifting the philosophy of our current social work practice away from one of solution holder and preferred service delivery agent to one where Aboriginal peoples make the best decisions for themselves. Non-Aboriginal peoples must play a critical and active role in making space for those decisions and in ensuring that adequate resources are available to implement them.

As the following section argues, it will also require a critical analysis of other factors influencing the profession, such as the assumption of pious motivation and effect.

Understanding the Occasional Evil of Angels

The assumption of piety in social work blinds us from considering the need for anything along the lines of a Hippocratic Oath. The concept that we can do harm (or even evil) rarely appears on the optical radar screen of professional training, legislation, or practice as anything other than a tangential way through procedural mechanisms such as codes of ethics. This is particularly true for those of us who work with children—believing that those who want to do good and are trained to do good could cause harm to children is astonishing and upsets our sensibility of the world. Talking about it even seems too much, as it breathes life into its possibility so often we are silent.

On the rare occasions when there are discussions of harm in social work, and in helping professions more broadly, they are predominated by inaccurate assumptions that incidents of harm will be obvious, that harm is done by others, that social workers will act out against it, and that when it does occur we will learn from it. We also wrongly assume that incidents are singular rather than systemic and that codes of ethics, professional training and standards, and anti-oppressive social work paradigms can prevent their insurgence and persistence.

When evidence surfaces that harm has arisen directly from the actions or inactions of practitioners of social work or of other helping professions, we often default to rationalizing the occurrence as exceptional, using one of these predominant arguments: 1) they acted based on the sensibilities of the day—we know better now; 2) they did not know about the harm; 3) it was outside of their mandate, and; 4) if the harm is so appalling that it cannot be rationalized as coming from a place of good intentions, they were immoral or bad individuals who are exceptions to the group. We have also developed systemic approaches, such as the emphasis on culturally appropriate services, that, whilst holding great promise for supporting Aboriginal families, have also been misused as a means of limiting critical systemic analysis and professional action. This section deconstructs these rationalizations to try to understand why social workers and others have demonstrated very limited, if any, sustained activism against the multiple harms experienced by Aboriginal children.

- **Sensibilities of the Day**

Some people rationalize the lack of social work efforts to stop residential schools by noting that child abuse has just recently surfaced on the societal radar screen as a problem deserving attention. The argument goes that "we had different standards back then—no one talked about child abuse" and thus it went unnoticed. But as John Milloy (1999) notes, the reports of child abuse at residential schools were made by people of the period who, given the sensibilities of those times, found the treatment of these children unacceptable. And yet, despite having received the reports, government officials typically did little to stop the abuse, and in some cases the death, of children.

Today we have a significant evidence base to suggest that Aboriginal children and young people face pervasive risk in a way not experienced by other Canadians, and yet our professional response has been lukewarm (Blackstock, 2009; Blackstock, Clarke, Cullen, D'Hondt, and Formsma, 2004). We are now the people of the period who should find such disproportionate risk unacceptable—but our professional actions are not, in my view, in keeping with the crisis before us. It is as if we have edged our collective tolerance for the risks experienced by Aboriginal children upwards to a degree where it is difficult to imagine what threshold needs to be reached for the profession to take action in a meaningful way.

- **We Did Not Know**

Another way to rationalize the mediocre response of social work to residential schools is to argue that information on the deaths and abuse was not widely known until recently. As John Milloy (1999) notes, this argument is weak, as there was significant information on the abuse and deaths of children in residential schools, and this information was available to governments, academics, and the media. Nevertheless, the availability of this information failed to inspire progressive action to redress the abuse and murders at residential schools.

The Royal Commission on Aboriginal Peoples (Canada, 1996) found that social workers knew about residential schools and routinely served on admissions committees adjudicating child welfare placements in these schools (ibid.). In addition to serving on placement committees, social workers actually placed substantial numbers of Aboriginal children in residential schools. As the RCAP notes, "residential schools were an available and apparently popular option within the broader child care system" (Canada, 1996, Chapter 10, p.21). According to Caldwell (1967), child welfare placements accounted for over 80 percent of the admissions in six residential schools in Saskatchewan. Caldwell's report outlines a number of shortcomings in the residential school program but even he, a social worker by training, did not recommend the closure of these schools. Caldwell did, however, go further than most other social workers of his time by recommending improvements to the residential school system.

The temptation to believe "if we had only known—we would have acted differently" may provide some false comfort, but in the case of the social work profession, it did know and acted largely in complicit support of the residential school system. The application of the "if we only knew, we could act differently" argument has little merit in today's context as well. Even with multiple sources of information documenting the relationship between structural risks (such as poverty, substance misuse, and poor housing) and child maltreatment (Auditor General of Canada, 2009; Blackstock, 2009; Trocmé, Knoke, & Blackstock, 2004), efforts by social workers and others to prioritize, protest, and redress the harms experienced by Aboriginal children continue to be inadequate and piecemeal.

We continue to confine our assessments of child risk to the family, which fetters our ability to identify risk factors that impact the child but that have their source outside of the sphere of influence of their parents. We have also done little to address the longstanding inequitable child welfare funding provided to First Nations children on reserves (Blackstock, 2009; First Nations Child and Family Caring Society et al. v. Attorney General of Canada, 2016 CHRT 2; Office of the Auditor General of Canada, 2009). In missing these structural risks, we set up a situation where Aboriginal parents are held responsible for things outside of their control, and we deprive Aboriginal families of the same access to services as other Canadians to redress risk to children.

- **We Are Needed**

So if information on its own is not enough to mobilize social workers, is it possible that by entrenching in the idea that social workers are positive agents for social well-being, we have unintentionally built a barrier that rebuffs or rationalizes information suggesting we are perpetrating harm? Take, for example, the assumption that social work is in the best position to respond to child maltreatment and neglect in Aboriginal communities. Increasing evidence suggests that Aboriginal communities, when provided with adequate supports, develop the most sustainable socio-economic improvements for children, and yet as a profession we continue to believe, almost at the exclusion of other options, that we are the best response. This should be a touchstone question for our profession, but it is rarely asked. Instead, we are busy developing programs and services to offer abused and neglected children and families instead of providing communities and families with the resources to implement their own best solutions (Blackstock and Trocmé, 2005).

- **Mandates and Borders**

Another way of rationalizing the harm is to claim it was outside of the mandate of the various helping professions or organizations to intervene. Take the case of Jordan, a First Nations boy from Norway House Cree Nation who was born in 1999 with complex medical needs. His family placed him in child welfare care—not because he was abused or neglected but because that was the only way the provincial and federal governments would provide the money required for Jordan's special needs (Lavallee, 2005). (In a policy that baffles common sense, the federal government will not provide adequate support for special needs children on reserve—unless they are in child welfare care.) Shortly after Jordan's second birthday, doctors agreed to allow him to return home, however, as Noni MacDonald and Amir Attaran (2007) of the Canadian Medical Association Journal note, "bureaucrats ruined it." Jordan was a First Nations boy whose family lived on reserve, and unfortunately, provincial and federal governments do not agree on who is responsible for payment of services for children on reserve. The standard practice by both levels of government has been to defer or deny First Nations children the government services that are routinely available to other Canadian children until the dispute can be resolved, with little consideration for the child's safety or well-being. For Jordan, provincial and federal bureaucrats argued over every item related to his at-home care, while he stayed in hospital at about twice the cost (Lavallee, 2005). Days turned into weeks, weeks turned into months, and Jordan saw the seasons change through his hospital window. All the while, bureaucrats met somewhere, likely feeling good about "doing something about Jordan's situation" while privileging their respective government's desire to not pick up the tab. It seems that they became ethically blind to Jordan's fate, and sadly, Jordan died waiting at five years of age, having never spent a day in a family home.

This sad example shows just how easy it is for something as insignificant as a mandate to overshadow the precious life of a young boy. This astounding story is not unique. A recent study found that in 12 sample First Nations agencies, there were 393 jurisdictional disputes between governments around children's services in the past year alone (Blackstock, Prakash, Loxley, and Wien, 2005). Governments put their needs ahead of children's needs far too often. Jordan's passing prompted the development of Jordan's Principle, which is a child-first principle aimed at resolving government jurisdictional disputes. It is supported by over 9,900 individuals and organizations, including growing numbers of social work organizations and governments, and the Canadian Human Rights Tribunal recently ordered the federal government to immediately cease applying its narrow definition of Jordan's Principle. However, the reality is that no provincial/territorial or federal government in Canada has fully implemented this principle. I continue to receive reports of First Nations children who are being denied life-saving and wellness government services available to other children because of jurisdictional wrangling.

I have often wondered what the provincial and federal officials involved were thinking when they allowed Jordan to languish in hospital. I have decided to believe that they were not evil people, and yet their collective actions had devastating consequences for Jordan. I have no good answers, as every rationale I come up that would help me understand what the bureaucrats were thinking seems so very weak in the face of Jordan's needs.

Mandates are both a necessary act of pragmatism and a cop-out. They are pragmatic because no profession or institution can manage it all, and they are a cop-out because they allow for inaction in the face of gross and demonstrated immorality. Perhaps part of the reason that good people can do such immoral things in the name of mandates is explained by the work of Zygmunt Bauman (1989), who argues that too often, our personal morality is usurped by our need to comply with what is deemed morally good by the institutions we are affiliated with or work with. He argues that there is a reason why whistle blowers are the exception—because they accomplish what is too rare, to break through the institutional moral code calling for company/professional loyalty to act on the basis of their moral conscience. In social work, we talk about social change, but we do not talk as honestly about how our bureaucracies often prefer conformity versus courageous conversation and innovation in child welfare (Blackstock, 2009). Social change is what we do externally—but not as often internally.

The power of mandates and borders can also be more subtly shaped by interfaces between our national, professional, and personal ideologies and assumptions, which locate harm outside of what has already been deemed to be good. This partially explains why Canada, considered a bastion of human rights, was able to sign the Universal Declaration on Human Rights in the same year it was operating residential schools, did not recognize Indians as people under the law, and invited South African apartheid delegates to learn about its Indian pass system without any public protest by human rights organizations or institutions. It also partially explains why the government of British Columbia was able to run a referendum on Aboriginal treaty rights in 2002 while refusing to educate the public on the treaty process. This, the first referendum on minority rights, was held with only moderate intervention by human rights groups and only the modest disapproval of the federal government. As these examples illustrate, too often, non-government organizations (NGOs) and human rights organizations do not think to look within Canada for human rights transgressions; instead they focus abroad. As Aziz Choudry explains, "many social justice campaigns, NGOs, and activists in these countries operate from a state of colonial denial and refuse to make links between human rights abuses overseas, economic injustice, and the colonization of the lands and peoples where they live" (Choudry, 2001).

It is easier to believe that some other society is perpetrating human rights abuses than to believe your own country and society are—because that frames the accountability on a more personal level to either do something or own the responsibility of remaining silent and still. There are few things more courageous than to stand up to people or a government that you respect and care for—especially for an interest outside of oneself. Bryce did it and should be celebrated as one of the great Canadian heroes.

• Evil: A Domain of the Well-Intentioned?

Another rationalization hinges on the propensity to believe that if we as social workers are well-intended in our actions, we are essentially absolved from moral responsibility, regardless of consequences. As Zygmunt Bauman (1989) notes, the idea that evil is obvious and perpetrated only by bad apples serves to absolve us all of being evil and affords a false security that we will know evil when we see it. As a child-protection worker, I have seen evil in its many faces, and it has rarely been obvious or predictable. It is more often grey than black and white. It can be multi-dimensional, rationalized, normative, and carried out by many instead of one. It often has benefits for someone, and those benefits can seductively legitimize the costs experienced by another. As John Milloy (1999) noted, the motivations of staff at the Department of Indian Affairs and those of the churches were not always evil in the way they understood evil to be—they used words like "civilizing," "integrating," and "educating" to describe what they were doing. The Royal Commission on Aboriginal Peoples echoes Milloy's findings, noting that "[P]olitician, civil servant, and perhaps most critically, priest and parson felt that in developing the residential school system, they were responding not only to a constitutional but to a Christian 'obligation to our Indian Brethren' that could be discharged only 'through the medium of children' and therefore 'education must be given its foremost place'" (Canada, Chapter 10, p.3). This created a moral cushion that blinded them to the end result of their actions, which some of their contemporaries, such as P.H. Bryce and S.H. Blake, found repugnant if not criminal.

This moral cushion was strengthened by limited acts that workers carried out to try to redress the harm. These acts were often perfunctory and unmonitored, but served to liberate workers from the moral responsibility to do something. For example, upon hearing reports of child deaths and maltreatment, staffers would often issue edicts that said it was not to happen again, but nothing was done to ensure these edicts were followed up—even in the face of substantial evidence that the abuse was continuing.

These cushions have served to comfort thousands of Canadians, including those active in human rights, the voluntary sector, and academia who either contributed to the harm or stood silent in its wake. Some lived near the residential schools, some read P.H. Bryce's article in the magazine *Saturday Night*, and others saw the graveyards on residential school grounds or the buses collecting children from reserves to be placed in foster homes, and yet, except for some courageous instances, there was silence.

Evil happens in degrees—there are those who beat children to death, those who issued edicts without following up, and those who lived next door and said nothing (Neiman, 2002). Are they all accountable? If so—how, and why? To what standard of courage and compassion should we hold social workers—are we willing to support them when they identify acts that upset our sensibilities, or are we as a society willing to tolerate their silence in the face of atrocities? These are difficult questions that have remained underground in social work and need to be unearthed if we are to deconstruct our professional past in a way that makes obvious the thinking that fuels colonization.

- **Culturally-Appropriate Services: A Step Forward?**

In the absence of the recognition of Aboriginal child welfare laws, a subsidiary movement has developed to deliver "culturally-appropriate" services. This sounds good—it feels like we are moving in the right direction as a profession, but the problem is that few of us really understand what being culturally appropriate means. This is partly because few services are analyzed for their underpinning cultural value in order to determine what program elements are culturally predicated and on what culture. Too often, services are proclaimed culturally neutral, often by those whose cultures are embodied in the service, in the absence of any thorough analysis or search for perspective from other cultural groups. In the absence of this analysis, social workers can wrongly assume that nothing needs to be changed about the fundamental elements of the service—it just needs to be made "culturally appropriate" by adding in Aboriginal symbols or ceremonies. I am open to debate on this issue, but in my own experience, I have yet to see a Euro-Western program of any stature deconstructed from a value perspective by Aboriginal and non-Aboriginal peoples and then reconstructed on an Aboriginal value base.

What we do know is that this movement toward culturally-appropriate services has gained increasing authority. Governments are amending their internal operational guidelines and contract service guidelines to require child welfare service providers ensure that Aboriginal children receive culturally-appropriate services. As a result, large numbers of organizations have begun to redefine their services as culturally appropriate. However, as there is an absence of guidelines and monitoring bodies for culturally-appropriate services, what began as an earnest attempt to better support Aboriginal children has largely degenerated into a movement that gains culturally-ascribed organizations social capital and funder recognition without having to critically evaluate the cultural efficacy and relevance of their programs. I argue that the focus on culturally-appropriate services takes attention away from the real need to affirm Aboriginal ways of knowing and caring for children. After all, the basic assumption underlying culturally- appropriate services is that one can adapt a mainstream model for application to Aboriginal children—without compromising the basic integrity of the service—including the values and beliefs that drive it. As Aboriginal values and beliefs respecting children are very divergent from Euro-Western understanding, marrying the two into a coherent and effective program for Aboriginal children is difficult. This difficulty has been well recorded by Aboriginal child welfare agencies, who describe the problems inherent in delivering child welfare services to Aboriginal children within the realm of Euro-Western legislation. Until there are effective evaluation and monitoring mechanisms developed to measure the efficacy of culturally-appropriate services, we need to be vigilant about the usage of such terms and any conclusions we may draw between said services and the well-being of Aboriginal children.

Reconciliation and Social Work

After former Prime Minister Stephen Harper's apology for the wrongs done by the Government of Canada during the residential school era, reconciliation between Aboriginal and non-Aboriginal Canadians sounds like just the thing social work should be involved in—and it should. But not before it courageously engages in reconciliation itself. This means that social work must look in the professional mirror to see its history from multiple perspectives, including the perspectives of those who experienced the harm. We must look beyond our need to not feel blamed so we can learn and change our behaviour. It sounds trivial to write about the power of blame and shame among social workers, but I have seen its power. I have seen many bright and compassionate non-Aboriginal social workers raise walls of rationalization and distance to insulate themselves from it. As ostensible doers of good, we have not been trained to stand in the shadow of our harmful actions, so we ignore or minimize them. It is a privilege to put up those walls—to be able to insulate yourself from what happened. When Aboriginal people put up the walls, they are left alone to deal with the harm. When social workers put up the walls, they can pretend the pain does not exist at all and go about their daily business. The problem is that putting up the walls does not change the reality—Aboriginal peoples lost in colonization and social work did, too.

Social work misplaced its moral compass and in doing so perpetrated preventable harms to Aboriginal children. It denied itself the opportunity to learn from Aboriginal cultures and make a meaningful contribution to the safety and well-being of Aboriginal children. As social workers, we must understand that our failure to engage in an internal process of reconciliation has immobilized our strength and efficacy.

It is not enough to issue a statement on Aboriginal peoples from time to time or tinker with services if what social workers really want are justice, respect, and equality for Aboriginal children and young people. We must courageously redefine the profession using reconciliation processes and then move outward to expand the movement into society. In 2005, over 200 Aboriginal and non-Aboriginal experts in child welfare came together to develop a process for reconciliation in child welfare and five principles to guide the process, known as *Reconciliation in Child Welfare: Touchstones of Hope for Indigenous Children, Youth, and Families* (Blackstock et. al., 2006). The reconciliation process is described as having four phases (truth telling, acknowledging, restoring, and relating) and five principles to guide the process (self-determination, holistic approach, structural interventions, culture and language, and non-discrimination). The Touchstone principles are constitutional in nature in that they are intended to be interpreted by both Aboriginal peoples and social workers within the context of the unique culture of different Aboriginal groups. To be effective, entire systems of child welfare need to engage in the process and embed the principles in all aspects of the work. To date, a number of First Nations and provincial state child welfare authorities in the U.S. and Canada have begun implementing the Touchstone framework, but social work more broadly has done little to embed the Touchstones process in its own work.

Conclusion

So although there has been some marginal progress, the lived experience of Aboriginal children and youth in Canada continues to be predominated by social exclusion, discrimination, and oppression. The significant body of evidence regarding the disproportionate risk faced by Aboriginal children has been inadequate to motivate social workers and social work organizations to implement the many solutions proposed by Aboriginal peoples. Nor has it promoted substantial internal reflection within social work or other helping professions on what our role has been in perpetrating the harm and our consequential responsibility to understand and reconcile the harm. There is a need to affirm and support the traditional ways of helping that have sustained Aboriginal communities for generations.

I look forward to a time when talking about justice for Aboriginal peoples is no longer an unusual or courageous conversation but is instead one that is encouraged and recognized by all Canadians as being important and necessary to affirm our national values of freedom, democracy, justice, and equality; a time when the conversation of reconciliation is just as likely to be initiated by non-Aboriginal people as by Aboriginal people themselves. This will only occur when we as Canadians share what Michael Walzer (1983) describes as a "collective consciousness." When we can create a common understanding of culture, history, and language through conversation and political action, we can then challenge the inconsistencies in our professional social work values and concepts of justice. This will ensure that democracy, freedom, and equality become the real experience of every Canadian—not just a privileged few standing on one side of a one-way mirror of justice (Blackstock, 2003).

To get there, we must collectively call out the legislation, values, regulations, systems, and actions that perpetuate colonization and its concordant impacts on Aboriginal children and their families, including those harmful and colonial philosophies and practices that are embedded in social work itself. It means understanding the harm from those who experienced it; it means setting aside the instinct to rationalize it or to turn away from it because it is too difficult to hear—or because we feel blamed. It means having conversations about some of the basic values and beliefs that shape our concepts of social work. It means working *with*, versus working *for*, Aboriginal peoples. It means understanding that good intentions and conviction are not enough; it is our actions that are most important. It is about embedding the reconciliation process set out in the Touchstones of Hope document throughout the social work profession.

Most of all, it means not standing still—or moving just a little; it means social work taking the long journey of reconciliation. And as we walk and grow tired of the journey, let the images of children like Jordan flash across our consciousness and urge us firmly forward.

Endnotes

1. This version is based on an original article published by Blackstock, C. (2005). "The occasional evil of angels: Learning from the experiences of Aboriginal peoples with social work. *World Indigenous Nations Higher Education Consortium Journal, Volume 2*. New Zealand.
2. The term "Indian" used in this article to describe Aboriginal peoples who are defined as Indian pursuant to the *Indian Act*.
3. Duncan Campbell Scott, Superintendent of Indian Affairs for the first three decades of the twentieth century.
4. Special Joint Committee of the Senate and the House of Commons to examine and consider the *Indian Act*. Evidence given by the CASW and the CWC (1946). Ottawa, Edmund Cloutier, p.158.
5. Lands set aside by the Crown for the use of Indians pursuant to the *Indian Act*.
6. Refers to a child who is registered or is entitled to be registered pursuant to the *Indian Act*.

The Late Twentieth Century: The Erosion of the Welfare State

In 1980, the Liberal Party of Canada, led by Prime Minister Pierre Trudeau, resumed office during a period of double-digit inflation and a severe economic recession. The social policy field was dominated by efforts to restrain public expenditure (Guest, 1997: 190). In 1984, the Conservatives, led by Brian Mulroney, took office. Their cost-containment measures led to a decline in the living standards of low- and moderate-income Canadians. Following the 1980s, advanced capitalist countries such as Canada systematically began to dismantle the welfare state, as responsibiltiy for the well-being of citizens shifted from the community to individuals and families. Much of the social welfare foundation established in Canada after World War II began to unravel.

Health and social service workers protest against cuts to health care and austerity policies outside the office of Québec Premier Philippe Couillard.

"Starve the Beast"/"Death by Deficit "

The rise of what has been coined "neo-liberalism" characterized this period. Advocates of neo-liberalism supported extensive privatization, fiscal austerity, deregulation, free trade, and reductions in government spending to enhance the role of the private sector in the economy. Overall, the period from around 1980 to the present has been characterized by greater global economic integration, sweeping cutbacks in social services, and increasingly strong, ideological arguments for greater fiscal restraint.

American President Ronald Reagan's slogan of the day was to "starve the beast"—meaning the government—and to provide tax breaks for the wealthy. They would, in turn, reinvest their wealth and grow the economy, or so the argument went. This argument was not lost on Canadian politicians at the time. In Canada, this era was referred to as "death by deficit." The economic downturn of 2008—the fault of corporate greed—served to encourage still further cutbacks in government spending on health, education, and social welfare.

This period saw increasing income inequality, with the rich getting richer and the poor getting poorer. In many nations, especially poorer ones, economic restructuring and cutbacks to social programs have been imposed by international agencies, such as the World Bank and the International Monetary Fund, in the form of so-called "structural adjustments." The Canadian government was not immune to these pressures. It reduced its own income security programs to meet the new economic order and to compete with other nations to be "investor-friendly."

Less Power to the People

Unfortunately, the impact of globalization on Canada's income security programs was felt mainly by the most disadvantaged members of our society—people who are impoverished and homeless. They were also the ones who were least able to fight back. Cutbacks and strict eligibility criteria meant that many people were often left without the bare necessities of life.

And for the middle class, high-paying jobs were moving offshore to corporate tax havens or export processing zones. Welfare cutbacks meant that ordinary working Canadians might not be able to depend on the traditional social protection offered by such programs as Employment Insurance and Old Age Security.

Globalization also meant that national and local governments had less and less freedom to act on behalf of their citizens, especially on the big economic and social questions of the day. The fight to gain and maintain global human rights in the face of economic globalization became, in many respects, the modern epic struggle. And advocacy for equality within and between nations became an integral part of social welfare.

Changes in Social Work Practice

Overall, changes in government policy were reflected in changes of emphasis within the social work profession. During this period of cutbacks and restraint, welfare programs became less universal and more targeted toward specific categories of individuals and families. There was increased emphasis on demonstrating quantifiable, measurable results and on justifying every public dollar spent. Scientific management techniques and tighter control of public funding imposed new ways of thinking onto the health professions, including social work, where the client's needs were no longer necessarily at the top of the list. To be sure, some of the efficiency measures were for the better, but the severity of the cutbacks was detrimental to those most in need and resulted in increased pressure on already-overburdened social workers.

Major Influences and Shifts in the Profession

Meanwhile, the aging of the baby boom generation (people born between 1945 and 1965) caused social work to expand and enhance services for older adults. These included services to prevent elder abuse; interventions for people with dementia; palliative care; and services that promote independence for seniors. Trauma treatment expanded from care for military personnel returning from war to care for clients experiencing severe traumatic events that left them feeling depressed and anxious. Post Traumatic Stress Disorder (PTSD) became an increasingly common diagnosis. And finally, new waves of refugees arriving from war zones, such as Syria, presented new challenges and new opportunities for social workers.

New technologies such as desktop computers and the Internet were integrated into social work practice in the 1990s, and the impact of technology intensified in the 2000s. Online education and counselling, Telehealth, and practice-based databases increasingly affected how social work was organized and carried out.

As another noticeable shift in practice, social workers became increasingly involved in bullying prevention programs throughout Canada. A highly significant turning point in this area took place in the mid-1970s with the work of Dan Olweus. The 1999 Columbine High School shooting in Colorado, the high-profile suicides of young persons who had been bullied, and increasing reports of cyberbullying caused schools to take notice of this serious issue. Government legislation followed, with the *Bullying Act* of 2012 in Ontario and Bill 56 in Québec.

Anti-oppressive practice became more prevalent in schools of social work. It was well understood that some groups in society were excluded from social resources and had fewer choices than other groups. Women, Indigenous people, youth, older adults, racialized Canadians, people with disabilities, and members of the LGBTQ+ community all possessed a less powerful voice in Canadian society compared to white, male, middle-aged, able-bodied heterosexual individuals. Anti-oppressive practice emphasized social justice, social change, and empowerment through analysis and advocacy at both the macro and micro levels of oppression.

Similarly, social work interventions increasingly focused on risk assessments and structured treatment protocols, which were accompanied by the emergence of practice-focused micro-level theories such as systems theory, narrative therapy, and crisis intervention models. More recently, new theoretical practice models such as mindfulness-based interventions and evidence-based practice have emerged. Other trends that affected social work included a greater focus on the field of children's mental health, treatment for gambling, Internet-based social work education, and treatment of substance use disorders .

The Twenty-First Century—What Lies Ahead?

In February 2006, Stephen Harper became the twenty-second prime minister of Canada, and the first prime minister representing the "modern" Conservative Party of Canada, which was formed when the Progressive Conservative Party and the Canadian Alliance (the origins of which were in the Reform Party of Canada) joined forces. In 2008, a major economic recession occurred. This global financial crisis has had serious and costly repercussions to this day. What followed was a drastic continuation of the systematic dismantling of social programs. This leaner, meaner approach to social policy changed Canada for the worse, claimed former Saskatchewan premier Roy Romanow, and chipped away at programs that had helped define the compassionate and caring Canada that had evolved over several generations.

Romanow, who had headed a royal commission on health care in 2002, predicted that the cuts the Harper Conservative government made would result in a more inequitable nation. Federal health-care spending was reined in, the age of eligibility for Old Age Security was increased by two years, Employment Insurance eligibility criteria were tightened, Indigenous and environmental organizations received less support, and advocacy groups for child care, women's health, and support for immigrants were all adversely affected. NDP Leader Thomas Mulcair stated that, "Families are getting hit three times at once: they're getting fewer services, a bigger share of the tax bill, and declining incomes." In short, Mulcair stated "we're becoming the first generation in our country's history to leave our children and grandchildren with a lower quality of life than we inherited from our parents."

In 2015, one in seven people in Canada lived in poverty; 250,000 people were homeless and emergency shelters were at maximum capacity; socio-economic disparities accounted for 20 percent of total annual health-care spending; food bank usage had Increased by 25 percent since the 2008–2009 economic recession; there were only enough child-care spaces for 20 percent of young children; and precarious employment (insecure, unpredictable, low wage, and few benefits) had increased by nearly 50 percent over the last 20 years. And yet, there was still no national poverty plan.

Growing the Middle Class

In 2015, Justin Trudeau (the eldest son of former prime minister Pierre Trudeau) led the Liberal Party of Canada to a majority government on a platform dedicated to "growing the middle class." The 2016 federal budget defined a new vision for Canada's economy: "Canada as a centre of global innovation." It proposed creating jobs through infrastructure planning, investing in public transit and green infrastructure, and sustaining healthy communities through new clean water and waste-water infrastructure.

The budget expanded affordable housing, housing for seniors, and shelter for victims of violence, as well as projects such as the Housing First Initiatives that help homeless Canadians secure stable housing. In addition, $500 million was dedicated to supporting a National Framework on Early Learning and Child Care, of which 20 percent was allocated for Indigenous child care on reserves. Investment in Indigenous Community Infrastructure was a clearly announced priority in the 2016 budget, with a historically high investment of $3.5 billion over five years for green and social infrastructure. The budget appeared to respond to the underlying social determinants of health. Only time will tell whether increasing the deficit will work, and whether these priorities will decrease social and health inequities among Canadians.

The Environmental Justice Movement

Embraced primarily by African Americans, Latinos, Asians, Pacific Islanders, and Indigenous peoples, the environmental justice movement protests the fact that people who live, work, and play in the world's most polluted and damaged environments are most often people of colour and the poor.

Struggles for environmental justice include conflicts over deforestation to allow expansion of the agricultural frontier throughout the Amazon region; mining activities; oil and gas extraction; infrastructure (roads, mega-dams); and pollution by pesticides.

Emerging Social Movements: Finding Allies

Social workers have an ethical responsibility to advocate for social justice, and many social workers focus on influencing public policy, participating in political action, and organizing group activism. In the first decades of the twenty-first century, many traditionally oppressed groups, whose members are politically astute and adept at using social media, have found a distinct voice and are mobilizing for social change.

These modern social movements focus on global and environmental issues, and they collaborate with grassroots organizations to respond to the oppressive political, economic, and social contexts of our daily lives. Rather than simply building coalitions across single issues or lowest-common-denominator politics, these movements are effecting a deepening of interconnected and intersectional analysis that draws strength from each movement and that represents more than the sum of its parts.

Idle No More

The Idle No More (INM) movement was initially a series of teach-ins to protest parliamentary bills in Saskatchewan that threatened to erode Indigenous sovereignty environmental protection. The movement quickly became one of the largest Indigenous mass movements in Canadian history—sparking hundreds of rallies and protests across the country. The INM's vision is to build sovereignty and a resurgence of nationhood, to pressure government and industry to protect the environment, and to build allies in order to reframe the nation-to-nation relationship by highlighting grassroots perspectives, issues, and concerns.

Anti-G20 Mobilization

Anti-G20 mobilization in Toronto in 2010 marked a resurgence in coordinated movement organization. The logistics involving the coordination of billets and food and creating infrastructure, including legal support, communications, and medics, was a victory in itself. This mobilization linked global anti-capitalist movements in an era of austerity with local community resistance. It brought multiple vulnerable groups together (people of colour, trans folks, racialized and immigrant people, and Indigenous peoples) to form a grassroots anti-colonial migrant justice group protesting against the indignity of poverty, a lack of inclusive services, repressive immigration policies, and environmental degradation.

"Leave coal in the hole, leave oil in the soil, leave tar sands in the land"

Environmental justice movements are on the upswing in Canada. Many Canadians and Indigenous communities are proclaiming themselves to be ardent environmentalists. Active resistance against the Alberta Tar Sands and the Enbridge Pipeline is ongoing in British Columbia. Localized movements have protested corporate development and environmental degradation. For example, Mohawks in Kanesatake, Québec, rejected a niobium mine; the Okanagan Indian Band in British Columbia staged a blockade against Tolko Industries logging in their watershed; fishers in Prince Edward Island filed a lawsuit against British Petroleum for the Deepwater Horizon oil spill that interfered with the northern migration of tuna; the Halalt First Nation blockaded the Chemainus River to protect their aquifers; environmentalists repeatedly opposed the Raven Underground Coal Project in the Comox Valley of British Columbia; Innu communities erected a blockade against New Millennium Capital and Labrador Iron Mines Holdings; and highway developments from Gateway in British Columiba to the Humbolt Highway in Saskatchewan have met with organized resistance.

Future Challenges for the Social Work Profession

Today there is an unprecedented demand for the skills and knowledge of social workers. And a number of factors are contributing to the challenges social workers and other caring professions will face over the coming years.

- **Information technology.** Technology is good, for it enhances our ability to act, but social work is also a hands-on, caring profession where personal interaction is important. Computerized, matter-of-fact solutions to difficult individual problems, in the absence of a caring social worker, can make a bad situation even worse. Moreover, workers will need to be aware of the implications of this technology for client needs as well as client privacy.
- **Income inequality.** Social inequality is on the rise. Upward social mobility for young people in particular is more difficult nowadays. This is causing stress for those in the middle and at the bottom, for many of those new to Canadian society, and for those who need social support services the most.
- **Demographic changes.** Population changes and service demands are rapidly shifting. The population is growing older; common-law and lone-parent families are increasing, as is the proportion of children living in poverty; and immigration is creating cultural shifts.
- **Economic globalization.** Social workers and social activists will increasingly confront the seemingly relentless integration of our world at the global level—economically, politically, and socially. This trend means that national and local governments will enjoy less freedom to act on behalf of their citizens, especially on the big economic and social questions of the day. Thus, local communities and individuals will need to discover new pathways to power.
- **Immigration and multiculturalism.** Canada is one of the most multicultural nations in the world. As Canada continues to welcome people to this country, the difficulties and the excitement associated with new families integrating into Canadian society will continue to dominate the field, changing Canadian society as this process unfolds.

Future Challenges for Social Work Practice

It seems likely that social workers, like many professionals, will continue to be expected to do more with less. Likely, they will face greater caseloads and work-related demands. As members of the baby boom generation of social workers retire, future generations will continue to build an understanding of ethical and meaningful practice in the middle of the twenty-first century. This practice will, we hope, differ from the scientific, risk-averse, and accountability-driven social work typical of the late twentieth century. Ideally, government organizations will become more collaborative and Integrated, rather than "stove-piped" (arranged in vertical hierarchies), as was typical of the late twentieth century. Aspects of a newer, more contemporary, and more caring and inclusive practice would include the following:

- **Relationship building.** The focus on accountable and technocratic practice has relegated the relationship-building practices of early social workers to the background. However, as vulnerable people have been oppressed and disenfranchised, their anger, frustration, and powerlessness are often directed at the social workers attempting to engage with and support them. Social workers will need more advanced relationship-building skills to offset the distrust, cynicism, and powerlessness that people we work with may have experienced.
- **Collaborative practice.** Working "with" individuals, families, and communities is increasingly important as social workers recognize their privilege of social location compared to vulnerable people. Listening to, attending to, and empowering clients cannot be practised from a "power over" others stance.
- **Interdisciplinary practice.** Interdisciplinary teams that pool resources (social workers, psychiatrists, substance use counsellors, family-care workers, and so on) can enhance social work practice. Nevertheless, social workers and others will need to be attentive to the potential dangers, perhaps inherent in large-scale practice settings, of a lack of attention to the often specific and complex needs of individuals and families.
- **Evidence-based practice.** There will be pressure for social workers to show measurable results in relation to the interventions they use with their clients. They will need to keep in mind, as will their superiors, that resolving intractable personal and family problems usually takes time and patience and often requires various attempts and creative approaches.
- **Community-based practice.** Indigenous communities are increasingly taking responsibility for a range of social, health, and economic programs within their communities. Policy, programs, and practice can then be adapted to the unique needs and capacities of those communities. Social workers can learn from examples of Indigenous knowledge in action, and mutual learning can replace the imposition of Western world views.
- **Mobility.** Information technologies make geographic boundaries meaningless. International social work, national disaster relief, and critical incidence support (for example, after a school shooting or teen suicides) mean social workers may work outside the province in which they are regulated. To ensure ethical practice, however, regulators must continue to explore cross-jurisdictional and international mobility in relation to regulation.

Despite these challenges, it is an exciting time to begin a career in social work. As our country's 150th anniversary approaches, a new socio-political context is taking shape in Canada. More jobs are predicted, as are more possibilities to provide leadership through change at the macro level. Social workers have been influential in advocating for equality and social justice and in caring for vulnerable and marginalized people for more than a century. They will continue to adapt to and thrive in the new environments in which they find themselves.

National and International Associations
Regulating our profession

Ensuring the highest standards of practice within Canada and internationally

The profession of social work in Canada is regulated by ten provincial associations and one territorial organization, each with its own name, policy, and regulations. Each association is mandated by provincial legislation to regulate and monitor professional social workers and social work practice in their jurisdiction.

Each province has established regulatory bodies (sometimes referred to as Colleges) to govern the profession in accordance with the legislation. Social workers become registered or licensed by becoming members of the regulatory body in the province or territory where they work.

The associations come together under the umbrella of the Canadian Association of Social Workers (CASW), which provides national leadership in strengthening and advancing the social work profession. The education of social workers is monitored by the national Canadian Association for Social Work Education (CASWE).

The Canadian Association of Social Workers (CASW)

The Canadian Association of Social Workers was founded in 1926 after close to 60 social worker representatives from Winnipeg, Toronto, Ottawa, Halifax, and Montréal met and agreed to form a Canadian association. On September 1 of that year, the constitution for the Canadian Association of Social Workers was approved.

At first, social workers joined individually; there were 197 initial members. Today, the CASW is a federated organization with member organizations across the country. The first edition of its professional journal, *The Social Worker*, appeared in 1932. A simple code of ethics was adopted in 1938 and a significantly revised code was adopted in 1956 (revised or amended in 1963, 1983, 1994, and 2005). The 2005 Code of Ethics is included in an Appendix to this book.

The CASW has jurisdiction over some issues, while the provincial and territorial associations maintain jurisdiction over others. Because social services are primarily a provincial or territorial responsibility in Canada, the provincial associations assume great importance in the development, administration, and day-to-day advocacy of social work. The CASW also assesses foreign social work credentials to evaluate equivalency with Canadian standards; Québec and British Columbia have separate provincial evaluations.

Data on the membership of the CASW is an indication of the rapid growth of the profession: in 1939, CASW had 600 members; by 1966, it had 3,000; and by 1986, there were 9,000 members. Today, there are about 16,000 CASW members across the country, all with some formal credentials in social work.

CASW supplies members with relevant professional documents, a national journal, activities and events, access to benefits, representation nationally and internationally, and an opportunity to participate in professional development panels and organizations.

CASW also influences governments through consultations, position statements, and the presentation of briefs. The main benefit of belonging to the CASW is being part of a group of like-minded people who share the same goals and work together to improve their profession.

The Canadian Association for Social Work Education (CASWE)

The Canadian Association of Schools of Social Work (CASSW) was established in 1967, replacing the National Committee of Schools of Social Work, which, since 1948, had been the forum for professional education in social work.

Since 2008, CASSW has been called the Canadian Association for Social Work Education (CASWE). CASWE is a national association of university faculties, schools, and departments offering social work education at the undergraduate, graduate, and post-graduate levels. There is no association representing college-level social service work education.

The purpose of the CASWE is to advance the standards, effectiveness, and relevance of social work education and scholarship. CASWE is responsible for reviewing and approving social work education programs. It also publishes a quarterly journal, the *Canadian Social Work Review,* and undertakes research relevant to the profession.

The International Federation of Social Workers (IFSW) and the International Association of Schools of Social Work (IASSW)

The International Federation of Social Workers is a successor to the International Permanent Secretariat of Social Workers, founded in Paris in 1928. In 1950, the IFSW was created, with the goal of becoming an international organization of professional social workers. The IFSW represents over half a million social workers in 55 countries. The IFSW promotes social work as a profession, links social workers around the world, and promotes social policy and planning at the national and international levels.

The International Association of Schools of Social Work is an association of educators and institutions involved in social work education worldwide. The IASSW adheres to all UN Declarations and Conventions on human rights, while recognizing that respect for the inalienable rights of the individual is the foundation of freedom, justice, and peace.

The 1933 graduating class of the Montréal School of Social Work.

Louise Carignan

Louise Carignan, Ph.D., is the director of the Social Work Education Unit at the University of Québec in Chicoutimi. She is also an associate professor at the school.

During my years of social work practice, I worked primarily with children and adolescents, as well as with their parents, their immediate and extended families, and their social networks, both one-on-one and in small groups. Currently, I teach courses in methods of individual intervention and preparatory intervention courses for student field placements. I also run seminars for students during their placements to facilitate the integration of theory and practice. From time to time, I offer preliminary and advanced training for supervisors in the field to help them prepare for student placements. From 2008 to 2011, I was responsible for the coordination of the field program, as well as all activities surrounding field work, including the development of educational tools to support supervisors and students.

Having worked with children, youth, and families in schools and in child protection for more than 15 years, my main research interests concern the social and individual adaptation of children and youth, the parent–child attachment, families in social distress, social exclusion, and the trajectory of youth marginalization through the child welfare system. During my doctoral studies, I completed a research project involving both quantitative and qualitative methods with youth who were placed in care until they reached adulthood. Since then, I have included both types of research methods in my training of masters' degree students at our university and in my own research.

Currently I am the principal investigator on a joint France–Québec research project. Five social work training institutes in the region of Paris are measuring the impact of the new public management and core competency practice requirements on professional social workers. This research aims to analyze the impact of social work reforms and the introduction of core competencies and practice behaviours on the professionalization of social workers in three generational groups (under 30 years old, 31 to 50 years old, and over 50 years old) to determine whether there is a difference in the practice of social workers trained before or after the introduction of core competencies and to analyze whether the new public management approach changes professional practices.

I am also interested in the emergence of new social work practices based on evidence and on community initiatives. For example, in partnership with several community organizations, I am working on a research project to develop alternative means of prescribing medication for people with a diagnosis of attention deficit hyperactivity disorder (ADHD) in the Saguenay–Lac-St-Jean region. This collaborative research aims to better understand the problem of ADHD; to draw a picture of the current situation in the Saguenay–Lac-Saint-Jean region; to improve knowledge of the overall vision, best practices, and alternative means to the use of medication; and to document the most appropriate alternative to addressing the multiple challenges of ADD/ADHD.

In addition, I work with the Addiction Rehabilitation Centre (Centre de réadaptation en dépendance) in Jonquière, Québec to evaluate the effectiveness of the opioid substitution program. The project focuses on an evaluation of the current program, designed to reduce the consumption of opioids by using methadone. Our research aims to analyze the effectiveness of the services offered to meet the needs of service users; to examine the short-term and long-term impacts of the program, along with their sustainability and relevance with respect to the initial goals of the program; to highlight the strengths and weaknesses of the impact of the intervention methods; and, finally, to compare the program with other programs worldwide and to offer recommendations that will help improve program effectiveness.

I have been involved with the Canadian Association for Social Work Education since 2004, first as executive director for three years, during which time I had the pleasure of managing the main activities of the association, including three annual conferences on various topics affecting the advancement of social work in Canada. Since 2011, I have been an evaluator and the francophone vice-president of the Commission for Accreditation, which oversees the accreditation of bachelor's and master's degree programs in social work for the Canadian Association for Social Work Education (CASWE), representing the 42 schools of social work in Canada.

Chapter 2 Review

Review Questions

1. Identify some key themes that differentiate the era of moral reform from the era of social reform.
2. How did the purpose of Charity Organisation Societies differ from that of settlement houses?
3. Compare and contrast the concepts of public welfare and poor relief.
4. Explain how the concepts of a social minimum and scientific philanthropy contributed to the birth of social work as a profession.
5. What were the aims of the Social Gospel movement at the beginning of the twentieth century?
6. How did the Great Depression leave an indelible mark on the development of the social work profession?
7. Using a simple timeline, identify some key events in the progression of social work in Québec from domination by the Catholic church to secular bureaucratization.
8. Identify some factors underlying the expansion of social services and social work in the mid-twentieth century.
9. What major shifts in social work practice occurred in the late twentieth century, and why?
10. Identify several future challenges for social work practice and for the social work profession.

Exploring Social Work

1. Cindy Blackstock wrote: "To what standard of courage and compassion should we hold social workers—are we willing to support them when they identify acts that upset our sensibilities, or are we as a society willing to tolerate their silence in the face of atrocities? These are difficult questions that have remained underground in social work and need to be unearthed if we are to deconstruct our professional past in a way that makes obvious the thinking that fuels colonization." Write a brief personal response to this stance that reflects the main ideas in Cindy Blackstock's article, included in this chapter.
2. Propose ways in which the social work profession might incorporate the Touchstones of Hope principles.
3. Make some predictions as to future directions of social work in Canada, and justify your thinking.

Websites

Canadian Association of Social Workers (CASW)
www.casw-acts.ca
Founded in 1926 to monitor employment conditions and to establish standards of practice within the profession, CASW has evolved into a national voice. The CASW Board of Directors determines and oversees general and financial policies. With each provincial/territorial partner organization appointing one member to the Board, a unified voice for the Canadian social work profession is assured. The Board of Directors works from a national and an international perspective to benefit the social work profession.

Canadian Association for Social Work Education – l'Association canadienne pour la formation en travail social (CASWE-ACFTS)
www.caswe-acfts.ca
CASWE-ACFTS is a national charitable association of university faculties, schools, departments, and modules offering social work education in Canada. The Association's primary mandate is to support the promotion of excellence in social work education, scholarship, and practice through research, a journal, an annual conference, and the accreditation of B.S.W. and M.S.W. social work programs.

International Federation of Social Workers (IFSW)
www.ifsw.org
The IFSW is a non-governmental organization of national associations of social workers. It thus acts as a global voice for the social work profession. Its 100-plus member countries strive for social justice, human rights, and social development. The Federation partners with organizations and agencies such as WHO and UNICEF to promote social work, best practice models, and the facilitation of international cooperation. This website provides resources such as international social work policies and resolutions, as well as information on the Federation's current campaigns, e.g., World Social Work Day.

Social Work Theories and Practice Models

"An ounce of practice is generally worth more than a ton of theory."
E.F. Schumacher, author of *Small Is Beautiful* (1973)

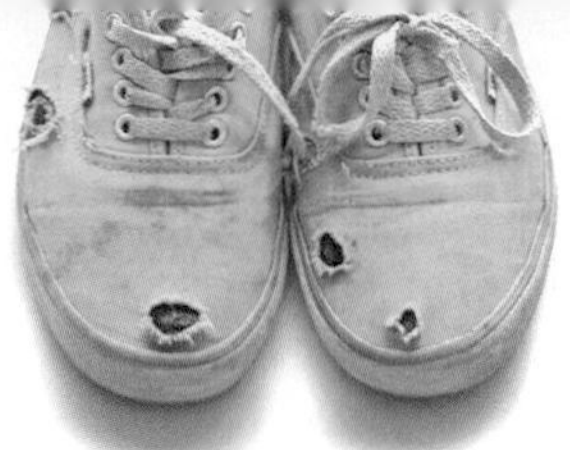

Daniel W.L. Lai

Conventional and Progressive Approaches

3

Personal problems are often social problems with underlying causes.

Social work is a multi-faceted, unique, and specialized profession. The scope of practice is wide, and although many of the theories encompass elements of psychology, sociology, community development, and socio-political change, social work theories understand individual and social problems from a multifactorial perspective. Social workers have a particular interest in the needs and empowerment of people who are vulnerable, oppressed, and/or living in poverty. Standardized best practices are readily available, yet new ideas and new techniques continually emerge in the search for effective interventions that help the welfare and self-realization of individuals, families, communities, and society. Indeed, it is this potential for innovation that makes social work so exciting for those fortunate enough to be involved in it.

A solid grasp of social work theory is important for effective practice—the more ideas brought to bear on a particular situation, and the smarter they are, the better the likely outcomes for the client. Coming to grips with theory can be a challenge for beginning students, however. This chapter provides a broad survey of some of the main theories and practice models in social work. When trying to make sense of theory in social work, it may be helpful to keep in mind that most front-line, direct-service practitioners are "generalists"—that is, they are professionals who can draw from the various theoretical strands and apply them to meet the client's unique needs as the situation demands. Social workers with advanced qualifications and training (at the master's and Ph.D. levels, for example) may specialize in one area of practice or another.

In this chapter, you will learn how to...

- define what is meant by "theory" in social work
- understand the dynamic interaction between social work theory and social work practice
- situate and make sense of various theoretical perspectives in social work
- distinguish between various classical practice models used in social work
- understand some of the more recent and innovative practice models
- analyze some creative and exciting practice tools (e.g., creative arts therapy, play therapy) being used by practitioners in the field of social work today

Key Concepts

- Foundational theories/perspectives
- Practice theories/models
- Ecological theory
- Cognitive theory
- Systems theory
- Structural theory
- Critical theory
- Anti-oppressive theory
- Generalist social work practice
- Empowerment
- Cognitive behavioural therapy (CBT)
- Mindfulness
- Mindfulness-based stress reduction (MBSR)
- Solutions-focused practice model
- Narrative therapy
- Creative arts therapy
- Digital storytelling
- Play therapy
- Photovoice

Focusing Question

"Theory feeds practice, and practice feeds theory." How does this aphorism apply specifically to social work?

Social Work Theory and Social Work Practice

A social work theory, like any other theory, is a set of ideas that attempts to explain and make predictions about a particular issue or phenomenon. A theory tries to capture the essence of a phenomenon or problem. For example, Abraham Maslow's theory of the "hierarchy of needs" asserts that we have certain basic needs to fulfill: "physiological," "safety," "belongingness," "love," "esteem," "self-actualization," and "self-transcendence." Maslow asserted that these needs progress from the basic necessities of survival through a hierarcy toward spiritual requirements for life satisfaction and self-realization. From this theoretical understanding, certain practical interventions can follow, and outcomes can be tested in real life.

In Western social work, it is helpful to distinguish between two broad categories of theory:

- **Foundational theories/perspectives.** These theories comprise general explanations about the underlying makeup and workings of our society. They can focus on personality and behaviour, people in society, or social, political, and economic relationships. They draw from foundational disciplines such as psychology, sociology, economics, political science, and the allied health professions. Examples include ecological theory, cognitive theory, systems theory, structural theory, and critical theory (discussed later in this chapter).
- **Practice theories/models.** These models are built on foundational theories, but they are specific to how social work is practised in real-world contexts. While they are based on foundational theories (e.g., human development theory), practice theories or models focus on factors that are important for practitioners in assessing a client's situation and working with a client to determine the most effective intervention. Examples include client-centred models, task-centred models, strengths-based models, cognitive behaviourial therapy, mindfulness, and narrative therapy—all of which are explained later in this chapter.

Social work theory focuses on explaining, understanding, and predicting human behaviour in different socio-economic and cultural contexts and on identifying patterns to guide interventions. Some theories are foundational, and some are more specific to social work practice.

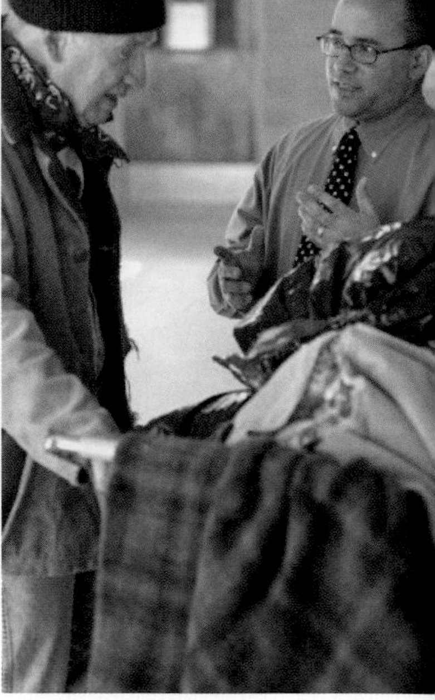

Individual-Level and Structural-Level Theories

Social work theories are sometimes classified into two broad groupings:

- Individual-level theories focus on individuals and their interactions with others.
- Structural-level theories emphasize social structures, processes, and systems and how they shape people's experiences, both positively and negatively.

The Integration of Theory and Practice

Social work is an applied professional field. Its theories inform action (practice), provide a framework for the main tasks of social work (assessment, planning, intervention, and follow-up), and help identify gaps in knowledge about practice (Gentle-Genitty et al., 2014).

The reverse is also true. Theoretical knowledge is developed and enhanced through hands-on practice—that is, through social work research, interaction, and dialogue (Fook and Victoria, 2000; Parton, 2000). Just as in the natural sciences, research (comparable to practice) is used to test hypotheses that in turn lead practitioners to deeper theoretical insights and higher levels of knowledge. Indeed, it has been suggested that social work is distinguished from other applied fields precisely because of this close relationship between theory and practice (Parton, 2000). Evidence-based practice is explored further in Chapter 4.

Social work theory can also legitimize voices and ways of knowing that traditionally may have been been minimized, ignored, or excluded (Fook and Victoria, 2000; Parton, 2000). Innovative theorizing can bring to the forefront issues not normally addressed, or not adequately addressed, by more customary approaches. This, in turn, can result in more effective practice outcomes for clients.

Theoretical Knowledge, Professional Judgement, and Creativity in Social Work

A social worker's day-to-day interventions with clients will always be influenced, to some extent, by his or her theoretical preferences (that is, by his or her most valued underlying philosophy or perspective). Social work professor Ben Carniol at Ryerson University suggests that this relationship can best be understood if we categorize theoretical perspectives in terms of broad clusters or groupings. These perspectives range from "conventional" (e.g., ecological, cognitive, and systems approaches to social work) to "progressive" (e.g., structural, critical, and anti-oppressive approaches). Table 3.1 summarizes this way of categorizing the different perspectives and approaches. Keep in mind that this general categorization is not exhaustive or all-inclusive, but rather represents one useful means of organizing and understanding some predominant social work theories.

It would likely take an entire course to teach students the nature of any particular theory in all its complexity—for example, an ecological (conventional) or an anti-oppressive (progressive) approach. However, while commonalities may exist between certain theoretical perspectives, social work practice recognizes that no one solution fits all client situations. Each client and situation are unique. Social workers need to be "generalists"—they need to learn about and understand a wide array of theories and practice models. Over time, they combine their knowledge with professional judgement and creativity.

For a generalist social worker, it is the problem at hand that determines the approach, not the other way around. A practitioner might use an individual-level approach when counselling a child who has been sexually abused or when working one-on-one with an individual with a substance use disorder. On a different occasion, in a different context, the same social worker might use a structural-level approach to help a family access child services or to advocate to improve public funding for mental health services. An ecological (or systems) approach will likely not bring about the desired outcome if an anti-oppressive intervention is called for. Likewise, a structural solution will not prove effective if a one-on-one intervention is called for.

Table 3.1
Selected Foundational Theories/Perspectives in Social Work

Conventional Approaches	Progressive Approaches
Ecological	Structural
Cognitive	Critical
Systems	Anti-oppressive

Ecological, Cognitive, and Systems Perspectives

When trying to make sense of the major theoretical perspectives in social work, it is helpful to refer to Table 3.1. This table represents one possible way to organize selected theories in social work into coherent, comprehensible categories. The categories are elaborated more fully later in this chapter in a comprehensive chart entitled "Perpectives on Social Work Practice: A Teaching/Practice Overview."

Ecological Theory in Social Work

Ecological theory places the individual within a series of interdependent relationships. This theory is based on the concept of an ecosystem in nature in which every organism is affected by and influences other organisms within the system.

Ecological theory is a reaction to approaches that locate the cause of problems solely within the individual (as in certain branches of psychology) or solely within the structures of the wider society (as in certain branches of sociology). While the idea of the individual existing within a series of systems has a long history, in the 1980s social work professors Carel Germain and Alex Gitterman used ideas from ecology and biology to develop the "life model" of social work. This approach is considered a conventional one in social work, as Ben Carniol (2010) has noted, and it still tends to guide much of social work practice today.

According to ecological theory, individuals exist in particular social environments, and problems arise when there is a lack of "fit" between people and their environments. People interact in complex relationships and at different levels, such that problems at one level can create difficulties at another level. For example, if an adolescent is having trouble in school, this situation may cause conflict to emerge within the family. This conflict might lead the family to turn for help to a social agency offering services for youth, which can then support the teen in making positive changes in academic performance and relationships at school. Using an ecological approach, social workers examine what might be causing problems in different areas of a person's life, and then work clossely with the client to craft solutions to these problems at different levels.

The ecological approach draws upon knowledge of human behaviour as well as knowledge of the influence of social environments on behaviour. When assessing a situation with a client, the social worker maps out the context and decides which component of the situation to focus on first. The goal is to understand how people and their environments mutually influence each other in shaping responses at both individual and social levels. Social workers who rely on this perspective also incorporate aspects of humanist philosophy into their practice, as their work typically involves a strong element of empathy and reflection.

The ecological approach has obvious strong points. Clearly, individuals do not exist on an isolated island, so some level of systems-based analysis is required to make sense of any situation. However, the approach will be limited in situations in which , for example, systemic factors also play a prominent role—for example, prejudice and discrimination based on gender, race, or ability. Ignoring the effects of systemic factors when they are present can limit a social worker's ability to intervene on behalf of a client or group of clients.

Using an ecological approach, the practitioner and the client can begin to separate the various and intricate relationships and components in a client's life that are causing problems and then address them individually or all together.

The Components of the Ecological Perspective

The ecological perspective is widely accepted within social work. It provides a relatively straightforward way to identify and understand the complexities of personal and social networks.

- In this model, the emphasis is on the interrelationships between individuals and their immediate environments.
- The ecological metaphor can be expressed in an ecomap that attempts to depict all the elements of a client's situation.
- The ecomap shows the patterns of positive and negative interactions that comprise the client's familial and social situations.

Cognitive Theory in Social Work

Cognitive theory underlies a range of potentially effective intervention strategies, e.g., psychotherapy, cognitive behavioural therapy (CBT), and mindfulness, which have roots in the psychodynamic perspective most often identified with Sigmund Freud's work of the 1920s. Psychodynamic theory and Freud's views are historically important, since they helped to uncover the complexity of the human mind and moved social work practice toward a more open, therapeutic approach, rather than simply instructing people how to live "moral" lives.

For example, Freud argued that the norms and values of a society put limits on the extent to which people can actively pursue their basic needs. He suggested that the id, the ego, and the superego work together to fulfill these needs, but only in ways that are acceptable to the society in which we live. There is, he argued, a constant conflict between human desires and the limits set by society, which in turn can lead to anxiety and can cause an individual to act in seemingly irrational ways. Early conscious and unconscious experiences that create these anxieties and the ways in which people manage them are critical in shaping human personality.

According to the cognitive perspective, the goals of social work are to (1) understand the cognitive roots of anxiety to determine what is fuelling a person's irrational or troubling behaviour, (2) use specific techniques such as "talk therapy" to expose the source of the problem, and (3) use these insights to resolve the issue, which can then help people manage their anxieties and develop more effective coping behaviours.

Systems Theory in Social Work

Whereas the ecological approach focuses on intricate relationships established at the individual level, **systems theory** (sometimes referred to as "ecological systems theory") focuses more on the working (or lack thereof) of wider social systems or structures, such as family, community, school, place of worship, workplace, and so on. (See Figure 3.1.)

There have been many iterations of systems theory over the years. The key idea is that these systems comprise interrelated parts and constitute an ordered (or disordered) whole, and each part influences other parts of the whole. A breakdown in one system will affect other systems and the persons involved in those systems.

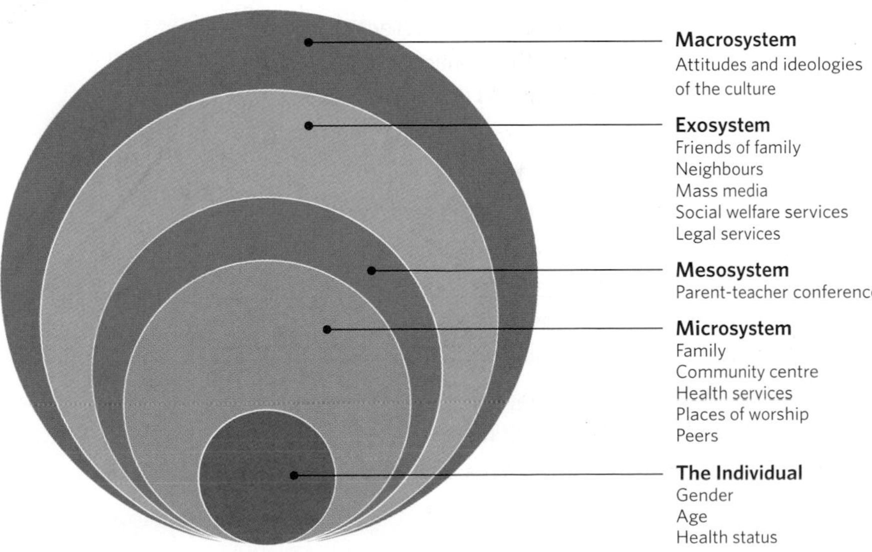

Figure 3.1
Systems theory is premised on the idea that individuals are part of wider social systems that can be identified and "mapped." The proper functioning of these systems is critical to the satisfactory resolution of a person's or a group's problem.

Structural, Critical, and Anti-Oppressive Perspectives

Now let's briefly survey structural, critical, and anti-oppressive theoretical perspectives, widely viewed as relatively "progressive" compared to some other approaches.

Structural Theory in Social Work

Structural theory is largely a Canadian development and can be traced to the work of Maurice Moreau at Carleton University in Ottawa beginning in the 1980s. Structural social work can take several forms. The skills involved in structural social work are similar to the ones used in ecological systems theory. They draw on the same sense of empathy, reflection, and a belief in the basic goodness of people. It is the way in which the social worker analyzes problems—and the resulting range of actions—that distinguish the structural approach from traditional systems theory.

Practitioners of structural social work consider all dimensions of personal problems, while being particularly attuned to the less "visible" structural elements of these problems, such as social class, race, gender, and ability. While every problem that a client experiences is not entirely caused by societal structures, "there is always a structural element in any experienced problem," according to Jan Fook (1993: 74–75). The structural social worker is concerned with helping the individual deal with a difficult problem, typically resulting from discrimination of some kind, but he or she is also concerned with changing the overall situation that is causing the problem in the first place, as much as possible.

Structural social work thus goes beyond an analysis of the immediate family and community, and looks to the broader socio-economic factors that underlie personal dilemmas, such as class, gender, age, and ethnicity. Advocates emphasize the links between the client's feelings and behaviours and structural aspects of the larger society. This approach requires the social worker to be skilled in casework, family counselling, group work, and community organizing, as well as knowledgeable about social policy and social welfare issues.

Critical Theory in Social Work

Critical theory, broadly speaking, covers a number of more specific structural theories, including feminist theory, anti-racist theory, and post-colonial theory. Critical theory involves an analysis of socio-economic structures that oppress and exploit people, whether these structures are based on class, race, age, gender, ability, education, or sexuality. Critical social work theory moves beyond understanding and interpretation to criticism of the structure or structures being studied and engagement in action for social transformation (Leonardo, 2004).

Both as a broad-ranging perspective and as a strategy that acknowledges the client-worker power imbalance, critical social work draws upon the notion of empowerment. Empowerment at an experiential level has three aspects: (1) explicitly identified power elements in the client-worker relationship; (2) explicit experience of control by clients; and (3) explicit support by social workers of clients' efforts to gain greater control over their lives and promote change.

Horkheimer (1993), a key contributor to the early development of critical theory, stressed the explanatory and practical aspects of this perspective. Critical theory, he argued, should explain the drawbacks of the current social reality, identify the people who can contribute to change, and provide a clear picture of anticipated social transformation, including detailed norms and achievable goals.

Anti-Oppressive Theory in Social Work

Anti-oppressive theory is not so much a single theory but rather a cluster of theories that share the goal of understanding and responding to oppressive social conditions and relationships. Feminist and anti-racist social work are two major types of anti-oppressive social work. (These approaches are discussed in greater depth in Chapter 8 and Chapter 10 respectively.)

- **Feminist social work.** Feminist perspectives in social work emerged in the 1960s and 1970s alongside a growing feminist movement. Feminist theories offer different ways of seeing, asking questions about, and understanding women's lives and experiences, the nature of inequality between the sexes, and gender relations in society. Some theorists have called this a "gender-conscious practice" (Orbach, 1990). Social workers advocating a feminist approach to practice provide women-centred support and deconstruct how social, economic, and political structures create and sustain gender inequality. Mutual support, respect for diversity, and an emphasis on women's lived experiences guide their work with clients.
- **Anti-racist social work.** Anti-racist social work focuses on how racial prejudice and racial discrimination—as structural characteristics—affect the lives of people of colour. Racist attitudes sustain a system of exclusion and marginalization based on observable, physical human features, such as skin colour or hair texture (Henry and Tator, 2006). An anti-racist approach decries the harm that racism does to individuals, families, and entire communities, supports individuals and families who are experiencing racial oppression, and advocates on their behalf. It calls for a wholesale deconstruction of social structures based on racial categorizations of all kinds.

Anti-oppressive theory focuses on how systemic forms of discrimination affect the daily lives of individuals and families. Anti-oppressive social work practice supports clients while simultaneously addressing the root causes of the oppression they experience.

The Components of the Anti-Oppressive Perspective

Anti-oppressive practice (AOP) seeks to address power imbalances in society. Anti-oppressive social work theory draws on many traditions with several common ideas, as outlined below.

- People's everyday experiences are frequently shaped by multiple oppressions.
- Social justice-oriented social work practice assists individuals while addressing causes of inequity and oppression.
- Social work needs to build allies and work with social causes and movements.
- Participatory approaches are essential to anti-oppressive social work.
- Self-reflexive practice and analysis are critical to social justice-oriented social work.

Reflecting anti-oppressive theory, feminist perspectives in social work respect the lives and experiences of all women, regardless of their circumstances, professions, or socio-economic status.

Generalist Social Work Practice

When it comes to practice, social workers tend to be generalists. That is, while they may (and should) hold strong views and conduct their work broadly on the basis of those views, they are at the same time flexible in their dealings with clients. Each situation is unique. Social workers apply their extensive knowledge and skills creatively and deliberately. They work collaboratively in teams with other health professionals to serve their clients. They adapt their interventions to the situation at hand, drawing on vast professional knowledge and best practices in the field. The interests of their clients are always paramount.

Generalist social work practice takes place at multiple levels:

- **Micro-level practice** focuses on individuals, families, or small groups, aiming to promote healthy personal functioning, social relationships, and interactions with resources.
- **Meso-level practice** focuses on formal groups, organizations, and service delivery networks, aiming to promote change in group dynamics, structures, and practices.
- **Macro-level practice** focuses on social problems in community, institutional, and policy-related contexts (Kirst-Ashman and Hull, 2009; Miller et al., 2008; Miley et al, 2013).

Social work practitioners also recognize the interactions between these micro, meso, and macro levels of practice (Kirst-Ashman and Hull, 2009). They take advantage of and apply practice manuals and standardized procedures, but they are not unduly limited by these protocols when they appear not to work. Nor is their practice driven solely by rigid, a priori ideas about how things are supposed to work, in theory.

The Generalist Intervention Model

The generalist intervention model is first and foremost tailored to the needs of the client, taking into account how differences in the personal backgrounds of the worker and client may also affect treatment outcomes (Cameron, 2014; Drisko, 2013). This model involves deliberate and "planned change." Interventions are based on a careful assessment of the client's situation (problems, needs, and strengths), planning (identifying priorities and objectives), implementation (monitoring progress and revising plans), evaluation of goal attainment, and termination and follow-up (Kirst-Ashman and Hull, 2009).

Social work practitioners are also attuned to issues and developments in the wider society and within the social work profession itself. These include issues related to professional identity (e.g., licensing and regulation, interdisciplinary relationships) and service delivery (Pearson, 2015). They have knowledge of social work values and ethics, diversity and oppression, cultural competence, social and economic justice, human behaviour, and social welfare policies and programs. They possess a range of skills necessary for micro-, meso-, and macro-level practice, such as communication and interviewing, group facilitation, administration, community mobilization, and research skills (Kirst-Ashman and Hull, 2009). Social work practitioners also demonstrate an aptitude for critical self-evaluation and ongoing self-reflection and assessment (Cameron, 2014; Dorfman, 2013).

Social work practitioners understand the importance of strong therapeutic client-worker relationships based on empathy, warmth, genuineness, and trust (Cameron, 2014; Dorfman, 2013). Indeed, many studies show the overriding influence of the client–worker relationship on successful outcomes, regardless of the technical aspects of the intervention (Drisko, 2013). The client–worker relationship is discussed in greater detail in Chapter 4.

Person in Environment

Social work practice is rooted in a "person in environment" perspective. This perspective aims first and foremost to enhance interactions between individuals (particularly individuals who are vulnerable or marginalized) and society, as well as to promote social justice and ensure equality of opportunities, access, and participation (Kirst-Ashman and Hull, 2009; Miley et al, 2013). The focus is on **empowerment**—the enhancement of personal power that enables individuals to take action to improve their situations. Empowerment is achieved by building on client resources, capabilities, strengths, and resiliency.

Empowerment
The process of increasing the capacity of individuals or groups to make choices and to transform those choices into desired actions and outcomes

Social work practitioners support clients in finding solutions to challenges they are facing and in developing plans that will bring about lasting change. They provide guidance and counselling through clinical intervention and group facilitation, and they support organizational and program development and social planning (e.g., needs assessments/inventories). Generalist practitioners facilitate access to available resources, provide case management, advocate for clients in service delivery and policy systems, mobilize groups for resource or service development and distribution, and engage in activism (e.g., coalitions, legal action, and lobbying) for social change (ibid.). The immediate needs of the client are first and foremost.

Social workers also function as educators, facilitating the exchange of information, knowledge, and ideas through teaching or training in organizational or institutional settings, through community outreach and awareness raising, and through research (ibid.).

Each client situation in social work presents its own unique issues and typically requires an individualized solution. Generalist social workers, working alone or in teams, apply their professional knowledge and experience to help their clients get through challenging times.

The Components of Generalist Social Work Practice

A basic goal of generalist social work is to facilitate the social well-being and social functioning of the person in environment.

Generalist social workers apply knowledge from the humanities and social sciences to advance human rights and social justice, and to provide sufficient supports for individuals, families, and communities.

Generalist social workers rise above personal preferences to advance the social well-being of others through their practice.

They constantly monitor and evaluate personal and professional influences that affect how they use themselves as change agents.

In addition, they are expected to integrate the relevant codes of conduct that apply to their activities and adhere at all times to explicit standard-of-care tenets.

Perspectives on Social Work Practice
A teaching/practice overview

Social workers are influenced by different theoretical perspectives, ranging from conventional to progressive. This chart links different perspectives to a sampling of social work practice skills. For further discussion of progressive practice approaches, see *Case Critical: Social Services and Social Justice in Canada*, 7th edition (forthcoming) by Banakonda Kennedy-Kish Bell, Ben Carniol, Donna Baines, and Raven Sinclair, Toronto: Between the Lines. (Chart reproduced courtesy of Ben Carniol.)

	Assessment Skills	Empathy Skills
CONVENTIONAL PERSPECTIVES **Ecological, Cognitive, and Systems Theories**	Use ecological, cognitive, and systems theories to • analyze dysfunctional interactions among individuals, families, groups, communities, and formal systems; • identify areas for new beliefs, new behaviours, new services, and new policies; and • prioritize professional interventions appropriate to meeting clients' needs.	• Communicate an understanding and appreciation of clients' feelings, subjective experiences, and narratives (as part of developing trust within a professional relationship). • Use these skills in working directly with individuals, as well as with individuals in families, groups, and communities. • Develop anticipatory empathy by "tuning in" emotionally, as part of preparing to work with specific client systems.
PROGRESSIVE PERSPECTIVES **Anti-Oppressive, Anti-Racist, Structural, and Critical Theories**	Use structural, critical, and liberation narratives to • analyze power and privilege associated with whiteness, neoliberalism, racism, sexism, colonialism, classism, heterosexism, ableism, and other forms of systemic oppression, as well as social and environmental barriers harming service users; and • identify urgent survival needs and next steps toward goals of emancipation.	• Communicate efforts to learn about and appreciate the service users' feelings and meanings (as part of trust evolving within a non-elitist professional relationship). • Honour individuality but not individualism. • Widen focus on emancipatory empathy, i.e., engage in dialogue about subjective and systemic barriers faced by others similarly oppressed and find courage to name and address such barriers.

Reframing Skills	Communication Skills	Spiritual Sensitivity Skills	Advocacy Skills
• Aim to reduce clients' sense of hopelessness by encouraging new, more hopeful ways of thinking about and re-storying the situation. • Congratulate clients for achievements that are ignored or devalued by others. • Invite clients to identify unrecognized strengths within themselves and in their interactions with other systems, and help empower alternative, harm-reduction responses that contribute to emotional growth and systems change.	• Listen. • Encourage options for crisis dissipation and stress reduction. • Explore ways that clients could function better with family members and others. • Focus on access to available services/resources while affirming clients' strengths. • Offer respect, and support client self-determination. • Mediate/guide client systems in their problem-solving and solution-finding processes.	• Validate religious/ meditative/spiritual pluralism. • Support clients' spirituality as a strength to cope with stress (e.g., life transitions, trauma, and crises caused by painful losses). • Honour/appeal to spiritual/ meditative/religious values, including compassion, charity, and generosity of spirit to support clients and others within/across multi-cultural communities.	• Work at persuading formal and informal systems to better meet client needs by urging more generosity and good will toward disadvantaged populations. • Act with others in lobbying governments for better policies, co-ordination, integration, and delivery of social programs. • Seek support from private, public, and charitable sectors for access to additional resources to alleviate social problems.
Aim to reduce self-blame by co-investigating the following with service users: • external and internalized oppression • external and internalized privilege • systemic change and service users' growth Facilitate new, more hopeful (e.g., decolonized, feminist) ways to build on service users' resilience in light of social justice inspirations, initiatives, and solidarities.	• Listen. • Encourage options for crisis dissipation and stress reduction, using narratives that explore ways in which clients may be victims and survivors of oppression. • Model power-sharing with service users. Focus on unmasking illegitimate privilege. • Support and suggest narratives pointing to personal and political emancipation.	• Validate religious/ meditative/spiritual pluralism. • Oppose religious beliefs and practices that are oppressive. • Learn about/honour spirituality rooted in diverse cultures, including its role in Indigenous people's helping and healing. • Find spiritual/meditative/ religious inspiration for personal/political/ economic/global liberation.	Become allies with Indigenous people, service users, and other oppressed populations in challenging • neo-liberalism, colonialism, racism, and other systemic oppression; and • environmental decisions that harm people and communities. Participate in social movements that demand local/ global human rights, justice, and democracy.

Reclaiming an Indigenous World View
Implications for social work practice

By Dr. Patti LaBoucane-Benson

Patti Laboucane-Benson (pictured on the right) is a Métis woman and Director of Research, Training, and Communication at Native Counselling Services of Alberta (NCSA). She has a Ph.D. in Human Ecology, focusing on Aboriginal Family Resilience. For more than 20 years, she has researched the healing and reconciliation of gang-affiliated and incarcerated Aboriginal men. Here, she explores how reclaiming and building on a traditional Indigenous world view can provide a practice model informing historic-trauma healing programs for Aboriginal offenders.

A world view is the overall perspective from which one sees, experiences, and interprets the world. As one example of an Indigenous world view, Cree beliefs about creation teach that the Creator gave the people sacred gifts as a result of the sacred relationship between the people and the Creator. The first gifts were physical in nature and included the people, land, animals, and plants. The second gifts were metaphysical in nature, including the laws, rules, and values that guide our many relationships. These laws include the irrefutable laws of nature, as well as the Creator's laws that govern relationships between all things (*wahkohtowin*) and the laws that direct us to have good relationships between people. Living within the boundaries of these laws will ensure that the people feel safe, secure, and able to live "the good life." These laws are informed by and based upon the values that were gifted to the people. The most common values that are referred to are kindness, caring, sharing, respect, humility, honesty, and freedom.

The spiral is used as a symbol of the Cree interconnected world view and the nature of the relationship between the people and all of the beings in their world view. The spiral is supported and is kept beautiful and whole by the strength of the rules that govern the relationships, represented by the spaces between the rings. By observing the rules of *wahkohtowin* and Natural Laws, the people keep in place the scaffolding that ensures we have equality, harmony, and balance in all relationships throughout the spiral.

Indeed, this spiral is the actualization of the best possible life we can attain. The ongoing act of building, strengthening, and renewing our relationships is thus the essence of seeking the good life.

Colonial Policies of Domination and Assimilation

Colonial policies have caused chaos in many Aboriginal communities across Canada and, for the Cree, have disrupted the teaching of *wahkohtowin*. The result has been devastating, leaving Indigenous people feeling disenfranchised and demoralized.

Between 1763 and 1867, the concept of Indian Nations as autonomous political entities began to give way to legislation that focused on usurping the power to define who was Indian and who could live on Indian reserves, as well as on the "civilization," control, and assimilation of the First Peoples. Acts of government legislated the inferior status of Indian identity—an assault on the Aboriginal psyche that created an environment whereby only Indians who renounced their communities, cultures, and languages could gain the respect of colonial (the Crown) and later Canadian society. By the time Confederation occurred, control over all Aboriginal peoples and their lands had been transferred to the office of the Chief Superintendent of Indian Affairs.

In 1876, the first Indian Act was passed. The Royal Commission on Aboriginal Peoples concluded that, "while protection remained a policy goal, it was no longer collective Indian tribal autonomy that was protected: it was the individual Indian recast as a dependent ward—in effect, the child of the state." The Indian Act was amended in 1884 to protect Indians from their own cultures, prohibiting ceremonies such as the Potlach and the Tamanawas dance, and, later, the Sundance.

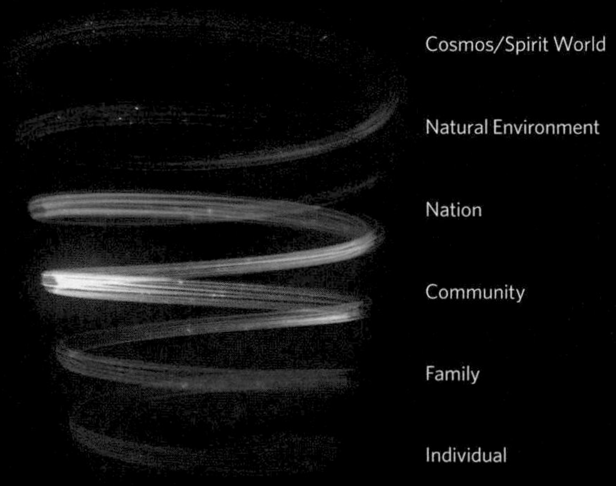

The Impact of Colonization—Historic Trauma

For the Cree, colonization has had devastating, pervasive, and multi-dimensional effects. Colonization has interfered with the creation of a positive Cree identity, both individually and as a collective. Many Aboriginal, First Nations, and Métis children have been raised in environments that reinforce the inferior status of Aboriginal identity, creating a deep shame in or denial of being an Aboriginal person. Many live in impoverished families that are still burdened by the intergenerational transmission of family violence and by parents who are the third and fourth generation of survivors raised "in the system" with very little knowledge of how to be parents. The loss of connection and communication between children and their parents and grandparents has severely damaged these essential family relationships, blocking the transmission of cultural, ethical, and normative knowledge between generations.

The image shown here is a spiral, illustrating an interconnected world view that was supported by the Cree teachings of *wahkohtowin* and Natural Law. When the Cree people were prevented from teaching these values, rules, and way of life, the scaffolding that ensured healthy, respectful relationships was severely damaged, and the spiral collapsed upon itself; the critical relational boundaries were transgressed.

For some families and communities, the spiral has become a tangled, chaotic knot. The intergenerational effect of colonial policies is a pervasive sense of hopelessness, helplessness, and powerlessness. As a result, Aboriginal people remain over-represented in the child welfare, justice, and correctional systems in Canada.

Programs to Promote Healing from Historic Trauma

Effective correctional policies can be an important aspect of the untangling of the chaotic spiral. Drawing on the Indigenous model of building family and community resilience, the process must include three interconnected dimensions: (1) reclaiming our *wahkohtowin* (an interconnected world view); (2) reconciling our damaged relationships; and (3) repatriating the power to respectfully self-determine.

The cornerstone to recovering an interconnected world view is the reclamation of our ceremonies as an educational instrument. Within the correctional institutions, Elders' ceremonies are the milieu in which traditional teachings are imparted in the context of prayer and connectedness to the land and the cosmos. Indeed, the work of the Elders in correctional institutions and community correctional centres is one of the most effective strategies to build a positive sense of Aboriginal identity and develop pro-social values in Aboriginal offenders.

Furthermore, effective healing programs need to be offered in the institutions that deal specifically with historic trauma. If correctional programs are developed in collaboration with Aboriginal peoples, grounded in the world view of local Aboriginal peoples and taking into account the effects of historic trauma, the core criminogenic issues can be addressed. The voicelessness and powerlessness of Aboriginal peoples can only be transformed through dialogue and relationship. While there will always be differences in opinions, common ground in our collective beliefs and goals is achievable and can drive the development of programs that will make a significant difference in the lives of Aboriginal offenders and, eventually, their families.

A Treasure Trove of Practice Models
Classical intervention strategies

The Functional Practice Model in Social Work

The functional approach was introduced in the 1930s by Jessie Taft and Virginia Robinson and is based on the work of Otto Rank, a psychologist who once worked closely with Sigmund Freud. The introduction of the functional approach to social work practice coincided with new ways of understanding the relationship between the client and the social worker.

In previous approaches to practice, the therapist was seen as the "expert" who diagnosed a person's problem and developed a course of action in response to it. The functional approach, however, emphasized the importance of the client's role in directing change. This new approach signalled an early shift away from the "medical model" or "diagnostic approach" and the beginning of an approach to practice whereby the client and the worker engage together in a "helping relationship" aimed at achieving certain goals.

Whereas Freud believed that a person's problems were often due to negative childhood experiences, Rank emphasized the importance of life events in the present. For Rank, all human beings are engaged in a struggle between a desire to create a unique, individual identity and a desire to stay connected to, and dependent upon, others. Individual problems, therefore, can only become resolved when a person is assertive and acts as her or his own force for change (Taft, 1948).

With functional theory, the goal of practice is to enhance social functioning in individuals, families, groups, and communities by assessing the problem at hand and using the client's personal power to effect change in a structured way.

The Client-Centred Practice Model

Taking the functional model one step further, the client- or person-centred approach is based on the idea that clients are the experts in understanding and resolving their own problems. The client-centred approach was introduced by psychotherapist Carl Rogers in the 1950s.

Rogers was greatly influenced by the philosophy of humanism, which has as its central belief the idea that all human beings are good, worthwhile, and guided by a search for meaning and purpose in life. When personal growth is impeded—usually by difficulties in relationships with others—people experience problems. The goal of therapeutic practice is to help clients empower themselves and take responsibility for making changes in their own lives. Rogers viewed the therapeutic relationship as central in this process, and believed that the therapist should strive to be genuine, empathize with clients' world views, and provide them with unconditional positive regard (Rogers, 1951). He believed that a non-judgemental, non-directive approach, characterized by mutual respect, would help people to tap into their own personal power to stimulate and sustain change.

While a client-centred model of practice can be effective, agencies offering social work services are often pressured to produce measurable results in a short period of time. Social workers often draw on cognitive behavioural approaches as more practical, time-limited practice models with clearer guidelines. These shorter-term approaches focus on modifying behaviours by changing the way we interpret our world. The results can be quantified and measured more easily.

The Rational-Emotive Practice Model

The rational-emotive model, introduced by psychologist Albert Ellis in the mid-1950s, blended ideas from two key areas in psychology: cognition and behaviourism. Ellis believed that the way we think (our cognition), how we feel (our emotions), and how we act (our behaviour) interact to produce outcomes (Ellis and Dryden, 1987). Irrational and dysfunctional ways and patterns of thinking, feeling, and behaving contribute to self-defeatism and social defeatism. Rational-emotive psychotherapy (RET) was the earliest form of a cognitive behavioural approach to social work practice.

Using this model, the therapist aims to help a client see that the negative emotions being experienced are due to a distorted perception of reality. For example, if an individual believes that she is not likeable, she might experience a level of anxiety that makes it impossible for her to meet and socialize with others. With counselling, the client can gain a more accurate perception of reality, allowing her to challenge her troubling emotions, and work to change the undesirable behaviours that her thoughts and emotions have produced. This process should take place in a supportive, nurturing relationship that is directed largely by the client.

Rational-emotive therapy differs from other interventions in that it places less emphasis on exploring the hidden past and more emphasis on changing the client's current emotional state of mind. Many social workers are drawn to this form of therapy, since it encourages clients to exercise control over their own throughts and effect change in their own lives.

As with other forms of cognitive therapies, some critics argue that this approach gives undue weight to clients' psychological and emotional responses. Interventions tend to minimize the importance of the conditions in which such personal problems arise and largely ignore the structural or systemic context within which a client's emotional problems occur.

The Task-Centred Practice Model

Developed in the 1980s, the task-centred practice model is a short-term intervention with a measurable outcome and proven effectiveness. Social workers assess and clarify the target problem and desired outcome, and create a list of tasks that must be accomplished in order to resolve the problem.

The task-centred practice model is based on the assumption that people experiencing particular problems typically possess the resources and motivation to resolve them (Reid and Epstein, 1977). The task-centred model is particularly helpful in dealing with persistent problems such as interpersonal or relationship conflicts, problems with role performance, difficulties in making decisions, and reactive emotional stress.

Critical to the success of this practice model is the extent to which personal, family, and environmental contexts support or impede the client's problem-solving efforts.

The Strengths-Based Practice Model

Currently, many social workers approach practice from an individual-level, strengths-based perspective. This approach avoids pathologizing people and helps to create a foundation for future personal growth (Saleebey, 2012).

The strengths-based approach was introduced by University of Kansas professor Dennis Saleebey and his colleagues Charles Rapp and Ann Weick. Saleebey's work with people experiencing serious mental illness helped him to recognize that each person has unique strengths and abilities and, accordingly, the capacity for individual growth and change.

Practitioners working from a strengths-based approach begin by encouraging the client to recognize her or his assets. The worker and client collaborate and draw on available strengths and resources in order to work toward change. The therapeutic relationship is an optimistic and empowering one.

Using Practice Models in Social Work Today

Social work practitioners are often on the lookout for new ideas and new practice models that will lead to positive outcomes for their clients. They have adapted practice models from psychology and other health-care fields and have also conceptualized new ones. When adapting or integrating new approaches to practice, social workers should always ensure that these approaches align with the profession's mission and values and are grounded in a non-judgemental, anti-oppressive, and empowering philosophy.

Described below are some empowerment-driven models of practice that have proved helpful to social work professionals in recent years.

The Cognitive Behavioural Therapy Practice Model

Cognitive behavioural therapy (CBT) is based on the idea that psychological, mental, and emotional distress or disorders are maintained by an individual's cognitive factors. That is, a person's thoughts and beliefs determine their emotional and behavioural responses to life events or situations. Thoughts and beliefs are affected by individual traits, interpersonal relationships, life events, and environmental factors (Miller, 2005).

Cognitive behavioural therapy differs from traditional psychoanalytical approaches, in which therapists seek the unconscious meaning underlying human behaviour. CBT focuses on using cognitive change as a means of supporting emotional and behavioural change, leading to a person's healthy functioning and goal attainment. CBT involves modifying distorted, irrational, or maladaptive thoughts and beliefs about the self, world, and others, and developing social and behavioural skills that can be applied to all areas of life (Beck Institute for Cognitive Behavior Therapy, n.d.; Gonzales-Prendez and Brisebois, 2012; Hofmann et al., 2012).

CBT is a frequently used psychotherapeutic intervention tool, and its effectiveness in treating various conditions (including anxiety, stress, anger, and eating disorders) is generally supported by research evidence (Gonzales-Prendez and Brisebois, 2012; Hofmann et al., 2012). While treatment techniques for specific disorders may differ, CBT models share the same core approaches to treatment. CBT generally involves brief, time-limited, present-focused, and problem-solving approaches (Beck Institute for Cognitive Behavior Therapy, n.d.; Gonzales-Prendez and Brisebois, 2012). CBT approaches have been developed for individual, group, couples, and family counselling practice (Gonzales-Prendez and Brisebois, 2012). CBT may be limited, however, by its primarily Eurocentric nature: less evidence exists for its efficacy with cross-cultural approaches involving diverse populations (ibid.).

Practitioners using cognitive behavioural strategies work with clients to understand the thought patterns that lead to certain behaviours, as well as factors that sustain these patterns or behaviours. The goal is to help the client re-interpret events in her or his environment and reshape the conditions that are sustaining the negative behaviours. Practitioners and clients collaborate in identifying needs, planning treatment, and identifying and challenging negative thoughts and beliefs. Clients are seen as being able to actively shape their lives and determine problems and goals.

Techniques that may be used in CBT include systematic questioning and inductive reasoning, reattribution of negative outcomes to external influence rather than internal causation, challenging "general rules" shaping perceptions of experiences, and confronting anxious responses to specific triggers (e.g., phobias) (Miller, 2005).

CBT and Social Work Values

CBT aligns well with key social work values that emphasize client strengths and empowerment, self-determination, the importance of human relationships, respect for individuals' dignity and worth, practice competence, and social justice (Gonzales-Prendez and Brisebois, 2012).

CBT focuses on the client's specific behaviours and does not view her/him as inherently pathological or flawed. Key elements include establishing collaborative relationships and conducting cognitive behavioural assessments, including identifying problem onset, triggers, and impacts (Miller, 2005).

CBT's Effectiveness in Treating Common Mental Health Disorders

Although some clinicians, researchers, and scholars have raised questions about cognitive behavioural therapy's overall effectiveness, many believe that CBT works to alleviate a variety of conditions (e.g., mood disorders, anxiety, personality disorders, eating disorders, and substance use disorders). During cognitive behavioural therapy, the client works with a mental health counsellor in a structured way, attending a specific number of sessions.

Cognitive behavioural therapy (CBT)
A form of psychotherapy originally designed to treat depression and now used for a number of mental disorders. It works to solve current problems by changing unhelpful thinking and behaviours.

The basic steps in a CBT intervention are outlined below.

- Identify critical behaviours.
- Determine whether such behaviours are excesses or deficits.
- Evaluate behaviours for frequency, duration, and intensity (in order to obtain a baseline).
- Attempt to decrease the frequency, duration, and intensity of behaviours if there are excesses or attempting to increase such behaviours if there are deficits.

Clients are often expected to complete homework in order to apply the skills they learn in therapy sessions to their everyday lives.

CBT is a structured, goal-oriented treatment that emphasizes the "here and now" rather than the past. Clients learn skills and strategies to manage current symptoms and prevent relapses. CBT is widely used for group treatment of social anxiety disorder, generalized anxiety disorder, obsessive compulsive disorder, panic disorder, and major depressive disorder/dysthymia. There are many variations, including exposure therapy (exposing the individual to his or her painful memories) and relaxation training (e.g., progressive muscle relaxation).

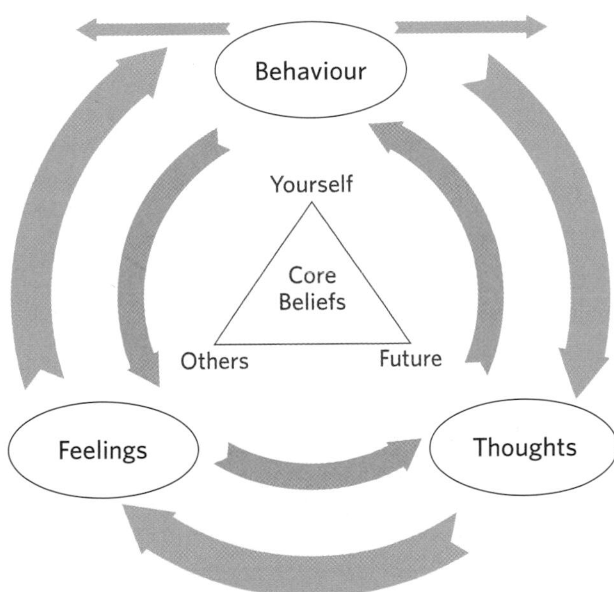

Figure 3.2 A graphic depiction of how feelings, thoughts, and behaviours influence each other. The triangle in the middle represents the idea that core beliefs can be summed up in three categories: self, others, and future. This is a main tenet of cognitive behavioural therapy.

Mindfulness-Based Practice

Mindfulness has become widespread as an intervention strategy, and it has well-researched applications in social work. With roots in Eastern Buddhist traditions, mindfulness has been effectively adapted as (1) a treatment intervention, (2) a mode of self-care, and (3) a way to enhance the client-worker helping relationship (Hick, 2009; Hick and Bien, 2008). Mindfulness involves purposefully paying attention to the present moment with an attitude of openness, non-judgement, and acceptance.

Mindfulness as a social work intervention strategy with individuals or groups is commonplace today. Mindfulness represents a shift from a "doing" mode to a "being" mode. A "being" mode accepts what is happening in the present moment and incorporates experiencing the present directly and unconditionally without asking ourselves "Is it good?" or "Is it bad?"

A number of benefits have been identified in the research literature (Hick, 2009: 9–10):

- a clear awareness of one's thoughts and emotions,
- an ability to relate in new ways to pain and difficulties,
- healthy emotional processing and regulation,
- facilitation of a mental "space" where creative solutions can arise,
- the development of self-awareness and a positive self-image,
- a greater sense of well-being and ease in the world,
- an ability to respond to stress more effectively, and
- an ability to make choices with greater clarity and awareness.

A primary practice or skill cultivated in mindfulness interventions is meditation. Meditation allows us to develop the capacity to pay attention in a controlled environment with less sensory stimulation than is normally present in our daily lives. Once meditation is cultivated in this environment, it can more easily be transferred to our everyday lives. Both formal and informal meditation practices and nonmeditation-based exercises such as tai chi are currently used to cultivate mindfulness. Formal meditation involves sustained attention on a particular object (e.g., the breath) or choiceless awareness (of whatever thoughts arise). An example of this kind of meditation is an exercise called Awareness of Breathing. The best way to understand formal meditation practice is to meditate. This can be done while sitting, lying down, moving (yoga is meditation in motion), or standing. Informal mindfulness is the application of mindful attention in everyday life.

Social worker self-care is a growing area that is benefitting from mindfulness practice. Several studies have found that mindfulness can build a practitioner's resilience, protect the brain against the damaging effects of stress, and produce the same effects on mood and the brain as anti-depressant medications. Within the client-therapist relationship, mindfulness is a way of paying attention with empathy, presence, and deep listening that can be cultivated, sustained, and integrated into the work of therapists.

This is particularly important, since research has consistently shown that it is the strength of the therapeutic relationship itself that accounts for a large proportion of effective therapeutic outcomes. Virtually all mindfulness-based interventions insist that practitioners take part in their own daily mindfulness practice before they consider using mindfulness with clients, and that they practise for a significant period of time—often two years or more—before doing so.

Mindfulness Interventions

Mindfulness techniques or strategies include meditation, transformative breathing, stream of consciousness, intuitive writing, yoga, and tai chi.

Client populations described in literature on mindfulness include those affected by substance use disorders, illness, bereavement, violence, trauma, anxiety, stress, and depression. Aboriginal and multicultural communties have benefitted from mindfulness-based interventions.

For these clients, mindfulness approaches can address issues related to finding meaning in life, roles and purpose, and helplessness and resilience (Birnbaum and Birnbaum, 2008; Lynn, 2010; Turner, 2009).

Interventions Drawing on Mindfulness

Mindfulness is being used in group settings in programs such as **mindfulness-based stress reduction (MBSR)**, the most widely used mindfulness intervention. MBSR has been shown to be effective in dealing with chronic pain, stress, caregiver stress, anxiety, depression, disordered eating, psoriasis, cancer, and suicidal behaviour. Such interventions aim first of all to gain insight into how stress and distress are increased by automatic and habitual patterns and by cognitive reactivity to sensations, thoughts, and emotions. Second, they aim to reduce vulnerability to these mind states, eventually leading to lasting improvements in emotional well-being.

Building on MBSR, mindfulness-based cognitive therapy (MBCT) was developed as a treatment approach to reduce relapse and recurrence of depression (Segal, Williams, et al., 2002). MBCT focuses on teaching people to notice the effects of negative thoughts and how to change their relationships to them. Clinical trials have found that MBCT can reduce the likelihood of relapse by 40 to 50 percent in people who have suffered three or more previous episodes of depression.

Other variations on mindfulness include dialectical behaviour therapy (DBT) and acceptance and commitment therapy (ACT). Originally developed to treat people with borderline personality disorder, DBT integrates behavioural therapy with mindfulness practices (Linehan, 1993). ACT therapy takes an overall wellness approach and is not targeted at a particular illness or disorder but rather aims to alter the harmful effects of unwanted thoughts and feelings by modifying the psychological contexts in which such feelings are experienced by the client.

Mindfulness
Mindfulness in the context of social work involves being present, through attention and awareness, "in the moment" without judgement, moving beyond what human senses can directly experience and everyday states of awareness and taken-for-granted perceptions. It is linked to a holistic conception of social work practice that integrates spiritual approaches and mind-body techniques reflecting equal attention to mind, body, emotional, and spiritual experiences.

Mindfulness-based stress reduction (MBSR) has become a popular and effective intervention strategy in groups designed to help clients manage a wide variety of disorders affecting the mind, body, and spirit.

The Solutions-Focused Practice Model

A **solutions-focused practice model** is based on the belief that people have the necessary inner resources to resolve their problems and contribute to their own growth and change (Corcoran and Pillai, 2009; Kim et al., 2010; Lee, 2013). The key to this approach is encouraging people to visualize the goals they would like to achieve—how they would like their lives to be—and what is needed to make that happen, focusing on the present and the future rather than the past. It focuses on asking "how" to attain goals, rather than asking "why" problems have originated (Grant and O'Connor, 2010).

A solutions-based practice model aligns with social work values and goals, including a strengths-based perspective, collaborative therapeutic relationships, client empowerment and resilience, and a systems perspective focusing on the context of individual behaviour (Corcoran and Pillai, 2009; Kim and al., 2010). This model is based on the assumption that people do not need to know the cause of a problem in order to identify and attain solutions and goals, and that people should be held accountable for solutions rather than responsible for problems (Grant and O'Connor, 2010; Lee, 2013).

A solutions-focused approach is "constructivist" insofar as knowledge about reality and experiences is constructed through social interactions, language, and dialogue. In this sense, solutions-focused practitioners use language, questions, and dialogue to shape how clients perceive their problems, potential solutions, goals, and expected change.

Solutions-focused practitioners ask clients to think about possible solutions to problems and to identify ways in which they can move toward creating a viable solution . Practitioners may use a range of questions to help clients identify their strengths, resources, and solutions, including exception questions (e.g., about times when the problem was absent or less intense), miracle questions (e.g., describing what ideal or perfect solutions to problems would look like), coping questions (e.g., about times when clients successfully coped with problems), and relationship questions (e.g., about how significant others might react to solutions and changes) (Corcoran and Pillai, 2009; Grant and O'Connor, 2010; Lee, 2013).

Solutions-focused approaches can be effective in various contexts, including crisis intervention, child protection, family therapy, and school settings, addressing issues such as behavioural problems, substance use, mental health, and family or marital conflict. Such approaches can also inform management and supervision practices . Solutions-focused approaches are generally brief or time limited, and may be used with individuals, couples, families, and groups (Corcoran and Pillai, 2009; Lee, 2013). Specific solutions-focused clinical approaches have been developed and assessed, such as Solution-Therapeutic Brief Therapy (SFBT) (Kim et al., 2010).

Typically, solution-focused therapy (SFT) is a short-term, strengths-oriented intervention that identifies and enhances clients' resources in coping with life's difficulties. Recent research generally supports the efficacy of solutions-focused approaches, suggesting that they contribute to increased self-efficacy, a positive outlook, and psychological well-being. Interventions based on solutions-focused approaches appear to increase clients' understanding of the nature of the problem affecting them and support client goal attainment (Corcoran and Pillai, 2009; Grant and O'Connor, 2010).

The Components of Solutions-Focused Therapy (SFT)

Solutions-focused therapy encourages clients to identify their own competencies, skills, and support networks.

Typically, SFT seeks to empower clients by way of probing questions.

- **Scaling questions.** These types of questions invite clients to find ways to measure and track their own experiences in a non-threatening way.
- **Problem-free talk.** These types of questions are designed to uncover hidden resources that can help the client relax and become more naturally proactive in tackling problems.
- **Exception-seeking questions.** These types of questions are designed to encourage clients to identify times when the problem is less severe or absent and to maximize the frequency of such occasions.

Narrative-Based Practice Models

Narrative-based practice models view storytelling as an integral part of the way in which we communicate with one another and make sense of our experiences (McLeod, 2006). Narrative approaches focus on the meanings that people can find and create in their life stories, as well as the extent to which people feel their lived experiences are represented within their own stories, as told by themselves or by others (White and Epston, 1990).

Underlying **narrative therapy** is a view that a person's beliefs, skills, principles, and knowledge can be the means to help them reclaim their lives in the face of problems. A narrative therapist aims to help clients examine, evaluate, and change their relationship to a problem by acting as an "investigative reporter" who is not at the centre of the investigation but who is nonetheless influential; that is, the therapist poses questions that help people externalize the problem and then investigate it as thoroughly and reflectively as possible.

Clients are encouraged to describe their life stories, reflecting their subjective lived experiences. They are then encouraged to re-tell stories in a way that represents how they wish to live their lives, integrating current experiences and future goals (Phipps and Vorster, 2009; White and Epston, 1990). Through this process of telling and re-telling their stories, clients are encouraged to explore the different, and changing, meanings associated with events, people, or issues in their lives (Phipps and Vorster, 2009). This process is intended to empower clients by strengthening skills, beliefs, commitments, and resources that can be used to reduce the impacts of problems or challenges in their lives (Dulwich Centre Publications, 2009).

Narrative therapy can be adapted for practice with individuals, families, and groups, as well as with different age groups (Ricks, Kitchens, Goodrich, and Hancock, 2014). In general, narrative approaches suggest that a client's challenges or concerns are not simply "personal" problems. Rather, they are "external" to the client (whether individual or family), rooted in their community, socio-economic status, and political histories and contexts (Cobb and Negash, 2010; Hoffman, 2002; Payne, 2006). Drawing on this perspective, narrative approaches support clients in "externalizing" the problem (that is, in separating the problem from the person), and in understanding the problem and exploring possible responses to it within a broader socio-political context (White and Epston, 1990). The primary focus in narrative therapy is on the relationship between clients and their broader contexts (Dulwich Centre Publications, 2009).

Narrative therapists support the exploration of life stories and the identification of possible responses through careful listening and attention to the whole story, attempting to understand the client's intentions and goals rather than focusing on understanding the causes of life problems (Hibel and Polanco, 2010). A number of tools have been developed to facilitate narrative therapy approaches, drawing on various creative techniques. These include visual arts, photography, videos, and music, as well as memoirs, journaling, and scripts (Ricks et al., 2010). These techniques can facilitate the construction and reconstruction of life stories, including the examination and reframing of meanings or consciousness associated with life events and experiences (Wallis, Burns, and Capdevila, 2011).

In a narrative approach to practice, the therapist aims to adopt a collaborative therapeutic posture rather than imposing ideas on people by giving them advice. Both the therapist and the clients who consult them are seen as having valuable information, in terms of both the process of the therapeutic conversations and the content of these conversations.

Narrative therapy

A form of psychotherapy that seeks to help people identify their values, skills, and knowledge so that they can confront whatever problems they may face. In essence, the therapist seeks to help the client co-author a new narrative about themselves. Narrative therapy challenges the dominant discourses that shape people's lives. The approach was developed during the 1970s and 1980s, largely by social workers Michael White of Australia and David Epston of New Zealand.

Creative and Arts-Based Tools in Social Work Practice

A high degree of creativity lies at the core of generalist social work practice. Unique situations often demand creative and imaginative solutions, and the social work practitioner is frequently called upon to take risks, learn from mistakes, draw on unusual intervention techniques, and display flexibility. "The introduction of imaginative techniques into the daily practice of social workers in a structured and systematic manner can greatly enhance the performance of practice," notes Gelfend (1988).

In the field of social work today, there has been no shortage of creative and innovative approaches to helping individuals, families, and communities. Linda Turner has observed that creativity comes into play in social work in five main areas: (1) creative expression, (2) creative presentation of self by the social worker, (3) creative conceptualization at the direct practice level, (4) creative conceptualization at the community practice level, and (5) a "creative cosmology" paradigm. She concludes that imagination, creativity, and innovation will continue to be in high demand in social work as new situations unfold with clients and as social work practice adapts to respond to these new situations (Turner, 1999). Below, a few creative, arts-based techniques are discussed.

Creative Arts Therapy

There is no debate about the need for scientifically-validated and evidence-based approaches to social work practice. However, much of social work practice involves creative initiatives that recognize the unique history, strengths, and culture of the client. **Creative arts therapy** in its many forms offers a way to reach clients and validate their experiences by allowing them to "tell their stories" in powerful ways. The use of creative arts therapy aligns perfectly with the overall social work strategies of empowerment and building on clients' own strengths.

Art therapy involves the integration of art and psychotherapy (Vick, 2003), and has been defined as the "use [of] art media, the creative process, and the resulting artwork to explore [clients'] feelings, reconcile emotional conflicts, foster self-awareness, manage behaviour and addictions, develop social skills, improve reality orientation, reduce anxiety, and increase self-esteem" (American Art Therapy Association, 2013: 1). Art forms used during the therapeutic process might include drawing, painting, sculpture, and other media. Although individual art therapists may draw on different approaches and favour different areas of therapeutic focus, they use art practice to promote individuals' mental, physical, and emotional well-being and development (Vick, 2003).

Art therapy can engage people from diverse backgrounds, supporting individuals and groups as well as couples and families. During the art therapy process, clients can share their thoughts and feelings through both individual and group art activities, and art forms can represent new means of expression and communication with partners or family or group members (Vick, 2003). Art therapy is widely adapted in different settings, including community services, schools, hospitals, rehabilitation or wellness centres, and other clinical facilities. Art therapy can respond to an array of therapeutic needs, including social and psychological needs as well as developmental, medical, and educational challenges (American Art Therapy Association, 2013). Four primary theoretical orientations in contemporary art therapy have been identified, each having a particular emphasis or area of focus: (1) psychodynamic approaches, (2) humanistic approaches, (3) learning and developmental approaches, and (4) family therapy approaches (Vick, 2003).

Digital Storytelling

Digital storytelling involves the use of digital technologies (e.g., computers, cameras, recorders) to communicate with others and to express life stories, experiences, events, emotions, information, and so on (Burgess, 2006; Robin, 2008).

Widely used in social work education, research, and daily practice, digital storytelling can facilitate more engaging and more proactive relationships. For example, the use of digital storytelling with refugee communities provides an opportunity for them to share their life experiences (Lenette, Cox, and Brough, 2015).

Similarly, the use of digital storytelling in social work courses on oppression and social justice can encourage students to reflect on practice issues in relation to oppression and diversity (Walsh, Shier, Sitter, and Sieppert, 2010).

Play Therapy

Play therapy uses "the therapeutic powers of play to help clients prevent or resolve psychosocial difficulties and achieve optimal growth and development" (U.S. Association for Play Therapy, 2013). While play therapists may work with couples or families, they focus on children, providing them the opportunity to share and explore their feelings, and to interact positively with others and develop social skills (Gaikwad, Lalitha, and Seshadri, 2015; Peterson and Boswell, 2015). Play therapists observe children's behaviours in order to better understand and support them and improve their health and well-being. Play therapy is based on the development of healthy and trusting relationships between therapists and children and on encouraging children to express themselves in their own ways.

Play therapy has been widely used with children who have been traumatized (e.g., through abuse, domestic violence, or disaster) or who have experienced loss, as well as with children in adoptive care or foster care. Research indicates that play therapy is indeed effective in helping children, who can develop the ability to deal with difficulties in constructive and healthy ways when they are given positive feedback, using appropriate modes of communication (e.g. play), in safe and healthy situations (Bratton and Ray, 2000; Bratton, Ray, Rhine, and Jones, 2005; Gaikwad et al., 2015).

"Any child that has any sort of problem they need to discuss or be able to process would make a good candidate for play therapy," says Elena Mazza, M.S.W., L.C.S.W., an assistant professor in the play therapy program and coordinator at the School of Social Work at Monmouth University in West Long Branch, New Jersey. "If it's too hard to put into words, they can work on it with play," adds Dr. Theresa Aiello, co-director of the Advanced Certificate in Child and Family Therapy at New York University's Silver School of Social Work.

Photovoice Therapies

Photovoice is a participatory intervention technique that combines photography with social action (Schwartz et al., 2007). It is "a process by which people can identify, represent, and enhance their community through a specific photographic technique" (Wang and Burris, 1997: 369), aiming to support personal and community change (Wang, Yi, Tao, and Carovano, 1998).

The photovoice process involves documenting individual, family, and community realities (including strengths, concerns, and needs) through photographs, using these images to communicate experiences and knowledge. Photographs are used as a starting point for group discussions, to promote critical dialogue and knowledge about important social issues, and to engage with policy makers to promote broader change (Wang, 1999; Wang and Burris, 1997).

The photovoice intervention is centred on principles of individual and community strengths, capacity building, empowerment, and action (e.g., policy influence) (Catalani and Minkler, 2010; Wang et al., 1998). Elements of the photovoice process, such as participation in research, training, critical dialogue with other community members, and a role as a community change agent can play a key role in empowerment (Catalani and Minkler, 2010) . For people with varying degrees of power, photovoice participation can contribute to the development of new relationships; increased awareness through the exchange of ideas; improved status (peer status, as well as political, social, material, and academic status); increased credibility through affiliation, collaboration, and recognition; and enhanced self-esteem, sense of control over life and relationships, and access to power. Photovoice approaches can also contribute to broader social change and innovation.

Creative arts therapy
The creative arts can often draw ideas from individuals that they may not otherwise be able to put into words. Creative arts therapy in social work involves the use of visual art, music, dance, drama, and poetry to facilitate therapeutic goals with clients.

Digital storytelling
People inherently need and want to communicate. Digital storytelling is a way for social work practitioners to help clients tell their own story as part of the healing process. Through websites, blogs, and social media, stories can be disseminated more widely and quickly than ever before.

Play therapy
Playtime can be an opportunity for adults to reach children on their own level. Play therapy is a specialized area of social work practice and a way to relate to clients, especially young clients, who may be unable to verbalize their feelings.

Photovoice
A form of participatory action research involving photography and narrative, used by practitioners to empower communities so as to include the voices of individuals who otherwise may be marginalized

Shabnam Janani

Shabnam Janani stays grounded in her job as a mental health therapist by valuing each client's unique perspective and their need to be heard.

Human beings are members of a whole / In creation of one essence and soul / If one member is afflicted with pain / Other members uneasy will remain

These words by the thirteenth-century Persian poet Saadi can be found at the entrance to the United Nations building in New York City. They inspired Shabnam Janani to pursue a career in social work after immigrating to Canada in 1999.

I was passionate about choosing a career path that stemmed from my personal philosophy. To me, one's purpose in life is to be proactive, compassionate, and loving toward all human beings—not just our friends and family members, but everyone who needs a helping hand. Motivated by this vision, I completed a master's degree in clinical social work at Wilfrid Laurier University. I attained my degree after writing a thesis titled *The Words beyond My Accent: A Closer Inspection of My Canadian Identity.* Applying a social-creative constructionist theoretical framework, my research explored the process of identity formation experienced by an immigrant to Canada. Incorporating autoethnography and poetic expression, my thesis offers the reader a lens into my experience as an immigrant to Canada. As a result of its innovative methodology, my thesis was nominated for an academic gold medal.

After graduation, I was employed as a mental health clinician in a variety of settings, including hospitals, counselling agencies, and community organizations where I could apply a range of therapeutic modalities and interventions. These included cognitive behavioural therapy (CBT), problem-solving solution-focused therapy, mindfulness-based cognitive therapy (MBCT), psychodynamic therapy, play therapy, and family system therapy.

I am currently a registered social worker with the Family Association for Mental Health Everywhere (FAME), providing both one-on-one and group support to family members concerned about a relative who has a mental health issue. I also run my own private practice for individuals, couples, and groups. As a mental health clinician, I encounter a wide range of psycho-emotional difficulties, including depression, anxiety, and addictions.

Both my national and international social work experience have allowed me to integrate various theories, modalities, and social work perspectives into my practice. Each individual has hidden treasures within themselves, and theories and modalities help social workers to understand the whole person in his or her environment and to determine where, when, and how the best intervention can take place. In particular, systems theory guides my social work practice; it enhances my understanding of a person's needs in the context of the systems in which he or she is involved. Furthermore, I often use a solutions-focused approach along with strengths-based theory to draw upon individuals' untapped resources during the intervention process.

In social work, a gap between theory and practice is sometimes inevitable because human experiences are so complex and settings vary a great deal. This is not necessarily a disadvantage, since this complexity creates aspirations on the part of social workers to fill that gap with creativity and innovation.

Theories and therapeutic modalities provide a pathway that brings together all that you have learned to create a foundation for assessments and interventions, but it is your kind heart and caring soul that enable you to truly help another human being.

For that to occur, the formation of an effective therapeutic relationship with each client is essential. Building a relationship with clients based on trust, rapport, and respect; being an empathetic active listener; asking relevant questions at the right time; and being truly present in conversations with clients are indispensable skills for social workers.

Furthermore, practising social work in Canada means interacting with people from diverse backgrounds, including many immigrants who are in a new environment facing a number of challenges. Cultural sensitivity, digging deep into your sense of self, and assessing your own personal biases are additional skills that must be exercised at all times.

I see social work not just as a profession, but as a way of living in which helping others, human rights, and social justice intersect. My spirit becomes a bit richer every day when I open my heart to someone else's pain and help them to find the strength to pull through situations in ways they never thought possible.

Chapter 3 Review

Review Questions

1. What are the differences between individual-level and structural-level practice theories in social work? Why is each type important?
2. Use the main ideas of ecological/systems theories and the structural approaches to analyze the problem of homelessness among Canadian youth. What are the similarities and differences between these perspectives?
3. Develop a concise definition of "generalist social work practice." Explain what the terms means to a fellow student or friend.
4. Select three of the social work practice models discussed in this chapter. What are some of the strengths and limitations of these intervention strategies?
5. Which one of the various practice models discussed in this chapter feels the most natural to you now, and why? Give examples of how your preferred approach to practice might be applied to a specific social work problem.

Exploring Social Work

1. Research current issues related to oppression and discrimination faced by various vulnerable groups. From an anti-oppressive practice perspective, how can the issues and challenges faced by these vulnerable groups be explained? What are the key issues that anti-oppressive practice could address if this approach is used?
2. Imagine that you are a practitioner working in a community health centre, located in an economically disadvantaged part of the city. Recently, you have noticed that there is an increase in the number of older women of colour seeking services for anxiety and depression. Using cognitive behavioural therapy, what are some of the issues you might consider when assessing and working with these clients? On the other hand, to what extent might the use of a mindfulness approach be relevant to helping your clients?

Websites

Association for the Development of the Person-Centered Approach
www.adpca.org
The Association for the Development of the Person-Centered Approach is an international network of individuals who advance the person-centered approach. This site offers an excellent collection of articles on this approach, which seems to be making a comeback among social workers.

Critical Social Work
www.criticalsocialwork.com
Critical Social Work is an online journal with articles on how social work can contribute to social justice. In part, the goal of the website is to assist in collectively recognizing the current potential for social justice, as well as future possibilities.

Beck Institute for Cognitive Behavior Therapy
www.beckinstitute.org
This non-profit institute was established in 1994 by Dr. Aaron Beck and his daughter, Dr. Judith Beck. The website consists of information about CBT as well as a training program and services provided to clients.

Mindfulness
www.psychologytoday.com/basics/mindfulness
The Psychology Today website provides some basic information about mindfulness and its related techniques.

Canadian Art Therapy Association
www.canadianarttherapy.org
The Canadian Art Therapy Association (CATA) was founded in 1977 by Dr. Martin A. Fischer, a psychotherapist practising art therapy. This website provides basic information about the use of art therapy in Canada.

PhotoVoice
www.photovoice.org
This website shares information about projects using photovoice and resource manuals for those who are interested in using this approach.

Individuals, Groups, and Communities

"Knowing is not enough; we must apply. Willing is not enough; we must do."

Johann Wolfgang von Goethe (1749–1832)

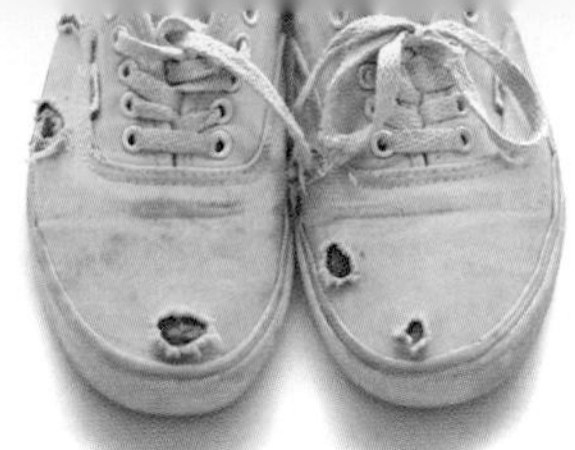

Stewart J. Smith

Applying Direct Practice Skills

4

Social workers require multiple skills and a broad-based perspective.

Social work practice can be thought of as both a science and an art. To be effective, social work interventions must be evidence-based according to the latest research and thinking in the field, but the effectiveness of social work interventions is also rooted in the social worker's judgement and creativity, and on a fundamental trust between the individual practitioner and the client or clients. Some might even argue that it is the strength of the worker–client relationship that is the most important factor in fostering positive outcomes. Most schools of social work distinguish between three categories of direct social work practice: (1) individuals and families, (2) group work, and (3) community work. Most social workers and social service workers will find themselves practising in one or more of these areas, and may be involved in all three over the course of their careers. As "change-makers," social workers must acquire multiple skills and a broad-based perspective. This chapter introduces the main skills that a social worker is likely to need in each of the three areas of direct practice.

In this chapter, you will learn how to...

- explain the importance of evidence-based practice in social work
- identify the three areas or fields of direct social work practice
- describe important attributes of social workers in a helping relationship
- explain the process of reflection-action-reflection in direct social work practice with individuals and families
- analyze skills needed when working with individuals and families
- discuss the importance of critical self-reflection in social work
- describe the four broad stages of the direct social work process
- explore the concept of "group dynamics" and describe different types of groups and their purposes
- analyze group facilitation skills
- describe the stages of group development
- outline several models and approaches to social work with communities

Key Concepts

- Evidence-based practice (EBP)
- Casework
- Helping relationship
- Reflection-action-reflection
- Critical self-reflection
- Group dynamics
- Community
- Community capacity building

Focusing Question

After reading this chapter, which area of direct social work practice seems most appealing to you, and why?

An Overview of Direct Social Work Practice

Social work practice consists of a series or a process of interventionist actions. Workers call upon their repertoire of knowledge, skills, and values and apply it in particular ways in specific situations to help clients achieve purposeful change. While each situation will require different interventions, the step-by-step process is essentially the same.

A useful analogy is that of a skilled dancer who knows the steps involved in a particular dance, but to be truly excellent, must recombine the movements into new patterns. To respond to the unique needs of the client—whether individual, family, group, or community—competent social work practice requires this kind of artful improvising, or the ability to "think on one's feet," in combination with the knowledge and value base associated with the profession.

Social work practice is fundamentally related to decision making along a continuum of services from first encounter to the conclusion of the working relationship with a client. Decisions might pertain to questions such as the following: Is this person eligible for services? Which services might be a good match to the client's needs? Which theory best applies to the unique needs of this individual or family? Which interventions would be most appropriate? Is individual work or group work best suited to this situation? Are there circumstances that should be reported to a legislated authority? How will the worker know when to end the working relationship?

Decisions in social work are often made in the midst of complex and uncertain conditions with information that may not be reliable or consistent. However, to provide fair and impartial services, the decision-making process must be transparent, purposeful, and free of bias. Simply adopting a "go with your gut" or intuitive approach to helping others is not sufficient. On the other hand, relying solely on empirical research to validate decision making and subsequent actions may also be difficult given the varied and unique circumstances of each situation. What is indisputable is the centrality of the helping relationship to positive outcomes. Studies have found that the helping relationship may account for as much as 30 percent of positive outcomes, regardless of the different therapies or interventions used (Norcross, 2002).

The Vital Importance of Evidence-Based Practice in Social Work

Social workers strive to draw upon the best available knowledge and research to guide their direct and indirect practice. The concept of **evidence-based practice (EBP)** is central to effective social work practice. Based on the work of Sackett, Richardson, Rosenburg, and Haynes, evidence-based decision making has been defined as "the integration of the best research evidence with clinical expertise and patient [client] values" (cited in Glasner-Edwards and Rawson, 2010). In this model, research evidence alone is not sufficient to determine a particular intervention. Similarly, worker experience and judgement alone are not sufficient; nor can the client's wishes serve as the sole decision-making factor. Evidence-based decision making depends on the integration of factors such as scientific knowledge, the social worker's experience and judgement, and the client's preferences, values, and circumstances. Evidence-based practice helps clinicians to collect and critically appraise the best evidence (from literature, self, and client) in order to guide an intervention or treatment decision.

Gitterman and Knight (2013) employ the term "evidence-guided practice," as it integrates the science and the art of social work. Evidence-guided practice, from this perspective, incorporates research findings, theoretical constructs, and a repertoire of the profession's values and ethics. It also takes into account the individual social worker's distinctive style.

Evidence-Based Programs in Action

Programs based on evidence-based practice are run all across Canada. In Manitoba, for example, Communities That Care (CTC) is an evidence-based cornerstone of Reclaiming Hope: Manitoba's Youth Suicide Prevention Strategy. Each community appoints a facilitator who takes the lead in developing the CTC board and strategy. The board chooses from a list of evidence-based programs to suit that community's particular needs and implements those programs using existing community resources.

The Saskatchewan Ministry of Health, in partnership with the University of New Brunswick's College of Extended Learning, offers training to support workers in providing services to individuals with autism spectrum disorders in Saskatchewan. Program components include evidence-based intervention strategies.

The Three Areas of Direct Social Work Practice

Regardless of the approach taken to social work, it is important to have a basic understanding of all three areas (or fields) of direct practice, shown in Figure 4.1.

Working with vulnerable individuals and families draws many practitioners to social work. However, it has long been recognized that the blend of support and empowerment that occurs in a group in which people with similar life situations share stories and hear about one another's experiences can be equally or even more powerful than individual support. Generalist social work, rooted In the "person in environment" or ecological approach, recognizes the interdependency between individuals and their communities (whether geographic or identity-related), and, therefore, direct practice also involves a third area: building on community strengths to enhance the social determinants of health and well-being.

As Figure 4.1 indicates, each field influences the other fields and reveals that a primary intervention in one field may involve some level of intervention in another. For example, working in the area of substance use may entail working with the family; accessing AA and Al-Anon groups; and working with schools or communities to promote skills for healthy living. Another example of overlapping fields of practice is the Garden Gate project in Kamloops, B.C. This project provides rehabilitation, skills training, and vocational training for persons with mental health disabilities on a horticultural site that includes a greenhouse, a vegetable garden, and a kitchen/classroom. Participants and volunteers increase their own food security by taking home organic produce in exchange for their help in the garden, while at the same time increasing the community's food security by producing fruits and vegetables for local food charities.

Evidence-based practice (EBP)
A process in which the practitioner combines well-researched interventions with clinical experience, ethics, and the client's preferences and culture to guide the delivery of services. This approach ensures that treatment and services, when used as intended, will have the most effective outcomes as demonstrated by the research. It also ensures that programs with proven success will be more widely disseminated and will benefit the greatest number of people.

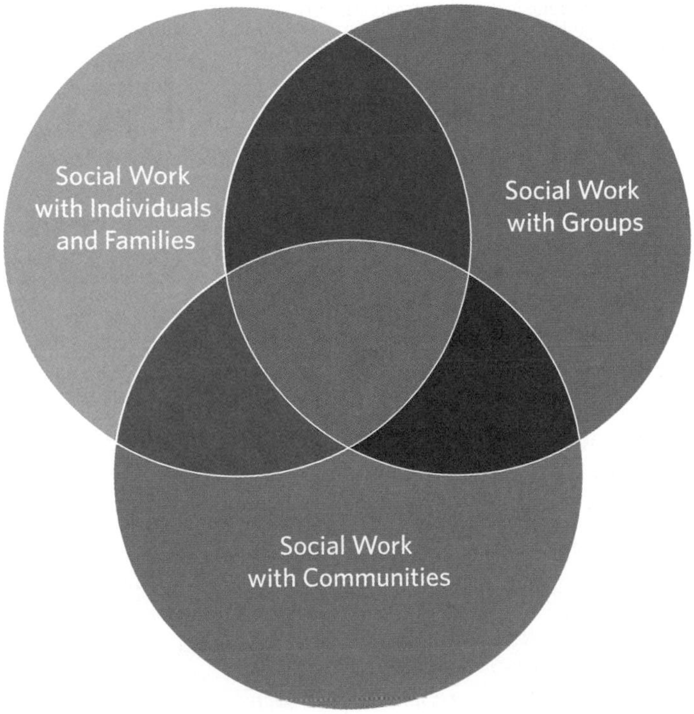

Figure 4.1 This graphic shows the three areas of direct practice. A social worker's career might span all three of these areas, sometimes all three simultaneously.

Social Work with Individuals and Families

The process of helping individuals is sometimes called **casework**. A majority of social workers spend their time with individuals in private or public agencies or in private practice, although the latter is still comparatively less common. Although other areas of social work are expanding, the practice of social work with individuals still predominates.

Social work with individuals is primarily aimed at helping people resolve their problems or change their situations on a one-to-one basis—for example, helping unemployed people obtain work or job training, providing protective services for children who are being abused, counselling people dealing with mental health issues, providing parole or probation services, supplying services to homeless and impoverished individuals, coordinating services for people with AIDS, or coordinating discharge services for individuals being released from hospital.

The Helping Relationship Is Central to Work with Individuals and Families

A social worker works collaboratively *with* the client, not *for* the client, in a **helping relationship**. In this relationship, the client will likely confide personal information to the social worker. The practitioner listens attentively and becomes involved in a manner that benefits the client.

The helping relationship involves certain key elements: deep listening, an emotional bond between client and worker, and eventual agreement on treatment goals and tasks. Psychologist Carl Rogers emphasized three important attributes in the client–practitioner relationship:

- **Warmth.** Social workers rarely believe that they should keep clients at a distance. Too much emphasis on diagnostic labels and professional objectivity can interfere with developing a warm relationship. Warmth is especially important during the early stages of intervention as trust and acceptance develop. Warmth communicates to clients that the worker is approachable and genuinely cares about them. Warmth might involve simple courtesies such as offering a comfortable seat or making appropriate eye contact. It means taking time to show a caring attitude about the client's needs, despite busy or overbooked schedules.
- **Empathy.** Empathy is the capacity to relate to another person's subjective experience and frame of reference by means of listening focused on deep understanding. Such understanding can generate powerful bonds of trust and rapport. Often, this understanding begins with acceptance of the client as a person and the suspension of judgement. A non-judgemental stance requires an intention on the part of the social worker to be aware of their own emotions, assumptions, and reactions. It can take time to hone this kind of open and accepting attitude. It is important not to become trapped in the suffering of the client, but at the same time a social worker must be able to perceive and acknowledge the client's pain.
- **Genuineness.** To be genuine is to behave in a real and authentic way. Central to this characteristic is the awareness of one's own feelings, attitudes, and physical responses. In action, genuineness means that a social worker is trustworthy and honest with clients. The goals are to be truthful and timely in all communication with clients and, above all, to do no harm.

The helping relationship is also central to social work with families, which might involve working with a couple, a child and a parent, or entire families to help them address specific situations or achieve purposeful change. Often, the work focuses on communication or relationship difficulties, or on stressful life transitions. It can also focus on family crises, such as violence within the family, relationship breakdown, care for older family members or those with disabilities, issues at school, help for immigrant families, and/or economic instability.

The Reinstatement of the Long-Form Census

High-quality data are the backbone of research and policy making. The primary source of data about Canadian individuals and families is the census, conducted every five years by Statistics Canada.

Because of a 2010 decision by the federal government, however, the 2011 census consisted only of a "mandatory short-form questionnaire" and a voluntary National Household Survey (NHS).

The Conservative government's cancellation of the mandatory long-form questionnaire was highly controversial. Nearly 500 organizations, including the Canadian Medical Association, the Canadian Chamber of Commerce, and the Canadian Catholic Council of Bishops, protested the decision.

One of the first things the new Liberal government did when it took office in October of 2015 was to reinstate the long-form census.

Core Elements when Working with Individuals and Families

Beginning students may be somewhat confused by the different ways in which various textbooks introduce social work practice with individuals and families. Some outline a series of steps, others emphasize a set of skills, and still others stress theories or models of practice. This textbook does not focus on any one of these aspects, but rather introduces all of them—stressing the helping relationship as a core element.

The profession of social work has a long history of addressing the needs of individuals and families, predating that of many other professions. Social work models tend to emphasize empowering individuals and developing more secure relationships between family members. When working with vulnerable families, such as families in transition (e.g., immigrant families or divorcing parents) and families living in poverty, the emphasis is on stabilizing connections with social institutions, such as schools, churches, child welfare agencies, and hospitals.

Social work practice is grounded in theories and evidence-based practices that inform the steps or skills that social workers employ with clients. These steps are common to most social work interventions with individuals and families. Although assessment precedes intervention, and intervention precedes evaluation and termination, the overall process is often cyclical. For example, during intervention, the client and worker may discover new information that raises the need for more planning. In fact, each step can take place at any point in the process. The steps are guideposts that involve combining and recombining actions into new ways of looking at things—in other words, **reflection-action-reflection** occurs. Stepping back to look, listen, and reflect are closely linked to improvements in practice.

Casework
Social work involving direct consideration of the problems, needs, and adjustments of an individual case in working with a person or a family

Reflection-action-reflection
Reflecting on our practice in such a way that our personal beliefs, expectations, and biases become more evident. This self-understanding increases our awareness of the assumptions that we might make automatically or uncritically as a result of our views of the world.

A social worker asks questions and listens attentively to understand family dynamics—the relationships between family members—and to assess a family's social supports and immediate needs.

Skills for Working with Individuals and Families

Social work practice with individuals and families involves a set of skills that can be continually improved. Often, social work students will engage in role-playing exercises, which afford an effective way to practise these skill sets. The skill set for direct intervention should include the following techniques:

- **Active listening.** Also known as "deep listening," this skill may be the most important one, since it underlies many of the other skills. Without genuinely and actively listening, the social worker cannot fully appreciate the messages, feelings, and needs of the client.
- **Validating feelings.** A social worker validates a client's feelings by conveying an understanding of these feelings. This validation builds rapport and helps the client to identify and sort out a variety of emotions. The social worker must also consider non-verbal emotional responses in developing this understanding.
- **Interviewing or dialoguing.** Open-ended and closed-ended questions are often used to elicit and elaborate on information. Open-ended questions allow the client to explain in greater depth certain aspects of a problem that they see as important. These questions often begin with "how" or "what." Closed-ended questions are often used to check for accuracy.
- **Paraphrasing.** Social workers use paraphrasing to confirm that the meaning the worker has attached to a client's message is the meaning intended by the client. This skill also provides feedback to the client. Beginning social workers need to be aware that overuse of paraphrasing can give the client the impression of being mimicked.
- **Clarifying.** This skill is used to determine if the worker and client are on the same "wavelength." It is often used to probe an issue that is not clearly understood by the social worker. It involves asking for specific details about an event, experience, or state of mind. Clarification often becomes a reciprocal process between the social worker and the client, as each tries to understand the essential meaning of what the other is saying.
- **Summarizing.** This skill is used when attempting to capture or pull together the most important aspects of a problem or situation. It provides focus for the next interview and can assist in planning. Both the feelings and content of the client's message should be reflected in a summary statement. Summarizing can also signal that it is time to move on to another topic.
- **Giving information.** Without overwhelming people with too many details at one time, the social worker often shares information about resources in the community (e.g., women's shelters) or information showing that the client is not alone in experiencing the problem. The social worker takes care to ensure that the client realizes they can choose not to act on the information, and provides pamphlets, brochures, or websites when possible.
- **Interpreting.** This skill enables the social worker to delve into the presented problem and "read between the lines." By using this skill, you may be able to "reframe" the issue, giving it your own unique angle. The worker's insights may help the client develop a deeper understanding of what is really going on, and not just what appears to be happening. Always check the client's verbal and non-verbal responses to your interpretations.
- **Building consensus.** Consensus building attempts to work out an agreement as to what should be done to address a problem. Consensus may be easily attained, or there may be discrepancies between what a client says they want and their behaviour, or between separate messages communicated by a client. Confrontation may be used to challenge a client to examine discrepancies. Such confrontation should be non-adversarial, respectful, and used only when a safe and trusting relationship exists between the worker and the client.

Essential Dialoguing Skills

- Being open to the client's lived experience, especially at the beginning of the relationship.
- Exhibiting warmth, empathy, and genuineness.
- Listening and speaking in a way that benefits the client.
- Defining problems from a broad perspective.
- Demonstrating a non-judgemental and accepting attitude.
- Reflecting on the sociological dimensions of an apparently individual problem.
- Eliciting the information and feelings required to understand a client's problem.
- Relating to the client's and one's own emotions.
- Developing an egalitarian relationship as opposed to an authoritarian one.
- Allowing silences between the words to be a part of the dialogue.

The Role of Critical Self-Reflection

Social work scholars, such as Bob Mullaly (2002), also emphasize the importance of what is sometimes called "**critical self-reflection**" or "knowledge about oneself." This self-reflection helps social workers understand how their own identities and beliefs, as well as their professional and personal lives, are shaped by forces in society such as parental influences, cultural influences, the media, educational institutions, political movements, and social structures.

Critical self-reflection
A frame of mind which recognizes that a social worker's identity and beliefs are shaped not only by unique traits and personal experiences, but also by societal forces and social structures

Critical self-reflection is an ongoing process in the lives and careers of social workers. Self-reflection can pave the way to early identification of latent or overt emotional issues experienced by a social worker that might need exploration and attention. For example, identifying the sensation of being overwhelmed by clients who are struggling with a particular type of dilemma can prompt a social worker to acquire new skills related to that issue and to focus on improved self-care. Examples of such professional and personal growth might include participating in further training in how to deal with clients struggling with a substance use disorder.

Social workers can often struggle with deciding whether it is appropriate to share personal feelings or stories with clients. It is important to understand the triggers and underlying motivations that might lead a social worker to self-disclose. There are definitely times when beginning social workers should exercise caution in spontaneously expressing personal feelings. On the other hand, such sharing can help demonstrate that certain feelings are common and emphasize our shared humanity. In adopting a feminist approach, for example, social workers often share personal experiences with clients in order to establish a sense of solidarity and to draw a link to social structures that act as barriers to self-realization.

The helping relationship requires empathy; without judging or even liking a client, a social worker tries to understand the person's unique needs and challenges. This requires the worker to be keenly aware of his or her own emotions, assumptions, and reactions.

Working with Individuals and Families

Empowerment as both a tool and a goal

The direct social work process outlined below consists of four broad stages: (1) intake, (2) assessment and planning, (3) intervention, and (4) evaluation and termination.

The Intake Stage

From the first encounter with the person seeking help to the last, the social worker is mindful of the vital importance of the working relationship. Some identify this relationship as a "therapeutic alliance." A therapeutic alliance exists when both the social worker and the client feel that theirs is a positive working partnership.

Intake is a process whereby a request for service is put forth either by or for a person, and a social worker responsible for intake then determines whether and what kind of service is to be provided. The social worker attempts to gather initial information to determine what assistance is needed and whether the agency and worker are the appropriate providers. If it is mutually determined that the agency can be of service, then some sort of agreement or contract is drawn up. If it is determined that the client's needs cannot be met by the agency, then a referral to a different service or agency is made or a decision is made to pursue another route to help.

During the intake phase, the client makes a personal request for help, or someone from the community directs the client to a particular social work agency. The social work relationship can be either voluntary or involuntary. The intake step is voluntary when a client willingly seeks help from a social work agency. For example, a lone parent struggling to care for a child may approach a child welfare agency for assistance. In contrast, an involuntary client is ordered to see a social worker or is required to do so by law. For example, a social worker is required by law to assist a child in danger when the child's situation has been reported as unsafe by a physician, hospital worker, police officer, or schoolteacher. In such cases, families are often uncooperative, especially if allegations of child abuse have been reported. Working with involuntary clients can often place more demands on a social worker due to resistance and lower motivation on the part of the client(s).

In the intake stage, the social worker acknowledges the client's need for help, collects information from the client, assesses the client's problem or situation and, based on the agency's resources, determines if the social work agency can help the client. In essence, when they first meet, both the worker and the client want answers to specific questions. The applicant or potential client wants to know: Can I get the help I need here? Can this person help me? The worker will ask: Can I help this person, or would it be more appropriate for someone else in this or another agency to offer help?

It is important in this phase for the social worker to clarify his or her role and purpose, as well as the agency's role. The context of practice is particularly important during the intake phase. In some cases, an agency-mandated intake form or checklist is used. The social worker should ensure that there is some congruence between the mandate of the agency and the issues that are important to the client. In the case of an involuntary client, this congruence is assumed. Finding this similarity forms a kind of contract between client and agency, with the worker as the intermediary. The worker's function in this initial phase is a form of mediating an engagement between client and agency—a finding of common ground.

The social worker might start the intake process with an opening statement such as the following:

"My name is Lorraine, and I am a social worker here at the social work department. Your doctor has asked me to see you regarding your recovery from your operation and challenges you might be having. This can be a difficult time and, if you wish, I would like to offer some assistance."

This straightforward statement sets the groundwork and then leaves it open to the client to clarify what the role of the worker might be from his or her perspective.

The Assessment and Planning Stage

During assessment, the social worker and the client analyze what help is needed based on the client's ideas, thoughts, and feelings. Once the assessment is complete, the social worker formulates a plan in collaboration with the client. The plan is not set in stone but provides an initial course of action, which is reviewed and updated throughout the process. The client is viewed as a partner rather than simply a consulted party.

Many textbooks describe a process that involves problem definition, data collection, and "objective" recommendations. In this section, we are emphasizing a social work process that stresses reflection-action-reflection, in which the social worker continually thinks things through while acting on the problem at hand and always in consultation with the client. She or he adapts the intervention based on dialogue, reflection on prior experience, and judgements about past actions.

During the assessment stage, the social worker may also rely on other people who know the client personally, for example, a teacher, doctor, police officer, or Elder. Assessment involves the art of asking questions. Purposeful and well-timed questions are the cornerstone of this phase. Social workers may prefer a structured interview in which they pose a predetermined set of questions. This is usually the case in agencies that require specific forms to be completed as part of the assessment. In other cases, unstructured interviews are the norm. This type of interviewing is still focused, but takes a more conversational tone and is relatively flexible. With the latter approach, beginning social workers must ensure that the interview does not wander too far off topic.

The planned actions may occur at a variety of levels: individual, environmental, multi-person, systemic, or structural. For example, actions might involve therapeutic, educational, and social action-oriented approaches. What varies between practice models is the focus of attention. A behavioural therapy approach would tend to focus on changing individual behaviours, whereas a social action or structural approach may focus on examining behaviours within a wider context, perhaps exploring how they might be changed, and working toward changing systems in order to shift power relations. There can also be a combination of these approaches. In any event, the social worker assesses the client's problem with the client and negotiates a plan with the client that includes

- the type of actions or interventions deemed viable,
- the length of the intervention,
- the frequency of meetings and the desired outcomes, and
- the intervention plan (a contract is made with the client).

The concept of empowerment is crucial in the planning phase. The foundation of empowerment is the notion that clients have the right to self-determination and are capable of discerning the best course of action for themselves. Often, clients come in with a negative self-image and a feeling of powerlessness. Sexism or racism may feed into this. This poses a challenge in substituting an attitude of empowerment.

One response is to use a mindfulness approach to explore clients' thoughts, feelings, and physical sensations. Clients are encouraged to see self-deprecating thoughts as just thoughts and not who they are. They are able to learn that they possess an effective intuitive sense and an inner resilience that can be called upon to face and surmount life's difficulties.

Other approaches might use consciousness-raising to promote empowerment. Consciousness-raising encourages people to gain insight into their circumstances with a view to changing them. This notion is often associated with progressive, feminist, or structural approaches to social work, but it is increasingly becoming part of many other approaches.

Consciousness-raising can involve one or more activities, including the provision of information concerning the social structures implicated in the person's situation, reflection based on the client's lived experiences, sharing of experiences in common with the worker (if this is appropriate), or conscious-awareness exercises that cultivate insight.

Part of the consciousness-raising process involves normalization. Normalization highlights the notion that any particular difficulty that a person experiences is universal and not unique to any one person—that many difficulties are a normal part of being human or being part of a particular social group that is being oppressed or marginalized.

The Intervention Stage

The worker, the client, or both may initiate the intervention stage. The actions may be directed toward the client, other individuals, family members, groups, communities, institutions, social policies, or political and social structures. Intervention does not always focus on the treatment of the individual alone. For example, in situations where the social worker is using a structural or feminist approach to practice, the intervention will usually include some kind of organizational, community, or social action measures in addition to working with a client.

It is through the process of intervention that the worker and the client implement the assessment and the plan that emerged after completing the assessment. The intervention undertaken is directed at meeting the client's needs as determined by the worker and the client together. In the intervention stage, the client shares with the social worker any information regarding what progress has been made in resolving the problem that is confronting the client.

During this stage, the social worker

- establishes a rapport with the client,
- accompanies the client to meetings with other support personnel as needed (e.g., employment counsellors),
- provides advice and support to the client,
- adjusts the intervention based on further information from the client, and
- helps the client to resolve the problem or situation by providing new knowledge and skills that assist in alleviating the problem or that shift the client's relationship to the problem in beneficial ways.

The intervention phase should focus on creating an ongoing dialogue between the client and the worker and perhaps others involved in the situation. In cases where the uncertainties loom large or are numerous, it is advisable to take small, cautious steps and then reflect on the intervention. This will allow for an enhanced understanding of the situation and an opportunity for the worker and the client to alter the course of action to suit current realities as they come to light.

The Evaluation and Termination Stage

In this, the final stage, the client and the social worker achieve a resolution or a partial resolution to the problem, preferably one that prevents the situation from occurring again. The social worker evaluates the following items with the client:

- the choice of intervention
- the length of the intervention
- the frequency of the meetings between client and worker
- the outcome or outcomes of the intervention
- the need for any follow-up meetings or actions
- when to terminate the intervention

Evaluation is an ongoing part of the process. Evaluation should identify a rationale for the actions chosen, whether or not a client's needs were met, the expected and unexpected effects, and alternative courses of action that may need to be taken.

Increasingly, there is recognition of the benefits of client participation: clients can have an insider's perspective on agency functioning; information can be validated; confidentiality can be examined; plans can be adjusted; knowledge can be gained; the client–worker relationship can be strengthened; and clients can be empowered.

Termination, or the ending of the client–worker relationship, occurs ideally when the action plan has been completed and the client's goals have been met. In this stage, essential records are organized and stored in a place of safekeeping.

The use of records raises concerns about the confidentiality of sensitive information: What constitutes the ethical disclosure of information about a client? In addressing this question, social workers are obligated to follow the guidelines of the agency or organization employing them. They must also obey legislation and association policy. The CASW *Code of Ethics* stipulates, at length, the requirements for collecting, recording, storing, and accessing client records.

Social workers must ensure that appropriate supports are in place before the intervention is ended. A client who has become dependent on assistance and interaction with the social worker may have difficulties with termination. Helping clients build their own support network is crucial. Such support may come from family and friends, informal helpers, self-help groups, or through community or voluntary activities. If an empowerment perspective is embraced, termination often proceeds more smoothly.

The Direct Social Work Process

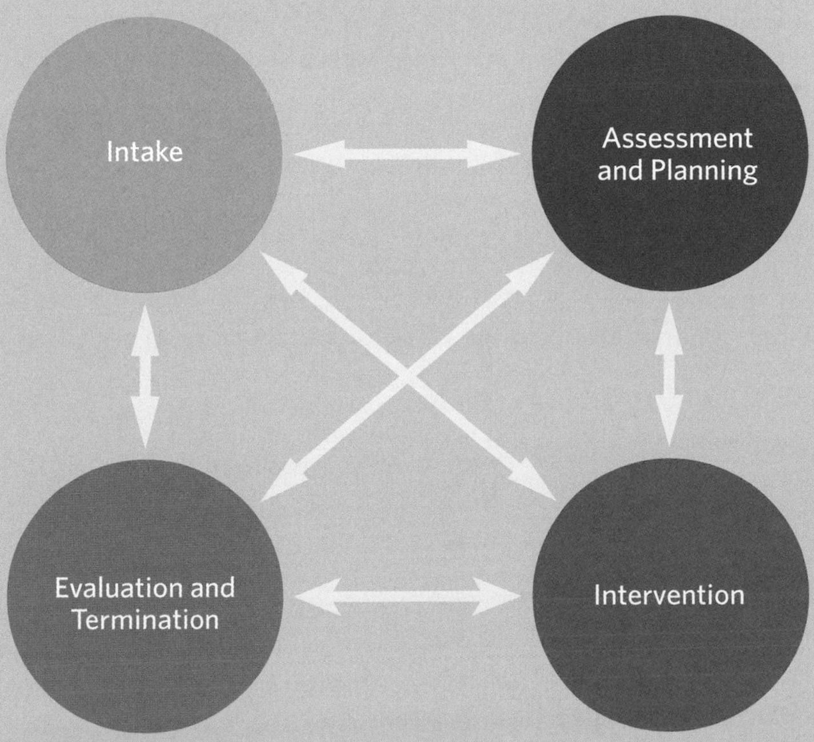

Social Work with Groups

While casework had been defined as a method by the early twentieth century, *group work* and *community work* (or *community organizing*) were latecomers to the profession. Group work was basically seen as an informal and unstructured activity and not part of the profession (Goldstein, 1973: 26). The focus was on helping people participate collectively in grappling with common problems. Ellen Mesbur (2002) notes that it was not until the 1930s that group work was considered a method of practice. During the Great Depression, social action came to be viewed as a significant and accepted part of the social work profession, and it involved helping and supporting destitute farmers, unemployed labourers, and orphaned children. This was also the period when self-help groups started to develop; people dealing with similar issues came together to support and aid each other. Over the past 50 years or so, the profession has identified group work as one of the models of practice in social work, with a growing body of literature and research available on the subject.

Group Dynamics

Although there are many similarities between helping people in a group setting and assisting them one-on-one, there are some significant differences. These elements are sometimes referred to as **group dynamics**. Group dynamics include how people talk and interact with each other in the group (communication and interactive patterns), a sense of belonging to the group (cohesion), and the influence that a group has on individual members to conform to certain behaviours, practices, and beliefs (Toseland and Rivas, 2005: 65). The purpose for which a group is established will in large measure influence its dynamics.

- **Communication patterns.** Depending on the overall objectives of the group, a facilitator will seek to establish a particular communication pattern. For example, in an educational group, the facilitator will have a central role in conveying information to the group; in many parenting groups, the facilitator will systematically present course materials followed by group discussion; in a support/therapeutic group, the facilitator generally aims to have free-floating communication rather than setting up the group so that it is leader-centred.
- **Cohesion.** Cohesion is an important component to be aware of when working with a group. When group members feel connected to the other members in the group, they are more likely to benefit from the group experience. A sense of cohesion in a group provides safety and sets the stage for group members to interact in an authentic way with each other. This sense of connectedness is possibly the most important ingredient in making a group a valuable experience for its members. It is also what motivates people to continue participating in the group.
- **Group influence and conformity.** Group influence and conformity will affect how well a group will function and whether it will be able to achieve the purpose for which it was established. Groups in which members have many common characteristics and hold shared values and expectations are groups that tend to move forward more quickly in achieving group goals. For example, a group of parents of adolescents who have dropped out of school might have many similar goals and will thus be able to support one another. However, part of the strength of groups also lies in members' differences. Different experiences and backgrounds can provide perspectives and insights that are new to other group members. The balance between homogeneity and heterogeneity in a group's membership will affect the functioning of the group and how influential it will be on individual members.

Principles of Group Work

A facilitator generally takes an active role during the initial stages of establishing the structure and format of a group. It is at this stage that ground rules are established, and group members demonstrate their level of commitment to the group.

The optimum group size depends on the following:

- the age of the clients
- the type of group
- problems/issues to be explored
- the needs of the members
- the experience level of the social worker

The following should be kept in mind when selecting group members:

- common experiences/ common problems
- motivation
- age, gender, and socio-cultural factors
- clear expectations that the group members will help solve a problem

Kinds of Groups

Group work can be defined as assisting a collection of people who are dealing generally with a similar problem or issue. Groups can be peers, a family, or a therapeutic group. Group work approaches range from therapeutic to educational to activist. Similarly, some communities want to take a healing or therapeutic approach to their problems, others want to learn skills, and some want to head to the streets in protest.

A wide range of groups operate in most communities. Whether a group considers itself a community or not, the approaches that are described in this section are helpful for working with any collective of people as they try to create change in their lives.

Groups generally fall into the following five categories: self-help, educational, support/therapeutic, task, and social action groups.

Cohesion within a support/therapeutic group provides a sense of safety, which allows the facilitator to encourage group members to interact in an authentic way and offer support and encouragement to each other.

- **Self-help groups.** Self-help groups are ones that do not have a professional facilitator and may be either leaderless, have a rotating leader, or designate a leader from within the group. Alcoholics Anonymous is one of the most well-known and longest running self-help groups. Many others have been established, such as PFLAG (Parents, Families, and Friends of Lesbians and Gays) and CanSurmount, a peer group for cancer patients and their families. There is also a growing number of web-based support groups, which can be useful for people who are not able to connect with a community group. However, online groups do have limitations—for example, health information online is not subject to the same scrutiny as information in printed medical journals. There are also privacy concerns related to Internet-based groups.
- **Educational groups.** Educational groups have a primary focus on education, but might also have a support aspect. Examples are groups for heart and stroke victims, parenting groups, and groups for families in which there has been a recent diagnosis of diabetes. These groups usually have a leader who has expertise on the topic.
- **Support/therapeutic groups.** In support/therapeutic groups, the primary purpose is supporting people dealing with specific problems. These are groups that have a professional facilitator. Examples are groups for victims of sexual abuse, women empowerment groups, and groups for people dealing with mental health issues or substance use disorders.
- **Task groups.** In task groups, the primary focus is to accomplish a specific mandate. Although social support may be a side benefit, it is not the primary purpose for which the group was designed. Some examples are a group that coordinates settlement services for newcomers in a community or a personnel committee charged with the task of hiring an executive director for a non-profit organization.
- **Social action groups.** Social action groups tend, as the name implies, to focus on broader social issues, although they may have a personal dimension to them as well. For example, a group organized to ban the use of pesticides on lawns may have been sparked by a personal concern around a child's cancer diagnosis. These groups are part of community organizing. A premise for social action groups is often the need for equitable distribution of resources, whether locally or globally.

While task groups and social action groups share common aspects with self-help, educational, and support/therapeutic groups, and although many of the skills involved in leading these groups are similar, the focus and emphasis are different for each type of group.

Group Facilitation Skills

The skills related to working with individuals (mentioned earlier in this chapter) are also the skills required when working with groups: active listening, expressions of empathy, questioning, paraphrasing, reflecting, summarizing, providing information or suggestions, building consensus, and interpreting or reframing ideas. In addition to these skills, however, there are specific group facilitation skills that are important to learn. Some of the main group facilitation skills are described below.

- **Connecting.** This skill involves linking what one person is saying or doing to what another member in the group is experiencing. The facilitator listens for common themes in people's specific stories and draws meaningful connections. For example, one person's story about losing a job may lead to a discussion of how others in the group have dealt with similar losses that they have experienced. Connecting is an especially important skill in terms of building group cohesion. Part of the effectiveness of groups lies in the support that people receive from recognizing that they are not the only ones dealing with a particular concern. Drawing connections dispels feelings of isolation and helps build group cohesion, moving the group toward mutual aid.
- **Focusing on process.** Process is critical in group work, but it often gets overlooked when the facilitator becomes too engaged in the content of the discussion. While the content may be interesting and important, it is frequently the process that is the most important issue to attend to in a group. Groups are a microcosm of the larger society. How members react to one another can serve to reveal how they treat others outside the group. Helping people to examine their interactions and reactions in the here-and-now can provide an opportunity for gaining insight into the self. Focusing on process includes pointing out patterns to the group and reframing issues. Shulman (1992) notes that the group facilitator has to consider two clients at all times, both the individuals in the group and the group as a whole. This requires the worker to use a microscopic lens and a wide-angle lens simultaneously, metaphorically speaking.
- **Cueing.** Cueing is another skill that is specific to group work. Here, the facilitator scans the group, takes its pulse, as it were, and becomes instrumental in inviting silent or non-participating members to engage in the group process. This might be done non-verbally through body language (e.g., by making appropriate eye contact with the person you are inviting into the conversation). At other times, it can be done verbally (e.g., by specifically inviting someone to make a comment). When one member is dominating the discussion, it is often useful to take the time to invite members to take turns contributing to the discussion. Engaging with all members will help bring about the attainment of the group's objectives.
- **Supporting.** The facilitator's judgement is required to determine when to support a group member. Jumping in too early might prevent the member from fully exploring a situation and learning from it. This skill also incorporates encouraging group members to support each other. For example, many people come to treatment groups because they feel powerless, hopeless, or isolated. The phenomenon of feeling like you are all "in the same boat" is one of the healing aspects of a group. In a cohesive and healthy group, members will frequently support each other by sharing similar feelings, thus making the feelings less frightening or overwhelming. The social worker can also encourage empathic statements by asking the group, for example, "Has anybody else in the group had similar feelings?" or "Can anybody else relate to what was just said?"

The Talking Stick

A talking stick is often used by First Nations to ensure that everyone's message and opinions are heard by the group, but it can be used in a variety of social work groups.

The group usually positions itself in a circle without any obstructions in the middle. A stick or feather (or almost any object) serves as the talking stick. Each group member can speak only when he or she is holding the stick. The speaker passes the stick to the next person who wishes to speak.

This method ensures that everyone can contribute without interruption, and encourages shy members to participate.

- **Blocking.** In addition to supporting, a facilitator must also decide when to challenge a group member. Harmful things can be said in groups and, as much as possible, the group facilitator must try to block certain comments or activities in order to maintain the safety of the group. This requires sensitivity and the ability to use power effectively without disempowering group members. Situations in which the facilitator should block discussion include the following: if a member is betraying confidences; making racist, sexist, homophobic, or other discriminatory comments; or being abusive and disrespectful. It is the responsibility of the group facilitator to ensure the safety of all members of the group by establishing rules of conduct prior to each group session and ensuring that the rules are upheld by everyone.
- **Demonstrating social empathy.** While expressing empathy means understanding and validating a client's feelings, social empathy takes this notion a step further. Here, the facilitator makes links between personal troubles and structural issues. Connecting the personal and the political can be very affirming for clients. By providing a social and political context for group members' experiences, the facilitator reframes their issues so members can shift from feeling worthless or frustrated (for example, with being unemployed) to feeling empowered. Generally, the facilitator will ask questions that help individual group members make those larger connections in their own lives, for example: "In whose interest is it that women stay at home and care for their children (or older parents)?" or "What seems to get in the way of you getting what you want?" The expression of social empathy highlights various oppressions, but it also underlines the fact that the same circumstances may affect individuals in the group in different ways. Context is everything. This is an example of what is meant by the social work phrase "person in environment."

An understanding of group work is a critical part of social work practice knowledge, since group dynamics can help to shape individual behaviours, practices, and beliefs.

Social Work with Groups
Coming together to get results

Groups do not proceed systematically or in a linear manner through stages. Rather, they typically move back and forth between stages. For example, while conflict is usually associated with the early stages of group formation, conflicts may arise during the later phases as well, if members challenge each other or the basic framework of the group.

Different theoreticians have conceptualized group development in various ways, although there is substantial agreement. Shulman (1992), for example, has outlined group development as having three general phases: beginning, middle, and end. Others have suggested that groups go through five or six stages consisting basically of orientation, conflict, negotiation, functioning, and termination (Toseland and Rivas, 2005: 87).

Bruce Tuckman's (1965) early work on the stages of group development continues to be a useful approach. He outlined the stages in an easy-to-remember way: forming, storming, norming, and performing, and he later added adjourning to that list (Tuckman and Jensen, 1977).

The Forming Stage

The forming stage has two primary components: planning the group and getting the group started.

In planning a group, it is vitally important that the purpose is clearly defined (e.g., to provide support, to educate, or to accomplish a specific task). The purpose should be broad enough to attract a sufficient number of people with somewhat varying needs, and yet specific enough to define the common nature of the group. The facilitator should also think about whom the group is intended to attract. In other words, for whom is the group designed? Knowing the group's objective helps the social worker in the screening process to determine who is appropriate to join the group.

Part of planning also includes issues such as the length of the group meetings, the frequency with which the group meets, and the duration of the group. It is also important at this stage to consider whether the group will be open to new members along the way or whether it will be a closed group.

The Storming Stage

The storming stage occurs when conflict emerges in the group. Differences in members' understanding of the group's purpose and the group members' roles and expectations can lead to friction. If it is a voluntary group, members may decide not to return at this stage.

This is the time when members test and challenge the authority of the facilitator. Although this can be a difficult phase in the life of a group, it is also a time when growth can occur and when relationships can be established and strengthened.

By anticipating conflict, group leaders can help members to view conflict as a natural or helpful part of group development and as an opportunity to gather information and share views and opinions rather than as a personal attack.

It is at this stage that the facilitator can be highly influential in establishing a tone for the group and modelling the essential ground rules. This modelling might involve encouraging members to own their statements, listen without interrupting others, ask questions or take time to reflect before reacting in a "knee-jerk" manner, and addressing and responding to each other in a respectful manner.

The Norming Stage

In the norming stage, group norms (expectations, standards, or common practices) and roles become more clearly defined, and members establish a sense of trust with each other. Group cohesion increases, and the group moves toward working on the agreed-upon objectives. One example of a useful norm to establish is that everyone has a right to be heard. It is also useful to encourage members to talk directly to each other rather than communicating through the facilitator.

The Performing Stage

In this stage, the group members work toward achieving the outlined goals. Trust and a sense of confidence with each other are evident. Members might disclose painful personal issues from their past and seek assistance and support from each other. Group cohesion is strong, and group participation is lively, with attendance at sessions generally high.

During this stage, individuals begin to consider other group members as friends and feel a sense of connectedness to each other and to the group facilitator. The role of the facilitator is largely one of maintaining a safe and supportive environment for the group members. The facilitator will refocus the group should members get off track. This is the stage in which both the members and the facilitator feel rewarded for their efforts.

The Adjourning Stage

The adjourning stage occurs when the group moves toward termination. Group members may start disengaging from each other. Some members may express increased anxiety about the group ending, while others might deal with the group's termination by participating less actively or attending group sessions more sporadically.

Groups come to an end for a variety of reasons. For example, some groups have a fixed timeline, and when the eight or twelve sessions are completed, the group is finished. A group may also terminate because its goals have been met and people are ready to move on. A group may also fall apart and disintegrate because members are no longer committed to the purpose for which the group was established. Part of the work of the facilitator is to assist the members in ending the group together positively.

One of the tasks of termination is evaluating the group experience. Evaluation can be done either in a formal way, in which the facilitator systematically collects information at the beginning, middle, and end of the group, or in an informal way. For example, group members might be asked in the final session to identify what was valuable about the group and what they found to be less helpful.

Social Work with Communities

In social work, we generally think about **community** as a group of people who share either a geographic space (e.g., a neighbourhood), an identity (e.g., people with disabilities), or an interest (e.g., social activist communities) (Lee, 1999). Communities also require a consciousness of themselves as a community. For example, while people may share a geographic space or an identity, if they do not think of themselves as a community, then generally we regard them as a group of people who lack a sense of community.

As social workers, we are very interested in helping people organize into communities because we know that a sense of community is often helpful for decreasing isolation, sharing resources, and facilitating a sense of self-efficacy, and because communities are often an effective defense against oppression and exploitation. People who have a greater sense of community tend to have a better overall sense of health and well-being.

People, Acting Together

As you read previously, one of the first and most well-known community organizers was Jane Addams, who helped to bring the idea of the settlement house to the United States from Britain. Those involved in the settlement house movement helped to ensure that social work included social activism and bringing people together to meet their own needs more effectively. Jane Addams's work at Hull House in Chicago reflects much of what continues to be integral to community practice today. The women of Hull House created a community space where people could come together, share their concerns, and begin to develop solutions to their problems. The work of Hull House also included research with communities to obtain empirical evidence regarding their challenges, which was in turn used to pressure politicians and city officials to create change and to fulfill people's needs more adequately. Many of the programs at Hull House focused on meeting the needs of women and children, who were considered the heart of the community. When traditional pathways for creating change were not available, the women of Hull House worked with the citizens of east downtown Chicago to hold public protests calling for legislative and policy changes.

Underlying community work is the belief that people acting together have the capacity to improve their own circumstances. Those involved have first-hand knowledge of their situation and what is needed to change things for the better. This belief reflects the fundamental values of the social work profession itself. Community social workers are engaged in expanding community awareness, in leadership development, in building alliances, in education, in collaboration, and in building community capacity. They are often involved in social movements and issues such as homelessness, and in various social programs and research.

Today, this balance of developing programs, creating community space and resources, completing research, and agitating for political change remains central to community work. It often takes place in community health centres, within city governments, or in various non-profit agencies in a community. Even larger bureaucracies such as Children's Aid Societies often employ a community worker to help build more effective community relations.

There are a number of different approaches to community development. Each tends to work better in particular situations, with particular people, and around specific issues. It is helpful to know what approaches are available so that you can find one that fits your personal style and the community with which you are working.

Preserving Neighbourhoods

Trefann Court began as a working-class neighbourhood in the mid 1800s. Its future was threatened in 1966, when Toronto city planners recommended that Trefann Court's deteriorated housing stock be demolished and the entire neighbourhood be rebuilt from scratch.

The city's plans were vigorously opposed by Trefann Court residents, led by a young lawyer named John Sewell—who later became mayor of Toronto.

The battle over Trefann Court was historically significant in that it brought forth new urban planning ideas that advocated greater community involvement, less government interference, and an enlightened interest in rehabilitating and preserving Toronto's historic neighbourhoods.

Rothman's Model of Community Work

In the 1960s, Jack Rothman summarized community work as fitting into three distinct types.

- **Locality development.** Locality development includes those approaches to community organizing that focus on issues relevant to a particular neighbourhood or geographic space. Its focus is on engaging a wide number of community participants. Consensus is built by establishing common interests, and community members are encouraged to become leaders. This approach is exemplified by the settlement house movement and, today, by community health centres. The focus of change tends to be municipal governments, external developers, and sometimes provincial and federal governments. Social workers who use this approach often see their role as one of educating people, facilitating conversations, and organizing community members to pursue specific goals.
- **Social planning.** Social planning is an expert-driven approach to community work, which can often be found in social planning councils and city planning departments. While community members are involved to varying degrees in making this process work, the experts (social workers, public health workers, or social planners) tend to facilitate meetings and write any reports that emerge from the process. This approach focuses mainly on the technical aspects of achieving tasks and allocating resources. It is not about changing society, but about how to meet immediate needs. Social workers in this type of community work often take on the role of researcher, proposal writer, or communications manager.
- **Social action.** Social action is an activist approach to community work seen in many social movements, such as the anti-globalization movement, the feminist movement, and the anti-racist movement. This approach often uses social protest to challenge injustices. A social action approach to community work aims to redistribute power, resources, and decision making. Generally, it involves organizing people who are marginalized from the decision-making process, but it can also focus on the general public. The aim is to build political power and to create institutional change. Social workers who engage in this type of community work are often advocates, facilitators, organizers, and researchers.

Community
A group of people with diverse characteristics who are linked by social ties, share common perspectives and a common identity, and engage in joint action in specific geographical locations or settings. A community is often an effective defense against oppression and exploitation.

Saul Alinsky's Approach to Community Activism

Saul Alinsky is sometimes called "the father of community organizing." Alinsky was very effective in organizing communities in the United States from the 1930s to the 1960s. He also travelled to Canada to work with Aboriginal peoples.

Alinsky's approach was confrontational and strategic. Alinsky was largely concerned with strategies to win battles for marginalized communities. He spoke of community organizing as a process of going to war (Alinsky, 1971). This masculine language often alienated women and peace activists, but many groups have successfully adapted his methods to fit their own agendas. Alinsky was not only concerned with battling the power holders to demand distribution of resources, but he was also very effective at building community organizations, which he saw as instrumental in making community work sustainable. Thus, his approach is a balance between creating long-term activist organizations and planning short-term, exciting challenges to power holders.

One of the most helpful insights that Alinsky brought to organizing is the notion that community work needs to be fun—people only like to get involved with tactics that are enjoyable and do not drag on too long (Stall and Stoeker, 1998).

He was also well aware that an organizer needs to plan tactics that are within the experience of the community members and outside the experience of those people that you are organizing against. He understood how powerful the element of surprise is for communities who challenge power holders.

Alinsky did not feel that democratic capitalism itself needed to be challenged, but he did believe in creating confrontation to redistribute resources within that system (Alinsky, 1971). He was disdainful of idealistic approaches to community work, feeling that it was important to start where people were at, and to create a vision that was fundamentally built within the existing social structures. His approach to organizing is still widely used in North America today.

Saul Alinsky (1909-1972)

Saul Alinsky is generally considered to be the founder of modern community organizing. In the 1930s, he organized the stockyard workers of Chicago and founded the Industrial Areas Foundation (IAF).

Alinsky helped organize Mexican-Americans after World War II. In the 1950s, he turned his attention to the African-American ghettos. He is often credited with inspiring the grassroots movements of the 1960s.

Alinsky's most famous work, *Rules for Radicals* (1971), was published just before his death in 1972. Alinsky's tactics were often unorthodox. In *Rules for Radicals*, he wrote that the job of the organizer is to "maneuver and bait the establishment so that it will publicly attack him as a 'dangerous enemy.'"

Idle No More, a national and worldwide grassroots movement, protests alleged legislative abuses of Indigenous treaty rights by Canada's former Stephen Harper-led Conservative federal government.

Paulo Freire's Approach to Community Mobilization

Paulo Freire was an educator in Brazil in the 1950s, and his work is significant in the shaping of contemporary community work, not to mention education theory and practice. In Brazil he worked to develop a national education system at a time when poor Brazilians were starting to realize that they needed to challenge the oppression they were facing. In this revolutionary context, Freire developed a radical approach to education that is applicable to community practice.

Freire criticized the "banking" approach to education, whereby an educator stands in front of a group of people who stay silent and quickly copy down everything the educator says. Freire argued that this makes people into passive objects. Instead, he developed an approach to education in which the educator asks the community members questions about their lives; in critically exploring their lives, people also learn to read and write.

When the questions asked by a facilitator are relevant to people's lives, they learn easily. At the same time, they develop a collective, critical consciousness of their lives and the challenges they are facing.

Freire's education system was highly effective, but it was perceived as a threat to the country's power holders, many of whom relied on the peasants' acquiescence to being exploited. As a result, Freire was exiled in 1964 after a military coup in Brazil. In the 1960s and 1970s, Freire taught at universities in the United States and Britain and helped with education reform in former Portuguese colonies in Africa. He returned to Brazil to continue his work in the 1980s.

A Freirian approach to community work begins with a listening survey. The community organizer goes into the community and talks to people, knocking on doors and visiting people at bus stops, in laundromats, and at other common gathering places. While doing this, the organizer tries to find out what community members feel strongly about—either positive aspects of their lives or negative ones.

Next, the organizer and a small group of community members—called a learning group—gather together to go through the findings of the listening survey, making *codes* from the ideas they have heard. Codes can be pictures, films, images, or plays that represent the issues the community feels strongly about. These codes are then presented to the community to stimulate discussion about what is going well or badly in the community and to stimulate action planning with a view to creating change (Hope and Timmel, 1984).

Freire's Concept of "Praxis"

What is integral to a Freirian approach to social change is a process of reflection and action called "praxis." Freire believed that a successful action for social change must be reflected upon both in advance of the action and afterward, thereby creating new and more effective actions, which are also then reflected upon.

Freire argued that his approach would encourage thoughtful actions rather than reactive responses to injustice, which are often contradictory and difficult to sustain. For example, when some revolutionary movements achieve power, they can be just as oppressive as the power holders they overthrew.

Freire's approach to community work and community education is fundamentally committed to people becoming empowered to create a social justice revolution.

Paulo Freire (1921–1997)
Brazilian educator and social critic Paulo Freire studied law and philosophy. In the 1940s, he worked with illiterate and impoverished people in Brazil. In 1962, he had the opportunity to apply his educational theories to 300 sugar cane workers, teaching them to read and write in 45 days.

Freire is best known for his attack on what he called the "banking" concept of education, which views knowledge as a gift to be bestowed by the knowledgeable upon the ignorant. This concept attempts to control people's thoughts and actions, leads men and women to adjust unthinkingly to the world, and inhibits their creative power. Freire's work laid the foundation for what is now called "critical pedagogy."

Community Capacity Building

Community capacity building is an approach that originated in the United States and that was spearheaded by John McKnight and John Kretzmann. It is a contemporary approach to community organizing that has become popular both nationally and internationally. McKnight and Kretzmann believe that it is vitally important to develop an approach to community work that builds upon the strengths and assets of a community rather than focusing on the community's needs. They also argue that communities should develop their own resources to meet their needs rather than relying heavily on state programs, which are stigmatizing and create a destructive dependency (McKnight and Kretzmann, 1993).

This approach involves assessing the strengths and resources in a community in terms of social relationships, people's gifts and skills, local businesses, places of worship, and community space. Generally, organizers using this approach create a map of these strengths and resources, which is the foundation from which community members work to further develop their assets. This approach is particularly powerful for communities in which people need to become more aware of their potential.

One possible limitation of this approach is that some communities are so resource-poor that they are unable to deal with their problems without state support. Some argue that a more rights-focused approach to community work is necessary, one that demands state institutions be accountable for meeting the needs of marginalized communities, rather than simply encouraging communities to meet their own needs (McGrath et al., 1999).

A Community Capacity-Building Peer Model

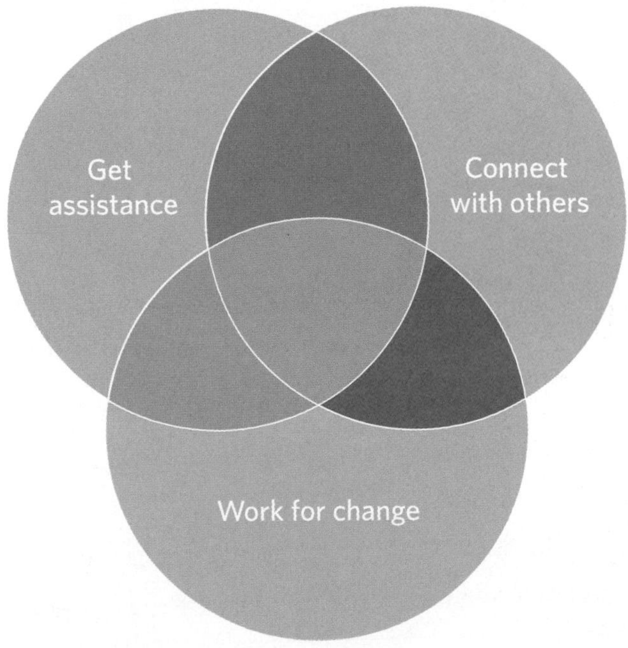

Figure 4.2 This community capacity-building peer model underlies the work of organizations such as the Centre for Gender Adocacy in Montréal. It shows how all aspects of the Centre's work are interconnected.

Margaret Mead (1901–1978)
American cultural anthropologist Margaret Mead made this now-famous statement about community empowerment:

"Never doubt that a small group of thoughtful, committed citizens can change the world; indeed, it's the only thing that ever has."

Feminist and Women-Centred Community Work

Feminist and women-centred approaches to community development are not linked to a particular person, but rather are ways of organizing that have been identified with feminist and women's organizing throughout the twentieth century. This style of organizing was developed by working-class women, Black women activists, lesbian activists, and middle-class white women. While it does not necessarily exclude men, it often focuses on women as key to their communities and on the notion that meeting women's needs impacts positively on families and the community more broadly (Stall and Stoeker, 1998).

Community capacity building
A popular approach to community work that builds upon the strengths and assets of a community rather than focusing on the community's needs. Its ultimate goal is self-sufficency rather than dependence on state programs.

Feminist and women-centred approaches to community organizing tend to rely on consensus decision making, shared leadership, and a process orientation (Adamson et al., 1988). To achieve its ends, the activist group uses methods that are consistent with their goals. This model tends to focus on creating concrete changes in the experiences of women and communities and is often used to establish community kitchens, playgrounds, co-operative childcare, shelters for abused women, and sexual assault centres. This approach usually involves a great deal of peer education, or consciousness raising. One of the limits of this approach is that it can take some time, so it is not always the most appropriate approach when decisive action is needed. It is also geared to more long-term changes involving small groups of citizens coming together.

As one example of vibrant, feminist-based community work, the Concordia University-based Centre for Gender Advocacy in Montréal is an independent, student-funded advocacy organization that promotes gender equality and empowerment, especially as it relates to marginalized communities. Its programs include Missing Justice (for Missing and Murdered Indigenous Women); a Sexual Assault Centre Campaign; Reproductive Justice; and Trans Health Advocacy. The Centre believes that gender oppression is inextricably linked to social and economic justice. The Centre works within a feminist framework to challenge these systemic oppressions by

- facilitating social action through ongoing programming and campaigns, as well as building coalitions and working in solidarity with grassroots social movements;
- providing respectful, confidential, peer-to-peer support, advocacy, and resources for those who seek it with a focus on harm reduction, empowerment, and self-determination;
- providing a multimedia resource centre and library, both open to the public; and
- providing an accessible space to facilitate community organizing and action. (See Figure 4.2.)

Another approach to community work looks at the building of community as a healing practice (sometimes linked to spirituality). From this perspective, community members draw on community traditions and values as part of a process of healing. This reconnection to traditional values and practices is seen as an important way to deal with problems such as family breakdown, suicide, substance use disorders, and histories of abuse.

This healing approach is often used by Indigenous groups and spiritual communities. Members of these communities are encouraged and supported to find a path to wellness. This approach to community work can help people remove internal obstacles to meaningful participation in society and bring about genuine healing for the individuals involved, but it tends not to focus as much on the structural inequalities that may also exist in a particular context.

Social Work with Communities
Mobilizing to effect social change

Bill Lee (1999) breaks down community work into a series of discrete phases. While these phases do not always occur in a linear fashion, they provide an idea of the process that constitutes community work. The following phases are similar to those outlined by Lee in his book, *Pragmatics of Community Organizing* (2011).

Pre-Entry

The job of a community worker begins even before entering a community, in a process identified as pre-entry. Often before having contact with a community, a social worker is hired by a funder to complete a project. While it is preferable to begin work at the community's direct request, it is rare that communities have sufficient resources to do this. As a result, there are tasks that the social worker can do to help prepare to collaborate effectively with community members.

A social worker who is hired by a funding organization to work in a local community needs to spend time learning the general history of the community and its relationship with the funder before entering the community. He or she also needs to have a sense of the politics of the community, how the community's problems are perceived by a diverse group of its members, and whether this differs from the funder's understanding of the problems.The social worker also needs to understand the length of time available to do the work and what outcomes are expected (and whether the community has any input into these outcomes). This type of preparation work is vital to ensuring that an organizer is able to create a helpful beginning for the community process.

Contact and Engagement

The next stage of community work is contact and engagement. It is in this phase that the community organizer starts to meet community members, listens to how they feel about their community, and begins to engage them in a process of change.

Engagement is often a long and challenging process in which the organizer works to build trusting relationships with as representative a sample of the community as possible. In this phase, the worker also tries to support people in developing a sense of hope that things can change.

The most challenging part of this and of later stages in community practice is that rather than doing all the work necessary to organize and create change, a social worker is always trying to support the community to do the work themselves. This often requires that the worker take a slow and often winding approach to reaching goals.

The key issues in contact and engagement are significantly shaped by whether the community worker is perceived as an insider or an outsider to the community and by the amount of trust that develops between the organizer and community members. Being a community outsider presents a different set of challenges in this phase than those presented when one is a community insider. In either situation, the building of trust, broad participation, and hope that change is possible are key.

Community Analysis

Since the days of the settlement movement, it has been clear that in order to create lasting social change, a community must understand itself and develop a process to gain information about what is happening to its members. The most common approach used to achieve this is participatory action research (PAR), where community members are involved in deciding the research questions, determining the research process, and analyzing the research data.

Through this process two important things happen: first, community members develop skills, and second, the community gets the evidence they need to encourage power holders to listen to their demands and create change. It is far harder to ignore a community group armed with data to support their position than it is a group that is simply presenting opinions or their unique perspective.

Organizational Development

The next important phase of community work is to help the community get organized and develop roles and responsibilities that people can take on to facilitate change. For example, a community association may elect board members through biannual elections in which anyone who lives within certain community boundaries can vote. Sometimes communities hire a part-time staff person to help develop community programs. Other communities rely on a large number of volunteers who make decisions as a collective. In either situation, the roles, responsibilities, and decision-making processes need to be clear and agreed upon.

It is important in this phase (and in all phases of community practice) that social workers work *with* people, not *for* them. If we support community members in doing the work to create change, they learn skills and become more confident, and this can often help build solidarity. If a community worker does everything, then all the community learns is to be dependent on that worker. Working with people, not for them, can be difficult at times. It requires patience, and sometimes we have to let people make their own mistakes, but it is only by doing so that communities can do the learning that helps them become more confident in their decisions and processes.

Action Planning and Mobilization

After a group has become organized, it is time to begin to plan actions and mobilize. The most important predictor of success at the action planning and mobilization stage is the amount of community support for any action.

Any plan for moving forward relies upon people building consensus around a clear plan in which everyone knows what goals are being pursued, how long it will take to achieve these goals, and how the community is going to attain these goals. If a community is deeply divided, it is difficult to launch a successful action. There are usually three approaches to action planning. The first involves co-operating with power holders. If that approach is unsuccessful, groups can launch various types of issue-raising campaigns. If such campaigns don't effect change, the third approach is confrontation.

Key to any successful action is media coverage. Again, this requires substantial work prior to an action. Relationships need to be built with the media, and care has to be put into ensuring that the action is, in itself, media-worthy. Are there visuals for television cameras and social media? Does the group have a clear message that is easily grasped by an audience who is unfamiliar with the issue? Are the community members prepared to speak to the media? Does everyone know how to stick to the message? Do you have information for reporters so that they have the facts and the background?

Conflict Resolution

Another key component of community work is trying to mediate conflicts either within the community or with parties outside the community. In this process, a community worker needs to be aware of what is at stake in a conflict in terms of process, emotions, and content. To resolve conflict, an impartial person may need to be brought in to help each side clarify its position and to search for possible compromises. There are many different resources, workshops, and certificate programs to help social workers develop their conflict resolution skills.

Evaluation

One of the final stages of community practice involves evaluation, which allows a community to reflect upon whether they were able to achieve the goals that they set for themselves. A final evaluation is most effective when evaluation has been an ongoing component of the community work. Sometimes it is driven by a funder who wants a report on outcomes, but evaluations can also provide a useful opportunity for communities to reflect upon what they have achieved and to enhance their enthusiasm and confidence for future projects.

Social work with communities often addresses the same problems that individual- or family-focused counsellors deal with, but it takes a slightly different approach, looking at problems as something that a group of people experience. Community social workers go to great effort to identify people's common experiences and to build upon them to create effective community groups capable of creating change for themselves. As they do so, community groups often gain valuable skills and are more able to effect change. And increasingly, they develop a sense that they can influence their environment and improve their lives. With this lived experience, they are armed with the skills and confidence to challenge those who exploit them, and to imagine and create a better future for themselves.

Susan Macphail

Susan Macphail was one of the founders of a women's resource centre in London, Ontario. It was an idea so new to the city at the time that "We actually didn't know what we were going to do. I got hired as a feminist counsellor and I had no idea what that would be."

My Sisters' Place is a day shelter, counselling service, and agency for change for homeless and at-risk women. At My Sisters' Place, the women who seek assistance—as well as those who offer it—are empowered by programs that build on women's many strengths.

Susan Macphail is the director of My Sisters' Place, a women's program centre located in London, Ontario. The centre offers more than two dozen programs for marginalized women. These services are provided by staff, by volunteers, and sometimes by outside agency personnel.

Those individuals offering services at My Sisters' Place range from having no formal training to having extensive professional training, including social work education. The helping relationship—which includes warmth, empathy, and genuineness—is centrally important to effective social work with individuals. A helping relationship can be demonstrated by volunteers, peers, and professionals. My Sisters' Place provides an excellent example of effective social work with individuals, groups, and the larger community.

At My Sisters' Place, social work that benefits individuals includes clinical mental health counselling, case work, First Nations counselling, information sharing about resources, and physical health services. Women who visit the centre can have lunch, take a shower, sleep in a day bed, use the house telephone, meet with a support worker, access the services of a social worker, and see a nurse practitioner. Staff and volunteers who engage with the women often conduct either formal or informal intakes, assessments, and collaborative planning to help the women reorganize their lives.

The centre offers groups focused on anger management, healthy relationships, mindfulness, gardening, and art therapy. Women have the opportunity to both give and receive support from each other. Educational, support, task, and social action groups are all available at My Sisters' Place, and social action groups connect the agency with the larger community.

My Sisters' Place liaises with the community in a number of ways. There are 27 community partners, including businesses that support a micro enterprise at the centre that makes jewellery. This cooperative group meets behind the main building in what was once an old coach house. This building has been restored, and is now used to give women the opportunity to create jewellery and accessories to sell to customers.

Other community services include engaging the east-end London neighbourhood in community development and capacity building focused on affordable housing and day care.

The centre's work is informed by a number of converging ideas, such as feminism, strengths-based practice, a pro-LGBTQ+ orientation, women-centeredness, anti-oppressive practice, respect for First Nations, a rational-cultural model, an emphasis on community development, and a focus on social determinants of mental health. Various theories inform the work, and vice versa.

Working with, and not for, people is a centrally important principle at My Sisters' Place. The so-called "expert" who attempts to diagnose clients and devise solutions has no place in this agency. Working with the women, who already have many strengths, empowers those who seek assistance as well as those who offer it.

Because the centre has engaged for many years with numerous marginalized women, it has identified some common issues that affect the lives of these women. Concerns related to housing, violence, children, and poverty are uppermost.

An important part of the centre's role is to advocate for a national housing strategy, a national plan for violence prevention across the lifespan, national child care, a poverty reduction strategy, and a national minimum wage.

Chapter 4 Review

Review Questions

1. Explain what is meant by "evidence-based social work practice."
2. What are the three areas or fields of social work practice, and how do they differ?
3. What steps does a social worker usually follow in providing help to an individual or family? Identify and describe each step.
4. Select four direct practice skills and describe their importance for working with individuals and families.
5. Why is the helping relationship important?
6. Briefly describe the three attributes identified by Carl Rogers that are needed to develop a helping relationship. Why are these attributes important?
7. Why do you think community capacity building has become a popular approach to community organizing?

Exploring Social Work

1. Graphic organizers known as "genograms" can be helpful in beginning to understand family dynamics. Do some research about genograms, and then create one for your own family, showing the complex relationships between family members—today and over generations. Show how you and various members of your family interact with people and institutions in ways that might be relevant to a better understanding of your family today.
2. Social work with individuals and families involves the skill of active listening. You have the opportunity to practise this skill every day. Choose a period of time in your week when you are in dialogue and consciously practise active listening. Notice how your perception shifts when you consciously listen. How is it different from your usual form of listening? How would this benefit you in your role as a social worker or social service worker? Record your experience in a two-page report. Be sure to indicate how this technique might be employed in a practice setting.
3. Do some research or draw upon your own experience to describe Bill Lee's phases of community work in a real-world context. By what means can a social worker try to ensure that community work is effective, positive, long-lasting, and respectful of the needs and goals of community members?

Websites

Success and Innovation in Social Work Practice
www.casw-acts.ca/celebrating/innovation_e.html
The Canadian Association of Social Work (CASW) shares stories of creative and innovative practice from across Canada. By sharing these stories, the CASW hopes to facilitate further innovation and to celebrate the social work practice of our colleagues.

Information for Practice
www.nyu.edu/socialwork/ip/
IP's mission is to help social service professionals throughout the world conveniently maintain an awareness of news regarding the profession and emerging scholarship. It is sponsored by the New York University School of Social Work, the Division of Social Work and Behavioral Science, Mount Sinai School of Medicine, the Institute for the Advancement of Social Work Research, and the Society for Social Work and Research.

The Vanier Institute of the Family
www.vifamily.ca
The Vanier Institute of the Family is a national, charitable organization dedicated to providing leadership on issues affecting the well-being of Canadian families. Its work includes collecting and analyzing information on changing patterns of family formation and function; advocating social change to create more supportive environments for families; and advising government, corporations, and religious organizations on matters of family policy.

My Sisters' Place
www.mysistersplacelondon.ca
My Sisters' Place is a diverse group of women supporting each other through experiences with homelessness, mental health issues, and substance use. Every self-identifying woman is welcome through its doors. This agency offers a safe space to be off the streets for women experiencing homelessness, and it provides the necessities of home, such as healthy food, showers, laundry, phone, and access to the Internet.

Social Work and Child Welfare in Canada

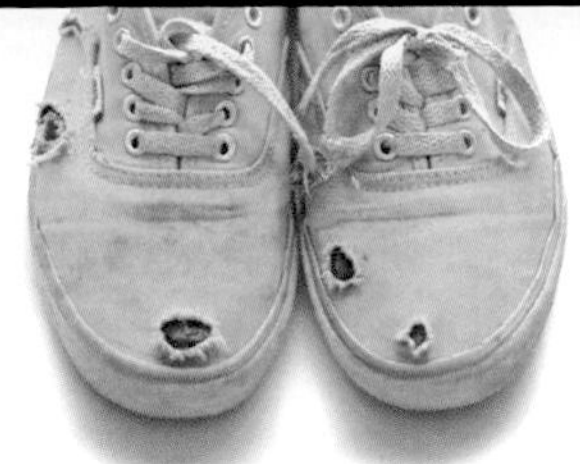

Jackie Stokes

5 Child Protection and Family Support

"The child is the central figure in all social reform."

J.J. Kelso (1864–1935), child welfare pioneer

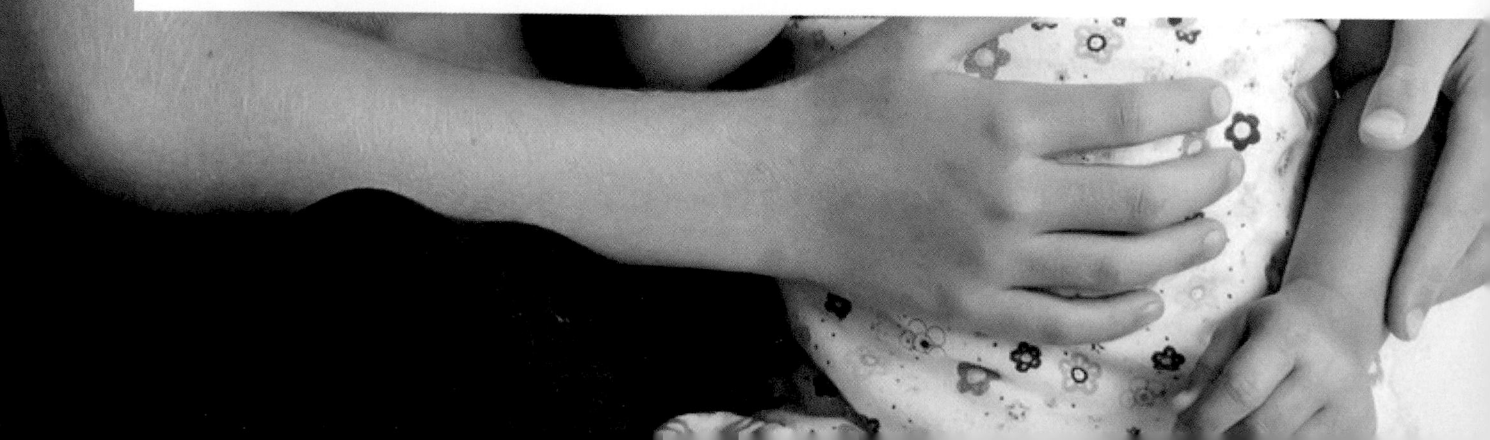

There is no centralized agency across Canada to coordinate child welfare.

In all the provinces and territories of Canada, governments and non-profit agencies provide a broad range of indispensable services to ensure the well-being of children, youth, and families. These family support and child protection services are collectively known as the child welfare system. The aspects of child welfare most often associated with social work are the legislative and mandated responsibilities related to protecting children and youth from harm. Child protection services include investigating and assessing the abuse and neglect of children and youth; collaborating with family members, other professionals, and often elders to devise safety plans; and providing in-home and out-of-home services.

Child welfare is a common field of work for graduating social work students. The field is changing rapidly, and workers continually need to update their skills and learn new approaches. Despite its difficult conditions and high rates of attrition, work with vulnerable children, youth, and their families can be highly rewarding and contributes greatly to a civilized and just society.

In this chapter, you will learn how to...

- identify six key activities related to service provision by social work practitioners on behalf of children and families
- explain evidence-based child welfare practice
- describe the historical evolution of child welfare in Canada
- explain the goals and characteristics of emerging collaborative approaches to child protection
- define child maltreatment and analyze the prevalence of child maltreatment and child neglect in Canada
- identify systemic risks and structural interventions associated with the maltreatment of children, including Indigenous children
- explain some psycho-social processes and decision making related to placing children in substitute care
- analyze current child-welfare dilemmas
- explain the steps in providing child-welfare services in ways that demonstrate effective social-work practice
- identify the key elements of a Family Group Conference

Key Concepts

- Child welfare system
- In-home services
- Out-of-home services
- Evidence-based practice
- Battered-child syndrome
- Badgley Report
- Risk assessment
- Duty to report
- Collaborative approaches
- Family Group Conference (FGC)
- Best interests approach
- Least restrictive approach
- Child maltreatment
- Canadian Incidence Study of Reported Child Abuse and Neglect (CIS)
- Foster homes
- Group homes

Focusing Question

What factors must social workers consider when assessing a child's safety and a possible need for substitute care?

An Overview of Child Welfare Services in Canada

Canada currently has no national **child welfare system** to address the needs of disadvantaged children. Child welfare is highly regulated across the country, however, through provincial and territorial laws and regulations. Each province and territory assumes responsibility for its children and youth and has different organizations and legislation governing their welfare. For example, there are 53 separate child welfare agencies in Ontario alone. In addition, First Nations child welfare services are provided by the provincial agency, by a First Nations agency delegated by the provincial authority, or directly by First Nations agencies as negotiated under the federal government's policy on Aboriginal self-government.

Kinship Care

Kinship care can be provided by a child's grandparents, aunts and uncles, other relatives, or even close family friends. This option allows children to maintain a family connection even though they cannot live with their birth parents. It also allows for the maintenance of a child's cultural identity.

Child welfare is a major area of employment for social workers. In 2008, just under one quarter of a million Canadian children (a rate of 38 per 1000 children) were investigated by child welfare agencies due to child protection concerns. Of those investigations, approximately 8 percent (a rate of 3 per 1000 children) resulted in a change of residence for the child (Public Health Agency of Canada, 2010).

This field is also one of the most difficult areas for practitioners because of the heart-wrenching cases that can arise and the often-complex moral, legal, and ethical issues involved. The work of child welfare practitioners involves much more than simply removing children from unsafe home environments. Provincial services for children and youth, provided by a branch of the provincial government or by a private or non-profit agency, involve six key activities:

- **Child and family investigation.** Protecting children at risk of abuse and neglect by investigating their family's capacity to ensure a safe environment for them
- **Family support.** Providing a range of family programs and services in order to maintain healthy families, support families at risk, and protect children
- **Child placement.** Finding temporary substitute care, such as kinship care, foster care, and group homes, for children who cannot continue to live with their parent(s) or guardian(s)
- **Foster care.** Recruiting foster-care providers and providing training and support, as well as monitoring foster homes
- **Guardianship.** Delivering services to children who are in government care on a long-term or continuing basis
- **Adoption.** Finding permanent homes for children who cannot live with their biological or legal parents

Acting in these many ways through provincial agencies and non-profit centres, social workers and child welfare advocates support and intervene on behalf of children and their families.

Comprehensive Social Services for Children and Youth

The services that social workers provide for children and youth can be either "in-home" or "out-of-home."

- **In-home services** are provided to help family members live together harmoniously in a secure and safe environment. The main categories of in-home services include family counselling services, parenting supports, and family educational services.
- **Out-of-home services** are implemented when the home situation becomes unsuitable for the child. They include foster care, kinship care, residential care, reunification services, and adult transition programs.

Evidence-Based Child Welfare Practice

As explained in Chapter 4, **evidence-based practice** (or evidence-informed practice) refers to a process designed to ensure that social work interventions have the best possible outcomes and benefit the greatest number of people. Practitioners combine the latest research with their own experiences and client preferences to help guide service provision.

In an attempt to group and classify factors that might have an impact on service provision, Regehr, Stern, and Shlonsky (2007) outlined a practice model in relation to child welfare (shown in Figure 5.1 below). It takes into account not only the immediate situation of the client, but also the wider community, the social services agency itself, and the larger political context.

For example, Fallon and Trocmé (2011) examined the *CIS*-1998 data on how social workers' characteristics contributed to the provision of services. Some of the findings were:

- Metropolitan agencies provided ongoing services to 27 percent of cases (the lowest proportion), whereas rural agencies provided ongoing services to 45 percent of cases.
- Investigations involving workers with a generic caseload had a higher rate of ongoing services (46 percent) than those with only intake responsibilities (29 percent).
- Investigations by workers who had either a B.S.W. or M.S.W. had a lower rate of ongoing service provision (31 percent) compared to workers who did not (38 percent).
- The characteristics of the social worker had little effect on decision making; however, workers' attitudes made a difference—those who were "pro-removal" rated risk more highly and were more likely to recommend removal than those who were "anti-removal."

Child welfare system
A group of public and private services focused on ensuring that all children live in safe, permanent, and stable environments that support their well-being

Evidence-based practice
A process aimed at ensuring that social work interventions have the most effective outcomes and benefit the greatest number of people. Practitioners combine the latest research with their own experiences and client preferences to help guide the delivery of their services.

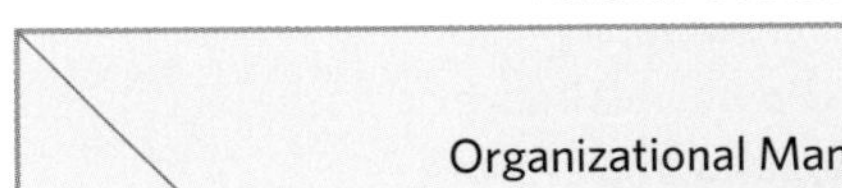

Figure 5.1 This diagram represents a practice model for effective decision making related to child protection that identifies the complex, interrelated variables in their various contexts.

Source: Regehr, C., Stern, S., and Shlonsky, A. (2007). Operationalizing evidence-based practice. *Research on Social Work Practice*, 17(3), 408–416.

The Historical Evolution of Child Welfare in Canada

Each province and territory in Canada now has a well-established system of child welfare services to prevent or help remedy problems that may cause children to be neglected, abused, exploited, or in trouble with the law. For much of our history, however, children were often regarded as chattel to be bought, sold, or even put to death. The evolution of child welfare demonstrates a radical shift in societal views of children. Once treated as property or a source of cheap labour, children are now seen as valuable human beings entitled to legislated rights and protection.

Pre-Industrial Child Welfare—Pre-1890

The problems of child abuse and neglect did not suddenly appear in the twentieth century. The children of rural settler families in British North America typically worked at farming alongside other family members, and a strict division of labour was enforced. The mother was responsible for family-care needs, such as cooking, cleaning, and nursing, while the father was responsible for the family's economic survival needs. The wife and children existed as dependants of the family patriarch. Patriarchal authority was reinforced through a variety of state laws and practices.

By contrast, Indigenous communities had rather more inclusive ideas concerning children. Most Indigenous peoples of Canada believe that a child belongs to his or her people, and that a child is a gift from the Creator. They believe that this connection of child to community is non-discretionary—it is the responsibility of all to meet the child's needs.

In 1792, the Province of Upper Canada proclaimed that the Common Law of England would be enforced in the new province. This law was exceedingly harsh toward children. Then, in 1799, Upper Canada introduced the first act concerning children. Known as the *Orphans Act*, it gave town wardens the power to bind a child under 14 to an employer as an apprentice. In 1827, this act was replaced with the *Guardianship Act*, which allowed guardians appointed by the court to bind the child as an apprentice. Poor families were viewed as moral and economic threats, and to avoid tainting the children of such families with parental failure, the children were "bound out" to proper self-supporting families.

The period from 1867 to 1890 saw new laws that began to change the exalted position of husbands and fathers, but times remained difficult for children and women. The legislative right of men to inflict arbitrary and severe punishment on their wives and children was beginning to be challenged. In 1874, Ontario introduced compulsory education, the regulation of work hours, the right of women to hold property, and the rise of new and improved social agencies. For the first time, courts would decide whether a child's best interests would be better served with his or her family, one parent, or an employer. Until this time, however, children generally were not seen as needing special care or nurturing. In fact, their needs were often ignored.

This period also saw the beginning of a campaign to assimilate Indigenous children into mainstream Canadian society. The *Indian Act* (1876) exemplified the colonizers' views toward First Nations and their children. Besides outlawing traditional ceremonies, such as the potlatch, the laws attempted to eradicate Indigenous cultures by taking children out of First Nations homes and communities and placing them in residential schools. These schools were administered by Christian churches in association with the government. (For more on residential schools, see Chapter 9.)

John Joseph Kelso (1864–1935)

J.J. Kelso (at right in photo) was an Irish immigrant to Toronto and a child welfare pioneer. He helped found the Toronto Humane Society in 1887, which at the time aimed to prevent cruelty to children and animals. Kelso served as Superintendent of Neglected and Dependent Children in Ontario until retiring in 1934. During his tenure, Kelso helped establish Children's Aid Societies throughout Ontario—60 by 1912—and in four other provinces. Kelso's influence led to the Ontario Children's Protection Act, the first such legislation in Canada. He was a tireless promoter and advocate of children's rights who firmly believed that wide community mobilization is required for social change.

Child Welfare Legislation in the Late 1890s and Early 1900s

In the late nineteenth and early twentieth centuries, there was a marked increase in government involvement in children's issues. In particular, federal and provincial legislation was enacted that allowed the state to remove children from the care of their parents or guardians. The federal *Juvenile Delinquent Act* of 1908 and the *Ontario Act for the Prevention of Cruelty to Children* of 1893 were both aimed at the protection of children. The legal mandate for promoting the "best interests" of children was given to the state, and the state could decide whether parents were good or bad. It had the authority (through legislation and the courts) to remove children from homes and place them in care.

In the 1890s, Canadian provinces began to establish commissions to inspect the working conditions for children in factories. Many children as young as eight and nine years of age were employed, and inspections often revealed a callous disregard for the welfare of these children by factory owners. For example, there were repeated reports of poor ventilation and a lack of sanitary equipment. As well, the children were receiving no education while working in the factories, which contributed to the large number of illiterate adults across the country. As a result, new legislation was passed to regulate working conditions and hours of work. Eventually, the age at which one was no longer considered a child was raised to 16.

The passing of the 1893 *Children's Protection Act* in Ontario ushered in a new era of child welfare legislation protecting children from abuse and neglect. For example, a child found sleeping in the open air was now considered to be neglected. Those found guilty of mistreating a child were sentenced to three months of hard labour. The idea of foster homes, supervised by Children's Aid Societies, also originated with this act. In 1908, the *Child Welfare Act* provided for procedures to rehabilitate mistreated children. Between 1891 and 1912, sixty Children's Aid Societies sprang up in Ontario. In 1912, they amalgamated and are now known as the Ontario Association of Children's Aid Societies (OACAS). In other provinces as well, a new idea began to crystallize about the obligation of society to protect children. Following the lead of Ontario's first child protection law in 1893, other provinces developed laws and practices based on the doctrine of *parens patriae* (parent of the nation).

The Role of Women's Organizations in Furthering Children's Protection

Several important women's organizations emerged in the late nineteenth century that affected the rights of children. These organizations played an important role in the development of child and family welfare in this country, not to mention the status of women.

The Women's Missionary Societies that had formed in most Canadian churches in the 1870s and 1880s began addressing the needs of women and children. The Women's Christian Temperance Union, established in 1874, originally emphasized the prohibition of the sale of alcohol, but broadened its social goals to helping children. This included ensuring child protection, establishing reformatories for juveniles, and building cottage-style homes to replace institutional care facilities. The Young Women's Christian Association (YWCA) addressed the needs of urban working women, including assisting them with their children.

Additionally, the National Council of Women, formed in 1893 as an alliance of women's organizations aimed at coordinating policies at a national level, considered many women's issues to be "mothering" issues, and their goal was to bring private mothering practices to public and national attention.

Child Welfare Laws in Québec

Québec was the last province to develop child welfare legislation: in 1977 the *Youth Protection Act* (*YPA*) was passed to govern the child welfare system. Until then, responsibility for child protection in Québec had resided with the Catholic Church. French Civil Law, the governing tradition in Québec, gave the Church the power to step in when parents failed. Thus, Québec did not initiate child protection as a separate provincial service until 1933, and the Church's influence on child welfare was strong up until the early 1960s.

The *YPA* defines the range of situations that can endanger a child's safety or development to the point where intervention is required. The *YPA* also specifies that all citizens, and especially professionals who work with children, are responsible for reporting suspected child maltreatment to a Director of Youth Protection (DYP).

Changing Paradigms of Child Welfare in the Twentieth Century

Describing the evolution of child welfare legislation and practice in Canada is complicated because each province and territory has individual jurisdictional responsibility for the well-being of children, and no national framework for child welfare exists.

In general, however, child welfare was originally entrenched in a child-saving paradigm—that is, in the perceived need to rescue children from abusive and neglectful parents. This approach was based on principles related to investigation by an agency and resulted in the provision of either meagre support for "deserving parents" or foster care for children whose parents were deemed unfit (Swift, 2011: 40). Exceptions occurred in Québec, where the Catholic Church was relied upon to step in when parents could not care for their children, and for Aboriginal children, where the primary form of "child protection" was residential schools.

By the 1920s, however, a new notion of "childhood" was emerging. The idea that family care, even flawed family care, was better than institutional care, and that a natural family was better than a foster family, took hold. In 1927, Charlotte Whitton's seminal report on child welfare in British Columbia painted a compelling picture of the negative effects of institutions on children's well-being. This report endorsed preventive work with families and set the stage for the training of skilled social workers.

By the 1960s, various treatment regimes for children emerged in social work, ranging from strict discipline to a more permissive approach that concentrated on free expression and creativity.

Research-Based Revelations of the Extent of Harm Being Done to Children

The post-World War II period saw an expansion of research and of empirical knowledge related to child welfare and child maltreatment in particular. American pediatrician Dr. C. Henry Kempe published a landmark article in 1962 on the **battered-child syndrome**; for the first time, a medical professional identified child abuse as a clinical condition. Kempe's paper established child abuse as a regular and recurring aspect of family life in many households rather than a sensational exception. Recognizing that children may be frightened to "disclose" and that parents may describe injuries as "accidents," legislators developed laws that required professionals and members of the public to report suspected child abuse and neglect (Bala, 2011: 3).

In 1951, the federal government amended the *Indian Act*, transferring responsibility for the welfare of First Nations children to provincial governments. The resulting removal of thousands of First Nations children from their families claimed national attention in 1983 in Patrick Johnston's *Native Children and the Child Welfare System*. In the book, he coined the now-commonplace term "the Sixties Scoop." Although the practice of removing Aboriginal children from their families and communities had existed prior to the 1960s, this era saw an acceleration in the rate of removal and in the placement of these children, in most cases, into middle-class Euro-Canadian families. This practice eventually led to a massive over-representation of Aboriginal children in care (in 1951, only 1 percent of children in care were Aboriginal, compared to 34 percent in 1964). The over-representation of Aboriginal children in care continues today.

In 1984, the **Badgley Report** (so called because Robin F. Badgley was the chairman of the authoring committee) brought to light the disturbing extent of child sexual abuse in Canada. The report revealed that one out of two females and one out of three males had at some point in their lives been the victim of unwanted sexual acts, and that four out of five of these acts took place during childhood or adolescence. The report concluded that all systems for reporting sexual abuse were flawed and ineffective and that children needed considerably better protection from sexual predators.

New Thinking about Children and Child Welfare

During the post-war period, hundreds of pieces of new child welfare legislation were introduced across the country, altering the way we think of children and how child welfare workers can best perform their roles. While each province passed distinct and separate pieces of legislation, several overall trends became apparent:

- First, there was a shift from volunteers to a more professionalized service delivery system.
- Second, provincial governments themselves began to accept direct responsibility for the delivery of child welfare services.
- Third, social work agencies began to develop and implement risk-assessment models and standardized record-keeping methods.
- Finally, there was a move from institutional and protection-oriented services to non-institutional and prevention-oriented services.

By the end of the 1960s, the number of foster homes had begun to decline, and two alternatives to foster homes and large-scale institutions had emerged: treatment regimes for troubled children and youth were established, and group homes were launched.

The shocking revelations of the extent of child abuse, along with legislation aimed at protecting vulnerable children and young people, led to important improvements in the child welfare system in Canada as the twenty-first century drew near. However, many deep-rooted structural problems, such as poverty and insufficient government funding, continued to present difficult challenges for child-welfare practitioners and advocates, as they do to this day.

As a result of underfunded and understaffed child welfare agencies, social workers often have 30 or more cases at any given time, despite the fact that best practices are half that number. (*The Globe and Mail*, December 9, 2015)

Emerging Approaches to Child Welfare—1990–Present

The 1990s saw heightened media attention on the deaths of children known to child protection authorities. The most prominent of these was the death of Matthew Vaudreuil in British Columbia, which led to the 1995 *Report of the Gove Inquiry into Child Protection in British Columbia* (named for the report's commissioner, the Honourable Judge Thomas J. Gove). Emphasizing the safety of children over family support, the report recommended that a comprehensive "risk-assessment" approach be adopted by child protection agencies. The report instigated an overhaul of the child protection system in British Columbia.

Those changes were replicated across the country. In Ontario, similar reviews occurred in the late 1990s, resulting in new legislation and the implementation of risk-assessment tools designed to prevent harm to children. By 2002, eight Canadian provinces had adopted some form of risk-assessment tool (Swift, 2011: 52).

Risk-Assessment Models

Models for **risk assessment** estimate the likelihood that a child will be maltreated and, if a harmful event should occur, the potential severity of that harm. Child protection authorities hoped that the implementation of standardized risk-assessment models would promote more reliable, more accurate, and less biased decision making related to child welfare (Hughes and Rycus, 2007). Although these models purport to have a research base that correlates risk factors with the abuse and neglect of children, they vary greatly in their scope and purpose, with differing weights assigned to the various risk factors. While it is true that the risk factors identified in most of the risk-assessment systems are associated with child maltreatment, "causality has not been established" (Krane and Davies, 2000: 37).

Importantly, risk-assessment approaches were never intended to be used in isolation from clinical judgment and expertise; they were intended to complement these, not replace them. Over time, however, the approaches became increasingly bureaucratic and used as technocratic tools that child welfare authorities relied upon to address the apparent problem of accountability in the child welfare system. Many opponents of risk-assessment approaches argued that in practice, these approaches contributed to the erosion of professional practice in favour of managerialism (Callahan and Swift, 2007).

By the turn of the twenty-first century, the verdict was in. Most provinces had begun to look at alternative practice paradigms, and many began adopting a range of collaborative approaches to use alongside risk-assessment tools. Under the broad category of alternative responses, these paradigms offer two simultaneous pathways that enable social workers and child welfare agencies to protect children more effectively:

- an investigative track that assesses safety and risk factors
- an assessment track that focuses on family strengths and needs, as well as on voluntary support services available to the family

In many ways, the pendulum is swinging more visibly toward the second, family-centred model of practice, which allows for more collaborative and flexible services and responses to the needs of children and families, while encouraging all parties to seek alternatives to court disputes. Increasingly, amendments to legislation related to child and family services emphasize engaging with family and kin to strive to keep children within permanent family structures.

Risk assessment
In the area of child protection, risk assessment is used to estimate the likelihood that a child will be maltreated, based on a careful examination of pertinent data. The goal of risk assessment is to take action to prevent future abuse or neglect.

Social workers have always assessed risk for future maltreatment as part of their jobs by applying clinical judgement and experience. Structured risk assessment can improve accuracy and consistency in identifying children at high risk for future maltreatment.

A Duty to Report Child Abuse and Neglect

Maltreated or neglected children may be afraid to disclose their abuse because they think no one will believe them. In addition, abusers frequently warn children not to tell anyone about their actions. They may even convince the child that the abuse is the child's fault and that telling someone will only cause more trouble.

For this reason, people in professions that bring them into contact with children have a duty to report if they have reasonable grounds to suspect that a child is, or may be, in need of protection. But it is not only child protection workers who have a duty to report suspected instances of child abuse or neglect. Every member of society has a responsibility to report if there is reason to believe a child may need protection.

Collaborative Approaches to Child Protection

Today's emerging **collaborative approaches** to child protection are based on developing constructive and positive working relationships between social work professionals and family members. Some examples of collaborative approaches include the following:

- **Family Group Conference (FGC).** An FGC is a formal meeting facilitated by a child-welfare worker, at which members of a child's immediate family, extended family members, close friends, and community members develop the best plan to ensure the child's safety and well-being. (See Figure 5.2.)
- **Mediation.** When family members and child-welfare workers disagree on the best way to meet a child's needs, mediation can break the impasse. In this alternative dispute resolution process, a mediator encourages both sides to focus on common goals and interests and to work toward a mutually acceptable solution that will benefit the child.
- **Cultural and/or Traditional Decision Making.** Participants in these processes follow community- or culturally-based models and practices to formulate child-protection plans or resolve disagreements. For example, Elders in some Indigenous communities can guide family members and a child-welfare worker through the stages of reaching a decision.
- **Signs of Safety.** Designed in Western Australia and adopted in Alberta and British Columbia, this approach is a strengths-based program that involves collaboration between family members and child-protection workers in order to focus on safety planning.

Collaborative approaches
Give-and-take partnerships between social workers and clients that de-emphasize the role of the professional as helper, establish a relationship based equality, and engage clients on their own terms

Child-welfare practitioners usually try to seek a balance between two types of approach. The **best interests approach** emphasizes the protection and well-being of the child above all else. The **least restrictive approach** emphasizes the course of action that will cause the least disruption or change for the child, preferably leaving him or her with the family.

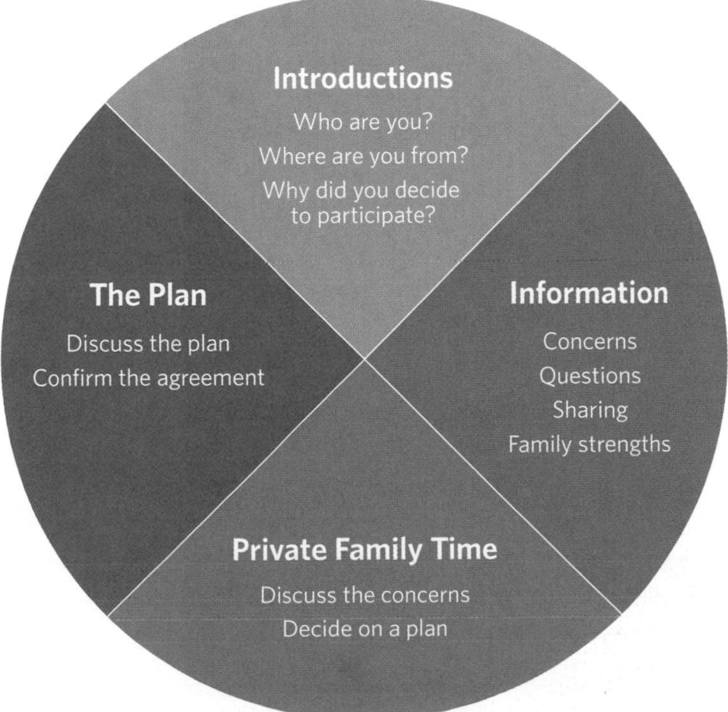

Figure 5.2
The Stages of a Family Group Conference

This diagram represents the typical stages of a Family Group Conference, beginning with "Introductions" of all individuals participating in the conference and proceeding clockwise.

Child Maltreatment and Neglect in Canada

Child maltreatment is an umbrella term referring to multiple forms of child abuse and neglect. Child maltreatment includes acts of *commission* or *omission* by a parent or other caregiver that result in harm, potential for harm, or threat of harm to a child. Different jurisdictions have differing definitions of child abuse, and maltreatment can take many forms. Nevertheless, child maltreatment has five broad categories:

- **Physical abuse** includes any non-accidental action that causes, or could cause, physical harm to a child, such as hitting, shaking, or the unreasonable use of force to restrain a child.
- **Sexual abuse** includes using a child for sexual purposes, such as through sexual contact, inappropriate exposure to sexual activity or material, or exploitation through prostitution and related activities.
- **Neglect** includes the failure of a parent or guardian to provide a child's basic needs, such as food, education, health care, or supervision.
- **Emotional maltreatment** includes behaviours that harm a child's development or sense of self-worth, such as humiliation, rejection, or withholding love or support.
- **Exposure to domestic violence** includes directly witnessing violence between parents or caregivers, or being indirectly exposed by hearing the violence or seeing the after-effects, such as bruising or other physical injuries. (Some provinces and territories include exposure to domestic violence under "emotional maltreatment.")

Canadian Incidence Study of Reported Child Abuse and Neglect (CIS)
The CIS is a national initiative to collect data on children who come to the attention of a child welfare authority due to alleged or suspected abuse and/or neglect. The CIS examines the incidence of reported child maltreatment and the characteristics of the children and families investigated by child-welfare authorities in the year the study is conducted.

Former Public Health Minister Carolyn Bennett (shown here) released results of the CIS for 2003 at a news conference in Ottawa in 2005.

The Prevalence of Child Maltreatment

How extensive is the problem of child maltreatment in Canada? The **Canadian Incidence Study of Reported Child Abuse and Neglect (CIS)** reports national data on the incidence of child maltreatment in Canada and has completed its third cycle of data collection. "In 2008, an estimated 235,842 maltreatment-related investigations were conducted across Canada, representing a rate of 39.16 investigations per 1000 children" (Public Health Agency of Canada, 2010).

According to the *CIS*, "the two most frequently occurring categories of substantiated maltreatment were exposure to intimate partner violence (34 percent) and neglect (34 percent)." Physical abuse was the primary concern in 20 percent of the substantiated cases, emotional maltreatment in 9 percent of substantiated investigations, and sexual abuse in 3 percent. Figure 5.3 shows the extent of substantiated child maltreatment in Canada in 2008.

Of the estimated 235,842 investigations, 92 percent resulted in no out-of-home placement. Of the almost 20,000 investigations that did result in a child's change of residence, 4 percent resulted in an informal arrangement with a relative, 4 percent resulted in a move to foster or kinship care, and fewer than 1 percent resulted in a move to a group home or residential/secure treatment.

In an Ontario-specific *CIS* report published in 2013, it was revealed that 125,281 investigations were conducted in the province that year (a rate of 53.32 per 1000 children); 78 percent of these were maltreatment investigations that focused on a concern of abuse or neglect (an estimated 97,951 investigations, or 41.69 per 1000 children) and 22 percent of the investigations were based on concerns about the risk of future maltreatment (an estimated 27,330 investigations, or 11.63 per 1000 children) (Fallon et al, 2013).

Child Neglect: The Least Understood Form of Maltreatment

Child neglect is a major social problem and the most pervasive form of child maltreatment in high-resource Anglophone countries such as Canada. Approximately one third of all substantiated cases of child maltreatment in Canada are due to child neglect. Whereas reported rates of physical and sexual abuse have declined over the last two decades, the rate of child neglect has remained fairly constant.

Child maltreatment
All forms of physical and emotional ill-treatment, sexual abuse, neglect, and exploitation that result in actual or potential harm to a child's health, development, or dignity

Child neglect is the least understood form of child maltreatment. In part, this reflects differing definitions and understandings of the term *child neglect*. However, the consequences for children who are neglected are well documented and are as severe as those associated with physical and sexual abuse. These include the child not meeting developmental milestones, poorer school achievement, increased problems with attachment and subsequent personality disorders, and increased internalizing behaviours (withdrawal, anxiety, and depression). Neglect is the form of child maltreatment that is most likely to require medical treatment and that is most associated with child fatality. Child neglect also often occurs alongside other forms of maltreatment.

Cases of child neglect are notoriously difficult to resolve. Once a case of child neglect has been assessed by child welfare authorities, the response is complex and requires more interventions than other forms of maltreatment. Once closed, a case of child neglect is more likely to be re-opened, compared with cases of physical or sexual abuse. This chronic opening, closing, re-opening, and re-assessing of cases—through a succession of social workers and foster home placements—contributes to poor outcomes for children who are experiencing neglect.

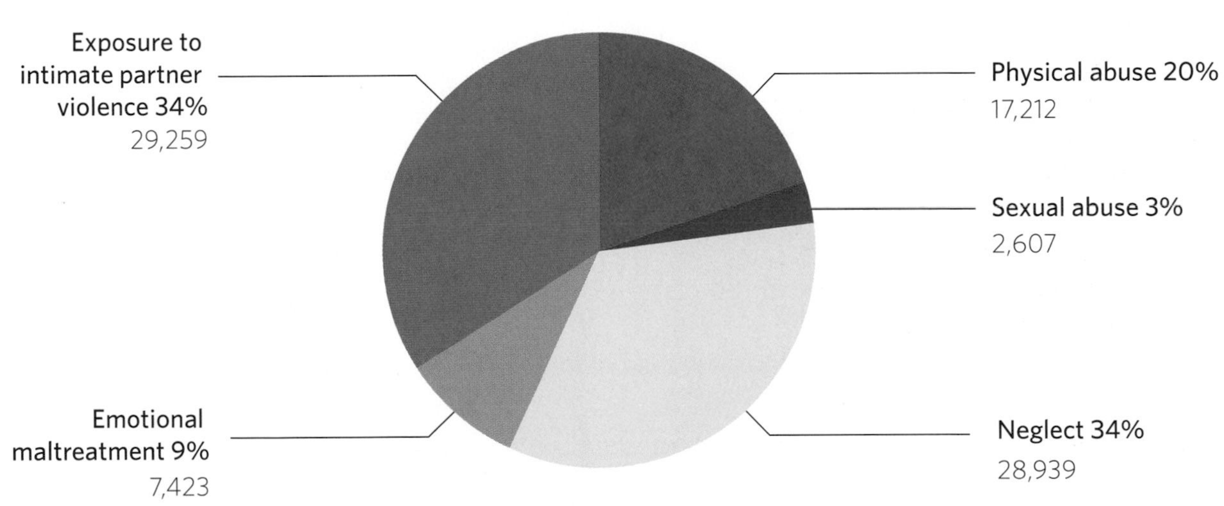

Figure 5.3 This pie chart shows the primary categories of substantiated child maltreatment in Canada. Child neglect and exposure to intimate partner violence constitute the most predominant categories.

First Nations Child Welfare
Addressing systemic risks

Aboriginal children in Canada are over-represented in out-of-home care—making up just 15 percent of the total child population, but 40 percent of children in care.

The number of investigations into the maltreatment of Aboriginal children is more than four times higher than those involving non-Aboriginal children. Furthermore, over-representation occurs at all stages of these investigations: Aboriginal families are more likely to be investigated, cases are more likely to be substantiated, and children are more likely to be removed from the home. As well, once a file is opened, it is also more likely to stay open.

The First Nations component of the *Canadian Incidence Study of Reported Child Abuse and Neglect* (Sinha, Ellenbogen, and Trocmé, 2013) analyzed child protection information for First Nations children. It showed that First Nations famiiles were disproportionately investigated for all forms of child maltreatment—twice as frequently for physical abuse and three times as often for sexual abuse. The highest disproportionality was in situations of suspected neglect. First Nations children were the focus of investigations for neglect six times more often than non-Aboriginal children.

Sinha, Ellenbogen, and Trocmé (2013) examined caregiver and household risk factors associated with the investigation and substantiation of child neglect among First Nations families. They found that the most commonly identified risk factors for First Nations children were substance abuse, domestic violence, and a lack of social supports. The most commonly identified risk factor concerns were low income and caregiving resource strain.

Systemic Risks

The persistent over-representation of Aboriginal famillies in investigations of child maltreatment cannot be adequately understood through the dominant individual and forensic perspectives. It can be tied to the low incomes and poor housing conditions of many First Nations families (Sinha, Trocmé, Blackstock, MacLaurin, and Fallon, 2011), and is exacerbated by social issues of substance use and domestic violence. These issues are structural factors that "place children and families at risk [and] that are largely beyond their ability to control" (First Nations Child and Family Caring Society of Canada, 2013).

Some of these systemic risks are related to federal and provincial jurisdictional disputes, the underfunding of services on reserves, and a failure to provide adequate resources for family support programs (Sinha, Trocmé, Blackstock, MacLaurin, and Fallon, 2011).

Aboriginal overrepresentation in child abuse and neglect investigations can also be linked to historical practices, in particular, the period of the "Sixties Scoop" and the placement of First Nations children in residential schools.

Recently, there have been changes to Indian and Northern Affairs Canada's Directive 20-1 to shift funding models away from in-care options to programs and supports that help First Nations families keep their children at or closer to home. But the systemic risks must also be addressed.

Structural Interventions

Blackstock et al. (2006) make the point that it is important for child-welfare workers to differentiate between family risk and structural risk, and to respond meaningfully to both. The First Nations Child and Family Caring Society of Canada (Martel, 2013) has identified some promising structural interventions and practices:

- **Housing.** Inadequate housing is a structural risk factor often correlated with poverty. Safe housing is often not accessible (e.g., there is often overcrowding, a lack of clean drinking water, and mould in First Nations housing on-reserve). Developing safe and affordable housing options and/or connecting clients to housing option resources are structural interventions that mitigate the unnecessary removal of a child from the family home. An example is the Native Child and Family Services of Toronto (NCFST), which offers apartments to women and children up to the age of 16 for a stay of up to 18 months. Support services augment the housing stability.
- **Substance use.** Substance use is a significant contributory risk factor. In order to protect the health and well-being of families and to prevent child maltreatment, substance misuse services must be available and accessible to families. This requires improving training and awareness, as well as collaboration to ensure that substance misuse workers and child welfare workers act together to meet the needs of children and their families. *Understanding Substance Abuse and Facilitating Recovery: A Guide for Child Welfare Workers* (Breshears, Yeh, and Young, 2009) is a useful resource outlining tools and skills to support child safety in the context of substance misuse.
- **Poverty.** Poverty is the leading structural risk factor associated with the removal of all children, and particularly First Nations children. The employment rate and employment income rate for Aboriginal people are substantially lower than for non-Aboriginal people. Improving Canadian child tax benefits and employment opportunities are pathways to reducing this structural inequity.

Understanding Disparity in Representation: A Hypothetical Example

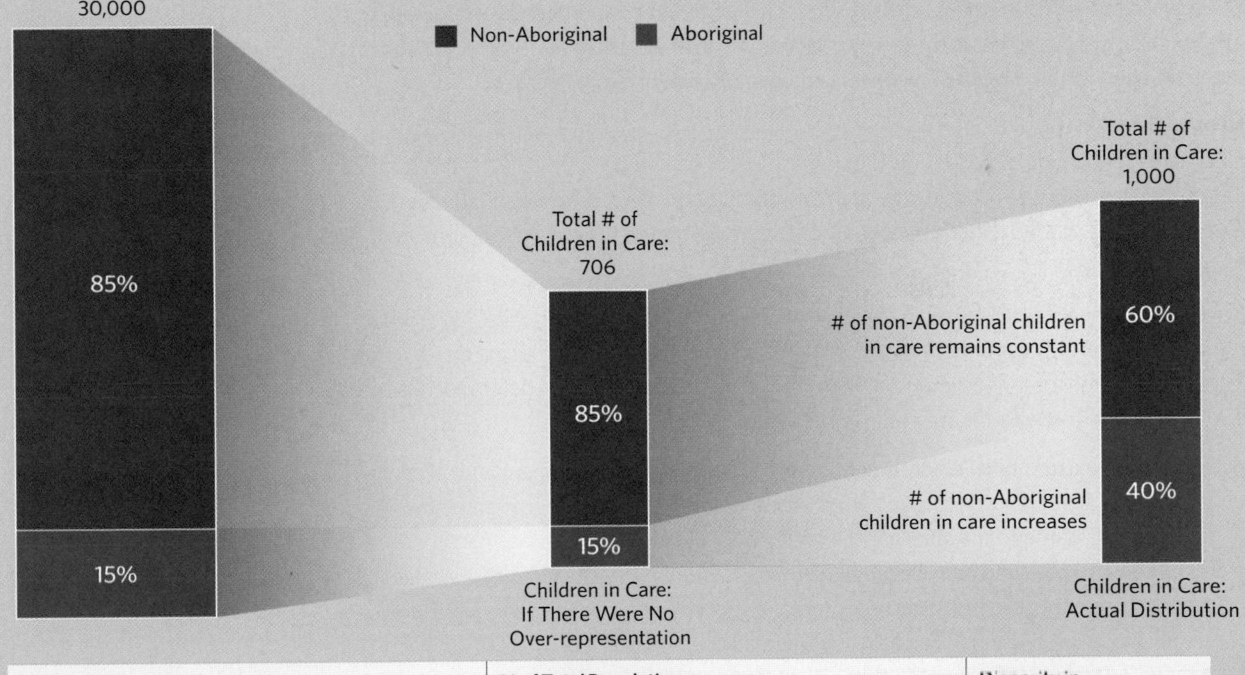

% of Children in Care		% of Total Population		Disparity in representation of Aboriginal and non-Aboriginal children in care
Aboriginal children	Non-Aboriginal children	Aboriginal children	Non-Aboriginal children	
40%	60%	15%	85%	3.8

Source: Sinha, V., Trocmé, N., et al. (2011). *Kiskisik Awasisak: Remember the Children, Understanding the Overrepresentation of First Nations Children in the Child Welfare System.* Ottawa: Assembly of First Nations.

Social Work and Substitute Care

If a child protection agency or a court decides that maltreatment of a child has been substantiated, substitute care may be required. Taking children into care is typically seen as a last-resort measure in cases where the risk to the child is assessed to be significant. However, if substitute care becomes necessary, and since "family" is seen as the ideal setting for childrearing in the Western world, foster care is normally the "placement of choice" for younger children who are deemed to be in need of substitute care (Kufeldt, 2011: 157). For older children, the placement of choice is a group home.

Foster Care

Foster homes provide substitute parenting for children who cannot safely stay with their own families, for children whose families have asked for help with parenting during times of crisis, or for children whose families need specific or periodic help in caring for their children. In the foster home, the child is entitled to receive

- physical care, such as clothing, food, and shelter;
- emotional care, including love and inclusion in family events;
- nurturing of both intellectual and emotional development;
- guidance and supervision; and
- positive role modelling.

Placement in a good family, combined with sound social work services, are key factors leading to positive foster care experiences. Factors that contribute to negative outcomes include frequent changes in placement (and subsequent changes in school), intensive damage associated with early experiences in the family of origin (which affect education and social relations), and little attention paid by social workers to the importance of family contact.

Group Homes

Despite a significant decrease in residential care for children and youth since the 1970s, most jurisdictions continue to provide at least a minimal number of **group homes**. Staffed group care residences accommodating generally between two and eight young people are preferable to large institutions.

In response to scathing critiques and revelations of institutional abuse, Anglin (2011) undertook a research study to construct a theoretical framework for well-functioning group homes. Three interwoven threads emerged as important psychosocial factors in determining whether a young person's experience in a group home is positive or negative:

- **Creating an extrafamilial environment** relates to the overall development and ongoing operation of a group home. Group homes strive to create a home-like environment while removing the intimacy and intensity of a family environment.
- **Responding to pain and pain-based behaviour** is a primary challenge for care workers. So-called "acting out" behaviours and internalizing processes, such as depression, are frequently the result of internalized pain and traumatic personal backgrounds.
- **Developing a sense of normality** within the "abnormal" living environment of a group home provides a bridging experience in terms of the resident's readiness to engage successfully in more normative environments.

In 2015, 18-year-old Alex Gervais (shown here) was found dead outside an Abbotsford, B.C. hotel.

Gervais had been living in a group home, which was shut down by B.C.'s Ministry of Children and Family Development. Gervais and the other residents were moved to locations such as the hotel where Alex lived alone and allegedly unsupported for several weeks before his death.

The Need to Monitor the Quality of Out-of-Home Care

As remarkable as it may seem, over 200,000 children and youth come into contact with child welfare authorities every year in Canada, and on any given day of the year, over 67,000 children and youth are living in out-of-home care. Although this is clearly one of the most high-risk groups of children in Canada, there is no accepted framework for tracking how well they are doing. In an effort to address this issue, Nico Trocmé and his colleagues put forward an "outcomes matrix" that can be used by child welfare managers and policy makers to track trends and evaluate programs and policies (Trocmé et al., 2009).

The National Child Welfare Outcomes Indicator Matrix (NOM) was developed through a series of consultations initiated by the Provincial and Territorial Directors of Child Welfare and Human Resources Development Canada. In the absence of any national benchmarks, the proposed indicators can be used to measure the degree to which child welfare services are working effectively on behalf of Canadian children and families. The NOM takes into account the balance between a child's immediate need for protection, a child's long-term need for nurturing and a stable home environment, a family's potential for growth, and the community's capacity to meet a child's needs.

The NOM framework consists of four nested domains that capture the key indicators: the child's safety, the child's well-being, permanence, and family and community support. (See Figure 5.4.) The permanence indicator tracks a child's out-of-home placement(s) and the number of moves made by a child who is in out-of-home care.

Foster homes

Households in which a child is given parental care by someone other than his or her birth parent or adoptive parent

Group homes

Homes where a small number of unrelated people in need of care, support, or supervision can live together. Typically, there are no more than six residents, and there is at least one trained caregiver on site 24 hours a day.

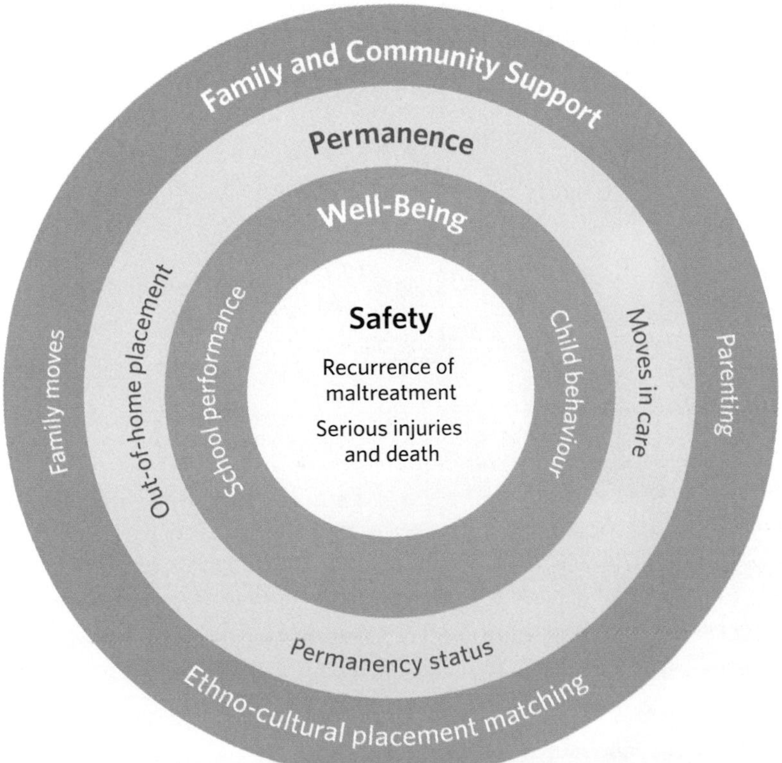

Figure 5.4
The National Child Welfare Outcomes Indicator Matrix (NOM)

This matrix provides a framework that can be used to track outcomes for children and families who are receiving welfare services.

Re-Examining the Foster-Care System
Aboriginal girls at greater risk for violence

"There are more First Nations children in foster care today than at the height of residential schools."

As the mandate for the inquiry on murdered and missing Indigenous women takes shape, the government ought to consider the role systemic disadvantage plays in placing women and girls at higher risk for violence.

The recent revelations in Val-d'Or, Québec [allegations by Aboriginal women of assault and sexual abuse at the hands of provincial police officers], for example, suggest that racism is more prevalent than we would like to think.

As a recent series in *The Globe and Mail* reported, a number of the murdered and missing women and girls were in foster care. A child-welfare system is an essential public service. On those rare occasions when parents are unable to ensure the safety and development of their children, the state must step in and provide alternative arrangements that will safeguard the interests of the children.

However, as the Truth and Reconciliation Commission pointed out, the system is not well-suited to the needs of Indigenous children. It does not account for the multigenerational impacts of residential schools and inequitable services on reserves. This means First Nations families have less support to care for their children than other Canadians. This entails a dramatic over-representation of First Nations children in foster care. The problem is so severe that there are more First Nations children in foster care today than at the height of residential schools. Too often, Indigenous children removed from their families are placed in non-Indigenous foster homes and experience multiple placements. When that happens, Indigenous children are not only separated from their families, but also from their culture and from their communities. Taken together, these circumstances place First Nations girls and women at greater risk for disadvantage, including violence.

The First Nations Child and Family Caring Society brought a human-rights challenge against the federal government to correct the inequalities in on-reserve child welfare and give First Nations an equitable chance to care for their children. In the evidence before the tribunal, we learned that

- the federal funding formula puts an incentive on the removal of children from their families by inequitably funding family support services;
- rigidity in federal government mandates results in First Nations children being denied or delayed receipt of public services available to all other children;
- federal policy prevents the adaptation of provincial child-welfare systems to First Nations cultures and community needs; and
- the federal government pays non-Aboriginal child-welfare providers more money than it pays First Nations to deliver the same services.

Instead of remedying the inequalities First Nations children experience, the previous federal government failed to implement evidence-based solutions to address the problems and spent at least $5 million trying to derail the human-rights case on legal technicalities.

This regressive approach got in the way of implementing proven strategies to help First Nations children and families, and in doing so perpetuated the long, dark shadow of federal-government discrimination against First Nations children.

Tragically, Canadian governments have not paid enough attention to the well-being of children. The KidsRights Index ranks Canada 57th in the world when it comes to respecting children's rights in proportion to its wealth. That means the Canadian economy is doing about five times better than Canadian kids are. Saving money on the backs of kids is fool's gold. As the World Health Organization notes, for every government dollar invested in children, taxpayers save $7 in downstream costs, such as policing, addictions, and social assistance. Thus, it makes good economic and moral sense for the federal government to end inequalities in First Nations education, health, and child welfare.

When an inquiry gets underway and explores how these tragedies can be prevented, it should turn its attention to the long-standing gaps in children's services in First Nations communities. The federal government simply can't afford to continue to use racial discrimination as a fiscal-restraint measure. Our children deserve better.

[*Note*: The Canadian Human Rights Tribunal ruled on January 26, 2016 that the federal government is racially discriminating against First Nations children on reserves.]

- *Source:* Blackstock, Cindy. (2015). A MMIW inquiry must examine the child-welfare system. *The Globe and Mail* (December 2).

Percentage distribution of the population aged 14 and under in private households by living arrangement for selected Aboriginal identity categories

Living arrangements	Total Aboriginal identity population	First Nations single identity	Métis single identity	Inuit single identity	Non-Aboriginal identity population
Total population aged 14 and under in private households	100.0	100.0	100.0	100.0	100.0
Children of both parents[1]	49.6	45.0	58.0	61.6	76.0
Stepchildren	8.5	8.7	8.6	6.3	5.8
Children of lone parent	34.4	37.1	29.8	25.8	17.4
—of male lone parent	6.0	6.7	4.3	6.1	2.9
—of female lone parent	28.4	30.4	25.5	19.7	14.4
Grandchildren in skip-generation family	2.7	3.3	1.4	2.3	0.4
Foster children	3.6	4.5	1.7	2.8	0.3
Children living with other relatives[2,3]	1.2	1.4	0.5	1.1	0.2

[1] Includes children in a two-parent family where there may also be step siblings or half-siblings present. Also includes children in a two-parent family for whom it cannot be determined if they are stepchildren. [2] Non-relatives may be present. [3] This category includes foster children.
Source: Statistics Canada, National Household Survey, 2011.

Campaign 2000: Working to End Child Poverty in Canada

As stated earlier in this chapter, poverty is the leading structural risk associated with the removal of children, especially Indigenous children, from their homes. Hunger and food insecurity, a dearth of affordable housing, and a lack of sustainable full-time employment all place enormous stress on parents and can destabilize families. In 1989, in response to this troubling reality, all Canadian political parties resolved to end child poverty in Canada by the beginning of the twenty-first century.

Campaign 2000 arose as a non-partisan, cross-Canada, public education movement to build awareness and support for this all-party House of Commons resolution. The campaign began in 1991 out of concern for the lack of government progress in addressing child poverty.

Campaign 2000 Declaration

On November 24, 1989, a Canadian House of Commons unanimous all-party resolution stated that the House "seek[s] to achieve the goal of eliminating poverty among Canadian children by the year 2000."

The Campaign 2000 Declaration states: "We are committed to promoting and securing the full implementation of the House of Commons Resolution of November 24, 1989."

The Campaign's Primary Goals

The campaign now encompasses a network of more than 120 national, provincial, and community partners. Additionally, hundreds of other groups across the country are working to advance Campaign 2000's goals, such as children's aid societies, faith organizations, community agencies, health organizations, school boards, and low-income people's groups. These goals include the following:

- To raise and protect the basic living standards of families in all regions of the country so that no child in Canada must ever live in poverty. [Poverty is measured using Statistics Canada's Low-Income Cut-Off Lines (LICOs).]
- To improve the life chances of all children in Canada to fulfill their potential and nurture their talent, and to become responsible and contributing members of Canadian society.
- To ensure the availability of secure, affordable, and suitable housing as an inherent right of all children in Canada.
- To create, build, and strengthen family support, child care, and community resources to empower families to provide the best possible care for children.

How Are We Doing?

Campaign 2000's annual national *Report Card on Child and Family Poverty in Canada* measures the progress, or lack of progress, of the unanimous all-party resolution. Its *Report Card on Child and Family Poverty in Canada, 2014* states: "As Campaign 2000 issues its 23rd monitoring report, we are saddened and distressed by the abysmal lack of progress in reducing child poverty in Canada." Over the past 25 years, child and family poverty has actually increased to 1,331,530 children (19.1 percent) from 1,066,150 children (15.8 percent) in 1989, according to taxfiler data (see Figure 5.5).

The report points out that the Canadian economy has doubled in size, yet the incomes of families in the lowest decile have stagnated. The gap between rich and poor remains extremely wide, leaving average-income families imperilled as well.

What needs to happen, the report asks? One key recommendation is to increase the Canada Child Tax Benefit/National Child Benefit (CCTB/NCB) for low-income families to a maximum of $5,600 per child. This enhanced benefit, when coupled with full-time work, would enable a lone parent with one child to lift her family out of poverty. The report stresses our country's urgent need for decent, full-time jobs with benefits to replace low-waged, precarious, and part-time employment.

The Unique Situation of Indigenous Children and Their Families

As stated earlier in this book, term "Indigenous" includes the three primary groups with Aboriginal rights as outlined in Canada's constitution: First Nations or Indian, Métis, and Inuit. The impoverished conditions that Indigenous peoples now experience are rooted in a legacy of colonialism and harmful policies that for decades separated children from their families.

Research confirms that the average child poverty rate for Indigenous children is 40 percent, in contrast to the average child poverty rate for all children, which is 17 percent. The status of Indigenous children, as well as their location, is linked to their poverty rate. One in two (50 percent) of Status First Nations children lives in poverty in a First Nations community. First Nations child-welfare agencies are chronically underfunded, despite a complaint first filed in 2007 by the First Nations Child and Family Caring Society and the Assembly of First Nations against the government of Canada at the Canadian Human Rights Tribunal. This complaint alleges discrimination in the provision of child and family services in First Nations communities. A landmark decision favouring this complaint was rendered by the Canadian Human Rights Tribunal on January 26, 2016.

In its 2014 report, Campaign 2000 made two recommendations in response to the grinding poverty that remains a major barrier to well-being for Indigenous children: (1) "a plan to prevent, reduce, and eventually eradicate family poverty in Indigenous families developed in conjunction with Indigenous organizations"; and (2) "a commitment by the federal government and by provinces and territories to implement **Jordan's Principle** to ensure that Indigenous children's needs are met expeditiously."

Jordan's Principle

Jordan's Principle calls on all government institutions and departments to ensure that children's needs are met first and jurisdictional disputes are resolved later.

The approach was named for Jordan River Anderson, a child from Norway House Cree Nation in Manitoba. Jordan had to be hospitalized for his first years of life, but after his medical team recommended his discharge, Jordan remained in hospital for two more years because neither the federal nor the provincial government would take responsibility for funding his at-home care.

In 2005, Jordan died in hospital at the age of five.

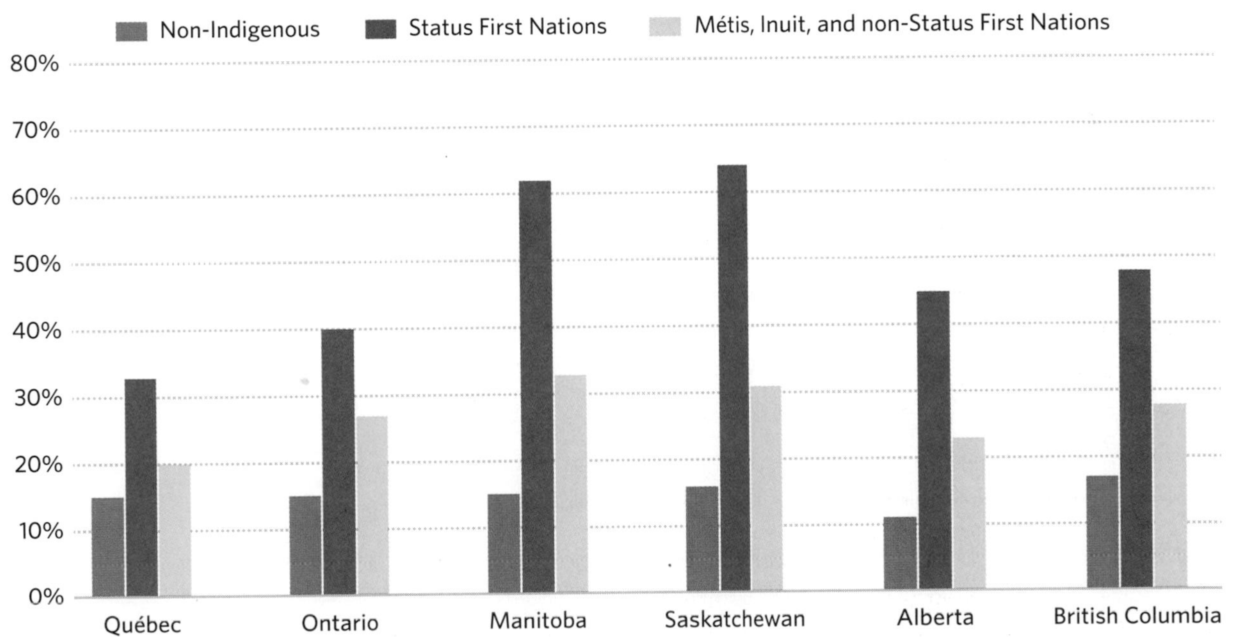

Source: Macdonald, D., and Daniel Wilson. (2013). *Poverty or Prosperity: Indigenous Children in Canada*. Ottawa: Canadian Centre for Policy Alternatives.

Figure 5.5 Child poverty rates for Indigenous children vary by identity and status, with the highest rates for Status First Nations children. Métis, Inuit, and non-Status First Nations child poverty rates follow a similar pattern across the country.

Child Welfare Dilemmas

In Canada, child welfare legislation and policy have been organized around two primary frameworks: child protection and family support. The former focuses on applying resources to the investigation of child maltreatment. Generally a highly legalistic and bureaucratic process, it emphasizes a social control function. A family support orientation places greater emphasis on providing early intervention and additional supports and resources to vulnerable families (Mackenzie and Shangraux, 2011: 328).

"Best Interests" versus "Least Restrictive" Approaches

As stated previously, the "best interests" approach emphasizes the protection and well-being of the child, whereas the "least restrictive" approach emphasizes the course of action that will cause the least disruption for the child, leaving him or her with the family if possible.

Deciding what is in the best interests of a child is often extremely difficult. When provinces have had "best interests" legislation in place, the number of children taken from their families generally increased, sometimes dramatically. A few high-profile cases in which children were harmed as a result of being left in a dangerous situation at home have led several provinces to change their "least restrictive" legislation. Of course, the state must also consider the emotional and spiritual damage that may be caused by removing children from their families and placing them in group homes.

"Urgent Protection" versus "Chronic Need"

The concepts of "protection," "safety," "harm," and "risk" are relatively clear in the context of child sexual abuse and severe physical abuse. The meaning is less clear in relation to the predominant forms of child maltreatment—neglect, emotional maltreatment, and exposure to intimate partner violence. Clearly, child sexual and physical abuse are acts of "commission" associated with acute harm, and are readily observable and can be documented. Child neglect and intimate partner violence, on the other hand, are situations of "omission," whereby the parent fails to provide for the child's needs, thus leading to long-term psychological harm (Trocmé, Kyte, Sinha, and Fallon, 2014).

The distinction between urgent protection and chronic need is clear in an examination of the *Canadian Incidence Study* (*CIS*) data. The rate of "urgent protective investigations" (those involving severe physical injury, sexual abuse, or victims under four years of age at high risk of serious injury) has remained relatively constant, at a little over six investigations per 1000 children. In contrast, other maltreatment investigations have more than doubled, increasing from a rate of 15.39 investigations per 1000 children in 1998 to 33.13 investigations per 1000 children in 2008. As a result, the proportion of investigations that meet the urgent protection classification dropped from 28 percent in 1998 to 15 percent in 2008. The vast majority (85 percent) of child maltreatment reports, investigations, and open file services in Canada involve "non-urgent" situations of child neglect, emotional maltreatment, and family violence that threaten the well-being of children (Trocmé, Kyte, Sinha, and Fallon, 2014).

Understanding the complex factors associated with the continuing increase of child maltreatment and children's chronic needs requires further study. Some researchers hypothesize that two decades of education about childhood physical and sexual abuse may be helping to reduce the incidence.

Adapting to Changing Realities

As our understanding of child maltreatment changes, the responding service systems will require adjustment as well. Fundamentally, the assessment of "risk" is a necessary but insufficient response when considering the long-term development and well-being of children.

Some promising responses are emerging, however, e.g., the development of Indigenous community-based child-welfare practices, attention to structural policies, and the creation of child-welfare systems that embrace trauma-informed policies and practices.

Individual versus Structural Orientation

Another source of debate within child-welfare practice and policy involves "individual" versus "structural" explanations and solutions. Child-protection legislation tends to take a more individualistic approach, that is, responsibility rests with the parent(s) to provide a safe and supportive environment. Child maltreatment is constructed as an individual parental failing. However, this perspective can obscure broader socio-economic conditions and structural and ecological factors that may be contributing to a child's neglect and abuse.

Many researchers and practitioners argue for a more comprehensive approach to child welfare, one that addresses the systemic issues, such as poverty and discrimination, that can jeopardize a child's well-being. This perspective acknowledges the relationship between personal struggles and the degree of adequacy of social conditions (or "structural imperatives"). We know, for example, that social and economic inequality based on gender, race, ability, and length of time in the country are reflected in disproportionately high child poverty rates. Lone mothers and their children are one of the most economically vulnerable groups, with almost one in every two female lone-parent families (47 percent) living in poverty. Low income among new immigrants is more than three times higher than among people born in Canada. Compared to people of European background, racialized people are more likely to be unemployed or in low-paying occupations. Along with a broad national poverty-reduction strategy, policies are needed that address these systemic barriers to equality.

Addressing Child Neglect in Québec

Child neglect is viewed as a breakdown of the parent-child relationship

In 2009, the Québec Department of Health and Social Services advocated for the development and implementation of province-wide integrated services for families affected by child neglect. The program that emerged was the Ecosystemic and Developmental Intervention Program for Children and Families—Second Generation (EDIP-CF2).

This program's theoretical foundation is an ecosystem approach that recognizes that child neglect is characterized by children "in need" and occurs due to the collapse of the social organization surrounding the children and their parents. Lacharité (2014) asserts that rather than viewing child neglect as a consequence of a parent-child relationship (predominant in residual child welfare), it should be viewed as a breakdown of the family-community relationship.

Furthermore, the EDIP-CF2 incorporates a developmental model which understands neglect in terms of the developmental needs of the child, but also considers parenting as a developmental challenge for adults. The goals are to ensure that children are surrounded by adults (including parental figures and family members) who are attentive and responsive to the child's developmental needs with a vision of the capacity, resources, and obstacles in the child's environment.

Service planning requires an understanding of the social conditions necessary for the adults to fulfill the child's needs; parental and child (if old enough) involvement in the analysis of the situation and the plan of action; parental awareness of their role in the child's development; and a recognition that community systems (daycares, schools, etc.) are involved and must be in step with the plan to ensure positive developmental outcomes. This appears to be a hopeful and innovative practice, which the rest of Canada will be watching with much interest.

Social Work and Child Welfare in Canada
A duty to support and protect

Child-welfare service procedures are outlined in detail in the various provincial standards manuals. Specific criteria for determining whether a child needs protection are found in provincial child-welfare acts. What follows are the general steps for providing child-welfare services in Canada.

Initial Response to Reports of Abuse and Neglect

The person receiving a report of child abuse and neglect must exercise careful judgement. Workers should collect accurate information from various sources, such as the child, other family members, and neighbours, and from persons with well-meaning intentions as well as from persons intending to make malicious accusations. Even though decision making may be difficult and emotional, workers must make decisions in the best interests of the child. The response steps are as follows:

- receiving the report
- obtaining complete information from the informant
- assessing the motivation and credibility of the informant
- checking records
- determining if an investigation is necessary
- developing an initial investigation plan
- documenting the reported abuse or neglect

Investigation

The social worker should obtain detailed and complete information using interviews, observations, and assessment and service reports from professionals, checking all available records. All decisions must be based on detailed, accurate, and documented evidence. Crucial decisions must be made at this juncture in response to the following questions:

- Has the child been abused?
- What are the immediate safety needs of the child?
- Is there a risk of future harm?
- What is the capacity of the family to protect the child?
- What services are required by the child and family?

All provincial child-welfare acts empower child-protection workers to enter premises to remove children whom they deem to be in need of protection. Workers will frequently interview children at school, as this is considered a safe and familiar environment. Interviewing children requires considerable skill and interpersonal sensitivity.

While each province and, indeed, each local agency has its own policies and procedures, general investigative guidelines are common. A typical investigation would include

- conducting a telephone interview with the person who reported the alleged abuse and with any other individuals who have pertinent information;
- searching existing agency records for any present or past contact with the family, the alleged abuser, or the child;
- contacting the Child Abuse Register to ascertain if the alleged abuser is registered, and if so, why; contacting any child-welfare authorities that previously registered the alleged abuser;
- seeing the child who is alleged to have been abused and conducting an interview using methods appropriate to the child's developmental stage and ability to communicate;
- ensuring that the alleged abuser is interviewed by the police or an agency worker pursuant to the protocol established between the agency and the police;
- interviewing the parent or person having charge of the child, if he or she is not the alleged abuser;
- interviewing other potential victims (e.g., siblings, other children in the home, classmates);
- gathering evidence from other professionals involved in the investigation (e.g., medical, law enforcement, educational); and
- gathering information from other witnesses.

Assessing the urgency of a response is critical. The child who is the subject of a report of abuse must be seen as soon as possible, generally not later than 12 hours after the report is made. To assess urgency, the social worker should consider the child's age, the nature of the alleged abuse, the known injury to the child, the potential for the child to suffer physical harm, the availability of possible evidence (e.g., visible marks), and the immediate need for counselling or support. The worker should ensure that a medical examination is performed by a qualified medical practitioner when there is a need to document the child's condition. A medical examination may also be necessary to ascertain whether the child has been harmed. This can be arranged by obtaining the cooperation of a parent. If cooperation cannot be obtained, it may be necessary to apprehend the child and conduct the examination without parental consent.

Substantiation

Agencies generally have established policies and procedures outlining how a protection substantiation decision occurs. This decision must be made at a formal meeting in consultation with the social worker's supervisor or higher authorities. The worker should record the process of substantiation and the standards of proof for making the decision in the case file.

There are generally four possible investigative outcomes:

- The complaint is not substantiated.
- A protection concern is substantiated, but the child remains in the home.
- A protection concern is substantiated, and the child remains in the home but may be in need of protection. With this option, a plan must be developed to ensure the child's safety, including a schedule of visits and restricted access by some family members. This approach is consistent with the philosophy of taking the "least restrictive" course of action to protect the child.
- A protection concern is substantiated, and the child is removed from the home.

Assessment Report and Service Plan

If abuse is verified, the law requires a complete assessment and a plan of service for the child and family. The assessment report should address the following: the nature of the abuse, precipitating factors, the nature of the dispute, family dysfunction, family background, parental capacity, family relationships, family strengths, service needs, child development, and the risk of further abuse.

The service plan should include the specific risk factors, service needs, strategies and service providers, ongoing care responsibility and coordination, expectations, review dates, and client involvement in the service plan.

Case Management

Case management is the coordination of services for clients by allocating a professional to be responsible for the assessment of need and implementation of service plans. It involves coordinating the various system components in order to achieve a successful outcome.

Case management activities include (1) assessment, (2) planning, (3) linking clients and services, (4) monitoring the quality of the services provided, and (5) advocacy. The primary goal is service provision for the client, not management of the system or its resources.

Careful record keeping is mandatory in child welfare agencies. A case worker must be able to substantiate the decisions made. Supervision, consultation, review, and decision making occur frequently during the management of all child abuse cases. All agencies have strict documentation requirements.

Agencies must also evaluate the effectiveness of their case management approach and make adjustments as needed. What outcomes are expected for effective service delivery to children and families?

The Child Protection Process in British Columbia

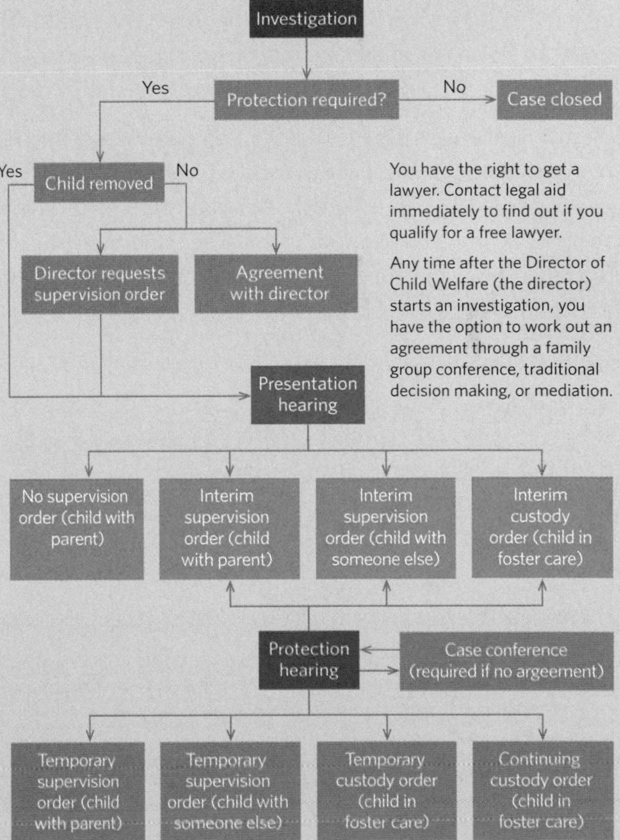

Source: Adapted from a flowchart published by Crown Publications, the Queen's Printer for British Columbia.

Family Group Conferences

Social work with families and children at risk

A central challenge in child protection social work is to achieve a safe balance of parental or kin responsibility while ensuring the child's safety. It is not easy. An innovative, collaborative approach that has emerged in recent years is the Family Group Conference (FGC).

A Family Group Conference involves a formal meeting between family members and social workers (and possibly other interested parties, such as the police or elders) with respect to the care of a child or adolescent. This method appears to have originated in New Zealand, where it was developed to facilitate social work practice that respects the values and culture of the Maori, New Zealand's Indigenous people. In this model of practice, immediate and extended family members, with the support of child and family practitioners, work together to make decisions that best meet the needs of the child.

The Key Elements of a Family Group Conference

The Family Group Conference process has four main stages: (1) a meeting where professionals inform the family of the concerns they have; (2) private family time, where the family alone develops a plan that addresses the concerns; (3) a meeting where the plan is presented to the professionals; and finally (4) the implementation and review of the plan itself.

"Family" in this case includes the children, parents, extended family, and even significant friends and neighbours who may not be blood-related. This group is given "private" time to develop a plan that will ensure the safe care and protection of a child or children in need. The social work professional is involved at the beginning of the process and in the assessment of the plan following a decision. Professionals are excluded from the private time, which is attended by family members only.

The principles that underpin the Family Group Conference process are as follows:

- The child's interests are paramount.
- The child should have the resources for his or her voice to be heard.
- The child's views, feelings, and solutions are as valid as those of the participating adults.
- Children are generally best looked after within their families. Services should seek to promote this wherever possible.
- Working in partnership with families is beneficial for children.
- Families have the ability to make rational and sound decisions about their future and the future of the children involved.
- Given the right environment and the correct information, families instinctively know what is best for their children.

The Family Group Conference emerged as an alternative and progressive way to work with children and families at risk. The approach can be used in a number of different contexts: child welfare, youth offences, domestic violence, children as young carers, foster care breakdown, adoption, and so on. The successful outcomes where this method has been applied demonstrate that the approach has great potential, as the adjacent case study shows.

Reflecting on Darlene's Story

1. How do you think Darlene experienced this process?
2. How did Sally balance caring, respectful, non-judgmental processes with ensuring that the children were safe?
3. How might this story have gone differently if a non-collaborative, directive approach had been taken?
4. What organizational and environmental factors were likely in place for successful planning?

Darlene's Story... Facing grief and addiction

Sally, a child protection social worker with six years' experience in a Delegated Child Welfare Aboriginal Agency in British Columbia, is called in to help a family plan ways to support a young mother struggling with grief and addiction.

On Monday morning, Sally received a call from Darla, who is very concerned about her sister, Darlene Luis, a lone parent to Lia, aged 4 and May, aged 2½. Darlene's boyfriend and father of her children, Mike, committed suicide three months ago. On the previous Saturday night, Darlene called her 17-year-old niece Natalie (Darla's daughter) to babysit Lia and May. Darlene didn't return home until Monday at 5:00 a.m.

This is not the first time Darlene has disappeared for several days. Darla told Sally that Darlene's house is in disarray and there are empty liquor bottles everywhere. There is little food in the house and unwashed laundry lies in piles. The girls watch TV most days while Darlene sleeps or drinks. Sally thanked Darla and agreed to meet Darlene later that day.

When Darlene met with Sally, Darlene admitted that she had been drinking daily since Mike had died and that she wasn't coping well. Respectfully, Sally explained to Darlene that because of her drinking, the lack of food, and the state of the family home, she did not think it was safe for the girls to stay with Darlene. Sally recommended that she make a referral to the Aboriginal Family Group Conference (FGC) Coordinator. Darlene agreed with Sally's assessment and consented to participate in a family conference.

The First Priority: Safeguarding the Children

When Darlene met with Shari, the FGC Coordinator, Shari asked Darlene which family members she wished to attend the meeting with her. Darlene specified Darla, Natalie, and her Auntie Molly, who is an Elder in the community. She also asked that Nicole, the counsellor she had seen after Mike died, attend. Other people included her best friend and neighbour, Roberta and Roberta's husband, George, her dad, and Mike's mom. The family group conference was arranged for the following Wednesday afternoon. On the day of the conference, Shari brought cookies and juice. She arranged the chairs in a circle and greeted everyone when they arrived. She had taped pictures of Lia and May to the wall and on the table she had placed a family photo of Darlene, Mike, Lia, and May. Shari opened the meeting by stating that Lia and May were the primary reason that they had gathered together. Everyone agreed that they needed to collaborate to develop a plan to ensure that the children were safe while Darlene sought help for her drinking problem. Shari asked the group to brainstorm ideas that might spare the children from being placed in foster care. Sally explained that she would take part in the discussions at first and then go outside to give the family some private time. Shari stayed to help the family and to take notes. Darlene cried when she saw the family photos. Roberta held her hand and told her they were all there to support her. Molly suggested they pray to the Creator for guidance and led the group through a smudge.

Sally waited outside while Shari helped the family write out a plan on a flip chart. An hour later, Shari joined Sally at the picnic table outside to give the family and friends some privacy to complete the plan.

When Sally and Shari were invited back, the family explained the plan. Darlene would go to an alcohol treatment centre, and Lia and May would stay with Darla and Natalie until she returned home. Molly agreed to help with household tasks when Darlene returned to the community. Darlene's dad offered to take her to a sweat lodge when she returned from treatment. Roberta and George promised to maintain the house and yard while Darlene was in treatment. George also said that he would work with the band council to make sure that Darlene's freezer was stocked with food for the winter. Mike's mom offered to drop by when she came to town on Saturdays to look after the girls for a few hours. Darlene asked Sally if the agency could cover daycare costs three days a week so she could get alcohol and drug counselling and attend a bereavement support group.

Sally suggested that the family try the plan for two months and then reconvene to review it and modify it if necessary. Shari typed up the plan for everyone to sign. Darlene thanked everyone and expressed relief that her girls could stay with family rather than go into foster care. She entered a treatment centre the following Tuesday.

A Family Group Conference recognizes the fact that people are usually experts on their own situation.

Growing Up in Foster Care

Social-work practice in substitute care

At times, risks to a child's safety become so significant that either short-term or long-term substitute care is required. Taking children into care is usually a last resort, occurring only after deliberation with the social-work child protection team and their supervisors.

Although kinship care is the preferred form of substitute care, non-kin foster families are very common. Despite the stereotype that foster parents are "in it for the money" and sensationalized stories of foster parents abusing children, the majority of these parents provide an invaluable resource for children requiring alternative, family-based care. Across Canada, governments are paying heed to the recruitment and retention of foster parents, particularly those of Indigenous ancestry.

Meeting the Needs of Foster Children

Foster parents face daunting challenges: foster children have complex needs requiring special attention and skills. The foster-care system itself needs upgrading, too. As Peter Dudding, executive director with the Child Welfare League of Canada (CWLC) points out, "there are problems in the current system with overcrowding, placement mismatches, and lack of training and support, all of which can result in placement breakdown and harm for these children" (CWLC press release, March 30, 2010). Foster parents may end their relationship with a child for multiple reasons, but lack of support from placement agencies is a primary complaint.

Foster parents need support around "breakdowns or disruptions [of placements], allegations, relations with birth parents, family tensions, 'tug of love' cases, and other disagreements with social services" (Wilson et al., 2000: 193). Notwithstanding these difficulties, however, most foster parents step forward because they care about vulnerable children and want to make a difference. In Selishia's Story, Selishia's foster parents provide a safer environment for her than her birth parents could. However, Selishia feels that the money associated with her care differentiates her from her foster parents' birth children. Her foster family provides a stable environment, but when some normal teenage rebellious milestones occur, the consequent challenges and conflicts lead to a traumatic replacement for Selishia.

Social workers can help provide stability and continuity for a child in substitute care by facilitating a good relationship between the child and the foster parents, supplying information about normal developmental milestones, providing parenting support, and promoting conflict resolution to repair normal, everyday tensions that occur in all families.

Like many children in her situation, Selishia had no warning that her life would change drastically. While social workers may have visited the foster family, Selishia has no memory of such visits. She now knows that a decision was made for her safety, but she was either not told the reasons for the decision, or they were not explained so that a five-year-old could understand. If we consider Selishia's story in the context of Maslow's "hierarchy of needs," we see that her physiological and safety needs were met and that some of her love and belonging needs were met, but not all. This made her feel excluded and different. Her self-esteem improved after connecting with the Métis community and meeting other youth in care.

Reflecting on Selishia's Story

1. Consider the developmental stage of a five-year-old child. Even when it is necessary to remove a child due to safety issues, how can the child be supported?
2. What do you think should be told to a child about his or her family history?
3. What do you think of Selishia's move at age 16 for being rebellious? What might her behaviour have been signalling?

Selishia's Story... Part one

This is a true account of one individual's experience of being removed from her biological family and placed in substitute care. Selishia was interviewed by the author and has consented to share her experiences publicly. Selishia's real name has been used because she believes that telling her story authentically is part of her process of personal healing.

Selishia's early years were spent with her mom, dad, and older sister. One day, when she was five years old, there was a knock at the door. With no warning, a woman she had never seen before removed Selishia and her nine-year-old sister from their home and took them to live with a foster family. Selishia remembers that day clearly, and recalls that she had absolutely no idea what was happening or why. She also vividly recalls crying every night for eight months.

Selishia and her sister lived with the same foster family until she was 16 years old. She received good marks in school, played soccer, stayed away from drugs, and found full-time employment. Despite these signs of stability, however, she came home from school one day, and a social worker—again, someone she had never met—told her that she was going to be moved elsewhere. Having been labelled a "rebellious" teen, she was placed in a rural foster home for youth with extreme behavioural problems. Selishia recalls falling into a major depression at this time. However, she told no one about her depressed emotional state.

During the 11 years that Selishia spent in her first foster home, the foster mother worked outside the home and the foster father was on a disability pension. Selishia and her sister were permanent foster children, and two other children eventually became permanent. Three or four short-term foster children also came to stay at intervals, and the family had two biological children. Thus, throughout most of Selishia's stay, there were seven to nine children in the home.

Selishia's Family History

The foster family had forbidden Selishia to speak openly about being a foster child. Nevertheless, if the family was out in the community, they would introduce Selishia as a foster child. When the family went to Mexico for a holiday when Selishia was 12, she and the other foster children were left at home. Selishia's physical care was good, and there was a sense of permanency. However, when she was removed from this foster family at the age of 16, there was no prior discussion at all. During her 11-year stay in this home, she had had only rare contact with her biological parents and had only pieced together her family of origin's history by overhearing conversations. When she reached adolescence and learned of her mother's drug addiction, her father's criminal history, and the poverty in which her biological family had been living, Selishia's developing sense of self was eroded.

Struggling to Achieve a Sense of Connectedness

A Métis woman, Selishia was unaware of her cultural identity until the age of nine or ten. When she did learn of her cultural background, she asked to be included in local Métis community activities. Developing a healthy sense of self and belonging was a struggle for Selishia. At school, for example, any lessons associated with "family" were painful exercises in fabrication for her. Unable to acknowledge that she was a foster child and having little knowledge of her own family meant concocting a series of lies that piled up over time.

Selishia yearned to "fit in," but she felt isolated and alienated. While in foster care, she had contact with approximately 14 social workers, but never developed a relationship with any of them (even though they were, in all likelihood, her appointed guardians). She didn't even understand what a social worker did. She knew only that her foster family was required to contact them in order to grant her permission for a school field trip, to have a sleepover with her best friend, or to get a navel piercing.

Selishia sometimes missed out on field trips and sleepovers because her social workers did not return phone calls in time. The navel piercing was vetoed by a social worker whom Selishia had met only once, who recommended that she get a nose ring instead. Another social worker whom she had met only once told Selishia that she must have poor hygiene because she had acne. Selishia cannot remember the names of most of the social workers who were involved in making the major decisions that affected her life over a significant period of time.

Selishia yearned to "fit in," but due to her experiences as a foster child, she often felt isolated and alienated.

Transitioning Out of Foster Care

Social-work practice with youth "aging out of care"

Every year, as many as 6,000 youth in Canada "age out" of, or leave, government care and must move out on their own because they have reached the legal age of majority (Mann-Feder, 2011). These youth are expected to live independently at an earlier age than other Canadians, despite their often-compromised development as a result of being victims of abuse, neglect, or abandonment. Leaving home for any young person is fraught with difficulty, but leaving care for these young people often means leaving the only safe place they have ever known.

Best Practices in Discharge Planning

Youth "aging out of care" do not fare as well as other youth. Studies indicate that they are more likely to be undereducated and under- or unemployed; live below the poverty line; and experience incarceration, homelessness, and dependency on social assistance. They are also at higher risk for early parenthood, substance abuse, and mental health issues (Mann-Feder, 2007).

Canadian youth aging out of care have cited the following requirements as being crucial to ensure a better transition to adulthood: ongoing supportive relationships; peer support and independent living training; increased access to financial support; and support in gaining access to education, employment, and training programs.

In several studies, youth who have aged out of child welfare have spoken of their experiences and highlighted areas where they could have been better prepared for their transition from care. Best practices suggest that strong youth participation in discharge planning is an important factor in developing resilience and continuing aftercare (Tweddle, 2005). A current example in Québec, *le Projet de Qualifications des Jeunes*, stresses the importance of a stable, long-term relationship with one adult for the highest-risk youth who are exiting care. In this program, each young person is assigned a youth worker prior to discharge, and this relationship continues for a year after discharge (Mann-Feder, 2007).

Nineteen U.S. states have extended foster care support to age 21. Ontario recently adopted the same policy, and its youth advocate has penned a cost-benefit study arguing that it would be economical for the province to boost the age of support even higher, to 25. "If (foster care) and other supports are extended for four additional years, fewer youth will likely become involved with the criminal justice system. Fewer youth will likely access social assistance. More youth will likely finish high school and post-secondary education, thereby increasing their earnings and the taxes they will pay." (Provincial Advocate for Children and Youth, 2012).

More must to be done to address the needs of this small but significant—and very vulnerable—population. The next story (Selishia's Story, Part Two), a continuation of the previous story, shows youth participation and resilience at their best. Selishia not only transitions successfully out of care, seemingly with minimal support, but moves on to study to become a social work practitioner herself. Her insider advice to practitioners dealing with youth aging out of care, based on personal experience and deep reflection, is all the more relevant for that reason.

Reflecting on Selishia's Story

1. What kind of personal difficulties might a person leaving substitute care and returning to his or her birth home likely face?
2. In the absence of strong social supports, what kinds of social factors might lead such a person to a life on the streets or in a correctional facility?
3. Do you think the age at which young people are transitioned out of care is too early? Why or why not?

Selishia's Story... Part two

"Leaving home" can be daunting for young people who have grown up in foster care. Here, Selishia narrates her journey out of care and suggests ways in which social workers can support youth undergoing this transition.

After spending six months with a new foster family and participating in a family mediation meeting, Selishia returned to her original foster home. However, this reunification quickly broke down, and Selishia went to live with an aunt and uncle in another community during her Grade 11 school year.

She does not recall exactly when and how she became a continuing custody order (CCO) child in care. However, at the age of 17 while she was in Grade 12, she signed a youth agreement and began to live independently in a basement suite. She worked full time while also attending classes full time. She graduated from high school, and at the age of 19 signed an agreement that provided her with a living allowance if she pursued studies at a college or university. She was also promised a partial grant for academic fees if she continued her studies.

Finding One's Own Voice and Identity

A pivotal event in Selishia's life has been her involvement with "Voices of Experience," an after-school educational program that features accomplished women role models from diverse backgrounds speaking about their lives, education, and careers. For most of her life, Selishia felt alone and different from her peers because of her status as a foster child and then as a continuing custody order child. After joining the Voices of Experience, she was able to see her experiences in a larger context and no longer felt that she needed to hide her identity, but rather could acknowledge it openly. For Selishia, telling her story at this stage of her life is "not about receiving pity or getting attention, but about sharing knowledge and being able to have others relate to her [experiences and challenges]."

Currently, Selishia is a 21-year-old university student with an A average who wants to be a social worker. She also trains to enter body sculpting competitions. Despite being separated from her family of origin and feeling lonely and alienated for many years, she has developed resilience and self-sufficiency and describes herself as a "survivor" of government care.

When she finds herself struggling with adult transitions and decisions, Selishia contacts her sister. She does not have a home where she can spend Christmas, or someone to ask about how to make medical appointments, or relatives with whom she can swap family recipes. She has no safety net other than the one she has determinedly woven—and continues to weave—for herself.

Selishia identifies four areas that social workers should focus on when intervening with children and youth in care:

Explain the child's rights. Selishia was labelled as a rebellious teenager when she started to learn more about her rights and to question authority. For example, she learned that her foster parents had been receiving money to clothe her, despite the fact that she had been working since the age of 12 to earn money to buy clothes.

Recognize that "acting out" and "manipulation" signal that young people are searching for their own voice. Children and youth in care rarely have role models to teach them how to advocate for themselves appropriately, and they must learn to fend for themselves early in life compared to most children. Acting out and yelling are often protective devices against further emotional pain—and sometimes the only way that young people know how to get their voices or opinions heard.

Assign consistent social workers who are willing to forge a positive and understanding relationship. There was no social worker in Selishia's life to whom she could relate until she was 16; she remains in contact with this individual. However, prior to this, social workers whom Selishia did not even know could exert control over her friendships and her activities.

Acknowledge the insidious and ever-present experience of trauma and neglect. Being removed from a parental home and/or having multiple placements is traumatizing. Extensive emotional damage occurs when a child or youth lacks nurturing and safety. Not knowing in advance that a move is about to occur, or why a move has been arranged, compounds the trauma unnecessarily. All children should be provided with age-appropriate information about their own situation.

Selishia has developed reslience and self-confidence by determinedly creating a safety net for herself.

Marian Anderberg

Marian Anderberg has been a professional social worker in British Columbia since 1999. She attained her B.S.W. from Thompson Rivers University and her M.S.W. from UBC.

As Marian describes below, social work practice in the area of child protection presents many unique challenges and frustrations—as well as rewards. It is demanding but important work that benefits society in countless ways.

Although child protection is one of the most complex and challenging areas of social work, many social workers begin their careers in child welfare. At the age of 25, I was hired by British Columbia's Ministry of Children and Families as an auxiliary child welfare worker with a generalist caseload.

I had graduated in social work post-Gove, so my focus was on child-centredness and prioritizing children's needs. I was completely unprepared, however, for the many cases that involved extreme violence, murder, and suicide that are now seared into my memory. I also didn't anticipate the bureaucratic hurdles. At times, it seemed like there were more people ensuring my paperwork was complete than front-line social workers helping families.

Balancing Personal Life and Professional Life

Despite the horrors I encountered, I have fond memories of assisting many families. I am especially proud of my focus on "concurrent planning," which entailed working on permanency planning while completing an investigation.

For example, one of my cases involved a 12-year-old boy whose mother had passed away when he was two. He lived with his father and step-siblings and was sexually abused by his father, who was eventually convicted and jailed. In the course of the investigation, I was able to access information that helped reconnect the boy with his previously estranged maternal family. They created a scrapbook for him and provided information about his mom and her family members.

During the 13 years that I worked for the Ministry of Children and Families, I experienced personal and professional growth. Professionally, it took me two to three years to understand the job fully. Eventually, though, changes in my personal life affected my ability to work in the area of child protection. I got married and thought about having children. However, I was so used to seeing maltreated and traumatized children and their resulting special needs that I worried about having children of my own. Over time, as my friends and family started having babies, my concerns were balanced by seeing the joy of raising healthy children. I had a beautiful son and returned to work after my maternity leave.

But I had changed. In particular, I found that my objectivity had eroded and it was much more difficult not to personalize situations. Within a couple of months of my return to work, I went out on a case in which a mother was struggling with mental health issues and had attempted suicide. Her nine-month-old baby was removed for safety reasons. The baby, similar in age to my own son, coincidentally had the same name. This case completely overwhelmed me and was a turning point in my career. Within 18 months I had transferred into work in child and youth mental health.

Burnout and compassion fatigue are realities for many social workers in child protection. Yet, despite the rigours of learning the job and the rigidity of the bureaucracy, I have absorbed valuable lessons into my ongoing social work. I remain committed to collaborative community work in child welfare, support changes that enable working together with Aboriginal children, families, and communities, and continue to advocate for children. I am a better parent as a result of my experiences in child welfare. This type of work is difficult for new social work grads, but it is vital work that really matters.

For the child protection system to continue to improve, we need new eyes, fresh thinking, and strong beliefs to offset entrenched, bureaucratic processes. I don't at all regret my practice in child protection, as it continues to be a strong foundation for my evolving career in social work.

Chapter 5 Review

Review Questions

1. Identify and describe the main phases in the history of child welfare in Canada.
2. Explain what is meant by the "best interests" and "least restrictive" approaches to child-protection cases.
3. What constitutes child maltreatment in Canada? Why are Indigenous children at greater risk for maltreatment?
4. Discuss the pros and cons of foster care and group homes as forms of substitute care.
5. What are the steps to be followed in providing child-welfare services?
6. What is the role of the social worker in a Family Group Conference?
7. Give an example from this chapter of how empirical research can inform child-welfare practice.

Exploring Social Work

1. According to Gaetz, Donaldson, Richter, and Gulliver's *The State of Homelessness in Canada 2013*, youth account for approximately 20 percent of the homeless population in Canada (i.e., 6,000 young people on any given night). Consider why some young people might choose a life on the streets. What societal conditions make this choice more likely? What can social workers do both at the practice level and the policy level to help prevent this?
2. Research how child-welfare legislation in your province or territory has changed over the past several years. What *positive* policies have been implemented? What laws might *restrict* a social worker's ability to apply best practices? What areas are still in need of improvement?
3. Suggest some possible self-care strategies by which child welfare workers might reduce burnout and compassion fatigue as a result of work-related pressures and sometimes overwhelming caseloads. What might indicate whether these strategies are successful in mitigating signs and symptoms of burnout and fatigue?

Websites

Child Welfare League of Canada
www.cwlc.ca
This organization is active in Canadian policy, research, and advocacy. The site contains an issue-specific search engine.

The First Nations Child and Family Caring Society of Canada
www. fncaringsociety.com
This non-profit organization provides research, policy, professional development, and networking to support First Nations child and family service agencies (FNCFSA) in caring for First Nations children, youth, and families. It is the only national organization serving Aboriginal children and families.

The Canadian Child Welfare Research Portal (CWRP)
www.cwrp.ca
This portal gives child welfare professionals, researchers, and the general public a single point of access to Canadian child welfare research on children who are abused and neglected and on the programs and policies developed to protect these children and to support their families.

Youth in Care Canada
www.youthincare.ca
Formerly known as the National Youth in Care Network, this organization is driven by youth and alumni from care. It voices the opinions and concerns of youth in and from care and promotes the improvement of services for them. It is the only national constituency-driven, consumer-focused organization in the child-welfare sector and the oldest national youth-directed organization in Canada.

Campaign 2000
www.campaign2000.ca
This website posts information on current issues, new legislative and court rulings, and updates about what Campaign 2000 and its 120 partner agencies are doing to end child poverty in Canada.

Projet de Qualification des Jeunes (PQJ)
www.publicsafety.gc.ca
Targeting 16- to 18-year-olds living in youth centres, this program provides not only a support network for those transitioning out of care, but also practical training and opportunities for successful integration into the community.

Social Work and the Health of Canadians

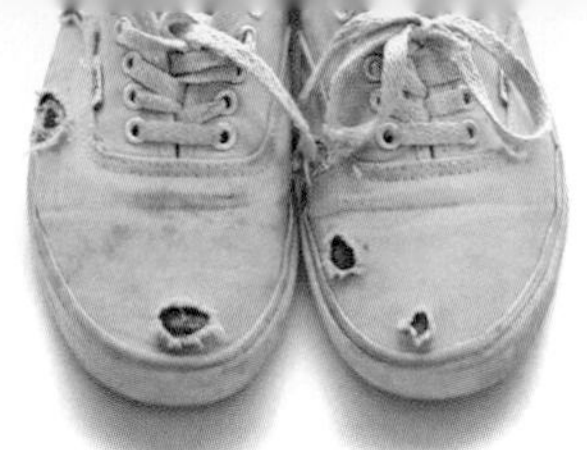

Sandra Loucks Campbell

6 Client-Centred Health Care

"People should be able to get whatever health services they require irrespective of their individual capacity to pay."

Tommy Douglas, father of Canadian medicare

A holistic perspective involves the promotion of wellness.

ocial workers play a key role in the provision of health services in Canada. In hospitals and other health-care settings, social workers are often part of multidisciplinary teams that provide a unique holistic perspective related to health care. This holistic perspective is concerned not only with the treatment of illnesses, but also with the promotion of wellness and the social, psychological, spiritual, economic, and cultural needs of the health services client.

This chapter provides an overview of the history of public health care in Canada. Several key issues are discussed, including universality, privatization, health-care expenditure, and the future of health care. The chapter also looks at the major social determinants of health in this country and the critical role of the social work practitioner in hospitals, in community health centres, and in other settings dedicated to promoting the all-round health of Canadians.

In this chapter, you will learn how to...

- identify some key events in the history of health-care policy in Canada
- describe some unique features of Canada's current health-care system
- identify the five principles by which the provinces qualify to receive health-care funding from the federal government (the "five principles of medicare")
- analyze trends in health-care expenditures in Canada
- compare the advantages of a publicly funded health-care system to a privatized system
- explain how the social determinants of health help us understand why some Canadians are healthier than others
- explain the general contributions made by social workers to Canada's community-based health-care system
- describe several important roles performed by social work health practitioners (e.g., in hospitals or in palliative care settings)
- identify the principles of effective social work practice related to the health of Canadians

Key Concepts

- Universal public health care
- Hall Report
- Medical Care Act (1968)
- Canada Health Act (1984)
- Romanow Commission
- Medicare
- Privatization
- Contracting out
- Community health centres
- Canadian Association of Community Health Centres
- Medical social work practice
- Interdisciplinary teams
- Holistic approach to health and healing
- Hospice and palliative care

Focusing Question

Social work health practitioners play an important role in Canada's public health-care system. What would the system look like without them?

A Brief History of Health-Care Policy in Canada

Universal public health care, the system all Canadians know and benefit from today, came about as a result of a great deal of deliberate work on the part of citizens, advocacy groups, and policymakers. The Canadian health care system is not perfect by any means, but certainly it is one of the best—and arguably the best— in the world. Prior to the late 1940s, before the fight for universal health care began in earnest, access to health care was based solely on one's ability to pay. Most Canadians had no access to health care whatsoever.

Pressure to Implement Universal Health Care

The British North America Act of 1867 established the jurisdictions of the federal and provincial governments in delivering health-care services. The division between the two was simple. The larger tax base of the federal government allowed it to exert a strong influence on Canadian health policy, as it continues to do today. The management of health fell to the provinces.

From 1880 to the 1950s, there were a variety of pre-payment health plans in place across Canada, sponsored by local governments, industries, and volunteer agencies (Vayda and Deber, 1995), but that was all that was available to average citizens. By 1934, for example, there were twenty-seven hospital-sponsored pre-payment plans in six provinces. Medical associations and hospitals also developed health insurance plans in Ontario, Manitoba, and Nova Scotia. In 1939, the first Canadian Blue Cross plan was formed in Manitoba, with most provinces following suit in the 1940s. But these voluntary plans did not cover all medical services, and were available only to those who could pay the premiums.

Provincial governments were slow to move toward universal health care and they only reacted under pressure from non-governmental groups. For example, in British Columbia, relief workers, the One Big Union, and the Co-operative Commonwealth Federation (CCF) put intense pressure on the government of Thomas Dufferin ("Duff") Pattullo to institute comprehensive health insurance in the 1930s. In 1933, the Pattullo government included health care as a key component of its election platform. The health-care legislation passed a third reading, but because of opposition from doctors, the government refused to enact it. Health insurance plans were also blocked in Alberta by the powerful Alberta Medical Association.

The Marsh Report, 1943

The lines of opposition were not always clear-cut even within the field of social work itself. For example, the 1942 Heagerty Report and the 1943 Marsh Report both recommended state-funded health insurance. The Heagerty Report proposed a federally funded, two-stage health insurance scheme. The report received widespread support, including from the labour movement and the Canadian Medical Association, but foundered because of federal-provincial disagreements. The more conservative Social Service Council, on the other hand, led by Ottawa mayor Charlotte Whitton, opposed the idea of state-funded health insurance.

The Marsh Report of 1943, which detailed the need for comprehensive and universal social programs, including health care, can be regarded as a critical event in the history of social welfare. Indeed, Canadian historian Michael Bliss described the Marsh Report as "the most important single document in the history of the Welfare State in Canada." The report recommended that the country establish a "social minimum," a standard aimed at protecting the disadvantaged through policies such as social insurance and children's allowances. By 1966, most of Marsh's recommendations had become law in Canada.

Charlotte Whitton

A femininst who held strong views on women's equality, Charlotte Whitton (1896-1975) was at the same time a strong social conservative for whom the notion of state-funded health insurance was unacceptable.

As mayor of Ottawa from 1951 to 1956 and again from 1960 to 1964, Whitton was the first female mayor of a major city in Canada. She became the founding director of the Canadian Council on Child Welfare from 1920 to 1941 (which became the Canadian Welfare Council, now the Canadian Council on Social Development) and helped bring about new legislation to aid children.

Canada's Unique Health-Care Model

In 1947, the first public insurance plan for hospital services was instituted in Saskatchewan. By 1961, all provinces and territories had signed agreements with the federal government for limited, in-patient hospital care with federal cost sharing. In 1962, Saskatchewan was the centre of a hard-fought struggle between the provincial government under the leadership of Tommy Douglas on the one hand, and the medical establishments on the other. The Saskatchewan universal health care program was finally launched by Douglas's successor, Woodrow Lloyd, in 1962.

In 1964, Conservative Prime Minister John Diefenbaker (also from Saskatchewan) appointed Justice Emmett Hall to chair a Royal Commission on Health Care. The resulting Hall Report disclosed that 7.5 million Canadians did not have medical coverage and recommended a comprehensive health service patterned on the Saskatchewan model. Women's organizations and organized labour were particularly strong supporters. The Liberal minority government that followed, supported by the newly established New Democratic Party (now led by Tommy Douglas), continued to push for universal health care.

The *Medical Care Act* was passed in 1968. By 1972, all provinces and territories had extended their plans to include physicians' services, although physicians were permitted to "opt out" and extra billing was permitted.

Subsequently, the **Canada Health Act** (1984) changed the funding structure, prohibited opting out and extra billing, and further strengthed the universal nature of the public health-care system in Canada.

Thomas Clement ("Tommy") Douglas (1904-1986) led the first social democratic government elected in Canada (the CCF in Saskatchewan in 1944). He became the first leader of the newly formed New Democratic Party in 1961.

Debating the Future of Health Care in Canada

In 2001, Allan Rock, the federal Minister of Health, announced the formation of the Royal Commission on the Future of Health Care in Canada, under the leadership of Roy Romanow. Its mandate was to engage Canadians in a national dialogue on the future of health care and to make recommendations to preserve the long-term sustainability of Canada's universally accessible, publicly funded health-care system.

The Romanow report has been the backdrop for the major debates and disagreements between the federal and provincial governments over health care in recent years.

The Romanow Commission

The final report of the **Romanow Commission** was released in 2002. In his work, Romanow said he was guided by two things: Canadian values of fairness, equity, and solidarity; and by the evidence. This approach led him to recommend expanding public, not-for-profit **medicare** to include home care and pharmacare, and to introduce a genuine system of primary health care. "In the coming months, the choices we make, or the consequences of those we fail to make," declared Romanow in his final report, "will decide medicare's future. I believe Canadians are prepared to embark on the journey together and build on the proud legacy they have inherited" (Romanow 2002, 247).

The Commission's final report, *Building on Values: The Future of Health Care in Canada*, comprises 47 detailed, costed recommendations. Romanow 's recommendations were premised on three main themes: (1) strong leadership is needed to maintain Medicare, (2) the system should become more efficient and responsive, and (3) both short-term and long-term strategies are needed to maintain universal health care. The Commission's report also addressed such diverse issues as Aboriginal health care, culturally sensitive access to health care, and the impact of globalization and applied research on the health of Canadians .

Medicare Under the Microscope

Canadians are justifiably proud of the health care system that they have inherited and, by any standards, the system is unique. It is "universal" insofar as it covers all "medically necessary services." Doctors cannot charge individual Canadians for such services, nor are there any private hospitals. Undoubtably, this is what provides Canadians with a sense of personal security and even pride. But just what is "medically necessary" is unclear. For example, special services (e.g., MRIs, certain blood tests), dental care, drugs required outside the hospital setting, and long-term care—all medically necessary—typically involve a fee.

Critics of the current system want to increase the private, for-profit component. They want to bring Canadian health care more in line with other models, such as the National Health Service in Britain. They argue that a "two-tier system," with private and public medicine offered side by side, will make the system more cost-efficient and provide more medical choices for consumers. There is no such thing as "free" health care, they argue, it is just a question of who pays.

The system's supporters, on the other hand, argue against a two-tier system. If anything, they insist, what is needed are renewed efforts to defend and even extend the system—to include more "medically necessary" procedures, not fewer—and to make it more cost-efficient and more equitable for Canadian citizens.

This debate over the future of health care occurs in real time—major groups align themselves on one side or the other. Who will win out? Time will tell, but the stakes are certainly high.

The Health Council of Canada

In 2014, Roy Romanow, former NDP premier of Saskatchewan and one-time chair of the Royal Commission on the Future of Health Care, lamented the end of the Health Council of Canada and the 10-year health accord that led to its creation.

"It's a blow to nation-building because it's a blow to one of our revered, if not most revered, social programs, which is medicare," commented Romanow.

The 2004 accord was intended to enact reforms and set national standards in areas such as primary care, wait lists, and electronic health records, with the council acting as watchdog.

The Five Principles of Medicare
In search of the perfect health system

Medically necessary health care on the basis of need, rather than the ability to pay

Today, Canada's health-care system—commonly referred to as medicare—is funded by government insurance, and is publicly delivered by hospitals and other health-care settings and privately delivered mainly by physicians (who are self-employed or employed by physician-owned corporations). Each province must meet the following five principles to receive funding from the federal government:

- **Public administration.** According to section 8 of the *Canada Health Act*, the health care insurance plan in each province must be administered and operated on a non-profit basis by a public authority responsible to the provincial government, and be subject to an audit of its accounts and financial transactions.
- **Comprehensiveness**. According to section 9, the plan must cover all insured health services ("medically necessary services") provided by hospitals, medical practitioners, or dentists, and, where permitted, cover services rendered by other health care practitioners.
- **Universality.** Section 10 requires that 100 percent of the insured persons of a province be entitled to the insured health services provided for by the plan on uniform terms and conditions.
- **Portability.** In accordance with section 11, residents moving to another province must continue to be covered for insured health services by the home province during any minimum waiting period imposed by the new province, not to exceed three months.
- **Accessibility.** By virtue of section 12, the health care insurance plan of a province must provide for: (a) insured health services on uniform terms and conditions and reasonable access by insured persons to insured health services unprecluded or unimpeded, either directly or indirectly, by charges or other means; (b) reasonable compensation to physicians and dentists for all insured health services rendered; payments to hospitals in respect of the cost of insured health services.

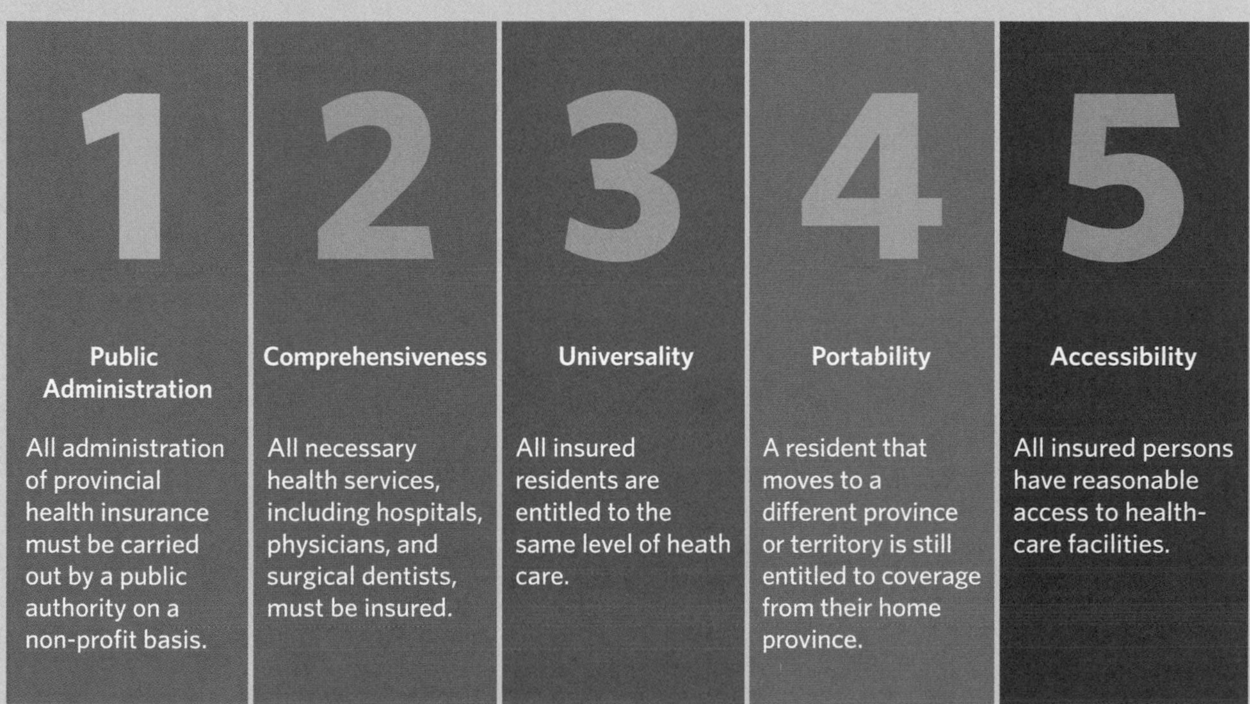

An Overview of Health Expenditure Trends

Both the public and the private sectors contribute to the financing of Canada's health system (see Figure 6.1). Public-sector funding includes payments by governments at the federal, provincial/territorial, and municipal levels and by workers' compensation boards and other social security schemes. Private-sector funding consists primarily of health expenditures by households and private insurance firms.

Total Health Expenditure in Canada

The latest data available put health spending in Canada at approximately $214.9 billion or $6,045 per Canadian (2014). The rate of growth in health spending (2.1 percent in 2014) continues to be less than inflation and population growth combined. Health spending decreased by an average 0.4 percent per year in the previous four years after adjusting for these factors.

Since the start of the global economic recession in 2008, the ratio of health spending to GDP has stabilized or fallen in most OECD countries. A new period of slower growth is emerging. It reflects, in large part, Canada's modest economic growth and fiscal restraint as governments focus on balancing budgetary deficits. Health expenditure, on average, accounts for about 40 percent of provincial/territorial government budgets. Hospitals (29.6 percent), drugs (15.8 percent), and physician services (15.5 percent) continue to account for the largest shares of health dollars (more than 60 percent of total health spending).

While Canadians aged 65 and over account for less than 15 percent of the Canadian population, they consume more than 45 percent of all public-sector health dollars spent.

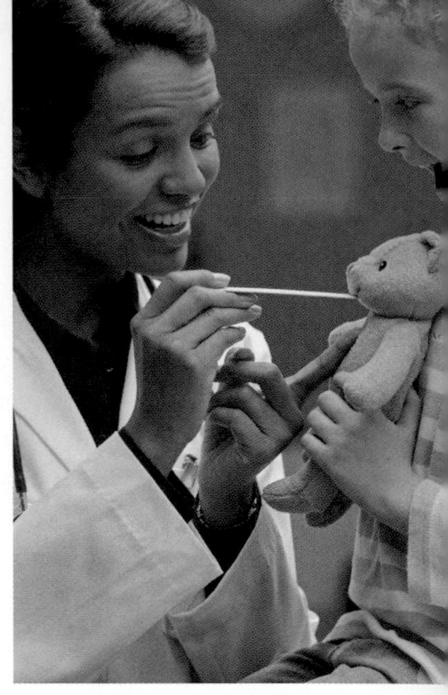

Average salaries of physicians in Canada in 2015 ranged from $263,000 in Nova Scotia to $368,000 in Ontario. (Canadian Institute for Health Information, 2015)

Health Expenditure by Source of Finance

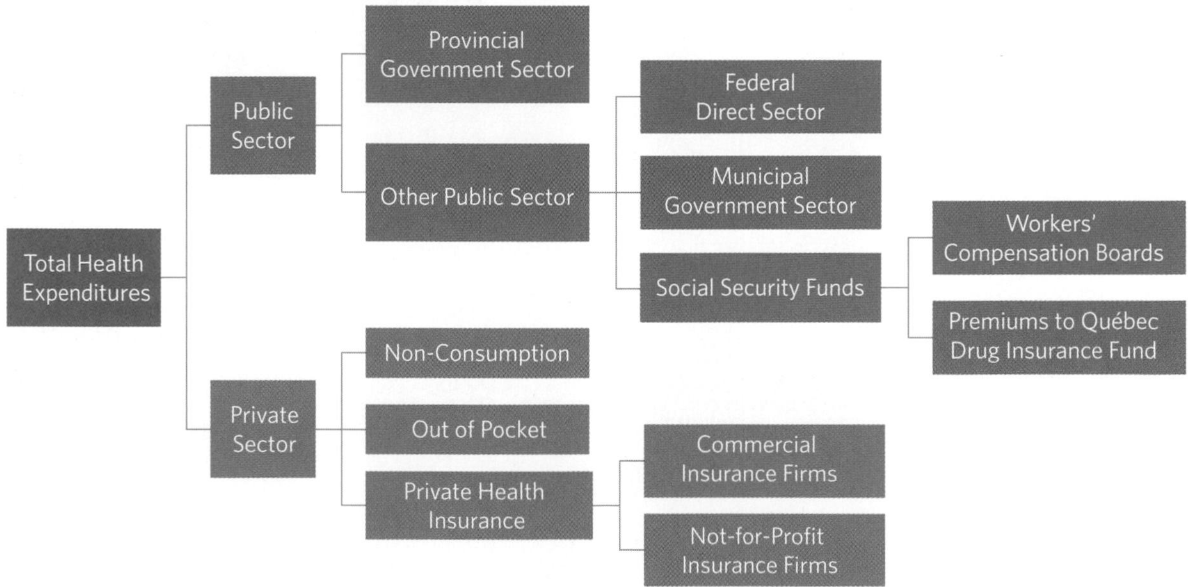

Figure 6.1 This flow chart provides an overview of both public and private funding sources that underpin the financing of Canada's health system expenditure.

Provincial and International Variations

Health spending per person varies among provinces and territories. Total health spending per person is highest in Newfoundland and Labrador ($6,953) and Alberta ($6,783) and lowest in Québec ($5,616) and British Columbia ($5,865). The amount spent per person reflects the population of each province and territory and its health-care needs, as well as the organization of health services, personnel compensation, and the sharing of costs between public and private sectors. Per person spending on health might be expected to be higher in the territories due to their small, dispersed populations. Hospitals (29.6 percent), drugs (15.8 percent) and physician services (15.5 percent) continue to account for the largest shares of health dollars (more than 60 percent of total health spending). Although spending continues to grow in all three categories, the pace has slowed in recent years.

Among 30 countries that had comparable accounting systems in the OECD in 2012, the latest year for which data are available, spending per person on health care remained highest in the United States (US$8,745). Canada was in the top quartile of countries in terms of per person spending on health, with spending at US$4,602, which was similar to several other OECD countries, including Germany (US$4,811), Denmark (US$4,698), and Luxembourg (US$4,578).

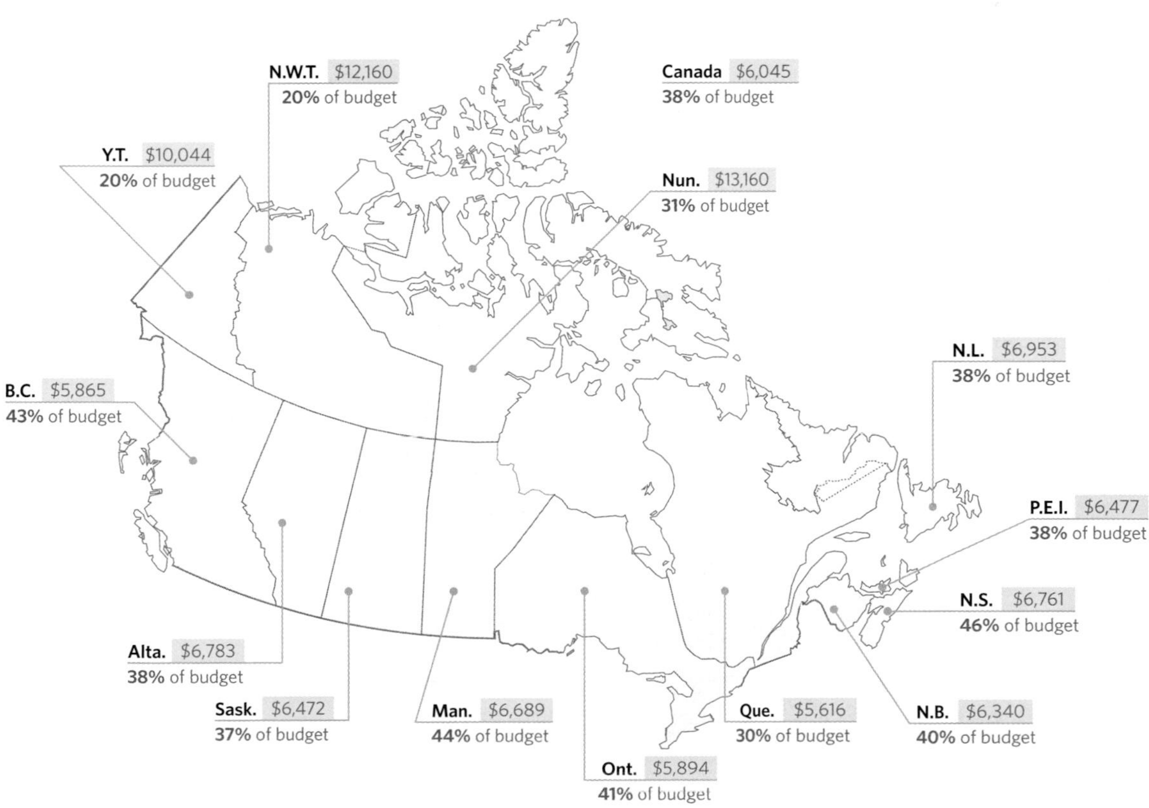

Figure 6.2 Health-care spending per person and as a percentage of budget varies between provinces and territories, depending on factors such as population size and needs and the organization of health services.

Source: Canadian Institute for Health Information. (2015). *National Health Expenditures Trends, 1975-2014*. CIHI: Ottawa, Ontario. Per person data (public and private) shown are projected for 2014 and provincial/territorial percentages are projected for 2013.

The Advantages of a Public Health-Care System

In reality, "free" health care does not exist anywhere; it is a question of who pays how much, and for what services. However, the case for some form of publicly funded health care is accepted by most countries in the world. Apart from being an effective delivery method, public medicare has important advantages over a private health care system.

- First, public financing spreads the cost of health care across society, rather than only to those who are unfortunate or sick.
- Second, financing health insurance through taxation is efficient, since it does not require the creation of a separate collection process.
- Third, medicare encourages Canadians to seek preventive care services and to treat problems before they worsen and treatment becomes more costly.
- Fourth, the government can cut costs, as it is largely a single buyer of health care supplies and services.

Many Canadian businesses also recognize and support Canada's universal medicare system. Lower employee benefit costs and a healthy and mobile workforce are competitive advantages. Also, the portability principle of medicare ensures that workers can move from province to province and still be covered by health insurance. Provincial governments have also begun to address preventive medicine and community-based care.

Public vs. Private Health Care

Nevertheless, public health care in Canada is not entirely secure. An aging population and ever-spiralling costs will require defenders of universal care to be even more alert. Some of the potential dangers are indicated below.

- **Universality**. One of the biggest threats to our public system of health care is the current movement to privatize care in some provinces, particularly in Alberta and Ontario. Saskatchewan recently passed legislation that allows patients to pay privately for MRIs. Québec also introduced legislation that will allow physicians to bill for a range of "ancillary" products and services, ranging from eye drops to colonoscopies. Several trends indicate increased **privatization** in our health care system:
  - the "de-listing" of services covered by medicare (e.g., specific medical procedures, support services, and drugs)
  - the transferring of care out of areas covered by medicare (e.g., acute care in hospitals) to areas that are not (e.g., home care)
  - the contracting out of "non-core" medical services (laboratories, ambulances, and rehabilitation services) to private firms
- **Comprehensiveness.** Some provinces have attempted to reduce costs by reducing comprehensiveness—that is, the range of what are considered to be "medically necessary" services. Because the *Canada Health Act* states that the provinces should determine which services are "medically necessary," there is some room for provinces to limit that range.
- **Contracting out.** There are also concerns regarding the administration of hospitals. Governments are **contracting out** the management of some hospitals to private companies. Also, some services, such as catering, laundry, and cleaning, have been contracted out to private, for-profit organizations.

Health-Care Spending

"You can't talk about health care without talking about money," Terry Lake, B.C.'s health minister (shown here) remarked during discussions between provincial and territorial health ministers and the federal government in early 2016.

Today, Ottawa covers about 22 percent of publicly funded health care ($34 billion of $155 billion).

The provinces and territories want Ottawa to increase that amount to 25 percent of their health budgets. They also want to revisit equalization to ensure fairness across the country.

Improving Health Care for All Canadians
There is no such thing as "free"

Which country has the world's best health system?

That is one of those unanswerable questions that health-policy geeks like to ponder and debate. There have even been serious attempts at measuring and ranking.

In 2000, the World Health Organization (in)famously produced a report that concluded that France had the world's best health system, followed by those of Italy, San Marino, Andorra and Malta. The business publication Bloomberg produces an annual ranking that emphasizes value for money from health spending; the 2014 ranking places Singapore on top, followed by Hong Kong, Italy, Japan and South Korea.

The Economist Intelligence Unit compares 166 countries, and ranks Japan as No. 1, followed by Singapore, Switzerland, Iceland and Australia. The Commonwealth Fund ranks health care in 11 Western countries and gives the nod to the U.K., followed by Switzerland, Sweden, Australia and Germany.

The problem with these exercises is that no one can really agree on what should be measured and, even when they do settle on measures, data are not always reliable and comparable. "Of course, there is no such thing as a perfect health system and it certainly doesn't reside in any one country," Mark Britnell, global chairman for health at the consulting giant KPMG, writes in his new book, *In Search of the Perfect Health System*. "But there are fantastic examples of great health and health care from around the world which can offer inspiration."

As a consultant who has worked in 60 countries—and who receives in-depth briefings on the health systems of each before meeting clients—Mr. Britnell has a unique perspective and, in the book, offers up a subjective and insightful list of the traits that are important to creating good health systems.

If the world had a perfect health system, he writes, it would have the following qualities: the values and universal access of the U.K.; the primary care of Israel; the community services of Brazil; the mental-health system of Australia; the health promotion philosophy of the Nordic countries; the patient and community empowerment in parts of Africa; the research and development infrastructure of the United States; the innovation, flair and speed of India; the information, communications and technology of Singapore; the choice offered to patients in France; the funding model of Switzerland; and the care for the aged of Japan.

In the book, Mr. Britnell elaborates on each of these examples of excellence and, in addition, provides a great précis of the strengths and weaknesses of health systems in 25 countries. The chapter on Canada is appropriately damning, noting that this country's outmoded health system has long been ripe for revolution, but the "revolution has not happened."

Why? Because this country has a penchant for doing high-level, in-depth reviews of the health system's problems, but puts all its effort into producing recommendations and none into implementing them. Ouch. "Canada stands at a crossroads," Mr. Britnell writes, "and needs to find the political will and managerial and clinical skills to establish a progressive coalition of the willing."

The book's strength is that it does not offer up simplistic solutions. Rather, it stresses that there is no single best approach because all health systems are the products of their societies, norms and cultures. One of the best parts of the book—and quite relevant to Canada—is the analysis of funding models. "The debate about universal health care is frequently confused with the ability to pay," Mr. Britnell writes. He notes that the high co-payments in the highly praised health systems of Asia would simply not be tolerated in the West.

But ultimately what matters is finding an approach that works, not a perfect one: "This is the fundamental point. There is no such thing as free health care; it is only a matter of who pays for it. Politics is the imperfect art of deciding who gets what, how and when."

The book stresses that the challenges are the same everywhere: providing high-quality care to all at an affordable price, finding the work force to deliver that care and empowering patients. To do so effectively, you need vision and you need systems.

Above all, you need the political will to learn from others and put in place a system that works.

- *Source:* Picard, André. (2015). Canada needs "coalition of the willing" to improve health care. *The Globe and Mail* (November 18).

The Social Determinants of Health
The components of well-being

> A health care system—even the best health care system in the world—will be only one of the ingredients that determine whether your life will be long or short, healthy or sick, full of fulfillment, or empty with despair.
>
> The Honourable Roy Romanow, 2004

The primary factors that shape the health of Canadians are not medical treatments or lifestyle choices but rather the living conditions they experience. These conditions have come to be known as the social determinants of health.The importance to health of living conditions was established in the mid-1800s and has been enshrined in Canadian government policy documents since the mid-1970s. In fact, Canadian contributions to the social determinants of health concept have been so extensive as to make Canada a "health promotion powerhouse" in the eyes of the international health community. Recent reports from Canada's Chief Public Health Officer, the Canadian Senate, and the Public Health Agency of Canada continue to document the importance of the social determinants of health.

But this information—based on decades of research and hundreds of studies in Canada and elsewhere—tells a story that is unfamiliar to most Canadians. Canadians are largely unaware that our health is shaped by how income and wealth are distributed, whether or not we are employed, and if so, the working conditions we experience.

Furthermore, our well-being is also determined by the health and social services we receive, and our ability to obtain quality education, food, and housing, among other factors. And contrary to the assumption that Canadians have personal control over these factors, in most cases these living conditions are—for better or worse—imposed upon us by the quality of the communities, housing situations, our work settings, health and social service agencies, and educational institutions with which we interact.

There is much evidence that the quality of the social determinants of health Canadians experience helps explain the wide health inequalities that exist among Canadians.

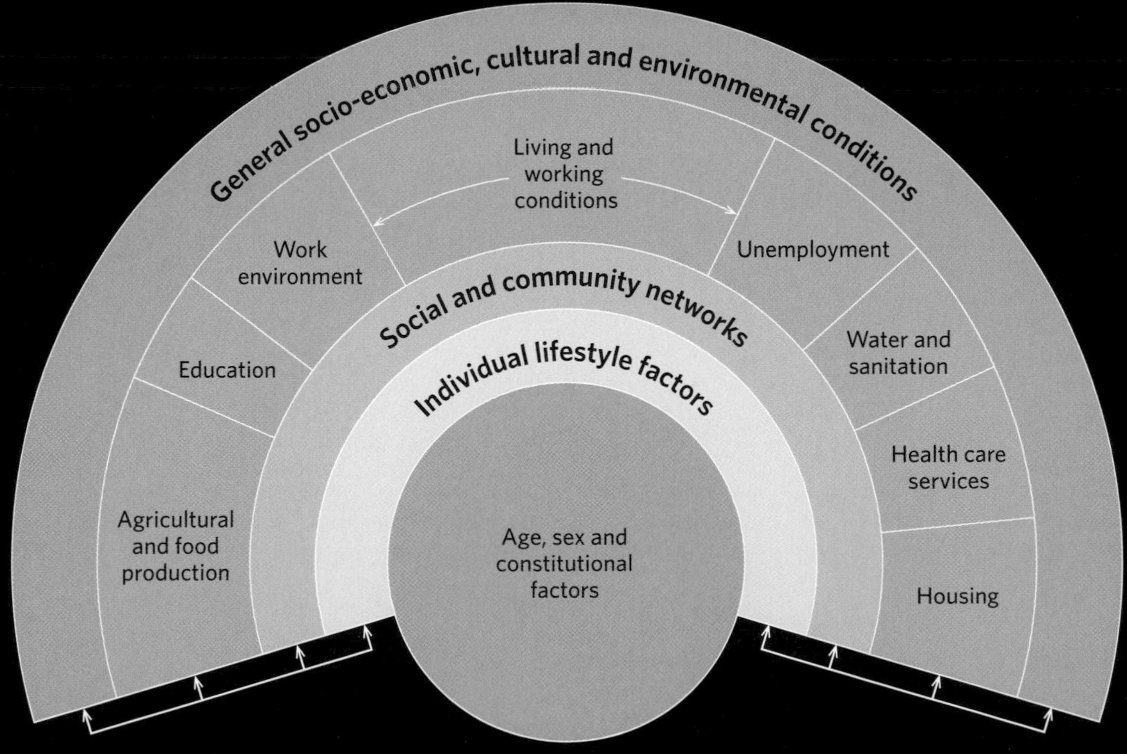

Source: Dahlgren, G. and Whitehead, M. (1991). *Policies and Strategies to Promote Social Equity in Health.* Stockholm: Institute for Future Studies.

How long Canadians can expect to live and whether they will experience cardiovascular disease or adult-onset diabetes are very much determined by their living conditions.

The same goes for the health of their children: diifferences among Canadian children in their surviving beyond their first year of life, experiencing childhood afflictions such as asthma and injuries, and whether they fall behind in school are strongly related to the social determinants of health they experience.

Research is also finding that the quality of these health-shaping living conditions is strongly determined by decisions that governments make in a range of different public policy domains.

Governments at the municipal, provincial/territorial, and federal levels create policies, laws, and regulations that influence how much income Canadians receive through employment, family benefits, or social assistance, the quality and availability of affordable housing, the kinds of health and social services and recreational opportunities we can access, and even what happens when Canadians lose their jobs during economic downturns.

These experiences also provide the best explanations for how Canada compares to other nations in overall health.

Canadians generally enjoy better health than Americans, but do not do as well compared to other nations that have developed public policies that strengthen the social determinants of health. The World Health Organization sees health-damaging experiences as resulting from "a toxic combination of poor social policies and programmes, unfair economic arrangements, and bad politics".

Despite this evidence, there has been little effort by Canadian governments and policymakers to improve the social determinants of health through public policy action. Canada compares unfavourably to other wealthy developed nations in its support of citizens as they navigate the life span. Our income inequality and poverty rates are growing and are among the highest of wealthy developed nations. Canadian spending in support of families, persons with disabilities, older Canadians, and employment training is also among the lowest of these same wealthy developed nations

Improving the health of Canadians is possible but requires Canadians to think about health and its determinants in a more sophisticated manner than has been the case to date.

- *Source:* Mikkonen, J., & Raphael, D. (2010). *Social Determinants of Health: Canadian Facts.* Toronto, ON: York University School of Health Policy and Management.

A Model of the Social Determinants of Health

Among the variety of models of the social determinants of health that exist, the one developed at a conference held at York University in Toronto in 2002 has proven especially useful for understanding why some Canadians are healthier than others. The 14 social determinants of health in this model are as follows:

Aboriginal status	Gender
Disability	Housing
Early life	Income and income distribution
Education	Race
Employment and working conditions	Social exclusion
Food insecurity	Social safety net
Health services	Unemployment and job security

- *Source:* Mikkonen, J., & Raphael, D. (2010). *Social Determinants of Health: Canadian Facts.* York University School of Health Policy and Management, Toronto, Ontario.

Ethnic Differences in Health
Vulnerabilities revealed for certain groups

A study of 220,000 Canadians found that health problems affect four major ethnic groups at different rates

It is widely known that rates of obesity, type 2 diabetes, and high blood pressure are on the rise. But a new Canadian study shows that certain ethnic groups—specifically, South Asian men and Black men and women—get these chronic health problems more often than the rest of the population.

The study, published on Monday [August 10, 2015] in the journal *BMJ Open*, found that overall, the heart health of South Asian men and Black people in Canada has deteriorated significantly in the past decade. For instance, diabetes in South Asian men has doubled to more than 15 percent of the population in 2012 from 6.7 percent in 2001.

Among Black women, the rate of diabetes grew to just over 12 percent from 6.3 percent during that same time period. Rates of obesity rose in each of the ethnic groups studied, but the largest increases were found in Black and Chinese men. Given that obesity is often a precursor to chronic health problems, these findings should be sounding an alarm, said Dr. Maria Chiu, scientist at Toronto's Institute for Clinical Evaluative Sciences and lead author of the study. The obesity trends "paint a really scary picture" of what could happen to type 2 diabetes rates in the future, she said.

The study looked at data from nearly 220,000 Canadians who took part in Statistics Canada's Canadian Community Health Survey. The researchers focused on individuals belonging to Canada's four major ethnic groups: white, South Asian, Chinese, and Black.

The results add to a growing body of evidence suggesting health problems affect ethnic groups at different rates. While genes certainly play a role, they do not tell the entire story, Chiu said. "I like to think of it as genes load up the gun and environment pulls the trigger," she said.

Her study helps explain why some ethnic groups appear to be more vulnerable to certain health conditions. Overall, the ethnic minority groups included in the study had household incomes that were as much as $30,000 lower than those of their white counterparts.

Those groups also reported that they ate fewer fruits and vegetables. At the same time, smoking rates among all of the groups studied fell, with the exception of Black women and Chinese men.

"This is another wakeup call," said Dr. Sonia Anand, professor of medicine and epidemiology at McMaster University in Hamilton and a spokeswoman for the Heart and Stroke Foundation. "We have to get going or we're going to end up with an epidemic of obesity and type 2 diabetes in the next 20 years."

Anand was not involved in this study, but much of her research focuses on the causes of heart disease in ethnic groups. She said the evidence is clear the differences exist, but there is no clear strategy on how to solve this complex problem.

The important question for researchers and policy makers, according to Chiu, is how to bridge the gap and reverse the trends.

One solution will be to tailor campaigns to ethnic groups, Chiu said. They need to know they are at risk and what changes they can make to reduce their vulnerability, such as quitting smoking or eating more fruits and vegetables.

And, as Anand noted, "we move less, we commute by car, we don't live in walkable neighbourhoods."

That means the necessary solutions are going to require a lot of time, co-ordination, funding and commitment, she said.

- *Source:* Weeks, Carly. (2015). Some minorities more likely to see heart health deteriorate. *The Globe and Mail* (August 10).

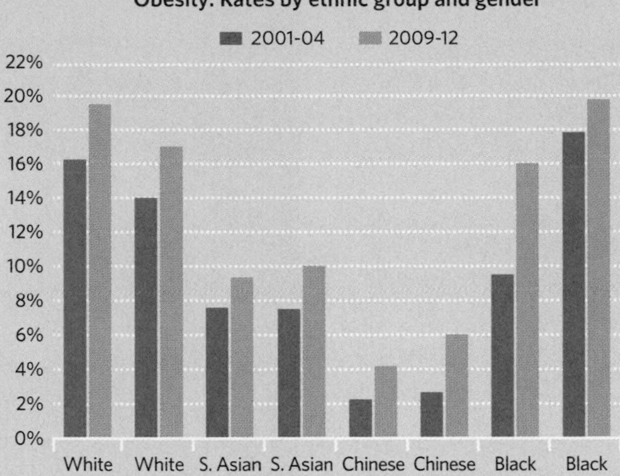
Obesity: Rates by ethnic group and gender
2001-04
2009-12
22%
20%
18%
16%
14%
12%
10%
8%
6%
4%
2%
0%
White (M)
White (F)
S. Asian (M)
S. Asian (F)
Chinese (M)
Chinese (F)
Black (M)
Black (F)

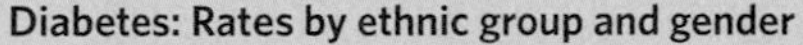
Diabetes: Rates by ethnic group and gender

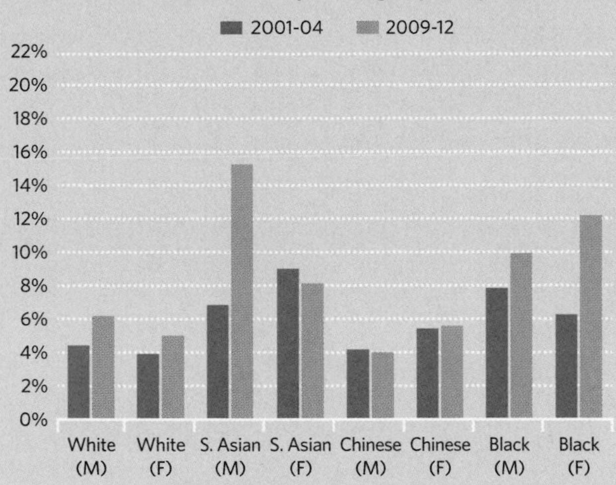
2001-04
2009-12
22%
20%
18%
16%
14%
12%
10%
8%
6%
4%
2%
0%
White (M)
White (F)
S. Asian (M)
S. Asian (F)
Chinese (M)
Chinese (F)
Black (M)
Black (F)

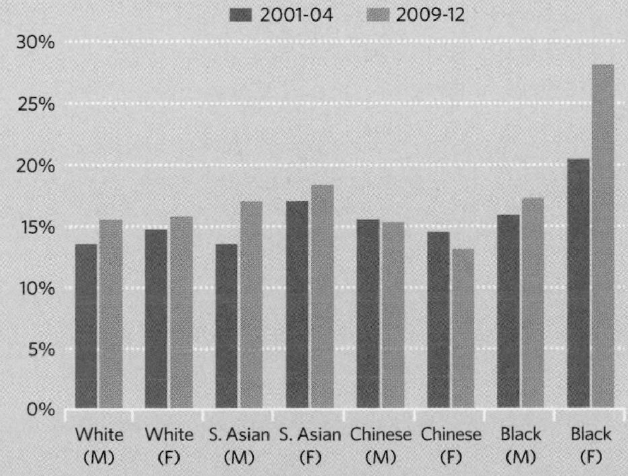
Hypertension: Rates by ethnic group and gender
2001-04
2009-12
30%
25%
20%
15%
10%
5%
0%
White (M)
White (F)
S. Asian (M)
S. Asian (F)
Chinese (M)
Chinese (F)
Black (M)
Black (F)

Social Work and Community-Based Health Care in Canada

The idea of community-based health care as an alternative to individual physician care has existed since early in the twentieth century, with the first examples appearing in the United Kingdom and the United States. Canada's first community-based centre—the Mount Carmel Clinic in Winnipeg—opened over 90 years ago, in 1926, and is still in operation. Ontario's first **community health centre (CHC)** opened in Sault Ste. Marie in 1963.

Each province currently offers its own unique collection of community-based organizations and access points for health care in their province. Among the services offered are: primary care, maternity care, home support, family care clinics, community care access centres, Aboriginal health centres, family health teams, nurse practitioner-led clinics, interdisciplinary teams, midwifery, and community-based palliative care.

The Advantageous Role of Community Health Centres

The **Canadian Association of Community Health Centres** is the federal voice for community health centres and community-oriented, people-centred primary health care across Canada. The association was established in 2012 to replace the previous Canadian Alliance of Community Health Centre Associations, which was first established in 1995. Once considered the "poor cousins" of the mainstream health-care system (because of their association with low-income and disadvantaged populations), CHCs have grown in number and size as provincial governments recognize their role in preventative medicine and health promotion. Since the mid-1980s, they have offered an ever-broadening range of client services to the general public, as well as to parents, seniors, women, and ethnic and immigrant populations.

The underlying premise of the CHC system is that community residents, in partnership with providers and funders of health services, need to be involved in identifying the needs of their community and in designing and overseeing service delivery, and evaluating health services programs. CHCs tend to network with other health and social services agencies and are accountable to their communities through community boards. They operate on the principle that communities should work together to "own" health care services. They frequently address issues pertaining to the social determinants of health, such as housing, literacy, and poverty through programs and social action.

CHCs are funded primarily by provincial grants. Additional funding is often obtained from the United Way, other foundations, and federal government programs. Funding is allocated either through a global budgeting process, based on services directed at populations, or through capitalization funding, where fixed sums are established for each registered client based on need as a reflection of age, sex, key demographic factors, and prevalence and severity of chronic illness. The use of CHCs (centres locaux des services communautaires) is most widespread in Québec. Ontario comes second. There is, however, a growing interest in the CHC model across the country, both as a way to cut costs and as a community-based approach.

An important advantage of the CHC model is the focus on prevention, education, community development, social action, and health promotion. CHCs tend to address four main determinants of health—living and working conditions, available social support, individual behaviour, and genetic makeup. Located as they are between the patient and medical practitioners, social workers are central to the provision of both direct care and community development in the CHC model of health-care delivery.

Major Health Care Reform

Ontario has signalled sweeping changes to community health care with a view to eliminating duplication and inefficiency.

Community Care Access Centres (CCACs), which were set up in 1996 to co-ordinate access to home and community care services, will be wound down starting in 2016. The province's Local Health Integration Networks (LHINs) will play a larger role in these service areas.

Regional Differences in Health Outcomes
Averages can be misleading...

Canada needs to find a solution to serious regional health inequalities

Canadians, on average, are fairly healthy. Life expectancy continues to rise, fewer of us smoke and more of us are becoming physically active. That's the problem with averages. They are misleading. In Ontario, for instance, average life expectancy is 81.5 years—a pretty decent number. It's only when you look beyond the big picture that you see the cracks. The life expectancy of a baby born in Brampton is 84. A child born the same day in Sault Ste. Marie, less than 700 kilometres away, is 79.

Another telling metric is potentially avoidable deaths—how many people likely died unnecessarily because they didn't receive proper care after a heart attack, weren't vaccinated against a disease, or suffered another preventable or treatable ailment. According to the Ontario average, 163 in 100,000 people die from a potentially avoidable death a year. But in reality, the numbers vary wildly across the province, from a low of 114 per 100,000 in cities such as Richmond Hill and Vaughan, to a high of 258 in Thunder Bay, Marathon, Dryden and the surrounding area.

These numbers are from a report released last week by Health Quality Ontario, a provincial agency mandated to improve the province's health care system. But this isn't just an Ontario problem. Across the country, the situation is much the same: startling, persistent regional health inequalities that, quite literally, are sickening and killing countless Canadians before their time.

Often, stark inequalities exist between urban and rural or remote communities, which is why northern parts of the country are so often struck by much higher rates of disease and premature death. There are many reasons behind these differences, such as the fact that in northern communities, people tend to smoke more, be less physically active, have a much more difficult time accessing specialized medical care, have higher Aboriginal populations and have lower education and income levels compared with large urban centres. Of course, many of these same problems can be found within cities, where pockets of vulnerable individuals can live just a few blocks from affluence.

But none of this explains why we as Canadians have allowed these problems to persist for so long. Why we consider it acceptable that, depending on where you live, how much you earn or what education level you have achieved, you are much more likely to die from a chronic illness or have to wait weeks longer for a loved one to get a spot in a long-term care home.

The answer, quite possibly, is that many of us have never really stopped to consider that these differences exist. That, in 2015, Aboriginal peoples in Canada are being infected with and dying of tuberculosis. Or that many patients with chronic diseases living outside of urban centres often have few resources to help them manage their conditions. Or that many communities throughout Canada face crippling doctor shortages that close emergency rooms and delay treatment.

Joshua Tepper, president and CEO of Health Quality Ontario, says that many people simply don't "understand how dramatically different health outcomes are across the province." After all, most politicians and policy-makers live in and around the urban areas where health outcomes tend to be the best. It's all too easy to forget about the people living in remote cities or rural areas.

Some will argue that it's up to people to take charge of their own health. That's true. But when the realities of daily life set them up for failure, it's a sign that change is needed from a higher level. An excellent example of this is cited by Connie Clement, scientific director of the National Collaborating Centre for Determinants of Health. She notes that the Liquor Control Board of Ontario is able to tightly regulate the price of alcohol throughout the province. Yet nothing is done about the fact that milk or fresh produce can be priced so high that few families in remote communities can afford them.

It's heartening to hear experts such as Tepper and Clement put these serious health inequality issues on the table. Now, it's up to the politicians and policy-makers to listen up and pledge to do something about it. Canada needs to find a solution to serious regional health inequalities.

- *Source:* Weeks, Carly. (2015). Canada needs to find solution to serious regional health inequalities. *The Globe and Mail* (October 18).

The Health-Care System in Québec
Sweeping changes to health-care delivery

By Adje van de Sande

Today, 147 CLSCs continue to serve as the point of entry for the Québec population to the province's Health and Social Service Networks

With the death of Premier Maurice Duplessis in 1959 and the election of the Liberal government under Jean Lesage (shown here) in 1960, Québec entered what is generally referred to as the Quiet Revolution. This period was marked by a radical transformation of Québec society in which the State took over control of health and social services.

Up to the time of the Quiet Revolution, at least for the French-speaking population of Québec, health and social services were under the control of the Catholic Church.

The Castonguay-Nepveu Report

In 1966, Premier Jean Lesage mandated Claude Castonguay and Gérard Nepveu to chair a commission of inquiry into health and welfare (*Commission d'enquête sur la santé et le bien-être social, CESBES*).

The report, known as the Castonguay-Nepveu Report, was published in 1970 and provided a blueprint for the reorganization of health and social services in Québec.

As a first step, the Québec government, under Premier Robert Bourassa, created the Ministry of Social Affairs (*Ministère des affaires sociales*) and appointed Claude Castonguay as its first minister.

Then, in 1971, even before the ink on the Castonguay-Nepveu Report was dry, the Québec government passed a law (*la Loi sur les services de santé et les services sociaux*) commonly known as Bill 65. This law called for six structures:

- regional health and social service councils, *les conseils régioneaux de la santé et des services sociaux, CRSSS;*
- community health departments, *les départements de santé communautaires, DSC;*
- residential centres, *les centres d'accueils, CA;*
- hospital centres, *les centres hospitaliers, CH;*
- social service centres, *les centres de services sociaux, CSS;* and
- local community service centres, *les centres locaux de services communautaires, CLSC.*

Three New Structures and Twleve New Regions

As stated in the law (Bill 65), each of the structures were to be administered by a board of directors that was required to include community representation.

Three of these structures—namely the residential centres, the hospital centres, and the social service centres—already existed, while the regional health and social service councils, the community health departments, and the local community service centres were totally new structures.

The Québec Government divided the provinces into twelve regions, each of which would be administered by a regional health and social service council (CRSSS) whose role it was to organize the health and social services programs based on the needs of the population within its region. The community health departments were integrated within the hospital centres and were responsible for epidemiological studies on health concerns and the evaluation of programs with a focus on preventative care.

The Innovative Nature of the CLSCs

The most innovative of the new structures was the CLSCs. Québec, which has been described by Shah and Moloughney (2001), as being in the forefront in the development of community health centres in Canada, created the CLSCs to provide a multi-service "one-stop" agency for the provision of basic health and social services throughout the province.

As explained by Ives, Denov, and Sussman (2015, p. 47), "CLSCs were mandated to provide the delivery of preventative, restorative and ongoing health and social services at home, school, work or in a clinic to older adults with loss of autonomy, at-risk children and families, persons with physical disabilities, children with learning disabilities, persons living with mental health challenges, and persons in need of family physicians." However, as stated by Gaumer and Fleury (2008), the development of the CLSCs was not without controversy. Many of the CLSCs in the various communities evolved from the grass-roots initiatives of community organizers who wanted to maintain community control.

"Although few in number, the community organizers were to play a particularly important role in developing and supporting community organizations, and the CLSCs emerged as bona fide laboratories for social innovation especially when they were first created" (p. 91).

During the mid-1970s, some Québec politicians were nevertheless concerned about the role of the community organizers, suggesting that the CLSCs had become sites of left-wing protests and "revolution."

New Health and Social Service Networks

In response, the Government launched *l'Opération bilan* and commissioned a panel of experts to evaluate the functioning of the CLSCs. Robert Mayer (2002) explained that the formal report of *l'Opération bilan*, which included the majority of the panel members, recommended that the CLSCs should spend less time engaging in social activism and more on providing basic health and social services to be offered by multidisciplinary teams of professionals. At the same time, a smaller dissenting group of panelists prepared a minority report and insisted that the CLSCs should "at all cost" preserve its social action role (ibid., p. 296).

By the early part of the 1980s, the Québec Government, trying to regain control, gradually forced the CLSCs to tailor their services to the unique needs of each local community but standardize their practices and focus on priority areas such as home care for the elderly and mental health. For example, in the Québec City region, the CLSCs were the only organizations to offer psycho-social counselling for people living with mental health problems (Gaumer and Fleury, 2008).

More recently, in 2005, the CLSCs lost even more of their autonomy when the Québec Government passed a new law, *la Loi modifiant la Loi sur les services de santé et les services sociaux*, or Bill 83, that modified the 1971 law and grouped health and social services into eighteen regions to be administered by Health and Social Service Networks, *Centres de santé et de services sociaux, CSSS*.

In each of these regions, the CLSCs, residential long-term centres, and general and specialized hospital centres were merged and were required to co-ordinate their services with other suppliers in the regions (Gaumer and Fleury, 2008). As explained by Ives, et al. (2015), today the 147 CLSCs continue to serve as the point of entry for the Québec population to the Health and Social Service Networks.

The Health of Canada's Indigenous Peoples

As a result of the *Indian Act*, the federal government has declared self-appointed jurisdiction over Indigenous peoples' health care. The health status of some Indigenous peoples lags far behind that of other Canadians. Some communuities are healthy and thriving, but others face many challenges, often stemming from the residual impacts of colonization.

The Assembly of First Nations (AFN) points out that the **health gap** between First Nations people and the general population is widening. Sixty-two percent of adult Canadians over the age of 15 reported their health as being excellent or very good, whereas only 58 percent of Métis, 53 percent of First Nations people living off reserve, and 50 percent of Inuit adults identify their health as excellent or very good (Canadian Community Health Survey, 2005; Aboriginal People's Survey, 2006).

The AFN's Health Secretariat, the National First Nations Health Technicians Network (NFNHTN), and the Chiefs Committee on Health (CCOH) have identified seven health priorities in relation to closing the health gap:

- sustainability
- health research
- jurisdictional issues
- mental health
- children's health/gender health
- smoking, and
- environmental health and infrastructure

These priorities have been, and continue to be, urgent.

The prevalence of risk factors and chronic conditions varies significantly between Aboriginal and non-Aboriginal populations, with Aboriginal people generally having less favorable outcomes. Obesity and being overweight, for example, are more common among Aboriginal people. Also, the likelihood of having at least one chronic condition and conditions such as cardiovascular disease and diabetes is higher among Aboriginal people, even when sociodemographic characteristics are taken into account.

The Importance of Traditional Indigenous Approaches to Health and Healing

Current health disparities are linked to the historical impacts of colonization and cannot be understood in isolation from the structural determinants of health. Insufficient funding for Indigenous programs and services, inadequate health system infrastructure in Indigenous communities, economic exclusion, and educational inequities along with overcrowded housing, particularly in remote communities, affect the overall social determinants of community health (Greenwood et al., 2015).

As one of 94 calls to action, the Truth and Reconciliation Commission (2015) has urged the federal government to establish mechanisms to narrow the health-care gap between Aboriginal peoples and other Canadians, including building Aboriginal healing practices into the health-care system and spending more on Aboriginal healing centres.

While improvements in health-care services have eased this situation somewhat, they have also contributed to the gradual erosion of traditional Indigenous holistic approaches to health and healing. Indigenous leaders wish to see an integrated, holistic, interdepartmental, and interorganizational strategy to address the inequities in health and social service delivery. They believe that jurisdictional issues between the federal and provincial governments with respect to responsibility for Indigenous health care need to be removed.

Adverse Living Conditions
While the housing conditions of some Indigenous peoples have improved in the past decade, others are living in overcrowded conditions and in homes needing major repair. This is particularly true of First Nations peoples on reserves and Inuit peoples in the North.

Inuit live in some of the most crowded living conditions in Canada. (Crowding is defined as more than one person per room in the dwelling.)

Most Inuit live in Inuit Nunaat, the northern region spanning the Northwest Territories, Nunavut, Québec, and Labrador. In that region, more than 15,000 Inuit—38 percent of the total Inuit Nunaat population—lived in crowded conditions in 2006, down from 43 percent in 1996.

Indigenous Food Sovereignty

Indigenous peoples of Canada have harvested and eaten traditional food sources from the land, water, and air since the time of creation. These traditional foods provide ample nourishment to support optimal health and have been of fundamental importance to culture. Eating patterns depended on seasons and where people lived: coastal peoples ate seafood, inland peoples ate game foods and, in other regions of Canada and the Midwest, communities relied heavily on corn, beans, and squash.

Today, dietary patterns are much different compared to those in previous generations, which is one factor contributing to poor health outcomes for Canada's Indigenous population. Land dispossession, poverty, environmental contaminants, climate change, and food insecurity have all had a significant impact on dietary patterns and access to traditional foods.

Indigenous Food Sovereignty is the right of peoples, communities, and countries to define their own agricultural, labour, fishing, food, and land policies, which are ecologically, socially, spiritually, economically, and culturally appropriate to their unique circumstances. The First Nations Health Authority (FNHA) in British Columbia has developed *Healthy Food Guidelines for First Nations Communities*, not only to guide First Nations communities in making better food choices, but also to begin to regain sovereignty over their food systems. Participation in harvesting activities such as gathering berries, hunting, or fishing, and eating traditional foods at social and cultural events nourish bodies and spirits while protecting against illness. Another way to change the nutrition environment that has proved successful is to bring people together to participate in community gardens.

These guidelines support community members in educating each other about better food and drink choices to offer in schools, homes, and restaurants, and at cultural and recreational events.

Indigenous traditional foods provide substantial amounts of important vitamins and minerals to support good health and wellness.

Social Work and Client-Centred Care
A holistic approach to health promotion

Advocating on behalf of clients and for a more effective health-care system

Medical social work practice is wide-ranging. It includes direct casework, group work, discharge planning, family consultation, patient advocacy, counselling for terminally ill patients, training of other professionals, and policy and administration. Almost every hospital in Canada has social workers employed in its departments, including emergency services, oncology, pediatrics, surgery, intensive care, rehabilitation, gerontology, and orthopedics.

Social workers in the health-care field not only work with the immediate impact of disease, injury, disability, and trauma but also with the integration of the client with the support system. This work is complex and multifaceted—incorporating education, team building, and relationship enhancement

Social work health practitioners generally are required to hold a graduate degree in the field, such as a Master's degree in social work.

Achieving Better Outcomes for Clients

The social worker's main goal is to assist the client so they can get the help and care they need prior to their recovery, adaptation, and return home. They help the client through the support system, provide education related to clients' health concerns, and facilitate communication with other health professionals, particularly as they deal with issues of grief, depression, sadness, and anxiety.

Social workers typically will scan the client's environment both inside and outside the hospital facility, on the lookout for helpful people, organizations and programs, and helping the client and system meet current and predicted future needs. The worker may negotiate with specific health-care providers on behalf of their client to ensure the best service for their client.

The social worker will also work more generally with the hospital to build client-supportive programs and policies, taking part in ethics initiatives, group development, proposal writing for new program funding, and other such tasks.

In the hospital context, social workers work with other professional groups with skills and values that may differ from their own (doctors, nurses, physiotherapists, etc). There are times when social workers mediate conflict, intervene in crises, or counsel and educate clients, family, and team members.

Assessing Client Needs

This is one of the most rewarding aspects of social work in the health-care field. A well put-together assessment and plan for moving forward can help a social worker assess all elements of concern to the client, select the best intervention point, and plan an effective strategy to enhance the client's health and well-being.

The psychosocial and environmental factors that social workers take into account when performing a needs assessments of a client are listed below:

- What is troubling the client?
- What social, health, and education services are available to this client and their family?
- Are there other systems that exist nearby but which are not available to the client?
- What is the client's employment, level of education, and income?
- What are the client's financial resources?
- Is the client's housing adequate and affordable? What is their neighbourhood like?
- How much stress is the client coping with and are they coping well?
- What are the client's strengths?
- Does the client have a secure source of food?
- Is the client connected with a social network including family, friends, and others?
- What was the client's childhood like?
- What is the client's age?
- What is the client's ethnic backgroundl?
- What is the client's gender/sexual identity?
- How is the client's overall health? Are they living with a disability?

The social worker's psychosocial assessment will include these considerations, in addition to other key components such as the client's unique emotional, social, physical, and cognitive context. When a social worker carefully documents and analyzes these aspects of a person's life and their health status, the relationship and interaction between the elements can be seen more clearly.

Interdisciplinary Team Work

In a hospital setting, the social worker is often a member of an interdisciplinary team that includes members of other health professions, such as general medicine, nursing, nutrition, phsyiotherapy, occupational therapy, and psychiatry.

The role of social workers is becoming more central in this holistic approach to health and healing, which addresses not only the physical aspects of health, which have commonly been addressed by physicians and nurses, but also the social, cultural, mental, and spiritual aspects. Social workers in such teams possess a distinct skill and value set. Their primary role is to prepare and represent the client at team meetings with other team members. They often throw new light on a situation to help the health-care facility provide even better care for their clients. Their goals might include helping a client do the following:

- Cope with a new diagnosis, such as diabetes or cancer
- Face and cope with a diagnosis of a terminal illness
- Enter a parenting role successfully
- Interface with providers of long-term care
- Adjust to being discharged from hospital and benefit from appropriate post-discharge supports for recovery

Social Work in Other Health-Care Settings

In addition to hospital work, social workers are involved in other health-care settings, such as hospices, local medical clinics, community health centres, and specialized care agencies (such as HIV/AIDS clinics, substance use disorder treatment centres, family planning, prenatal care, long-term care, home care, nursing homes, and services for people with disabilities).

Keenly aware of the social determinants of health, social workers are also active as health promoters, community developers, and policy advocates in the field of health care. For example, a social worker may work with a community health centre to promote a particular aspect of healthy living in the community. Through this work, social workers are at the forefront in addressing a preventative approach to primary health care, health promotion, and client self-care.

Social workers are also among the staunchest supporters and advocates of universal health care. Efficiencies and improvements are definitely needed to secure medicare and to make it work better for Canadians, but such changes must be made in the context of continuing efforts to ensure full access to quality health care for all citizens of Canada.

Stories from the Field

Hospital Discharge Planning

Social work practice with clients concluding a hospital stay

One of the primary roles of social workers in hospitals is discharge planning. Ensuring that patients are discharged from hospital in a timely manner with appropriate supports in place once they return home requires numerous skills. Social workers must be able to

- work cooperatively with other staff as part of a multidisciplinary treatment team,
- apply sharp analytical and assessment skills,
- communicate clearly, patiently, and compassionately with patients and staff,
- initiate a therapeutic relationship with the patient in a timely manner,
- process paperwork efficiently, and
- advocate for the patient's best interests.

Discharging a patient may involve ensuring that home care services or other follow-up services are set up. An individual's discharge can become complicated, for example, when dealing with a previously homeless person with multiple psychosocial and addictions issues. Perhaps a bereaved couple have lost a child and will require either follow-up grief counselling or marital counselling. Or perhaps an older adult cannot return home but must be put on a waiting list for transfer to an assisted-living facility. Sometimes even simple issues need attention; for example, a patient's discharge could be delayed because they do not have a winter coat.

Facilitating Post-Hospitalization Recovery and Supports

As mentioned previously, a team approach is used increasingly in health care to ensure that each patient's needs are being met as completely and effectively as possible. This approach can prove beneficial during a patient's hosptial discharge planning stage as well.

Social workers bring a unique perspective to health care in this respect. Their assessments help establish a "big picture" context for each individual's life circumstances, and their empathy, insights, and recommendations can increase chances for recovery. Many patients are living with concerns about employment, housing, child rearing, marginalization, social supports, and, most of all, poverty. Affordable, high-quality child care, employment insurance for part-time workers or workers suddenly faced with a disability, improved working conditions for those in high-stress, low-income positions, and increases in affordable housing—all these factors have a direct effect on health outcomes. Social workers are especially aware of the importance of such factors on wellness and they are prepared and able to address them in the interests of their clients, some of whom may be overwhelmed at the prospect of returning home after a period of hospitalization.

In Sam's story, a young man undergoes a traumatic injury and loses the use of his legs. His initial reaction to this loss is one of intense anxiety verging on panic, followed by bouts of anger and depression. The hospital social worker called in to support the man and his young family must first support them in coming to terms with their grief. The social worker then helps the family adapt to their changed circumstances, avail themselves of financial and community supports, and move forward with a sense of renewed hope for their future.

Reflecting on Sam's Story

1. Evaluate the effectiveness of Richard's role in Sam's discharge planning.
2. In your view, what are the two most important actions that Richard undertook to help Sam? Explain your answer.
3. Identify one concern that Sam must face when he moves back home. How might a community-based social worker help him with this issue?

Sam's Story...
Adjusting to altered life circumstances

Sam, 35, is an avid motorcyclist. One spring evening, he and his friends were out riding in a rural area and it started to rain. The roads were slippery and Sam's cycle went out of control and hit a bridge abutment. Once safely in hospital, Sam underwent a series of tests. He had no sensation in his arms or legs. After being referred to the rehabilitation team for assessment, he began to recover sensation and use of his arms but none in his legs. It was at that time that Richard, the team's social worker, was called into the case.

Richard met with Sam to conduct a psychosocial assessment. Apart from the recent injury, Sam was in good physical health. He was married and he and his wife Sue had two young children, Alyson, 3, and Jake, 4. Sam's mother and father were retired and lived nearby. Sam and his family lived in a modest home with a mortgage in the suburbs of a large city.

Sam worked in construction as a bricklayer but during the winter he was not always able to find work. Sam also volunteered at a local public school coaching children in volleyball. Sue had returned to school to complete a degree in accounting. Sam played an active role as a father, tending to the needs of the children while his wife attended classes in the evenings. Sue was usually at home with the children during the day. When Sam was working and Sue had academic assignments to do during the day, his parents or a babysitter cared for the children.

Sam was experiencing an intense emotional reaction to the accident. He described his anxiety as "skyrocketing" when the rehabilitation team and his doctor concluded that Sam would not likely regain the use of his lower body. He panicked about his possible inability to work to support his family, especially while his wife completed her studies. He was also worried about his current inability to control his bowel and bladder functions and the possible effect of his disability on his sexual functioning. He faced many problems in the face of these drastic changes in his life and their implications for his family's future.

Richard began by working directly with Sam to provide him with emotional support, encouraging Sam to talk about his sadness, grief, and anger. After a few weeks, Sam's emotions became less volatile. Together, Richard and Sam identified the issues in Sam's life that needed the most urgent intervention. They decided to prioritize Sam's strong desire to get back to work. As a result, he increased time spent with the occupational therapist and the physiotherapist so he could build up his capacity to return to some form of work. The rehabilitation team worked with Sam for several months.

Richard and Sam began to focus specifically on discharge planning. They met with Sue to discuss concerns such as child care, Sue's wish to complete her education, financial stresses, Sam's incontinence, and his sexual functioning. Richard reassured the children that their father would get better and would return home soon but that he would need to use a wheelchair.

Richard worked with Sam to navigate and mobilize community resources to help the family apply for disability benefits, subsidized child care, and other similar supports. Sue applied for and received a scholarship. Sue and Sam were relieved because this would allow her to complete her studies and re-enter the workforce to help support the family.

After discussions with Richard, Sam admitted it was unrealistic for him to return to his former job. However, he expressed an interest in helping out in elementary schools. He began to phone school-based contacts that Richard had provided to see what opportunities might be available. He decided to volunteer at an elementary school down the street from where he lived. This would give him a chance to explore future career options while completing rehabilitation from home. He was now using an electric wheelchair both at home and on sidewalks. Richard found a mechanic who reconditioned vehicles previously used by others with disabilities similar to Sam's. The mechanic kindly offered to adapt a vehicle for Sam free of charge after his rehab treatment was complete. Sam and Sue began to feel hopeful for their family's future and seemed to be adapting to the jolting changes in their lives fairly well.

Subsequently, Richard referred the family to a community social worker with expertise in working with persons with issues such as those Sam was facing as he began a new life back in the community.

For a hospital-based social worker, detailed discharge planning is the key to a client's successful transition home.

Community Health Care

Social work practice in community health care

The goals of social work in community health care include mobilizing clients' strengths; offering a holistic perspective; identifying support networks; helping clients navigate through complex bureaucracies; providing information; and sometimes counselling. Many of the goals and interventions are similar regardless of the health-care setting. But there are some differences. How do social work skills translate when a worker interfaces with a community health-care system?

Social workers in community health care assist clients as they adjust to illness or disability, incorporating community strengths in the wellness plan they construct with a client. Practitioners in this area often follow up on previous discharge planning work if the client has just come home from the hospital. This responsibility for follow-up allows the community worker to monitor the client's emotional responses to their situation; explore various options in terms of medical treatment, employment, or housing; seek out essential resources; and offer ongoing support. The worker can help the client explore their own role in recovery and seek ways to build up their confidence and optimism.

Perhaps one of the most important client-centred roles for a community social worker is their work with family members. Family members may offer invaluable support or pose a risk to the client's recovery and well-being. In an ideal situation, however, the individuals who can offer the most help to recovering clients are members of the person's own family. In fact, three in ten people in Canada are family caregivers, providing care to a parent or grandparent, spouse, or child. In 2012, caregivers spent 4 to 14 hours per week providing this kind of care. Caregivers often report spending less time with their own children and their caregiving can have negative effects on family relationships and on the caregivers' own health. They frequently report feeling depressed and in need of financial assistance. Some provide care on a full-time basis.

Social workers interface frequently with caregivers as they provide care to a family member. This social work role is very important because they see first-hand the burden felt by caregivers and are often able to provide helpful links to community supports.

Moreover, social workers are trained to recognize and intervene effectively when relational stressors, intergenerational conflict, and precursors to abuse arise. As skilled facilitators, counsellors, and system navigators, social workers strengthen community health-care programs. Collaborative multidisciplinary models that have been advanced in health-care circles, efforts to improve the social determinants of health, and work designed to empower marginalized groups are central goals in the delivery of community health care.

Kicho's story demonstrates how social workers can intervene with a client, the client's family, and community health-care resources simultaneously on the client's behalf. The story underscores the fact that the most powerful resource a community has to offer is often the collective lived experience and wisdom of the members of that community—especially if they are given an opportunity to support one another in a safe and caring environment.

Reflecting on Kicho's Story

1. What are some advantages of running a breast cancer support group rather than offering one-on-one counselling?
2. What guidelines might help ensure the success of a community health-based support group?
3. How might the success of such a group be assessed?

Kicho's Story...
Benefitting from a cancer support group

Sally has been a social worker at a community health centre for eight years. The health centre is located in the heart of the Southeast Asian community in Vancouver. Sally runs support groups and offers individual and family counselling as well, receiving referrals from health care workers in the community. Individuals can also self-refer for access to services offered by the community heath centre.

Sally has received 15 files of women recently diagnosed with breast cancer. After reviewing the list, Sally decides to offer a breast cancer support group at the CHC. She telephones each person on the list and arranges to meet with them individually to assess their suitability and their interest in joining the group. One woman does not wish to be part of a group but requests personal counselling from Sally instead, and Sally complies. Ultimately, eight women, four of southeast Asian descent, would like to participate in the group.

Among the participants is Kicho, a 37-year-old woman who has been advised by her medical team to undergo aggressive treatment for breast cancer to increase her odds of survival. Kicho has two young children and she is terrified that she will die as a result of her illness. Kicho's husband, parents, brother, and friends do not yet know about her diagnosis.

Sally structures the group to be held for two hours once a week for ten weeks in the early evening to allow women who are working to attend. All eight women attend the first meeting. The women enter the room tentatively and sit in a circle of comfortable chairs. Sally introduces herself, talks about the need for confidentiality and active listening, and sets forth other norms such as having only one person speak at a time. She then invites the members to introduce themselves. When it is Kicho's turn, she shares how alone she feels as she struggles with her diagnosis. Others in the group ask her about her family and she tells them about her children, her husband, her other family members, and her friends. As she speaks, she becomes teary and says she cries a lot now. Other members of the group then share their stories. Some are similar to Kicho's story and others differ. One older woman says that she, too, is alone with her fears as she has no one to share them with. She encourages Kicho to talk with her husband. Kicho nods, but says that she is not sure whether that would be a good idea. The weeks unfold as women continue to tell their stories and support each other.

During the fifth group meeting, Kicho tearfully reveals her marriage problems to the other women. Her husband had had an intimate affair that ended when Kicho found out about it two years ago. Although the affair is over, Kicho is worried that her husband will abandon her again after she has undergone breast surgery.

Sally looks around the room and notes that some other women also have tears in their eyes. She comments, "It seems that Kicho's story is troubling for many of you around the circle. Does anyone have anything they wish to say?" Silence follows as members look at the floor or wipe their eyes with tissues. After a few minutes, which seems like an eternity to Sally, Mary speaks up.

Mary explains her fear of ending the treatment process with a less-than-perfect body. She said, "My appearance has always been so important to me. Isn't it important to every woman?" Kicho replies, "Well, yes, but living is more important to me than my appearance. But I am not sure my husband feels the same way." Others in the group nod and express their understanding.

Sally listens intently but does not speak, waiting for other comments. A deep discussion about women and beauty ensues. Comments follow about wanting to live, yearning to see children and grandchildren grow up, being proud of their good health and their bodies. The discussion then turns to intimate partners and their responses to their female partner's disease. Kicho says she is surprised that the other women seem to understand her fears. She reports that she often gets blank stares from people on the few occasions when she shares her private concerns.

The following week, the women decide they want their partners to have an opportunity to participate in a support group as well. Sally promises to speak with her supervisor to find out if there are space and resources at the centre for her to run a partners' support group in parallel with the breast cancer support group.

Cancer and other support groups are now a common feature of the community health-care landscape.

Hospice and Palliative Care

Social work practice with persons who are dying

Social work is prominent in palliative care and hospice settings in hospitals, community residences and agencies, and private homes. **Hospice and palliative care** is focused on reducing the severity of disease symptoms, rather than providing a cure, for people at the end of life. It can also include bereavement support for family members and caregivers.

The essence of palliative care is holistic, collaborative, and client-focused. The comfort of the dying individual is the first priority. Social workers assist the dying individual, family, and team members as they help each other to make the process of dying meaningful. Expertise in collaboration, facilitation, communication, system navigation, and psychosocial assessment makes the social work role crucially important in palliative care.

Generally, hospice social work includes one or more of the following services.

- **Pain management.** Often, life-threatening illness causes pain. Social workers consult with other health-care providers to determine what is causing the pain and the best ways to relieve it. Pain may be managed with narcotics and other drugs, but also by means of massage therapy and relaxation exercises, including mindfulness meditation.
- **Symptom management.** Social workers report symptoms such as loss of appetite, nausea, weakness, difficulty breathing, bladder/bowel problems, and confusion to the medical team.
- **Social, psychological, emotional, and spiritual support.** Social workers often focus on the well-being of the person in the final days of their lives. People in such circumstances confront a variety of psychological and spiritual issues. Different kinds of support to both the individual and the family may be helpful in these instances.
- **Caregiver support.** Social workers work closely with family and other caregivers, providing necessary support, not only during the patient's last stages of life, but also during the bereavement process.

Social Work in Palliative Care Settings

Palliative care is health care for individuals who are living with a life-threatening illness, usually at an advanced stage. The goal is to provide the best quality of life for the critically or terminally ill person and ensure their comfort and dignity. Hospice palliative care focuses on holistic care by offering a wide range of health, emotional, and spiritual support services.

Palliative care is provided in a variety of places—at home, in long-term facilities, in hospitals, and in hospices. The Sunnybrook Health Sciences Centre in Toronto, for example, has a palliative care unit that serves cancer patients. Other centres, such as the Maison Michel Sarrazin facility in Québec (the first such facility opened in Canada in 1985), offer a network of services, providing both care at the facility and support in the home.

Social workers offer hands-on support and assistance in such situations. They provide instructions on how to care for the person, administer medication, and recognize signs of impending problems that might require emergency assistance. They may also help family members work through emotions regarding the illness or death of a loved one, as Sidney's story shows.

Reflecting on Sidney's Story

1. Which aspect(s) of this case do you think the social worker found most difficult? Explain your answer.
2. What do you think is the greatest advantage of palliative care, and why?
3. Identify one other action the social worker might have taken in helping Sidney and explain why you identified this action.

Sidney's Story...
Facing death with courage and dignity

Sidney, a 38-year-old computer technician, is at risk of dying from non-Hodgkin's lymphoma. His wife, Josette, recently gave birth to an infant daughter, Chantal. Sidney's family lives in England and is seldom able to travel to Canada. Josette's family lives in Québec.

As is often the case with complicated diagnoses, Sidney's diagnosis takes time to complete. Meanwhile, Kevin, a social worker employed as an occasional consultant with the hospital and who has a part-time position with a community health centre, is asked to meet with Sidney to see if he can help. Kevin agrees to accept the case.

Over time, Sidney has encountered many turning points in his illness and treatment. Sometimes a treatment made him feel better and doctors gave him positive reports. At other times, he received only bad news. At first the treatment worked, and then it didn't. Sidney tells Kevin that he feels as though he has been on an out-of-control rollercoaster ride. Kevin and Sidney develop a rapport with each other and agree to meet regularly.

After a few months, doctors are especially concerned about the results of one particular medical test. Sidney is feeling more tired and cuts and bruises are taking longer to heal. He is losing weight. He feels worried and depressed. Sidney tells Kevin that he fears he is dying and he asks Kevin what he should do. Kevin asks him: "What do you need?" Sidney responds, "I need to know what is going on with my body." Kevin offers to sit down to talk with Sidney and his doctor. Sidney and Kevin draw up a list of questions that Sidney needs answered, including "Am I dying? Is there anything you can do to help me?" They discuss the possibility of having Josette attend the meeting, too. But Sidney wants to wait until he feels stronger emotionally in order to deal with Josette's reaction. The meeting with the doctor is emotionally draining but helpful overall. The doctor answers all Sidney's questions. Sidney learns that he is indeed dying.

Sidney and Kevin spend many hours talking about Sidney's impending death. Finally, Sidney asks Kevin to help him break the news to his wife.They all sit together in Sidney and Josette's home after Chantal has gone to bed. Kevin helps support Sidney as he tells Josette that he is dying. Sidney comforts Josette and answers as many of her questions as he can. Sidney asks Kevin if he thinks the doctor would be willing to meet with the three of them together. Kevin sets up a meeting.

Meanwhile, Kevin asks Sidney and Josette what their major concerns are. Naturally, they are concerned about the progress of the illness, about the actual experience of death, and if there will be pain. Kevin teaches the couple about palliative care and the goal of ensuring comfort for the dying individual and for the family. They decide to ask the doctor what death might be like for Sidney. Sidney begins to cry and then asks two questions: "How will my family survive without my income? And what about our wonderful little girl—how will she know who her father was?"

Kevin is able to help ease these worries. They discuss financial issues and set up a budget. They discuss Josette's earning potential. Sidney has some creative ideas about ways in which Josette can juggle her career as an ultrasound technician while caring for Chantal. Finally, they talk about Sidney's relationship with Chantal. Sidney confides to Kevin that he deeply wishes his daughter to know about him as she grows up. Kevin helps Sidney develop some ideas aboout how to achieve this goal. Sidney is an amateur musician. He decides to compose and record a series of songs. Each song would be planned for Chantal to hear at a different stage of her life. The songs would reveal Sidney's love, hopes, and dreams for his daughter.

Ultimately, composing and listening to these songs together help Josette and Sidney face Sidney's death more calmly. The members of the palliative care team succeed in easing his pain and ensuring his physical comfort in his final days.

Not long after the songs are completed and recorded, Sidney and Josette plan his funeral. Sidney dies peacefully as soon as the planning is complete.

Kevin meets with Josette to offer her grief counselling. He helps her get through the first six weeks following Sidney's death and he introduces her to a bereavement support group at a local community centre for people who have lost their partners.

Social workers in palliative care help their clients to confront various complex issues related to death and dying.

Marg Hancock

The ability to listen empathetically is a key skill in Marg Hancock's role as Care Coordinator for a community health-care agency.

Marg Hancock works as a Care Coordinator for a provincial agency that delivers a range of health-care services to clients in their homes.

As a Care Coordinator, I manage a caseload of individuals who need support in order to recover from a health-related incident or to remain living as independently as possible at home.

A large part of my job is assessment and partnering with the client to devise the best possible plan to meet specific goals. We use a consistent assessment tool and conduct assessments in the individual's home, taking up to two hours on the initial visit. Another aspect of my work involves "navigation" and I get a great deal of satisfaction from helping individuals find their way through the local health network. Many of my clients are older adults. Mobility issues may have begun to detract from their ability to access community services. I have some younger clients, too. Some of my peers work exclusively with children. I work in the community now, but I also have hospital experience. I work in a multidisciplinary team consisting of health professionals and a manager.

I arrived at my graduate social work studies with an interest in older adults and palliative care. I selected the "family and individuals" stream, picking up all the courses on working with seniors as I studied. I benefitted from a placement in a continuing care hospital setting with excellent supervision and I enrolled in community palliative care courses. Upon graduation, while working on a contract in long-term care, a social worker friend told me how much she enjoyed her work as a Care Coordinator. Her agency advertised a position involving work with older adults with a potential for work in palliative care. I applied and was hired.

My work offers significant opportunities to influence the lives of others for the better. I am often introduced to an individual or a family at a time of dynamic life changes when the gateway to intimate conversation is open. This is where the skill of listening has been my biggest ally and the source of greatest satisfaction in my work. I recall, for example, an angry, depressed senior who had alienated her family. Quiet, empathetic listening opened the door to a constructive conversation with her primary support person. I recall a 20-something man with a young family who had sustained permanent injury from a sporting accident. His grief and guilt were barriers to healing. Constructive listening at his bedside helped him accept that ongoing counselling support should be a part of his care plan.

Conversations can become "critical," and I have enhanced my skills to take part in those "critical conversations" constructively. I frequently find myself in situations where I face an ethical dilemma and am given resources to formulate a model of ethical decision making. There is opportunity to consult with other professionals on behalf of a client. I meet people from all walks of life and provide individualized access to the health care community. My agency's vision of "outstanding care—every person, every day" is a great fit with social work values. I value the dignity and worth of my clients and I value my own integrity and competence as well.

My job is rewarding and offers tremendous opportunities for learning. It is a secure environment from the perspective of job security, retirement pension, and so on. However, the health care field is under pressure to spend limited health care dollars wisely and Care Coordinators are not immune to those pressures. We handle large caseloads and are held accountable for all the resources we use. We are challenged to work faster and to adopt "lean" approaches that are not always compatible with spending time with a client.

Care Coordinators must be tolerant of bureaucracy and have skills for stick-handling creative ideas through established policy networks. While organizational and time-management skills are an asset, attention to self-care is essential, too—and what better setting for keeping your own health and well-being at the forefront than in the health care field!

Chapter 6 Review

Review Questions

1. Briefly outline the history of Canada's health-care system.
2. Describe some unique features of Canada's current health-care system.
3. What are the five fundamental principles of medicare in Canada?
4. List some advantages of a public health-care system compared to a privately funded system.
5. What are some signs that universal public health care is being eroded in Canada?
6. What does the "health gap" in Canada mean, and why should it concern us?
7. Describe the social worker's role in palliative care.
8. What are some key challenges facing medical social workers today and how might they be overcome?

Exploring Social Work

1. In 2015, the UN Human Rights Committee criticized Canada's federal government for failing to meet the basic health needs of Indigenous peoples in Canada. How might social work practitioners influence the creation of policies designed to address the lowered life expectancy and higher rates of diabetes and numerous other conditions among Canada's Indigenous peoples?
2. Research one community health program in your area or province that is designed to address a health issue related to the social determinants of health. Discover the benefits that social workers in this program bring to the community. Present your findings in a brief report.
3. Write a brief response to the following excerpt by Jeffrey Simpson from *Chronic Condition: Why Canada's Health Care System Needs to be Dragged into the 21st Century* (2012): "The Canadian health-care system was originally designed around hospitals and, to a fault, it remains so today—a system whose hospitals struggle to cope with changing patient demand, an aging population, higher costs, global budgets imposed by provincial capitals, fast-developing technologies, rigid rules, new drugs and the social inequities that lead to poor health.'"

Websites

Health Canada
www.hc-sc.gc.ca
Health Canada is the federal department responsible for helping the people of Canada maintain and improve their health.

Canadian Health Coalition
www.healthcoalition.ca
The Canadian Health Coalition is dedicated to preserving and enhancing Canada's public health system for the benefit of all Canadians. Founded in 1979, the coalition includes groups representing unions, seniors, women, students, consumers, and health care professionals from across Canada.

World Health Organization (WHO)
www.who.int
World Health Organization (WHO) is an agency of the United Nations and is based in Geneva. WHO was established in 1948 and is "the directing and coordinating authority on international health work."

Public Health Agency of Canada
www.publichealth.gc.ca
The Public Health Agency's website contains information about the health of Canada's population, including the government's response to the WHO Commission on the Social Determinants of Health. Key determinants of health include income/social status, education and literacy, and the physical and social environment.

The First Nations of Québec and Labrador Health and Social Services Commission (FNQLHSSC)
www.cssspnql.com
The FNQLHSSC is a non-profit organisation that is responsible for supporting the efforts of the First Nations of Québec and Labrador in order to, among other things, plan and deliver culturally-appropriate and preventive health and social services programs.

National Aboriginal Health Organization (NAHO)
www.naho.ca
The National Aboriginal Health Organization is a knowledge-based organization that excels in the advancement and promotion of health and well-being of all First Nations, Inuit, and Métis individuals, families, and communities.

Mental Health and Social Work Practice

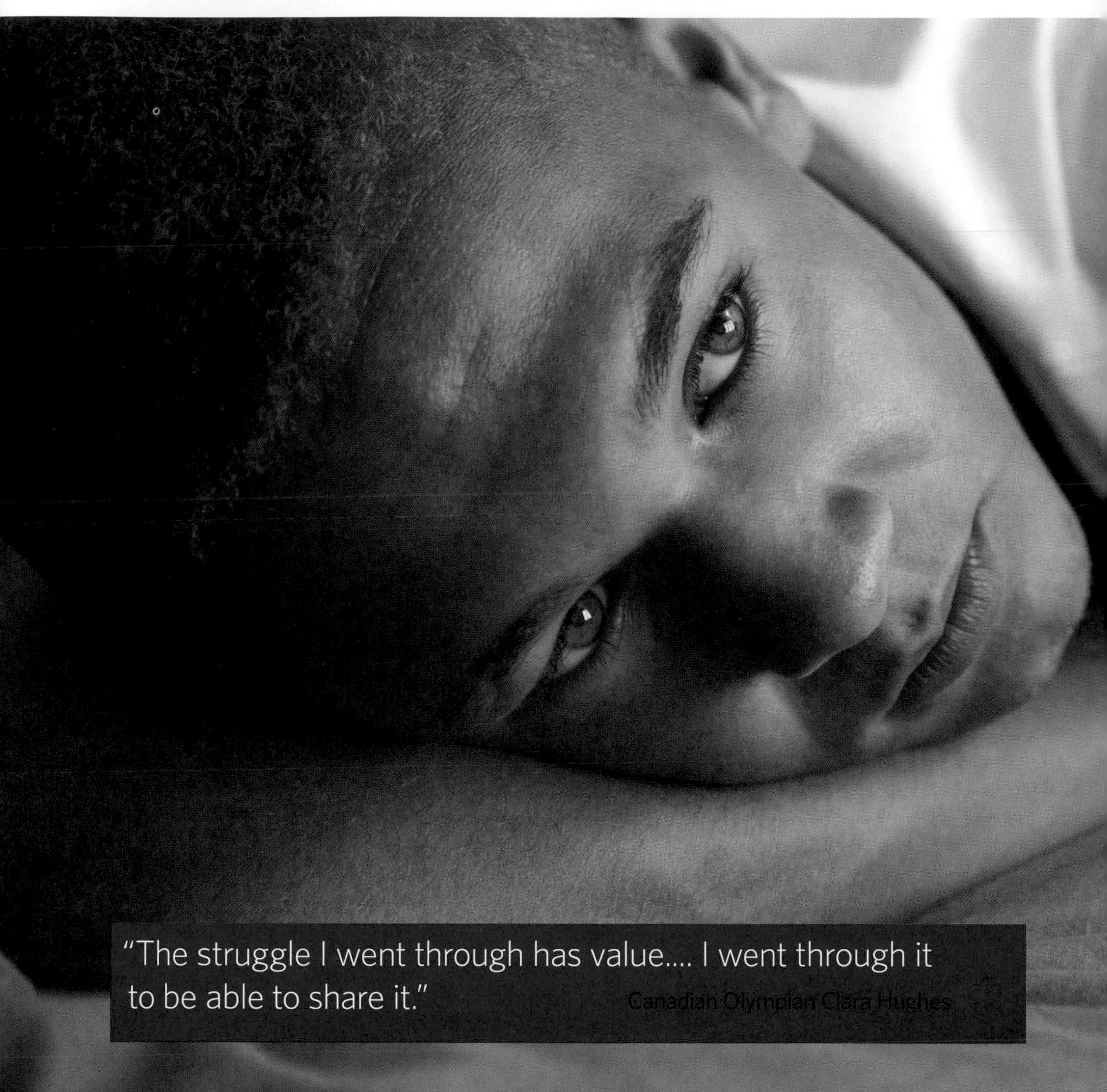

"The struggle I went through has value.... I went through it to be able to share it."

Canadian Olympian Clara Hughes

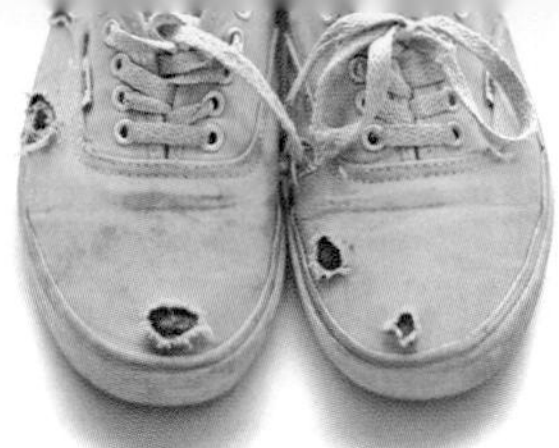

Sharicka Reid and Jackie Stokes

Promoting Wellness and Recovery

7

One in five Canadians will experience some form of mental illness.

he Public Health Agency of Canada (PHAC) defines mental health as "the capacity of each and all of us to feel, think, and act in ways that enhance our ability to enjoy life and deal with the challenges we face. It is a positive sense of emotional and spiritual well-being that respects the importance of culture, equity, social justice, interconnections, and personal dignity" (PHAC, 2014).

Organizations such as the Canadian Mental Health Association (CMHA) exist to promote the mental health of Canadians, and they employ an increasing number of social workers who provide services at the community level. These workers operate on the principles of empowerment, peer and family support, participation in decision making, citizenship, and inclusion in community life. They dedicate themselves to helping people who are experiencing mental illness and their families to develop resilience as they embark on a journey of recovery together. Their mission is accomplished through advocacy, education, research, and service.

In this chapter, you will learn how to...

- distinguish between mental wellness and mental illness
- describe some risk factors and protective factors associated with mental wellness and mental illness
- identify major types of mental disorders (risk factors, signs/symptoms, impact on one's life, and treatment or coping strategies)
- describe the mandate and some initiatives of the Mental Health Commission of Canada (MHCC)
- articulate the importance of destigmatizing mental illness and ways to end stigma and discrimination against persons with a mental health concern
- explain the efficacy of the recovery model in sustaining mental health
- analyze characteristics and treatment of substance use disorders and concurrent disorders
- analyze how to apply suicide prevention and risk-reduction strategies
- describe signs, symptoms, support, and treatment related to post-traumatic stress disorder (PTSD)
- explain effective social work responses to mental health issues

Key Concepts

- Mental health
- Mental illness
- Mental Health Commission of Canada (MHCC)
- Stigmatization
- Substance use disorder
- Concurrent disorder
- Post-traumatic stress disorder (PTSD)

Focusing Question

What understandings of mental health and mental illness must social workers acquire to ensure that service delivery is as effective as possible?

What Distinguishes Mental Wellness from Mental Illness?

The World Health Organization (WHO) defines **mental health** as "a state of well-being in which the individual realizes his or her own abilities, can cope with the normal stresses of life, can work productively and fruitfully, and is able to make a contribution to his or her community."

The WHO considers mental wellness an integral part of the general definition of health. In the WHO Constitution, for example, health is defined as "a state of complete physical, mental, and social well-being and not merely the absence of disease or infirmity."

As with physical health, the best way to understand emotional health, or mental wellness, is to view it as a continuum. All of us lie somewhere on this mental health continuum, depending on our unique genetic makeup, environmental factors, and family dynamics. Our position on the continuum may shift from time to time, depending on events and stressors in our lives.

- **Mental wellness.** At one end of the continuum is "mental wellness" (also referred to as "mental well-being"). Mental wellness exists when there is a reasonable balance in all aspects of one's life—physical, intellectual, social, emotional, and spiritual.
- **Mental illness.** At the other end of the continuum is "mental illness," a term referring to a range of emotional and mental health problems that may be long-lasting and that may interfere with normal family, school, social, or work-related activities.

Developing Resilience
Positive mental health is closely related to the development of psychological and emotional resilience—the ability to recover or "bounce back" from crises or change. Resilience depends on many things: individual characteristics and lifestyle, family circumstances, ties to community, and environmental factors. Some of these factors can increase our resilience by protecting us from psychological harm, but some can expose us to psychological risk. We can learn to manage certain factors to strengthen our resilience.

The factors that contribute to mental well-being are not entirely understood. Clearly, some factors are related to an individual's life circumstances at any given time. In the case of severe mental illness, the causes are usually deeper, and medical professionals generally intervene to provide diagnosis and treatment.

In the same way that physical illnesses can take many different forms, so too can mental illnesses. Unfortunately, in the wider community, mental illnesses are still feared and misunderstood by many people. Myths and misconceptions concerning mental illness abound in popular culture and in mass media. In contrast to exaggerated stereotypes, mental illness can be treated, and most individuals with a mental illness can lead a normal and fulfilled life.

Safeguarding Mental Wellness: Risk Factors and Protective Factors

Various factors influence an individual's emotions and state of mind at any stage of life. Some such factors, called "risk factors," include physical illness, family problems, physical or sexual abuse, childhood trauma, difficult relationships, and heredity. When present, these factors can predispose a person to greater levels of stress and more complex unsettling emotions.

There are also "protective factors" that work in the opposite way, to stabilize our emotional well-being. As the name suggests, these protective factors—strong family ties and close interpersonal relationships, for example—can reduce or minimize the likelihood of undue emotional hardship.

When a person experiences a number of unfortunate events all at once, the combined effect can take its toll on that individual's mental health. In extreme cases, the sheer weight of circumstances can overwhelm an individual, to the point where he or she will need to seek professional help in order to deal with the problems at hand.

Just as with physical illness, the prognosis of mental illness is better if the illness is detected as early as possible and if early remedial action is taken. Social workers play a critical role in helping to prevent mental illness while at the same time promoting mental well-being.

Table 7.1
Risk Factors and Protective Factors Associated with Mental Wellness

	Risk Factors	**Protective Factors**
At the individual level	Risk factors in this category can include • genetic influence • having a long-term physical illness • experiencing discrimination based on race, sexuality, gender, or religion • being easily angered • communication difficulties • low self-esteem • childhood abuse/neglect/trauma	Protective factors in this category can include • a sense of humour • spiritual faith • good social skills • a positive attitude about life • respect for authority • personal goals • high self-esteem • good problem-solving skills
At the relationship level	Risk factors in this category can include • family problems • having been severely bullied or physically or sexually abused • acting as a caregiver, taking on adult responsibilities • living in poverty or being homeless • associating with friends who engage in high-risk behaviours, such as experimenting with drugs • witnessing family conflict and violence	Protective factors in this category can include • at least one close relationship • a stable family environment • involvement with extended family • parents who spend quality time with their children • parental warmth, support, and clear expectations • parental support for education
At the school and community level	Risk factors in this category can include • having a learning disability or long-standing school difficulties • having few recreational activities for children and youth • lack of basic services (e.g., housing, water) in the community • easy access to alcohol and other substances • few economic opportunities • being a refugee or asylum seeker • violence or war in the community	Protective factors in this category can include • feeling connected to school • strong relationships with teachers • teachers who express high expectations • participation in a range of sports/leisure activities • involvement in community activities • peers who have conventional values • having a positive role model • stable housing

Signs and Symptoms

Although symptoms may vary according to the type of mental illness and the individual, the following are some common symptoms to watch for:

- Depression lasting for longer than a few weeks
- Confused thoughts, delusions, and/or hallucinations
- Extreme fears or anxiety that seem "out of proportion" to circumstances or events
- Lack of motivation for a prolonged period of time
- Persistent feelings of helplessness or hopelessness
- Loss of interest in activities previously enjoyed
- Extreme mood swings between depression and mania, sometimes with overly reckless behaviour
- Difficulty concentrating and/or sudden irritability
- Disruption in sleep patterns
- Talk or thoughts of suicide

Source: Canadian Mental Health Association (www.cmha.ca).

The Characteristics of Mental Illness

Mental illness
A spectrum of diagnosable mental disorders—health conditions that are characterized by alterations in thinking, mood, or behaviour (or some combination of these) associated with distress or impaired functioning in one or more areas (school, work, social, family, and community interactions)

Mental illness is a condition that involves disturbances in a person's thoughts, emotions, moods, and behaviours, which decrease that person's capacity to cope with the challenges of everyday life. The term "mental illness" is generally used to refer to serious mental health problems that are diagnosed and treated by mental health professionals. The terms "mental health problem," "mental illness," and "mental disorder" are often used interchangeably. Diagnosis criteria and treatment protocols for mental illnesses are contained in the *Diagnostic and Statistical Manual of Mental Disorders, DSM-5*, published by the American Psychiatric Association.

All of us are vulnerable to mental health problems. As mentioned earlier, the state of our mental health, at any given time, can lie anywhere along a continuum between well and not well. The first signs of a serious mental illness often appear between the ages of 15 and 30. The signs and symptoms of mental illness differ according to the illness and the individual.

Factors Contributing to Mental Illness

We do not know exactly what causes mental illness, but it is believed that a combination of factors contribute to its onset and severity. These factors include the following:

- **Genetic factors.** It is believed that some mental health problems occur more often in families in which there is a history of mental illness.
- **Biological factors.** Age and gender, for example, are believed to affect the rate and prevalence of mental illness, especially when combined with other factors.
- **Environmental factors.** Stresses due to finances, relationships, family background, and lack of access to health care and social supports are all believed to affect mental health.
- **Physical factors.** Symptoms of mental illness can occur in people with a physical illness—for example, people who experience a physical illness may also experience severe depression.

In one important respect, mental illness is no different from physical illness—professional help is often required to relieve the symptoms and alleviate or reverse the problem. For many years, it was thought that mental health problems would keep coming back or would never go away. It is now known that many people recover from such challenges. With careful treatment and appropiate support, the symptoms of these disorders can be managed in much the same way that diabetes can be managed, for example—with lifestyle changes and medication. In many cases, the individual can experience complete recovery.

People with continuing emotional and mental health problems will often have difficulties in other parts of their lives, such as employment, housing, or relationships. While medical professionals can do a great deal to diagnose and treat mental health conditions, the consequences of mental illness can be far reaching, for the individual as well as for his or her family and friends.

Social workers today recognize that "whatever makes it difficult for the individual, the group, and the environment to interact effectively and justly (for example, poverty, prejudice, discrimination, disadvantage, marginality, or poor coordination of or access to resources) is a threat or barrier to mental health.... Our interactions with others take place within a framework of societal values; therefore, any definition of mental health or mental illness must reflect the kind of people and the type of society we aspire to be and the goals we consider desirable. Social workers do not isolate ideas about mental health from such wider social values as the desire for equality among people, the free pursuit of legitimate individual and collective goals, and equitable distribution and exercise of power" (CASW website, 2016).

Table 7.2

An Overview of Selected Mental Illnesses and Disorders

	Risk Factors	Signs/Symptoms	Possible Impact on Life	Treatment/Coping

Anxiety Disorders	• parental depression or anxiety
	• children who cannot tolerate uncertainty
	• extremely shy children and those likely to be the target of bullies
		• restlessness (inability to relax, feeling uptight, apprehensive)
		• disturbed sleep
		• pounding or racing heartbeat
		• upset stomach (including stomach pains, diarrhea, and nausea)
		• light-headedness/dizziness and/or headaches
		• breathlessness
		• difficulty concentrating
		• fear of losing control
		• extreme need for reassurance
			• can be stereotyped as chronic "worry wart"
			• can lead to social isolation and avoidance of many situations (e.g., public speaking, eating/dressing in public, school activities)
			• can limit ability to function in various areas of daily life:
			  • self care: bathing, dressing, eating
			  • family relationships
			  • going to school or work
			  • doing household tasks and fulfilling responsibilities
				• education and counselling to help the person understand his/her thoughts, feelings, and behaviours
				• cognitive behavioural therapy
				• relaxation techniques
				• biofeedback to control muscle tension

Autism	• appears to have a genetic link, but there are no known environmental causes	• ability to respond does not develop normally in the first three years
		• will often respond bizarrely to their environment
		• seem to lack interest in others, acting as if hard of hearing
		• often unable to sustain eye contact
		• seem not to care whether they are cuddled or held
		• failure to develop language, or a tendency toward repeating or echoing what is said to them
		• unable to form two-way, give-and-take social relationships
			• failure to develop useful speech or trouble with starting/continuing conversations
			• may have distinct skills in specific areas, such as music or math, while simultaneously experiencing difficulty in other areas of mental processing
			• large physical and emotional demands on parents caring for autistic children
			• children identified early and given specific support are often able to live almost normally
				• Autism is not a disease in the true sense and generally does not need treatment; however, medication can be prescribed for specific problems associated with autism, such as
				  • hyperactivity,
				  • obsessive behaviour, and
				  • epilepsy.
				• Educational management and parental support are helpful during an autistic child's development.

Attention-Deficit/Hyperactivity Disorder (ADHD)	• genetics
	• viruses
	• harmful chemicals in the environment
	• problems during pregnancy or delivery
	• anything that hurts brain development
		Inattentive Type
		• short attention span
		• easily distracted
		• no attention to detail
		• failure to finish things
		• trouble remembering things
		• poor listening skills
		• unable to stay organized
		Hyperactive-Impulsive Type
		• often fidgets or squirms
		• runs/climbs when they shouldn't
		• talks too much, interrupts
		• trouble taking turns
			• difficulty managing situations that require lengthy and quiet focus
			• disruption in family, social, and school life
			• at risk for many other mental disorders (conduct disorder, anxiety disorder, depression)
			• at risk for developing personality and substance abuse disorders in adolescence or adulthood
				• Early diagnosis is crucial.
				• Treatment can include
				  • medication,
				  • behavioural therapy,
				  • classroom modifications, and
				  • counselling.
				• Parents and teachers find it helpful to get instruction on how to manage and modify behaviour, such as rewarding good behaviour.

	Risk Factors	Signs/Symptoms	Possible Impact on Life	Treatment/Coping
Major Depression	• heredity (history of depression among family members) • being raised in an abusive environment • stressful life events (e.g., parental death or divorce) • sensitive, perfectionist personality	• fatigue/loss of energy • loss of interest in usual activities and/or pleasure in life • sadness that won't go away • unexplained irritability or crying • sense of worthlessness, guilt, hopelessness • low self-esteem and lack of self-confidence • difficulty thinking and concentrating • can have thoughts of suicide and death	• misses school or has poor school performance • can have difficulty making it through daily activities • may also have alcohol or other substance use disorder • difficulties with home life and withdrawal from friends • risk of suicide	• "talk" treatments (often used with adolescents) • Medications can be prescribed, but they tend to work better for adults. • Young people may need a "plan of care" to help with daily life. • Lifestyle changes, such as increased exercise and physical activity, can help.

Schizophrenia	• genetic link
	• biological factors—abnormal brain structure and activity
	• environmental influences (e.g., family factors may be involved in onset of schizophrenia)
	• substance use (e.g., cannabis) can worsen symptoms
		• delusions (beliefs not founded in facts)
		• hallucinations (hearing, seeing, feeling, smelling, or tasting something that does not exist)
		• disorganized thoughts, odd speech
		• declining ability to take care of personal hygiene and grooming
		• altered sense of self (sense of self or personal identity may be greatly reduced)
		• withdrawn and preoccupied—no contact with outside world
			• affects all aspects of a person's daily life
			• Educational progress is often disrupted, and young people may be unable to finish school or hold down a job.
			• requires much family and community support
			• Society often excludes people with this illness due to a lack of understanding and a fear of the risk of suicide.
				• Often, medication is required to control the most troubling symptoms.
				• When symptoms are controlled, psychotherapy and self-help groups can assist people with
				  • developing social skills,
				  • coping with stress,
				  • identifying early warning signs of relapse, and
				  • prolonging periods of wellness.

Bipolar Mood Disorder	• Men and women are equally at risk of developing this disorder. • genetics, chemical imbalance in brain • stress may play a part • mania more common in spring, depression in winter • usually begins in adolescence or in twenties	**Mania** • individual feels extremely high, happy, full of energy • reduced need for sleep • irritability • rapid thinking and speech • lack of inhibitions • big plans and schemes • may not see own behaviour as inappropriate **Depression** • loses interest in activities • may stop seeing friends • loss of appetite • may attempt suicide • may develop false beliefs of guilt or feel that he/she is evil or being attacked	• can have difficulty making it through the daily activities of life • may experience significant weight loss or gain • possible difficulties at school, work, home life • may withdraw from social activities • risk of suicide	• In the manic phase, the person may not see a need for treatment. • Medications can be effective (e.g., antidepressants for depressive phase, medications such as lithium to help control mood swings) • Counselling along with medication is considered the most effective treatment. • With access to appropriate treatment and support, the person can lead a full and productive life.

What Are the Different Types of Mental Disorders?

Among mental health professionals, the clinical term "mental disorder" is used to describe a mental health condition that matches a defined list of signs and symptoms. Table 7.2 summarizes some commonly occurring types of disorders identified by mental health professionals, the risk factors associated with each condition, manifestations, possible impacts on a person's life, and treatment and coping mechanisms. Serious mental disorders take many forms; the following major classifications are described in the *DSM-5*:

- Neurodevelopmental disorders
- Schizophrenia spectrum and other psychotic disorders
- Bipolar and related disorders
- Depressive disorders
- Anxiety disorders
- Obsessive-compulsive and related disorders
- Trauma- and stressor-related disorders
- Dissociative disorders
- Somatic symptom and related disorders
- Feeding and eating disorders
- Sleep-wake disorders
- Sexual dysfunctions
- Gender dysphoria
- Disruptive, impulse-control, and conduct disorders
- Substance-related and addictive disorders
- Neurocognitive disorders
- Paraphilic disorders
- Personality disorders

Having agreed-upon definitions makes it easier to create a program of treatment that is most likely to help a person cope with the disorder.

The Mental Health Commission of Canada

Formed in 2007, the **Mental Health Commission of Canada (MHCC)** grew out of a recommendation in the first (and , for some, long overdue) comprehensive report on mental health, substance use, and the state of mental health care in Canada, titled *Out of the Shadows at Last.* The report was prepared by the Standing Senate Committee on Social Affairs, Science, and Technology and was released in May, 2006. Michael J. L. Kirby, who had been appointed by the committee as its first chairperson, co-authored the report.

Mental Health Commission of Canada (MHCC)
The MHCC is a catalyst for improving the mental health system and for changing the attitudes and behaviours of Canadians around mental health issues. Funded by Health Canada, the MHCC brings together leaders and organizations from across the country to accelerate these changes. Its work includes Canada's first mental health strategy, stigma reduction, knowledge exchange, and ways to help people who are homeless and living with mental health problems.

Funded by Health Canada, the MHCC is a national non-profit organization that operates at arm's length from government. It has been endorsed by all provincial and territorial governments except Québec's. It does not provide services directly, but is rather a catalyst for action. Initially, the commission received a ten-year mandate (2007–2017), but on April 21, 2015, then-Minister of Finance Joe Oliver announced that the 2015 federal budget called for the renewal of the MHCC for another ten years, starting in 2017–2018.

The organization is governed by a board that includes both governmental and non-governmental directors. Since 2013, the board has been assisted by an advisory council and a network of ambassadors. From 2007 to 2012, the board was assisted by eight advisory committees. The commission is not responsible for undertaking service delivery or advocacy for mental health services. Its aim, rather, is to provide relevant jurisdictions and stakeholders with the tools and information required to improve the quality of mental health care and access to it for all citizens in Canada.

The MHCC was tasked originally with three major objectives:

- To develop a national mental health strategy
- To oversee the development and implementation of an anti-stigma and anti-discrimination campaign
- To create a Knowledge Exchange Centre, with the aim of mobilizing evidence-based knowledge to improve best practices and increase dialogue about mental health issues across Canada

The MHCC's Main Initiatives and Accomplishments to Date

On May 8, 2012, Canada became the last of the G8 nations to create a national mental health strategy. A document entitled *Changing Directions, Changing Lives: The Mental Health Strategy for Canada* set out six strategic aims related to the implementation, prevention, diversity, access, and delivery of services.

The commission's "At Home" research project ("Chez Soi" in French) looked to address homelessness for people with mental illness by combining treatment with places to live, and is the largest experiment of its kind in the world. Operating in Vancouver, Winnipeg, Toronto, Montréal, and Moncton, the project is based on the Housing First model of the Pathways to Housing program in the United States, which has reported positive results in cities such as New York, Philadelphia, and Washington.

Another important MHCC initiative is called "Opening Minds," launched in 2009 to combat stigma against mental illness. This program has been involved with 65 partners and 45 active projects. The directors of the commission decided that the projects would focus on four target groups, namely, health-care providers, youth aged 12 to 18, the media, and the workforce.

MHCC Initiatives of Relevance to Social Work

Mental health problems are widespread and have a major impact on the workplace and the economy. There are many sources of stress, yet there seem to be some common causes. In a survey of over 1,500 working adults, 30 percent of Canadians point to finances as their top stressor; 17 percent say family matters and 6 percent say lack of time is their biggest stressor. In the same survey, 19 percent of Canadians say work pressure causes them the most stress (The Psychology Foundation of Canada and Desjardins Financial Security, 2007).

Partly in response to the prevalance of workplace-related mental health concerns, a Mental Health First Aid (MHFA) course was launched by the MHCC in 2010. The course has been thoroughly evaluated and has been found effective in improving participants' knowledge of mental disorders and increasing the amount of help provided to others. On January 16, 2013, the MHCC released the *Psychological Health and Safety in the Workplace Standard*, a framework aimed at combatting mental illness and identifying mental health hazards in the workplace.

MHCC has also initiated *Informing the Future: Mental Health Indicators for Canada* to paint a picture of mental health in our country. These indicators provide information on the mental health status of children and youth, adults, and older Canadians, as well as information on how the mental health care system responds to mental illness.

Patrick Dion, vice chair of the Mental Health Commission of Canada's Board of Directors, launched the final report of the national At Home/Chez Soi research project in Ottawa on April 8, 2014.

Stigma and Mental Illness

Stigmatization is the expression of negative attitudes and behaviours toward individuals who share a certain characteristic. In the wider community, persons with a mental illness are often stigmatized and outcast, even though they need the same understanding and support as persons with a physical illness. People who stigmatize others cast uninformed judgements on them and form fixed ideas about their illness. Stigma worsens the suffering that results from having a mental health problem.

Stereotyping, another harmful reaction to the occurrence of mental illness, often goes hand in hand with stigmatization. It is often expressed through demeaning labels, such as "psycho," "insane," "addict," or "junkie." Negative words as well as negative actions can inflict further emotional damage upon a person who is mentally unwell.

The Importance of Destigmatization in Mental Health

Presuming that people with a mental illness can never hold a job or that the problem is "all in their head" are forms of stigma. So are attitudes based on the misconception that all people who have a mental illness are a danger to society. These prejudices, negative attitudes, and discrimination can affect the ways in which people with mental health issues are treated by others. The effects of stigmatization can be both detrimental and debilitating.

To make matters worse, those who are suffering from mental health issues often internalize the stigma and the negative stereotypes imposed on them by others, which can damage their self-image and self-esteem.

Stigma can also diminish an individual's quality of life by

- reducing the person's ability to maintain relationships or acquire new relationships, which can lead to social isolation;
- inducing reluctance and/or avoidance in seeking help for mental health issues;
- causing a person to keep symptoms a secret from others;
- reinforcing belief in the negative attitudes that are expressed by others and/or by the media, which can lead to self-stigmatization; and
- setting up obstacles to acceptance and support from family members, friends, and community.

Stigma affects everyone involved in the mental health system. To support individuals who are struggling with a mental illness, it is important for social workers to recognize the various forms that stigma can take, the many negative ways in which it can affect individuals, and some effective strategies to decrease stigmatization.

Developing awareness of how stigma and stereotypes affect others and questioning our own attitudes and feelings are ways to decrease stigma on an individual basis. This is especially important for social workers to understand and practise. They may find themselves interacting with health-care professionals who lack competence and training in assessing and treating individuals who express suicidal ideation, for example, which may contribute to stigma and poor outcomes. It is also essential for social workers to recognize that many consumers of mental health services may have had a negative experience involving stigmatization at some point in their lives.

Ending Stigma

As a first step to ending the stigma associated with mental illness, we as individuals can take personal responsibility to decrease our own tendency to stigmatize individuals who experience mental illness. We can try to empathize with those who are being stigmatized, paying more attention to the language we use to describe mental health problems, questioning why labels are attached to others, and maintaining awareness about our own attitudes and feelings.

Five Ways to End Stigma
Changing how we see mental illness

Everyone can do their part to eradicate myths and negative stereotypes

One of the biggest hurdles for anyone suffering from mental illness is overcoming the stigma. Across Canada, many individuals, organizations, and initiatives are striving to decrease stigma in relation to mental health.

For example, Stop the Stigma is a partnership between the Mood Disorders Association of Ontario and the Toronto District School Board that trains students to serve as leaders during mental health awareness weeks in their schools. Students give presentations on topics such as youth mental health and how to access support services.

As another example, the Schizophrenia Society of Ontario has implemented an initiative called Sound Off (Turtert, 2014). This campaign was founded by University of Toronto student Mona Abadi in 2011, in an attempt to reach out to youth across Ontario to create open discussions surrounding mental health. The goal was to give youth an opportunity to share their stories and have their voices heard in a public forum.

The Mental Health Commission of Canada (MHCC) strongly advocates for the abolition of stigma within the context of mental health. In June 2012, the MHCC and the World Psychiatric Association hosted the fifth international conference on stigma reduction, titled "Together against Stigma: Changing How We See Mental Illness."

The largest stigma-related event ever, the conference invited 670 researchers, practitioners, policy makers, advocates, caregivers, and people with lived experience to Ottawa to share research, programs, best practices, and personal stories. The conference's main purpose was to encourage citizens everywhere to talk about how to bring about positive change in the way people view mental illness.

Bell's "Let's Talk" Campaign

Stigma is the number one reason why two thirds of those living with a mental illness do not seek help. Bell Canada's "Let's Talk" is a multi-year charitable program dedicated to mental health. Bell has committed over $100 million to support a wide range of mental health organizations, large and small, from coast to coast to coast. (Bell Let's Talk, 2015).

Talking is the first step toward creating meaningful change and building greater awareness, acceptance, and action.

- **Language matters.** Pay attention to the language being used around you. Explain to people that labelling individuals who are dealing with mental health issues as "psycho" or "crazy" has detrimental effects. Suggest alternative language that is more respectful of others.
- **Educate yourself.** Learn the facts about myths that exist concerning mental health to help combat stigma.
- **Be kind.** Small gestures can have a huge impact. Advocate for people who are being labelled, mistreated, or cyber-bullied. Treat people who suffer from mental illness like you would treat others who have different illnesses.
- **Listen and ask.** Sometimes people just need to be heard. Do not minimize or trivialize someone's illness. Try to empathize.
- **Talk about it.** Have a dialogue, not a debate. Break the silence; mental health affects everyone involved and is not confined to the person who is experiencing mental health issues. Sharing stories of lived experiences is one of the best ways to help eradicate stigma. Support mental health and anti-stigma programs within your community.

What Is the Recovery Model?
Sustaining mental health

The recovery model offers a distinctly life-affirming conceptual framework and an optimistic outlook

The recovery model is a concept that has been integrated into mental health services and treatments relatively recently. In the past, individuals experiencing mental health issues and their families were often told to lower their expectations in light of the fact that the individual's symptoms would probably worsen over time (Canadian Mental Health Association Ontario, 2015). Today, however, the idea of recovery is an important foundation for how social workers and other health professionals engage with individuals living with mental health issues and with their families.

The Essential Components of the Recovery Model

Recovery encompasses a holistic approach toward treatment. A holistic approach "embraces the interconnectedness of our body, mind, and spirit, and encourages us to cultivate physical, mental, and spiritual health" (Hong Fook Mental Health Association, 2008). This approach focuses on the person as a whole rather than on symptoms alone, and it avoids making assumptions based on an individual's diagnosis (Mental Health First Aid, 2010).

Hope is one of the main components of the recovery model. It is vitally important for workers in the field of mental health to relay a message of hope. Regardless of the symptoms that a person might experience, individuals living with a mental illness can avail themselves of every opportunity to lead fulfilling and satisfying lives. Championing hope involves adopting an open-minded perspective, cultivating a sense of life's possibilities, and learning to use the language of recovery—notions that stray markedly from past attitudes toward mental illness. Hope bolsters the idea that recovery is possible for anyone struggling with a mental illness.

"Recovery" in the Context of Mental Illness

The term "recovery" in relation to mental illness has a different connotation than when it is applied to physical illness or injury (Trainor et al., 2004). Moreover, in a mental health context, recovery does not necessarily mean absence of symptoms. The recovery model affirms the potential to lead a meaningful life *despite* co-existing symptoms.

There is no single definition for recovery, which is often referred to as a journey or a process (Mental Health Foundation, 2015). This journey involves devising ways to lead a satisfying, hopeful, and productive life despite limitations that may be associated with a mental illness. Furthermore, recovery involves redefining one's purpose in life and constructing new meanings that transcend the effects of living with a mental illness.

What Factors Influence Recovery?

Recovery is a highly personal and unique process (Trainor et al., 2004). In a mental health context, recovery is seen as person-driven; each individual defines what recovery means to him or her.

For some people, recovery might mean being symptom-free, while for others it could mean staying in control of their thoughts and behaviours despite their mental illness (Mental Health Foundation, 2015).

The recovery model implies that individuals, families, and service providers must often shift their view about mental health and mental illness. They learn to adjust to the notion that individuals play a key role in their own recovery.

Furthermore, recovery involves building upon strengths. It is essential to mobilize and tap into individuals' talents, resources, and potential instead of focusing on their illness, symptoms, and problems.

Recovery also means that individuals take responsibility for and control their own health-related choices. There is a shift in focus from illness to wellness, a lessened emphasis on symptoms, and diminished preoccupation with diagnosis, medication, and treatment in favour of focusing on more rewarding life experiences.

Factors that can influence recovery include access to education and employment opportunities, quality and availability of treatment, and supportive social networks (Mental Health First Aid, 2011). Individuals' ability and willingness to participate in their own treatment also influences recovery.

Recovery is aptly described as a deeply personal and unique process of transforming one's attitudes, feelings, values, skills, goals, and roles (Trainor et al., 2004). Because recovery is an individualized process, social workers must adapt to the remarkable diversity of persons living with mental illness.

The ultimate goal of countless mental health services and treatments is recovery. Therefore, workers who engage with individuals experiencing mental health issues are entrusted with supporting their recovery process. This process starts with the acknowledgement that recovery is possible in spite of the complex issues that arise from living with a mental illness.

Family Involvement: A Crucial Factor in Recovery

Families are the single largest category of caregivers of people who are suffering from a mental illness (Trainor et al., 2004). Family members thus play a pivotal role in an individual's recovery.

When a loved one is first diagnosed, his or her needs become paramount. Family members assume various roles, often providing significant financial, emotional, and social support. Their contributions may go unrecognized, however (Ibid., 2004).

Living with and/or supporting a loved one with a mental illness can impact the personal health and well-being of members of that individual's family. Family members often experience burnout, stress, and social isolation.

Self-care becomes extremely important in maintaining a family's overall health and wellness. Family members can learn a variety of coping skills to help them stave off burnout and exhaustion. Social workers can encourage family members to reach out and seek help for themselves through individual counselling or involvement in a support group.

Wellness Recovery Action Plan

A Powerful Tool Used in the Mental Health Journey

The Wellness Recovery Action Plan, or WRAP, is a peer-led mental illness self-management program that helps indviduals manage their illness and provides them with a plan when they are not well. WRAP is a best practice that is used worldwide.

The program involves an educational and planning process that is grounded in mental health recovery concepts such as hope, education, empowerment, self-advocacy, and interpersonal support and connection. Within a group setting, individuals explore self-help tools, such as peer counselling, focusing exercises, and relaxation and stress-reduction techniques. They share resources for keeping themselves well and helping themselves feel better during stressful times (Canadian Mental Health Association, 2015).

Shown here is Margaret Trudeau, former wife of the late Canadian prime minister Pierre Trudeau and mother of Canada's twenty-third prime minister, Justin Trudeau. Margaret has chronicled her own recovery related to bipolar disorder in her book *Changing My Mind*, published by HarperCollins Canada in 2010. She now advocates for better understanding of mental health issues and is an honorary patron of the Canadian Mental Health Association.

Substance Use and Substance Use Disorders

Inappropriate or excessive use of alcohol or drugs can result in various mental, physical, or social impairments (Kendall et al., 2008). There are several types of alcohol and drug use and different levels of risk associated with each type. Risks vary depending on the intensity of the drug and on the frequency, circumstances, and modality of use. People can move back and forth between various types of use. Individuals have an increased risk of developing a substance use disorder if they use alcohol or drugs compulsively, are unable to control their use, and/or continue despite negative consequences.

A **substance use disorder** is defined as a physiological and/or psychological dependency on a drug to sustain a sense of well-being and to avoid withdrawal symptoms (Kendall et al., 2008). Two essential characteristics of substance use disorders are tolerance and withdrawal. Tolerance occurs when larger doses of a drug are required over time to replicate the same physical or psychological effect that could originally be achieved with a smaller dose. Withdrawal is characterized by the various physical and psychological symptoms that are associated with the discontinuation of a drug.

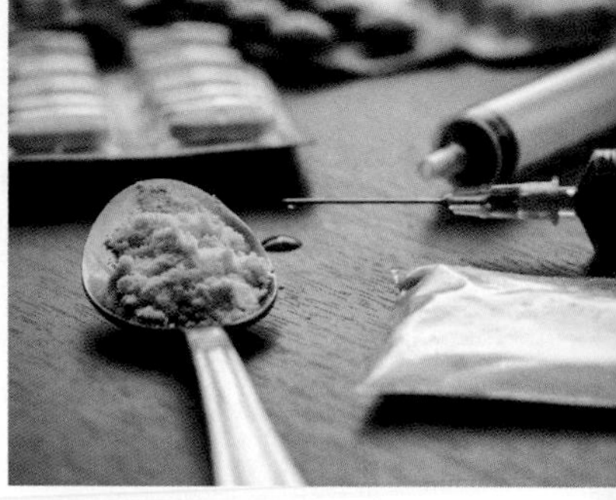

Licit and Illicit Drugs

It is a common misconception that people who engage in drug use will develop a substance use disorder. The fact is that individuals can struggle with drug use and never become dependent (CAMH, 2016). For example, many people drink alcohol without problem. Alcohol and tobacco are licit (legal) drugs (Kendall et al., 2008). Licit drugs have addictive qualities similar to illicit (illegal) drugs, and substance use disorders can result from use of either type of drug. Abuse of prescription drugs (licit drugs) is common, leading to increased tolerance and withdrawal effects when stopped (Tyyskä, 2009). Licit drug use can also lead to addiction.

Types and Symptoms of Substance Use Disorders

The overarching categories of substance use disorders are diagnosed based on the criteria described below.

- **Alcohol use disorders.** Issues controlling alcohol intake, continued alcohol intake despite problems resulting from drinking, increased tolerance, or development of withdrawal symptoms.
- **Cannabis use disorders.** Disruptions in functioning and development of withdrawal symptoms (difficulty sleeping, nervousness, anger, restlessness, and/or feelings of depression after a week of abstinence).
- **Stimulant use disorders.** Craving for stimulants, issues controlling use, use of larger amounts over time, development of tolerance, and development of withdrawal symptoms (tiredness, difficulty sleeping, increased appetite, and vivid and unpleasant dreams). Amphetamines, methamphetamine, and cocaine are stimulants.
- **Hallucinogen use disorders.** Cravings for hallucinogens, engaging in risky activities when using (e.g., driving), and continued use in spite of interference with obligations or social functioning. Lysergic acid diethylamide (LSD) and psilocybin mushrooms are hallucinogens.
- **Opioid use disorders.** Inability to control use, strong desire to obtain opioid, and withdrawal symptoms (nausea/vomiting, diarrhea, fever, negative mood, and insomnia). Heroin, oxycodone, and hydrocodone are opioid drugs.

Substance use disorders can have symptoms that reflect behavioural, physical, and social changes (United States Department of Health and Human Services, 2015). Behavioural changes may include decreased attention at work or school; substance use while driving; changes in appetite or sleep patterns; changes in personality or attitude without explanation; sudden mood swings; irritability; and engaging in suspicious behaviours. Physical changes may include abnormally sized pupils; red eyes; sudden change in weight (loss or gain); deterioration of physical appearance; unusual odours on breath, body, or clothing; and impaired coordination/speech. Social changes may include sudden isolation; unexplained financial need; use of substance despite problems with relationships; and sudden changes in hobbies or interests.

Factors Related to Substance Use Disorders

Substance use disorders have been attributed to a variety of biological, psychological, and sociological factors (Kendall et al., 2008). Biological factors may include a genetic predisposition to substance use and substance use disorders. Moreover, drugs such as alcohol, heroin, and cocaine directly affect the brain mechanisms that are responsible for reward and punishment. Psychological factors focus on personality traits and the effects of social learning on behaviours associated with substance use. As well, personality disorders and other mental illnesses may increase a person's risk of developing a substance use disorder. Sociological factors include the social determinants of health, such as poverty, unsafe communities, and low educational attainment. Patterns of substance use and substance use disorders vary by gender, race, social class, and ethnicity. Some populations appear to be more susceptible to drug use and substance use disorders than others. For example, as noted above, a population that may be more susceptible to substance use disorders are those who experience mental health issues.

Substance use disorder
A condition in which the use of one or more psychoactive substances leads to a clinically significant impairment or distress. In 2014, almost 18 percent of Canadians reported drinking heavily (*The Chief Public Health Officer's Report on the State of Public Health in Canada, 2015: Alcohol Consumption in Canada*). Others experience problems with narcotics, tranquilizers, sleeping pills, cocaine, LSD, and cannabis.

Substance Use Disorders and Social Work

Substance use has historically been—and will likely continue to be—one of the problems that social workers encounter most frequently, regardless of their role. In fact, in two studies conducted by the National Association of Social Workers (NASW), between 71 and 87 percent of social workers reported interacting with a client who had substance use issues (O'Neil, 2001; Whitaker, Weismiller, and Clark, 2006).

Adopting a Harm-Reduction Approach

Social workers are at the forefront of developing innovative ways and evidence-based practices to help people with substance use disorders. Social workers and others in Canadian substance use programs adopt a harm-reduction approach. Harm reduction forms one of the pillars of provincial and national drug strategies (the other three pillars being prevention, treatment, and enforcement). Harm reduction refers to "any strategy or behaviour that an individual uses to reduce the potential harm that may exist for him or her" (Csiernik, 2011: 183). Harm reduction may involve abstinence—although abstinence is not necessarily a goal. Rather, harm reduction includes a range of options, such as adopting safer drug use techniques, using licit rather than illicit drugs, and decreasing the amount and/or frequency of use.

Although harm-reduction strategies have been available for decades, the emergence of AIDS and HIV raised their profile, particularly in relation to decreasing injection drug use. Harm-reduction principles are congruent with social work values, which promote a non-judgemental approach to substance users, recognize the principles of self-determination, perceive that outcomes are in the hands of the client, and provide options in a non-coercive way.

Harm Reduction

CACTUS Montréal is a community organization for the prevention of blood-borne and sexually-transmitted infections (BBSIs). It works with injecting and inhaling drug users, sex workers, and trans people.

CACTUS promotes its clients' health, their well-being, and their inclusion in society. Staff members at CACTUS assist individuals through various prevention, awareness, and educational services and activities. They actively defend their clients' rights and give voice to their needs and concerns.

Harm reduction guides all their interventions: "Our approach, pragmatic and humanistic, places the participation of people at the core of our action."

The federal government is expected to approve an application for supervised, illicit drug injection sites in Montréal and Toronto, comparable to the two sites that currently exist in Vancouver.

Mental Health and the Justice System
Alternative intervention for offenders

CAMH's Toronto Drug Treatment Court

The Centre for Addiction and Mental Health's Toronto Drug Treatment Court (TDTC) program provides alternative intervention for some lawbreakers.

In most cases, clients in custody apply through their lawyers to the TDTC—a joint collaboration between CAMH and the Ontario Ministry of the Attorney General. The program is not available to violent offenders, so most applicants have been charged with crimes such as trafficking or simple possession, prostitution, or petty property crimes.

Specifically, the TDTC looks for people whose criminal behaviour is directly linked to their need to support their addiction to cocaine, crack, or opiates. TDTC focuses on harm reduction by providing treatment for the underlying cause of illness, something that would be ignored within the prison system.

The first step is a 30-day assessment. Throughout the client's stay with the program, he or she attends a TDTC session twice a week, while simultaneously receiving treatment three days a week at CAMH. This program, like many others, recognizes that relapse is a part of recovery, especially in the early stages, and it supports clients during that period of time.

Once the client is stable and a reduction in substance use is evident, the intensive stage of changing entrenched patterns of behaviour and thinking and living a healthier life begins. Clients are directed either to the Structured Relapse Prevention Program or to the Women's or Youth Program. Those who are really struggling are referred to a residential treatment facility.

In phase two, clients meet with CAMH caseworkers once a week; at this point clients are expected to be abstinent from their drug of choice (crack, cocaine, or opiates) and to be working on reducing use of secondary substances, such as marijuana or alcohol. Clients often discuss the root causes of their pain, such as childhood abuse, institutionalization, or child welfare experiences. They also attend a drug treatment course once a month.

Caseworkers prepare clients for re-entry into school, work, and long-term housing. Closer to graduation, clients attend a support group one evening a week. To graduate from the program, clients must be drug-free for three months, in school, working, or volunteering, and in stable housing.

The goal is to reduce the rate of recidivism among this population and to avoid the "revolving door" of crime and addiction that tends to exist when incarceration is used to deal with substance use disorders. CAMH's recovery model allows for more success because it keeps clients in the TDTC.

As one TDTC worker put it, "We're helping our clients to recover in their communities by facing real issues and pressures and walking with them as they struggle."

- *Source:* Adapted from the Centre for Addiction and Mental Health website, (www.camh.net).

Concurrent Disorders

Understanding and knowledge of concurrent disorders has increased over the last two decades in response to the growing number of individuals who experience both a substance use disorder and a mental illness. A **concurrent disorder** is defined as a condition in which a person suffers simultaneously from a mental health issue and a substance use disorder (Canadian Mental Health Association Ontario, 2015).

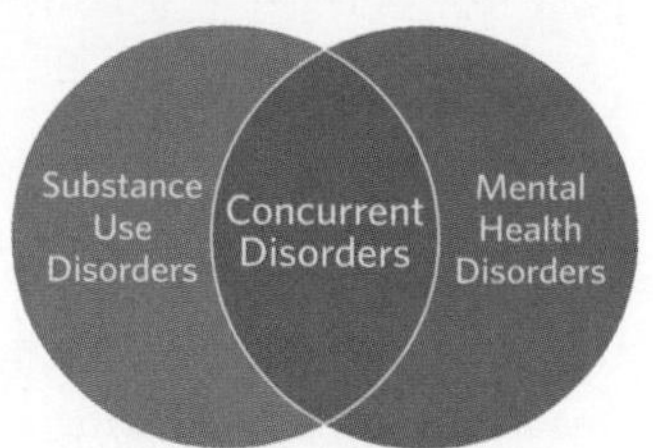

Concurrent Disorder or Dual Diagnosis

The term "dual diagnosis" is used interchangeably with "concurrent disorder" in some countries. In Canada, "dual diagnosis" is used when an individual experiences both a developmental disability and a mental health issue (Centre for Addiction and Mental Health, 2015).
The term "developmental disability" applies when an individual experiences significant limitations in cognitive functioning and adaptive functioning. Examples of developmental disability include autism, traumatic brain injury, and Down syndrome.

Combinations of concurrent disorders can be divided into five main groups (Centre for Addiction and Mental Health, 2015):

- Substance use accompanied by a mood or anxiety disorder (e.g., depression, panic disorder)
- Substance use accompanied by a severe and persistent mental health issue (e.g., bipolar disorder, schizophrenia)
- Substance use accompanied by a personality disorder (e.g., borderline personality disorder)
- Substance use accompanied by an eating disorder (ie.g., anorexia nervosa, bulimia)
- Substance use accompanied by a mental health disorder (e.g., gambling)

Specific examples of combinations are depression and alcohol use (disorder); schizophrenia and cannabis use (disorder); and anxiety disorder and sedative- or anxiolytic-related use (disorder), that is, opiod use (disorder).

According to the Centre for Addiction and Mental Health (CAMH, 2015), the following mental health issues are common among those who experience concurrent disorders:

- **Anxiety disorders.** Approximately 10 to 25 percent of people develop an anxiety disorder in their lifetime. Among the individuals diagnosed, 24 percent will also experience a substance use disorder in their lifetime.
- **Major depression.** Approximately 15 to 20 percent of people develop major depression in their lifetime. Among the individuals diagnosed, 27 percent will also experience a substance use disorder in their lifetime.
- **Bipolar disorder.** Approximately 1 to 2 percent of people develop bipolar disorder in their lifetime. Among the individuals diagnosed, 56 percent will also experience a substance use disorder in their lifetime.
- **Schizophrenia.** Approximately 1 percent of people develop schizophrenia in their lifetime. Among the individuals diagnosed, 47 percent will also experience a substance use disorder in their lifetime.

The Interplay Between Mental Health Disorders and Substance Use Disorders

Individuals who experience mental health issues have an increased risk of developing substance use disorders, as they find ways to "self-medicate" for any distress they may experience due to their mental health issues. Conversely, specific illicit drugs can cause individuals to experience symptoms of a mental health issue (United States Department of Health and Human Services, 2015).

Statistics show that 30 percent of individuals diagnosed with a mental health issue will also experience a substance use disorder at some point in their lives (CAMH, 2015). Comparatively, 37 percent of individuals who experience an alcohol use disorder will develop a mental health issue. And 53 percent of individuals diagnosed with a substance use disorder (other than alcohol) will experience a mental health issue at some stage of their lives.

Causes and Treatment of Concurrent Disorders

There is no simple cause for the development of concurrent disorders. Mental health issues and substance use disorders affect each other in several ways:

- Substance use may make mental health issues worse.
- Substance use can replicate or mask symptoms of mental health issues.
- Individuals often turn to substance use to relieve or avoid symptoms of mental health issues.
- Substance use may decrease the effectiveness of medications, and/or make people forget to administer their medications.
- If an individual relapses with one problem, the other problem can be triggered.

Concurrent disorder
The co-occurrence of a substance use disorder and a mental health disorder in an individual. Concurrent disorders can co-occur in a variety of ways—they may be active at the same time, in the present or in the past, and their symptoms can vary in intensity and form over time.

The Centre for Addiction and Mental Health (CAMH, 2015) has found that individuals who experience mental health issues are a vulnerable population, and experiencing substance use disorders simultaneously can make it more difficult to get help. An individual who experiences a concurrent disorder will often experience more serious medical, social, or emotional issues). Individuals who experience concurrent disorders must receive treatment for both issues. Therefore, treatment may take longer and prove more challenging. It is important for social workers to establish treatment for both issues to promote their clients' chances of recovery.

The treatment approach depends on the type and severity of an individual's issues. The individual may receive psychosocial treatments (individual or group therapy) or biological treatments (medications), or both. Although it is essential to consider both issues, depending on the severity of the substance use and the severity of the mental illness, it may be necessary to treat one issue first, rather than treating both concurrently.

A Model for Assessing a Client's Service Priorities

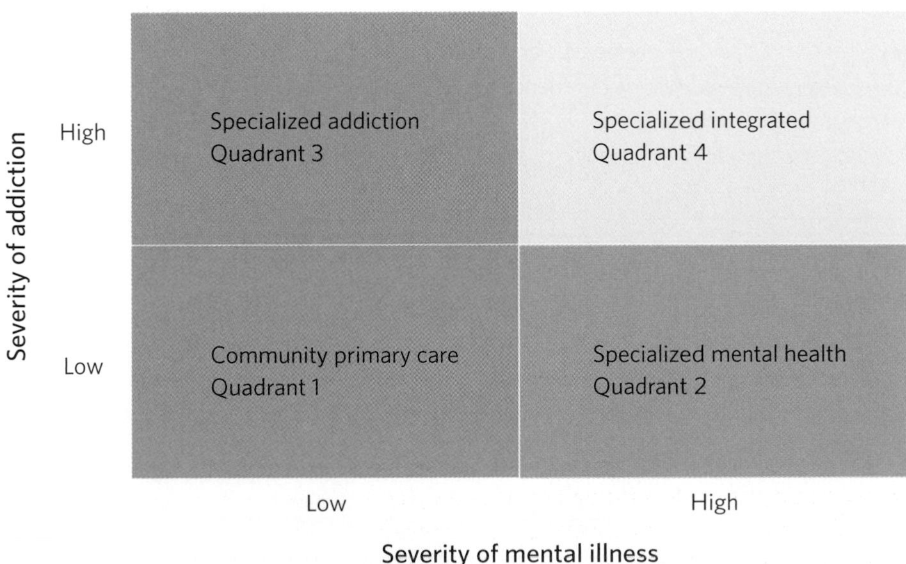

Figure 7.1 This four-quadrant model depicts the range and severity of concurrent disorders and can help service providers meet the needs of their clients as effectively as possible

Source: Ontario Centre of Excellence for Child and Youth Mental Health, "Pathways to care for youth with concurrent mental health and substance use disorders" by Gillian K. Watson, Charles Carter, and Ian Manion (April 2014).

Suicide and Suicide Prevention
Recognizing warning signs

The stigmatization of mental illness may prevent individuals who are contemplating suicide from seeking the support they need

For some time now, suicide has been a prevalent mental health issue affecting many people around the world. Suicide is non-discriminatory; it affects people of all ages, genders, ethnicities, and financial statuses. In Canada, 13.4 percent of people over the age of 15 have seriously considered suicide at one point in their lives (Mental Health First Aid Canada, 2011). Moreover, 3,500 to 4,000 Canadians of various ages die by suicide each year. Suicide is one of the leading causes of death of Canadians aged 15 to 24. Furthermore, Canada has the third-highest youth suicide rate in the industrialized world. Clearly, suicide is becoming an increasingly predominant mental health problem in Canadian society.

Individuals often turn to suicide when they experience deep feelings of hopelessness and helplessness over a prolonged period of time. In other cases, suicide can be an impulsive act. Suicide has a ripple effect; most often, after an individual commits suicide, their families, friends, and other social circles are heavily impacted and frequently devastated. The effect of stigma surrounding suicide can be especially damaging; it is a major barrier preventing people from engaging in conversations about suicide (Ibid, 2011).

Suicide Prevention: Warning Signs

Suicide does not necessary follow an escalating continuum. However, there are warning signs that an individual may be contemplating suicide. These warning signs include the following behaviours (Mental Health First Aid Canada, 2011):

- expressing suicidal ideations (thoughts)
- expressing the intention to die by suicide, followed by the description of a plan to execute suicide
- expressing negative thoughts about oneself
- constant expressions of hopelessness, desperation, or helplessness
- relaying final wishes to family members or friends
- giving away important possessions, creating and/or changing a will, or arranging financial affairs
- loss of interest in social circles, hobbies, or activities that were previously enjoyable
- loss of appetite
- loss of energy
- increased or decreased sleep
- unexpected changes in appearance or behaviour

This list is not exhaustive. Each individual can exhibit different signs of impending suicide. It is vitally important for family members, support workers, and mental health professionals to familiarize themselves with the warning signs and risk factors related to suicide.

Risk Factors and Risk Reduction

Risk factors that increase the possibility of suicide may include the following (National Suicide Prevention Lifeline, 2009):

- **Suicidal behaviour.** A history of suicidal ideations, suicide attempts, or self-injurious behaviour
- **Current/previous mental health issues.** Recent onset of illness may increase risk; illnesses such as mood disorders, psychotic disorders, alcohol/substance use disorders, attention-deficit-hyperactivity disorder (ADHD), traumatic brain injury (TBI), post-traumatic stress disorder (PTSD), and conduct disorders may also increase risk
- **Family history.** History of suicide within the family
- **Key symptoms.** Experiencing anxiety/panic, insomnia, or hallucinations
- **Precipitating factors.** Events that trigger feelings of humiliation, shame, or despair (e.g., financial burden, loss of a relationship); these feelings can be real or anticipated.
- **Related stressors.** Other medical issues can perpetuate more stress. Intoxication can also be a factor.
- **Interpersonal factors.** Family turmoil or chaos, history of physical or sexual abuse, or social isolation
- **Access to weapons and firearms.** Weapons increase the risk of self-inflicted harm, especially during a mental health crisis.

Protective Factors

Certain protective factors may reduce the risk of suicide. As mentioned previously, protective factors aid an individual's capacity to recover stability in the course of a stressful situation. Assessing an individual's protective factors can be an integral part of suicide risk reduction.

According to organizations such as the National Suicide Prevention Lifeline, protective factors can be internal or external. Internal factors may include a person's resilience and ability to cope with stress, their religious beliefs, or their levels of tolerance for emotional distress. External factors may include a feeling of responsibility toward others (e.g., children, partner, parents, siblings, friends, co-workers, pets); positive therapeutic relationships with mental health professionals, including social workers; and various social supports, such as an affiliation with a place of worship or a self-help group.

Safety Plans

Safety plans can be a key factor in suicide risk reduction. Such plans are completed by the individual, and they can be extremely helpful when that person is experiencing a crisis. Such plans are devised when the person is in comparatively good spirits and is able to reflect on how they behave when they are experiencing suicidal ideations.

An effective safety plan will result if the person is able to identify strategies that would reduce their risk of committing suicide during a crisis. A safety plan might include names and phone numbers of people and services to contact when a person is in distress. The people and services listed in the safety plan might include family members, close friends, crisis support agencies, emergency helplines, and contact information for support personnel, such as a psychiatrist and/or a social worker.

Organizations Seeking to Prevent Suicide

The Canadian Association for Suicide Prevention (CASP) is a Canada-wide, non-profit organization that is dedicated to suicide prevention. This organization aims to reduce the rates of suicide in Canada and to decrease the negative connotations associated with suicide and/or suicidal behaviour. CASP also provides certification courses for crisis workers and facilitates a yearly conference that brings together researchers and other health professionals to discuss the most effective methods of suicide prevention. (For more information, visit their website: www.suicideprevention.ca.)

The International Association for Suicide Prevention (IASP) is dedicated to the prevention of suicidal behaviour, the alleviation of the effects of suicide, and the promotion of a forum for academics, mental health professionals, crisis workers, volunteers, and suicide survivors. The IASP includes professionals and volunteers from more than 50 countries, and officially partners with the World Health Organization (WHO). (For more information, visit their website: www.iasp.info.)

The Centre for Suicide Prevention (CSP) is a branch of the Canadian Mental Health Association in Calgary, Alberta. The CSP is an educational centre that hosts the largest English-language library dedicated to the collection and distribution of suicide prevention, intervention, and post-intervention resources. (For more information, visit their website: www.suicideinfo.ca.)

The Jack Project was founded in 2010 by Eric Windeler and his wife, Sandra Hanington, after their son Jack died by suicide in his first year at Queen's University. Now known as jack.org, the project encourages youth to engage, raise awareness, and reduce the stigma around the topic of mental health issues. It is the only national network of young leaders focused on peer-to-peer engagement in mental health issues. (For more information, visit their website: www.jack.org.)

For a generation of young people raised on the Internet, social media, and text messaging, the traditional approach to mental health awareness and stigma reduction just isn't working. One of the most powerful ways to inspire students is for young people to share their experiences and spread the message that we all have mental health issues and that it is all right to reach out for help.

Eric Windeler displays a photo of his son Jack, a Queen's University student who died by suicide in 2010.

Social Work Practice in Situations of Trauma

A traumatic event is often defined as an event in which a person experiences, witnesses, or is confronted with a situation that involves actual or threatened death, serious injury, or a threat to one's physical integrity or that of others. In response to these stressors, an individual's reactions may include fear, helplessness, shock, and/or denial (Wilson and Keane, 2004).

Examples of traumatic events include the following:

- Physical and/or sexual assault
- Domestic violence and/or child abuse/neglect
- Witnessing someone else being seriously harmed
- Car accident, fire, or explosion
- Unexpected death in the family, including suicide
- A serious or terminal illness, e.g., cancer, in oneself or a family member
- A natural disaster (e.g., hurricane, flood, earthquake)

When an individual is beset by constant thoughts and/or memories of a traumatic experience, and if these thoughts and memories persist or worsen over time, the person may develop **post-traumatic stress disorder (PTSD)**. Individuals who are especially susceptible to experiencing PTSD are emergency personnel (firefighters, police officers, and paramedics); correctional officers; military personnel; victims of war; refugees; and immigrants. The criteria used to diagnosis this disorder are constantly reviewed due to its impact on people worldwide and the many ways in which traumatic events can damage individuals.

Signs and Symptoms of Post-Traumatic Stress Disorder

PTSD usually appears within three months of the traumatic event, but sometimes symptoms may not appear for years after the occurrence. Common general symptoms include reliving the event, avoiding reminders of the event, losing emotional control, and always feeling that something bad is going to happen. Specific symptoms may include recurring nightmares about the event; unwanted, disturbing memories of the event; avoidance of activities, places, or people that are reminders of the event; isolation from family and friends; loss of interest in previously enjoyed activities; difficulty displaying affection; inability to feel pleasure; constant worrying; difficulty concentrating; shortened temper; changes in sleep patterns (trouble falling asleep and staying asleep); experiencing sudden attacks of dizziness, increased heartbeat, or shortness of breath; and fears of death.

Risk Factors and Protective Factors Associated with PTSD

Women are more likely than men to develop post-traumatic stress disorder, and the disorder can occur at any age. Although a correlation has been established between traumatic events and post-traumatic stress disorder, not everyone who experiences a traumatic event develops PTSD (Centre for Addiction and Mental Health, 2010). Risk factors include inadequate social support following the traumatic event; feelings of guilt, shame, or responsibility for the event; or encountering other stressors after the event, e.g., the loss of a spouse, job, or home. Risk factors specific to the traumatic experience also include the severity, duration, and proximity of exposure to the event (Statistics Canada, 2013).

Protective factors that mitigate against developing PTSD include finding support from friends and family; participating in a support group following a traumatic event; applying coping strategies; and being able to learn from a traumatic experience.

Treating Post-Traumatic Stress Disorder

Jen Chouinard (shown here) is a social worker in Saskatoon. She specializes in trauma cases and developed a support group for individuals experiencing PTSD after her own lived experience involving this disorder (CBC News, 2015). Jen uses her own insights into treatment and recovery to reach out to others who are suffering in silence.

Support and Treatment for PTSD

Early detection of PTSD is a key component in recovery. Support for individuals who have been diagnosed with PTSD may include family service agencies; community mental health agencies; counsellors or therapists; family doctors; community health centres; settlement agencies; and workplace Employee Assistance Programs (EAPs). Because relationships can become strained when an individual experiences PTSD, families may also seek support.

Post-traumatic stress disorder (PTSD)
A condition of persistent mental and emotional stress occurring as a result of injury or severe psychological shock. PTSD typically involves disturbance of sleep and constant vivid recall of the experience, with dulled responses to others and to the outside world.

Counselling, one-on-one or group therapy, and medication for depression, anxiety, and sleep problems are common treatments for individuals diagnosed with PTSD (Wilson and Keane, 2004). A holistic approach encompassing several treatment options may lead to improved chances of recovery. One common therapeutic approach is cognitive behavioural therapy (CBT), in which individuals learn to change their thought patterns to overcome their anxiety and other symptoms (Statistics Canada, 2013).

Another approach that is proving effective is cognitive processing therapy (CPT). In 2015, through a grant from the Canadian Institutes of Health Research, and with help from Veterans Affairs Canada, Ryerson professor Candice Monson began to conduct research and training of front-line providers who deal with veterans who are experiencing PTSD. Monson is advancing CPT as a trauma-focused therapy that allows individuals to work through their past experiences by confronting the emotions related to traumatizing events.

Throughout Canada, 134 clinicians who traditionally treat veterans have been recruited to assist in Monson's study by delivering CPT to people affected by PTSD. As of 2015, more than 500 veterans had been treated using this therapeutic approach.

In 2013, Veteran Affairs Canada unveiled the "PTSD Coach Canada" mobile app to help veterans, Canadian Forces personnel, and civilians with post-traumatic stress disorder manage their symptoms.

Social Work and Mental Health
Prevention, treatment, and rehabilitation

Effective social work responses to mental illness

Social workers have always played a critical role in the Canadian mental health system, addressing a range of issues that encompasses both mental health and mental illness. Social work's historical perspective of viewing the person within his/her environment sets it apart from other professions.

Social work is founded on long-standing commitments to

- respect the inherent dignity and worth of all persons (lifestyle, gender, spirituality, race, culture, and beliefs);
- respect the person's right to make choices consistent with their capacity and the rights of others; and
- pursue social justice (e.g., combat discrimination and promote equitable access to services).

Social workers practise in diverse sectors of mental health, such as community mental health programs, adult psychiatric inpatient and outpatient services, children's mental health services, primary health care, and private practice. Additionally, social work services include, but are not limited to, assertive community treatment (ACT), early intervention, specialized geriatric psychiatry, corrections, treatment for substance use and concurrent disorders, and education and training.

Social Workers' Contributions to Mental Health

Social workers have contributed two key ideas to the mental health field. First, they have expanded the understanding of mental health. Social work has highlighted the influence of social and economic factors, family and other relationships, and the physical and organizational environment on individual mental health. The role of physiological processes, human biology, and experience are now viewed within the wider social context. Second, although social workers must understand and refer to the DSM-5, they avoid overusing labels such as "depressed," "schizophrenic," "manic," or "hyperactive" because stigmatizing labels are a barrier and discourage individuals and their families from getting the help they need.

Many individuals involved in mental health systems have reported feeling that they are being stigmatized by staff (Perlman et al., 2011). Social workers must be mindful of their own biases, therefore, when interacting with clients. Social workers are in a unique position to help decrease stigmatization. When social workers maintain openness, acceptance, and willingness to examine and perhaps discuss their own liabilities, these attitudes may help minimize feelings of guilt, shame, and stigma that a person affected by a mental illness may experience (Ibid., 2011).

The education, skills, and knowledge required by social workers in mental health include, but are not limited to,

- theories of communication and human development, family functioning, group behaviour, advocacy and the broader socio-political context, practice-based research, and interviewing skills;
- relevant legislation impacting service delivery;
- specialized knowledge of mental disorders, including the psychiatric classification system and major syndromes;
- theories and knowledge of etiology (origins of mental illness) and current methods of intervention, treatment, risk assessment, and rehabilitation; organizational structures of mental health services within community and institutional settings, including awareness of socio-political processes; knowledge of the paradigms, perspectives, and practices of other mental health disciplines; and
- an understanding of current research and best practices in order to maintain professional practice standards.

A Three-Pronged Approach

Social workers are playing an increasingly important role in promoting the mental health of Canadians with respect to prevention, treatment, and rehabilitation. Social workers may specialize in one of these areas or work across all three.

- **Prevention** aims to reduce the number of people with mental illness through awareness raising, standards development, and identification and avoidance of risk factors.
- **Treatment** aims to reduce the prevalence (number of existing cases) of mental illness through counselling, intervention, therapy, and/or advocacy.
- **Rehabilitation** is intended to reduce the after-effects of a mental illness and maximize the use of the client's strengths, capacities, and hope. Rehabilitation activities may focus on clients who are disabled by mental illness and may include building knowledge and coping skills or the provision of specialized residential, vocational, and leisure services.

Specific Services Provided by Social Workers

Social work in the mental health field requires the ability to work collaboratively with family members and the community. Social workers in the mental health field may deliver any of the following services:

- **Psychosocial assessment.** Performing a comprehensive assessment of individuals, families, groups, and/or communities in response to identified needs and strengths/coping capacities; assessing formal and informal support networks; and recommending an action plan.
- **Direct services.** Providing counselling, crisis intervention, advocacy, and management of resources to individuals, couples, families, and/or groups.
- **Case management.** Coordinating interdisciplinary services for a specified client, group, or population.
- **Community development.** Working with communities to identify mental health needs and issues, as well as to develop the capacity to deliver services.
- **Administration.** Putting systems in place and direct supervision to maintain effectiveness of mental health.
- **Program management.** Developing, implementing, and evaluating a mental health program.
- **Teaching and research.** Providing university and college courses or other workshops, conferences, and professional in-services.
- **Policy analysis.** Analyzing mental health policies.
- **Social action.** Organizing people to change mental health policies or advocate for changes to systems or programs.

What Interferes with Recovery?

- The misconception that recovery is only possible with medication
- Stigma surrounding mental illness
- Focusing on symptoms, not strengths
- Lack of motivation or unwillingness on the individual's part to participate in treatment
- Fear of change and unpredictability
- Feelings of hopelessness about the future and helplessness about one's illness
- Inequitable access to services, employment, and resources
- Lack of a social support network
- Isolation from family, community, and peers

What Facilitates Recovery?

- Building hope in order to get better
- Promoting a positive attitude, looking at strengths, and viewing the individual as a whole person, beyond his or her diagnosis
- Finding a balance of treatment, wellness, and health promotion (e.g., building relationships with family/friends)
- Advocating for changes to the design and delivery of mental health services
- Advocating for equitable access to services, employment, and resources
- Creating partnerships between the individual, family, and service providers

Culturally Competent Practice

Forging therapeutic relationships with culturally diverse clients

Growing numbers of immigrants and refugees are settling in Canada. The stress of adapting to a new society in the face of language and cultural barriers places immigrants and refugees at risk for anxiety, depression, and other mental health concerns. These problems can worsen when immigrants and refugees must also overcome challenges such as illness, poverty, and geographic isolation. Older adults who have limited English proficiency and are experiencing difficulties resettling are especially at risk because they cannot easily understand or access social services.

Social work with immigrants and refugees involves developing an understanding of the unique aspects of immigrants' and refugees' lives. Older immigrants and refugees in particular may feel overwhelmed. They may have experienced the trauma of war or persecution, separation from family and homeland, and the loss of loved ones. They may lack any sense of control over their lives, and experience cycles of crisis followed by boredom and hopelessness.

The role of social workers serving immigrants and refugees is to work with clients to identify and help them overcome any barriers to the resettlement process. There are many strategies that social workers can apply to ensure that their interactions with such clients are beneficial. According to social workers who have extensive experience with immigrant and refugee populations, the most important factors to consider include the following:

- **The need for culturally competent practice.** Social workers must educate themselves about a client's cultural background and determine how the person's culture tends to view issues such as aging, mental health, gender roles, and power relations within families. Simultaneously, social workers must remember that each client is an individual with unique experiences that will shape his or her interactions with the social services system.
- **Family dynamics.** A social worker serving a client who is an immigrant or refugee must often interact with a large number of family members. Thus, understanding the dynamics among family members provides clues as to how to best help the client. The worker must get to know the family's structure. For example, if a worker spends time with only female family members but the men in the family hold the power, the worker's efforts may be misdirected.
- **The value of social connections.** Because isolation is often a concern of immigrants and refugees, it is important for a social worker to assess clients' social connectedness and link them with community organizations, places of worship, and other support networks.
- **The need for patience and respect.** These qualities are necessary in any social work interaction, but they are especially important when working with older immigrants and refugees because these clients may be particularly reluctant to access services. A trusting relationship with such clients may take time to build, and a comment or action that a client perceives as disrespectful could cause irreparable damage. If a client is made to feel needy or "talked down to," he or she may retreat. Facilitating a therapeutic alliance based on respect for both the individual and the individual's cultural norms is essential to a positive outcome, as the next story demonstrates.

Reflecting on Anwar's Story

1. Do you think the social worker demonstrated cultural competence in her work with Anwar? Explain.
2. How did the social worker exhibit respect for Anwar, his family dynamics, and the need for social connections? How could she have improved on these aspects of practice?
3. Do you think it was a good idea for the social worker to offer Anwar the option to work with a male social worker? Why or why not?

Anwar's Story...
Seeking help for depression and anxiety

Mood disorders such as depression and anxiety span all age groups and cultures and are the result of a complex mix of social, environmental, and biological factors. Cognitive behavioural therapy (CBT) can help relieve the symptoms of a mood disturbance.

Anwar is a 58-year-old man from Turkey who immigrated with his family to a city in Canada two years ago. He has been married for 28 years and has three daughters aged 23, 19, and 14. For the past month, Anwar has been spending much of the day in bed, which has led to quarrels with his wife. She pleads with him to visit a community mental health centre.

Reluctantly, and after much emotionally-charged persuading from his wife and daughters, Anwar books an appointment with Lorraine, a social worker at the mental health centre. During the initial appointment, he tells Lorraine that he has a ten-year history of depression and anxiety. He was diagnosed with a mood disorder by a family doctor back home. His symptoms include low energy, poor concentration, shortness of breath, sweaty palms, and feelings of helplessness and hopelessness regarding the future. These symptoms occur mainly when he is alone. He does not have thoughts of suicide and has never made an attempt.

Anwar lost his job three months ago and has been struggling with the resettlement process. He feels isolated both culturally and socially, and is beset by feelings of worthlessness. He holds traditional cultural views about gender roles; he sees men as strong providers and women as nurturers. Thus, it is a source of shame to him that he is out of work and is so unable to control his moods that he must seek professional help.

During their first session together, Lorraine asks Anwar if he would be comfortable answering some questions about his background and personal history as part of a psychosocial assessment to help her understand his situation better. She reassures him that he is under no obligation to answer these questions and that he may stop the interview at any time if he feels uncomfortable for any reason. Lorraine poses a series of questions to Anwar about his family history, upbringing, medical history, education, employment status, and current family dynamics. It becomes clear to Lorraine that Anwar holds a negative view of himself as worthless and inadequate and that he believes there is little hope for improvement in his life.

Lorraine explains to Anwar that our experiences can be viewed from four perspectives: our moods, thoughts, behaviours, and physical reactions. Small changes in any one of these areas can result in changes that help reverse the downward spiral of depression. She explains that in CBT sessions, the therapist asks a series of questions designed to help a client gradually discover different ways of thinking about themselves and their situation, and to consider how their behaviours and thoughts are related.

As an example, Lorraine asks Anwar to rate his mood today on a scale of one to ten. When he says, "Six," she asks him how he remembers yesterday, and he responds, "Four." She asks him what is different between yesterday and today. He laughs and replies, "I had to get out of bed and come to see you." Lorraine connects how Anwar's behaviour has affected his mood as an example of CBT. Anwar then comments, "I definitely feel more hopeful today that my life can get better," and Lorraine is able to connect his thinking patterns to his overall mood.

Lorraine asks Anwar if he would be open to meeting with her on a weekly basis to work together to develop some cognitive behavioural therapy goals for him. Alternatively, Lorraine offers to refer Anwar to a colleague of hers at the clinic, a male social worker who is highly skilled in cognitive behavioural therapy. Lorraine senses that Anwar is embarrassed at appearing "weak" as a man and infers that he might feel less emotionally guarded with a male social worker. She suggests that he take time to reflect on this option and to let her know by the end of the week.

Because CBT for depression is often most effective when complemented by drug therapy, Lorraine also refers Anwar to a GP to assess the suitability of using an antidepressant to help relieve some of Anwar's symptoms. At the end of the week, Anwar calls Lorraine to thank her and to say that he would like to engage in weekly CBT sessions with Lorraine's male colleague. Lorraine thanks Anwar and then contacts her colleague to set up his first appointment with Anwar.

Cognitive behavioural therapy teaches clients that they can exert at least partial control over their moods.

Social Work with Transitional Youth

Issues surrounding services for transitional youth

The term "transitional youth" describes youth aged 15 to 24 who are transferring from children and/or youth mental health services to adult mental health services (Mental Health Commission of Canada, 2015). Approaching adulthood is hard for any young person, but it is particularly difficult for young people who are experiencing mental health issues. Various factors account for the tendency of this vulnerable population to "slip through the cracks" of the mental health system.

Some youth disengage from services altogether due to a lack of transition management between different sectors of the mental health system (Ibid., 2015). In fact, this is one of the most pressing problems affecting transitional youth, who are often left to seek out services and supports on their own, with little help from the services and supports with whom they were previously engaged.

Traditional mental health services assist youth and adults through separate systems of care with no bridge between them. Given the lack of support in transitioning to adult services, many youth find their progress toward recovery becoming jeopardized.

Supporting Transitional Youth

A number of supports and strategies can be implemented when a social worker assists a youth who is transitioning from youth mental health services to adult mental health services. Interventions during this transition can positively impact the individual's trajectory of mental health (Mental Health Commission of Canada, 2015).

Effective planning on the part of the social worker is a key characteristic of effective transitions. Transitional planning should be initiated as soon as possible prior to discharge of services, and care plans developed as part of this plannning should be flexible enough to adjust to different service environments and the unique needs of the youth (Davidson et al., 2011). If the social worker invites the youth to participate in transitional planning prior to discharge as well, this partnership can help align the young person's needs with the supports available in adult mental health services. Such an alignment serves to promote recovery.

Transition is most effective when improving transition is an important goal across sectors and between systems (Davidson et al., 2011). A social worker is most effective when connecting individuals with other agencies in a supportive manner. Making these connections involves more than providing contact information or a business card. An effective transition entails a case conference among those providing current supports and those providing desired supports to help ensure as seamless a shft as possible into the adult mental health sector.

In Mike's story, a young man's transtiion from youth mental health services to adult services is complicated by several problems, including the threat of homelessness. Acting as case manager, the social worker takes steps to liaise with the new case manager to ensure that Mike continues to engage with mental health services and to ensure as well that Mike's needs, goals, and priorities are kept at the forefront of his care plan.

Reflecting on Mike's Story

1. How did the case manager implementing the discharge/care plan enhance the referral to adult mental health services?
2. What is an essential aspect of referring an individual to another organization?
3. How did the family dynamic play a role in Mike's transition and discharge/care plan?

Mike's Story... Transitioning into adult services

Devising an effective discharge/care plan is key when a social worker facilitates an individual's transition from youth mental health services to adult mental health services.

Mike is a 17-year-old male who lives with his parents in an urban community. He is the oldest of three children; his siblings are aged five and seven. At 15 years old, Mike was diagnosed with schizo-affective disorder induced by marijuana use. One day he was smoking with his friends and experienced a hallucination. He went home and described it to his parents, who became frightened and brought him to the nearest hospital. Mike was in hospital for eight months, diagnosed, treated with antipsychotic medication, and then discharged.

Two weeks after he was discharged, Mike was admitted for services at a youth agency. Phil was assigned as Mike's case manager. Mike's parents expressed concerns about his illness and how it would affect their other children. Phil has been working with Mike for the last two and a half years. In this time, Mike has received peer support, vocational skills training, substance use support, and counselling for his illness and his familial dynamic.

Mike is turning 18 in six months, and Phil is responsible for helping him enter into adult mental health and addiction services. Mike is currently studying for his GED and will take the test in eight months, after he is discharged from services. Over the last few months, tensions with his parents have escalated. His parents don't understand his illness and how it affects him. Moreover, their fears of his illness affecting their other children are increasing. His parents have even kicked Mike out of the house a few times and he has had to stay at a shelter.

Phil starts working on Mike's discharge and care plan, which will be submitted to his new case manager in adult mental health and addiction services. Phil schedules a discharge/care plan meeting with Mike to gain his input in co-creating his plan.

After conducting various assessments and one-on-one counselling sessions, it becomes clear that Mike is at imminent risk of homelessness. Due to the tensions between Mike and his parents, Phil feels it is best that he find more stable housing. As part of his discharge/care plan, Phil identifies that Mike is willing to use emergency housing (a shelter), if necessary. Also, Phil and Mike identify other family members and friends who could fulfill temporary respite needs. Moreover, Phil has made an application for supportive housing, and Mike has been put on the wait list. Because wait lists can be lengthy, Phil completed the application immediately. This is highlighted in Mike's discharge/care plan so that his new case manager can follow up with his status during his transition to adult care.

Working collaboratively, Phil and Mike decide that Mike would continue to benefit from substance use support. He is put on an adult substance use services wait list, which is identified in his discharge/care plan. His discharge/care plan also states that he is working to complete his education to supplement the vocational skills he has acquired over the last couple of years. Phil identifies that the new case manager can continue to support him in his educational accomplishments.

Mike identifies a new goal that he wants to see included in his discharge/care plan. He wants to be involved in a day program that promotes and supports peer support groups, psychosocial rehabilitation, vocational skills, life skills, and activities of daily living. Mike identifies that he would like this support to commence after he attains his GED (General Education Diploma). Phil outlines this goal in Mike's discharge/care plan for his new case manager. Mike is pleased that he is able to contribute to his plan. He feels empowered that he has a say in what happens to him when he transitions into adulthood services.

Over the next six months, Phil and Mike meet regularly to update Mike's progress and to review his discharge/care plan to see if it is still viable or if he would like to make any changes. The week Mike is scheduled to meet his new case manager, Phil suggests that if he is comfortable with the idea, Phil could attend the intake session with him. Mike is relieved to know that someone he has trusted for the past three years will accompany him through this transition. Phil attends the intake with Mike and helps him present his discharge/care plan to his new case manager. Moving forward, Mike will be supported in identifying and articulating his goals as he engages in adult mental health and substance use services.

More Canadians aged 15 to 24 are developing mental health issues, but services for this age group are lacking.

Indigenous Mental Health

The First Nations Wellness Continuum Model

The social determinants of health are important in maintaining strong mental health. This is particularly true for Indigenous peoples. Historical determinants such as the residential schools legacy also play an important role in Indigenous mental health. An Aboriginal Healing Foundation survey found that 75 percent of residential school survivors had received a mental health diagnosis, the most prevalent being post-traumatic stress disorder, substance use disorders, and major depression (Research Series, 2003). Thirty percent of First Nations people have experienced depressive symptoms for two or more weeks (First Nations Regional Longitudinal Health Survey, 2005), and suicide and self-inflicted injuries are the leading causes of death for First Nations youth and adults up to 44 years of age (Health Canada, 2003).

Non-Indigenous social workers must be sensitive to the cultural values and perspectives of Indigenous peoples; similarly, First Nations, Inuit, and Métis people acknowledge the diversity of practices and values among other Indigenous people in different regions of the country. Just as there are no pan-Canadian Indigenous world views, there is no uniform understanding of mental health and wellness on the part of Indigenous peoples.

The First Nations and Inuit Health Branch of Health Canada and the Assembly of First Nations have jointly developed the First Nations Mental Wellness Continuum Framework. In this model, cultural values and sacred knowledge are understood as intrinsic ways of living with the land, which provides for the "good life," or *Mino-pimatasiwin*.

The model emphasizes purpose, hope, meaning, and belonging: "Mental wellness is a balance of the mental, physical, spiritual, and emotional. This balance is enriched as individuals have purpose in their daily lives, whether it is through education, employment, care-giving activities, or cultural ways of being and doing; hope for their future and those of their families that is grounded in a sense of identity, unique Indigenous values, and having a belief in spirit; a sense of belonging and connectedness within their families, to community, and to culture; and, finally, a sense of meaning and an understanding of how their lives and those of their families and communities are part of creation and a rich history" (www.hc-sc.gic.ca).

Holistic Wellness

Many Indigenous communities draw on this model to develop a holistic wellness framework. The Wet'suwet'en people in northern British Columbia have embraced the concept of "Yinta," meaning "people connected to the land." This concept is embodied by the statement, "We are the land and the land is us." Five key related themes are 1) Being Seen/Being Heard; 2) *Hiltus* (Strengths); 3) Spirituality; 4) Sustainable Livelihood; and 5) Social Responsibility.

Indigenous peoples have experienced lifelong intergenerational trauma, and social workers must ensure that their services do not recreate or reproduce structural violence. In Donna's story, Donna's reconnection with the land eventually provided a "breakthrough" in her recovery when her social worker recognized the validity of adopting practices based on complementary approaches, cultural competence, and cultural safety.

Reflecting on Donna's Story

1. What aspects of cultural safety were demonstrated in Donna's experience?
2. What elements of holistic wellness were missing for Donna, and how did her connection with the land help fill this gap?
3. In what ways do you think the social worker was implicated in structural violence?
4. For you, what is the most important lesson to be learned from this story?

Donna's Story... Reconnecting with the land

Building on strengths-based, solutions-focused, multicultural counselling can enhance cultural competence for non-Aboriginal social workers working with Aboriginal clients.

Donna is a 45-year-old First Nations woman living in a small urban community. A single parent to two sons, aged 10 and 14, she has been sober for seven years. She worked for the local health authority for five years and is currently employed as an Aboriginal educator and liaison worker. Her children attend the local school and are involved in youth soccer. The children have some contact with their father, but his sobriety is transitory.

Donna has recently accessed a community counselling agency, presenting with work stress that has been exacerbated by her sister Carlie's recent death from a drug overdose. Donna is having more frequent intrusive thoughts about drinking, and she is worried about losing her sobriety.

Initially, Donna's social worker adopted a strengths-based approach using a number of CBT techniques. These included reviewing Donna's supports for sobriety, finding ways to reduce her work-related stress, particularly through reframing techniques (reducing her self-expectations), and reaching out for family support to facilitate some of her sons' extra-curricular activities. Although a referral to a physician for antidepressants was discussed, Donna was reluctant to use psychotropic medication. After six counselling sessions, Donna had not experienced any relief, and if anything, her anxiety and depression were increasing. When she wasn't working, she stayed in her pajamas and lay in bed. She was isolating herself from her friends and family, and experienced a setback when she went on a weekend drinking binge. Her 14-year-old was beginning to act out, and she had a call from the school because he had been in a fight, which was unusual for him.

It was time for the social worker to reconsider her interventions with Donna. Trust had been built, but the question of whether the approach was working had to be re-evaluated. Troubling questions as to whether Donna was being retraumatized through structural violence emerged for the social worker. At the next session, the social worker returned to Donna's presenting problem, which was work stress. This provided an opportunity for Donna to reflect on the difficulties of integrating the demands of employment in a health bureaucracy with her own needs and those of the Aboriginal clients with whom she worked. This opportunity for reflection allowed the social worker to raise the question of whether the approach to counselling had been effective. Donna liked the social worker and didn't want to offend her, but she acknowledged that the sessions were not helping. This honest appraisal opened the possibility of working more "with" each other, and exploring a more holistic wellness model.

A pivotal question to ponder was what gave Donna strength and energy? What replenished her? And what had she done over the years to overcome the significant adversities she had experienced? After a long silence, Donna started talking about her need to find time to walk outside, away from the concrete buildings. She recalled the peace she had felt as a child sitting beside a creek just outside her village. As she talked more about this memory, her energy lifted and she became brighter. She concluded the session with the worker by announcing a commitment to take a week off from work to return to her village and reconnect with her community. She saw this retreat as a way of honouring her deceased sister as well. Donna developed a solid plan that promised to be a strengthening journey for herself, rather than a journey to support others.

Two weeks later, Donna came back to see her counsellor. She was back to work and looked much better. During her time away, she had walked endlessly in the woods with no direction. One day, she was sitting by the creek and two eagles circled overhead, eventually swooping down as if watching her. She felt the presence of her sister and her mother, and she knew her sister was being cared for again.

Although Donna came in for support periodically after her time away, a turning point had occurred. She found more ways to connect with nature, at least on weekends, and she reconnected with her spirituality more frequently as well. Donna continued to teach her social worker about holistic wellness and the importance of listening and accepting a different world view, one that avoided reinforcing structural violence.

Reconnecting with the natural world can help stave off depression, restore hope, and sustain balance in one's life.

Sharicka Reid

In her role as a family support worker, Sharicka Reid provides counselling and education to families of individuals struggling to cope with a mental health issue.

Sharicka Reid helps families understand that they did not cause a family member's mental illness and cannot cure it, but that they can learn to cope with the illness.

As a child, I always knew that when I grew up, I wanted to help people. At the age of 21, fresh out of the University of Ontario Institute of Technology with an Honours Bachelor of Arts degree in Criminology, I landed a job as a mental health worker with the Canadian Mental Health Association. Based at Partnership Place, a clubhouse in Brampton, Ontario, my job involved organizing social, vocational, skills-based, and daily living activities for adults with mental health issues. My background in criminology provided me with a strong rehabilitative perspective—I viewed my clients holistically rather than in terms of labels, and I believed that they were all capable of getting better.

I left that job to work for the Peel Halton Dufferin Acquired Brain Injury Services. As a team leader, I oversaw programming for individuals with either dual diagnosis or acquired brain injuries—the latter involving high medical or behavioural needs—and the families of these individuals. I was responsible for behaviour management programs related to personal care activities, as well as for the integration of individuals in a supported living environment into the broader community.

Currently, I am a family support worker with the Family Association for Mental Health Everywhere (FAME). I provide direct support to families in which one or more members are affected by a mental health issue. This work is unique because there are few resources available for family members struggling to support a loved one who is experiencing a mental health problem. Families are an integral part of an individual's recovery process, but they often feel overwhelmed and anxious about what lies ahead, and they need guidance and reassurance.

Using print and online materials, I help educate families about mental illness—its origins, symptoms, and treatment. I also help families develop communication strategies, coping strategies, and self-care strategies. I provide counselling to individuals, families, and groups. Families often experience burnout, and they need a safe environment in which they can vent their frustrations and learn that they are not facing an uncertain future alone.

Cultural sensitivity is an important aspect of the work that I do. Mental health is viewed differently across diverse cultures, genders, religions, ages, and abilities. People from some cultures perceive mental illness as a "disgrace," and they need help in reframing their attitudes so that their illness does not cause them to feel diminished as human beings. Coping strategies differ from culture to culture as well. Being able to understand each family's unique situation and cultural context, and to adapt my working style accordingly, is an absolute necessity in the work that I do each day.

Staying informed about resources in the community is also essential, as I help families navigate an often confusing mental health system. I maintain a caseload that continues to grow; time management and organizational skills are therefore key.

Community outreach is another vital aspect of my job. I give presentations about mental health and the importance of family support to schools, seniors' groups, hospitals, police associations, and other agencies.

Sometimes conversations with family members can be emotionally draining, as their dilemmas are often complex and distressing. Because I run a small satellite office on my own in Brampton, Ontario, I frequently debrief with co-workers either by phone or in our monthly team meetings.

When a person who has been ill finally receives a diagnosis, accepts therapy and/or medication, and learns to manage their symptoms, I celebrate those "mini-milestones" with the individual and his or her family. Seeing families progress from crises to more stable relationships is very rewarding and gives me hope. Nothing is more fulfilling than when a client tells me at the end of a session, "You don't know how much you have helped me." At the end of the day, if I have had a positive influence on one family, I've done my job. The reason I chose social work as a profession was to make a change. And change happens one person at a time.

Chapter 7 Review

Review Questions

1. List five characteristics of a mentally healthy person.
2. Identify three ways to prevent or reduce stress in your own life.
3. Explain why good mental health is not quite the same as having no mental health problems. Explain the difference between a bad mood and a mental health problem.
4. Identify three typical symptoms of mental health problems.
5. Explain the WRAP model for managing one's mental health.
6. Describe three components of effective social work practice in the area of mental health.

Exploring Social Work

1. Conduct research on whether mental health problems among young people are increasing. Do you think young people are under more stress compared to twenty years ago?
2. Various mood-altering substances (e.g., alcohol, cannabis, ecstasy) have been linked to mental health problems. Research the connection between one of these substances and mental health.
3. Stigma is a major barrier to dealing with mental health problems for individuals and communities. Devise a campaign theme and a message for fighting stigma in your school or community.
4. Keep a journal of times when you are feeling stressed, as well as times when you are calm and relaxed, and describe what you learned from keeping a journal.
5. Find out what support services are available in your community to help a person who is contemplating suicide.
6. It is said that having high but reasonable expectations placed on you as a young person can promote your mental health. Do you agree? Why or why not?

Websites

Freedom Center
www.freedom-center.org
Freedom Center is a support- and activism-oriented community run by and for people diagnosed with severe mental disorders. Freedom Center calls for compassion, respect for human rights, self-determination, and holistic options. The Center is based on a pro-choice, harm-reduction philosophy regarding medical treatments, and it supports people whether or not they are taking medication.

Mental Health Recovery
www.mentalhealthrecovery.com
Founded by Mary Ellen Copeland, the Wellness Recovery Action Plan site is rich with recovery resources and articles available for download, including wellness tools, crisis planning, ways to renew hope, strategies for dealing with symptoms, and hope-inspiring recovery stories.

Mind Your Mind
www.mindyourmind.ca
This organization helps youth and emerging adults to access information, resources, and various tools to use during tough times. Its interactive website offers uplifting stories of recovery and useful tips.

National Network for Mental Health
www.nnmh.ca
Run by and for mental health consumers and survivors, this organization's purpose is to advocate, educate, and provide expertise and resources that benefit the Canadian consumer/survivor community. It networks with Canadian consumers/survivors and with families and friends of consumers/survivors to provide opportunities for resource sharing, information distribution, and education on issues impacting persons living with mental health issues/illness/disability.

Social Work with Women in Canada

"I think we should be feminists in order to build a better world."

Nathalie Provost, École Polytechnique survivor

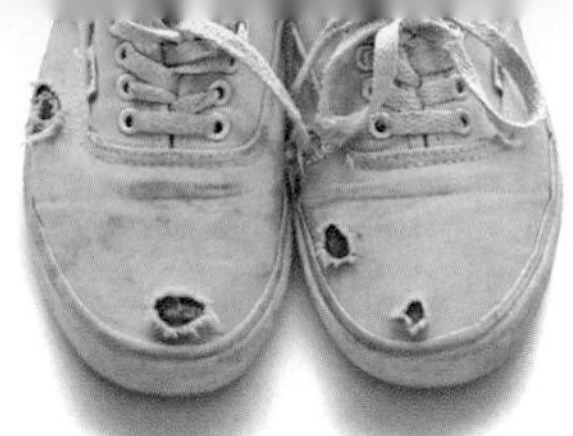

Kathleen C. Sitter

A Feminist Approach

8

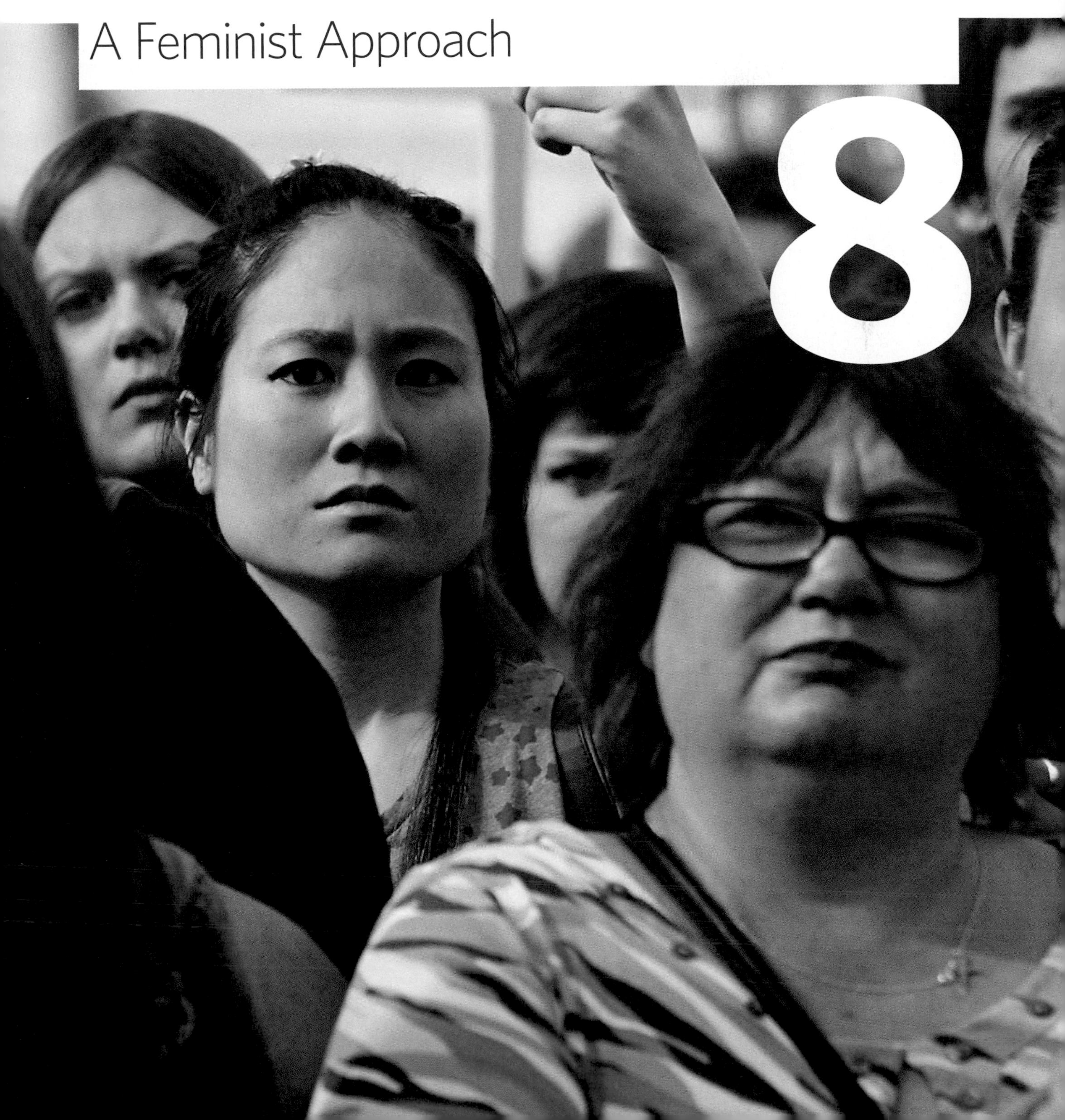

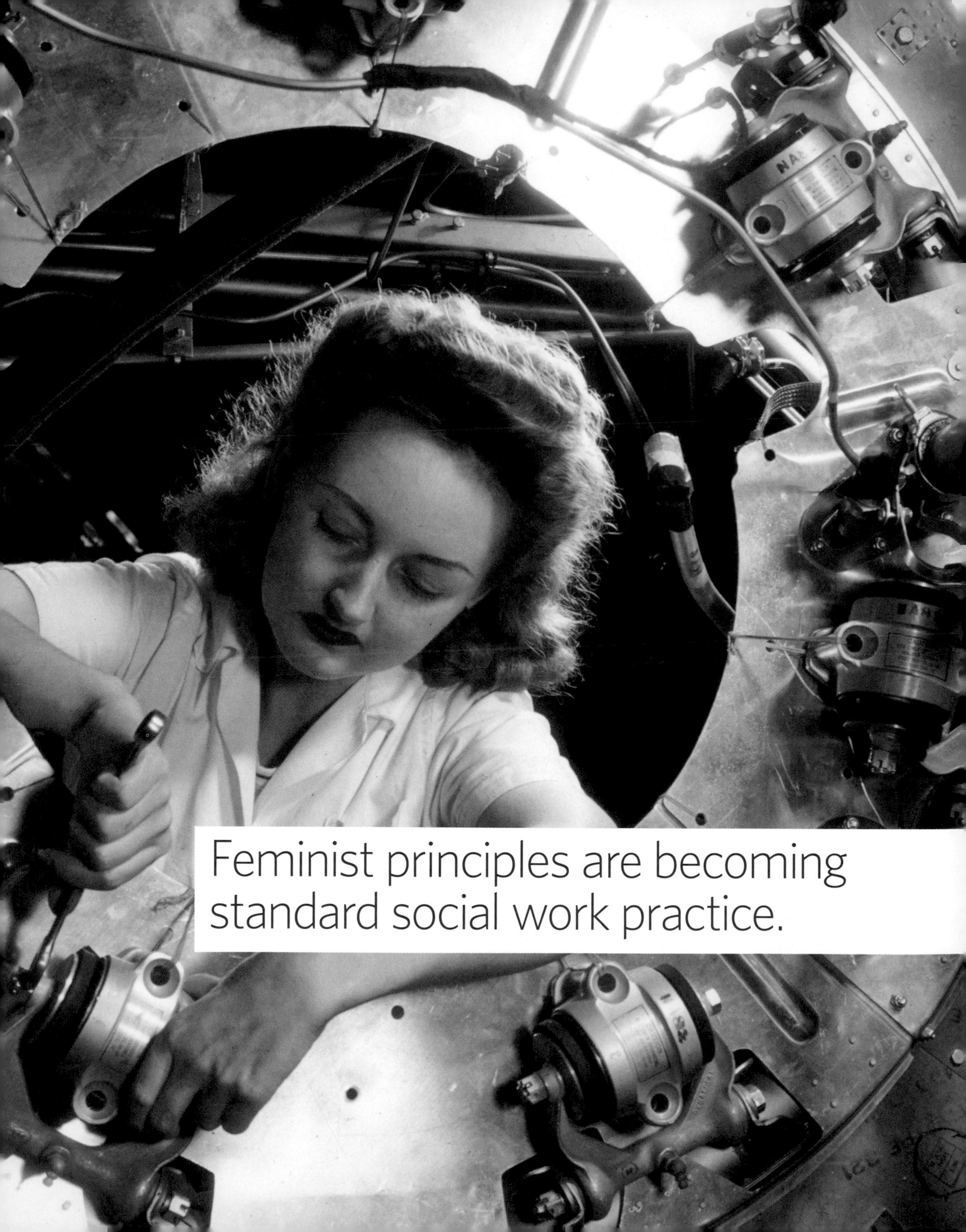
Feminist principles are becoming standard social work practice.

ne of the defining social characteristics of the second half of the twentieth century was the increased participation of women in the labour force. The implications of this economic fact were phenomenal. It gave rise to the two-earner family and precipitated an increase in the demand for child care, part-time work, flexible work arrangements, and pressure for greater equality between men and women.

What feminist author Betty Friedan referred to in the 1950s as "the problem with no name" very soon received a name and a proposed solution—women's inequality and women's liberation. Gender inequality persists to this day, however, and harm and violence against women take many forms. The death and disappearance of hundreds, if not thousands, of Indigenous women in Canada is just one of many issues causing concern among social workers, policy makers, and the country as a whole about the treatment of women and girls in our society.

In this chapter, you will learn how to...

- describe the four waves of feminism and their influence on social work
- explain "the feminization of poverty" and other persistent problems affecting women in Canada
- identify women's double burden and the implications for social services
- explain the theories that help us understand and stop systemic and pervasive forms of violence against women
- identify principles of feminist social work practice
- recognize that sexual violence reflects wider social and structural dimensions of oppression that take place in both online and offline contexts
- identify types of crisis support services and the competencies required in social work when supporting women who have experienced sexual assault
- describe how to support survivors of abuse through various interventions
- recognize the role of transition housing and emergency shelters in supporting women and their children who are survivors of abuse
- explain how the restorative justice approach can be used when working with men who use violence against women

Key Concepts

- Suffragette movement
- Consciousness-raising groups
- Intersectionality
- Gender
- Gender equality
- Sexism
- Patriarchy
- Equal-pay policies
- Equal employment
- Employment equity
- Feminization of poverty
- Sexual assault
- Sexual harassment
- Consent
- Power theory
- Learning theory
- Anger-control theory
- Cycle-of-violence theory

Focusing Question

What barriers to women's equality exist in Canada today, and how can the social work profession help to break down these barriers?

Social Work and the Struggle for Women's Equality

The modern movement for greater participation by women in public life first arose toward the end of the nineteenth century. Its subsequent history is frequently described as appearing and re-appearing in three or four different waves.

The First Wave of the feminist movement (approximately 1840s–1920s) had a number of strands, including the temperance movement, women's missionary and charitable activities, and the **suffragette movement**. The temperance movement focused on the prohibition of alcohol (because of its devastating effects on male breadwinners, and therefore, on women and children). Missionary and charitable activities provided an opportunity for women to become involved in public life, and the suffragette movement fought for and ultimately won women's right to vote. Women became involved in the Women's Christian Temperance Union, the National Council of Women, the Young Women's Christian Association (YWCA), and church missionary societies and charities (the Protestant Orphans Homes, homes for unmarried mothers, homes for the aged, and settlement houses). These groups were also the forerunners of the social work profession. Women were involved in campaigns to improve conditions for nursing mothers, in organizations that provided care for people with tuberculosis and other illnesses, and in providing assistance to families of veterans. For example, when the federal government agreed to pay an allowance to support the families of men who had died in the First World War, a group of Manitoba women (including suffragette Nellie McClung) campaigned for a similar benefit for the families of men who died in peacetime. In 1916, Manitoba introduced the Mothers' Allowance—Canada's first legislated welfare program.

A Pioneer of Feminism

Helen Levine (1923–) is a radical feminist and former social worker. In her writings, she challenged traditional views of mothering, critiqued psychiatry for defining women through a patriarchal lens, and offered an alternative way of working with women through feminist counselling. At the School of Social Work at Carleton University, Levine pushed the parameters of structural social work to include a feminist analysis, introducing women's issues and feminist perspectives into the curriculum for the first time.

Levine received the Governor General's Award in Commemoration of the Persons Case for advancing the equality of women in Canada. She is still an enthusiastic advocate for women's rights.

The Second Wave of the feminist movement occurred during the 1960s–1980s, when inequality in the wider society became a focus of concern. The phrase "the personal is political" emerged during this period, identifying the impact of sexism and patriarchy on women's lives. A core focus involved the breaking down of gender stereotypes. This Second Wave had a profound impact on social work through the rise of **consciousness-raising groups** that questioned gender roles and traditional power relations in society. However, there were a few limitations. One was that women were treated as a homogenous group, and attention was therefore focused mostly on the concerns of white, middle-class women. For example, in bell hooks' book *Ain't I a Woman*, the author notes the devaluation of racialized women within the feminist movement.

This changed with the Third Wave (1980s–2000s), which drew more attention to the multiple forms of feminism. The idea of **intersectionality** arose during this period, calling for a recognition that gender, ability, age, race, sexuality, class, and nationality intersect in shaping women's experiences. This more inclusive approach continues to influence social work practice today.

According to Phillips and Cree (2014), we are now entering a Fourth Wave, defined by the proliferation of new technologies that have major implications for social work practice. Information Communication Technologies (ICTs)—texting, social media, blogs, and online platforms—have transformed how people discuss critical issues, with young women aged 18–29 being the highest users of social networking sites (Pew Research Center, 2011). While some question whether the increased use of ICTs represents a clear Fourth Wave, these new platforms are certainly facilitating participation in feminist organizations and advocacy. The Canadian Association for Social Work Education (CASWE) is actively considering some of the effects of new media on social work practice.

Gender, Gender Equality, Sexism, and Patriarchy

Before continuing, it may be useful to identify several key terms:

- **Gender.** Gender has come to refer to the characteristics that identify the social relations between men and women, or the ways in which this relationship is socially constructed. Gender is a relational term similar to the concepts of class and race, and it is an analytical tool for understanding social relations and processes.
- **Gender equality.** Gender equality means women and men live in a society that affords them equal opportunity to realize full human rights; to contribute as equal citizens to national, political, economic, social, and cultural development; and to benefit from the results.
- **Sexism.** Sexism refers to prejudice or discrimination based on a person's sex. It is a system of discriminatory physical and social controls, derogatory beliefs, and institutional- and societal-level policies. Sexism can be blatant or subtle; it can take the form of derogatory language or lead to the denial of career opportunities based on a person's sex.
- **Patriarchy.** Patriarchy literally means "rule by the father," but in a broader sense, it has come to mean the domination of society by men and male interests. Men continue to be represented in higher numbers in positions of authority, and male interests continue to take precedence over those of females.

Suffragette movement
The campaign for women's right to vote, begun in 1903 by Emmeline Pankhurst and others in Britain

Intersectionality
An approach used in critical social work that takes into account the complex interplay of race, class, gender, sexuality, and other factors that impact life experiences

Rosemary Brown (1930–2003) was a highly regarded Canadian social worker and feminist. Elected to the B.C. legislature in 1972, Brown was the first Black female member of a Canadian parliamentary body. She championed gender equality throughout her career.

Equal Pay and Employment Equity

While women were becoming more engaged in public life in the twentieth century, they were not doing so on equal terms with men. "Excluded in large part from the male-dominated fields of business, government, and the professions, a new generation of college-educated women after the turn of the century provided a large pool of available labour for the emerging fields of nursing, teaching, library science, and social work" (Struthers, 1991: 128). Delegates to a 1929 conference on equal pay pointed out that women were generally paid less than men for work of equal value. This is often still the case today.

Moving Very Slowly toward Employment Equity

The economic crisis of the 1930s—also known as the Great Depression—did little to improve women's employment prospects. From the 1950s onward, however, more and more Canadian women entered the labour force, although rarely on equal terms with men. In addition, the industries and occupations initially open to women were generally less prestigious. Women's incomes were inferior to those of men in the same occupations, and all sorts of justifications for this fundamental inequality seemed to be readily available. Furthermore, patriarchal norms were still in force within the family: women were expected to tend to their children, husband, and household affairs, as well as earn an income outside the home. In the 1960s, salaries for women did begin to improve somewhat, with the expansion of employment opportunities in the social services sector.

Many legislative changes and policy initiatives in the post-World War II period were aimed at fostering greater equality for women at work. These included the following:

- **Equal-pay policies.** During the 1950s and 1960s, every Canadian province enacted legislation requiring equal pay for similar or substantially similar work. During the 1970s, both Québec and the federal government introduced pay equity legislation that required equal pay for work of equal value (allowing comparisons between occupations). In the 1980s, most jurisdictions followed suit, at least with respect to public sector employment.
- **Equal employment and employment equity.** All Canadian provinces now have equal employment legislation in place, usually as part of their human rights code, which prohibits discrimination on the basis of race, age, religion, nationality, or sex. Employment equity legislation, which requires or encourages proactive hiring practices in regard to identified groups, such as women, was not introduced in Canada until the 1980s. In 1996, employment equity legislation was expanded to include the federal public service, and this legislation became (and still is) required of federal contractors. Employment equity may also be required of cities and municipalities.
- **Equity-driven legislative and policy changes.** Under pressure from women's organizations, many other changes were introduced in the postwar period to help put Canadian women on an equal footing with men in the labour market. These included changes in divorce laws, policies against sexual harassment at work, extended maternity leave, policies to protect part-time and temporary workers, and policies to ensure that women have equal access to higher education.

Such policies have helped to equalize employment opportunities for women, although there is still the overriding concern that women leave work at the end of the day only to find that they must still assume the "double burden" of work at home and in the family. Much more needs to be done to ensure wage parity and equal job opportunities for women in Canada.

Equal Pay Day

It seems unbelievable that in the twenty-first century, in developed countries around the world, women still only earn about 70 cents for every dollar earned by men.

This fact is the origin of Equal Pay Day, observed every April in several countries. The date on which Equal Pay Day occurs symbolizes how long a woman must work into the next year to earn as much as a man earned in the previous year.

Gender Equality and Employment Equity
How Canada scores

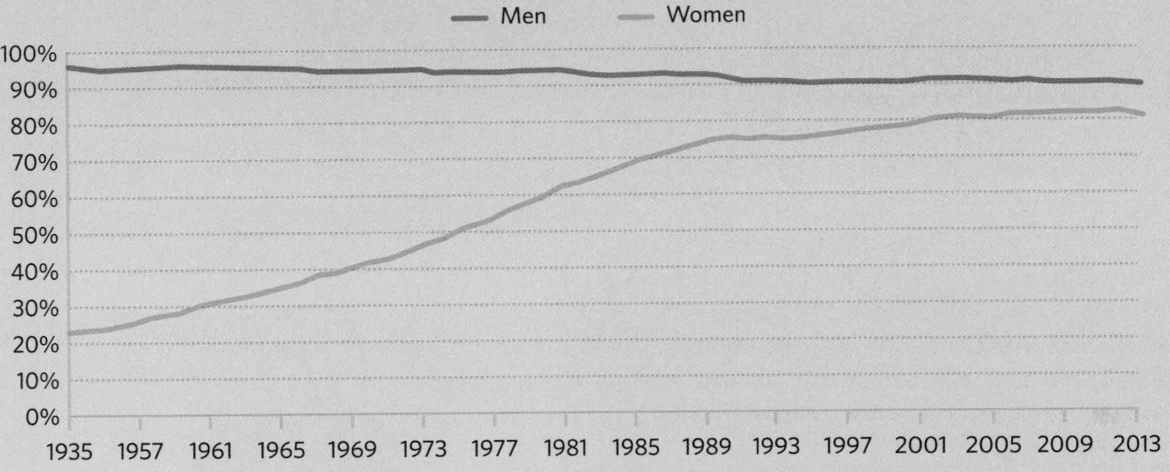

Labour force participation rates of men and women aged 25 to 54, 1935 to 2013.

Source: Statistics Canada. Labour Force Survey (LFS), 1976 to 2014, and Labour Force Survey, July 2015.

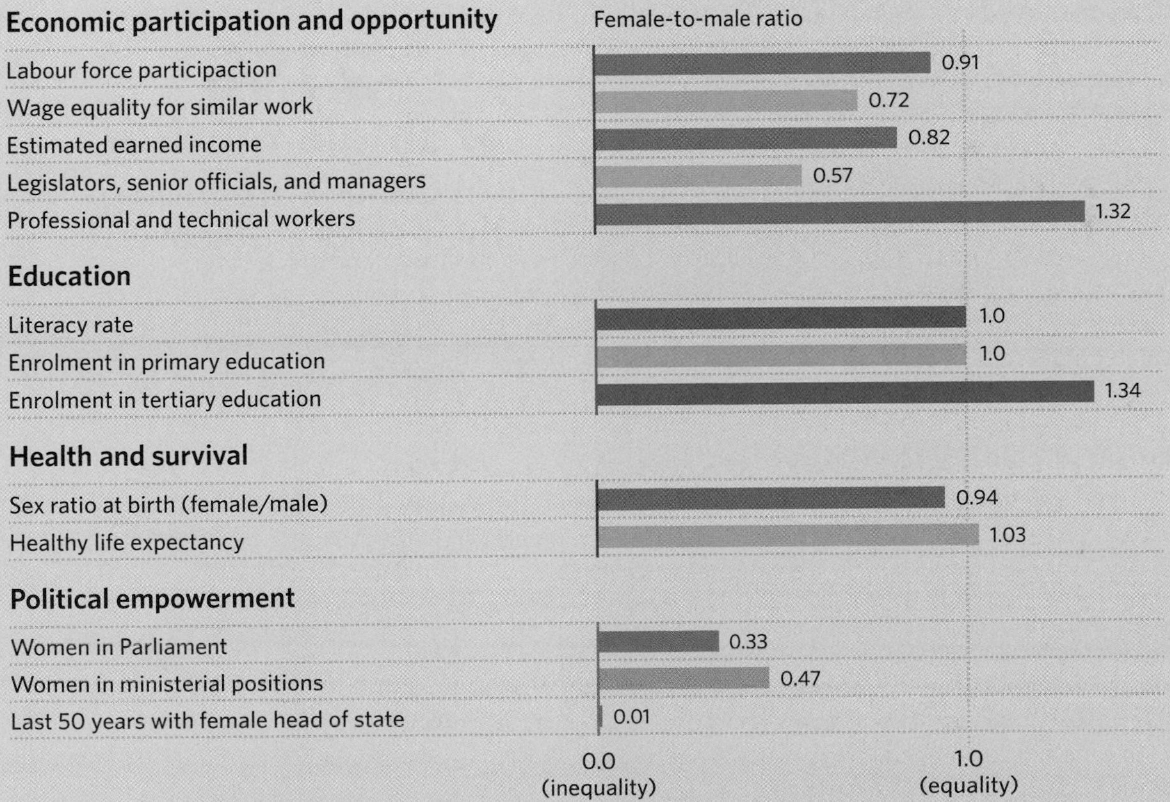

Source: World Economic Forum. (2014). *The Global Gender Gap Report, 2014.* Geneva, Switzerland.

The Feminization of Poverty
Two thirds of the adult poor are women

Mounting numbers of women—especially lone-parent mothers—are receiving social services across Canada. So disturbing is the problem that a phrase has been coined to capture it: "the feminization of poverty."

The factors of gender, race, and social status all play a critical role in determining who is poor. Across Canada, women are more likely to live in conditions of poverty than men. The infographic below, produced by the Canadian Women's Foundation, displays some disturbing facts about the high rate of poverty among women.

Single Mothers

The infographic shows that 21 percent of single mothers in Canada live in poverty. Women on their own are the poorest of the poor, especially those raising children single-handedly. The children of single mothers are almost four times more likely to be poor than those in two-parent families.

Many factors create a situation in which one in five mothers is impoverished. Women spend more time than men doing unpaid work, such as child care, meal preparation, and housework. The lack of affordable child care in Canada also forces mothers to limit their career and education opportunities. In order to balance their work and home responsibilities, many women have no choice but to take employment that is precarious (positions that are part-time, seasonal, or contractual). The gender wage gap is another factor that contributes to increased rates of poverty among women rather than men. Jobs traditionally occupied by women pay less than jobs traditionally occupied by men.

Children growing up in poverty are far more likely to experience food insecurity, poor health outcomes, and difficulty succeeding in school. Over the long term, boosting women's economic status will benefit their children as well.

Visible Minority Women

Twenty-eight percent of women belonging to visible minority groups live in poverty and are likely to face additional stressors and barriers, including difficulty obtaining employment. Unemployment rates for immigrants are higher than those for Canadian-born individuals at every level of education—despite the fact that there are similar participation rates in the labour market. The high rate of poverty among women belonging to visible minority groups is likely the product of an interaction of factors associated with being a woman and being a member of a minority group. There are similar interactions between (1) being a woman in Canadian society and (2) unique factors associated with being Aboriginal, living with a disability, or being a single older woman.

Source: Infographic and text by the Canadian Women's Foundaiton with data from Statistics Canada.

Aboriginal Women

The infographic also shows that 37 percent of Aboriginal women in Canada live in poverty. An argument is sometimes made that the direct effects of colonialism and discrimination against Aboriginal peoples have worn off by now. This kind of argument makes light of the intergenerational impact that systemic racism and widespread policies of assimilation have had on Aboriginal peoples. It also ignores present-day policies and practices that negatively impact the health and economic well-being of Aboriginal women.

Women with Disabilities

In Canada, 33 percent of women living in poverty have a disability. While a number of services, benefits, grants, and tax deductions are designed to support people living with disabilities, these programs do not adequately address the employment and economic barriers that women with disabilities face.

Older Women

The Organisation for Economic Co-operation and Development reported that in 2013, "the biggest increase in old-age poverty occurred among older women, especially those who were divorced or separated" (OECD, 2013). Older women who do not have job security, pension funds, or retirement savings risk finding themselves living in situations of poverty.

Addressing the Feminization of Poverty

When the economy is weak, as it is now and as it is likely to be in the coming years, the poverty rate for women tends to rise even more. This is because women's poverty is caused by different factors than men's poverty.

Men's poverty is usually more directly related to low-wage employment, whereas women's poverty arises from additional factors, such as divorce and separation, as well as their responsibilities as mothers, homemakers, and caregivers.

Social workers should challenge governments at all levels to develop specific strategies to deal with women's employment, child care, old-age security, family law, Social Assistance rates, and general income security. Investing in education and career-training programs for women can be of great aid to those who may be struggling to find adequate, full-time employment. Changes in policy that address employment discrimination against Aboriginal women and women belonging to minority groups can directly improve their living conditions.

We can support specialized programs that target the aforementioned gaps in our social safety net. Spreading awareness about the scope of the problem is itself a critical step toward helping Canadian women move out of poverty.

Other Persistent Problems Affecting Women in Canada

While new legislation and strategic initiatives in the postwar period undoubtedly helped to improve the position of women in Canadian society, a closer examination reveals persistent problems in many areas of economic life.

- **Under-representation in management roles.** The proportion of women in senior management positions has virtually flatlined over the past two decades or so, even though there has been a steady increase in overall female labour-force participation. Since 1987, men have been two to three times more likely than women to be senior managers, and one-and-a-half times more likely to be middle managers. Contrary to popular assumptions, women have not made significant progress toward gender equality at the middle-management level in either the private or public sector. After decades of striving for equality, women still have not reached the executive level in organizations at the rates once predicted, despite early assurances that time would remedy the disparity. The few women who do become top managers often attract media scrutiny, which may create a false sense that barriers to women's advancement no longer exist (The Conference Board of Canada, 2011).
- **Part-time work.** Women constitute a large proportion of the part-time workforce, and as such, usually earn less and therefore are particularly vulnerable to economic downturns. Seventy percent of all part-time workers are women. Over 20 percent of these women would take full-time employment if it was available.
- **Minimum-wage legislation.** Because women hold 64 percent of minimum-wage jobs, they are the group most in need of minimum-wage legislation. Providing a decent living wage for women could be a major step on the part of governments toward promoting greater wage equity and anti-poverty policy goals.
- **Maternity and parental leave.** Women still perform double duty: even if they work outside the home, they are most often the primary caregivers for dependent children and relatives, so that work-life balance continues to act as a major barrier for working women.
- **Dependent care.** Because women are most often the primary caregivers of dependent children, Canada's lack of universal child care programs is a significant barrier to women's full participation in the labour force. Daycare is a necessity for many employed mothers.
- **Free trade and globalization.** These global trends, involving competition from cheap labour markets overseas, particularly affect women who find themselves in low-wage jobs.
- **Pension programs.** These programs are of special significance to women because women are often employed in jobs that do not give them access to private pension plans.
- **Recessions.** Economic downturns affect women disproportionately. Forty percent of employed women hold part-time, casual, or temporary jobs, which are the first to be cut during a recession.
- **Employment insurance programs.** Programs designed to assist workers can place women at a disadvantage. Increases in the required eligibility periods make it more difficult for women than men to collect Employment Insurance; for example, women who work part-time because they care for children may not have worked enough hours to qualify for EI.

In short, despite all the changes in the areas of pay equity and employment equity, the problems Canadian women face in (and out) of the labour market are widespread and persistent. The stress resulting from these inequalities takes a toll on women and their families, and social workers are often called upon first to deal with the unfortunate consequences.

Women's Labour Activism

For over three decades, labour rights activist and scholar Winnie Ng has championed women's rights, labour equity, and anti-racism. From 2011–2016, she was Ryerson University's Unifor–Sam Gindin Chair in Social Justice and Democracy, the first union-endowed chair at a Canadian university. Previously, Ng was the acting executive director of the Labour Education Centre, and for eight years, she was the Canadian Labour Congress's Ontario regional director after working with immigrant garment workers and hotel workers as a union organizer in the early years. She is the labour co-chair of the Good Jobs for All Coalition and an executive member of the Asian Canadian Labour Alliance. Ng has received the Urban Alliance on Race Relations' Leadership Award, the United Farm Workers' Cesar Chavez Black Eagle Award, and the YWCA's Woman of Distinction Award.

The Daycare Crisis

There has been much discussion about the daycare crisis in Canada. Besides a lack of government funding for child care, costs are prohibitive and spaces are limited (with the exception of Québec, which has a public childcare system in place).

The parents who most need help, often single mothers, face long waiting lists and struggle to find alternatives. One option is turning to unlicensed home daycares that have no standard of quality of care. While many home daycares are safe and nurturing, others are overcrowded, unsanitary, and undersupervised.

With no child care in place, women are sometimes unable to return to work or school.

Affordable Child Care Urgently Needed

Advocating for government help

Child-care fees across the country are high and getting higher, particularly in Toronto, and advocates say the federal government should take action to lessen the burden on families that are struggling to cover the costs.

A new study from the Canadian Centre for Policy Alternatives finds that child-care costs are highest in Toronto, where the median monthly cost of full-day care for an infant is $1,736.

The increasing fees are tantamount to "a second mortgage," said Carolyn Ferns, public policy coordinator with the Ontario Coalition for Better Child Care. "It's something that I don't think we can afford to ignore anymore."

For a child between the ages of one-and-a-half and three, the median monthly cost of care is $1,325; parents of children aged three to five can expect to pay $1,033 for a month of care, according to the study.

Adjusting for inflation and using federal data from 2010 for families in which the youngest child is under six, the CCPC says a Toronto family with a median income can expect to spend 48 percent of their after-tax income to pay for a year of child care for two children.

Subsidies for low-income families can render expensive child care affordable—at least in theory.

"Once subsidies are counted, the cities in Ontario where child care would otherwise be most expensive become the least expensive, with fees of $87 a month," the authors write.

The catch, co-author David Macdonald said, is that a family's eligibility for a subsidy does not guarantee that they will receive it.

The *Star* has reported that there are roughly 17,000 children waiting for child-care subsidies in Toronto. And proving eligibility can be an onerous task, Macdonald says, that guarantees you nothing but a spot in line behind 17,000 others.

Not only are spaces scarce, but fees are climbing, as well.

The study, which focused on licensed child care, found that "fees have increased by five percent [per year] on average," well above the rate of inflation. In Toronto, monthly fees have jumped by $56 since last year, the largest cash spike in Canada.

Kitchener and Windsor saw three-percent decreases in monthly fees, the study notes.

For Safra Najeemudeen, a Ryerson graduate student in Markham, child-care costs are a fact of life, like paying rent.

"You just have to suck it up," said Najeemudeen, a mother of two. "And whatever it is, you just have to live with it."

Najeemudeen's children attend child care before and after school at Mt. Joy Public School. The cost for each child is around $375, Najeemudeen said.

Najeemudeen believes a cultural shift is necessary so that people view raising children as a societal responsibility and not an individual one.

"Eventually, [our children] are going to support the entire society," Najeemudeen said. "The main thing is...how children are viewed and how they're not valued in society."

The study also highlights the low pay among child-care workers. Low wages for workers, high fees for parents, and the irrefutably high cost of providing child care point to a need for greater government involvement, Ferns said.

"If you're going to pay the workforce decently, and you're going to have affordability for parents, right, we need to have more government intervention. We need to have more government funding to child care," Ferns said.

"That appears to be the most effective way of reducing fees," said Macdonald, who believes a similar plan nationwide would keep fees low. "What it means, in essence...is that it's only really in Québec that parents can afford to raise children."

Québec has recently changed its child-care system to charge families according to their income.

The study suggests "federal coordination and funding" would lower costs and increase availability. Martha Friendly, executive director of the Child-care Resource and Research Unit, believes the government's role should be a nuanced one.

"What we need is more money. We also need more policy," said Friendly, who co-authored the CCPC's 2014 study on child care. "It's not just producing more shoes. It's a social program that has a lot of components."

This includes answering questions about staffing and maintaining good quality, Friendly said.

"The lack of policy driving even the money that there is makes it inefficient," Friendly said. "It's in fits and starts and, we always say, a patchwork."

- *Source:* Davis, Stephen Spencer. (2015). Toronto most expensive in Canada for daycare: Report. *The Toronto Star* (December 10).

Sexual Assault and Sexual Harassment

Sexual violence is a major social problem in Canada today. Indeed, the level of violence against women, in whatever form it takes, is one of the strongest indicators of prevailing societal attitudes toward women.

- **Sexual assault** is any form of unwanted sexual activity, including fondling, touching, and penetration, that is forced upon another person without that person's consent. It includes a wide range of criminal acts ranging from rape to sexual harassment. All forms of sexual assault are crimes under the Criminal Code. Lack of consent is a key component of defining an act as sexual assault. Consent is an active choice and the voluntary agreement of adults to engage in sexual activity. Someone who is under the influence of medication, drugs, or alcohol is not considered to be in the position to give consent (Status of Women, 2002: 19).
- **Sexual harassment** is any unwanted behaviour, comment, gesture, or contact of a sexual nature that treats the person receiving it as a sexual object.

Women make up the majority of victims of sexual assault (92 percent) and other types of sexual offences (Statistics Canada, 2008). However, most sexual assaults are not reported, either because women feel afraid, don't want to go to court, or know that the probability of conviction is low.

The Aftermath of Sexual Assault: How Social Workers Can Help

Many sexual assaults occur when women are on a date. In fact, acquaintance sexual assault accounted for 45 percent of reported cases in 2007. The perpetrators were current or former partners, friends, or acquaintances. In addition, 37 percent of sexual assaults on women were perpetrated by a family member or an authority figure).

Women who are assaulted by someone they know often struggle with trusting others and with trusting their own ability to stay safe and make good decisions. They may also struggle with blaming themselves, even if they know that the assault was not their fault. The recovery process can be more complicated when the assailant is known to the victim. It is important for social workers to be aware that this type of assault is common and can happen to anyone.

Recovering from a sexual assault can be a long and painful process. Women often feel as though they should have done more to prevent the situation, and they may be worried that people will not believe them. Many women seek support to help them deal with ongoing nightmares, distrust, fear, anxiety, fatigue, difficulties with sex, depression, guilt, and shame—and social workers are often the professionals to whom these women turn.

Social workers play an important role in sexual assault crisis centres, sexual assault helplines, sexual assault and domestic violence care and treatment centres, sexual assault survivor centres, and shelters or transition houses (see Figure 8.1). They arrange counselling, legal, and medical services that victims and survivors might need. They sometimes accompany women to the hospital, to the police, and through court proceedings, as well as to appointments with lawyers and financial aid workers, providing emotional support and advocacy.

In addition to providing counselling and other types of support, social workers educate the public about sexual violence, advocate for women, and campaign for policy and systemic change. Social workers in this field recognize that sexual violence is not only an individual problem, but also reflects wider societal and structural problems.

The Vancouver Rape Relief and Women's Shelter

The Vancouver Rape Relief and Women's Shelter provides a range of services for women who have experienced abuse and/or sexual assault:

- a 24-hour emergency help line
- a safe place for women and their children to stay so they can escape or prevent an attack
- support groups to help counter feelings of isolation, including a group for former residents
- information for interacting with the Ministry of Social Development and Social Innovation, the police, the court, and/or the hospital

The shelter staff believe that sharing emotional support and knowledge helps all women join together to act for change.

How Much Do Canadians Know about Consent?

The results of a study by the Canadian Women's Foundation revealed that the definition of **consent** can become blurred when it comes to new versus existing partners and online versus offline sexual activity (Canadian Women's Foundation, 2015). The study revealed that

- almost all Canadians (96 percent) believe all sexual activities should be consensual, yet only one in three Canadians understand what it means to give consent; and that
- one in ten Canadians believe consent to sexual activity is not needed between long-term partners and spouses.

"Over the past year, sexual assault has been pushed into the spotlight, causing greater awareness about the importance of consent," says Anuradha Dugal, Director of Violence Prevention at the Canadian Women's Foundation. "The fact that most Canadians agree sexual activity should be consensual is a positive sign that people understand the critical importance of consent. However, it's alarming that so many people don't understand what consent actually looks like. This gap can increase the risk of unwanted sexual activity and assault, and is a clear sign that Canadians desperately need more education on the meaning of consent."

The survey also showed that many young Canadians have a blurred understanding of consent when technology is involved. One in five (21 percent) people aged 18 to 34 believe if a woman sends a man an explicit photo via text or email, this always means she is inviting him to engage in offline sexual activity. According to Dugal, "As we embrace the digital age, it is important that younger Canadians fully understand the meaning of consent and how it applies in both online and in-person settings."

Consent
According to Canadian law, sexual consent should be both *positive* (e.g., saying "yes," initiating and/or enjoying sexual activity) and *ongoing* (i.e., continues during sexual activity). Only one in three (33 percent) respondents to a recent survey identified both of these traits as requirements for consent.

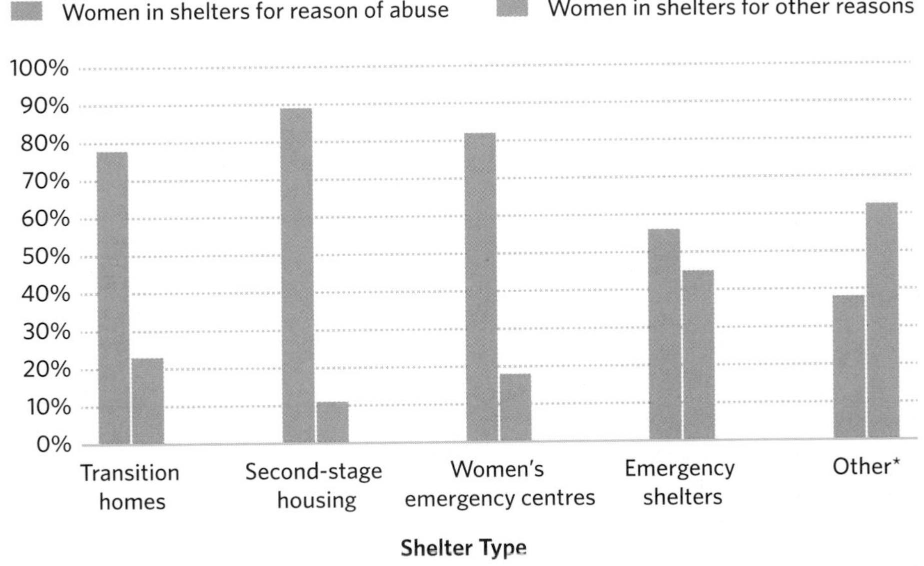

Source: Statistics Canada. (2015). *Canadian Transition Home Survey.* Centre for Justice Statistics, Ottawa.

Figure 8.1 These data compiled by Statistics Canada and the Centre for Justice Statistics clearly show that the majority of women seeking refuge in shelters in Canada have experienced some form of abuse.

The Role of a Social Worker in Supporting Survivors of Abuse

The role of social workers in helping women who are survivors of abuse may include crisis intervention, emotional support, empowerment, support group facilitation, and the provision of information. A social worker in a shelter will frequently be the first person a woman meets after she leaves a violent situation. At this critical time, it may be necessary for the social worker to explain the cycle of violence and emphasize that the abuse is likely to occur again. The social work process will be aided by conveying the message that the abuse is not the woman's fault and that she is not the only woman to have experienced this kind of trauma.

After providing the woman with the relevant information she needs to make a decision, the social worker should ultimately support the woman in whatever decision she makes. While it may be difficult for a social worker to see a woman go back to an abusive relationship (sometimes several times), the worker must be sure not to take the power of decision making away from the woman.

In all such situations, the first priority is the safety of the woman. Within this context, the social worker may partake in one or several of the following activities:

- Intervene in a crisis, which may involve the identification and assessment of danger to the woman and perhaps her children.
- Facilitate an empowerment approach with the woman.
- Listen to what the woman has to say and empathetically respond, sharing one's personal experience if appropriate.
- Connect the woman to a support group of individuals who have had a common experience.
- Make an appropriate referral if, for example, the woman has immediate financial needs.
- Advise the woman of her legal rights and link her to appropriate legal resources, in the event that she decides to press charges and appear as a witness in a criminal court.
- Mobilize safety, legal, and community resources effectively (e.g., linking children to a protective service, arranging admission to a shelter for abused women, finding a translator, or linking a sexual assault victim with an advocate).
- Implement agency policies regarding documentation and keep accurate records, including dental and other X-rays, as these may aid later legal action (if a woman decides to pursue such action).
- When writing case notes, be careful not to record anything that might be misinterpreted or used against a victim if her records are subpoenaed by a defence lawyer.
- Use the consultative process (know whom to call under what circumstances, and do it) and review one's referrals and interventions with other health-care providers.
- Complete the crisis management and follow-up referral or treatment steps while withholding judgement or imposing values on the woman and her significant others.
- Provide full follow-up and counselling with the woman to help prevent the onset of isolation and depression—these are risks for survivors of abuse or sexual assault.

Again, in carrying out these activities, the social worker should ensure that the woman feels empowered to make important decisions about her own life. Moving forward, a social worker can help a woman recognize abuse, name the problem and its source, and avoid self-blame. A social worker can also help a woman who is at risk of further violence to assess the assault/homicide potential in domestic and other situations, and take appropriate action.

Keeping Accurate Records

For all their cases, social workers are expected to keep records or written documents that detail the client's situation, the intervention(s) used, and the outcomes. However, practitioners who work with abused women often find this requirement to be troublesome. They find it difficult to keep accurate records because they know that these records might be entered as evidence in court proceedings.

For example, Bill C-46, the Rape Shield Law, is intended to protect women from character attacks by defence lawyers and restricts the questioning of victims regarding their sexual histories. To compensate for this restriction, lawyers can subpoena victims' counselling and medical records. Social workers must be mindful of this possibility.

The Women's Centre of Calgary

"I feel like the Centre is my second home"

The Women's Centre of Calgary is every woman's place for support, connections, and community. It is a street-level storefront, an accessible gathering spot for all women. The heart of the Women's Centre is a large open room with comfortable seating and a welcoming atmosphere. Women can simply drop by for a cup of coffee, talk with other women, and seek help for any concern they might have.

The Women's Centre is a place where women from all walks of life can feel safe to get and to give help, without time restrictions, cost, or judgment. Services include peer support, information and referrals, legal advice, discussion groups, workshops, basic needs assistance, and access to computers and other equipment.

The work of the Women's Centre is founded on a peer-support model of service delivery, whereby women are supported and trained to help other women. This means that all services are provided by and for women, with the backup and support of staff. As women talk, work, and help each other at the Centre, it is often difficult to distinguish between service user, volunteer, and staff member. The peer-support model also reflects a feminist, anti-oppressive, strengths-based, and community development approach.

The Centre works to recruit a diverse base of staff and volunteers, conduct ongoing diversity training, and develop inclusive policies and practices. Programs are based on the requests of women who use the Centre, and deliberate efforts are made to offer programs that will engage a wide range of women, as well as promote their participation in the community and their involvement in issues that affect them. There are community groups for women with disabilities, English practice groups, and after-school programs and camps for girls. The Centre participates in coalitions, organizes community events, and contributes to social action initiatives.

While the Centre does not keep individual client files, it does keep track of program contacts, and it aims to assess its work in various ways, such as through focus groups and surveys. For example, one survey found that 88 percent of women that come to the Centre reported they experience inclusion, finding someone to talk to at the Women's Centre.

"I feel like I belong to a strong community. I've been able to meet many women from different walks of life," one woman explained.

The Centre strives to ensure that women's voices are present in dialogues around various social, political, and economic issues. They work for change by spreading awareness and focusing on critical issues that matter to women. Women have the opportunity to become involved in the Social Issues Committee and the Social Policy Committee where they can discuss issues affecting women in Calgary. Each month, the Social Issues Committee holds a discussion night and invites community partners to present on topics of interest. Women are then encouraged to collaborate and brainstorm how they can create change in their communities. The Social Policy Committee works to contribute a gendered lens to policy by partnering with other non-profit organizations and coalitions to strategically influence policy change at the municipal and provincial levels. The Social Policy Committee is currently focused on the issues of poverty, child care, income, transportation, and women's leadership.

With incredible support from the community, funding, and over 690 volunteers and 14 staff, the Women's Centre continues to be a place for support, connections, and community for thousands of women. As one woman said, "Sometimes I feel like the Centre is my second home."

- *Source:* Women's Centre of Calgary. (2016). Copyright © 2016. Reprinted with permission. Website: www.womenscentrecalgary.org.

Violence against Women
The continuing patriarchal legacy

Seeking an understanding of intimate partner abuse and how to prevent it

It was not until the late nineteenth and early twentieth centuries that women were recognized as having legal and political rights. With respect to domestic violence, however, what happened behind closed doors was considered to be no one else's business. Police were reluctant to respond to domestic disputes, and the courts did not take such matters seriously. In fact, the prevailing view was that men should have complete authority in the home, and this view met with general acceptance. Insofar as they were financially dependant on their husbands, many women historically had little recourse if their husbands became abusive.

As a result, most assaults on women were not reported to the authorities. But in the 1980s, mandatory charging by police against accused assailants took effect across Canada. Formal training was established to assist police officers in determining a proper course of action when responding to domestic disputes, as well as to help them recognize chargeable assaults.

Findings of Victimization Surveys

Many social workers take exception to the phrases "family violence" and "domestic violence." They believe that these generalized terms gloss over the reality that it is usually men who are violent against women. The facts are certainly clear.

According to a Statistics Canada report containing police-reported data for 2010, there were almost 99,000 victims of family violence that year, accounting for one quarter (25 percent) of all victims of violent crime (Sinha. 2010). Almost an equal proportion of these victims were spouses (49 percent) or other family members, such as children, parents, siblings, or extended family members (51 percent).

Unlike for other forms of violent crime, females had more than double the risk of males of becoming a victim of police-reported family violence (407 victims per 100,000 people versus 180 victims per 100,000). This increased risk was primarily attributed to females' higher representation as victims of spousal violence.

In 2010, there were over 102,500 victims of intimate partner violence, including spousal and dating violence. This translates into a rate of 363 per 100,000 people aged 15 years and older and was almost 2.5 times higher than the rate recorded for family violence against a child, parent, or other family member (150 victims per 100,000).

A victimization survey carried out in 2003 by the Canadian Centre for Justice Statistics aligns with these facts. At the time, Canada had 606 victim service agencies: 41 percent were police-based, 19 percent were community-based, 17 percent were sexual assault centre-based, 10 percent were court-based, and 8 percent were system-based.

A survey conducted on one day in 2003 demonstrated that over 75 percent of the individuals who sought help from these agencies were victims of violent crime, and the majority were female. In fact, of the 4400 individuals helped on the day of the survey, almost three quarters were women or girls.

Even when sexual assault centres are removed from the total, women seeking assistance still represent 70 percent of those who seek help. And of the 4400 individuals surveyed, more than 1300 females were victims of violence by a spouse, an ex-spouse, or an intimate partner.

Theorizing Violence against Women

Violence against a woman by a man is a social act, a behaviour for which the perpetrator is accountable to the community. A variety of theories have been advanced to explain why this phenomenon occurs in Canadian society. Each of these attempts to conceptualize violence against women contains a great deal of truth. Below are four of them.

- **Power Theory.** This theory argues that violence against women is a societal problem which occurs mainly because of the power imbalance between men and women, and more specifically because of the dominance of men and traditional male roles. The violence has continued because there has been historical acceptance of men's right to control women, even by force. Those who hold this theory emphasize that society must change its attitudes, values, and responses with respect to women if violence against women is to be eliminated. This theory is consistent with a structural or feminist approach to social work.
- **Learning Theory.** The main idea behind this theory is that violence is a behaviour learned in childhood. Boys learn that it is okay to be violent, and girls learn that is it okay to be on the receiving end of violence and that this is what relationships are about. This theory holds that all children in our society are socialized to accept violence and that this, coupled with other roles into which boys and girls are socialized, supports

and perpetuates abuse. Accordingly, children who witness violence in the home are much more likely to become abusers or be abused. The emphasis of this theory is on changing behaviour through education and counselling.

- **Anger-Control Theory.** This theory emphasizes that men must be held accountable for their violent behaviour. That is, they must learn to deal with and control their anger or suffer the consequences. This theory does not attempt to explain the root cause of violence against women, and in this respect, is different from the two theories above. Instead, it focuses on anger control—if men can learn to control their anger, violence will stop. This is a behaviourial change model. Those who hold to this theory tend to favour a criminalization and punishment-based social work approach.
- **Cycle-of-Violence Theory.** This theory also avoids trying to explain why violence occurs; rather, it uses a three-step process to describe what happens in individual relationships.
  - The first phase is the tension-building phase. In this phase, the woman sees that tension is building in the relationship and that there is going to be an explosion. The man is expressing more anger every day. He may be kicking the dog or yelling at the children.
  - The second phase involves an acute battering incident. The tension reaches a point where the man becomes physically violent toward the woman. She may be verbally abused as well as hit, bruised, and battered. This is usually a shorter phase than the first, lasting between two and twenty-four hours.
  - The third phase is called the honeymoon period. In this phase, the man says he is sorry; he should not have done it; he loves her; he begs her not to leave him; he promises it will never happen again. The man calls relatives to ask them to convince the woman to return to him. If the woman has left during the second phase, she might return to him during this phase. Statistics show that a woman is usually abused and leaves many times before she leaves for the final time. Women want to believe that their partner has changed; they may also feel that it will be their fault if the marriage breaks down, as they perhaps didn't work hard enough at the relationship. Some women stay for the sake of the children or believe that a bad marriage is better than no marriage at all.

These four theories draw attention to different aspects of the problem of violence against women. Any social work assessment of a situation of violence enacted by a man against a woman needs to consider these major theories.

Social Work with Women in Canada
The principles of feminist practice

Different ways of seeing women's experiences and gender-based power relations

Social work, like many other fields of study and practice, was greatly influenced by the women's movement of the 1960s and 1970s. Students demanded that social work schools look more critically at social problems and develop programs that would be more responsive to women's issues.

Feminist theories offered different ways of seeing and understanding women's experiences, the nature of sexual inequality, and gender relations. Women's consciousness-raising groups began to question gender-based roles and power relations in society. By sharing experiences, women began to understand that their own experiences were not unique.

Incorporating Feminist Principles

Incorporating feminist principles into one's social work practice is a challenging and ongoing commitment. It should go without saying that it is important to value women's experiences and identities, and to recognize that women have been subjected to negative stereotypes. Social workers who incorporate these principles value the diverse experiences of all their clients.

Social work practice informed by feminist principles requires an awareness of power differences and how they affect both the therapeutic relationship and the client's life. While a client is recounting a bad experience, the worker may ask, "How do you think this experience relates to your gender?" or "How is your situation similar to that of other women?" Identifying and critically analyzing behaviours, rather than labelling them as "bad," helps women move from feelings of powerlessness and helplessness to confidence and determination. Focusing on the client's skills, agency, and resilience fosters self-esteem, as well as a healthy and egalitarian client–therapist relationship.

Giving voice to her experiences, especially those involving trauma, can be an important first step in a client's healing process. Listening and validating are therefore two of the most important aspects of applying feminist principles to social work practice. When appropriate, worker self-disclosure can bring comfort, validation, and a sense of connection, as it can help a client recognize that there are others who have faced similar challenges. It can also help her differentiate between individual and social problems and let go of self-blame. Worker self-disclosure can foster trust and egalitarianism.

The Components of Feminist Social Work Practice

There are numerous formulations and debates within feminist theory. There is, however, a core belief that social structures and gender stereotypes perpetuate women's subordination. Fundamentally, many feminist principles and concepts are similar to those of social work practice, such as empowerment and examining society through a critical lens.

In her 1995 book *Feminist Practice in the 21st Century*, Helen Land, a University of Southern California professor and accomplished feminist clinical practitioner, outlines the following thirteen components of feminist social work practice:

- **Validating the social context.** Feminist approaches emphasize the effect of social context or structures on the client, and the client and the worker assess them jointly.
- **Re-valuing positions enacted by women.** Social workers see the activities and stances ascribed to women, such as nurturing, cooperating, and caregiving, as important and valuable. Society and mainstream psychotherapies, however, typically assign more importance to behaviours and values ascribed to men, such as competition and upward mobility.
- **Recognizing differences in men's and women's experiences.** Feminist social workers maintain that mainstream social theories ignore women's experiences. To understand the emotional worlds of women, social workers must understand how the oppressive structures in society affect women.
- **Readusting perceptions of normality and deviance.** The need to readjust perceptions of normality refers to the fact that what is considered abnormal or dysfunctional is simply less common (or very common, but only within marginalized groups). For example, feminine behaviour, such as expressing emotion, is seen as weak or abnormal when exhibited by men. Similar attitudes exist about behaviour that is common among racialized groups and LGBTQ+ communities.
- **Taking an inclusive stance.** This requires social workers to challenge narrow assumptions—their own and others'— and to respect and affirm the experiences and values of clients from diverse communities.
- **Heeding power dynamics in the client–worker relationship.** This aspect ensures that the social worker develops professional, egalitarian relationships with clients. It also fosters a client's comfort, trust, and sense of empowerment.

- **Recognizing how "the personal is political."** This component acknowledges that personal difficulties faced by clients may reflect historical and political contexts, such as displacement and immigration. Such wider systems and ideologies influence how we think, feel, and experience events.
- **Taking a deconstructive stance.** The deconstructive stance attempts to uncover and examine how patriarchal social relations support and perpetuate a male-dominated world. The feminist approach therefore continually questions commonplace notions of what is "right" and "wrong," "normal" and "abnormal."
- **Taking a partnering stance.** This refers to the belief that disclosure of personal experiences by a social worker can be helpful to a client, especially if common experiences are apparent. This practice is quite contrary to traditional psychotherapy, which holds that professional distance between therapist and client is required.
- **Fostering inclusive scholarship.** In challenging the traditional notions of objective science, feminist scholarship frequently emphasizes both qualitative research methods (such as interviews or case studies) and quantitative methods (such as numerical frequencies and statistics). It also stresses centering on women's real-life experiences rather than on abstract theoretical models that claim to represent reality.
- **Challenging reductionist models.** Reductionism refers to the practice of reducing behaviours to simple cause-and-effect models, which often amount to stereotypes and which can severely limit one's ability to understand complex issues. For example, there is a stereotype of women as being naturally more emotional, and men as being more objective. Feminist social workers resoundingly challenge such views.
- **Adopting empowerment practice.** Empowerment practice means that the worker and the client develop goals together, with a focus on empowering the client to change his or her structures and environments, rather than on helping the client adapt to and cope with existing oppressive structures.
- **Countering the myth of neutral psychotherapy.** In general, feminist social workers reject the idea that a person can be neutral or value-free in their practice, and believe that workers must be explicit about their own biases and values. They also assist clients in discovering and taking ownership of beliefs and values.

These thirteen components offer a framework for understanding women's experiences and can help social workers support women through difficult times. These components seek to challenge wider structures and policies that foster gender inequality. Indeed, they are so important that they are becoming an accepted part of standard social work practice.

Can Male Social Work Practitioners Adopt Feminist Principles?

There are obviously many occasions when it is only appropriate that a female worker, rather than a male, support a woman in need. This is the case, for example, when working with women who have been sexually abused or raped, where the presence of a male social worker would be clearly inappropriate. It is widely recognized that women should counsel such individuals. This work normally takes place in settings such as rape crisis centres and women's shelters, where experienced staff members are trained to deal with emergency situations and to provide support and assistance.

However, male social workers can, should, and do incorporate feminist principles into their practice. Male practitioners working with the New Directions program in Ottawa, for example, use feminist principles when working with men who have abused women.

The program teaches men to take responsibility for their abusive behaviour and helps them see their behaviour within the wider social context of a male-dominated society. The history of abuse that many of the men themselves may have experienced is also addressed, and common experiences between the men are explored.

Male social workers can play a role in helping men change their attitudes and behaviours, including men who have used violence against women.

Stories from the Field

Stopping Violence against Women

Social work with men who use violence against women

Part of addressing intimate partner violence involves working with men who perpetrate the abuse. There are different approaches to working with men who use violence against women. One approach is restorative justice, in which a woman who has experienced abuse is invited to define what justice means to her, in this context. The rehabilitation process, therefore, is largely guided by the needs and perspectives of the person (or persons) affected by the partner's abusive behaviour. The process also involves the partner and the wider community in addressing these actions to restore the woman's sense of safety, respect, and integrity. The restorative justice process may or may not involve either restoring intimate relationships or arranging a face-to-face meeting with a woman and a partner.

The Bridges Institute in Nova Scotia is an organization that works with men and their families to stop abuse and build respectful relationships. Bridges integrates narrative therapy and restorative justice. Tod Augusta-Scott, a social worker and the executive director of the Bridges Institute, has identified several components in the therapeutic process whereby men take responsibility for the violence they have used against their female partners:

- **Exploring values and ethics:** Exploring the values and ethics that men deem important includes identifying what men perceive as important in relationships and in how they conduct their lives: respect, trust, safety, equality, taking responsibility, and accountability.
- **Studying the abuse:** Men study their own escalation and warning signs, and learn how doing so might prevent violence from happening in the future.
- **Studying the full effects of the abuse:** The goal is to prevent abuse from happening again.
- **Healing and repair:** Men come to understand how to heal and repair the effects of their abuse on their female partners, their children, and the wider community.

How the Restorative Justice Process Unfolds

Restorative justice does not involve a predictable approach but is based, rather, on the unique circumstances of each case. All men and women begin the process by meeting first with their own social worker, largely to determine issues of safety. A woman may choose to have no further contact with her partner. Many women, however, want to see clear evidence that the men who hurt them are learning to become accountable for their actions. Even women who wish to separate from their partners often want to see these men accept responsibility for their behaviour. Many of these women still have contact with their former partners because they live in the same community, have children together, or simply do not want their former partners to hurt other women. Women who do not wish further contact but who are invested in their former partner taking responsibility can still communicate what they want through counsellors or video-conferencing. Some women choose to speak with their partners or former partners directly in the controlled setting of a counselling office. These conjoint conversations hinge on issues of safety as assessed by the woman herself and by the social workers involved. The man is also offered an opportunity to take responsibility for his behaviour by attending group, family, and conjoint sessions if all involved decide that the conditions are safe.

Reflecting on Wade's Story

1. Discuss the factors in this story that are associated with restorative justice.
2. When might using a restorative justice approach not be appropriate?
3. What measures might be taken to help ensure that a man who has used violence against a female partner remains accountable for his actions in future?

Wade's Story...
A restorative justice approach

A couple damaged by the man's violence is guided by social workers in a restorative justice process to help regain dignity, equality, respect, and harmony in the relationship.

Susan and Wade have been yelling and swearing at each other in front of their children. When Wade pushed Susan, she called 911. The police arrived, charged Wade with assault, and removed him from the home. Child Protection Services became involved and insisted that Wade not return home. Wade and Susan are referred to the Bridges Institute, an organization that works with men and their families to stop abuse and build respectful relationships. Wade is mandated to attend counselling, while Susan's involvement is voluntary.

Susan and Wade each see their own social worker. With the couple's permission, the two social workers maintain contact with each other to monitor safety. The social worker who is seeing Susan adopts a therapeutic stance rather than making assumptions about her. Using a restorative justice approach, the social worker invites Susan to define what "justice" means to her. Susan defines both the effects of the abuse and what she wants from Wade and others so that she can start healing from the effects of domestic violence.

Susan reports that she loves Wade and wants to stay with him. She says that justice will be served when Wade stops his abuse and repairs the harm he has done. She wants Wade to treat her and the children with respect, and she wishes to feel safe. She would like Wade to repair the holes in the walls that he made when he lost his temper. She wants him to apologize to her parents for hurting their daughter and grandchildren. And she wants him to tell the children that inflicting violence on others is wrong.

Besides seeing a social worker on her own, Susan states that she wants to join a support group for women as well as attend counselling sessions with Wade. Susan says she wants the counsellor's support to tell Wade what the effects of the abuse have been and what she thinks he can do about repairing the damage. The social worker asks whether Susan would feel safe speaking freely with Wade in the room. Susan replies that she would feel safe. The social worker assesses the possible influence of dominant gender expectations on Susan, and considers whether Susan is prioritizing her own safety over comforting Wade. The social worker decides that Susan seems empowered and clear enough about her decision to recommend it as a possibility to the social worker who is working with Wade.

In a meeting with Wade, the social worker does not assume that Wade wants only power and control in his relationship with Susan. The worker is open to the possibility that Wade may also want mutual love, trust, respect, and safety in his family. The social worker engages Wade collaboratively by asking him to define his values and the type of relationship he wishes to have. The worker and Wade discuss values such as mutual respect, equality, safety, and responsibility. The social worker assesses whether Wade is willing to take responsibility for stopping his abuse by studying past incidents. By doing this, Wade can begin to spot the warning signs that precede his abusive outbursts and identify how he can prevent the escalation of violence by reminding himself of his values. The social worker invites Wade to consider the benefits of studying the effects of his abuse and how it might help him heal and repair those effects.

After several sessions together, Wade and his social worker determine that he is ready to take responsibility for his abusive behaviour in the next counselling session. Wade begins the process of openly studying and acknowledging his escalation toward violence. During a joint counselling session with Susan, Susan observes Wade becoming more accountable to her, and she witnesses his commitment to stop his abusive behaviour. Because she sees him taking the issue seriously, he begins to regain her trust. She decides that she wants to tell him the warning signs she notices that precede his abusive behaviour. She tells him how the abuse has affected her and what she wants him to do to address these effects. After three sessions over a five-week period, Susan reports that she feels more acknowledged, respected, and secure in Wade's commitment to repairing their relationship. The couple decide that they also want to focus on repairing the effects that Wade's abuse have had on Susan's parents. And finally, Wade decides that he wants to join a men's group to support the changes he is making.

A restorative justice approach with men who use violence against women can help men create safety, respect, and equality for women.

Providing a Safe Haven

Social work practice in women's shelters and transition houses

Each province and territory has a unique array of services dedicated to responding to the abuse of women. These services include transition houses and shelters, second-stage housing, safe houses, and family resource centres, all of which have varied funding arrangements and availability. They are all residential, meaning that they provide food and shelter for abused women and their children as required.

Transition houses are responsive to the needs of abused women and their children, are sensitive to the power relations within traditional family structures, and emphasize social change. Because of their success, the number of transition houses and shelters is growing. While they are becoming an increasingly important primary resource for women and their children, they also face serious funding problems.

In the 1970s, the women's movement struggled hard for the funding and development of shelters. Today they are the foremost resource for protecting assaulted women from violent partners and assisting women in moving on with their lives. An effective shelter provides the following kinds of services:

- emergency access to a safe place (including emergency transportation and overnight accommodation, particularly for those in rural and isolated areas)
- counselling and emotional support (immediately following a crisis and through follow-up and outreach on a residential or non-residential basis)
- information and referrals
- access to affordable and safe housing, and to legal and medical services
- employment and income support
- mental health and addiction services where required
- child care, child support, and counselling for children to overcome trauma
- safety planning
- assistance with the family law system (spousal maintenance, custody and access, child support, and accommodation)

Other available services may also include a crisis telephone line, crisis intervention, advocacy, and children's programs. Some centres provide former residents and non-residents with newsletters, walk-in services, or support groups.

As the next story shows, support groups are a key component of social work with women seeking to leave abusive relationships. They can support women in a number of ways: they help reduce isolation and allow women to meet others who share their experiences; they help women develop an understanding of issues of power and control and what actions they can take to change difficult situations; they can be a forum for women to exchange information, practical help, and emotional support; and finally, they allow women to explore their self-image and appreciate their strengths and accomplishments.

Reflecting on Marla's Story

1. What type of social work support was crucial to Marla and her family?
2. What other resources at the micro, mezzo, and macro levels could have further supported Marla and her family?
3. Peer support was and continues to be a core piece of Marla's experience. Are there times when peer support might not be appropriate?

Marla's Story...
Surviving intimate partner violence

Supported by social workers experienced in counselling women who have been physically, emotionally, and sexually abused by a partner, Marla found the strength to set out on a new life path for herself and her children.

My name is Marla. I want to share my personal experience as a survivor of intimate partner violence.

Over 20 years ago, I started suffering severe asthma attacks. At the time, I had six children ranging from 3 to 13 years of age, and I was working full-time in a hospital as a medical laboratory technologist. Needless to say, I was under a lot of stress. What wasn't so obvious to me was the secret stress that I couldn't even admit to myself: that I was being physically, emotionally, and sexually abused by my husband. My marriage was important to me, but the abuse was definitely taking its toll.

I thought back then that my husband had an excuse for his behaviour: he was struggling with the effects of alcohol addiction. And I loved him. I was married for 16 years before I separated from my husband.

Choosing to leave and then finally separating from my spouse was a very long and dangerous journey. I had endured years of abuse. I had also remained silent to ensure that my children would continue to love their father. But after repeated hospitalizations to treat my asthma attacks, I took the advice of a physician who said I needed help on an emotional level. My parish priest gave me the phone number for Catholic Family Services and suggested that I might wish to talk to someone there.

With the support of social workers at Catholic Family Services, I learned how to handle the unbelievable stress of being threatened, stalked, and deprived of funds by my estranged spouse, and I learned how to protect my children and myself from the man I loved. I learned how to organize and execute an escape plan, to keep clothes and supplies on hand in case we had to run, and to find safe houses where we could hide. I also learned how to enlist the help of schools and the police. All of these lessons were critical to our survival.

In order to keep my family under one roof, I began working 12-hour shifts at the hospital, including nights. Most mornings I would return home after working a night shift and care for the younger children while the older ones were at school. As a result, I became chronically over-tired, which sometimes landed me in the hospital.

Individual therapy, both for my children and myself, as well as my own group therapy with other women, were key to our survival. Through group counselling with other survivors, I learned that I was not alone. There was so much support provided by other women that a Sistering Program was developed at Catholic Family Services. This volunteer program for women who have experienced violence, trauma, or other forms of oppression began with seven women volunteers who were themselves survivors and who had moved forward in their healing journey. Therapists matched newcomers with women who were just beginning to make changes in their lives, and the newcomers benefitted from witnessing the healing process taking place in the lives of their "sisters."

Without the support, guidance, and financial assistance provided by Share Life and Catholic Family Services, my story may have been very, very different. Many women never make it, and I could not have done this alone. Given my limited financial resources, I would never have been able to protect my children without help. I do owe Share Life and Catholic Family Services my life.

Learning to live again without the threat of abuse, being a witness to women's rights, feeling validated, and being free—that's what life means to me now. How different things might have been for all of us! After six years on my own with my children following my separation and divorce, I married a good man with two children of his own. Today I am a grandmother to 13 beautiful grandchildren.

Now more than 17 years old, the Sistering Program is flourishing, and it remains an important part of my life. I continue to be involved in counselling other women who are living in abusive relationships, where I share my personal story while my own healing journey continues.

Marla recovered from the harm done to her and became a spokesperson for survivors of intimate partner violence.

Sexual Assault Crisis Intervention

Working with victims of sexual assault

Crisis-related services for victims of sexual assault include intervention and response, emergency crisis counselling, and crisis telephone-line assistance. Sexual assault crisis centres that function as community-based, non-profit agencies often have 24-hour crisis lines. Hospital-based sexual assault centres also have nurses and doctors on call 24 hours a day, seven days a week through emergency departments so that victims of sexual assault can receive specialized medical and emotional support services as soon as possible. Ontario also has a Victim Crisis Assistance and Referral Service (VCARS) made up of non-profit, community-based programs to provide on-scene, short-term support to help victims stabilize in the aftermath of an assault and to refer them to appropriate community services for long-term assistance.

Based on the 2011/2012 Victim Services in Canada survey, 76 percent of social service providers reported that they offer services to both urban and rural areas. Over half (57 percent) indicated that they service rural areas, and 24 percent reported that they service First Nations reserves (Allen, 2014).

At-risk rural women often face a unique set of challenges. These women may not have access to transportation or emergency shelters. Additionally, they may fear having their personal experiences revealed to others in close-knit communities, and protecting their children can also be more problematic in smaller communities. In the YMCA report *Life Beyond Shelter*, one core recommendation highlights the need for ongoing and accessible transportation to help rural women benefit from available social services (YMCA Canada, 2009).

Crisis Intervention: The Front-Line Worker's Role

When a worker takes a call on a crisis line, the first step is to ascertain the caller's immediate safety. Crisis counselling also aims to open a conversation about treatment planning and intervention. In any subsequent face-to-face meetings between a worker and a client, creating a supportive atmosphere by fostering collaboration builds trust and and a sense of safety.

The primary goal of the social worker in responding to cases of sexual assault is to express belief in the survivor's story, listen attentively, and validate the woman's feelings and concerns. Compassion, empathy, and interpersonal sensitivity are some of the core traits that social workers often draw on in this type of counselling.

As seen in the next story, a worker may need to provide a follow-up referral to a specific agency, so knowledge of organizational networks that can offer support is crucial. For example, the Canadian Resource Centre for Victims of Crime (CRCVC), a federal non-profit organization, functions as a broker of services for victims and survivors of serious crime in Canada, including sexual assault. All services are bilingual, free of charge, confidential, and socially inclusive. The Centre offers links to a wide range of agencies and resources that provide counselling, as well as information about victims' rights and services, women's shelters and transition houses, legal and financial help, and Internet and social media safety.

Reflecting on June's Story

1. What social work theories and principles does the worker apply in her interaction with June?
2. In what ways does the worker strive to help June regain a sense of control in an out-of-control situation?
3. Do you think it would be appropriate for the worker to self-disclose during her telephone conversation with June? Why or why not?

June's Story...
Getting help after a sexual assault

A 28-year-old woman named June calls the sexual assault crisis line in her community and tearfully informs the crisis line worker that her roommate's boyfriend has raped her. She also shares that she is a lesbian. June tells the worker that she is very worried about telling her roommate about the incident.

Having had specialized skills training in trauma counselling at the sexual assault crisis centre, the worker aims first of all to establish trust and respect between herself and the caller. Through active listening and validation, the worker strives to demonstrate compassion and a non-judgemental attitude in order to put June at ease, while creating a safe emotional space in which the worker can ask difficult yet important questions.

The worker begins by asking June about her immediate safety and well-being and her current location. June responds that she is alone at her cousin's house. June cannot stop crying and apologizes for her emotional state. Gently, the worker validates June's feelings by reassuring her that "it is okay to cry and to be upset. You have experienced a very traumatic event, and I am here to help you get through this."

The worker asks June about her health status and whether she has accessed a health centre or a hospital for medical treatment. These questions are posed because of the risk of sexually transmitted diseases (STDs) and other physical injuries that June may have incurred during the incident. The worker offers to accompany June to the hospital if she wishes, and explains both the agency's protocol in dealing with cases of reported sexual assault and the services that the agency can provide to support individuals who have experienced a recent assault. It is essential that the worker offer to accompany June to the hospital, as nurses may sometimes contact the police about a sexual assault without informing the victim beforehand. Having a social worker present to advocate and intervene on the woman's behalf is critical.

The worker talks to June about the option of reporting the sexual assault to the police, and describes the specialized services available for survivors and families who do file a report. June seems hesitant about officially reporting her assault and says that she needs to think about this option.

Clearly distressed, June expresses bewilderment as to why she was sexually assaulted and blames herself for the incident. She expresses shame and embarrassment and questions how this experience will impact her identity as a woman and as a lesbian. Drawing on feminist concepts, the worker further validates June's feelings, reminding June that the person to be blamed is the man who sexually assaulted her and that June is in no way at fault for this man's violent actions.

June asks the worker whether she should tell her roommate about the incident. The worker carefully explores the implications, risks, and potential responses that June might encounter should she choose to confide in her roommate. The potential responses include disbelief, acceptance, or anger and potential tension in the relationship—and perhaps even the termination of the friendship. The worker reminds June that it is June's decision and no one else's as to whether she informs her roommate of what has occurred. This reminder is intended to help June regain a sense of power and control in the midst of a high-stress situation.

As they continue to talk, June wonders about how she will fare in the aftermath of the assault. The worker explains that June may have trouble sleeping, eating, and feeling safe. She will probably feel anxious and sad. At this point, the worker asks if June would like to learn about options for long-term crisis support services in the community. They discuss resources such as survivors' support agencies, ongoing counselling services, and emotional support from family and friends. The worker asks if June's family is aware of her sexual orientation. June says that only her cousin is aware that she is gay. She also mentions that she has a strong connection to the LGBTQ+ community and expresses openness to accessing support through whatever LGBTQ+ community services might be available. The worker commends June for her willingness to reach out for help. She asks June what steps she would like to take next and what she thinks will work for her. As a first step, June books a face-to-face appointment with the worker for the next morning at the crisis counselling centre, with follow-up steps to be determined during the session.

Front-line crisis workers strive to allay self-blame on the part of women who have been sexually assaulted.

Diana Wark

One of the greatest lessons that Diana Wark has learned is that social workers must acknowledge and assess their own personal values and keep their values in check when working with clients.

Diana's work as a community development manager in Calgary, Alberta, has taught her to lead with curiosity and kindness, knowing that each individual is an expert in terms of his or her own experiences.

I began work at the Calgary Sexual Health Centre in 2007 as a community educator providing comprehensive sexuality education to junior-high and high-school students. Over time, my role has evolved into community facilitation on behalf of vulnerable youth and adult populations, including parents. I am now in a management position and am fortunate to work with dedicated, passionate, and feminist co-workers.

I completed a two-year degree in education at the University of Alberta and a two-year social work degree through Athabasca University. I am qualified as a registered social worker (RSW).

My journey in feminist practice was not planned. Early in my social work career, I was hired for an overnight position in a safe house for youth who had been sexually exploited and adults who needed a short-term respite from violence. My feminist perspective was shaped during those early days, as I encountered the powerful experiences of girls, women, trans women, and boys who were being victimized sexually. The realities of poverty, abuse in all its manifestations, addictions, violence, and the problems besetting First Nations peoples and women all collided, and I began to understand the interconnectedness of oppression and my role in it.

As a privileged, middle-class, white, able-bodied, cisgender woman, I have undergone a steep, terrifying, and ongoing learning curve. In the course of my work, my clients and colleagues have helped me understand my own experiences with sexual exploitation, addiction, unhealthy relationships, and patriarchal attitudes toward women.

At one point in my career, I became a doula and ran a pilot perinatal program to support young child-bearing women attempting to exit the sex trade. The barriers that these women faced from professionals and paraprofessionals in our health-care system were staggering. I am so grateful to those women who trusted me to be the best possible advocate for their reproductive rights. Not all of the outcomes were positive; some babies died, some were apprehended; some births were smooth and others complicated. These experiences taught me compassion and the fact that everyone deserves to be treated with dignity.

I also worked briefly with families and people with differing abilities in a HeadStart child-care program, where I witnessed the struggles of the working poor and single parents—mostly women—who were attempting to hold down jobs, go to school, and grapple with addictions and intimate partner violence while raising their children.

My path then led me to a group of ground-breaking women attempting to change community development in Edmonton, Alberta. I collaborated with this group, known as "Success by 6," in developing a model in which one staff person from various organizations was seconded to work as part of a team of professionals to provide quick, nimble, community-driven supports for children and families. Team members had backgrounds in child welfare, health care, policing, and community mapping. The "Success by 6" team launched community initiatives related to early literacy and FASD (Fetal Alcohol Spectrum Disorder) and trained me for feminist practice. This group of women believed in the power of women's voices to speak out for themselves and their families. Eventually, the fatigue involved in continually justifying our existence and the loss of our champion to retirement led to the dismantling of our group, and I assumed my current role at the Calgary Sexual Health Centre.

Issues related to reproductive justice and women's rights over their own bodies inform the work that I do. A core understanding that society still wants to control, manipulate, and coerce women in the realms of sexuality, birth control, abortion, pregnancy, parenting, work, and gender drives me to continue to learn and unlearn what is understood to be healthy sexuality. Exploring healthy sexuality in all its nuances and intersections with oppression, and working with people from all walks of life across the lifespan and in ways I could never have imagined—these experiences motivate me to live authentically according to my feminist roots and to strive for equality for everyone.

Chapter 8 Review

Review Questions

1. List and define five persistent problems that Canadian women confront in their daily lives.
2. What is meant by "the feminization of poverty"?
3. Distinguish between "online" and "offline" violence against women.
4. List and define five components of feminist social work practice.
5. Describe two ways in which social workers can put feminist principles into practice.
6. Expain two theories that provide insight into factors underlying men's violence against women.
7. What is the main role of a social worker when working with women who have been abused or assaulted?

Exploring Social Work

1. Re-read the section entitled "Other Persistent Problems Affecting Women in Canada" in this chapter and choose one of the identified issues to explore in greater depth. Write a brief paper that explains how women tend to be at a disadvantage in terms of programs and legislation related to minimum wage, pensions, or Employment Insurance. Suggest some changes that would increase equality in the area you've chosen to examine, and provide research to support your ideas.
2. The suicide of 17-year-old Rehtaeh Parsons in 2013 created renewed awareness of the issues of sexual assault, cyberbullying, and victim blaming. Explore the use of social media to perpetrate abuse against women and present an argument for some form of legislation to combat this phenomenon.
3. Gender-based analysis Plus (GBA+) is a tool that helps to assess the differential impact of proposed and/or existing policies, programs, and legislation on both women and men. Go to the Status of Women Canada website (www.swc-cfc.gc.ca) and search for "Gender-based analysis Plus." Write a two-page paper on how GBA+ can help inform social work practice. While the model was developed to inform policy analysis, you might find that it is just as relevant to direct practice. How could the eight steps of GBA+ be applied in direct practice?

Websites

Status of Women Canada
www.swc-cfc.gc.ca
Status of Women Canada (SWC) is the federal government agency that promotes gender equality and the full participation of women in the economic, social, cultural, and political life of the country. SWC focuses its work in three areas: improving women's economic autonomy and well-being, eliminating systemic violence against women and children, and advancing women's human rights.

The Family Violence Initiative
www.phac-aspc.gc.ca/sfv-avf/initiative-eng.php
The Family Violence Initiative has been the federal government's main collaborative forum for addressing family violence since 1988. The Family Violence Initiative brings together 15 partner departments and agencies to prevent and respond to family violence. The Initiative is led and coordinated by the Public Health Agency of Canada.

Canadian Health Coalition
www.healthcoalition.ca
The Canadian Health Coalition is dedicated to preserving and enhancing Canada's public-health system. Founded in 1979, the coalition includes groups representing unions, older Canadians, women, students, consumers, and health-care professionals from across the country.

Canadian Women of Innovation
www.women-innovation.techno-science.ca
This website allows the user to browse brief descriptions of Canadian women who have made a substantial contribution to science. It also lists various achievements by Canadian women in other fields, such as politics and sports.

Women's Art Museum Society of Canada
www.wamsoc.ca
"Dedicated to preserving women's visual heritage," WAM supports and showcases female artists through exhibits, publications, and the WAM website.

Social Work and Indigenous Peoples

"In the buzzword of the day, ***assimilation***; in the language of the twenty-first century, ***cultural genocide***." Chief Justice Beverley McLachlin

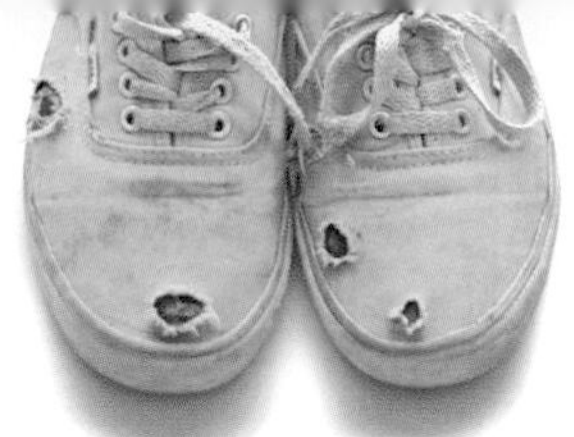

Elizabeth Fast and H. Monty Montgomery

Social Justice and Self-Determination

9

Indigenous peoples include the
Métis, the Inuit, and First Nations.

Indigenous peoples in Canada comprise 4.3 percent of Canada's total population. They include the Métis, the Inuit, and First Nations. Many endure conditions found only in the poorest countries of the world. A 2013 study by the Canadian Centre for Policy Alternatives and Save the Children Canada found that the poverty rate of status First Nations children living on reserves was triple that of non-Indigenous children (Macdonald and Wilson, 2013). The situation is not only unjust, it is a national disgrace.

Much remains to be done to reverse the damage done to Indigenous communities across Canada, which can be traced back to the history of colonialism by European settlers imposed upon the original inhabitants of this land. Social workers, Indigenous and non-Indigenous alike, will play an important part in this healing process. The urgency of addressing this national problem cannot be understated.

In this chapter, you will learn how to...

- identify the Indigenous peoples of Canada and give examples of their cultural and linguistic diversity
- explain the adverse effects of colonialism, the residential school system, the Sixties Scoop, and other negative events on Canada's Indigenous peoples
- analyze the meaning of "cultural genocide" in the context of Canada's Indigenous peoples
- explain the systemic factors underlying the serious problem of murdered and missing Indigenous women and girls in Canada
- describe attempts to address the historic trauma experienced by Canada's Indigenous peoples, including the Truth and Reconciliation Commission
- explain how the Touchstones of Hope movement offers a means of reconciliation in child welfare services across Canada
- describe some national organizations and grassroots movements dedicated to furthering Indigenous rights and self-government
- discuss the promise and the challenges related to post-secondary education for Indigenous young people
- describe how social workers can serve as advocates and allies to members of Indigenous communities
- explain key principles and approaches in social work with Indigenous communities in both urban and remote settings

Key Concepts

- Indigenous peoples
- Indian Act of 1876
- Colonialism
- Land-cession treaties
- Indian Agent
- Scrip system
- Disc list system
- Residential school system
- Assimilationist policies
- Sixties Scoop
- Royal Commission on Aboriginal Peoples (RCAP)
- Indian Residential Schools Settlement Agreement (IRSSA)
- Truth and Reconciliation Commission (TRC)
- Indigenous self-government
- Urban Aboriginal Peoples Survey (UAPS-2010)

Focusing Question

What does "reconciliation" involve in the context of social work practice with Indigenous peoples?

Who Are Canada's Indigenous Peoples?

Indigenous peoples (often synonymous with "Aboriginal peoples") are the original inhabitants of the portion of the North American landmass known as Canada. "Indigenous" and "Aboriginal" are collective terms which include the First Nations, Inuit, and Métis peoples. The term "Indian" is widely believed to have originated with the early explorers who thought they had reached India in their search for a passage to the east. Whether this is true or not, today the term is used to define a group of Indigenous people registered as such according to the *Indian Act*. Menno Boldt notes that the term Indian "serves the Canadian government as a convenient political, legal, and administrative categorization of the culturally diverse first peoples of Canada" (1993, 192). It is used in much the same way as "native," as a means of "outside-naming" those "who are descendants of the first inhabitants of what is now Canada." The term "Aboriginal" (and increasingly, the term "Indigenous") "appears to be associated with a general, emerging emancipation of Aboriginal peoples from domination of all sorts by the settler society" (Chartrand, 1991: 3–4). Of course, these peoples have their own names in their respective languages, such as Anishinabe, Inuit, Innu, Nuu-chah-nulth, and Métis.

Ill-Intentioned Policies
In the eighteenth and nineteenth centuries, newcomers to what is now Canada moved farther and farther westward, seeking land for agriculture and homesteads. This migration caused increasing displacement and conflict for the Indigenous peoples who lived on the land. The presence of Indigenous peoples on the lands desired by the settlers demanded a response from the European governments. The land's original inhabitants were seen as "the Indian problem," and impediments to "civilization." Government officials devised various schemes to address the problem, including land-cession treaties and assimilationist policies. Such schemes came at an exorbitant cost to the original inhabitants, in terms of the loss of Indigenous lives and ways of living.

First Nations, Inuit, and Métis

The First Nations include culturally, linguistically, and geographically diverse groups of people—some examples are the Cree, Dene, and Mi'kmaq peoples. The **Indian Act of 1876** sought strictly to define who would be considered an Indian so as to exert government authority over Aboriginal peoples. The *Act* fragmented the Aboriginal population into distinct groups with different rights, restrictions, and obligations. Because of the *Indian Act* and the significance of the Indian Register, the term "Indian" is still used in a legal context and usually defines a person as being either a Status or non-Status Indian.

Status Indians are persons of Aboriginal ancestry who are registered as Indians according to the *Indian Act*. Non-Status Indians are not, or have lost the right to be, registered as Indians as defined by the *Act*, but identify with the Indian community culturally and/or linguistically. Individuals who are "Indians" within this context are also First Nations people.

The Inuit are Aboriginal peoples of Canada "that have traditionally used and occupied, and currently use and occupy, the lands and waters ranging from the Yukon and Northwest Territories to northern Québec (Nunavik) and Labrador (Nunatsiavut) (INAC and Tungavik, 1993: 4). April 1, 1999, marked the creation of Nunavut, a new territory created from the eastern part of the Northwest Territories. The agreement between the Inuit of Nunavut and the federal government recognizes that the Inuit are best able to define who is an Inuk (or member of the Inuit peoples) according to their own understanding of themselves.

The term "Métis" is most often used to refer to descendants of the historic Métis—those whose origin can be traced back to the Red River in the early 1800s. Now located mainly in the prairies and the north, they formed a language and culture that was a unique blend of Indian and European cultures (Purich, 1988). On April 14, 2016, the Supreme Court of Canada ruled that both non-Status Indians and Métis are now considered "Indians" under the Constitution. This means that both groups are now the responsibility of the federal government and not the provinces. Although this decision is being hailed as a victory by those affected, its repercussions on new federal funding opportunities for Métis and non-Status Indians remain to be seen.

Contact with Europeans

When Europeans began to arrive on this continent, Indigenous peoples numbered between 500,000 and 2 million. They lived a wide variety of lifestyles, depending on the natural resources available to them. The oral traditions of some Indigenous cultures assert that the pre-contact population was even greater than the estimates of anthropologists and historians. Across Canada, there were approximately 50 Indigenous languages spoken, which made up 11 main language groups. Within each Indigenous language, there are several dialects. For example, the Algonkian (or Algonquian) language group includes the Ojibwa language, which in turn includes the Saulteaux, Odawa, Potawatomi, and other dialects.

Indigenous nations were also characterized by diverse systems of governance, health care practices, and cultural and spiritual rituals. These social aspects were not separated into functionally specialized institutions, but were organized holistically. Such social organization usually included some formal means by which different nations agreed to coexist. Some, such as the Haudenosaunee (Iroquois) or the Mi'kmaq, formed confederacies. Much of Indigenous history is based on unwritten oral accounts passed down over generations. These accounts often contain spiritual concepts foreign to European experience.

The relationship between Indigenous peoples and Europeans was initially friendly. During the sixteenth and seventeenth centuries, Indigenous peoples served as partners in exploration and trade. Later, as the English and French became locked in a struggle to control North America, the relationship with the Indigenous peoples evolved into military alliances. As European peoples and their governments exerted dominance over territories that had been inhabited by Indigenous peoples, they were no longer seen as military allies, but were gradually viewed as irrelevant, or worse, as an obstacle to imperial domination (Miller, 1989: 84).

Indigenous peoples
Collective term for the original inhabitants of Canada: First Nations, Inuit, and Métis. The terms "Indigenous" and "Aboriginal" are often used interchangeably.

Indian Act of 1876
Legislation that provides the Government of Canada with a legal framework of authority over Indians and lands reserved for Indians. The main purpose of the Act was to control and regulate Indian lives. An "Indian" is a person who is registered or entitled to be registered in the Indian Register (a centralized record), also referred to as a "status Indian."

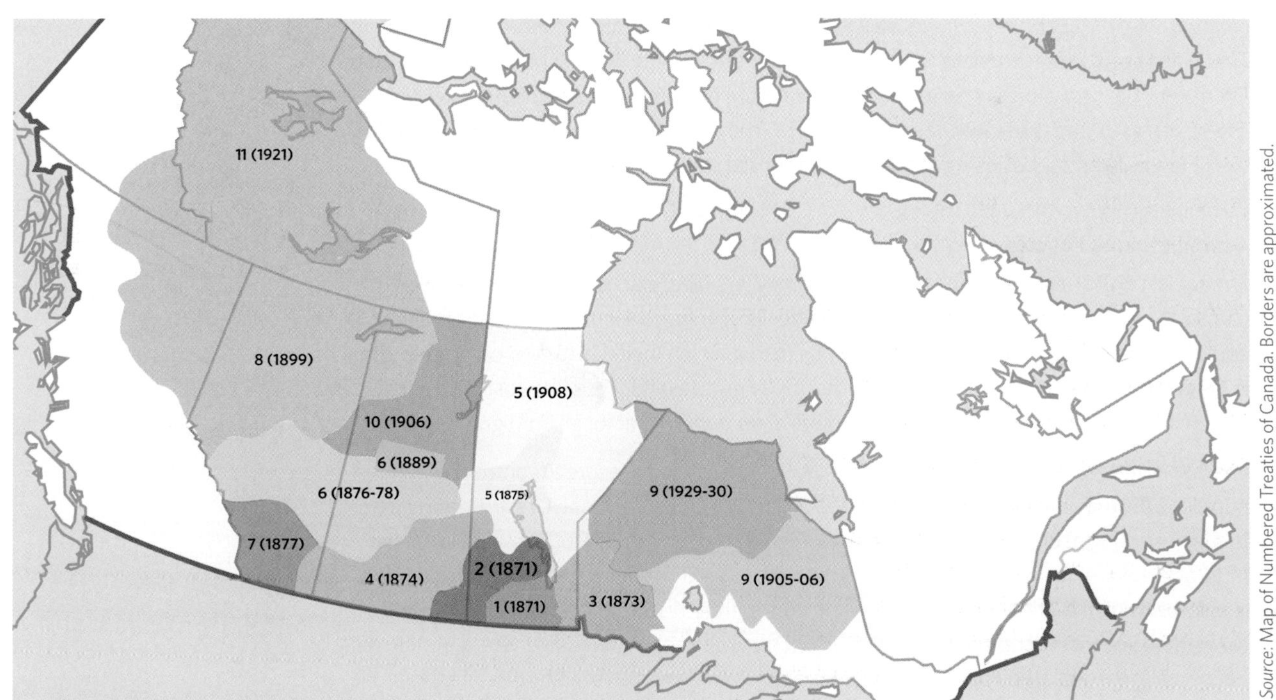

Source: Map of Numbered Treaties of Canada. Borders are approximated. Wikimedia Commons. Canada location map.svg. Modifications made by Themightyquill.

The "Numbered Treaties" are eleven treaties signed between 1871 and 1921. Numbers 1-7 (1871-77) were key in advancing European settlement across the Prairies and the Canadian Pacific Railway. For Numbers 9-11 (1899-1921), resource extraction was the government's main motive.

The Colonialization of Indigenous Peoples

The policy subsequently adopted by the settlers, best described as **colonialism**, amounted to an attempt to completely subjugate the Indigenous peoples and to annihilate their cultures.

The Indian Act

With the signing of **land-cession treaties** in the later nineteenth century, the government of Canada changed its relationship with the continent's first inhabitants. "The intention of the civil government, now that Indians no longer were militarily useful, was to concentrate Indians in settled areas, or reserves; to subject them to as much proselytization, schooling, and instruction in agriculture as 'circumstances' made necessary" (Miller, 1989: 100).

The legal instrument for colonialization was the *Indian Act*. Canada today is one of the few countries to still have separate laws for a specific group based on race or ethnicity. The *Indian Act* was, and still is, a piece of social legislation of very broad scope that regulates and controls virtually every aspect of the lives of Indigenous peoples.

Historically, an **Indian Agent** administered the *Act* in Indigenous communities. These agents were to displace traditional Indigenous leaders so as to institute a new way of living consistent with the intentions of the Canadian government at the time. The Indian Agents had extraordinary administrative and discretionary powers. In order to ensure this, Clause 25 of the *Act* established the government's guardianship over Indian lands. The *Indian Act,* still in force, certainly seems to be wildly out of step with the bulk of Canadian law. It singles out a segment of society (largely on the basis of race) removes much of their land and property from the commercial mainstream, and gives the Minister of Indigenous and Northern Affairs and other government officials a degree of discretion that is not only intrusive but frequently offensive.

Many want the *Act* abolished because it violates normative standards of equality; others want First Nations to be able to make their own decisions and see the *Act* as inhibiting that freedom. Even within its provisions, others see unfair treatment between, for example, Indians who live on reserves and those who reside elsewhere. In short, this is a statute of which few speak well. However, for fear of losing much-needed special status, some Indigenous groups seek to protect the *Act*.

Assimilationist Policies

The social control aspects of the *Indian Act* placed Canada's First Nations firmly in the position of a colonized people. The *Act* spelled out a process of enfranchisement, whereby Indians could acquire full Canadian citizenship only by relinquishing their ties to their community; that is, by giving up their culture and traditions and any rights to land. Thus, the cost of Canadian citizenship demanded of an Aboriginal person far surpassed that for an immigrant to Canada.

The Canadian government saw the *Indian Act* as a temporary measure to control Indigenous peoples until they had been fully assimilated through enfranchisement. (Assimilation refers to the absorbing of one cultural group into another.) It was not until 1960, however, that the federal government granted First Nations the right to vote in federal elections. This decision was important in that both enfranchised and non-enfranchised Indigenous peoples now had the right to vote in federal elections. For the first time, citizenship for Indigenous peoples was not conditional upon their assimilation into mainstream Canadian society. Despite this move, however, the federal government remained opposed to Indigenous self-government.

Colonialism
Forced political domination of one nation over another, including administrative, economic, and cultural control

Indian Agent
A government agent who administered the Indian Act, interfering in virtually every aspect of Native life. Indian Agents had extraordinary administrative and discretionary powers, and were meant to displace traditional Aboriginal leaders so as to institute a new way of living consistent with the assimilationist intentions of the Canadian federal government.

Land Treaties

While land treaties differed in their terms and complexity, they generally aimed to force Indigenous peoples to surrender land to the Canadian government. The major treaties were signed in the West, starting with Treaty No. 1 in 1871 and ending with Treaty No. 10 in 1906. (Treaty No. 11 was signed in the Far North.) These ten treaties allowed the vast territories of the West to be settled and the Canadian Pacific Railway to be constructed. It is important to note that no treaties were signed between the First Nations of Québec, the Maritimes, and most of British Columbia. In fact, almost half of the population of Registered Indians did not sign land treaties. Treaties and other land claims are now disputed across the country.

The Reserve System

Once land was ceded and Canadian settlements had been established, Aboriginal peoples were shunted aside onto small parcels of land largely devoid of any economic potential. This land could not even be used as collateral to develop business ventures, since that land was held "in trust" by the government. It has been argued that by confining Aboriginal peoples to reserves, Inuit communities, and Métis settlements

> the welfare of Aboriginal societies was systematically neglected. Famines and tuberculosis were allowed to virtually decimate Aboriginal communities, unaided except for relocation of survivors to state institutions. Housing provided was of the poorest quality, and health care and education were, until quite recently, left to the Church. (Scott, 1994: 7)

The federal government then established the Department of Indian Affairs as the main vehicle to regulate and control Aboriginal movement and ways of living. The modern equivalent of the department is known as Indigenous and Northern Affairs Canada (INAC), and its stated mission is to support Aboriginal communities in their quest to become healthy, safe, and economically self-sufficient.

The Métis and the Inuit

The situation among the Métis in the late nineteenth and early twentieth centuries was unique. The Métis in western Canada could seek to become status Indians by aligning themselves to certain treaty areas or they could "take scrip." The **scrip system** entitled the bearer of a scrip certificate to either land or money; in exchange, the person who took scrip gave up all further claims to land. Although the scrip system offered to the Métis was different from the treaty-making process for First Nations, the result was the same. Neither Métis nor First Nations were treated fairly (Purich, 1988).

The *Indian Act* also governed the Inuit. No land was formally set aside for their use, nor were any treaties signed with the Inuit peoples. However, because of the extensive mineral and oil exploration on their lands, many Inuit communities have been relocated, forcing a substantial change in their lifestyles.

One event that fostered deep distrust on the part of Inuit people toward the Canadian government was the 1950s Inuit relocation experiment from Northern Quebec's Ungava peninsula to Ellesmere and Cornwallis Islands in the High Arctic. In 1953 and 1955, the Canadian government forcibly relocated eleven Inuit families from the Port Harris region and four families from Pond Inlet to new communities at Grise Fiord and Resolute Bay. The relocated families suffered great hardship in the new region, however, despite the Canadian government's promises of improved hunting and trapping. Hunting and shelter were scarce, winters were darker, and because only a few youth were brought into the new community, partnership options were limited. Many Inuit individuals perished during the beginning of the relocation experiment, although most survived through fierce adaptation.

Another example of the paternalistic nature of state intervention in Inuit lives is the **disc list system**. As bureaucrats could not, or perhaps would not, acknowledge Inuktitut names, the disc list system assigned a numbered disc to each Inuk. Although originating as an administrative measure in the 1920s and not universally employed, the disc list system ultimately came to define a quasi-legal status that affected all aspects of Inuit life. By the 1960s, however, "it was evident that Government's attempts to implement a 'disc list' system was largely a failure" (Smith, 1992).

Scrip system
A system intended to extinguish the Aboriginal title of the Métis by awarding a certificate redeemable for land or money, depending on their age and status

Disc list system
A government-sponsored identification program for the Inuit that assigned a numbered disc to each Inuk, which ultimately affected all aspects of Inuit life

The Sixties Scoop
The massive removal of Indigenous children from their families and communities and their placement in non-Indigenous foster homes and adoptive homes, which took place primarily in the 1960s

Cultural Genocide—The Systematic Disruption of Indigenous Societies

Most Canadians are aware of the forced removal of Indigenous children from their communities and reserves and their placement in church-run, government-funded residential schools, which operated from the 1870s to the 1990s and were designed to assimilate the students into mainstream society. But fewer have heard the term "Sixties Scoop," coined by a social worker who reported in a government study that it was common practice in British Columbia in the mid-1960s to "scoop" almost all newborns from their mothers on reserves. Advocates say the removal of these children from their communities had devastating consequences, including high rates of depression, suicide, poverty, low education, unemployment, and incarceration.

The Residential School System

The now-infamous **residential school system** was established in the mid-1800s by Indian Affairs in conjunction with several Christian churches. By restricting Indigenous culture and language, the schools sought to fulfill the **assimilationist policies** of the federal government. The children were denied their language, spiritual rituals, and more importantly, access to their families. Indigenous children were regularly subjected to emotional and physical abuse, and many were also victims of sexual abuse.

As a result of having resided within an institution that regulated every aspect of their lives, these individuals had impaired decision-making skills: "residential schools were no preparation for life in any type of community" (Armitage, 1993: 142). Some struggled with drug and alcohol use and problems with mental health that arose from the psychological trauma they had endured. Many found themselves with a limited ability to parent their own children, as parenting models had been unavailable to them. While many individuals who emerged from these institutions retained a positive outlook, a true testament to their adaptability and resilience, it must be stressed that the residential school experience systematically damaged many Indigenous children and families. This legacy will take many generations to heal.

A Legacy of Harm
Indigenous people represent 4.3 percent of the Canadian population, yet in 2016 they represented 25 percent of the inmates in federal prisons. The percentages are even higher for females, and for most provincial jails. This over-representation occurs at virtually every stage of the justice system.

In 2015, the Truth and Reconciliation Commission called for the federal government to build more healing lodges and expand Indigenous-specific programs inside and outside our correctional institutions.

The Commission also called for the creation of Indigenous justice systems to deal with criminal conduct in ways that address the underlying causes of such behaviours.

The Sixties Scoop

In 1951, the *Indian Act* was amended such that provincial laws of application (and therefore child welfare legislation) applied to reserves (Timpson, 1990). With this legislative change, the government's approach to Indigenous assimilation veered from residential schools toward the apprehension and placement of Indigenous children in non-Indigenous foster homes. Child welfare agencies also assumed responsibility for services to Indigenous communities.

One result is what is known as the **Sixties Scoop**. In the 1960s, massive numbers of children were removed from their communities and placed in non-Indigenous foster and adoptive homes. By the late 1970s and early 1980s, at any given time, one in seven Status Indian children was not in the care of his or her parents, and as many as one in four Status Indian children was spending at least some time away from the parental home (Armitage 1993, 147).

The Sixties Scoop was widely condemned in the mid-1980s after ongoing criticism that included a judicial inquiry, headed by Manitoba Judge Edwin Kimelman. The inquiry led to policy changes signalling a need for more culturally sensitive legislation and a move toward Indigenous-controlled child and family service agencies. "Cultural genocide has taken place in a systematic, routine manner," Kimelman wrote. "The miracle is that there were not more children lost in this system run by so many well-intentioned people. The road to hell was paved with good intentions, and the child welfare system was the paving contractor."

Residential Schools

Children in residential schools were severely punished if they acknowledged their Indigenous culture or spoke their own language. Sometimes siblings were forbidden from even greeting one another. Additionally, residential schools provided Indigenous students with an inferior education, often only up to grade five.

From the 1990s onward, the Canadian government and the Anglican, Presbyterian, United, and Roman Catholic churches began to admit their responsibility for an education scheme that was designed not only to assert domination over Indigenous peoples but to eradicate their cultures.

On June 11, 2008, the Canadian government formally apologized in Parliament for the enduring damage done by the residential school system.

The Legacy of the Residential Schools and the Sixties Scoop

In 1981, the federal government entered into agreements with the provinces, insisting that child and family services for Indigenous peoples adhere to provincial standards and regulations. Under this legislative mandate, many Indigenous child welfare agencies came to resemble mainstream service providers. While it was recognized that a distinctive Indigenous approach was required in order to redress the damage done over generations, the provincial welfare system did not foster it.

Canadian child welfare authorities subsequently recognized the damage caused by this approach, and the federal government has made efforts to fund Indigenous child welfare agencies and to develop Indigenous child and family service standards.

Most Indigenous child welfare agencies have adopted placement protocols that specify placement preferences: first, with the extended family; second, with Indigenous members of the community with the same cultural and linguistic identification; and third, alternative Indigenous caregivers. As a last resort, placement is considered with non-Indigenous caregivers.

The Sixties Scoop has given birth to what some call the "Millennium Scoop," referring to the high rates of Indigenous children in care today. According to Statistics Canada, of the 30,000 children aged 14 and under in Canadian foster care in 2011, almost half were Indigenous. These children are part of the legacy of disrupted parent-child bonds caused by past assimilationist practices such as the residential school system, which robbed generations of Indigenous peoples of their language, their heritage, their personal histories, and their cultural identity.

Water Advisories on First Nations Reserves Ignored

Many people on First Nations reserves across Canada cannot trust the water they get from their taps. Contaminants include coliform, uranium, and carcinogenic trihalomethanes.

In a report issued on June 7, 2016, Human Rights Watch (an international non-governmental organization) says that, by not ensuring First Nations people access to safe water, "the Canadian government has violated a range of international human rights obligations."

Source: Matthew McClearn (2016). Ottawa has human-rights obligation to provide safe water on reserves. *The Globe and Mail* (June 7).

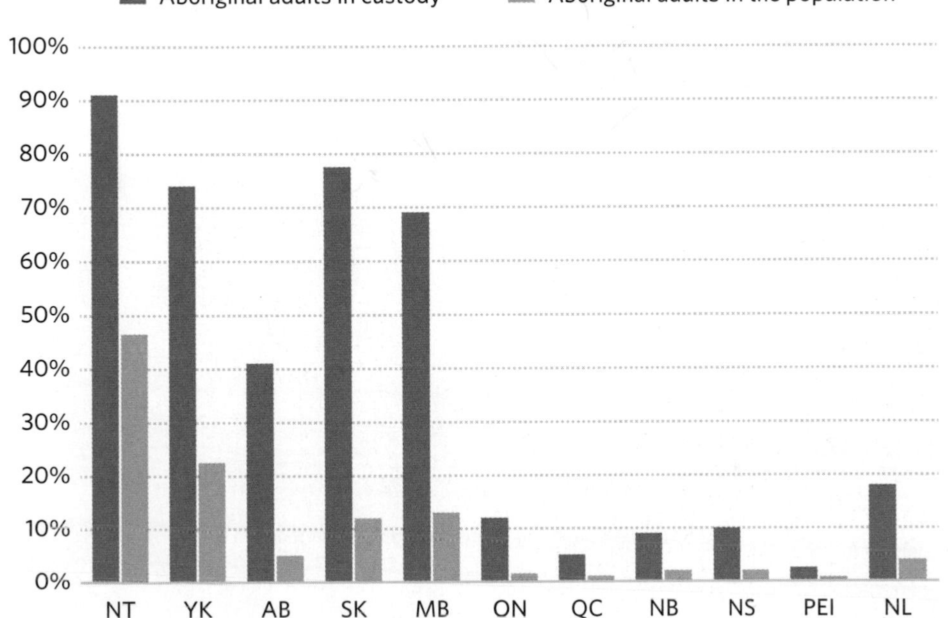

Source: Correctional Services Program. (2015). *Adult Correctional Statistics in Canada, 2013/2014*. Statistics Canada, Ottawa, Ontario.

Figure 9.1 Over-representation in the Canadian justice system today is one consequence of the residential schools, the Sixties Scoop, and the attempted systematic disruption of Indigenous societies. (Note: Graph excludes British Columbia and Nunavut due to the unavailability of data.)

Missing and Murdered Indigenous Women

Violence reflects systemic problems

Indigenous people six times more likely to be murder victims: Statscan

Canada's homicide rate has sunk to its lowest level since 1966—but Indigenous people are far more likely to be murder victims than other segments of the population.

In its first-ever complete analysis on homicides and Aboriginal identity, Statistics Canada said that last year [2014], Indigenous people were about six times more likely to be victims of homicide than non-Indigenous people. Almost a quarter of last year's 516 homicide victims were reported by police as Aboriginal, a group that accounted for just five percent of the Canadian population.

Indigenous women in Canada are roughly seven times more likely than non-Indigenous women to be slain by serial killers, a *Globe* analysis has found.

Both Indigenous men and women are more likely to be victims of murder. Aboriginal men were seven times more likely to be homicide victims than non-Aboriginal men, while the homicide rate for Indigenous women was six times higher than for their non-Indigenous counterparts.

The agency also recorded the number of Aboriginal female homicide victims between 1980 and 2014. It counted 1,073 in that time, accounting for 16 percent of all female victims (not including the number of missing Indigenous women).

The findings by a national statistical agency confirm what some have been saying for years: that an alarmingly disproportionate number of murder victims are Aboriginal.

"This is helpful and important because it confirms exactly what we've been saying," said Dawn Lavell-Harvard, president of the Native Women's Association of Canada, which has spent years collecting data and raising awareness on missing and murdered Aboriginal women.

"Until recently, people have said this is anecdotal, or there's no hard data to prove your accusations. This is important because our work has often been discounted as not valid. There is no way this can be ignored."

Indigenous Women at Higher Risk of Violent Victimization

A *Globe and Mail* investigation revealed this week that Indigenous women in Canada are about seven times more likely than non-Indigenous women to be slain by serial killers. Indigenous women are also at a far higher risk of violent victimization, a separate Statscan release on Monday showed. Aboriginal women had a rate of 115 sexual assaults per 1,000 women in 2014, more than triple the rate of non-Aboriginal women.

During a Parliament Hill rally on November 3, 2015, participants laid red dresses on the Peace Tower steps. The dresses symbolized missing, murdered, and abused Indigenous women in Canada, and the ralliers' ongoing fight for justice.

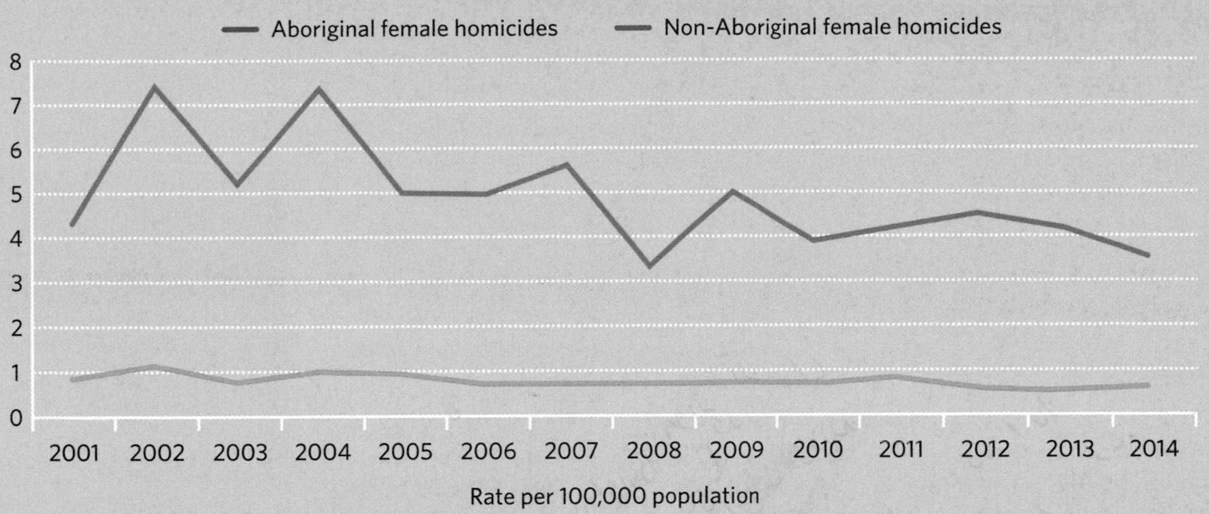

Source: Miladinovic, Zoran and Leah Mulligan. (2014). Homicide in Canada, 2014. *Juristat.* Canadian Centre for Justice Statistics.

National Inquiry into Missing and Murdered Indigenous Girls and Women

The release comes after a 2014 RCMP report, which found that 1,181 Aboriginal women were killed or went missing between 1980 and 2012. An update this year counted another 32 homicides of Indigenous women in RCMP jurisdictions during the previous two years.

The federal Liberal government plans to launch a national inquiry into missing and murdered Indigenous women in Canada by the summer [2016].

Statscan has been working with the RCMP to improve data quality on murdered Aboriginal women amid a growing public focus on the issue. As well, as of last year [2014], police services in Canada began reporting Aboriginal identity of all victims and accused people to the statistical agency. Statscan said it will continue to collect this data, adding that beginning next year [2016], it will also start tracking whether the victim was reported as missing to police prior to the homicide.

"In response to increasing efforts in Canada to address societal concerns regarding the prevalence of missing and murdered Aboriginal girls and women, the policing community has amended their policies which prevented the reporting of Aboriginal identity of victims and persons accused of homicide to [Statscan's] homicide survey," the agency said in an email.

The RCMP said they no longer plan to release annual stats on missing and murdered Aboriginal women. The data collected so far "provide us with enough information and insights on the issue of missing and murdered Aboriginal women to guide our investigations and prevention efforts," it said in an email to *The Globe*.

Aboriginal women account for a growing share of female homicide victims in Canada—21 percent last year, compared with 14 percent in 1991. That increase is because the number of Indigenous victims has held steady, while it has been falling among non-Aboriginal female victims since 1991.

This is the first time the agency has completed police-reported data on Aboriginal identity of victims and those accused of homicide. The 2014 homicide data show Aboriginal people are "over-represented as victims and persons accused of homicide," the agency said.

It found almost a third of people accused of these crimes last year were Aboriginal. The rate of Aboriginal people accused was ten times higher than the rate for non-Indigenous people.

The elevated rates of violence reflect complex and long-standing systemic problems that include poverty, racism and discrimination in the justice system, noted Dr. Lavell-Harvard.

Among provinces, the rate of homicides involving Aboriginal victims was highest in Manitoba, followed by Alberta, and lowest in Québec. For the population as a whole, there were four more homicides in 2014 than a year earlier. The homicide rate, however, was stable, which meant 2013 and 2014 tallied the lowest homicide rates since 1966. Among the total population, Manitoba had the highest homicide rate in Canada for the eighth straight year, though it saw a decline last year.

Among cities, Thunder Bay, in northern Ontario, had the highest homicide rate in Canada—nearly three times that of Winnipeg, which recorded the second-highest level in the country.

- *Source:* Grant, Tavia. (2015). Indigenous people six times more likely to be murder victims: Statscan. *The Globe and Mail* (November 25).

Attempts to Address Historic Trauma

Indigenous researchers have put forth the theory of "historic trauma" to describe the consequences of numerous stressors experienced by whole communities over generations, such as the trauma caused by residential schools in Canada. The theory argues that such traumatic events (and adaptive or maladaptive responses to it) eventually become imbedded in the shared memories of Indigenous communities and are passed on to successive generations through storytelling, community interaction and communication, and patterns of parenting.

The **Royal Commission on Aboriginal Peoples (RCAP)** of 1996 brought together six years of research and public consultation on Aboriginal issues (Canada, 1996). It was the most comprehensive distillation of such material ever published, and provided a factual basis for beginning to address the historic trauma inflicted on Canada's Indigenous peoples. Among other issues, the report examined the need for Indigenous peoples to heal from the consequences of domination, displacement, and assimilation. The RCAP concluded that the relationship between Aboriginal and non-Aboriginal peoples for the last 400 years has been built on "false premises": government policies, which were always presented as beneficial, have invariably resulted in harm. The foundation for a renewed relationship, according to the RCAP, involves recognizing Aboriginal nations as political entities. Unfortunately, many of the commission's recommendations were never implemented.

Records of Resilience

The newly opened National Centre for Truth and Reconciliation (NCTR) at the University of Manitoba preserves a vast collection of documents, oral history, and other records that detail the systematic and intentional attempt to assimilate the Indigenous peoples of Canada.

The Centre also contains incredible accounts of strength and resilience in the form of rich and dynamic stories from Indigenous cultures that resisted every attempt to eliminate them from the Canadian landscape.

The Indian Residential Schools Settlement Agreement

In 2007, another effort to address historic trauma was implemented. The settlement package between the Government of Canada, various Churches, and Canada's Aboriginal peoples, called the **Indian Residential Schools Settlement Agreement (IRSSA)**, is the largest class-action settlement in Canadian history. The agreement includes the following:

- A Common Experience Payment for all eligible former students of a recognized Indian Residential School, based on the number of years of residency ($10,000 for the first school year or portion thereof and $3,000 for each subsequent year)
- An Independent Assessment Process for claims of sexual and serious physical abuse;
- The Truth and Reconciliation Commission
- Commemoration Activities
- Measures to support healing, such as the Indian Residential Schools Resolution Health Support Program and an endowment to the Aboriginal Healing Foundation

To achieve resolution regarding the residential schools experience, the Aboriginal Healing Foundation proposed that four components were necessary:

- **Acknowledgement.** Naming the harmful acts and admitting that the acts were wrong.
- **Redress.** Taking action to compensate for the harms inflicted.
- **Healing.** Restoring physical, mental, social/emotional, and spiritual balance in individuals, families, communities, and nations.
- **Reconciliation.** Accepting one another following injurious acts or periods of conflict and developing mutual trust. Perpetrators ask for, and victims offer, forgiveness as they acknowledge and accept the past and recognize one another's humanity (Castellano, Archibald, and DeGagné, 2008: 385).

In 2008, the federal government formally apologized to Indigenous peoples for the residential school system.

The Truth and Reconciliation Commission

Following the announcement of the IRSSA, the newly-established **Truth and Reconciliation Commission (TRC)** spent six years travelling across Canada hearing from Indigenous persons who had been taken from their families as children and placed in residential schools. The TRC's mandate was to create an accurate historic record about residential schools and their impact on former students, and then share this record with the public. Once the truth had been determined, the process of reconciliation could begin. In other words, "Now that we know about residential schools and their legacy, what do we do about it?"

The TRC's final report was released in December 2015 and included 94 "calls to action": sweeping changes to child welfare, education, and health-care systems; recognition of Indigenous language and cultural rights; an inquiry into missing and murdered Indigenous women; and changes to public institutions to give greater recognition and visibility to Indigenous sovereignty and histories. In fact, one of the report's main messages is that

> too many Canadians know little or nothing about the deep historical roots of these conflicts. This lack of historical knowledge has serious consequences... In government circles, it makes for poor public policy decisions. In the public realm, it reinforces racist attitudes and fuels civic distrust between Aboriginal peoples and other Canadians (TRC, 2015: 8).

In 2015, Prime Minister Justin Trudeau promised to implement all 94 of the TRC's recommendations. This will require collaboration between provincial and federal governments, as well as a quick and efficient response by public institutions (McSheffrey, 2015). But it is a second chance to address the historic trauma caused by residential schools and to work toward reconciliation among former students, their families and communities, and all Canadians.

Lorna Standingready (left) was one of several residential school survivors in attendance at the closing ceremony of the Indian Residential Schools Truth and Reconciliation Commission in Ottawa in 2015.

Touchstones of Hope
Reconciliation in child welfare services

Re-Visioning Social Work Values and Services Related to Aboriginal Children

For thousands of years, Indigenous communities successfully used traditional systems of care to ensure the safety and well-being of their children. Instead of affirming these Indigenous systems of care, child welfare systems disregarded them and imposed a new way of ensuring child safety for Indigenous children and youth, which has not been successful.

Indigenous children and youth continue to be removed from their families and communities at disproportionate rates. In 2005, Indigenous and non-Indigenous leaders came together to develop principles to guide the re-visioning of child welfare services for Aboriginal children in Canada, Australia, and the United States.

Using the analogy of a journey down a river, the profession courageously reached within itself to look at what aspects of child welfare worked for, and against, the well-being of Indigenous children and youth.

The Four Steps of Reconciliation in Child Welfare

The Touchstones of Hope is a movement based on a set of powerful principles to guide a reconciliation process for those involved in Indigenous child welfare activities. It includes:

(1) Truth Telling

Begins with a full and truthful accounting of child welfare respecting Indigenous children, youth, and families. This would include identifying past and current harms experienced by Indigenous children, families, and communities, and must be told from both non-Indigenous and Indigenous perspectives. Truth telling gives voice to, and recognizes, past harm, obliges it to be heard, and sets the scene for restoration.

Requires non-Indigenous and Indigenous peoples to acknowledge and accept responsibility for redressing the wrongs done to Indigenous children, youth, families, and communities, regardless of their degree of direct involvement.

Touchstones of Hope lays out steps for hosting sessions to build a community-specific vision of healthy children. The Tool Kit includes culturally appropriate supports for all participants and celebrations. Elders are important participants in the visioning process.

Reconciliation in Child Welfare: Touchstones of Hope for Indigenous Children, Youth, and Families. Ottawa: First Nations Child & Family Caring Society of Canada.

(2) Acknowledging

Recognizes that child welfare practices imposed on Indigenous peoples, and the values that guided them, are not the right or best path to continue to follow.

- Affirms the child welfare practices of Indigenous people, and the values that guide them.
- Adopts equality, fairness, and balance as essential guidelines to child welfare.
- Respects the intrinsic right of Indigenous peoples to define their own cultural identity.
- Brings alive a new understanding about child welfare between Indigenous and non-Indigenous peoples.
- Asserts that Indigenous and non-Indigenous peoples can follow a new path in the future—a path that reflects learning from the past and a renewed sense of mutual respect.

(3) Restoring

- Provides an opportunity for those who have done past harm to work in a respectful and trustworthy way with those who have experienced the harm to design and implement earnest steps to redress past harms and set frameworks in place to prevent their recurrence.
- Involves an ongoing process whereby Indigenous and non-Indigenous people take mutual responsibility for child welfare and its outcomes.
- Guards against the human tendency to revert to past practices when something new becomes difficult or uncertain.
- Builds personal and community capacity for addressing past wrongs and current child welfare problems, and for promoting child and youth well-being.

(4) Relating

- Recognizes that reconciliation is not a one-time event or pronouncement but rather an investment in a new way of being and a relationship to achieve a broader goal: a child welfare system that supports the safety and well-being of Indigenous children and youth.
- Requires Indigenous and non-Indigenous people to work jointly to implement a set of core values, a vision, and a structure for best practice.
- Commits professionals and others to continue the journey of reconciliation—especially when energy and focus are diverted elsewhere.

Notably, the Touchstones of Hope process is also transferable across a variety of areas, including health care, education, research, and knowledge sharing in various contexts.

Reconciliation in Child Welfare: Guiding Principles

Five key principles must guide the process of reconciliation. They are essential to set in play a basis for a respectful and meaningful relationship between Indigenous and non-Indigenous peoples working in child welfare.

Self-Determination

- Indigenous peoples are in the best position to make decisions that affect Indigenous children, youth, families, and communities.
- Indigenous peoples are in the best position to lead the development of child welfare laws, policies, research, and practice that affects their communities.

Holistic Approach

- Child welfare approaches that reflect the reality of the whole child preserve the continuity of relationships and recognize the child is shaped by her/his culture, environment, social relationships, and specific abilities and traits.
- Effective child welfare services take a lifelong approach, and give due consideration to both the short- and long-term impacts of interventions.

Culture and Language

- Culture is ingrained in all child welfare theory, research, policy, and practice. There is no culturally neutral practice or practitioner.
- Language is the essence of culture, and child welfare knowledge, policy, and practice are most relevant when expressed in the language of the community served.

Structural Interventions

- Consistent with the United Nations Convention on the Rights of the Child, child welfare providers should not remove children or youth from their homes due to poverty. Impoverished families must be provided with the economic and social supports necessary to safely care for their children and youth.
- Social workers must learn to differentiate between structural risks and family risks to a child or youth, and develop meaningful responses to both.

Non-Discrimination

- Indigenous peoples are entitled to equal access to child welfare resources that are responsive to their needs, and the unique cultural context of their experience.
- Indigenous ways of knowledge must be given full credence when child welfare work is carried out with Indigenous children, youth, and their families.

Toward Indigenous Self-Government and Protection of Rights

Indigenous peoples across Canada are finding their own voice and, with that, pursuing the goal of establishing political, financial, and moral control over their lives. A dialogue and partnership with the rest of Canada in addressing the issues facing their communities is slowly evolving, whether those communities are on traditional lands or within urban centres.

Perhaps most important in this process is the reaffirmation of Indigenous rights to land, rights that are inextricably linked to the principle of **Indigenous self-government**. Such an affirmation is one of the key recommendations of the Truth and Reconciliation Commission and the foremost demand of Indigenous leaders. Indigenous peoples are seeking the formal recognition of rights that already exist, rights that existed prior to the European incursions.

An important factor today is the tenacious resistance on the part of Indigenous peoples, over a very long period of time, to all efforts to eradicate both them and their distinct ways of living. Also important are Indigenous economic development initiatives, the resurgence of Indigenous languages, the establishment of Indigenous education with a culturally based curriculum, the development of working models of Indigenous justice systems, and Indigenous control of social services that are no longer based exclusively on the mainstream social work model but are increasingly integrating an Indigenous approach to social work practice. All these developments create a path that will allow Indigenous people their rightful place in Canadian society.

The resurgence of Indigenous political activism that began in the 1970s has helped advance this process of redefinition. It has led to the development of several national organizations representing and uniting distinct constituent groups. Among these organizations are: (1) the Assembly of First Nations, which represents First Nations in Canada; (2) the Inuit Tapiriit Kanatami, representing Canada's Inuit population; (3) the Métis National Council; (4) the Congress of Aboriginal Peoples, representing off-reserve Aboriginal peoples; and (5) the Native Women's Association of Canada. These organizations are generally affiliated with provincial/territorial and local groups that lobby the Canadian government to develop policies to protect the rights and interests of Indigenous peoples—rights guaranteed in section 35 of the *Canadian Charter of Rights and Freedoms*. They also seek to educate governments and Canadians about the issues facing Indigenous peoples.

The Assembly of First Nations

The Assembly of First Nations (AFN) was founded in 1982. It is the national organization representing First Nations in Canada, advocating for treaty rights, economic development, education, languages and literacy, health, housing, social development, justice, taxation, land claims, and the environment.

The AFN is made up of elected Chiefs who meet annually and who elect a National Chief every three years. The AFN is funded mainly by Indigenous and Northern Affairs Canada.

Idle No More: A Grassroots Protest Movement

In addition to national organizations, grassroots movements strive to uphold Indigenous rights. One such movement is Idle No More, an ongoing protest movement founded in December 2012. It comprises the First Nations, Métis, and Inuit peoples and their non-Indigenous supporters in Canada, and to a lesser extent, internationally. It began in November, 2012, when three First Nations women and one non-Native ally in Saskatchewan—Nina Wilson, Sheelah Mclean, Sylvia McAdam, and Jessica Gordon—held the first community teach-in about proposed omnibus federal legislation, Bill C-45. This bill threatened protection of water and forests and proposed the leasing of First Nations territory—which protesters perceived to be in the interests of the Northern Gateway pipeline project. Idle No More has involved a number of political actions worldwide, inspired in part by the liquid diet hunger strike of former Attawapiskat (First Nations) Chief Theresa Spence and further coordinated via social media. While round dances in malls, marches, hunger fasts on Victoria Island, and calls for resistance to fast-tracked omnibus legislation have subsided, there is now more collective action led by Indigenous grassroots peoples throughout Canada than ever before.

Aboriginal Education
Reconciliation begins by closing the gap

Canadians have been called upon to contribute to a process of reconciliation with Aboriginal peoples. Increasing graduation rates for First Nations, Inuit, and Métis students at the postsecondary level is an important part of the challenge. This is a human rights imperative, and—as census evidence shows—a "no-brainer" policy priority for governments and post-secondary institutions.

Less than 50 percent of Aboriginal peoples aged 25 to 64 without a high-school education are employed. For Aboriginal high-school graduates, employment levels rise to 67 percent, to 75 percent for college graduates, and to 84 percent for those with bachelor's degrees. The employment rate for non-Aboriginal Canadians with a bachelor's degree? 83 percent. Gap, and case, closed.

Income results are similarly striking. Aboriginal peoples with a high-school certificate earn on average $36,000 per year. Those holding a bachelor's degree average $55,000 a year, while those with a master's degree average $67,000, rising to $71,000 for those with a Ph.D.

Put simply, post-secondary education (PSE) matters for addressing income inequality and fulfilling economic potential for Aboriginal Canadians, making all of Canada better off.

But despite growing numbers of First Nations, Inuit, and Métis university graduates, the gap with the rest of the population continues to grow. Only eight percent of Aboriginal adults aged 25 to 64 have a university degree, while that figure is 23 percent for the rest of the population.

We must build Aboriginal students' high-school graduation rates, ensuring effective financial, social, and cultural supports at the elementary and secondary levels, as well as supports for the transition to PSE. The level of federal funding to support Aboriginal students attending post-secondary institutions has increased only two percent a year since 1996—while tuition and the cost of living have been rising faster. And there are more Aboriginal students to support because of growth in the Aboriginal population. The cap on government resources must be lifted.

But the challenge and promise of reconciliation for the post-secondary sector is not just about enabling more Aboriginal students to graduate. A comprehensive approach is required, including taking responsibility for past actions and fundamentally challenging our institutions and practices to create possibilities for healthier relationships.

Curricula, programs, and the full range of university services must better promote and respect Indigenous knowledge, experiences, and world views so all students may learn and benefit from exchange and understanding. University faculties, administrative staff, and governance structures must evolve to better support participation and leadership by Aboriginal scholars and traditional knowledge holders.

Encouragingly, a growing number of universities and colleges across Canada are stepping up to the plate. The University of Saskatchewan, for example, has committed to rigorous programs for Aboriginal student success, inclusion of Indigenous knowledge and experience in curricular offerings, and intercultural engagement among faculty, staff, and students. The University of Manitoba has issued a formal apology to residential school survivors and established the National Centre for Truth and Reconciliation.

Fundamentally, as a sector, we must listen, talk, and listen some more. Dialogue and interaction between Aboriginal and non-Aboriginal students, faculty, and community members must underpin the co-creation of new futures.

- *Source:* Toope, Stephen. (2015). Reconciliation begins by closing the graduation gap. *The Globe and Mail* (August 31).

The University of Saskatchewan brings first-year Indigenous students to campus ahead of time for orientation.

Advocacy and Alliances
Healing and strengthening relationships

Government, school boards, and universities need to make reconciliation a priority

Many non-Indigenous social workers want to know how they can help advocate for Indigenous children, youth, and communities. There is no easy answer to this question because so many of the past attempts made to "help" Indigenous children and families have had disastrous results. The Truth and Reconciliation Commission (TRC) recommends that before entering the profession, social workers gain a thorough knowledge of residential schools and other ways in which Indigenous people have been—and continue to be—subjected to unfair government policies and programs (TRC, 2015).

It is also important to be aware of the current issues facing Indigenous communities. For example, Census 2006 data indicate that the First Nations unemployment rate was nearly three times the rate for non-Aboriginal people (18 versus 6.3 percent). It also shows that the median income was much lower for First Nations people than for non-Aboriginal people: in 2006, the median income for First Nations people was $14,477, but $25,955 for non-Aboriginal people. In reserve communities, the discrepancies were even more noticeable: the unemployment rate in 2006 was 25 percent, and the median income was only $11,223 (Statistics Canada, 2006).

In addition, First Nations peoples on reserve are four times more likely than non-Aboriginal people to live in a home needing major repairs (28 versus 7 percent). Many families live in unhealthy and crowded conditions, without basic resources such as clean drinking water or working toilets and sewage systems. Residents are thus exposed to infectious molds, bacteria, accidental injury, emotional stress, and health problems such as asthma, bronchitis, and tuberculosis (Allan and Smylie, 2015; Office of the Auditor General of Canada, 2008).

The fact is that poverty on reserves and in northern Inuit communities is not an individual problem. The living conditions are beyond the control of local leadership because access to funding and other resources necessary to make improvements is complicated by the existence of various government jurisdictions. For example, the provisions in the Indian Act make the federal government responsible for First Nations housing and infrastructure, including health care, but provincial governments are responsible for social assistance and other social services. Without a good system of coordination, projects to improve quality of life can often only be implemented in a piecemeal fashion (Allan and Smylie, 2015).

Advocacy Initiatives

Several advocacy initiatives have aimed to address the systemic factors that undermine the health and well-being of Indigenous families. One recent success is the 2016 Canadian Human Rights Tribunal ruling that the federal government has been discriminating against First Nations on reserve by supporting unfair funding models for child welfare services. For more information, visit the First Nations Child and Family Caring Society website (www.fncaringsociety.com).

Another example of advocacy work is an initiative by the Ontario Office of the Provincial Advocate for Children and Youth. With the support of First Nations leadership and federal and provincial members of the Intergovernmental Network, the Office brought together youth from 62 First Nations communities for five days in 2013 to discuss issues of concern (Office of the Provincial Advocate for Children and Youth, 2014).

Five of the youth wrote and implemented an action plan that stemmed from this meeting. They identified several themes to work on, including the impacts of residential schools, culture and identity, quality of education, suicide, youth opportunity and leadership, and sustainable funding (ibid.).

Indigenous communities have also done a great deal of work to advocate for culturally appropriate healing interventions. The Aboriginal Healing Foundation (AHF) worked with communities and other stakeholders from 1998 to 2014 to develop evidenced-based programming and frameworks that would address intergenerational traumas; "healing, in Aboriginal terms, refers to personal and societal recovery from the lasting effects of oppression and systemic racism suffered over generations" (Aboriginal Healing Foundation, 2006: 7).

The integration of an Indigenous world view into the planning and integration of activities—as well as the three pillars of legacy education, cultural interventions, and therapeutic healing—are listed as best practices in addressing intergenerational traumas among youth (ibid.).

Forming Alliances Through Reconciliation

To ensure that the Truth and Reconciliation Committee recommendations are implemented on a broad scale, all levels of government, as well as school boards and universities, will need to make reconciliation a priority.

A number of youth organizations have been leading the way by taking on the important role of bringing together Indigenous and non-Indigenous youth, their families, and their communities to discuss the impacts of residential schools and of other practices and policies that have harmed Indigenous communities.

For example, Canada Roots and the Assembly of Seven Generations use group theatre activities such as the "Blanket Exercise" (shown here) to help teach the impacts of colonization. Blankets on the floor represent Canada before the arrival of European explorers and settlers. Participants representing Indigenous peoples begin by moving around on the blankets. While a narrator reads from a script, other participants—representing European newcomers—interact with those standing on the blankets. At the end of the exercise, only a few people remain on the blankets, which have been folded into small bundles and now cover only a fraction of their original area.

The University of Winnipeg and Lakehead University have been the first to make learning about Indigenous histories and cultures a requirement of graduation. Several school boards in Manitoba, Saskatchewan, and Nova Scotia are adopting treaty education as part of their curricula as well.

How Can Social Workers Show Themselves to Be Allies?

In the context of reconciliation, it is important to understand the meaning of the word "allies" and how it relates to improving relationships with Indigenous peoples. The word "allies" has been defined as "people who recognize the unearned privilege they receive from society's patterns of injustice and take responsibility for changing these patterns" (from the Becoming an Ally website).

Respecting Indigenous sovereignty, learning about treaties, questioning and resisting racist stereotypes (including sports team names and mascots), learning about the people who are native to wherever you are, and learning about and supporting Indigenous programs and organizations are just a few of the ways that social workers can show themselves to be allies (Neighbours of the Onondaga Nation).

Working with Urban Indigenous Populations

Many people assume that being Indigenous and urban living do not go together; however, many Indigenous people have lived in cities for generations. According to the 2011 census, 53 percent of Indigenous people (those identifying as First Nations, Métis, or Inuit) now live in Canadian cities. As of 2011, the largest urban Indigenous populations were in Winnipeg and Vancouver with 78, 415 and 52, 375 people respectively identifying as Indigenous (Statistics Canada, 2012; StatsCan, 2005).

The largest survey of urban Indigenous peoples is the **Urban Aboriginal Peoples Study (UAPS-2010)**, in which interviews were conducted with 2,614 individuals aged 18 or older who self-identified as First Nations (Status or non-Status), Métis, or Inuit across ten cities in Canada, including Montréal. This comprehensive study surveyed participants about issues such as place of origin, reasons for moving to urban locations, the importance of culture, and experiences with Indigenous and non-Indigenous service providers in urban locations (Environics Institute, 2010).

Settler Racism in Montréal
A needs assessment survey of urban Indigenous individuals living in Montréal found that most participants were unable to access traditional services in that city, such as having access to Elders and ceremonies. Also, half of the service users were not satisfied with how services in Montréal are administered, and reported feeling that Indigenous peoples were not involved in the management of their health services or treated as partners in their relationship with health-care providers (Montreal Urban Aboriginal Health Committee (MUAHC), 2012).

The UAPS looked at generational differences among participants; Inuit (87 percent) were most likely to be first-generation residents, followed by Status First Nations people (75 percent), Métis (62 percent), and non-Status First Nations people (58 percent). Older people (77 percent of those aged 45 and older) were more likely than younger people (60 percent of those aged 18 to 24 and 64 percent of those aged 25 to 44) to be "first-generation" urban Indigenous peoples (Environics Institute, 2010). Among first-generation urban dwellers, the most frequently cited reasons that participants gave for moving to a city were to be closer to family and to pursue education and employment opportunities (Environics Institute, 2010).

The Development of Urban Indigenous Organizations

Urban Indigenous organizations first emerged as community clubs and then social service organizations in the 1950s. In the 1960s, there were only three "Indian and Métis Friendship Centres," but by 1968, there were 26, and by 2002, there were 117 such organizations. The clubs were said to provide a sense of community, a meeting place, and a more visible Indigenous presence in urban areas (Newhouse and Peters, 2001). In addition to Native Friendship Centres, many cities now have a number of Indigenous-specific cultural and artistic centres, healing centres, health and social service organizations, First Peoples' centres at universities, employment services, and other special initiatives and committees (Environics Institute, 2010; Montréal Urban Aboriginal Health Committee (MUAHC), 2012).

Social work with urban Indigenous populations might look very different depending on how long someone has lived in the city, the degree to which culturally-specific services are important to them, whether they speak an Indigenous language (and whether an interpreter is needed), and to what extent services for Indigenous peoples exist in any given city (Environics Institute, 2010; Fast, 2014; Montgomery, 2003). Some cities have a greater proportion of Indigenous peoples who are first generation, and therefore, so-called "culturally safe" and appropriate services may still be developing. For example, in a report exploring the need for culturally-specific resources for Nisga'a living away from their ancestral lands, Montgomery (2003) traced the development of the Native Friendship Centre movement and commented on some of the potential pitfalls of such a culturally diverse model of service provision for urban Indigenous peoples. He wrote that in 1972, the Canadian government officially recognized the long-term sustainability of Native Friendship Centres and implemented the Native

Migrating Peoples Program. An early evaluation of the Friendship Centres found that they had established a wide base of support among community members and were able to apply their funds creatively (Montgomery, 2003). However, despite the support received for the Centres, Montgomery asserted that due to the "liberal cultural pluralist" model employed by Friendship Centres, other local organizations may feel that they do not need to offer culturally relevant services to urban Indigenous peoples. Furthermore, certain cultural traditions tend to be favoured over others, in all likelihood based on the majority Indigenous culture(s) represented in a specific city. Thus, the relevance of some of the cultural programming or resources may be limited for Indigenous peoples who do not identify with those cultures.

Urban Aboriginal Peoples Study

The Urban Aboriginal Peoples Study is an extensive research study that sought to capture the values, experiences, and aspirations of Aboriginal peoples living in Vancouver, Edmonton, Calgary, Regina, Saskatoon, Winnipeg, Thunder Bay, Toronto, Montréal, Halifax, and Ottawa.

Speaking directly with a representative group of 2,614 First Nations peoples, Métis, and Inuit living in these major Canadian cities, as well as 2,501 non-Aboriginal Canadians, the Environics Institute released a study that offers Canadians a new perspective on their Aboriginal neighbours. Guided by an Advisory Circle, Aboriginal individuals designed the research themes and the methodology, and they executed the main survey.

Urban Peoples and Cultural Identities

The issue of cultural identity is important for all Indigenous peoples, but it may be further complicated when Indigenous individuals live in an urban environment. Early academic discourses on urban Indigenous peoples beginning in the 1940s and 1950s that coincided with increased migration to cities centered on the notion that urban life was incompatible with Indigenous cultures and identities. Migration to cities was seen as a decision to abandon Indigenous identities and assimilate into the mainstream culture. In contrast, a 2011 paper argued that emerging research has found that urban living is not at odds with a retention or emergence of positive Indigenous identities and communities (Peters, 1996, 2011).

Peters (2011) identified four main themes that impact urban Indigenous identities: (1) settler racism, (2) municipal settler colonialism, (3) the onus to search out opportunities to remain culturally connected ,and, (4) the cultural heterogeneity of cities.

Settler racism was defined as both blatant and more subtle forms of discrimination, where white privilege and ways of life were naturalized. For example, Indigenous healing practices were not even considered as options in mainstream health care.

Municipal settler colonialism was seen as a second, related theme in the emerging research on urban Indigenous identities . For example, Newhouse and Peters (2001) argued that research on urban Indigenous peoples often focuses on individuals and neglects the larger urban Indigenous community. Some legislation requires social workers to involve an Indigenous child's community in all decisions concerning placement of children (Sinha et al., 2011). Social workers may need to think more broadly about who makes up someone's community in an urban setting, especially if they have lived in the city for several generations, and they should always ask the family to determine who makes up their own community and support system.

The third theme that Peters found in the literature on urban Indigenous identities was the challenge of having to consciously decide to seek out opportunities to be involved in cultural activities or to be part of an urban community (Frideres, 2008; Lawrence, 2004). This might speak to the assumption that urban Indigenous persons have frequent access to the land or their home communities, when for many, this is neither a financial or logistical reality, especially if family members have been living in the city for several generations (Howard and Proulx, 2011).

The fourth emergent theme in the academic literature on urban Indigenous peoples is the cultural heterogeneity of cities. Tensions between providing culturally specific programs or opportunities and providing spaces where all Indigenous peoples are welcome are sometimes amplified by limited resources (Frideres, 2008; Proulx, 2003). Social workers must keep this in mind when working with Indigenous families.

Social Work and Indigenous Peoples
Redressing past injustices

"You want certainty? Knock at our door and ask our permission."
—Dean Sayers, chief of the Batchewana First Nation of Ojibways

Two factors make it difficult to formulate a comprehensive Indigenous approach to practice. First, the Indigenous peoples of Canada are exceedingly diverse, with many languages, cultures, and traditions, and Indigenous peoples have a variety of healing and helping philosophies and techniques. Second, a legacy of mistrust and animosity exists toward those in the helping professions, including social work. An Indigenous approach to social work needs to be flexible enough to incorporate a variety of healing methods and must avoid repeating the mistakes of the past. It is imperative that the approach is based on the wants of Indigenous peoples and that it gives power to Indigenous communities. Also, social workers must try to find interpreters that speak the same dialect as their clients, and respect a client's right to be served by either Indigenous or non-Indigenous service providers.

An Indigenous approach to social work does not mean that mainstream methods are of no value. Located in St. Albert, Alberta, the Nechi Institute: Centre of Indigenous Learning is a good example of a training organization that incorporates both traditional Indigenous and mainstream standards. Its holistic approach is based on the belief that true physical, mental, emotional, and spiritual healing occurs when an individual is in harmony with his or her environment. It also contends that problems must be understood within the context of history, community setting, personal experience, culture, and the social institutions that have had an influence on the individual.

Four Key Principles

The development of an Indigenous approach to social work practice should be consistent with four key principles:

- the recognition of a distinct Indigenous world view
- the development of consciousness regarding the destructive impact of colonialism on Indigenous peoples
- an emphasis on the importance of cultural knowledge and traditions
- the application of the concept of Indigenous empowerment

These principles need to be practised alongside adherence to a holistic approach, a belief in equity, Aboriginal self-control, and a respect for diversity (Morrissette et al., 1993: 91).

Recognizing a Distinct Indigenous World View

The first principle acknowledges the existence of a distinct Indigenous world view. The First Nations (as well as the Inuit and Métis) of Canada have a particular approach to healing and helping. While Indigenous peoples do not have one single philosophy, there are fundamental differences between non-Indigenous and Indigenous world views. For example, the concept of the circle captured in the Medicine Wheel illustrates the notion of balance prevalent in Indigenous societies, in contrast to the typically linear models of cause and effect common in Western societies.

Understanding the Impact of Colonialism

The second principle involves an analysis of the impact of colonization on Indigenous peoples. Colonizers attempted to subordinate Indigenous peoples and displace traditional spirituality, governance systems, leadership, and knowledge by means of missionaries, residential schools, child welfare, and artificial legal distinctions as set forth in the *Indian Act*. A recognition and analysis of colonialism can assist social workers in framing problems, in recognizing solutions that emphasize self-determination, and in seeing the importance of the reclamation of Indigenous cultures and identities in the social work process.

Even today, social work with Indigenous families is sometimes premised on the Western perception that individuals are members of nuclear families, and that individuals can turn to specialized institutions for problem-specific help. This is not consistent with an Indiegnous perspective. Indigenous peoples often perceive themselves to be members of a family network in which everyone is obliged to contribute resources and support to all community members. The discrepancy between Indigenous ways of helping and conventional social work is even more pronounced when the worker is an outsider. Conventional methods, in which community members turn to outside agencies for help, weaken internal bonds of mutual aid. Indigenous communities might begin to question their ability to help one another as they are unable to contribute to the external social work process that becomes the community's source of help. This fosters dependency and weakens the traditional community bonds of mutual aid.

Cultural Knowledge and Traditions

The third principle of reclaiming Indigenous culture emphasizes an awareness of and reflection on common aspects of culture and identity. By examining Indigenous history, culture, and traditions and dispelling the conventional views of Indigenous reality flowing from colonialism, Indigenous peoples can begin to see the underlying causes of their individual problems. There are differences in the extent to which individuals identify with traditional Indigenous culture and therefore in how much the reclamation of Indigenous culture will assist in social work intervention. Some will adhere to the teachings of Elders and follow traditional ways, while others may not.

Indigenous peoples today are healing from the ravages wreaked upon them by residential schools and the child welfare system, and from the results of the systemic racism and discrimination within Canadian society. They are in the process of redefining themselves in the context of their traditional cultural practices. Traditionally, Indigenous peoples have used some form of the "healing circle" to underpin their approach to healing. The circle captures the important notion that we are all one and that the entire universe is connected.

In many cases, traditional healing techniques and teachings are combined with mainstream methods at healing lodges in Manitoba, Alberta, Saskatchewan, British Columbia, and Québec, where the power of Aboriginal spirituality and traditional teachings are combined with crisis intervention techniques. Holistic healing is the healing of the mind, body, emotions, and spirit. Traditionally, this is done through sweat lodges, fasts, vision quests, herbal medicines, ceremonial healing with the eagle fan and rattles (in which sacred songs and the drum are key components), traditional teachings at the sacred fire, sharing circles, and individualized counselling.

Operated by Corrections Services Canada, the Waseskun Healing Centre located about an hour from Montréal, Québec works closely with different indigenous communities from across Canada, including the northern regions. It offers French and English holistic teachings. These teachings focus on an Indigenous offender's physical, emotional, mental, and spiritual health, to help them regain balance in their lives. Waseskun's overall aim is to empower residents to accept responsibility for their own actions and understand the consequences they have created for themselves, the people they have hurt, their families, and their communities.

Programs follow a community-based and holistic healing philosophy that incorporates both Western and traditional therapeutic approaches. The Centre strongly encourages Indigenous communities to participate in the healing journey and reintegration of their members.

The Principle of Empowerment

In the context of social work practice, the principle of Indigenous empowerment emphasizes the participation of community members in bringing about lasting social change. For example, the Native Women's Association of Canada (NWAC), a not-for-profit aggregate of thirteen Native women's organizations, was founded in 1974 with the collective goal to enhance, promote, and foster the social, economic, cultural, and political well-being of First Nations and Métis women within First Nations, Métis, and Canadian societies.

In the 1990s, when a substance use problem among young people arose within Innu communities in Labrador, leaders asked for help and the federal government spent millions of dollars to try to resolve issues in a Western way—but it didn't work. The tragedy of the Innu Nation of Labrador illustrates how important empowerment is to community healing. Chief Simeon Tshakapesh stressed the need to involve Innu members in finding long-term solutions to the problems of substance use and suicide among their children. He criticized the federal and Newfoundland governments for imposing unsuccessful programs on his community in the past: "We are here today because the solutions didn't work. We will never allow others to control our future."

At its most basic level, the principle of empowerment implies that services must be defined and shaped by those seeking help—and not controlled exclusively by service providers.

Wellness and Healing

Reclaiming traditional paths to holistic health

In urban areas of Canada, a range of medical and mental health services are provided to Aboriginal children, youth, adults, and seniors through universal healthcare programs provided by the provinces. In northern parts of Canada and on-reserve, medical services are funded by Health Canada, although the range of services varies from community to community, depending on remoteness and population. Rarely are health-care services provided in ways that are sensitive to Aboriginal cultures, languages, and ways of healing. And substandard services (e.g, starvation diets in residential schools, boil-water advisories lasting for decades, and other measures to minimize costs) have been well documented.

Aboriginal ways of healing typically follow more holistic methods of restoring wellness to individuals whose physical, emotional, mental, or spiritual health is out of balance. Aboriginal healing aligns with Aboriginal world views, Indigenous knowledge, and traditional roles that have enabled Aboriginal peoples to survive and thrive in their homelands for millennia.

Traditional Aboriginal peoples understand themselves as individual human beings who are connected to the other life forces that share and shape the lands where they reside. Many Aboriginal peoples understand that protocols for fostering good relations—and good health—are found within the teachings of Indigenous knowledge. Arising from traditional protocols, it is not uncommon for Aboriginal peoples to use some form of "healing circle" to underpin their approach to healing. The circle captures the important notion, often forgotten, that all life forces are one and that everything within the entire universe is connected.

Some Aboriginal cultural traditions conceptualize a healing circle in terms of the four sacred directions of North, South, East, and West. The circle and the four sacred directions are symbols of holistic healing that embody the four elements of whole health:

- Spiritual health, including gaining traditional knowledge and exploring the spiritual heritage of human beings in ways that may involve participating in prayer, rituals, and ceremonies
- Mental health, including engaging in formal and informal education processes, gaining knowledge of Aboriginal history and cultural contributions, being able to enact cultural roles, and having meaningful opportunities to demonstrate activities that promote self-determination
- Physical health, including taking steps to keep communities and loved ones safe, understanding the connection between what is ingested and the ability to undertake important functions, and participating in sports-related, recreational, and cultural activities
- Emotional health, including mastering self-discipline, establishing and maintaining good relations, and demonstrating and earning personal respect, especially as it relates to one's own cultural knowledge

Historic Aboriginal social systems that kept communities safe, cared for citizens, and educated children have been rediscovered and reclaimed. Aboriginal ways of healing that cannot be verified by Western scientific methods are also being reclaimed, as the story on spiritual healing illustrates.

Reflecting on the Story

1. Using words or artwork, summarize the Aborginal concept of human health and wellness as it is explained in this story.
2. Have you witnessed or experienced the healing power of a human-animal relationship? Elaborate on your answer.
3. Think of some other possible therapeutic benefits of animal-assisted interventions besides the ones described in this story.

A Story of Spiritual Healing... The power of "helping horses"

Within the cultural traditions of many Indigenous peoples of the Great Plains, the relationship between humans and horses holds much significance.

Many Aboriginal world views do not typically differentiate between energy forces found within the natural world in the same way as mainstream science does; in many cultural teachings, things are either animated with energy or they are not. The flowing currents of tides, winds, and weather patterns hold dynamic power, and because this same energy is contained within plants, it is that power that nourishes us. When we ingest food in the form of grains, roots, or meat, inhale air and the smoke of medicinal plants, and drink water and herbal infusions, the Earth's energy becomes manifest within our bodies and we can be well. Indigenous teachings call upon us to respect this power and uphold the relationships among living things. When we enter into respectful relationships with other beings in our environments—people we know and animals we share our lives with—our spirits and emotions become healthy. Within Western therapeutic methods, the healing power of human-animal interactions has been classified as animal-assisted interventions (Bachi et al., 2012).

One example of the healing power of relationships between human beings and animals can be found in the relationship between some Aboriginal peoples and horses. Horses represent strength, freedom, and an indomitable spirit that cannot be broken. When treated with respect, horses share their gifts with the human beings who seek relationships with them. So strong is this bond that some Aboriginal groups developed unique cultural ceremonies involving horses (e.g., the horse dance and the horse giveaway) as a means of respecting the mutually beneficial relationship that can develop when humans take care of horses, and horses take care of people.

Although the healing power of human-horse relationships has long been recognized among Aboriginal peoples, the phenomenon of equine-assisted learning has only relatively recently received attention from academic researchers. In 2013, a team of researchers from the University of Saskatchewan, the University of Regina, and the University of Calgary produced a study entitled "The Helping Horse: How Equine-Assisted Learning Contributes to the Well-being of First Nations Youth in Treatment for Volatile Substance Abuse" (Adams et al., 2015). This study involved a partnership between the White Buffalo Treatment Centre and the Cartier Equine Learning Centre located north of Prince Albert, Saskatchewan.

Girls from across the country, ranging between 12 and 17 years of age, come to the White Buffalo Treatment Centre because they have been sniffing solvents. They struggle with issues of identity, belonging, and acceptance. "They come to us with certain behaviour and learning challenges," said Ernest Sauve, executive director of the Centre.

A component of their healing journey is working with horses at the Cartier Equine Learning Centre. "The horses provide a real calming effect on the youth," added Sauve. Youth develop healthier relationships with people simply because they have learned to lead and respect the horse. "They have a lot of anger, resentment, and hostility toward themselves, others, and authoritative figures," said Sauve. "But that changes when they start working with a horse."

Principle investigator Colleen Dell, of the University of Saskatchewan, said the horse also helps make youth feel comfortable. "If you and a human go into counseling there will always be a barrier because it is human to human. With the horse that is gone because there is no verbal communication, which is often a barrier," she noted. "A child who has been physically abused only knows unhealthy touch, but a horse can teach you what healthy touching is. A counsellor can't," she added.

Dell said it's also important to recognize the significance of the horse in some First Nations cultures. Incorporating traditional teachings about the horse, she said, will help the teenage girls in their healing. "There is an exchange of spirits," she said. "The youth say they just want to be with the horse."

The research team, in consultation with Elders, organized a ceremonial horse dance to commemorate and bless the beginning of the study. "It gave the program the direction it needed. We honour the spirit of the horse and we honoured the girls in their healing." (Grebinski, 2010).

Animal-assisted interventions incorporate Indigenous traditions and honour the spirits of humans and animals.

Indigenous Social Work in Urban Centres

Decolonializing social work and incorporating traditional practices

As described previously in this book, social work and Indigenous peoples in Canada have had a long and tumultuous history. Deconstruction of Western pedagogies that have driven practice, and acknowledgement that oppression still exists, are vital to the formation of alliances between the social work profession and Indigenous peoples (Tamburro, 2013).

Mental health and substance use issues continue to cause harm to Indigenous populations, and they cannot be addressed from a purely Westernized social work perspective.Historically, the lack of traditional Indigenous practices in mainstream social work has meant that the experiences of Indigenous clients have been neglected. Just as our understanding of mental health and substance use disorders has changed and grown, so too must our understanding of these issues change and grow within an Indigenous cultural context. Social work traces its origins back to Euro-Western beliefs about alleviating social issues within societies. A more flexible, integrative framework will allow the inclusion of practices deriving from non-social work frameworks. Integrating traditional beliefs and customs into social work practice can better address the challenges faced by Indigenous clients. Social work education must reflect a commitment to this evolving framework. By drawing from the perspectives of Elders, teachers, and community members, social work educators can incorporate a revised understanding of the oppression of Indigenous peoples into their everyday practice (Sinclair, 2004).

The experiences of Indigenous individuals living in urban settings often reveal frequent misconceptions, assumptions, discrimination, and racist attitudes directed toward them . The Urban Aboriginal Peoples Study (Environics Institute, 2010) found that 70 percent of Indigenous people living in urban centres felt negatively portrayed by non-Indigenous people. Assumptions on the part of social workers that are fueled by historical racist connotations invalidate the voices and experiences of clients, much to the detriment of their mental health and overall social and personal well-being. Assumptive beliefs—about Indigenous history, culture, and current challenges faced by Indigenous peoples—that are held by social workers and Canadian society at large can impede the recovery of Indigenous clients.

Despite the existence of Indigenous services in urban settings, interaction with non-Indigenous service providers is often unavoidable. Social work practitioners and educators have a responsibility to work with Indigenous communities to challenge colonial pedagogy within Canadian society as well as within day-to-day social work practice.

Storytelling is an especially effective media included in traditional practices, as determined by both Indigenous and non-Indigenous researchers (Davis, 2014). Storytelling can lead to a deeper understanding of a client's own experiences, a dispelling of Westernized notions of barriers confronting indigenous clients, and a rejection of pervasive racist ideologies. Storytelling enhances understanding of past experiences of oppression within a present-day context to help gain helpful insights into current challenges. In Theresa and Sarah's story, a young woman gives voice to the painful aftermath of displacement from a rural to an urban setting by framing her experiences in the form of a personal narrative.

Reflecting on Theresa and Sarah's Story

1. Have you ever held an assumptive belief about a particular group in society? Elaborate on your answer.
2. Which key principles of effective social work practice with Indigenous persons does Derrick uphold?
3. Summarize the benefits of storytelling as a healing practice.

Theresa and Sarah's Story...
Framing experience through narrative

Both Indigenous and non-Indigenous practitioners who work with Indigenous individuals and families living in an urban environment must respectfully refrain from making prior assumptions about their clients' histories and lifestyles.

Theresa is a 52-year-old Indigenous woman who lives in Toronto, having moved there from a reserve in northwestern Ontario. Theresa has a 16-year-old son and a 21-year-old daughter who both reside with her. Theresa's 21-year-old daughter, Sarah, is living with a diagnosis of Bipolar Disorder type I and has struggled with alcohol dependency since adolescence. Sarah has an 18-month-old son, Jonah. Over the past several weeks, Theresa has become worried about Jonah's well-being and has called Native Child and Family Services of Toronto for assistance. The case worker appointed to the family encourages Sarah to seek mental health counselling. Sarah consents to this plan and the case worker sets up an appointment for Sarah with a social worker who will help determine which services Sarah might need.

Sarah's initial meeting with the social worker, Leah, does not go well. At one point, Leah makes unfavourable assumptive remarks about Sarah's family history. Leah alludes to the probability that Sarah had an abusive home life, a family history of alcohol misuse, and drug use within her home. Upon hearing these presumptuous and erroneous remarks, Sarah becomes upset and attempts to explain that her problematic behaviours do not originate from within her family, but rather, were encouraged by her peers. At the same time, Sarah's bipolar disorder symptoms were becoming worse. Leah is not fully convinced of this explanation, however, and persists with her line of questioning into Sarah's presumed family pathology. Sarah becomes angry and abruptly leaves the session, believing that her experiences and feelings of vulnerability have been invalidated.

Theresa learns about this incident from Sarah and encourages her to meet with a different worker. Sarah finally agrees to do so on the condition that Theresa attend the intake session with her. Theresa and Sarah meet with a new social worker, Derrick, who begins the session by explaining that he wishes to establish a mutual contractual agreement based on client-centered practice. Derrick and Sarah agree that discussions revolving around Sarah's mental health and substance use are to be the prime focus of Sarah's sessions with Derrick—and not Sarah's family history.

Derrick begins by asking Sarah to tell him about the current challenges she is facing in her relationships with family, friends, and others in her community. Sarah explains that her issues related to alcohol started within her social circle and not within her family. After moving to Toronto, Sarah began to drink to battle her bipolar symptoms, her feelings of alienation, and the racism she had experienced at school. She explained to Derrick that in the past, counsellors had made invaid assumptions about her substance use—but she is adamant that her dependency issues are not related to her First Nations heritage.

Derrick encourages Sarah to verbalize a narrative of her experiences with mental health challenges and substance use. He explains that her story does not need to follow a linear progression but rather can involve a recounting of her most difficult struggles and how she had managed at times to stabilize herself in ways that were empowering. Sarah narrates her experiences from her own perspective, looking to Theresa for verification of events, dates, and places about which her memory is somewhat unclear. As Sarah tells her story, Derrick engages only to acknowledge and validate Sarah's narrative. Through storytelling, Theresa portrays for Derrick the stresses endured by the whole family after moving to Toronto. Separation from their family, friends, and community while attempting to adjust to life in a large city had proved challenging for everyone.

Since moving to Toronto, the family has felt stigmatized by expressions of assumptive beliefs about First Nations people. Derrick encourages both women to continue to attend counselling sessions together and to feel confident in voicing their own story, rather than having it told to them by others. Derrick recommends various support groups for First Nations families living in the city, and provides a referral to these programs for both Sarah and Theresa. Both women agree to return for further counselling, having been reassured that Derrick will formulate no prior assumptions about them based on stereotypes.

Creating a safe and respectful space in which clients are encouraged to tell their own stories can aid recovery.

Social Work with Remote Populations

Community collaboration for northern well-being

Respectful social work practice in northern regions begins with an appreciation for a community's members; their ways of life, culture, beliefs, and values; and the land that sustains them. While some social work positions in these regions are rotational—involving travel in and out of the community—most Indigenous communities prefer workers to live in, engage with, and become part of the community. Demonstrating a genuine commitment to and respect for the community is central to gaining trust, building relationships, and providing meaningful services.

Many northern communities are small, isolated, and accessible only by long, rough roads, snowmobiles, boats, and/or small planes. This isolation promotes a feeling of community closeness and self-reliance that is not found in large urban centres. For a social worker, however, it can lead to a blurring of personal and professional boundaries: your clients are also your store clerks, neighbours, colleagues, and witnesses to—or even part of—your social life. Furthermore, clients often have interpersonal relationships with each other—both positive and negative—and the social worker may be providing confidential, individual services to more than one member of a social group or may become privy to information about a client by way of gossip, word of mouth, or social media. Finally, social service networks in northern communities are smaller, requiring outside-the-box thinking, flexibility, and collaboration on the part of service providers.

Indigenous communities in northern regions are struggling to achieve holistic wellness in a context of unmet basic needs and current and historic traumas. Approaches to addressing this challenge are multi-faceted and unique to each community. They include political processes for self-government and Indigenous-controlled services; recreational and wellness activities, including sports, sewing, drumming, and singing; and advocacy for the development of infrastructure and employment opportunities. Approaches also include community-building events, such as feasts and celebrations, as well as cultural and land-based programs that include sweat lodges, land-based treatment centres, and hunting/fishing/gathering mentorship activities. Finally, intervention services include counselling, family welfare services, and therapeutic groups, such as support groups and healing circles—all involving many people, from youth to Elders.

Many communities express a desire for partnerships in their efforts to achieve change; they do not want outsiders to "come and fix things for them," but rather to work alongside them, sharing knowledge, resources, and power in action. To become such partners, social workers entering northern communities can begin by engaging with community leaders, such as Elders, local service providers, the Chief, and the band council to learn about the strengths and needs of the community, its activities, services, and programs, and leaders' perceptions of your role. A genuine openness to understanding the perspectives of others, from the outset, is critical to providing meaningful services. Social workers from outside a community must be open to collaborating in the processes of Indigenous empowerment for culturally congruent services and programming.

Programming and services evolve with changing personnel and community needs. Thus, keeping up to date can facilitate appropriate connections for clients. Sustained communication also enables the pooling of resources for optimal programming, such as inter-agency committees and action groups. Programming might include Community Freezer services, youth land-based programs, and detailed case planning for vulnerable individuals. As Mark's story shows, clients are often willing to grant consent for social workers to engage with other services on their behalf.

Reflecting on Mark's Story

1. The lack of adequate infrastructure in northern Indigenous communities negatively affects the social determinants of health (e.g., housing shortages, limited employment opportunities, barriers to education, high food costs). How does this impact Mark's past, present, and future well-being?
2. In what ways does living in a small, isolated community impact the delivery of social services to individuals?

Mark's Story...
Overcoming loss and sustaining hope

Mark, aged 17, is from a small Indigenous community in northern Canada that is accessible only by plane. At the age of eight, Mark was removed from his parents' care due to domestic violence and neglect, compounded by alcohol misuse. He now wishes to live with his parents again.

As there were no foster homes in his community, Mark was placed with a foster family in another town. For the next eight years, he lived in five foster homes in three different communities. Due to high airfares, he saw his parents only once or twice a year. At the age of 16, Mark was legally entitled to terminate child protection services, which he did, and he decided to return to live with his parents. Adjustment to living at home has proved challenging for Mark: his parents are drinking heavily and getting into fights; the only family income is biweekly social assistance payments, often spent on alcohol; and there is rarely food in the home. Nor is there telephone, television, or Internet.

Consistent with Mark's cultural values, his extended family and friends help when they can, but they are struggling themselves. His paternal grandmother provides a home for her daughter and grandchildren and financial support to other family members. Mark often has meals at her house, but since she has only three bedrooms shared by seven people, he spends the night at his friends' houses when his parents are drinking and fighting.

Despite his chaotic home life, Mark usually attends school. He uses marijuana occasionally and smokes cigarettes once in a while, but he has sworn never to drink. Up until last week, he was dating a girl named Alice who was a major support to him. Today, however, Mark finds out that Alice is dating someone new. Distressed by this loss, upset with his parents' continued drinking, and feeling rejected for not having made the school hockey team, Mark posted on Facebook, "everythings wrong lifes not worth it." His aunt saw the posting and called the local health clinic, believing Mark to be suicidal. The RCMP brought Mark into the local health clinic for a suicide assessment.

Jane has lived and worked in the community for a year as one of two mental health social workers at the health clinic. She provides services ranging from crisis intervention to one-on-one counselling to coordinating Elder circles. When Jane meets Mark, she notices his dejected affect, monosyllabic responses, and air of hopelessness and helplessness. Seeking positives, she learns that his closest friends are James and Alex and that his favourite teacher is Mr. Collins. Mark tells Jane that he really likes playing hockey, going hunting, and playing with his younger cousins. Unfortunately, he didn't make the hockey team and he doesn't get to go hunting because his family cannot afford it.

Jane starts thinking about supports available to Mark in his community. These include his family and friends, a community youth support group, youth camping trips that feature cultural activities, outreach services for youth, a youth cooking program, and youth recreational activities. Jane suggests that she and Mark create a plan together, first to help Mark recover a sense of hope and then to address his immediate safety concerns.

After a discussion with Mark, Jane telephones an Indigenous youth worker, who invites Mark to participate in the upcoming youth camping and hunting trip and regular sports nights. Mark agrees to attend if his friends will go, and the youth worker offers to help Mark train for sports teams. Mark also learns that there is a Community Freezer where he can get basic food supplies such as pasta, canned milk, or fish and game. Having a plan to address some basic survival needs helps reduce Mark's anxiety level, and he and Jane then begin to develop an immediate safety plan.

With Mark's consent, Jane invites his grandmother and his aunt to join the discussion. Because his parents are drinking, he will stay with his friend James that night and James's mom will be told of the suicide concerns. The need for a consistent place to stay when his parents are drinking will be discussed at the next appointment. The people Mark identifies as being important supports to him will be invited to this appointment.

Mark's mood improves steadily during the appointment. He has a safe place to stay that night and a follow-up appointment booked for the next day. Jane concludes that Mark is no longer at immediate risk of suicide. To be on the safe side, she checks in with her manager (who is based in a larger city centre) and she consults with the clinic's nurse. James and his mom come to take Mark to their home, and Mark seems much calmer.

Helping young people in remote northern regions involves reaching out to the larger community.

Adolphus Cameron

Accepting responsibility for their own well-being and creating a history book have helped children and families in Adolphus Cameron's community understand their trauma and move forward with their lives.

I am Executive Director for the Wabaseemoong Child Welfare Authority. The province of Ontario mandated Anishinaabe Abinoojii Family Services (AAFS) (http://www.aafs.ca/) and we, in turn, work with AAFS. This arrangement is really a transfer of responsibility back to the community. It is the community that will build its own resources and then transfer that responsibility back to the kids, the parents, and the families. I think this transfer of responsibility brings back to the members of the community the dignity that they've lost [as a result of colonialism, the residential school system, and other past injustices].

For a long time, my goal as a social worker was always "helping, helping, helping" and I forgot that people are not just clients, but that they have responsibilities as well as rights. I learned from my grandkids, by just watching them. When I tried to help them, one of them said, "No, I have to learn!" and I knew he was right. He always found his own way. I thought that his self-sufficiency was great and I started using that example in my work. I knew that people had their own inner strengths and that they had to experience change from within.

So that's the kind of approach I'm taking now. I'm just trying to facilitate. All of our messes come from what I would call prescribed ways of thinking and doing : "This is how you do it, this is how you help," and I'm finding that we follow our processes and it justifies our actions—but it doesn't really build that person or family up. And that's where I'd like to go.

In my present work, I'm doing things in ways that differ from mainstream approaches. We're creating a history book of what it was like before things changed in the community and what happened with the flooding, the mercury, the residential schools, the Children's Aid Society, what was impacted, and who was impacted.

We're finding out that there is a layered effect to the experience of trauma, harm, and injustice. The community members who were affected immediately by trauma understand where their frustrations, resentments, hatred, and anger come from. We're now probably into the fifth or sixth generation of people who have experienced the same unsettling feelings but don't understand why. They don't realize that there was a system before this system came in, and that's what we're trying to revive—the old system that was based on responsibility.

When the Anishinaabe were hunting, there was no competition to see who the best hunter was. What they did was show each other how to become better because each of them relied on one another to feed the community, and each of them had to be as good as they could be. They all supported one another to help each other improve. Their goal was to make each other develop more fully, but it was not for themselves—it was so that others in the community could benefit. I can see something similar when my grandkids take their friends out into the wilderness with them instead of keeping it to themselves.

We had a conference a few days ago. A young man spoke and said, "I really want to go out and relearn all the things that our ancestors had, to go out in a canoe, to have an Elder tell me how to set up camp and what to look for, how to paddle properly, how to look after a fire." He told us, "I was diagnosed with Fetal Alcohol Spectrum Disorder and it's not my fault. But I don't want to be a victim or think of myself as a victim." So some things are getting better, and I think it's partly through young people reclaiming their Indigenous identity.

When I hear my grandkids pick up on an idea and get excited or hear about an idea and disagree with it, there's no holding them back. It's so free and so natural. I think that our younger people will carry that openness, that asking, that wanting to learn forward. It is a life-affirming process.

You have to go back into the past and you have to understand what happened, especially to yourself, as well what happened to our people. You need to understand what has happened to bring about changes, but also how to go back. The spirits are waiting and all the tools that are out there are waiting.

I was told, "You have such a pipe dream. It's so way out there. You're going to give up." That was back in the 1980s when I was talking about reviving our own laws. Now it's 2015 and we're almost there. We've moved toward people talking about reclaiming our laws and actually little bits at a time are bringing them back. My pipe dream is everybody else's pipe dream now.

Chapter 9 Review

Review Questions

1. What bearing does the history of the relationship between Indigenous peoples and the people of Canada have on social work with Indigenous peoples?
2. What were some long-term consequences of the residential school system and the Sixties Scoop for survivors and their families?
3. Describe the goals and guiding principles of the Touchstones of Hope movement.
4. Describe some beneficial initiatives to help close the gap in post-secondary education for Indigenous students.
5. How can social workers become advocates and allies with regard to Indigenous communities?
6. What are four key principles to incorporate into an Indigenous approach to social work practice?
7. Compare and contrast social work with Indigenous peoples in rural communities and in urban settings.

Exploring Social Work

1. Visit www.beststart.org, the Best Start Resource Centre website, and read the 2012 report titled "Why Am I Poor? First Nations Child Poverty in Ontario." In a two-page summary, describe the main contributing factors to First Nations child poverty in Canada's largest province as well as the report's key recommendations for the eradication of child poverty in First Nations communities.
2. The federal government formed the Truth and Reconciliation Commission (TRC) as part of IRSSA. Research the mandate and scope of the TRC and present your results in a three-page paper.
3. On September 13, 2007, the United Nations adopted the Declaration on the Rights of Indigenous Peoples. The Declaration establishes a universal framework of minimum standards, but Canada was one of four nations to reject it at the time. On November 12, 2010, the government of Canada finally formally endorsed the Declaration. However, some observers felt that the government's official statement fell short of actual endorsement. Beginning with the Assembly of First Nations website (www.afn.ca), research this issue and write a two-page paper summarizing your research findings.

Websites

First Nations Child and Family Caring Society of Canada
www.fncfcs.com
FNCFCS is a national non-profit organization founded to provide research, policy, professional development, and networking support in caring for First Nations children, youth, and families. It is the only national organization serving Aboriginal children and families. It championed Jordan's Principle and Shannen's Dream, two of the most widely supported child policies in Canadian history. Using a reconciliation framework that respectfully engages First Nation and non-Aboriginal peoples, the Caring Society provides high-quality resources to support First Nations communities to empower children, youth, and families. The website features news, events, programs, publications, access to the society's online journal, photo exhibitions, recommended reading, links to social media, and more.

National Centre for Truth and Reconciliation (University of Manitoba)
www.umanitoba.ca/nctr
The first stage of the journey of the Truth and Reconciliation Commission of Canada (TRC) is now complete. As of December 18, 2015, the TRC offices are now closed. But the journey of Truth and Reconciliation is far from over. The work of the TRC has now been transferred to the National Centre for Truth and Reconciliation at the University of Manitoba, which provides links to the TRC reports and findings and to resources of interest to students and educators.

Aboriginal Peoples Television Network (APTN)
www.aptn.ca
Founded in 1992 and headquartered in Winnipeg, Aboriginal Peoples Television Network is a Canadian broadcaster and cable television network. APTN airs and produces programs made by, for, and about Aboriginal peoples in Canada or the United States.

CBC Aboriginal
www.cbc.ca/news/aboriginal
Watch, listen, comment, and upload your own local news to this multi-platform website (offering access to TV, radio, live blogs, and more) that focuses on events, politics, and programming related to Aboriginal affairs and communities across Canada.

Racialized Canadians and Immigrants

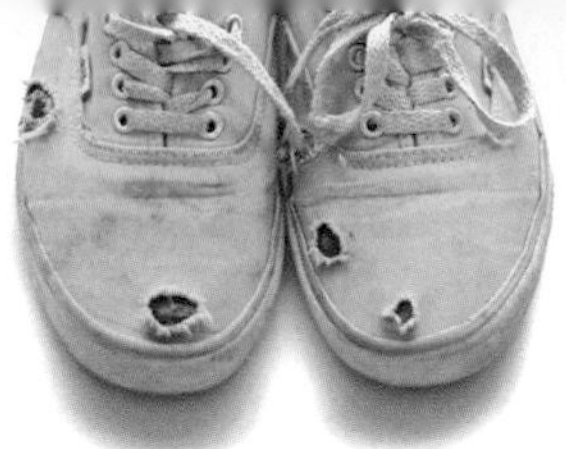

David Este and Christa Sato

Anti-Racist Social Work Practice Today

10

> "Above everything, we are Canadian."
>
> Sir George-Étienne Cartier (1814–1873), Father of Confederation

Canada sees itself as more of
a mosaic than a melting pot.

anada is one of the world's most ethnically diverse nations. It is also a country that tends to be highly accepting of cultural diversity, and the majority of Canadians pride themselves on that fact. Each new wave of immigrants adds to the richness of the Canadian way of life. Immigrants make positive contributions to our nation's economy, and they help to define us. Canada is, as has often been said, a mosaic rather than a melting pot.

Nothing can be taken for granted, however. The formal acceptance of racial and cultural diversity can be contrasted with the fact that many racialized minorities report that they frequently experience discrimination and unfair treatment. Perhaps nowhere was this more evident than during the 2015 federal election when the Conservative Party sought, unsuccessfully, to focus attention on so-called culturally barbaric practices and Muslim women in Canada who chose to wear the niqab.

The challenge ahead is clear. It is not to divide, but to find better ways to help new Canadians settle, raise children, and begin to make their imprint on the Canadian mosaic, free from discrimination of any kind.

In this chapter, you will learn how to...

- describe the history of Canadian immigration policy
- identify the trends in immigration policy that have led to the increasing ethnic and racial diversity in Canadian society
- explain current issues related to the settlement and integration of immigrants and refugees in Canada
- list recent changes in immigration policy that are hampering immigration settlement and integration
- explain the unique barriers to integration encountered by racialized Canadians, including second-generation Canadians
- identify the knowledge and skills that can help social work practitioners provide support for immigrant and racialized individuals and their communities

Key Concepts

- Racism
- Head tax
- Anti-Semitism
- Internment
- Anti-Black racism
- Immigration policy
- Immigration classes
- Racialized minorities/ Racialized groups
- Hate crimes
- Charter of Rights and Freedoms
- Family reunification
- Needs assessment
- Stage-of-Migration Framework

Focusing Question

Canada needs immigrants. They contribute to economic growth and enrich Canadian society in many ways. What can social workers do to welcome newcomers and help them to settle, integrate, and contribute to the Canadian mosaic?

A Brief History of Race Relations in Canada

Most Canadians take great pride in the ethnic and racial diversity of their country. Indeed, in comparison to many other countries, there is much to feel good about. However, we need not look too far back into Canadian history to see that ethnic conflict and racism are not completely foreign to the Canadian experience. Moreover, problems in this area continue to the present day.

Racism persists and even thrives in Canada, according to Lincoln Alexander (1922–2012), a former lieutenant governor of Ontario, former chair of the Canadian Race Relations Foundation, and the first Black member of Parliament:

> As Canadians, we are not doing a very good job. We're not making the grade. We get a failing grade when police officers in Saskatoon drive Aboriginal men to the outskirts of town and leave them in sub-zero temperatures without winter coats. We get a failing grade when 600 Chinese [citizens] arrive by ships off the coast of British Columbia looking for sanctuary in Canada only to be met with fear and even hatred.... We get a failing grade when our schoolyards become a war zone for some visible minority youth because they're bullied on a regular basis, sometimes with fatal results. We get a failing grade when new immigrants, especially non-white immigrants,... subsidize Canada's economy to the tune of 55 billion dollars each year... because skills acquired in their homelands are not recognized in this country (Alexander, 2001).

To begin with, then, let us briefly review the historical background that contributed to this troubling state of affairs. (For an exploration of the tensions between Aboriginal peoples and the dominant white Canadian culture, see Chapter 9.)

Chinese Immigration and the Head Tax

Between 1881 and 1884, some 15,700 Chinese workers were brought to Canada from China to work as contract labourers on the Canadian Pacific Railway (Isajiw, 1999). After its completion, however, a series of laws were put in place to exclude or limit the number of Chinese and South Asian immigrants to Canada: the *Chinese Immigration Act* of 1885; the **head tax** of $50 on Chinese immigrants set in 1885 (raised to $100 in 1901 and to $500 in 1904, an average two-year wage for a Chinese person in Canada); the *Immigration Act* of 1910 (which established "undesirable" classes of immigrants); and the *Chinese Exclusion Act* of 1923 (which admitted to Canada only certain specified classes of Chinese people and almost stopped Chinese immigration completely). William Lyon Mackenzie King, then deputy minister of labour, claimed in 1907 that it was "natural that Canada should remain a white man's country."

The head tax was eliminated in 1923, but other laws, that made it nearly impossible for Chinese men to bring their families to Canada and forced many to be separated from their wives and children for years at a time, remained in place until 1947. In 2000, the Canadian government was faced with a lawsuit by Chinese Canadians demanding compensation for the head tax and other racially motivated measures aimed at limiting immigration from China in the first half of the twentieth century; however, it was unsuccessful.

In 2005, the federal government signed a $2.5 million deal with the National Congress of Chinese Canadians and 14 other Chinese-Canadian groups to set up education projects to commemorate those who had paid the tax. On June 22, 2006, Conservative Prime Minister Stephen Harper formally apologized in Parliament for the head tax.

Racism
The belief that there are human groups with particular (usually physical) characteristics that make them superior or inferior to others. Racist behaviour can be not only overt, such as treating some people according to their race or colour, but also covert, such as society systemically treating groups according to some form of discriminatory judgement.

Head tax
A flat fee that each Chinese immigrant had to pay in order to enter Canada. The tax was levied between 1885 and 1923.

Anti-Semitism

Anti-semitism refers to prejudice against, hatred of, or discrimination against Jews as an ethnic, religious, or racial group. A person who holds such positions is called an anti-Semite.

The history of Canada contains various examples of anti-Semitism on the part of our own government. During World War II, for example, it refused entry to the St. Louis, a ship carrying Jews desperate to be admitted to Canada.

During and immediately after the war, the government was reluctant to admit European Jews as refugees to Canada. When asked how many Jews would be allowed in after the war, a senior immigration official issued his famous reply: "None is too many."

Anti-Semitism is a form of racism, and its beliefs and practices are still widespread today.

Japanese Canadians and Internment

During World War I and World War II, the Canadian government instituted a policy of **internment** of members of ethnic minority groups whom it defined as "enemy aliens." Immigrants from the Austro-Hungarian Empire, with which the Allies were at war, were relocated to prison camps in World War I. For the same reason, Japanese Canadians were uprooted from their homes and held in similar camps during World War II. In both cases, the basic human rights of these minority groups were violated. During World War II, the homes, businesses, and property of Japanese Canadians were confiscated, and their lives were turned on end (Isajiw, 1999).

Many historians claim that the forced eviction of Japanese Canadians from the Pacific Coast in early 1942 was the greatest mass movement in the history of Canada. It was not until 1949, four years after Japan had surrendered, that the majority of displaced Japanese Canadians were allowed to return to British Columbia. By then, most had begun new lives elsewhere in Canada. It took more than four decades, until 1988, for the Canadian government to announce a comprehensive settlement with surviving members of the Japanese wartime community. It also formally apologized. Japanese Canadians and the government announced compensation packages that included $21,000 for each individual directly wronged during this period.

The head tax was meant to discourage Chinese people from entering Canada after the completion of the Canadian Pacific Railway. In this photo, Lee Fum Suey shows his immigration certificate confirming that he paid his head tax.

African Canadians' Experience of Racism

The first account of the presence of Black people in Canada was in 1605. Mathieu da Costa, a Black man, is reported to have been travelling with the French explorers who landed in Nova Scotia (formerly Port Royal) in that year. Later, the French brought Black slaves to Canada. Slavery was officially introduced in Canada by the French in 1628 and was continued by the British until 1833–1834, when it was abolished throughout the British Empire.

The next significant migration was that of the "Black Loyalists," who arrived in Nova Scotia in 1784 following the American War of Independence. Hundreds of Black people who had fought for their freedom on the side of the British against the Americans were brought to Nova Scotia. They were emancipated and were promised education, employment, and citizenship, but were essentially left to fend for themselves. Many were forced back into slavery through abject poverty. The situation forced them to ask the British government in England to send them to Africa, and in the late 1790s, many of them were shipped to the British colony of Sierra Leone. In response to the need for cheap labour, however, the British deceived and brought Maroons (runaway slaves) from Jamaica to work on the fortifications at Citadel Hill in Halifax. The Maroons refused to be controlled as slaves by white Nova Scotians, who used them as forced labourers. Many were also shipped to Sierra Leone (Mensah, 2010; Walker, 1995). Another group of Black people taken to Nova Scotia consisted of refugees from the War of 1812 between Britain and the United States. Most Black Nova Scotians are descendants of these refugees. Between 1820 and 1860, Black people used what is known as the Underground Railroad to escape slavery in the United States. As fugitives, slaves, and freedmen, they formed sizable settlements, particularly in southwestern Ontario and the Maritimes. More recently, immigration from the Caribbean and Africa has accounted for the majority of Black Canadians.

Anti-Black Racism

The existence in Canada of **anti-Black racism**, racism toward Black people, should not be minimized. Canada actively practised slavery until the nineteenth century (Sheppard, 1997). Even the Black Loyalists who entered Canada as free persons were subject to racist policies. Black Canadians were subject to legislation that enforced segregated schools and communities and that limited property rights. In 1939, Canada's highest court found that racial discrimination was legally enforceable (Walker, 1997). Not until 1953–1954 did Canada delete from its statutes discriminatory laws that denied Black citizens the right to pursue formal education, respectable jobs, welfare assistance, and civil and humanitarian rights.

Despite this progress, many reports documenting the continuation of anti-Black racism suggest that much of the behaviour is not a matter of isolated events but is instead a systemic issue. According to Frances Henry, relations between police and the Black community have been "fraught with tensions" (1994). Similar conclusions were reached by the Commission on Systemic Racism in the Ontario Criminal Justice System (1995), which reported that discriminatory practices by police against Black men were widespread.

Many Black persons have shared their experiences of being stopped and questioned by the police while engaging in normal daily activities, such as driving or going to a movie theatre. The expression "driving while Black" emerged to describe this pattern of racial profiling of Black people. As well, James et al. (2010) provide many examples of how police officers in Halifax, Toronto, and Calgary negatively view Black men, which in turn shapes their regular dealings with this group of citizens.

Remembering Africville

Today, Canada is a country that prides itself on its multiculturalism and ethnic diversity. But in the 1960s, a different attitude was evidenced by a community named Africville in the north end of Halifax.

Africville was the result of segregation: not only were its Black residents separated from the white residents of Halifax, but their community was also on the outskirts of town.

To add insult to injury, between 1964 and 1969 Africville was bulldozed for expansion. Houses were demolished, and residents scattered.

In 2010, Halifax mayor Peter Kelly apologized to former residents of Africville and their families, and committed the city to rebuilding the Seaview Baptist United Church, which had been the focal point of Africville. The church now serves as a museum that pays tribute to the community.

Perceptions of Racism

According to new regulations effective January 1, 2017, police must tell people they have a right not to talk with them. Refusing to co-operate with or walking away from police cannot be used as a reason for an officer to elicit information.

However, the activist group Black Lives Matter has protested the fact that police can still gather personal information when a routine traffic stop occurs, when a citizen is being arrested or detained, or when a search warrant is executed.

The Skin I'm In
Combatting racism wherever it appears

"I've been interrogated by police more than 50 times—all because I'm Black"

For the May 2015 issue of *Toronto Life*, Desmond Cole, a writer for *Torontoist*, a project coordinator for City Vote Ontario, and a political commentator, wrote an article that completely shattered the notion of Canadian society as being "colour-blind."

The centrepiece of the article is Cole's exposé of "carding," an overt police practice of stopping people—disproportionately Black people—on the street and collecting information about them. These innocent individuals have committed no crimes. The information gathered by the police is kept in a secret database, presumably for future reference.

The Prevalence of Anti-Black Racism

Cole's exposé addresses a critical question for social workers who work with African Canadians and individuals from diverse racial communities: What is the impact of living in a society where racism and other forms of oppression prevail? Under sustained pressure from residents, community groups, and legal experts, the practice of carding has now been put on "pause," although this was never announced publicly.

As a third-generation African-Canadian male, I was not surprised by the contents of Cole's insightful writing. I have witnessed racism in virtually all sectors of Canadian society, as well as being the recipient myself of both subtle and overt forms of discrimination. Anti-Black racism has roots that date back to when people of African descent first arrived and settled in what eventually became the country of Canada.

Cole presents a consistent theme—that Black people and others experience racial profiling on a regular basis. It is imposed not only by police services but by an array of other major societal institutions as well. He noted in 2013 that 25 percent of the people carded in Toronto were Black. "At the time," he remarks, "I was 17 times more likely than a white person to be carded in Toronto's downtown core."

For Cole, the practice of carding is just one indicator of the systemic bias in Canada's justice system in relation to Black men and other racialized minorities. "Between 2009 and 2013," he states, "fifteen percent of Black male inmates were assigned to maximum security, compared to 10 percent overall." And racial bias is not limited to African Canadians. Today, 25 percent of inmates in federal prisons are of Indigenous descent, and the proportion is much higher for incarcerated females and for inmates in provincial jails.

A Role for Practitioners and Social Work Agencies

Racism and discrimination leave a deep scar on the emotional, psychological, and physical health of those on the receiving end (James et al., 2010). Cole recalls his own family being stopped by a white policeman when he threw an item from his father's car. The officer informed Cole and the rest of the family that they would need to watch their behaviour, as any future infraction could result in being stopped and interrogated by the police at will.

Given the deep, harmful effects of racism (which can be short or long term), social work practitioners have a professional responsibility to combat this type of oppression. At the micro level, they will likely find themselves working with African Canadians who experience this form of trauma.

At the macro level, it is imperative that social workers be in the forefront of advocating that the streets and our workplaces are free from racism and other types of oppression. This includes advocating that the agencies that we, as social workers, work for "walk the talk" and are themselves anti-racist entities, combatting racism wherever and whenever it appears.

- *Source:* David Este, Professor, Faculty of Social Work, University of Calgary, Alberta.

Desmond Cole (right, in orange shirt) puts questions to Chief Mark Saunders (far left) of Toronto Police Services.

Post-1976 Immigration to Canada

As might be expected in a country comprised largely of immigrants and their descendants, ethnic and race relations in Canada have been heavily influenced by **immigration policy**. Prior to 1967, when important new immigration legislation came into force, "nationality" was the main criterion for admission to Canada. Canadian immigration policy was undoubtedly Eurocentric—immigration was encouraged from white Europe and discouraged from the rest of the world. In 1967, new legislation introduced a system of **immigration classes** known as the "point system," whereby prospective immigrants had to qualify based on such criteria as education, work experience, language fluency, and age. "Country of origin" was no longer an explicit criterion in the selection process. The inevitable consequence of the new legislation was a new wave of skilled immigrants from Asia, Africa, and South and Central America.

The shift was dramatic. Prior to 1961, over 90 percent of all immigrants were from Europe, and over half of these were from Northern and Western Europe and the United Kingdom. Immigrants from Asia made up only a small percentage (3.1 percent) of all immigrants arriving in the country. By the 1990s, however, Europeans made up only about one fifth of all immigrants, while the largest number, close to 60 percent, came from Asia. The remaining proportion (16.6 percent) came from Central and South America, the Caribbean and Bermuda, and the United States. In addition, the largest proportion of European immigrants came not from the United Kingdom or Northern and Western Europe, but from Eastern Europe. (See Figure 10.1.)

According to the 2011 National Household Survey (NHS), in that year Canada had about 6,775,800 foreign-born individuals (Statistics Canada, 2011). They represented 26.6 percent of the total population, compared with 19.8 percent in 2006. In 2013, Canada admitted 258,953 permanent residents (Citizenship and Immigration Canada, 2013a). The top three source countries in 2013 were the People's Republic of China, India, and the Philippines. The proportion of the three major immigration classes was as follows: 51.2 percent were economic immigrants (along with their spouse/partner and dependants); 31.6 percent were in the family class; and 11.2 percent were protected persons and others.

"Visible Minorities"—An Outmoded Term

With this shift in immigration came a substantial increase in the so-called visible minority population in Canada. Although this term is still widely used in government circles, it has rightly come under criticism, even by outside organizations such as the United Nations. Many argue that the term "**racialized minorities**" or "**racialized groups**" is preferable, since these terms make clear that race is not a biological concept but a socially constructed one. Furthermore, the term "visible minority" supports a practice whereby non-white groups are categorized almost solely by race, whereas white groups are not.

In 2011, the racialized population in Canada was approximately 6,264,800 (Statistics Canada, 2011), or 19.1 percent of the total population. Of these, 30.9 percent were born in Canada, and 65.1 percent were born outside the country. A small percentage (4 percent) were non-permanent. The three largest racialized groups—South Asians, Chinese, and Blacks—represented 61.3 percent of the racialized population. The vast majority lived in Ontario, British Columbia, Québec, and Alberta. Seven out of ten lived in Toronto, Montréal, or Vancouver.

Statistics Canada projects that by 2017, one half of all racialized minorities in Canada will be South Asian or Chinese and that the size of each group will be around 1.8 million.

Multiculturalism

In 1971, Canada became the first country to adopt multiculturalism as an official policy. The policy aimed to create a more integrated Canadian society by providing our diverse ethnic minority groups with a sense of belonging to Canada.

In 1988, the Multiculturalism Act was passed, restating and reinforcing the 1971 policy and mandating that federal departments ensure equal opportunities in employment for all ethnic and racial groups. In order to implement the policy, the Canadian government created the Multicultural Directorate, which in turn developed a range of programs designed to help it fulfill the policy's objectives.

The Implications of Immigration to Canada

It is anticipated that the racialized population of Canada will continue to rise as a percentage of the total Canadian population. For example, the Black population is expected to reach one million by 2017. The groups that are expected to grow the fastest are the West Asian, Korean, and Arab communities. According to most projections, the size of each of these groups will more than double (Belanger and Malenfant, 2005).

The substantial increase in the racialized population in recent years has already affected public policy (e.g., multiculturalism and anti-racism policy) and will continue to do so. This increase in our ethnic and racial diversity has enriched Canada and the lives of its citizens, and the demographic changes need not result in ethnic and racial conflict. However, other factors, such as a serious downturn in the economy, and policies and institutional procedures that intervene and foster ethnic and racial divisions, may affect the social impact of this underlying demographic change. As a result, social workers and other front-line workers face a new set of issues today. They need to be sensitive to religious and cultural differences within the populations they serve. They also need to deal directly with the damaging effects of discrimination and racism on the personal well-being of their clients.

Immigration classes

Economic class includes skilled workers, business owners, and entrepreneurs.

Family class requires a sponsor to provide economic and personal support for three to ten years.

Refugee class includes individuals who need protection from persecution in their home country.

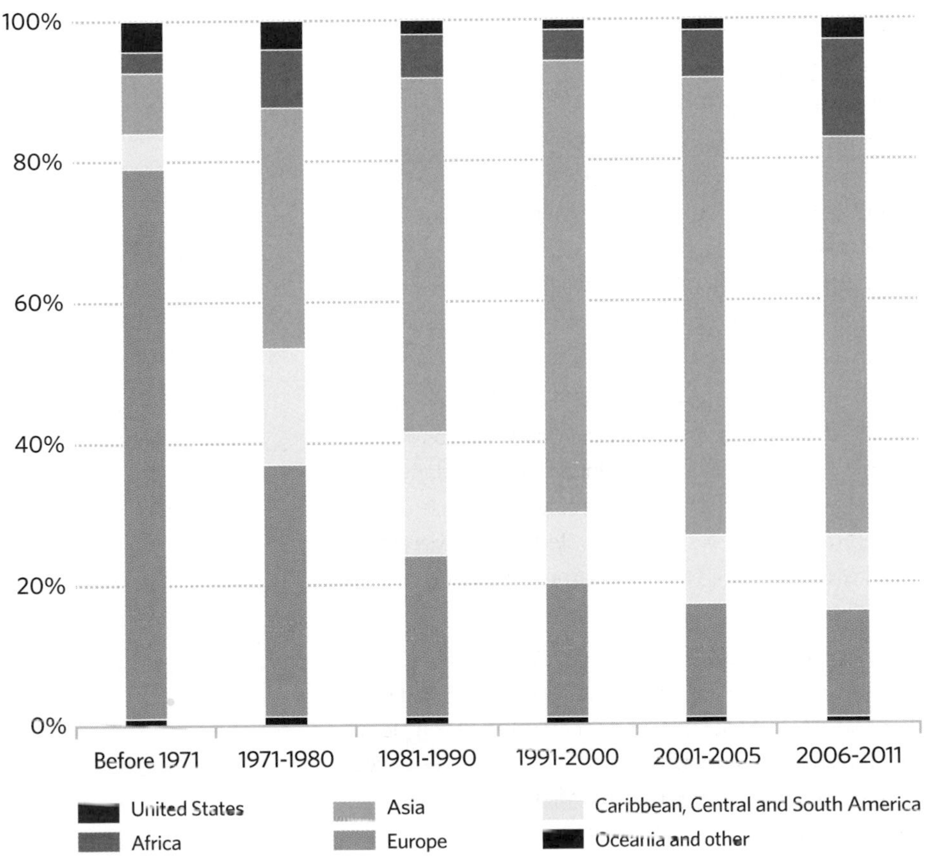

Figure 10.1 There has been a substantial shift in the countries of origin of Canadian immigrants since the introduction of the points system as the basis of immigrant selection in 1967.

Source: Statistics Canada. (2011). *National Household Survey, 2011*. Ottawa.

Combatting Hate Crimes in Canada

When people are the targets of violence because of who they are, or who they are thought to be, they are the victims of **hate crimes**. The promotion of hate based on race, religion, ethnic origin, or sexual orientation is widespread. There is a growing consensus about the need for consistent and firm policy responses from the criminal justice system at all levels.

Canadian Human Rights Legislation

National human rights legislation in Canada began with the passage of the Canadian Bill of Rights in 1960. Later in that decade, provinces enacted similar legislation, and by 1975 all provinces in Canada had human rights codes. In general, both federal and provincial human rights law prohibits the dissemination of hate propaganda and discrimination in all aspects of employment, the leasing and sale of property, public accommodation, services and facilities, and membership in labour unions and professional associations. Grounds of discrimination vary slightly depending on the jurisdiction.

In 1982, the Canadian Bill of Rights was superseded by the *Canadian Charter of Rights and Freedoms*. The Charter guarantees the fundamental freedoms of conscience and religion, thought, belief, opinion and expression (including freedom of the press and other media), and peaceful assembly and association. It guarantees democratic rights, geographical mobility rights, legal rights (including the right to life, liberty, and security of person), and equality rights that protect against "discrimination based on race, national or ethnic origin, colour, religion, sex, age or mental or physical disability." The *Charter* also reinforces official bilingualism in Canada by affirming the equality of the English and French languages and by affirming the rights of children to be educated in either language. It also affirms the multicultural character of Canada and recognizes the rights of Canada's Indigenous peoples. Finally, it emphasizes that all the rights and freedoms are guaranteed equally to male and female persons.

Police-Reported Hate Crimes in Canada

Passing laws is one thing; implementing them is another, however. All the provinces and territories and the federal government have human rights commissions charged with addressing human rights abuses. While these commissions have had some success, they have unfortunately often been hampered by limited resources and case backlogs. Furthermore, since such commissions are by their nature complaints-driven, it is generally felt that many victims of discrimination, perhaps because they are new to the country, do not have the financial resources or even the time to report discrimination and initiate the lengthy complaints process.

Our information on the extent of hate crimes comes only from anecdotal evidence and official police reports. For example, in 2013, the police reported 1,167 criminal incidents that were motivated by hate. Approximately half (51 percent) were motivated by hatred of a race or ethnic group. Another 28 percent were motivated by hatred of religion, and 16 percent were motivated by hatred of an individual's sexual orientation (Allen, 2015). (See Figure 10.2.)

With regard to hate crimes related to race or ethnicity, Black populations were the most frequently targeted (22 percent) in 2013. Of religion-motivated hate crimes, those targeting Jewish populations were the most common (16 percent). Four in ten (40 percent) police-reported hate crimes in 2013 involved violent offences, such as assault, uttering threats, and criminal harassment. Overall, the number of violent hate crimes increased 4 percent from the previous year, driven by increases in common assault and uttering threats.

Islamophobia

From 2010 to 2013, Muslim populations had the highest percentage of female hate-crime victims (47 percent). This may be related to the fact that the practice of wearing head coverings may make religious identity more visible for Muslim women than for men. For example, the National Council of Canadian Muslims noted that a particularly high percentage of attacks against individuals involved Muslim women wearing hijabs (National Council of Canadian Muslims, 2015).

A Role for Social Workers

The federal government demonstrated strong leadership in combatting hate crimes by amending the Criminal Code in 1996 to strengthen sentencing for any offence that is motivated by hate (Bill C-41). The move prompted community discussion, raised overall awareness of the issues, and helped to mobilize communities. It also highlighted the need for stronger responses in cases in which hate-motivated incidents occur and may go unreported.

For their part, front-line social workers are using innovative anti-racist approaches that emphasize community empowerment to combat hate crimes. Since hate crimes do not occur in a vacuum, education and community work can help prevent them and act as an important complement to hate crime laws. Social workers are involved in outreach and consultation, education, and awareness activities and in fostering the creation of advocacy and support groups. In struggling against overt racism of this kind, social workers also work closely with community organizations to promote an anti-racist perspective through education. This may involve producing brochures on anti-racism, going into schools and engaging students on the issues, or speaking out about adverse community conditions and the need for government action on unsatisfactory living conditions.

With their roots firmly in the locality, social workers and other community workers can also provide feedback on what works and what does not. This kind of collaborative, community-based approach to combatting overt racism can go a long way in helping to minimize the extent of hate-crime activity and to strengthen the resolve and solidarity of its victims. Hate-motivated crimes will not go away on their own—they need to be addressed head on, not only by those immediately affected but by all those who oppose such acts.

Hate crimes
Prejudice-motivated crimes, often violent, which occur when a perpetrator targets a victim because of his or her membership (or perceived membership) in a certain social group. Such groups can include but are not limited to: ethnicity, disability, language, nationality, physical appearance, religion, gender identity, or sexual orientation.

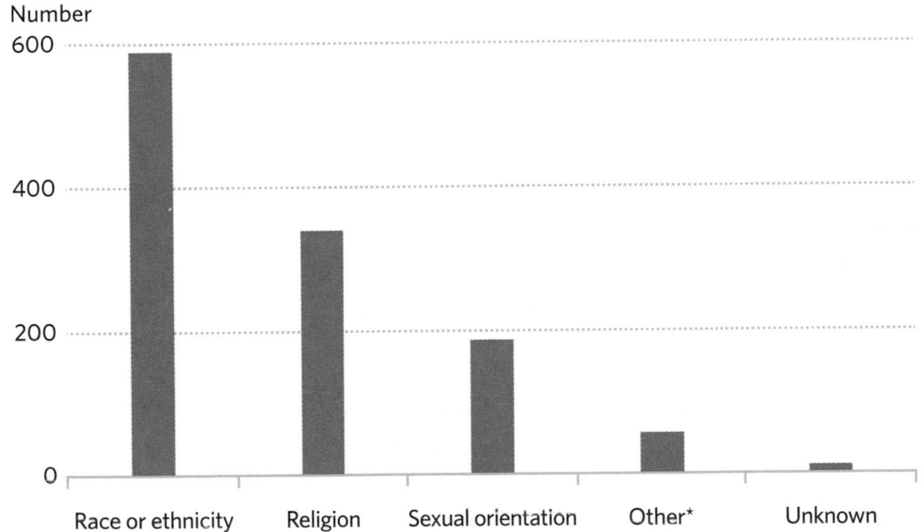

Figure 10.2 Police-reported hate crimes in Canada, by type of motivation. The information in this chart reflects data reported by police services covering 99 percent of the population of Canada.

Source: Allen, Mary. (2015). Police-reported hate crime in Canada, 2013. *Juristat.* Canadian Centre for Justice Statistics, Ottawa.

Current Issues Pertaining to Immigrant Resettlement

Canadian social workers play an indispensable role in the immigrant resettlement process at all levels. They not only provide direct support to the immigrants themselves, but also help create the broader conditions for their successful integration into Canadian society. A strong knowledge of immigration policy and recent shifts in this area is, therefore, essential.

Three issues that have risen to the surface in recent years that are likely to affect directly the kinds of work practitioners do with clients deserve special mention: skills recognition, family reunification backlogs, and Canada's foreign worker program.

Foreign Education and Skills Recognition

Historically, Canada's immigration policy has centred on attracting persons who are highly skilled and highly educated and who ultimately can contribute to the nation's economic growth. Many immigrants make the decision to leave their home countries with aspirations of living the "Canadian Dream," a chance at a better life with more opportunities. Unfortunately, the reality for highly skilled individuals is often closer to a "Canadian Nightmare" because their skills are often neither recognized nor valued. Many have no recourse but to accept lower-skilled, lower-paying jobs. This is known as underemployment. There is, according to Bhandari, Horvath, and To (2006), an underlying problem with an immigration policy that awards points based on education and skills if these skills are not ultimately valued as "Canadian experience." The result is what we see—namely, a lack of recognition of foreign credentials and experience (Guo, 2009; Ngo and Este, 2006; Wayland, 2006).

The lack of consistent, transparent, and fair assessment practices in relation to occupational and academic credentials is consistently identified in the literature as a major stumbling block for immigrants. Racism and other forms of discrimination also play a part—research consistently shows that newcomers often experience both subtle and direct forms of racism (Esses et al., 2007; Guo, 2009; Ighadaro, 2006). In addition, there is often an automatic assumption, not based on fact, that all foreign credentials are not up to Canadian standards and that therefore immigrant professionals must be required to upgrade their education if they want to work in positions that match their education level (Ngo and Este, 2006). That there would be such a problem likely did not even occur to these professionals when they first applied to immigrate to Canada. As a result, many qualified newcomers are not able to contribute fully to the Canadian economy and society, with all the accompanying hardships for them and their families.

What does this mean for the individual social worker? Many immigrant professionals are severely affected emotionally and financially by the lack of recognition of their prior educational achievements and previous work experience. Social workers must be able to provide the necessary information and support services to help guide them through this difficult period. In January 2016, the Government of Canada announced that it would invest $50 million over the next two years to develop a framework to speed up the assessment and recognition of foreign credentials.

Just as important, it is necessary to advocate on behalf of such newcomers—for example, with governments, professional associations, educational institutions, and employers. Such advocacy can address systemic and structural obstacles that prevent immigrant professionals and their families from seeking out jobs for which they are qualified so that they can begin to make a real contribution to Canadian society.

Welcoming New Canadians

Colleges and universities across the country have a long history of welcoming immigrants and refugees, for whom language training and skills upgrading are often a priority as they seek employment in the Canadian job market.

Many colleges and universities work in close partnership with community organizations to help coordinate the various tasks required to welcome newcomers to Canada.

Leveraging these resources will become especially important over the coming years, for example, if we are to ensure the successful integration of large numbers of Syrian refugees into our communities.

Family Reunification Backlogs and Delays

Although parents and grandparents make up only a small portion of immigrants in the family class (six to eight percent of all immigrants), this group continues to be the focus of Canadian policy debates. This is because the processing for **family reunification** is extraordinarily slow.

Family reunification
Under the Immigration and Refugee Protection Act and associated regulations, a Canadian citizen or permanent resident of Canada aged at least 18 is allowed, subject to certain conditions, to sponsor specific members of their immediate family for permanent residence in Canada.

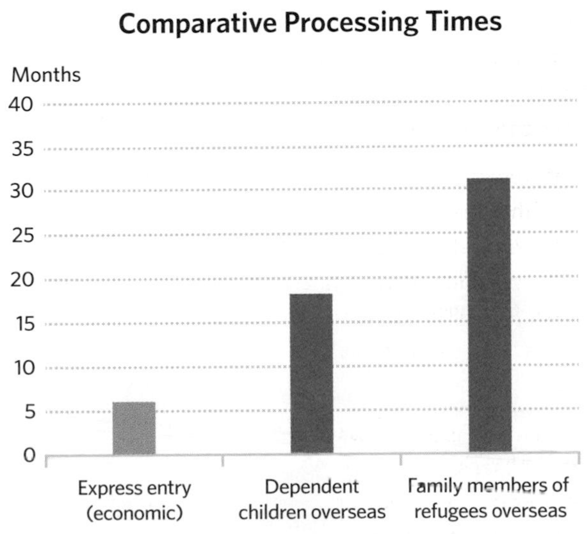

For refugees entering Canada, family reunification delays can be especially stressful:

- Long delays increase risks to family members overseas in conflict zones or refugee camps.
- Living conditions may endanger the health of family members and affect children's education, leading to increased social costs when they finally come to Canada.
- Long separations exact a heavy psychological toll. Prolonged family separation has its most negative impacts on children.

It seems obvious that people with relatives in Canada will be better able to settle here and contribute to Canadian society. Yet many children wait over two years before being able to reunite with their parents in Canada. For refugee families, the wait is 31 months.

Fulfilling an election promise, in early 2016 the new Liberal immigration minister, John McCallum, announced an increase to the number of applications the Canadian government would accept from parents and grandparents who want to immigrate to Canada, from 5,000 to 10,000 per year. However, with over 14,000 applications arriving within the first four days of the program in 2016, raising the cap a little still leaves a lot of disappointed families.

New approaches are definitely called for. For example, Immigration, Refugees and Citizenship Canada, or IRCC (formerly Citizenship and Immigration Canada), introduced an Express Entry program for economic immigrants. For immigrants with a valid job offer, IRCC will process applications within six months. For many professionals working to help immigrants settle in Canada, this has raised the question as to whether families' reunification applications should not be processed at least as quickly as those for economic immigrants, considering the enormous relief it would bring to the applicants themselves and their Canadian families.

Comparative Processing Times

Months
40
35
30
25
20
15
10
5
0

Express entry (economic)
Dependent children overseas
Family members of refugees overseas

Figure 10.3 Comparative processing times (in months) by class for immigrants to Canada.

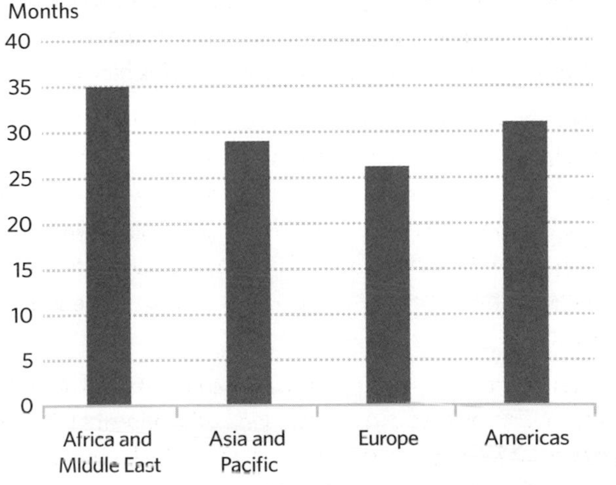

Figure 10.4 Comparative processing times (in months) by region for family members of refugees.

Source: Canadian Council for Refugees. (2015). Data from Immigration, Refugees and Citizenship Canada.

Temporary Foreign Workers in Canada

United, we stand...

Canadians have recently had their attention drawn to serious problems with the Temporary Foreign Workers Program. Time to fix it.

Over the past decade, Canada's immigration program has shifted significantly from permanent to temporary immigration. In 2008, for the first time, the numbers of Temporary Foreign Workers in Canada exceeded the numbers of Permanent Residents admitted. Since then the number of Temporary Foreign Workers has continued to grow.

This shift represents a radical change for Canada: previously, we were a country that welcomed newcomers on a permanent basis, with most becoming citizens. Immigrants have traditionally been understood to be contributing to building the nation and our communities, not simply contributing their labour. A notable exception to that practice, the expulsion of Chinese labourers after the construction of the railway in the nineteenth century, is a source of national shame. Countries that have developed "guest worker" programs, particularly in Europe, have learned by experience the disadvantages, for workers and for society, of relying on the labour of people who are not permitted to integrate into the community, creating a two-tier society.

The large-scale expansion of the Temporary Foreign Worker Program occurred without broad public discussion. Canadians were not given an opportunity to voice their opinions on the shift toward increased temporary migration, even though it represents a major change in Canadian immigration policy.

Low-Skilled versus High-Skilled Workers

The Temporary Foreign Worker Program is made up broadly of two parts. At one end, it provides a convenient way for high-skilled workers to come to Canada: they enjoy certain privileges (such as the right to be accompanied by family) and have avenues to permanent residence should they wish to stay.

At the other end, the program brings in low-skilled workers, who have very limited rights and usually no chance of obtaining permanent status. The workers are temporary (they have to leave after four years) but the labour needs they are filling are often not temporary.

These longer-term labour shortages being filled by Temporary Foreign Workers may be partly caused by the fact that it has been harder for immigrants willing and able to fill those jobs to come to Canada as permanent residents. Economic immigrants are increasingly selected based on advanced educational and professional qualifications.

When Canada identifies needs for workers in "high-skilled" professions, they are recruited with a clear path to permanent residence, but when we need people to work in food services, in greenhouses or on farms, they are recruited on a temporary basis, without the possibility of ever obtaining permanent status. This is discriminatory.

Another cause of this need for Temporary Foreign Workers is the unwillingness of some Canadian employers to pay wages and offer working conditions that would attract Canadian job seekers.

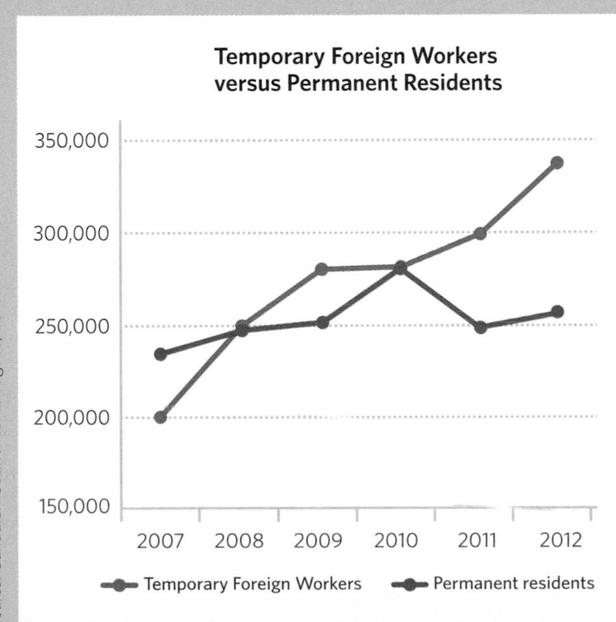

Source: Canadian Council for Refugees, 2015.

Pitted against Canadian Workers

By any account, the current situation is bad for migrant workers and bad for Canadians.

It is extremely unfortunate that Temporary Foreign Workers have too often been presented recently as if pitted against Canadian workers. The current situation should not be blamed on the migrant workers, on Canadian workers or on specific sectors.

At its root, the problem is a structural one.

Because of their temporary status, migrant workers are extremely vulnerable to abuse and exploitation. While many employers treat them fairly, it is easy for others to underpay them, overcharge them for substandard accommodation and expose them to dangerous working conditions.

There are many documented cases of abuse of these workers across the country. It is difficult for people with only temporary status to complain about mistreatment because they may simply be deported. At its most extreme, the exploitation of Temporary Foreign Workers has placed them in situations of human trafficking.

Having workers who are used and then discarded is bad for society as a whole. It is never good for our communities to have two-tier membership, where some people have limited rights and cannot integrate properly or advance themselves.

Our Own History Teaches Us the Benefits of Permanent Immigration

Throughout Canada's history, immigrants have started their lives here at the bottom of the ladder and worked their way into essential roles in our society, building businesses, creating culture, founding institutions, becoming political leaders, and raising families.

How many of us would not be here today if, in the past, immigrants considered "low-skilled" were forced to leave Canada after a few years? We should learn from our history about what works and makes the country strong.

While some things have changed in the labour needs in Canada, it remains true that we need people to work in a whole range of jobs, and that people have much more to offer than just their labour. We can only benefit from those contributions if people have a chance to make their permanent home among us, along with their families.

For more information about Canada's treatment of migrant workers, go to ccrweb.ca/migrant-workers.

- *Source:* Canadian Council for Refugees (2014). *Temporary Foreign Workers: The Broader Context*. Montréal.

Intake and Needs Assessment

Canada's Indigenous peoples were here first, and will always deserve first place, but the subsequent history of Canada is one of immigration. Successive waves of newcomers have come to Canada, settled, raised families, and contributed to Canadian society. Given the ongoing need for immigrants, it is highly likely that social workers, especially those who practise in large urban centres, will work with individuals or families from these communities.

Canadian social work programs, in recent years, have recognized the need to ensure that social work curriculum is complete with content related to newcomer populations, including immigrants, refugees, and temporary foreign workers. This was underlined in the recently revised Canadian Association for Social Work Education's Standards for Accreditation at both the B.S.W. and M.S.W. levels. However, several scholars, such as Herberg (1985) and Yan and Chan (2010), have posed this important question: How well are social workers today prepared for working with newcomers?

Accessing Health Care

In April 2012, the Conservative federal government announced changes to the Interim Federal Health Program, a program in existence since 1957.

All refugees lost access to medication coverage, vision care, and dental care. Those from "Designated Countries" lost all coverage, except in circumstances involving public health or security.

The cutbacks were initially directed at all refugees. After considerable public pressure, only Government Assisted Refugees (GARs) were spared from the cuts.

Assessing Needs and Advocating on Behalf of Newcomers

Effective practice with immigrants begins with a **needs assessment**. This process is continuous, and it is participatory. Essentially, it seeks to understand the client and his/her situation, and sets a framework for how change can be achieved (Coulshed and Orme, 2012).

As in other areas of social work practice, it is critical to gain a thorough understanding of process. A useful tool is Drachman's **Stage-of-Migration Framework**. This framework provides key questions that can be used to guide the assessment process with immigrants and their families. The outcomes of this inquiry process provide social workers (in consultation with the particular service users themselves) with clear guidance in determining the types of intervention that may be required to address prevailing concerns.

It is also imperative for social workers to be knowledgeable about the various kinds of challenges that immigrants experience in their efforts to settle and adapt to life in Canada. Some of these issues include language barriers, underemployment, unfamiliarity with the different systems available to them (such as education, health, and social services), lack of support, role reversals and family conflict, and, for some, making the transition from living in rural environments to large urban centres.

Quite frequently, and understandably, newcomers are simply not aware of what services may be available or which ones they are eligible for when they first arrive. Hence, being informed and being able to provide information, and following up on it with them, is critical when assisting immigrants in settling in and fully intergrating into mainstream Canadian society. Another important role is serving as brokers on behalf of new immigrants. This includes contributing to the development of programs and services that facilitate the settlement process.

Assessing Immigrants' Needs
A Stage-of-Migration Framework

The table below provides some background questions that can help to guide the assessment process with new immigrants and their families. The answers can guide social work practitioners as to the types of intervention that may be required to support these newcomers.

Stage of Migration	Areas of Exploration
Pre-Migration	What were your expectations within your home country? What roles did you play in your family? What socio-economic status did you hold in your country of origin? What was the size of your family? Who constituted your family? Where was your place of residency in your home country? (rural or urban) What level of education did you achieve in your home country? What was your occupation prior to coming to Canada? What was the nature of your employment status? What were your reasons for migrating? What (if any) decisions were made about which family members would migrate and who would stay in your home country? What challenges did you and your family (if applicable) encounter prior to departing? What prompted you to choose Canada as your country of resettlement? What knowledge did you possess about Canada prior to your arrival?
Migration	How did you arrive in Canada? What category were you admitted to? Is this your first place of residency? If not, where did you previously live?
Resettlement	What is your employment status? What type(s) of job(s) are you currently working? What are the dynamics within your family? How would you describe your relationship with your spouse? Children? What are your sources of support? What type of services or supports do you require? What challenges are you facing in settling into Canadian society? What has helped you to resettle into Canadian society? Who has assisted you in getting used to living in Canada? As you adjust to Canadian society, what health concerns (if any) have you encountered? What have been the major cultural changes you have experienced since arriving in Canada? What do you like best about living in Canada?

- *Source:* Adapted from: Drachman, Diane. (1992). A stage-of-migration framework for service to immigrant populations. *Social Work*, 37(1), 68–72.

Canada and the Syrian Refugee Crisis
Let's think big for once

Why Canada should take in many more refugees

The Syrian conflict has triggered the world's largest humanitarian crisis since World War II. In March 2011, civil war began in Syria and has not stopped since. Five years later, Syrians are becoming increasingly vulnerable as their savings are depleted and their assets liquidated. Half of the population is now dependent on humanitarian aid.

Eight million people are displaced within the country and over four million have fled. Shocking images in the media have revealed desperate scenes of families who have lost their loved ones. According to the United Nations Development Programme (UNDP), 75 percent of Syrians were living in poverty, as of March 15, 2015. Of this percentage, 55 percent are unable to access basic food and non-food items for survival. Twenty percent living in active conflict zones face abject poverty and are facing starvation and malnutrition.

The crisis intensified during Canada's 2015 federal election, giving party leaders and Canadians ample opportunities to voice opinions. Some seized the opportunity to try to instill fear in the Canadian public—that the refugees would bring terrorism to Canada. The reality is that if you were a potential terrorist looking to gain access to Canada, probably the last way that you would try to gain entry would be as a resettled refugee. It is a long and exhaustive security screening process.

Indeed, such "fear mongering" with security concerns about Syrian refugees plays right into the hands of the terrorists. Halting the resettlement of refugees would likely aid the terror group. Some experts even believe that the Paris terrorist attacks by ISIS in 2015, and similar attacks elsewhere, were attempts to foment hatred toward the Syrian refugees, thereby reinforcing a "them and us" mentality.

We Need to Do More

There are 60 million refugees globally, a number not seen since the end of World War II. The horrifying photos of dead children washing up on European beaches represent only a tiny fraction of the millions suffering in a dozen other conflict zones around the world.

The refugee crisis around the world has been mounting for a decade or more. Now it is at our front door and we need to address it seriously. The previous Conservative government did little by way of bringing in more refugees deserving a place to call their home.

The new federal Liberal government, elected in October 2015, carried through on its commitment to bring 25,000 Syrian refugees to this county. This achievement was significant but it can go further. We need to do more.

"Annually, we are letting in one quarter of one refugee for every 1,000 Canadian citizens," noted Scott Gilmore in *Macleans*. "By contrast, Germany is expecting 800,000 new arrivals this year, or 10 per 1,000 citizens. If one compares the economic ability of a country to accept refugees, Canada is accepting one quarter of a refugee per $1 of GDP per capita. Germany is accepting 80 times that amount, or 17.4 refugees per $1."

Combatting Xenophobia

The mayor of Calgary, Naheed Nenshi, one of the most high-profile Muslim figures in Canada, confesses that he has been "shaken" by the close-minded, even racist nature of some of the debate over the Syrian refugee crisis. Anti-Muslim hate crimes have increased since the 2015 Paris terrorist attacks. He said he is "very concerned" when Muslims "are asked to apologize for Muslims everywhere."

The Canadian Association of Social Workers Code of Ethics calls on social workers to act to prevent discrimination based on religion, race, culture, and other factors. Our Code of Ethics also calls on social workers to uphold the right of every person to be free from violence and the threat of violence.

As with the thousands of immigrants and refugees in the past, the task will be to resettle the newcomers from Syria, help them rebuild their lives, and encourage them as they begin to benefit from participation in Canadian society, as so many immigrants before them have done.

Social workers in Canada have a big part to play in that process. Opening up our doors to help out those in need around the globe will go a long way not only to building a stronger Canada but also to bringing stability back to the homelands they left behind.

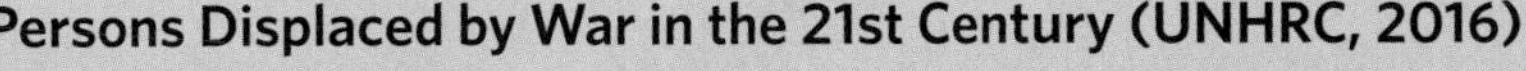

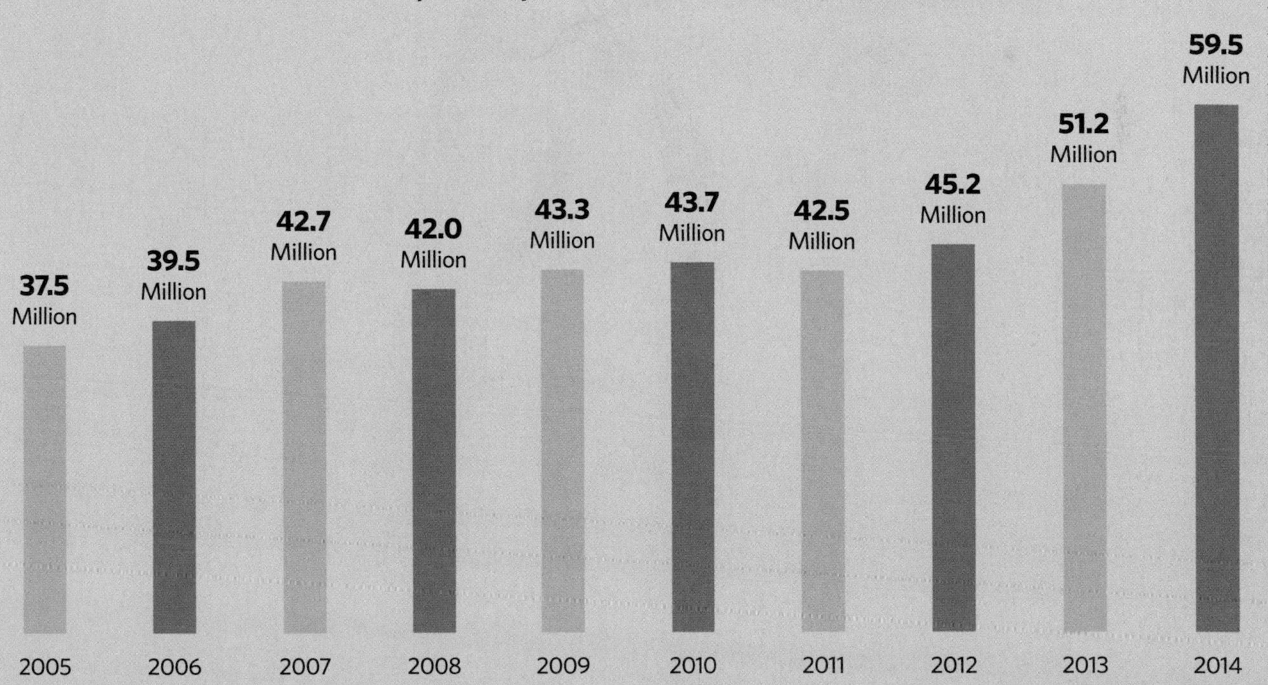

Source: United Nations High Commissioner for Refugees (UNHCR). (2015). Worldwide displacement hits all-time high as war and persecution increase. *Global Trends 2014*. UNHCR: New York, USA.

Toward an Anti-Racist Social Work Practice
Working from one's cultural lens

Reflecting on effective social work practice with racialized Canadians

Not long ago, racism was thought to be mainly the result of individual prejudice. Negative stereotypes were deemed to be "the cause" of racist discrimination; if individual attitudes were corrected through education and the sharing of cultures, racism would no longer exist. Much of federal multicultural policy is premised on this understanding.

Fighting Racism at the Personal, Institutional, and Societal Levels

More recently, in social work and in wider circles, we have seen the emergence of a comprehensive "anti-racist" approach. This has involved a shift from seeing the causes of racism only within personal prejudice and individual behaviour to seeing racism as interlinked with the larger structures and social systems in Canadian society.

Anti-racist social work practice today involves addressing racism at the personal, institutional, and societal levels, separately and simultaneously:

- At the personal level, social workers must ensure that their own practices are free of racism and challenge what are considered to be individual racist practices by others.
- At the institutional level, social service agencies and other organizations must pursue policies and practices that are non-discriminatory.
- At the societal level, legislation and government policies must be changed to remove barriers to racial groups. This includes working to eliminate unintentional racism in policy and procedures.

Community Action and Community Empowerment

Anti-racist social workers and social service workers often use an empowerment approach to elicit the participation of those vulnerable to racism. As one example, the Calgary Bridge Foundation for Youth (CBFY) is a not-for-profit organization that provides settlement services and support to immigrant youth and families in the Calgary region. Since 1990, CBFY has provided a welcoming and inclusive environment for over 12,000 newcomer families each year. It works to strengthen newcomer communities, primarily through the holistic development of immigrant youth by way of year-round programs. Its Afterschool Program, for example, provides opportunities for recreation, academic help, English language learning, and life skills development. The program is delivered at public and Catholic schools, public library branches, and Calgary Housing locations. Additionally, CBFY's RBC Youth Empowerment Program provides academic support for students in Grades 7 to 12 with varying ELL levels and academic abilities. The program seeks to help students improve their grades, promotes the importance of post-secondary education, develops critical thinking, and builds community-minded individuals, all within a safe and inclusive environment.

When mainstream community services are not fully meeting their needs, minority communities have sometimes seen the need to create their own separate social service agencies to act on their behalf. The Black Community Resource Centre in Montréal, for example, helps Black English-speaking youth and advocates for systemic change. The centre promotes the social, health, education, and economic needs of the youth by collaborating and partnering with Black community organizations, public agencies, and community-wide agencies.

The Black Community Resource Centre works with community organizations to monitor and review public policy that affects Black youth. The Centre attempts to improve the cultural and racial appropriateness of other public and government-funded agencies by organizing cultural and racial sensitivity workshops, and it works with other Black organizations in providing operational support and training. The Centre's approach is two-pronged: it has created a separate agency to address unmet needs, while also working to improve the cultural appropriateness and anti-racist perspective of mainstream agencies.

Social Workers as Advocates for Racialized Canadians

Anti-racist social work has an important role to play in creating a non-racist society. It demands that practitioners work to examine and perhaps change their own awareness and practices, the practices of those around them, institutional policies and procedures, and social relations and systems that operate, both overtly and covertly, to perpetuate racism.

The implementation of an anti-racist approach requires the employment of workers who have an ability to work across racial divides, and who have an empathy based on knowledge of the differences between people. It also means affirming the core values of being human—respect and dignity for all.

Anti-racist social work practice is a framework for analysis as well as a form of practice pertinent to all aspects of social work, including individual and group counselling, community work, social policy development, and advocacy. It is multi-faceted and relevant for practitioners from all backgrounds.

Below, David Este and Christa Sato, both contribuitors to this chapter, share their own backgrounds and experience working with immigrant, refugee, and racialized Canadians.

David Este's Perspective

"I am a third-generation African Canadian because my grandparents migrated to Canada between 1912 and 1928. They left their respective homes in Antigua and Barbados, settling in Montréal. As I became older, through conversations with my grandparents I cultivated interests in immigration as well as in the history of people of African descent. I completed a Master's degree in Black Canadian History and then changed focus and became a social worker. Since joining the Faculty of Social Work at the University of Calgary, I have taught courses on social work practice with immigrants and refugees, and in recent years, I have integrated content focused on the health and well-being of people of African descent into my courses.

"During the early years of my academic career, I played an active role in program development for Immigrant Services Calgary, including the Family Mosaic Centre and the Men's Program (focused on prevention of family violence and settlement issues). I provided a series of professional workshops for staff members and completed a series of program evaluations.

"The majority of my research has focused on immigrants, refugees, and people of African descent residing in Canada. Examples of these studies include the Racism, Violence, and Health Study among people of African descent; New Canadian Children and Youth; and Strengthening Social Services for Immigrants in Calgary. My co-author Christa Sato and I, along with members of our research team in Calgary, are involved in a research study entitled Strength in Unity (SIU). SIU is a community-based project that is attempting to build capacity among youth (males) and men from Asian communities in Canada and to mobilize participants to become Community Mental Health Ambassadors. These individuals are raising awareness about mental illness and health and working in their communities to develop anti-stigma initiatives. The study is being conducted in Vancouver, Toronto, and Calgary, and is led by Dr. Sepali Guruge, who is with the Daphane Cockwell School of Nursing at Ryerson University."

Christa Sato's Perspective

"Currently, I am completing a Master's of Social Work degree at the University of Calgary, specializing in international and community development. My passion for working with immigrant, refugee, and racialized populations emanated from first-hand experiences of social, economic, and cultural barriers encountered by my parents as a result of adapting to life in Canada. These experiences are reflected in my professional experience as a social work practitioner.

"My practicum experiences have been directly related to practice with immigrants and refugees. As a student intern with the City of Calgary, I was involved in community organizing with immigrant and racialized populations in an ethno-culturally diverse neighbourhood in Northeast Calgary. I helped to engage and mobilize residents to discuss and address local needs in their community. During my M.S.W. practicum with Citizenship and Immigration Canada, I was involved with the Local Immigration Partnerships (LIPs). LIPs are community-based partnerships that engage a broad range of local stakeholders to improve accessibility and coordination of services that facilitate immigrant settlement and integration, leading to economic, social, cultural, and civic inclusion of newcomers.

"Finally, over the past two years my professional experience as a research assistant has enabled me to build strong relationships with individuals from different immigrant and ethnocultural serving agencies from various communities."

Working within the Education System

Social work practice with immigrant youth in schools

In 2014 , Canada admitted 48,519 immigrant youth (Citizenship and Immigration Canada, 2015). The majority (74 percent) were admitted under the economic class; 12.3 percent arrived as refugees; and 11.7 percent were designated under the family class. The 2011 National Household Survey reported that since 2006, children aged 14 and under accounted for 19.2 percent of the newcomer population and that those aged 15 to 24 accounted for 14.5 percent (Statistics Canada, 2011).

As noted by Moreno and Chuang, for immigrant children, "schools are the primary institution that facilitates acculturation, socialization and second language acquisition" (2011: 239). Immigrant children and youth and their parents may find understanding and adapting to Canada's education system quite challenging. Este and Ngo (2011) maintain that linguistic and cultural barriers, socioe-conomic status, and patterns of acculturation can make it difficult to identify and assess the educational and social needs of immigrant children and youth. The inability to speak either English or French may constitute the most daunting obstacle. Immigrant or refugee students may require between two and five years of explicit English or French language instruction to develop basic communication skills. They need additional time to develop their academic language proficiency through ESL or FSL courses.

Those students who have limited education and poor literacy skills require concentrated academic support in order to achieve success in school. As Alejandra's story shows, children and youth who are inappropriately placed in classrooms with children who are several years younger may experience socio-psychological difficulties as a result (Este and Ngo, 2011).

Immigrant and refugee youth may experience racism from both teachers and students. It is vital that social work practitioners working in schools undergo anti-racist education and possess the skill set both to prevent racism and to intervene effectively when racist incidents occur. As well, social workers should provide in-service sessions to teachers and school administrators focused not only on what anti-racism is, but on strategies designed to decrease both overt and subtle racism in schools.

Social workers can also play important roles in helping parents understand the Canadian education system, including grading, school regulations, and school norms. As part of the assessment of immigrant families, it is critical that social work practitioners gain an understanding of the parents' language proficiency as well as their educational attainment. This information may shed light on the academic performance of their children. (To assist in this assessment process, the "Assessing Immigrants' Needs" feature earlier in this chapter will be helpful.)

Finally, schools should not adopt a passive stance and simply expect parents to attend parent-teacher meetings or curricular overviews. If the student's teachers and social worker function closely in tandem, both parties can share information and collaborate to ensure that immigrant and refugee children and youth have opportunities to succeed academically. And as time passes, immigrant and refugee parents can gain a greater understanding not only of the educational institution their child attends but of the broader education system as well.

Reflecting on Alejandra's Story

1. What are some challenges that immigrant youth might encounter when coming to Canada?
2. Although the immediate concern was Alejandra's academic performance, comment on the importance of gathering information about systems such as her family.
3. What skills can be used by school social workers to help develop a meaningful relationship with immigrant youth?

Alejandra's Story... From El Salvador to Calgary

Alejandra is a 14-year-old from El Salvador who recently arrived in Calgary with her parents and two younger brothers. After enrolling in a Canadian school for the first time, she appears to slip a little before a social worker intervenes with an assessment and a plan to help get her back on track.

When her parents register Alejandra for school in Calgary, the school board assesses her academically and determines that she should be placed in Grade 8. Alejandra is confused as she had already completed Grade 9 back home in El Salvador and had been among the top five percent of students in her school.

The school board did not provide a clear reason for her placement, saying only that she had arrived in the middle of the school year and needed to improve her English language skills. Since Alejandra's parents do not speak English fluently, they were unable to question the decision of the school board with regard to Alejandra's placement.

A School Social Worker Intervenes on Alejandra's Behalf

After several months, Alejandra's home-room teacher became concerned about her new student. Her grades were below average, and she had missed a number of classes. As well, the teacher observed that she was not involved in any school activities and was struggling to make friends. As a result of these concerns, Alejandra was referred to the in-school social worker.

Alejandra agreed to meet with the social worker, who subsequently conducted an assessment focused on her situation. Initially, Alejandra was reluctant to share any information with the social worker because she was afraid that revealing information about her family might impact her family's status in Canada.

After a series of meetings with the social worker, Alejandra eventually shared with her that she was bored at school and did not feel challenged. She discussed the significant responsibilities she had taken on as the eldest child since arriving in Canada, including acting as a language broker for her parents, taking care of her younger brothers, and helping them with their homework while her parents worked multiple part-time jobs. Alejandra worries a lot about her parents' situation as they are clearly struggling to adjust to life in Canada.

In order to help alleviate her parents' stress, Alejandra performs household tasks such as cooking, cleaning, and maintaining the home. Additionally, she does not feel a social connection with her peers, because they do not seem to understand the ongoing challenges she faces as a newcomer.

After processing the information that Alejandra has shared, the school social worker is concerned by the fact that Alejandra is experiencing ongoing high levels of stress and is beginning to show symptoms of depression. The social worker develops the following intervention plan for Alejandra and her family:

- meeting with all of Alejandra's teachers to gain a better understanding of (a) her academic performance, and (b) indicators of her mental health status
- arranging for a home visit with the goals of (a) sharing the school's concerns related to Alejandra's school performance with her parents; (b) gaining a better understanding of the family's situation; and (c) assessing the family's sources of financial and community support
- with the family's consent, making a referral for the family to visit a local immigrant-serving agency so that an assessment can be made that is focused specifically on the family's settlement needs
- working with Alejandra's teachers to develop a viable plan designed to assist her with school work
- developing an evaluation plan with Alejandra to assess the effectiveness of the intervention plan

It is still too early to evaluate the results of this intervention, but in the social worker's mind, this is not a simple case of a young person having difficulty coping with school work. By addressing Alejandra's home circumstances, engaging with Alejandra's parents, and providing some support and perspective for Alexandra herself, the social worker has increased the likelihood that Alejandra's issues will be temporary and that the situation will gradually normalize for her and her family.

Social workers can provide various home and family services to immigrant students that will help to ease their adjustment to new schools.

Working with Racialized Canadians

Social work practice with second-generation Canadians

Social work practice with immigrant and refugee populations is not limited to the first generation. Second-generation children encounter unique challenges, such as struggling for social acceptance, economic opportunity, and equal recognition in mainstream society (Arthur et al., 2008; Dion and Dion, 2004; Giguère et al., 2010; Reitz and Banerjee, 2007). Social workers need to be aware of the ways in which immigration impacts families and communities across generations. As Kobayashi (2008) notes, members of the second generation are agents of sociocultural change, therefore, and a prime locus for understanding the complexities of multicultural society.

One particular problem affecting second-generation Canadians of colour is racial discrimination. "Second-generation racialized Canadians are keenly aware of the changing nature and forms of racism in Canada," Brooks (2008: 76) asserts, "and this knowledge has been gained through stories told by their parents about their experiences of immigration." Research in this area underlines how systemic marginalization and exclusion based on one's race or cultural background is detrimental to creating a sense of belonging (Reitz and Banerjee, 2007; Stewart, 2014). "Despite being born in Canada, second-generation Canadians are often tasked with not only overcoming racial barriers within societal structure and institutions, but also proving their Canadian identity" (Brooks, 2008: 77). Such exclusion can make second-generation Canadians feel disenfranchised in their place of birth (Kobayashi, 2008).

Implications for Social Workers

What are the implications of issues affecting second-generation immigrants from a social work practice perspective? First of all, social workers cannot assume that all people from racialized backgrounds are immigrants, for this is clearly not the case. Canadian-born individuals from racialized backgrounds make up a significant portion of the Canadian population. Second, an awareness of the unique issues affecting racialized second-generation Canadians will allow social work practitioners to conduct more thorough assessments. This will put them in a better position to deliver interventions that address the unique needs of this group.

In working with second-generation Canadians, it is essential to take into account not only the individual himself or herself, but also the broader family dynamics. Services that emphasize strength and resilience are also critical. These kinds of supports provide individuals, families, and communities with a sense of agency and control. Rather than trying to fit them into either their parents' culture or the mainstream Canadian culture, encouraging second-generation Canadians to foster and embrace the duality of their cultures can often be an important step, not only in working toward a more inclusive society but also in creating one that validates and supports the unique needs of these often-neglected groups of Canadians.

In Christa's story, Christa, now a practising social worker in Calgary, explains the negative impact of marginalization in her own life. She relates her own personal feelings and experiences and goes on to emphasize the importance of proactive work that addresses the unique needs of second-generation racialized Canadians.

Reflecting on Christa's Story

1. In what ways can self-reflection enhance your social work practice?
2. What is the value of looking at the family as a unit during the assessment phase when working with second-generation Canadians of colour?
3. What are some of the unique challenges that individuals of biracial identities may encounter in Canadian society?

Christa's Story... Striving for a sense of belonging

A child of immigrant parents, a racialized Canadian, and now a practising social worker, Christa takes up the challenge of advocating with, for, and on behalf of new immigrants, refugees, and racialized populations.

As a Canadian-born child of immigrant parents, I can certainly relate to experiences of exclusion based on my ethnicity. One of the most salient forms of racism I encounter on a regular basis is being asked, "Where are you from?" When I say Calgary, I can almost always expect the follow-up question, "But where are you *really* from?"

While these questions may seem like an innocent indication of curiosity about my cultural background, it implies that as a racialized person, I do not fit conceptualizations of what it means to be truly "Canadian."

A Social Work Practice Rooted in Personal Experiences

Growing up, I struggled to feel a sense of belonging. Although I could identify with aspects of my mother's Filipino culture, my father's Japanese culture, and the Canadian culture in which I was born, I never truly felt a strong sense of belonging to any of these cultural communities.

Nor did any of these ethno-cultural communities truly accept me as an "insider." Being born in Canada and being a biracial female has undoubtedly presented challenges in coming to terms with my own ethnic identity.

During my childhood and especially during adolescence, I constantly felt competing pressures to meet the cultural and familial expectations of my parents in addition to pressures associated with wanting to fit in with the Canadian mainstream culture. Often, I felt that I could never measure up to these expectations and consequently felt I had either disappointed my parents or did not truly fit in with my Canadian peers.

This led to feelings of depression, as well as diminished self-esteem and self-confidence. These detrimental psychological effects manifested themselves as a result of the constant need to prove my Canadian and ethno-cultural identities.

After the long and arduous journey of discovering who I am, I have now come to a place where I can feel a sense of pride in my identity as a Canadian-born, racialized female.

Attending university and studying social work has enabled me to contextualize my own experiences and to situate them within broader issues related to structural and systemic discrimination. My practice as a social worker, particularly in community-based research with immigrant, refugee, and racialized populations, has been informed by my own experiences of injustice and it positions me to advocate with, for, and on behalf of other marginalized groups.

Creating Change for Others

Effective social work practice begins with taking a critical look at your own personal experiences, and using these experiences to address systemic barriers in order to create change for others who may be encountering similar challenges.

I can relate to feelings of alienation and dehumanization as a result of having been told that Canada is caring and accepting, despite the fact that people who do not fit the dominant mainstream culture continue to be marginalized and stigmatized. The consequence of such hypocrisies is merely to reproduce prejudice and vulnerabilities across generations.

If we deny that such racism occurs, and are unable to speak about it in the public realm openly and honestly, racialized Canadians will continue to be pushed to the margins and left to feel that this marginalization is due to personal and cultural inadequacies.

Social workers and others who are working in the health professions have a special role to play in supporting those Canadians who have been marginalized and in combatting discrimination, racism, and injustices wherever they appear.

Advocacy is especially critical in this area of social work practice. It provides a context in which to question, criticize, and change policies, laws, and practices that systematically prevent certain groups from full and equitable participation in society.

Many biracial citizens desire a sense of belonging, but can often feel like outsiders rather than participants in society.

Refugees and Displaced Persons

Social work practice with people displaced by war or disaster

Refugees and displaced persons are individuals who have left their home or country of origin unwillingly, often due to serious trauma and out of fear for their lives. According to the United Nations Commission on Human Rights , in more than 50 countries and in practically every world region—Africa, South and North America, Asia, Europe, and the Middle East—more than 25 million people are actually considered as displaced people just as a result of violent conflicts and human rights violations. This number increases by several millions when those who have been uprooted by natural or human-made disasters are taken into account.

In addition to the assessment questions presented in the discussion on social work practice with immigrants, the following questions need to be a part of the assessment process with such individuals and their families.

Critical Questions to Ask Refugees or Displaced Persons

- What forced you to leave your home?
- What types of violence did you experience or see in your country of origin?
- If you resided in a refugee camp(s), how did you get to the camp(s)?
- How much time did you reside in the camp(s)?
- Did members of your family spend time in the camp(s)? If so, which family members?
- What were the living conditions in the camp(s)?
- How did you spend your time in the camp(s)?
- Is there anything else that you would like to share about your experience living in the refugee camp(s)?

Assessing Emotional and Psychological States of Mind

The individual's responses to these questions will obviously affect the kind of support they will need during the resettlement process in Canada. It is well documented, for example, that as a result of their ordeal in getting to Canada in the first place, many such individuals will suffer from post-traumatic stress disorder (PTSD). Indicators of PTSD may include recurring recollections of past trauma, feelings of sadness, nightmares, social withdrawal, and memory impairment (Chambers and Ganesan, 2005).

The impact of displacement is felt more acutely by children, women with small children or those who are heads of families, and disabled and elderly people. As part of the assessment process with refugees and displaced persons, it is especially important simply to listen closely to those individuals and to learn about their histories. Gaining trust over time is especially important when working with refugees and displaced persons.

It is also important at the beginning to gain some sense of the emotional and psychological state of mind of the individual concerned. Such an assessment can serve as a starting point from which to enlist various support mechanisms, in the schools and in the community at large, that will facilitate the resettlement process.

Reflecting on Wek Deng's Story

1. Explain why it is important at first to listen and gain an understanding of the pre-migration and migration process experienced by immigrants and refugees.
2. What kinds of supports are initially most needed by refugees and displaced persons?
3. What additional challenges are refugees such as Wek Deng likely to encounter as they attempt to resettle into Canadian society?

Wek Deng's Story...
Escaping civil war in southern Sudan

A Canadian social worker employed by the Margaret Chisholm Resettlement Centre in Calgary provides front-line support for refugees of the civil war in Sudan who are anxious to settle into Canadian society and start a new life.

Wek Deng resided in the village of Nimule in southern Sudan with members of his family and neighbours. As an eight-year-old boy, he enjoyed playing with his friends and attending primary school.

During the fall of 1989, he could hear the sounds of armed conflict between forces loyal to the Government of Sudan and those under the leadership of General Omar al-Bashir.

The Ravages of Civil War

Within a couple of weeks, the government forces marched into Deng's village, destroyed it, and killed several members of the community. Deng and a small group of friends were fortunate because they managed to flee the village and hide in the forest. However, they witnessed friends and family members die at the hands of the government troops.

Deng and his friends spent the next several years searching for a safe place to live. They walked over a thousand miles, at times dealing with terrible conditions in addition to a lack of food and water. They eventually made it to a refugee camp in Kenya.

Wek Deng spent five years in the refugee camp. Being separated from family was painful and he experienced nightmares as a result of the violence he and his friends had witnessed.

Despite the challenges of living in an overcrowded refugee camp that at times did not have enough water and food, Deng felt relatively safe. He took advantage of the schooling that was offered at the camp and recalled his father's stories that stressed the importance of getting a good education. He remembered his father telling him that "the pen" would be his most important tool.

With the help of the United Natiions, he managed to travel to Cairo, where he continued his education. Not surprisingly, Deng found himself challenged by living in a completely new environment. However, over time, he seemed to adjust quite well.

First Cairo, Then Calgary

Wek Deng's first destination after leaving Cairo was Calgary, where he resided at the Margaret Chisholm Resettlement Centre.

The Margaret Chisholm Resettlement Centre provides temporary accommodation to newcomers as they begin the resettlement process in Calgary and assists them in overcoming initial obstacles in adjusting to a new country. The centre can accommodate up to 80 people. Government Assisted Refugees (GARs) who are destined for Calgary are brought from the airport to the centre, and they stay for up to 19 days until permanent accommodation is secured. The services provided by the centre for destined GARs include

- temporary accommodation;
- three meals a day, seven days a week; and
- Resettlement Assistance Program (RAP) services.

A Social Worker Facilitates Integration

During his stay at the resettlement centre, Deng was referred to a social worker employed by the organization. His social worker provided him with a list of resources that could help him begin to resettle in Canada. For example, Deng was interested in taking ESL classes.

The social worker helped Deng with some practical concerns such as opening a bank account, learning basic transportation routes using the bus and the C-train in Calgary, and very importantly, grocery shopping. The social worker also helped him get in touch with an immigrant-serving agency that provided different levels of ESL classes.

Deng stayed at the resettlement centre for three weeks. He was fortunate to have an uncle living in Calgary and was able to move in with him and his family. However, Deng kept the contact information of his first social worker, who reassured him that should he need any additional assistance, the worker would be available to help.

Social workers at resettlement centres help refugees and displaced persons to adjust to life in a new country.

Francis Boakye

Francis Boakye, who helps immigrants at the Centre for Newcomers, says the city of Calgary has made great strides in terms of welcoming immigrants.

Francis Boakye has been working as a social worker in management at the Centre for Newcomers for the last five years. He attained his Ph.D. from the University of Calgary.

My work with newcomers is influenced by my own experience coming to Canada 15 years ago. Completing my PhD in social work was a response to what was happening with newcomers and a desire to work in the field where you are in a position to influence ideas, people, and policies.

Our programs at the Centre are designed to help immigrants and refugees find ways of settling into the system. Our job is to support them in every way possible. As newcomers working with newcomers, we are equipped with knowledge that helps us reinterpret their frustrations and contextualize them in order to respond appropriately to their needs. It takes people who have understood these experiences to be more empathetic, and this understanding better positions you to apply social work methods and approaches that make sense to the people with whom we are working. Our work is not just for agencies. It is for all of us—and for Calgary to become a better place, each of us has to play a role.

As a social worker, I bring elements and principles of justice, equity, fairness, and equality to my practice. Social work is working with people and practising social work principles. It's not just for service users, but also for peers and colleagues. We need to implement just policies within management itself and let it run through the organization. That is critical. If at a management level we have just-minded approaches to policy development, then that affects what happens on the ground. That for me is social work—changing people's mindsets, attitudes, and behaviours toward others and ensuring a justice approach to the work we do.

What surprised me most in my work with immigrants and refugees? First, I thought that once you get into this work you would be in a position to transform people's lives in a very short time. Then you realize that this is not the case. The second thing that surprised me is the lack of cohesion among social workers in agencies. So many people feel isolated in their field and practice because they are standing on principles they feel very strongly about and these social work values they possess are so different from those of others. Finally, you want to make things happen quickly, but realize you are up against powerful institutional forces. Social workers can only reach a solution to problems if we come together and see issues at a big-picture level.

A Success Story

An immigrant youth at the Calgary Young Offender Centre was experiencing multiple challenges that others didn't know about. He sells drugs and brings money home so that his mom can help the family, feed them, and give them a place to sleep. This young man began telling me how he got involved in drugs, how he was beaten by the police, and how he landed in jail. Informally, I decided to mentor him and help build a support system for him.

I visited the young man and his mom. I talked to his soccer coach, and we went to the youth's home to talk about prospects for a soccer career. I advised him about his academics and he went back to school—he enrolled in college, began studying, and ended up with good grades. At one point he told me his GPA was 4.0! I mean, just look at his story, from being in jail to coming out of jail and saying, "I need to change my life." He came to me for help because he was participating in a program at the Centre. We had this deep conversation and then he made his decision to change his life. You see a whole new person... not only him, but also his family.

Words of Wisdom

What are some words of wisdom for social workers with aspirations to work with newcomers? First, I would tell students what attracted me to social work is the fact that it's one of the few professions that is value based, meaning that we must adhere to the values that guide our profession in our practice.

Second, sometimes the difference in how we treat newcomers lies in how we understand their experiences. Without that, it's difficult for you to provide meaningful support to people who turn to you for help. You are here to support newcomers and how you support them is critical. We need to do it in a way that respects these individuals.

Chapter 10 Review

Review Questions

1. Describe three major events in Canadian history that illustrate racial injustice.
2. What is meant by a "hate crime"? What is the extent of hate crimes in Canada? What is social work's role in addressing such crimes?
3. Explain what is meant by systemic racism and give some examples of systemic racism in Canada.
4. What is anti-racist social work? Describe three strategies that social workers can use to deal with racism in Canadian society.
5. Describe three major roles that social workers should perform in assisting immigrants and refugees to settle into Canadian society. Provide the rationale for your choices.
6. In recent years, changes in social policy have impacted the ability of newcomers to resettle in Canada. Discuss reasons why it is important for social work practitioners to be aware of policies that affect their practice with immigrants and refugees.
7. There is general agreement in the social work literature that advocacy is a critical skill for social workers to possess. Describe the different types of advocacy that practitioners can use to assist racialized Canadians in their struggle against the racism and discrimination they encounter on a daily basis.

Exploring Social Work

1. A story in *The Globe and Mail* included an account of a police arrest operation: "Parked directly outside his... office was a large, grey, cube-shaped truck and, on the ground nearby, he recognized one of the two brown-skinned young men who had taken possession of the next door rented unit...." Critics consider the use of the term "brown-skinned" to be racist. What do you think? Is this an example of racism in the Canadian media?
2. Some researchers have identified systemic barriers in our mental health care system for racial and ethnic minorities. Research systemic racism in the mental health care system and write a two-page report to summarize your findings.

Websites

Immigration, Refugees and Citizenship Canada (IRCC)
www.cic.gc.ca
Immigration, Refugees and Citizenship Canada is the department of the federal government responsible for dealing with immigration, refugees, and citizenship. The department was originally established in 1994 following a reorganization, and it was renamed from Citizenship and Immigration Canada to its current name with the swearing in of the new Liberal government in 2015.

Canadian Race Relations Foundation (CRRF)
www.crr.ca
The federal government proclaimed the *Canadian Race Relations Foundation Act* into law on October 28, 1996. The Canadian Race Relations Foundation (CRRF) officially opened its doors in November 1997. The Foundation is committed to building a national framework for the fight against racism in Canadian society. It operates at arm's length from the federal government, and its employees are not part of the federal public service. The CRRF has an excellent online media centre offering access to its publications.

Canadian Anti-racism Education and Research Society (CAERS)
www.stopracism.ca
The Canadian Anti-racism Education and Research Society (CAERS) is a Canadian non-profit organization that tracks hate groups and extremism, provides direct support to victims of racism and discrimination, and lobbies government and governmental agencies for the development of effective policy and legislation to stop racism.

United Nations High Commissioner for Refugees (UNHCR)
www.unhcr.ca
The United Nations High Commissioner for Refugees (UNHCR) is the world's leading organization aiding and protecting people forced to flee their homes due to violence, conflict, and persecution. Since its formation by the United Nations General Assembly in 1950, UNHCR has helped millions of refugees restart their lives and has twice received the Nobel Peace Prize. UNHCR's staff of 9,300 work in more than 125 countries.

Social Work with Older Canadians

"Aging is not lost youth but a new stage of opportunity and strength." Betty Friedan (1921–2006)

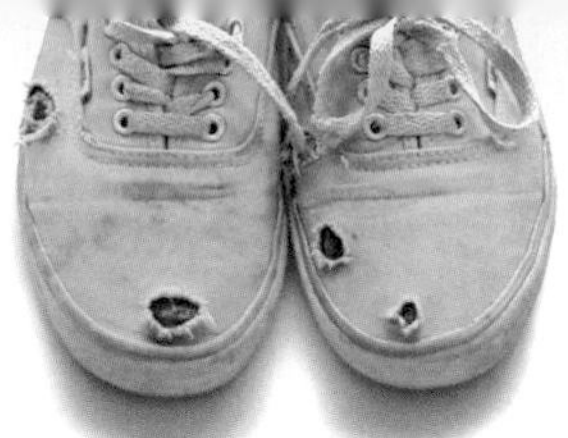

Sandra Loucks Campbell

The Implications of an Aging Society

11

Older adults are the most rapidly
increasing age cohort in Canada.

Statistics Canada projects that by 2021 almost seven million Canadians will be over the age of 64, comprising 19 percent of the total population. By 2041, there will be over nine million older adults, comprising 25 percent of the population. Twenty-eight percent of older Canadians are immigrants, which presents special issues for social work practice with this age group. Because of the sheer size of this older adult cohort, their concerns will likely be heard loud and clear.

In the coming years, these underlying demographic facts will increasingly affect most aspects of Canadian society, particularly in relation to health care needs and social service provision across the country. Already an important area of activity, social work with older adults may well become a veritable growth industry.

In its recent "World Report on Ageing and Health" (2015), the World Health Organization has called for "Ageing Well" to become a universal priority. "The greatest costs to society," the Report stresses, "are not the expenditures made to foster this functional ability, but the benefits that might be missed if we fail to make the appropriate adaptations and investments." It argues for strategies that extend beyond health care to include the development of communities where older adults are "healthier, happier, and more productive" members of society.

In this chapter, you will learn how to...

- describe the diversity that exists within Canada's oldest age cohorts
- identify some of the challenges facing older adults
- explain how federal and provincial/territorial governments can impact certain issues affecting older Canadians
- identify various types of elder abuse, and explain causes and preventative measures, both in private homes and in institutional settings
- describe the home care services available to older adults
- discuss the impact of dementia and what can be done about it
- compare various intervention approaches for social work with older adults
- explain the role of social workers in an aging society

Key Concepts

- Baby boom
- Ageism
- Medicalization
- Chronic illness
- Elder abuse
- Home care
- Respite care

Focusing Question

What are your preconceptions about older Canadians? What are the realities?

Portraits of Canada's Older Adults

Understanding a population's age composition can help policy makers plan for future social and economic challenges. This planning includes the funding of pension plans and health-care systems, as well as determining the number of immigrants needed to boost the labour force.

Figure 11.1 shows the projected population growth for children and seniors in Canada, comparing data from 1991 to the present with figures projected through to 2061. The graph shows that the numbers of older adults will continue to increase relative to children in our population.

Statisticians use data to calculate the median age of a population—the number signifying the halfway point in a group's age range. In Canada, the median age is about 40: about half of Canadians are under 40 and about half are over 40. The median age of women is higher than men (41.1 compared to 39.4) due to the persistent higher life expectancy of women (although the gap between genders has been narrowing). Overall, the median age of Canadians has been increasing, which means that the population as a whole is growing older.

The Canadian government typically classifies people aged 65 and over as "elderly." At this age, citizens are eligible for federal benefits, such as full Canada Pension Plan benefits and Old Age Security payments. The World Health Organization has no fixed standard but notes that 65 is the commonly accepted age for "senior" status in most core nations.

Gerontologists (scientists who study aging) often divide the older adult population into three subgroups: the young-old (approximately 65–74), the middle-old (ages 75–84), and the old-old (over age 85). People aged 90 and over are sometimes referred to as "the frail-old."

Why Is Canada Aging So Rapidly?

According to all projection scenarios, the Canadian population will continue to grow over the next 50 years, reaching between 40.0 million people and 63.5 million people by 2063 (Statistics Canada, 2014). "The greying of Canada" is a term that describes how larger and larger numbers of our population are getting older and older. (See Figure 11.1.)

Three main factors account for the aging of the Canadian population:

- **The baby boom.** Nearly one third of the Canadian population was born in the generation following World War II (between 1946 and 1966), when Canadian families averaged 3.7 children each (compared to 1.7 children per family today). This period is referred to as the **baby boom**. The so-called baby boomers began to reach the age of 65 in 2011.
- **A low birth rate.** The proportion of old to young will continue to increase because the average number of children per woman has declined. Many couples are postponing having families, or deciding not to have children at all. This trend reflects the increased participation of women in the labour force, the importance placed on women establishing their own careers, and the increasing economic demands placed on young families. A low birth rate contributes to the higher percentage of older people in the population.
- **Increasing life expectancy.** Statistics Canada data that group older Canadians by age show that we are living longer, primarily as a result of healthier lifestyles and universal health care. Between 1983 and 2013, the number of citizens over 85 increased by more than 100 percent. In 2013, the number of centenarians (those 100 years or older) in Canada was 6,900, or almost 20 per 100,000 persons, compared to only 11 centenarians per 100,000 persons in 2001.

Comparing Cohorts

A cohort is a group of people who share a statistical or demographic trait. People in the same age cohort, for example, were born during the same time frame.

As of July 1, 2014, for the first time in Canada, there were more people in the 55-to-64 age cohort than there were in the 15-to-24 cohort (Statistics Canada, "Population Projections: Canada, the Provinces and Territories, 2013 to 2063," 2014).

Older Adults—A Diverse Group

In Canada, as elsewhere, the population of those aged 65 and older is not a homogeneous group. For example, living arrangements vary: 56 percent live as part of a couple; 25 percent live on their own; 12 percent live with members of their extended family; and 7 percent live in a long-term care institution (Statistics Canada, 2011). Older adults living in rural areas as opposed to urban locations tend to remain in their home communities, where they support each other, despite fewer and limited services. In 2013, 67 percent of Canadians over the age of 85 were women. Seniors aged 85 and over are more likely than younger seniors to have serious medical conditions and disabilities, and therefore generally have a greater need for social support and health care.

Baby boom
The large number of individuals born between 1946 and 1966, who are now reaching their senior years. Canada's growing senior population will place increasing pressure on government services, particularly health care and the pension system.

Almost 21 percent of our current population was born outside of Canada, but 28 percent of the country's *older* adults were born elsewhere (Chappell, McDonald, and Stones, 2008). Older recent immigrants may face declining health, isolation, language barriers, discrimination, and other obstacles.

Current research estimates that up to seven percent of the senior population is openly LGBTQ+ (lesbian, gay, bisexual, transgender, or queer). That number is expected to double by 2030 (Sheldon, 2014; Fredriksen-Goldsen et al., 2011).

Becoming a senior does not automatically mean needing the services of a social worker, however. People age differently. Some remain physically and mentally fit; others face problems such as social exclusion, health crises, loss of mobility, inadequate income and housing, prejudice, crime victimization, and abuse. It is generally in these more difficult situations that the social worker and other social service professionals get involved.

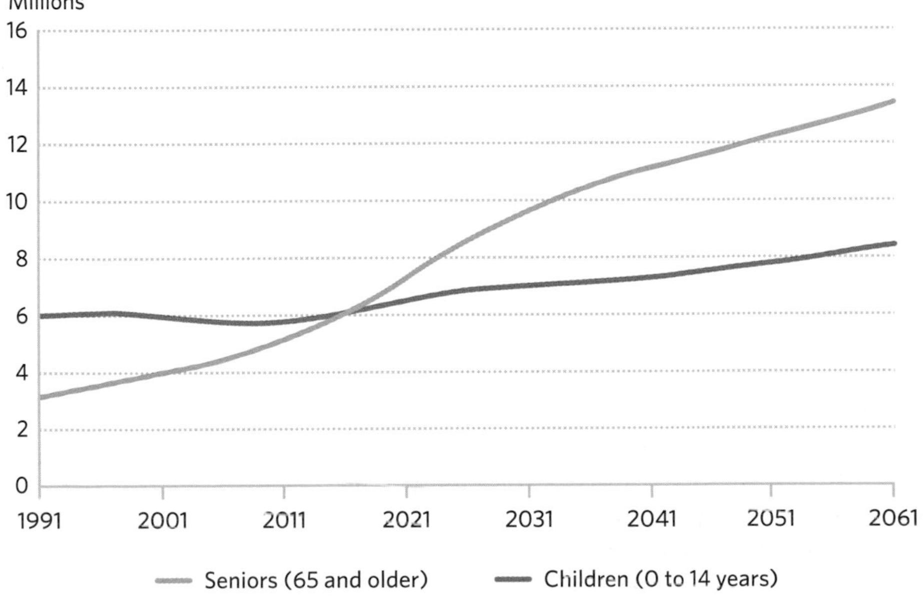

Figure 11.1 Seniors will become more numerous than children in Canada by 2017—a milestone in our history. Fertility has the greatest likelihood of either slowing or accelerating the aging of Canada's population over the next 50 years.

Source: Statistics Canada, CANSIM tables 051-0001 and 052-0005 (medium growth scenario).

Primary Challenges Confronting Older Canadians

Many adults face challenges as they grow older, including loss of independence, diminished physical and mental capabilities, discrimination, and financial insecurity. The aging process involves major biological, emotional, intellectual, social, and spiritual changes.

Ageism

Common phrases such as "over the hill" reveal North American society's frequently negative attitudes toward old age and older people in general. **Ageism** can be defined as any attitude, action, policy, or institutional structure that subordinates or oppresses a person or group on the basis of age. Some argue that ageism is different from other "isms," such as racism or sexism, because at some point everyone will grow old (unless, of course, a person dies young) and will therefore likely experience ageism. But the prevalence of negative attitudes toward an entire cohort of citizens serves to emphasize and condone ageist attitudes even further. Additionally, older persons may be part of more than one marginalized group. For example, an older individual may be female and living in poverty in addition to being old. In this situation, the individual may be subject to three societal "isms" simultaneously.

Every culture has a certain set of expectations and assumptions about aging. Lena Dominelli, a professor of Social and Community Development at Southampton University in England, believes that the decline in the economic status of older people in the West is part of the explanation for ageism (Dominelli, 2004: 135). In Dominelli's view, seniors in Western culture are often presented as a homogeneous group that is a burden to society. According to Dominelli, Western countries tend to regard people in materialist terms—people's worth or value to society is often based on how much they make, the size of their house, or the kind of car they drive. In retirement, the income of seniors usually drops. Furthermore, with urbanization, and especially with the breakdown of the extended family, the elderly have tended to lose their status in the family and in society as a whole.

Older persons have been inaccurately blamed for the high cost of health care. Also, they are sometimes portrayed in the press as "bed blockers" in health-care settings, particularly in hospitals. ("Bed blocking" is a term used to describe the long-term occupation of hospital beds, chiefly by elderly people, due to a shortage of suitable care elsewhere.) Older individuals identified as "bed blockers" can be abruptly discharged from hospital without adequate preparation. Government policies may unintentionally reinforce bias by using ambiguous language when establishing practices intended to enhance safety. In some provinces, hospital patients who do not require acute care are labelled as needing an "alternative level of care." This label could be leveraged by care providers to move the identified person out of the bed as soon as possible, but it also may put individuals at risk if they are discharged from hospital too soon.

North Americans generally seem to fear aging more (and be more ageist) than others. This is perhaps best exemplified by the high sales of beauty products and the common use of plastic surgery to restore a youthful look. Many media portrayals reflect dismissive and disrespectful cultural attitudes toward older adults. However, not all societies and cultures view older people this way. Many Aboriginal, Asian, and African societies (and many cultures within Western societies) place a high value on the wisdom and life experiences of the elderly. In many societies, older adults are traditionally viewed as sources of guidance and knowledge. Perhaps, as our population as a whole continues to age, some of our negative attitudes and perceptions will gradually begin to change.

Ageism
Any attitude, action, or institutional structure that subordinates or oppresses a person or group on the basis of age.

Former long-term mayor of Mississauga, Ontario Hazel McCallion stated in *The Globe and Mail* on June 6, 2016: "Canadians need to confront the reality that every day, its older citizens deal with the most widely tolerated form of social prejudice in the country: ageism."

First elected in 1978, McCallion oversaw the massive growth of Mississauga from farmland to Canada's sixth-largest city. Three months after retiring from office in 2015, she accepted a new job as special adviser to the principal of the University of Toronto Mississauga. She was 94.

Aboriginal Seniors Are Respected Elders

In contrast to various mainstream Canadian cultures, Aboriginal cultures tend to respect and even revere their seniors for their knowledge and experiences. Elders play an integral role in the well-being of families, communities, and nations, acting as key sources of traditional knowledge, wisdom, and cultural continuity.

Aboriginal peoples comprise only one percent of the overall senior population in Canada (compared with three percent in the total population). Manitoba and Saskatchewan have the largest proportion of Aboriginal peoples in their senior populations (Turcotte and Schellenberg, 2007).

Prevalent Myths about Aging and Older Adults

Some myths about old age depict aging negatively, while others portray an unrealistic picture of the joys of later life—travel, golf, dinner, and dancing. The following are a few of these myths.

- **Myth: "To be old is to be sick."**
  Reality: Most seniors are relatively healthy. Three quarters of Canadian seniors report that their health is good, very good, or excellent.
- **Myth: "Seniors and technology don't mix."**
  Reality: Seniors are the fastest growing group online, and they are capable of using digital technologies for more than just email. For example, seniors in the Seniors' Education program at Ryerson University developed, produced, and moderate an interactive website.
- **Myth: "Most seniors live in nursing homes."**
  Reality: Just five percent of men and nine percent of women over age 65 live in health-care institutions; most are 85 or older. And the percentages have declined.
- **Myth: "Seniors don't pull their own weight."**
  Reality: Up to one third of seniors provide help to friends and family, including caregiving for spouses and grandchildren, and giving financial assistance to children. Seniors pay taxes, too—just as they have done all their lives.
- **Myth: "Seniors increase the cost of medical care."**
  Reality: The increased cost to the health-care system due to aging is projected to be no more than one percent per year. The main causes of cost increases are inflation, a rising overall population, and advances in medical technologies (Evans, 2010).

Ninety-two percent of Canadians over the age of 64 lived in private homes at the time of the last census, while only 8 percent lived in seniors' residences or health-care facilities (Statistics Canada, 2011).

The Health Consequences of Inactivity

Physical inactivity may not appear to be a social work issue, but many emotional, spiritual, and mental health issues—perhaps especially among seniors—are directly related to it. Inactivity can lead to preventable health problems, such as heart disease, stroke, and osteoarthritis (along with the chronic pain associated with it). According to the Fitness and Lifestyle Research Institute, physical inactivity can also lead to depression, lack of energy, chronic disease, weight problems, disability, and premature death. The Canadian government estimates that billions of dollars per year could be saved if physical activity rates increased. For many seniors, walking, gardening, or taking part in low-impact sports could lead to a better physical and emotional state. Unfortunately, the majority of seniors are inactive: "More than 40 percent [of baby boomers] said they are not moderately active for 30 to 60 minutes at least three times a week." Given reduced strength and impaired physical fitness, Canadian seniors also face significant risks due to common accidents such as falling. Hospital admissions for unintentional injuries occur most often among older adults (Heart and Stroke Foundation, 2013).

Pension Reform

Canada's pension system needs urgent attention, according to a report released by the Canadian Centre for Policy Alternatives (CCPA).

- Old Age Security and the Canada Pension Plan provide only a modest income for people when they retire.
- Not everyone has a workplace pension—about 60 percent of Canadians must rely on public pension programs, supplemented by their own savings.
- Only about one third of Canadians take advantage of tax-assisted private savings through RRSPs.
- Almost $500 billion in unused RRSP contribution room is being carried forward.

The Erosion of Income and Financial Vulnerability

Canada's pension system is held in high regard throughout the world for the way it combines basic income security with public and private pension plans. The Canadian pension system has three tiers:

- **Old Age Security and the Guaranteed Income Supplement.** These plans provide income security for seniors independent of their prior participation in the workforce.
- **Canada Pension Plan (Québec Pension Plan in Québec).** The CPP provides pension benefits to individuals upon retirement or if they become disabled. It also provides benefits to the dependants of contributors who are disabled or deceased. The amount of the benefit depends on the level of contributions during the contributory period.
- **Private pension plans.** These consist of workplace plans and Registered Retirement Savings Plans (RRSPs), both of which result in tax breaks upon contribution.

Until recently, this three-tiered system has served seniors well. Canadian seniors' financial status improved significantly over the last 30 years. However, a 2013 report from the Bank of Montreal states that the average baby boomer falls about $400,000 short of adequate savings to maintain their lifestyle in retirement. The average senior couple spends approximately $54,000 a year, requiring accumulated savings of $1,352,000 in order to sustain themselves (not taking into account CPP and Old Age Pension payments). Individual Canadian boomers estimated they needed savings of $658,000 to feel financially secure in retirement but only saved an average of $228,000. Seventy-one percent of boomers said they plan to work part time in retirement. This will have a ripple effect on the economy as boomers continue to work but spend less (BMO Financial Group, 2013).

Victimization by Perpetrators of Fraud

Often isolated in their homes, seniors are the leading targets of fraudulent crimes, such as fake investment opportunities, phony contests, and false fundraising campaigns. Criminals are using more and more sophisticated techniques, often misrepresenting themselves as employees of a bank or other financial institution. In some cases, seniors have lost their life savings.

Medicalization of Older Adults' Problems

Medicalization describes our society's tendency to label the concerns of older adults as medical issues. Many older adults do experience **chronic illnesses** and discomforts and, in general, healing and recovery are slower when our bodies are old . But it is a mistake to assume that all older adults are physically and cognitively impaired in some way. And cognitive impairment is not necessarily a permanent condition—it can vary from day to day.

Current social work value systems shift the emphasis away from medicalization and toward self-empowerment and social engagement, which can reduce feelings of loss and depression—mental health issues commonly faced by older adults.

Medicalization
A process through which normal behavioural, emotional, and even physiological conditions (such as aging and menopause) become viewed as medical problems, to be treated by medical professionals

Chronic illness
An illness that lasts for a long time or that recurs frequently

Aging and the LGBTQ+ Population

An emerging field of study is how lesbian, gay, bisexual, transgendered, queer, and intersexed (LGBTQ+) people experience the aging process compared to mainstream groups. As they transition to assisted-living facilities, LGBTQ+ seniors carry the added burden of whether to disclose their sexual orientation and relationship identity to caregivers. In a long-term care setting, LGBTQ+ clients tend to conceal or "selectively disclose" their sexual orientation in order to feel safe.

A study titled *The Aging and Health Report: Disparities and Resilience among Lesbian, Gay, Bisexual, and Transgender Older Adults* found that older LGBTQ+ adults have higher rates of disability and depression than their heterosexual peers. For some LGBTQ+ people, aging in a care facility can mean a distressing retreat back "into the closet."

Despite Canada's legalization of same-sex marriage in 2005, LGBTQ+ seniors are less likely to have children who can provide care for them as they grow older (Fredriksen-Goldsen et al., 2011).

End-of-Life Issues: Complex New Legislation

After much legal and public debate, Canada now has its first doctor-assisted dying legislation. The law received royal assent on June 17, 2016 and sets out guidelines with respect to medical assistance in dying. But the details of the new legislation are not without controversy.

In June 2014, the Québec National Assembly had passed "An Act Respecting End-of-Life Care" (Bill 52). This legislation specified rights with respect to end-of-life care and regulates "continuous palliative sedation" and "medical aid in dying." In February 2015, the Supreme Court of Canada followed suit and ruled unanimously that Canadian adults in grievous, unending pain have a right to end their life with a doctor's help. The ruling established that the "sanctity of life" also includes "the passage into death." The court then suspended its ruling for 12 months to allow time for the Canadian Parliament to draft new laws.

In April 2016, the government introduced a more restrictive bill that requires a person seeking a doctor-assisted death to be a consenting adult, at least 18 years of age, in "an advanced stage of irreversible decline" from a serious and incurable disease, illness, or disability, and for whom a natural death is "reasonably foreseeable." It did not extend the right to assisted dying to those suffering from mental illnesses or to mature minors. Nor did it allow advance directives ("living wills"). This bill formed the basis of the new legislation that received royal assent on June 17.

Conflicting Viewpoints on Contentious Issues

In defence of the new legislation, the Minister of Justice and Attorney General of Canada and Minister of Health issued a joint statement that reiterated that the new law "strikes the right balance between personal autonomy for those seeking access to medically assisted dying and protecting the vulnerable." They emphasized that Health Canada will continue to work with the provinces and territories as provisions of the legislation come into force, and further study will be done with respect to medical assistance in dying in the context of mature minors, people for whom mental illness is the sole underlying condition and advance requests."

Some experts maintain that the end-of-life provision is unconstitutional because it narrows the eligibility criteria as established by the 2015 Supreme Court ruling that struck down the ban on assisted death.

The right-to-die movement has gained strength as a result of the "greying" of the population. New legislation seems to be driven less by the desires of older adults, however, than by the anxieties of a younger generation, whose members seek comfort in knowing that they can control the end of their lives.

In 2015, the Canadian Medical Association (CMA) produced a draft outline for a "principles-based approach" to physician-assisted death. The principles include the importance of patient consent and capacity, and respect for patient autonomy, as well as respect for a physician's personal ethical values. (The CMA conducted an internal survey in 2015 and found that 63 percent of its members would not give medical aid in dying to a patient who requested it.)

Gerontological social workers will find themselves handling complicated cases in which an individual's right to a dignified death must be balanced with a need to protect vulnerable members of the population, especially clients who have dementia. Most legal and medical experts agree that advance directives can serve as useful tools as long as they are frequently reviewed and updated, with current input from loved ones and primary health-care providers.

Canadian Support for Doctor-Assisted Dying

A Forum poll released on August 28, 2015, revealed that 77 percent of Canadians support doctor-assisted suicide for people who are terminally ill. This figure represents a 10 percent increase compared to a similar poll the firm conducted just four years previously. The survey of 1,440 voters found strong support across all age groups and political affiliations.

Accessing Quality Palliative Care

Each year, thousands of Canadians suffer because they do not have access to quality palliative care, according to a 2016 study by the Canadian Cancer Society.

With end-of-life issues now on the national agenda, the study says, it's time for governments to guarantee all Canadians access to quality palliative care.

Some parts of the country are already addressing the issue. Québec, for example, has included palliative care as part of its new law on doctor-assisted dying. Yet the study finds there is inconsistent and inadequate palliative care in most parts of the country.

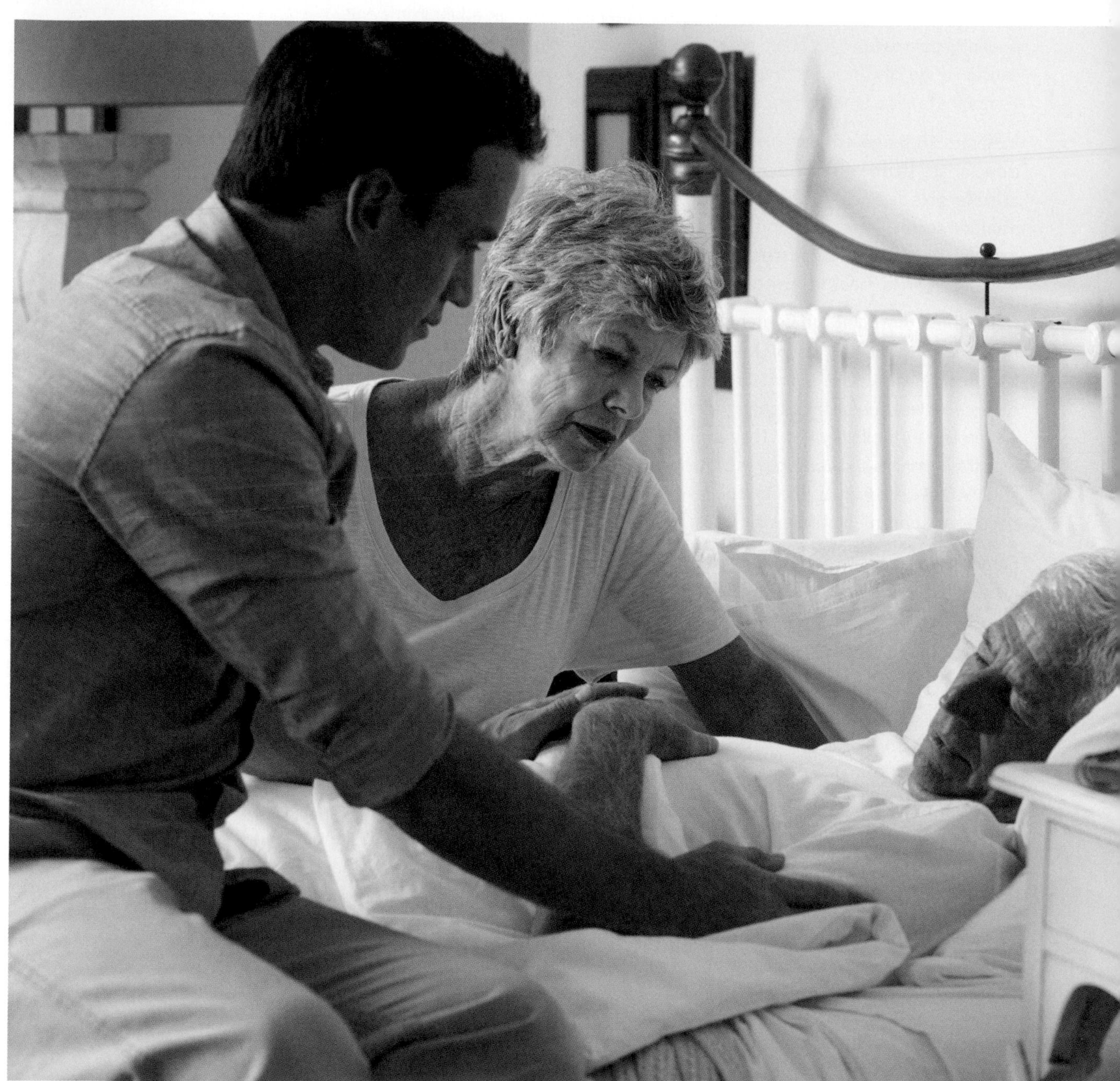

The Financial Realities of Living Longer
Unprepared for long-term care costs

"People tell me they worry more about money than they worry about cancer"

Every Thursday, Randy Filinski drives a group of seniors to one of two government-sponsored physiotherapy sessions in Toronto's Scarborough area and sees firsthand the realities of inadequate health-care coverage in the retirement years.

"When you watch the patients who go with benefits from work—they pay the $60 or $70—they actually get better, because they're actually getting the one-on-one care, versus the people I drive who are just dazed and confused after their 15-minute OHIP session."

The research confirms it. "A few years ago, we asked Canadians what they considered the biggest risk when planning for their retirement," says Chris Buttigieg, a senior manager at the Bank of Montreal in Toronto. "And the overwhelming response was that they were unprepared for unexpected costs."

Also, many Canadians are confused about what will be covered in retirement. Forty-four percent of Canadians expect to pay nothing for drugs, the 2014 Sun Life Canadian Health Index found.

But pay they will. Without private coverage, Canadians can expect to spend an average of $5,391 a year on out-of-pocket medical costs after age 65, according to a 2014 BMO Wealth Institute report. And these numbers will rise.

"Between 2004 and 2014, health-care costs rose by 54 percent, compared with shelter (41 percent), clothing (33 percent) and food (16 percent). Health-care costs are rising—from an inflation perspective—significantly faster," says Mr. Buttigieg. He says disability poses a large threat: "Between ages 65 and 74, 26.3 percent [of people] will become disabled."

If the disability is mild, there may be a need for modifications to a home, an electric wheelchair ($2,050 and up), a scooter ($1,000-$5,000), and/or a walker ($150 and up). But if a person is severely disabled, he or she may require a personal care worker—at a cost of $16 to $30 an hour—or a registered nurse ($24 to $76 an hour).

But the biggest sticker shock will be for long-term care. "Three quarters of Canadians have no long-term financial plan for long-term care if they need it," says Stephen Frank, vice-president of policy development and health at Canadian Life and Health Insurance Association.

According to Statistics Canada, there is about a 10-percent chance of needing long-term care by age 55, a 30-percent chance by 65, and about a 50-percent chance by 75. As long-term care isn't covered under the *Canada Health Act*, depending on an individual's province of residence and annual income, home care may be either covered, partly covered, or—most likely—not covered at all.

The bills can be steep, leading seniors to cash in retirement savings or rely on children or other family members for financial support. A nursing home in Ontario, for example, ranges between $14,000 and $132,000 annually, with long-term care averaging $20,800 to $29,300, according to Senioropolis, a virtual community for Canadian seniors.

In addition to long-term care, there are prescription-drug costs to consider, a reality that concerns 53 percent of Canadians, according to Sun Life. While provincial plans cover most prescription drugs for residents 65 or older, those who retire earlier are paying out-of-pocket for these medications.

And if an individual requires a drug that's not covered under the provincial drug formulary or under a catastrophic drug program—such as costly oral cancer medications, a specialty drug for a condition like rheumatoid arthritis, or a biologic drug in Ontario and the Atlantic provinces—he or she could be on the hook for thousands of dollars a year.

That's because Ontarians and residents of Atlantic provinces, unlike those in British Columbia, Alberta, Saskatchewan, and Manitoba, do not have their cancer treatments fully covered. That can be pricey. For example, the average cost of an oral cancer drug is $6,000 a month.

Pamela Bowes, manager of the Money Matters and workplace programs at Wellspring in Toronto, regularly meets people who've been diagnosed with cancer and are waking up to the financial realities of treating the disease.

"I have had people tell me they worry more about money than they worry about cancer."

- *Source:* Sharratt, Anna. (2015). Hidden health-care costs can be a shock for retirees. *The Globe and Mail*, November 18. [This copy has been shortened from the original article.]

Elder Abuse—A Serious, Ongoing Problem

Elder abuse is any action by someone in a position of trust or power that results in harm or distress to an older person. "Abuse can happen when the aggressor wants to intimidate, isolate, dominate, or control another person" (Government of Canada, 2015) . Abuse may take place in the home or in an institutional care setting. It can be a single event or a pattern of behaviour. Like other forms of family violence, elder abuse in the home is largely hidden from view. Isolated and often frail, older adults are highly vulnerable to mistreatment, sometimes by those closest to and/or responsible for caring for them.

In Canada in 2013, more than 2,900 seniors (56.8 per 100,000) were the victims of family violence. The perpetrator in 43 percent of cases was an adult child of the victim; in 28 percent of cases, it was the victim's spouse. The rate of family violence toward senior females was 26 percent higher than toward senior males (62.7 versus 49.7 per 100,000) (Canadian Centre for Justice Statistics , 2013).

Researchers have found that people over 85 years of age are most likely to suffer from dementia or other chronic illnesses and that this can render an individual physically or mentally incapable of reporting violence to the police (Welfel et al., 2000).

Besides physical violence, abuse can take other forms: emotional or psychological, sexual, and the most commonly reported form, financial (perpetrators of the latter form can be either close to the older adult or a complete stranger). Neglect is frequently associated with abuse.

Understanding and Preventing Elder Abuse in Families

The first step in preventing elder abuse within families is to understand the causes. Mia Dauvergne (2003) discusses several possible reasons: the stressfulness of the situation, especially if the family member has to balance a job, children, and other responsibilities in addition to caregiving; the fact that violence may be a learned behaviour for the caregiver and is now his or her way of responding to a stressful situation; the fact that the lives of the senior and the family caregiver are so intricately intertwined; and the possible effects of discriminatory attitudes toward the aging family member. Furthermore, "in some situations, the abuse may result from addiction issues (drugs, alcohol, or gambling) or mental health problems" (Statistics Canada, 2015).

The extent of informal caregiving is often understated. Most caregivers are looking after their own parents and their spouse's parents, and many are providing help to close friends and neighbours. "While the majority of caregivers (57 percent) reported providing care to one person during the past 12 months, assisting more than one care receiver was not uncommon. In particular, 27 percent of caregivers reported caring for two and 15 percent for three or more family members or friends with a long-term illness, disability or aging needs" (Sinha, 2013).

It is neither accurate nor fair, however, to ascribe most of the cause of elder abuse to caregivers. In households where abuse of an older person does occur, family relationships can sometimes be so complicated that the older person may have played a role in the development of an unhealthy dynamic, such as co-dependency. For example, the older person may have provided many years of care, housing, and food to an adult child who is coping with unemployment, mental health issues, and/or a substance use disorder. When the parent grows old, the caregiving can become especially difficult as both parties can become angry, frustrated, and abusive toward each other due to years of built-up tensions.

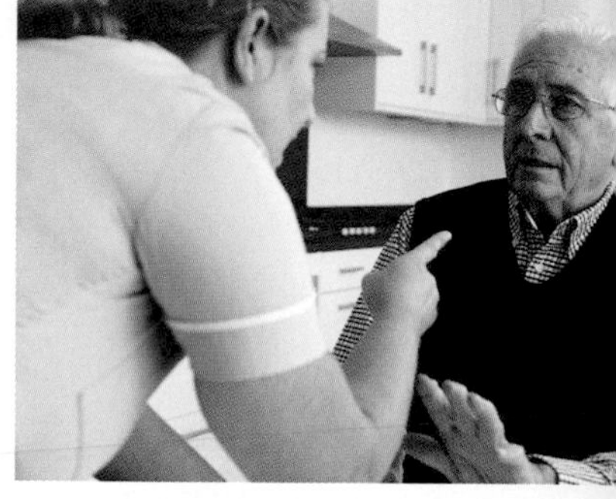

Caregiver Burnout

Caring for an older family member is often a long-term job that can become more difficult and complex over time. Exhaustion can put a great strain on family members who have the responsibility of caring for aging relatives, and can trigger frustration and resentment. For this reason, "self-care" is essential—before burnout occurs.

Moreover, women dedicate almost twice as much time to these types of tasks. Even working outside the home does not appear to reduce the amount of time women spend providing care—26.4 hours a month, versus 14.5 hours for men (Stobert and Cranswick, 2003).

There is an urgent need for social services that offer respite to informal caregivers.

Relieving Caregiver Stress Can Reduce Elder Abuse

It is troubling to note that fewer than one in five care providers reported that they received help if they needed a break. Yet when asked to identify the most useful thing to allow them to continue providing help, the most common answer (51 percent of those aged 45 to 64) was "occasional relief or sharing of responsibilities." Flexible work arrangements and financial compensation were also on the list.

There is the additional complication of seniors looking after seniors. Stobert and Cranswick report that over one in twelve seniors is also looking after at least one other senior: a spouse (25 percent), a close friend (33 percent), or a neighbour (19 percent). The gap between men and women with respect to giving care in this age group is higher than for younger caregivers. Moreover, only 18 percent of the senior caregivers indicated that someone else could take over should they need, or want, time off—pointing to an even greater need for support.

The physical and psychological effects of abuse against seniors are traumatic—if not completely devastating—for the senior, for the family, and perhaps even for the abuser. In the face of all these concerns and the growing older adult population, it is essential that governments at all levels, employers, other family members, friends, and social workers find more ways to provide relief and support to those who are giving care to seniors.

Elder abuse
The mistreatment or neglect of an older adult by a family member, a friend, a health-care provider in an institutional setting, or someone who provides assistance with basic needs or services. Elder abuse can be physical, emotional, sexual, medical, or (most often) financial. Any action that exploits an older person for personal or financial gain is a form of abuse.

Family caregivers may do a variety of tasks, including transporting their loved one to appointments, running errands, cooking meals, cleaning, making phone calls, and providing personal and medical care.

Abuse in Institutional Settings

Another issue of concern to social workers is abuse in facilities providing care to older people, including acute-care hospitals, nursing homes, and retirement homes. In this context, institutional abuse is any act or omission directed at a resident that causes the person harm, or that wrongfully deprives that person of her or his independence.

This definition focuses more on the consequences of acts on residents and less on the intent. The abuse could be of an individual nature, whereby a staff member at an institution directly abuses a resident. But often the abuse is systemic, whereby situations are allowed to develop that facilitate or permit abuse and neglect. It could also involve the failure to provide adequate safeguards for residents and staff. Guarding against such forms of abuse and neglect, both intentional and unintentional, is important not only for family members and relatives, but also for social workers associated with these older adults and the institutions in which they find themselves.

Combatting Systemic Abuse

Systemic abuse in institutional settings often results from policies, procedures, and processes that appear to be designed to maximize care and/or safety. For example, a facility may have a policy that permits staff members to search residents' rooms at any time for alcohol or medication. The intent of the policy may be to protect cognitively impaired residents from harm, but the outcome is an invasion of privacy.

Additionally, institutions typically have numerous policies regarding eating, wake-up, and sleep times. Often, these routines conflict with residents' lifelong eating and sleeping patterns. Residents also might find it difficult to question these policies as they are framed in terms of protection. One important way that social workers can assist with preventing abuse of seniors is by using various advocacy strategies, resident councils, and family councils. Ongoing staff training and policy reviews are also important.

The "home" or "residence" model for long-term care can help overcome some of the problems of abuse in institutional settings. Some facilities have found that developing a charter of rights works well in addressing abuse.

Awareness of the widespread abuse of older adults is growing, and social service agencies are responding with community-based initiatives that are proving effective in reducing the incidence of abuse and eliminating some of the causes.

As of 2011, the Government of Alberta, municipalities, and local non-profit and voluntary sector organizations are collaborating to offer a variety of services and supports to stop abuse from occurring and to restore older adults' safety if they have experienced abuse. These services and supports may include counselling, dispute resolution, legal aid, crisis response, shelter services, and safe and affordable housing.

Community members are encouraged to "see it," "name it," and "check it" as outlined in the "It's Not Right!" Neighbours, Friends and Families campaign developed under Canada's Federal Elder Abuse Initiative. "Seeing it" means noticing if something seems amiss, but also not jumping to conclusions. "Naming it" means letting the older adult know what you are observing. "Checking it" means asking the older adult if they are alright and offering to assist.

Charter of Rights and Freedoms for the Elderly

The charter for the Yvon-Brunet residence for older adults in Montréal includes five basic rights:

- information and freedom of expression
- privacy
- dignity and respect
- continuity
- responsibility and participation

These rights translate into a variety of procedures that ensure residents' needs are being met, such as a residents' council, flexible schedules, and consultation about medications and menu choices.

Lauren Colla, shown here, is a social worker with Baycrest Health Sciences in Toronto, a global leader in geriatric residential living, health care, research, innovation, and education.

Abuse and Neglect of Older Adults
Signs and symptoms

Elderly adults can be abused in their own homes, in relatives' homes, and even in facilities responsible for their care

As older Canadians become more physically frail, they are often less able to defend themselves against bullying and abuse. They may not see or hear as well, or think as clearly as they used to, leaving openings for unscrupulous people to take advantage of them.

Older adults can be abused in their own homes, in relatives' homes, and even in facilities responsible for their care. If you suspect that an elderly person is at risk from a neglectful or overwhelmed caregiver, or is being preyed upon financially, it is important to speak up. Learn about the warning signs of elder abuse, what the risk factors are, and how you can prevent and report the problem.

Neglect

- Dehydration, malnourishment
- Missing dentures, glasses, hearing aids
- Poor hygiene, lack of appropriate clothing
- Untreated medical problems
- Poor condition of skin
- Being left unattended or tied to a bed or chair
- Failure to monitor restraints
- Failure to allow outside services or medical appointments

Medical Abuse

- Reduced/absent therapeutic response
- Poor documentation of medical records
- Improper administration of drugs
- No reason for treatment given

Physical Abuse

- Unexplained injuries (fractures, bruises) or falls
- Unauthorized or inappropriate restraints
- Delay in seeking and receiving medical treatment

Sexual Abuse

- Pain, swelling, bleeding in the genital area
- Fear of specific persons or of being alone with them
- Sexually transmitted diseases
- Drawing back from touching

Emotional/Pyschological Abuse

- Feelings of fear, passivity, shame, or guilt
- Extreme passivity and withdrawal
- Symptoms of depression
- Exclusion from activity and family
- The use or threat of punishment
- Decisions made for resident

Financial Abuse

- Lack of money for necessities or comforts
- Unauthorized use of resident's money or property
- Disappearance of resident's property
- Unexplained changes in a deed or will
- Inadequate facilities to protect resident's property
- Lack of accounting for the way finances have been spent

Violation of Rights

- Difficulty visiting, calling, or contacting resident
- Resident not permitted to manage own financial affairs
- Lack of choices in life
- Lack of privacy
- Resident not permitted to participate in decision making about his or her own affairs
- Lack of confidentiality in use of health-care records

- *Source:* McDonald, L. and A. Collins. (2000). *Abuse and Neglect of Older Canadians: A Discussion Paper.* Ottawa: Health Canada.

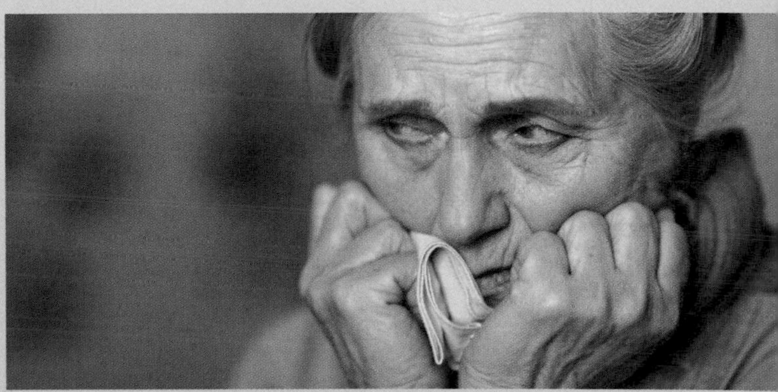

Home Care for Older Canadians: A Two-Tiered System

In the past three decades, there has been a devolution from institution-based services to community- or home-based services, given that more and more seniors are healthy and living on their own. Most older Canadians express a preference for remaining in their own homes, and it is estimated that between 85 and 90 percent of care for older Canadians is provided in the home by relatives. As Canadians age, informal caregiving is becoming increasingly important to the well-being of seniors. According to the 2008/2009 Canadian Community Health Survey (CCHS)–Healthy Aging, an estimated 3.8 million Canadians who were aged 45 or older (35 percent) were providing informal care to a senior with a short- or long-term health condition. In 2012, more than 5 million Canadians cared for an older family member, most of whom were living in their own homes (Statistics Canada, 2015). Informal caregivers—family and friends who provide unpaid assistance with tasks such as transportation and personal care—help seniors remain in their homes, thereby reducing demands on the health-care system.

Meals on Wheels
The Meals on Wheels program delivers low-cost, nutritious meals directly to the homes of clients who are unable to prepare such meals themselves. Hot or frozen meals are hand delivered, often by volunteers.

Caring for someone with a health condition or limitation, particularly a cognitive impairment such as Alzheimer's disease or dementia, can cause physical and emotional problems and create financial and social burdens for the caregiver. This may be especially true for caregivers who are seniors themselves. On the other hand, providing care can give individuals pleasure and pride, enhance their self-worth, and help them to build closer relationships with the care recipient.

Home-Care Services

Home care for older Canadians involves a range of services, including health promotion, curative medicine, end-of-life care, rehabilitation, support and maintenance, social adaptation and integration, and support for the informal (family) caregiver. Home-care programs also link formalized health-care delivery services in the home setting with community-based services (e.g., Meals on Wheels, respite care, recreational/social programs, and volunteer services).

Home-care services can include the following:

- assessment of a client's medical and social needs and determination of the best care setting based on the client's health, social situation, and support network
- development of an in-home care plan, which includes family involvement, teaching, interventions, and community support
- provision of nursing services, therapy services, and home support services
- coordination of medical supplies, equipment, pharmaceuticals, and assistive devices
- ongoing monitoring and evaluation of the client's, family's, and caregiver's status and needs
- **respite care** to assist informal caregivers and support families in their role as caregivers
- discharge planning and coordination of placement services to long-term care facilities (if required)

Additional services, such as long-term care placement, mobility clinics, home adaptation/maintenance, and help with activities of daily living are coordinated and provided through or in conjunction with home-care programs. Home-care services generally include the provision of health services by two tiers of workers: professionals (such as social workers, physicians, nurses, physiotherapists, occupational therapists, speech therapists, and dieticians) and unregulated workers (such as visiting homemakers, personal support workers, and personal care attendants).

A Provincial Responsibility

Home care falls within provincial jurisdiction. In Canada, there are at least 663 agencies providing home care services, with 93 percent of delivery agencies receiving some government funding and just over 50 percent receiving all of their funding from government sources. Under the *Canada Health Act*, home care is an extended health service, which is not insured and to which the principles of the act do not apply. The home care workforce is largely unregulated and largely composed of women. Many work part time and must hold multiple jobs to make an adequate income. They receive few fringe benefits and face limited career options.

Home care
A range of services for older persons, including health promotion, curative medicine, end-of-life care, rehabilitation, support and maintenance, social adaptation and integration, and support for family caregivers

Respite care
Temporary relief for an informal caregiver, either in the form of a substitute in-home caregiver or a short stay at a long-term facility for the person receiving care

The type of services, the amount of service, and the criteria for accessing services vary from province to province. The responsibility for home care has been delegated to a regional or local health authority in 10 of the 13 provinces and territories. Six provinces require an income test to obtain public funding for home care. Veterans Affairs Canada provides home care services to clients with wartime or special-duty area service when the service is not available to them through provincial and territorial programs. Home care services are also offered jointly by Indigenous and Northern Affairs Canada and Health Canada, which together have responsibility for on-reserve First Nations home care.

The slow pace and piecemeal development of home care services have left many older Canadians without programs that properly meet their physical, emotional, and social needs. Many social workers are convinced that nothing short of a universal and comprehensive national home care system is necessary. As hospital care is cut and people are sent home to recover, resources go to those with the most acute medical needs. This leaves frail older persons and those with disabilities at a disadvantage (Armstrong, Armstrong, and Neysmith, 2015).

"There is no information in Canada to tell us how many seniors may be falling through the cracks—people who don't have home care support, but probably should" (Health Council of Canada, 2012).

Dementia—A Growing Health Priority

Are we ready?

Rapidly rising dementia rates mean the disease will touch more and more people. But there is still time to act.

The tide of dementia is swelling, and no country will be spared. There are no effective drugs, no cure—and in Canada, no national strategy for a major public health issue that will only keep growing. This is not just a problem for old people. It is everyone's problem.

"I can think of no other disease that has such a profound effect on loss of function, loss of independence, and the need for care," Dr. Margaret Chan, director general of the World Health Organization, said in March 2015. "I can think of no other disease so deeply dreaded by anyone who wants to age gracefully and with dignity. I can think of no other disease that places such a heavy burden on families, communities, and societies. I can think of no other disease where innovation, including breakthrough discoveries to develop a cure, is so badly needed."

Dementia rates are rising because of how rapidly Canada's population is aging, and we will all feel the economic and social burdens of the disease.

- $33 billion: The annual cost of dementia in Canada today
- $293 billion: The projected cost of dementia in 2040

There is no question: if dementia doesn't already affect you, it will some day. You could become a patient or a caregiver, or a taxpayer increasingly burdened by dementia's spiralling costs. It is a growing public health crisis that will overwhelm countries like Canada if we are not prepared.

One in five Canadians aged 45 and older provides some form of care to seniors living with long-term health problems. If you are in your 30s, by the time you are ten years from retirement, your age cohort is even more likely to be part of this "sandwich" generation: balancing full-time work, child care, and caring for aging parents.

- 444 million: The unpaid hours family caregivers spent looking after someone with a cognitive impairment in 2011—the equivalent of 55.5 million eight-hour work days

- 1.2 billion: The unpaid hours family caregivers are projected to spend looking after someone with cognitive impairment in 2040—150 million work days.

- $1.3 billion: The cost in lost productivity in 2012. That year, 1.6 million caregivers took leave from work; nearly 600,000 reduced their work hours; 160,000 turned down paid employment; and 390,000 quit their jobs to provide care.

Because so much falls on families, dementia's toll on health ripples outward.

- 2008-09: 16 percent of people who care for sick loved ones at home reported feeling stress, anger, or depression.
- 2013-14: That number rose to 33 per cent.

The cost of dementia would rank as the world's 18th-largest economy:

- 17. Netherlands ($869,508 million)
- 18. Dementia ($818,000 million)
- 19. Turkey ($799,535 million)
- 20. Saudi Arabia ($746,249 million)
- 21. Switzerland ($685,434 million)

And it's not just happening in rich countries: poorer nations are experiencing a faster rise in dementia rates, too.

But there is still time. Dementia is finally becoming a global health priority: the world's first G8 dementia summit was held in 2013. Canada does not have a national dementia strategy, but it has committed to developing one and is investing millions of dollars in a major research network dedicated to neurodegenerative diseases, including dementia.

Alzheimer's Disease

Alzheimer's, the most common form of dementia, slowly destroys nerve cells in the brain. It affects primarily those over the age of 65, but it is considered to be an illness and not a normal part of aging. There are no drugs that cure Alzheimer's, but there are medications that can help relieve some of the symptoms.

- 1,120: The number of Alzheimer's drugs investigated between 1995 and 2014. Only four have made it to market, and all treat symptoms, not the disease itself.

Lifestyle Choices Affect Our Risk

The good news is that we can do something about dementia. Researchers have discovered that lifestyle choices affect our risk: one in three cases of Alzheimer's disease are attributable to risk factors that can be altered, such as smoking and physical inactivity.

Researchers believe that abnormal changes in the brain may begin up to 25 years before memory-related Alzheimer's symptoms start to appear. That means health choices you make in middle age can have a huge impact. For example, for each unit increase of body mass index (BMI) in a 50-year-old person, one study predicts the onset of dementia symptoms 6.7 months earlier. In another study, participants who engaged in physical activities at least twice a week in mid-life had half the dementia risk of sedentary people.

There is preliminary—and controversial—European research that suggests controlling risk factors has begun to affect how many people are getting dementia.

- 22 percent: The reduction in how many people 65 and older were living with dementia in 2011 than predicted in 1990 (according to one U.K. study), meaning that overall numbers are estimated to be stabilizing rather than rising.
- 43 percent: The reduction in how many men 65 and older were living with dementia in 1996 compared to 1987 in Zaragoza, Spain, according to another study.

The onset of dementia can cause emotional and financial stress for caregiving family members. They may become dependent upon physicians, other family members, friends, and a variety of health and social services. At the same time, caregivers may have mixed feelings about entrusting the care of a helpless relative to strangers over whom they have little control. Dealing with these situations and emotions is often the job of the social worker.

- *Source:* Yang, J., K. Allen, and A. Dempsey. (2015). The growing impact of dementia—are we ready? *The Toronto Star* (November 21).

Social Work with Older Adults
Toward hope and empowerment

The profession is moving from a deficit-based approach to a strengths-based practice

Aging well, maintaining dignity, and being treated respectfully are vitally important to older people, who may be dealing with new health concerns and feeling increasingly vulnerable. Social workers can help to ensure dignity and respect for their older clients, and at the same time address some of the ageist attitudes in our society.

Effective social work practice with older adults relies initially on a thorough bio-psychosocial assessment. Assessment is both a process and a product. During the process phase, the social worker builds a relationship with the older adult client. The product of this assessment becomes the basis of care planning and monitoring.

The major domains of assessment for older adults are physical health, competence in activities of daily living, psycho-emotional well-being, social functioning, spirituality, sexuality, and environmental safety.

Following the assessment phase, the social worker must help the individual and the individual's family examine various possible courses of action. Family members close to a situation may not see all the options available. In other cases, family members may think that they can do it all themselves and may not be open to a stranger's suggestions. The social worker needs to take into account the individual's bio-psychosocial status and the family's stance before making any recommendations.

The major theoretical approaches that inform social work interventions with older adult clients are outlined below.

Life Course Theory

Life course theory focuses on how individuals take various distinct pathways through life as they move through different periods. This approach does not view old age as any less satisfying than other periods of life, such as early parenthood. Rather, it views each period as having particular benefits, limitations, and characteristics. This approach is unique in that it discusses issues in terms of life events rather than age.

This theory has great potential with respect to informing effective social work practice. Glen Elder (Elder and Johnson, 2002), the originator of the theory, posits four principles for his approach:

- The life course of a person is shaped by his or her historical and geographic placement.

- The impact of a transition or event depends on when it occurs in a person's life.
- Lives are lived interdependently—the actions and relationships of one person can affect the lives of others.
- Individuals construct their own life course through choices and actions, but these are contingent upon the constraints and opportunities presented.

The life course theory has the advantage of addressing both the individual and the broader contextual issues surrounding aging. It also allows for the incorporation of ideas from feminist theory, critical theory, and political economy theory.

Strengths-Based and Solutions-Focused Approaches

The strengths-based perspective is a philosophical standpoint that focuses on the inherent resilience in human nature that underlies much of social work practice. This perspective is especially useful with older adults, who have a lifetime of rich experience to draw upon in order to confront current difficulties. Strengths-based and solutions-focused approaches are both rooted in the belief that capacity rather than pathology should be the primary focal point of the helping process.

A strengths-based approach focuses on individuals' potential and capabilities rather than on their limitations. In his popular book *The Strengths Perspective in Social Work Practice* (now in its sixth edition), Dennis Saleebey analyzes social work assessment and treatment. He writes about the language used in assessments and the power held by the assessor. The assessor wields considerably more power than the client and also controls the client's record of assessment.

Most professionals, particularly health professionals, are trained to search for problems or deficits so that the problems or deficits can be fixed. Saleebey sees this tendency as intertwined with the "lexicon of pathology." Traditional medical models of care impose a passive role upon clients. Problem-based assessment signals to the client that the social worker believes the client cannot cope. This messaging can instill an enduring lack of self-confidence in the older person.

The strengths-based model, by contrast, elicits an active role for clients—they interact with their social worker to achieve a positive outcome. Social workers base their practice on values that reflect a belief in each client's

- respect and dignity
- empowerment and self-determination
- full and equal citizenship and membership in society
- resilience (the capacity to recover over time)
- capacity to heal and to benefit from social engagement
- potential for positive "possibilities" (Saleebey, 2012)

Facilitating self-determination for older adults is key. Seniors have fundamental rights even if they are institutionalized, cognitively impaired, or unable to communicate. When we recognize the inherent competence of older adults, even when they are somewhat impaired, we can begin to help them envision a more satisfying future for themselves.

"Empowered practice" (Soniat and Michlos, 2010) and strengths-based theories reinforce social work advocacy for older adults. Critical approaches (e.g., Robbins, Chatterjee, and Canda, 2012) strengthen the capacity to empower individuals, families, and systems as social workers strive to tip the balance away from a deficit-based model and toward fulfillment of clients' needs and the maintenance of their dignity.

Other Approaches and Interventions

Cognitive behavioural therapy (CBT) and problem-solving therapy (PST) are often used to treat mild to moderate forms of depression and anxiety in older adults. The basic principles of these approaches have also been adapted to treat individuals with mild to moderate dementia.

Therapeutic reminiscence is a technique that encourages clients to summon memories involving positive affect in order to moderate negative emotional states. Life review encourages clients to retrieve both positive and negative emotional memories in order to help dispel current negative emotions.

One of the fastest-growing, innovative approaches to working with older adults is that of recognizing and mobilizing an older adult's spirituality. Such practice requires an ability to hear the grief, longing, joy, and hope in the stories that clients tell, and to help the client perceive important underlying spiritual themes in their stories, of which they may not be fully aware.

And finally, the power of the group process and family-centred methods can help alleviate stressors experienced by extended family members in caring for an aging adult. The importance of sustaining the well-being of caregivers is a vital part of a systemic approach to providing services to older adults.

The Role of the Social Worker

Today, social workers focus largely on the life stage and the assets of the older persons they serve, and they often find innovative ways to meet their clients' needs.

It is imperative that the social worker has a basic clarity about his or her task: to help the families of people with aging-related issues—as well as the individuals themselves—develop an understanding about the situation that enables them to act. This helps the family gain a sense of direction in the midst of what might otherwise appear to be a daunting situation.

Providing Relief to Caregivers

Supporting family members with caregiving responsibilities

In 2012, more than 5 million people in Canada provided care related to poor health, disability, or other aging-related problem for someone over the age of 64. These people provided care either in the recipient's home, in their own home, or in a care facility (Statistics Canada, 2015).

Most of the caregivers and care receivers were women. Some caregivers gave up their jobs to provide personal care for an ill parent or spouse, resulting in major financial, emotional, and health-related implications for the caregiver.

As mentioned previously, the extent of informal caregiving is often understated. It is estimated that between 85 and 90 percent of care for older Canadians is provided in the home by relatives. As Canadians age, informal caregiving is becoming increasingly important to the well-being of seniors.

Most older Canadians express a strong preference for remaining in their own homes. Informal caregivers—family and friends who provide unpaid assistance with tasks such as transportation, meal preparation, and personal care—help them to do so, while also reducing demands on the health-care system.

More Public Financial Support Is Needed

Caring for someone with a health condition or limitation, especially cognitive impairments such as Alzheimer's disease and dementia, can cause physical and emotional problems and create financial and social pressures for the caregiver. This may be especially true for caregivers who are seniors themselves.

Most working-age caregivers experience conflicting demands between paid work and caregiving and have to miss days at work or reduce their paid work hours. Clearly, caregivers bear a disproportionate share of the costs of caring for those with long-term health problems and disabilities. The issue of overburdened caregivers is prompting social workers, formal care providers, advocates for older adults, and family caregivers to call for more support—financial, educational, and practical—to give family caregivers a much-needed break.

Caring for older people at home puts an enormous strain on family members, yet studies have shown that caregivers believe the care they provide is better than the care that is available in institutions such as nursing homes. A strong case can be made that home care provision needs more public financial support if it is to reach all citizens and not just those who can pay for it.

Thomas and Eldrid's story describes how a social worker can collaborate with family members to develop a plan to help relieve some of the physical and emotional demands inherent in caregiving. In this case, the social worker acts as a sounding board and an empathetic listener.

Equally if not more importantly, the social worker can often function as a "broker" of additional home-care services that might be available to and affordable by the family members who are serving as caregivers. These additional services can make all the difference in alleviating the stresses experienced by the caregivers of older adults.

Reflecting on Thomas and Eldrid's Story

1. Identify the three issues in this story that you believe are the most important, and explain your thinking.
2. Briefly describe the challenges faced by each family member in this story. What types of supports and services might strengthen this family's ability to care for Thomas at home?
3. What social work values guided Shelley's professional behaviour?

Thomas and Eldrid's Story…
Helping older parents and their caregivers

Social workers can offer a fresh problem-solving perspective when informal caregivers feel exhausted and overwhelmed.

Thomas, aged 80, and Eldrid, aged 76, have been married for 58 years. Several years ago, Thomas suffered a stroke. Eldrid takes care of Thomas at home, with the help of two of her four children and occasional assistance from a home-care agency.

Partially paralyzed, Thomas becomes angry and verbally abusive when his immobility and incontinence frustrate him. Caring for Thomas is taking a toll on Eldrid's physical and psychological well-being. However, she would feel extremely guilty if Thomas were moved to a nursing home.

Veline, the older daughter, is worried about Eldrid's declining physical and mental health. Eldrid has arthritis and poor hearing. Veline would like to spend more time helping her parents, but her job as a manager of a restaurant chain keeps her extremely busy. When Veline does try to help her parents with household chores or transportation to medical appointments, she finds herself becoming angry and impatient with her father, who was often verbally abusive to her when she was growing up. The two sons, Paul and John, are younger than Veline and older than the younger daughter, Anne. Both sons live a long distance from their parents. Paul visits for two days every three months and tries to offer practical support during each stay.

Veline has contacted Shelley, a social worker in a family service agency, to talk about ways to get help for her parents. Shelley will need to conduct a psychosocial assessment and propose a plan that can support the family through this difficult period. Empathetic listening, compassion, and impartiality on Shelley's part will be essential in fulfilling her role.

Shelley sets up a meeting in the family home to pose assessment questions to Eldrid and Thomas. During the meeting, she notices Eldrid wince in pain as she bends to help her husband. In private, Eldrid admits to feeling downtrodden and discouraged. Upon completing the initial assessment and after speaking with each adult child (either in person or over the phone) to hear their uncensored thoughts, Shelley is getting a clearer picture of the family and the issues they are facing together.

Despite everyone's concerns about Eldrid, Shelley points out that Eldrid has the right to make decisions for herself and deserves respect and recognition for choosing to look after her ailing husband. Thomas, too, has a say in the type and quality of care he receives and he has voiced a strong preference to be cared for by his wife rather than by a stranger. But Eldrid has confided to Shelley that she "never has any time for herself" and that she is feeling "burnt out." With Shelley present, Eldrid has agreed to discuss her needs with each adult child individually. Shelley will also speak with Thomas separately.

As a first step, Eldrid and Shelley discuss an ideal plan that might include ways that each child can help relieve some of the pressure on Eldrid, regardless of where they live. Perhaps Anne can come to the house one morning, afternoon, or evening per week. Perhaps John, a successful entrepreneur, can pay for additional homemaking help, such as a cleaning service. Paul might extend his visits to five days so that Eldrid can enjoy restorative visits with her sister, who lives two hours away. When Shelley presents this plan to Thomas, he frowns but then replies curtly, "Whatever Eldrid wants is fine with me."

Eldrid and Shelley acknowledge the fact that the ideal plan might not work out. In that case, could the family afford more paid in-home help? Could they arrange regular respite care to relieve Eldrid's workload? Would they consider a move for Thomas to a long-term care setting? The family agrees to discuss further options if the need arises. Shelley knows that if that happens, the conversations will become more difficult. Her communication skills and family negotiation skills would be put to the test if a major shift of responsibility were required.

Shelley sets up appointments and arranges Skype sessions for the family members to discuss their roles in the ideal plan, first with each person individually and then with the entire family. Shelley prepares a list of community services (home nursing care, paid homemakers, Meals on Wheels, friendly visitors, and respite care) that could help the family cope as needed. She is relieved that the whole family, including Thomas, have agreed to implement a plan that could maintain stability in the home while giving Eldrid some much-needed time for herself.

Caregivers of seniors who are seniors themselves need support to avoid burnout, exhaustion, and illness.

Seniors in Long-Term Care Homes

Social work in institutional long-term care settings

At the time of the 2011 census, 7.1 percent of Canadians over 65 lived in special care homes, usually nursing homes. Among those Canadians over 85, however, the percentage was 29.6. Projections for 2031 are that the number of long-term care beds will triple or even quadruple.

More often than not, responsibility for looking after residents of long-term care facilities falls on other family members, many of whom themselves are in need of care. Family caregivers to seniors in long-term care homes help their loved one with personal care, medical treatments, banking, paying bills, and managing finances on a weekly basis. Over the past few years, the number of people in need of transfer to long-term care homes has increased. More long-term services and programming are now essential but not always available. Social workers play an important role in the provision of long-term care for older adults (Statistics Canada, 2011).

The Components and Phases of Long-Term Care

Social work in this field is multidisciplinary, allowing social workers to practise collaboratively and to join other health professionals in advocating for their clients. The components of long-term care are health care and social services to provide assessment, treatment, rehabilitation, and supportive care, as well as to prevent the increased disability of individuals of all age groups who have chronic physical, developmental, or emotional impairments. Social workers in long-term care settings are involved during all the phases of care, from pre-admission through residency to the termination of residency at the time of discharge, transfer, or death.

- **Pre-admission phase.** As the first contact with the resident and family, the social worker deals with client and family feelings about placement and provides information about the facility and services. This is an important phase, as the social worker can help the family deal with issues of immediate concern and identify potential future issues as well.
- **Admission phase.** Social workers are usually responsible for the admission process. During admission, the social worker helps the resident and family become familiar with the facility and its routines. The social worker is often the first liaison between the resident and family and any other community agency that was previously involved. Often, social workers engage in counselling during this phase as the resident and family members adjust to a new reality.
- **Residency phase.** A variety of interventions may occur during residency that involve the social worker. Social workers regularly work at the individual, family, community, and policy levels. Work at the individual level focuses on the social and emotional impacts of physical and mental illness or impairment and the prevention of further physical and mental health problems. Social workers work with families in discussing palliative care and end-of-life issues, dealing with family members who are feeling guilt related to the placement, or providing information about care and prevention issues. Commonly, social workers are involved in locating and arranging resources and in developing or implementing innovative programs and policy.
- **Discharge, transfer, or death phase.** Discharge and transfer planning is a key aspect of social work in long-term care. In the case of the death of the resident, social workers may provide grief counselling for team members and the family.

Reflecting on Claire's Story

1. Identify one idea from this story that is important to you as you build relationships with older persons in your life. Explain your answer.
2. Select one client-empowerment strategy applied in this story and explain why the strategy works.
3. Describe some advantages of a multidisciplinary team approach to social work with seniors in long-term care settings.

Claire's Story...
Adjusting to long-term care

In this story, a social worker helps an older client cope with a major life transition. The story provides insight into generalist practice with older adults.

For three months, 85-year-old Claire has been convalescing in the long-term care unit of a medical centre. She had suffered a fall while entering her daughter Daphne's home, where she had been living since moving from her own home two years before when managing a household became too challenging for her. Claire has been diagnosed with severe osteoarthritis and chronic obstructive pulmonary disease (COPD). She had been using a walker, but walking is now very painful. A long-term care social worker has been asked to help the medical team assess the viability of Claire returning to her daughter's home.

Facilitating Client Choices

It is clear that Claire is facing a major life transition—from being a relatively independent person who could look after herself to someone who is dependent on others and whose mobility is compromised. The team of workers assigned to Claire's case recognize that Claire is confronting several life stressors: declining health, the threat of losing her independence, and financial worries about the costs of residing in a long-term care facility.

Despite her setbacks, Claire is adamant that she wishes to return to her daughter's home once she is well enough to be discharged. The team respects Claire's determination and "fighting spirit," but they must investigate whether returning to live in this environment is a realistic goal for Claire.

To determine the feasibility of discharging Claire to Daphne's home, various team members carry out separate assessments. An occupational therapist conducts an evaluation with Claire to observe whether she has the necessary strength and stamina to prepare her own meals. (As it turns out, Claire does not have the physical capacity to reach into cupboards or to lift objects such as pots or a tea kettle.) Nurses take Claire for short walks around the unit at least twice a day as she pushes a wheelchair in front of her. They note that walking even a few steps causes Claire pain and anxiety as she fears taking another fall. To allay her anxiety somewhat and to offset the risk of blood clots, a physiotherapist demonstrates stretching and flexibility exercises that Claire can do while sitting in a chair or lying in bed. The social worker, Jo, sets out to help Claire and her family assess what resources and supports she would need if she returned to her daughter's home. Daphne and her husband work long hours far from where they live. Therefore, Claire would need daily visits from a personal support worker to help her get dressed and bathed. She would need Meals on Wheels, transportation to medical appointments, telephone check-ins, visits from neighbours, and a medical alert bracelet. Jo exercises respect and diplomacy in helping Claire realize that returning to live in her daughter's home would require many adaptations and a certain degree of risk to her well-being.

The social worker visits Daphne's home to assess the physical environment. The home is a multi-level dwelling with bedrooms on the top floor. The open-concept main floor plan precludes setting up a bedroom for Claire on ground level. The stairs leading to the top level are angled in a way that poses a serious hazard for Claire.

To help bolster Claire's sense of self-direction and autonomy, Jo encourages her to draw up a list of pros and cons related to moving back to Daphne's house. One major disadvantage would be social isolation and inactivity. Claire has expressed a high need for social stimulation, and admits that she would not enjoy spending long hours each day sitting by herself watching television. She is also nervous about getting back and forth to the bathroom on her own. Two advantages of remaining in the long-term care setting are the constant social interaction and the continual monitoring of Claire's needs.

Jo, Claire, and Daphne discuss the long-term care facility's monthly fees and decide that they are affordable.

Claire reflects on the list she has made and then decides on her own that the risks involved in moving back to her daughter's home outweigh the benefits. She makes up her mind to look on the bright side as she adapts to her new circumstances. Jo works with Claire and her daughter's family to set up a schedule of regular visitors each week and to arrange family get-togethers at Daphne's home twice a week to help ease Claire's transition to life in a long-term care facility.

Social workers in long-term care settings help older clients cope with a variety of life stressors and challenges.

Respecting End-of-Life Choices

Social work in palliative-care settings for older adults

As discussed in Chapter 6, palliative care is a specialized kind of holistic health care for individuals and families who are dealing with a life-threatening illness at an advanced stage. Those who provide palliative care strive to provide the best quality of life by ensuring that the dying individual's symptoms are managed while all possible steps are taken to maintain their comfort and dignity.

Palliative care offers a wide range of emotional, spiritual, and health-related support services. Madeleine Saint-Michel, a palliative care expert, emphasizes that a terminally ill person requires much more than physical comfort. They also need help in mindfully addressing the deep-seated emotions and feelings related to dying. While there are similarities in palliative care for all ages, palliative care for older adults presents some unique challenges, particularly for social workers.

Palliative care for older adults usually occurs in the person's home or in a long-term care facility where they have been living an average of two years before their death. In the latter case, teams are trained in basic palliative care strategies and they work alongside family members to ensure that the older loved one has a peaceful and dignified death. The Canadian Hospice Palliative Care Association acknowledges, however, that this collaborative approach has not been fully incorporated into the culture of long-term care homes. Achieving this cultural shift, combined with more advanced training in palliative care, will be a leading priority in long-term care facilities over the next few years (Canadian Hospice Palliative Care Association, 2015).

Palliative Interventions

Palliative interventions attempt to provide relief from suffering at the end of life, and may include pain medication, oxygen, intravenous or nasogastric (through the nose) feeding, anti-nausea medication, and anti-anxiety medication. Palliative interventions can also include psychosocial support, such as counselling provided by a social worker, and spiritual support for both the patient and the family.

Two categories of palliative interventions have the potential to cause death: opioid use and terminal sedation. Opioids—a group of drugs that act on receptors in the brain to reduce pain—include morphine, codeine, heroin, fentanyl, and oxycodone. Opioids can depress respiration (breathing), which in some rare cases can be fatal, even when the opioids are being used appropriately. Terminal sedation is the practice of total sedation combined with the withholding or withdrawal of potentially life-sustaining artificial hydration and nutrition. Terminal sedation might be requested if a patient is imminently dying (within hours) and physical pain cannot be controlled in any other way, or if a patient is expected to die within a week, is not suffering physical pain, but is suffering mental anguish that cannot be controlled in any other way.

In Helen and Josef's story, a social worker must keep the client's right to autonomous decision making in the forefront despite pressure from family members to sway the individual's decision toward their preferred course of action.

Reflecting on Helen and Josef's Story

1. Summarize the primary ethical dilemma depicted in this story.
2. What measures might encourage adults of all ages to organize advance directives that specify their wishes regarding end-of-life issues?
3. Who or what might verify that Josef is mentally capable of of making his own end-of-life decisions?

Helen and Josef's Story… Upholding the right to self-determination

From an ethics standpoint, a social worker must respect each mentally competent individual's right to self-determination right up until the moment of death.

Josef is 88 and his wife Helen is 84. They have three children. Susan is an administrative assistant who lives in rural Nova Scotia in the same town as Josef and Helen. George is a lawyer living in Toronto and Jim is an actor living in Vancouver. Josef has had a series of mini-strokes during recent years. About five years ago, he and Helen decided that he needed more care than Helen could provide, so he moved into a nursing home.

The most recent mini-stroke has left Josef unable to walk, speak, or write. He has been moved to the rehabilitation ward of a local hospital. Helen's health is comparatively good for a woman of her age. She has some hearing and vision loss but her cognitive abilities and mobility are good overall. She looks after herself with the help of a homemaker. She is able to continue living in the family home and she visits Josef every day.

A Complex Ethical Dilemma

Josef is not responding well to the treatment he is receiving for his latest mini-stroke. His doctor thinks it was likely a more substantial stroke than they had initially thought. Josef has had two choking spells in the last few days and a medical report indicates that he is at risk of having food lodge in his lungs if he continues to try to eat. This report has thrown the family into confusion regarding treatment for Josef.

A social worker, Nadya, is called in for a consultation with other interdisciplinary team members regarding Josef's inability to eat and Helen's distress in the face of this development. No one has yet contacted the couple's children to discuss their reactions to the latest medical report.

When this case is first assigned to her, Nadya thinks it seems quite straightforward—an older couple needs support to cope with a health-related difficulty. It gradually becomes clear, however, that this case involves complicated bioethical and psychological factors. Josef's level of care is now on the verge of becoming palliative, although no one has discussed this possibility with the couple or with the adult children.

Nadya is concerned about several issues. Is it possible for the doctors treating Josef to determine the likelihood of impending death? Is Josef willing to be fed intravenously or via nasogastric feeding? If not, will he consent to some level of sedation to offset both his physical and his mental suffering? Who holds power of attorney in deciding whether terminal sedation is administered to Josef? Has Josef documented his end-of-life wishes in the form of an advance directive?

To help address these questions, Nadya holds individual meetings with each family member as well as with some members of the health-care team. Josef is unable to communicate except by eye movement, but when he is told about the various medical reports, he indicates that he understands by blinking his eyes once for yes and twice for no.

Helen informs everyone that Josef has managed to tell her that he is ready to die and that he does not wish to have his life prolonged through artificial means. Understandably distraught, Helen and the adult children object to this decision and wish to persuade Josef to accept either intravenous or nasogastric feeding.

Decision-Making Power

This case raises the issue of decision-making authority. To what extent can or should the medical team influence decision making one way or the other?

Is the medical team ethically bound to make every attempt to prolong Josef's life, even if these attempts contradict his express wish to die a dignified death rather than continue to suffer when there is no hope of recovery?

The social worker must listen carefully to each participant's opinions and beliefs—remembering that the principal client is Josef and that his wishes and rights are paramount.

Ultimately, the social worker and the medical team sat down with Josef's family members to allow them to voice their fears and concerns. At the same time, they managed to gently guide the family to an understanding that Josef has an inviolable right to refuse invasive life-saving techniques and to choose how he spends his final days.

For everyone involved, end-of-life decisions involve navigating complex and challenging ethical questions.

Lorna MacGregor

Lorna MacGregor began her social work career in child welfare. She then moved from community work to management, and finally, to community and institutional care for older adults.

As this social worker re-examines her career, two interwoven themes emerge: the need for advocacy for various groups, and the constant challenges involved in balancing personal, family, and professional priorities.

I am currently chair of Care Watch, a senior-run organization that advocates for quality home care in Ontario. I am also an active member of Concerned Friends, an organization that provides a voice for quality in long-term care for older adults.

Time spent as a teenager in Canadian Girls in Training inspired my desire to make a difference. While studying math and physics at Queen's University, I met my husband-to-be along with his mother and aunt, both of whom had social work experience. Another social worker in the family had published a journal article titled "Reflections of a Radical Social Worker." Having learned about social work from knowing these women, I applied to the University of Toronto's School of Social Work after completing my undergraduate degree, and I was accepted at the age of 21.

Upon graduating from the M.S.W. program, I started work with the Children's Aid Society. Six years later, I left my job when I became pregnant. A year later, the YWCA hosted a "liberation school"—a day of workshops with childcare included! I joined the Board's Social Action Committee. It was focused on women's issues, including abortion, and I was soon appointed chair. The committee and the community were caught up in controversy; it was an exciting time. When the YWCA championed agencies' rights to determine their own policies independently, I found myself chairing a major YWCA-hosted meeting. Given my volunteer commitments at that time, juggling full-time work while raising small children was not an option for me.

When my younger child was in school full time in 1987, I received a phone call from the executive director of Meals on Wheels. She remembered me from my volunteer work with the YWCA and persuaded me to return to work full time. The salary I was being offered was attractive, and I could leave work early two or three days a week to be home after school with my children. I applied for and got the job, and ended up managing community services, including social work, transportation, meals on wheels, and community dining.

Several years later, around the time my younger child went off to university, I decided to do something different. After two interviews with the City of Toronto, I accepted a position as the manager of programs and services at Seven Oaks Long-Term Care Home, where I stayed for ten years before retiring. The job included management of a range of programs to benefit long-term care residents, including social work, recreation, physiotherapy , occupational therapy, spiritual and religious care, and massage/aroma/music/art therapies.

At Seven Oaks I particularly enjoyed my work facilitating staff development. I forwarded job postings to colleagues, offered staff members time off to attend professional development workshops, and encouraged staff to move beyond their comfort zones in pursuit of better positions. In this way, careers advanced and clients were better served. In hindsight, I view my efforts as backroom advocacy—I was doing my best work behind the scenes.

I enjoy applying my skills—administrative, management, leadership, organizational, playing "devil's advocate"—to advance important causes, but I am not comfortable performing in the spotlight. In retirement, as chair of Care Watch, I moderate meetings, organize agendas, and supervise a staff member. I depend on others to front appointments with politicians, write blogs, and facilitate events. With Concerned Friends, I review and analyze Ministry of Health inspection reports for long-term care homes in Ontario.

Gerontological social workers often find that end-of-life issues are at the forefront, but they deal frequently with a wide range of life issues as well. Workers have a chance to influence the environments in which their clients live—for the better. Although systemic change is necessary, complex, and slow, it does happen, thanks to the work of dedicated and persistent advocates for older adults.

Chapter 11 Review

Review Questions

1. What trends in Canadian society are likely to make working with older adults a "growth industry" in the future?
2. Describe some of the preconceptions that contribute to ageism in our society.
3. What are some of the issues of increasing concern regarding older Canadians? With which issues will social workers increasingly be involved?
4. Define and explore the causes of the abuse and neglect of older adults in family homes or institutional settings.
5. Explain why many older adults in Canada are not receiving the home care services they need.
6. What are the advantages of using the life course theory as a lens for effective social work practice?

Exploring Social Work

1. What kind of social work services do you believe are necessary for older adults to continue to live on their own? What are the roles of social workers in helping seniors "age in place"?
2. A major part of social work practice with older adults is helping them deal with end-of-life difficulties, including pain and spiritual and emotional questions. Discuss this topic in small groups and do a group presentation that depicts how social workers might assist older adults in hospice care. Include reflections on the kind of training that might help social workers in this type of work.
3. Write a brief response to the following comment by Dr. Chris Simpson, past president of the Canadian Medical Association: "We have emergency doctors treating patients in hallways because there are no beds. We have staff scrambling to free up beds. And we have social workers calling in favours to get a bed in a local nursing home.... We need a national seniors strategy to ensure that patients who are well enough to leave the hospital actually have some place to go. We need better home care and residential options so that we never again have to hear the term 'bed blocker.'"

Websites

Seniors Canada
www.seniors.gc.ca

This site provides access to information and services that are relevant to those 55 and older, their families, caregivers, and supporting service organizations. The publications section is excellent, and the listing of services available for seniors is a valuable resource for social workers.

Canadian Association on Gerontology (CAG)
www.cagacg.ca

Founded in 1971, the Canadian Association on Gerontology is a national, multidisciplinary scientific and educational association established to provide leadership in matters related to the aging population.

CARP: Canada's Association for the 50-Plus
www.carp.ca

Originally known as the Canadian Association for Retired Persons, CARP is an advocacy group dedicated to improving the quality of life for Canadians as they age. With an expansive membership and strong financial support, CARP is a powerful voice for seniors in Canada, promoting active lifestyles, financial security, access to health care, and an end to discrimination based on age.

The Alzheimer Society of Canada
www.alzheimer.ca

The Alzheimer Society of Canada's website is an excellent resource for information about Alzheimer's and how to work effectively with those affected by it.

Social Work and Sexual and Gender Diversity

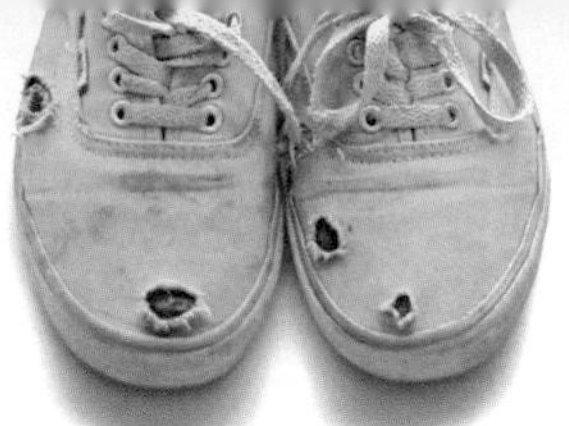

Sarah Todd

Celebrating Human Diversity

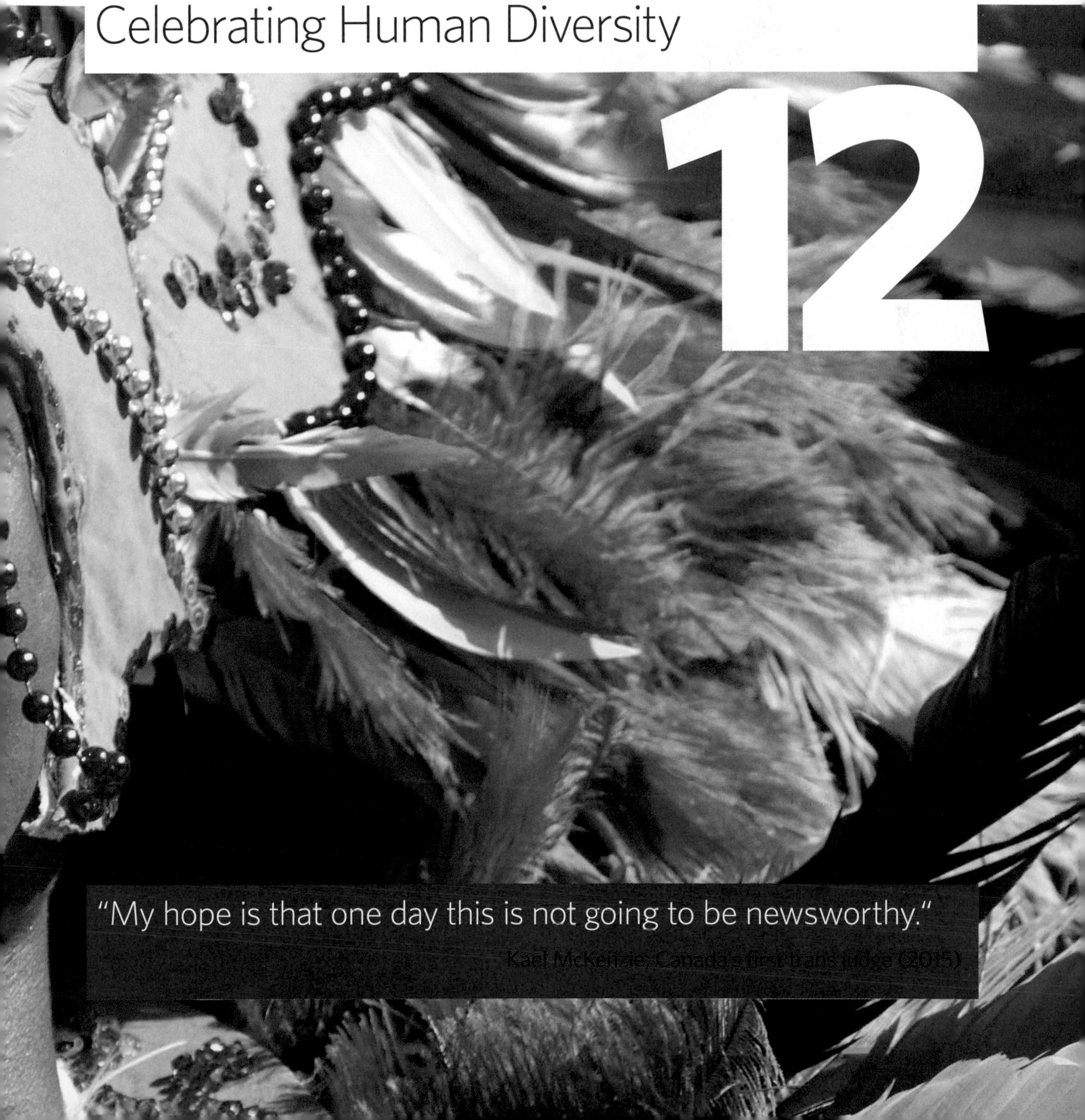

12

"My hope is that one day this is not going to be newsworthy."

Kael McKenzie, Canada's first trans judge (2015)

Social work is embracing fluid ideas about gender and sexual identity.

Sexually and gender-diverse social workers and clients enrich our profession and have challenged its complicity in the regulation of sexuality and gender. As a result, social work is increasingly able to embrace fluid notions of identity while drawing on more inclusive ideas about what is normal or healthy in terms of gender expression and sexual desire. This shift is a work in progress, requiring professionals to question heteronormativity, cisnormativity, and our own conceptualizations about sexual and gender identities and practices.

While many LGBTQ+ people (lesbian, gay, bisexual, transgendered, and queer, as well as two-spirited, transsexual, and intersexed) who reach out for social work services have needs similar to their non-LGBTQ+ counterparts, sexual orientation and gender identity may shape how they experience programs and resources. Social workers are also increasingly aware that sexuality and gender are not just issues for LGBTQ+ persons but are central to all our lives and the lives of our clients. As such, sexuality and gender are central to social work practice, and practitioners are challenged to interrogate their own identities and practices while also seeing all clients as sexual and gendered beings.

In this chapter, you will learn how to...

- understand the social and cultural experiences of sexually and gender-diverse communities in Canada
- become more aware of your own conceptualizations of sexuality and gender and how they influence your interactions with LGBTQ+ people
- promote an understanding of sexualities, gender, and identities as sometimes fixed, other times fluid, and always contextual
- unpack the social and material relations that privilege some genders and sexualities while marginalizing others
- expand and strengthen your understanding of human sexuality

Key Concepts

- Sexology
- Kinsey Report
- Heterosexism
- Biological determinism
- Social constructionism
- Queer theory
- LGBTQ+
- Sex and gender
- Sexual orientation
- Two-spirited
- Cissexual/Cisgender
- Transgender
- Transsexuals
- Intersexuals
- Homophobia, biphobia, and transphobia
- Stonewall Rebellion
- Queer activism
- Heteronormativity
- Cisnormativity
- Transmisogyny

Focusing Question

What are your beliefs about sexuality and gender, and how might they impact your role as a social worker?

Gender and Sexual Diversity: An Historical Context

Two major historical developments over the past 50 years have helped to shape our thinking about gender and sexuality. The first is **sexology**, a field of study that attempted to classify sexual desire and gender identity. The second is community activism—a creative and focused movement that evolved in response to a history of oppression and marginalization shared by persons embracing sexual and gender diversity. Community activism has led to growing recognition of sexual and gender rights in Canada.

Sexology Influences Perceptions of Human Sexuality

In the late nineteenth century, scientists and philosophers in Europe and North America increasingly applied notions of science and formal reason to explain and categorize the world around them. Part of that process of categorization involved documenting what was considered to be proper sexual attraction (Katz , 1995: 51). Thus, the science of sex—sexology—was invented, and the ideas of the "heterosexual" and the "homosexual" emerged. This is not to say that same-sex and different-sex desire did not exist before this time, but the turn of the century marked a shift in how people made sense of these desires and behaviours.

One aspect of the study of sexual identities that occurred at the turn of the century is often termed "medical colonization." The end of the nineteenth and beginning of the twentieth century was a time when medical authority began to replace pre-existing religious and judicial authorities. Prior to this transition, sexual and gender non-conventionality were most often understood as sinful or illegal. With the rise of professional "scientific medicine," sexologists were called into courtrooms to provide evidence that such transgressions were caused by biological or neurological abnormalities that required treatment, rather than punishment.

By 1900, much of the concern around sexual normality and abnormality was focused on whether people were engaging in sex primarily for reproduction (normal) or pleasure (deviant). One of the pioneers in creating categories of normal and abnormal behaviour was Richard von Krafft-Ebing (1840–1902). Krafft-Ebing's most famous piece of writing is a categorization of abnormal sexual behaviour entitled *Psychopathia Sexualis*. It is in Krafft-Ebing's work that the heterosexual begins to represent normality—Krafft-Ebing implicitly defined heterosexuality as reproductive sex between a man and a woman, and homosexuality as same-sex desire.

While some researchers were investigating the heterosexual, others were developing scientific theories of homosexuality. One of the first to do so was Karl Heinrich Ulrichs (1825–1895), a German lawyer who was vocal in the fight to decriminalize sodomy (anal sex). Ulrichs created categories of the *Urning* (a female caught in a male body) and *Urningin* (a male caught in a female body) to make sense of same-sex attraction. He viewed homosexuality as inborn and natural. Ulrichs was also one of the pioneers of the gay and lesbian rights movement.

In their efforts to provide ever-finer classifications of sexual differences, researchers sought physical markers. It was argued that one could determine a homosexual by the way he walked, the size of his hips, the shape of his penis, or his "womanly" behaviour. Female homosexuality was seldom explored scientifically until the end of the nineteenth century. Sexologists largely considered female homosexuality in relation to "abnormal" or enlarged clitorises, hermaphroditism, and gender-reversed body types. By the 1920s, lesbianism was linked with "inappropriate female behaviour," such as political activism or avoidance of motherhood. Many of the beliefs of early sexologists continue to influence common thinking about sexuality.

The Heterosexual Is Invented

In 1892, American doctor James Kiernan was the first to use the term "heterosexual." He used the term in a scholarly article to describe people who were seen as deviant because they had sex primarily for pleasure, not procreation, and were erotically attracted to people of both sexes.

Kiernan's article was also the first North American publication to use the term "homosexual," which described persons whom we would now think of as transgendered—people who bend or cross conventional gender roles (Katz, 1995).

Second-Generation Theorists

In the years following this early exploration of gender and sexual identity, a second generation of sexologists emerged. One of the most well known scientists of this generation was Alfred Kinsey (1894–1956). The Kinsey Report, published in 1948 under the title *Sexual Behavior in the Human Male*, surveyed a wide variety of people and their sexual habits and surprised the American public by revealing that 37 percent of the men in Kinsey's survey reported having had a homosexual experience to the point of orgasm. Most significantly, he showed that people's sexual behaviours combined so-called perverse behaviours with those considered normal. In 1953, he published a second report, titled *Sexual Behavior in the Human Female*.

Kinsey's research was groundbreaking because it suggested that everyday sexual behaviour often transgressed laws, public opinion, and social norms. However, with the rise of Cold War anti-communism in the 1950s, Kinsey's work was viewed with suspicion. Rumours spread that he was a communist, working to destroy American values. He lost his research funding and died of a heart attack in 1956. But Kinsey's research provided much of the basis for the political analysis developed by members of the gay liberation movement in the early 1970s.

The second generation of sexologists suggested that our social world plays a significant role in shaping our sexual desires and behaviours, and it also challenged **heterosexism**. This change in our understanding of sexuality was, in itself, a result of social and political changes. For example, second-generation sexologists were influenced by the feminist movement, which challenged the notion of a woman's "natural" place in society, suggesting that the "female" gender role is defined as much by social expectations as by any innate characteristics.

Heterosexism
A system of oppression that assumes heterosexuality is normal and superior

Discriminatory laws and practices are changing to ensure that people of all sexual orientations and gender identities have equal rights and protection in our society.

Such changes challenge what is sometimes called "heterosexual privilege"—the comfort and power accorded to people who are in, or are expected to be in, a relationship with a person of a different sex and who thus conform to dominant gender norms.

Alfred Kinsey received a doctorate in biology from Harvard University in 1919. Before the publication of his books on human sexual behaviour, he was a professor of zoology at Indiana University. He is shown here in 1948.

Shifting Theoretical Understandings of Human Sexuality

The following summaries of some modern Western responses to sexual diversity highlight a shift in theoretical understandings of human sexuality. Each of these theories attempts to solve the puzzle of sexuality, but none has been able to explain fully the complex and multiple ways in which we constitute our gender identities, sexual desires, and sexual practices, or how these identities, desires, and practices vary according to historical and cultural contexts.

Biological Determinism

Early sexologists attempted to explain sexuality in terms of biology. These explanations are known as **biological determinism**, which has traditionally focused on the organic causes of non-conventional gender and sexual identities and behaviours. This theoretical approach is still used today. Recently, Simon LeVay, former Harvard University researcher and founder of the Institute of Gay and Lesbian Education, argued that the brain structures of gay men differ from those of heterosexual men. We have also witnessed the search for the "gay gene." Such theories have been used to demand rights for queer communities on the grounds that queer persons are born queer and that their sexuality is not a matter of choice.

While it has a certain potential for liberation, biological determinism also has serious limitations. First, the argument that sexual diversity and gender identity are rooted in biology has not ended homophobia, heterosexism, and cissexualism. In fact, biological determinism has often been used to entrench inequality. Second, scientific "truths" related to gender and sexuality have consistently been shown to reflect current socio-political norms and values. The search for clear, identifiable differences regarding gender and sexuality also raises ethical concerns. For example, what if prospective parents want to test their fetus for the "gay gene" and choose abortion based on the result? This line of reasoning also accentuates the differences that heterosexual privilege relies upon, rather than exploring the similarities shared by people who desire those of a different sex and those who desire those of the same sex.

Social Constructionism

Another group of theories related to sexuality is known as **social constructionism.** These are predominantly the theories advanced by the second generation of sexologists. According to this perspective, sexualities are constructed by our social and cultural context and also by our cultural history. It is as a result of such theories that gender reassignment surgery at birth was introduced for babies determined to be intersexuals—persons whose sexual organs are not clearly male or female. It is also on the basis of such theories that psychotherapeutic approaches to "curing" sexual orientation (if an individual is attracted to people of the same sex) or reversing gender identity (if it is inconsistent with an individual's sex) evolved.

While it is clear that society does play a large role in our sexual and gender expression, social constructivist theory has a number of shortcomings. First, research has found that people cannot change their sexual orientation. While some individuals can decide not to act on their desires, the desires themselves do not disappear. Equally, babies who have been reassigned a gender at birth, either as a result of a botched circumcision or the development of ambiguous genitalia, have not easily reinvented themselves as the gendered subjects that doctors have chosen for them. Many face challenges once they enter puberty and find that their gender identity is incompatible with their sex. It seems clear that our sex, gender expression, and sexual orientation rely upon at least some biological factors.

Freud and Sexuality

Sigmund Freud (1856–1939) critiqued many of the biological explanations for homosexuality, coming close to arguing that masculinity and femininity are socially constructed. However, Freud also suggested that homosexuality is an immature stage of development compared to heterosexuality.

Freud's theories about sexuality marked an important shift away from biology to psychology, but his approach, as adopted by psychologists, was not necessarily liberating for gay men and lesbians. More often, Freud's theories were mobilized to further pathologize homosexuality as a mental illness that needed to be "cured."

Queer Theory

One significant theory that has emerged in the past 20 years or so to explain sexuality and gender falls largely within the social constructionist school of thought—**Queer theory**. This body of thought raises doubts about the feasibility of legislative changes within a capitalist democracy to bring about liberation for marginalized groups. Indeed, these theorists argue for a radical transformation of societal norms and expectations related to human sexuality.

By the late 1980s, people had begun to see the many ways in which women, people of colour, and members of **LGBTQ+** communities were still marginalized, discriminated against, and oppressed, despite hard-won legislative protection. Such observations led some activists to conclude that the existing social structures of Western society, while offering many benefits, also generate some fundamental problems that limit the possibility for freedom, equality, and justice for all.

Queer activists and theorists argue for a rethinking of the entire terrain within which we create categories of people and distribute power among them. In part, Queer theory responds to the realization that many people do not fit easily or neatly into the binary oppositions of man-woman, heterosexual-homosexual, and so on. Queer theorists suggest that identifying as gay or straight does not provide an unquestionable or complete description of who people are sexually attracted to, with whom they have sex, or with whom they share loving relationships.

Current Terminology Related to Sexual and Gender Diversity

Sex and gender refer to quite different aspects of our identities. *Sex* (usually male or female) is what doctors attribute to babies based largely on the shape and size of their genitalia. In fact, sex is determined by genetics, chromosomes, and hormones, which can combine to create an indeterminate number of sexes. *Gender* has two components: gender identity, which is the sense we have of ourselves as male, female, or transgendered; and gender role, which is our adherence to cultural norms of femininity and masculinity.

Sexual orientation is an emotional, romantic, sexual, or affectional attraction to another person. It is not dependent upon a person's gender identity or gender role.

Two-spirited is a First Nations terms that recognizes gender as a continuum and includes sexual or gender identity, sexual orientation, and social values.

Cissexual/Cisgender are terms used to define persons who are not transsexuals and who have only ever experienced their gender identity and physical sex as being aligned. The term "cisgender" is used to de-privilege those who consider themselves as having a "normal" gender expression and to validate an understanding of transgender identities as simply variants of gender expression. Cissexism refers to the belief that transsexuals' identified genders are inferior to, or less authentic than, those of cissexuals.

Transgender includes those who identify as bigender, gender benders, gender outlaws, cross-dressers, drag queens, drag kings, transvestites, and transsexuals. Some intersexuals also identify as transgender. Some transgendered persons understand their experience in dimorphic absolutes (e.g., a male trapped in a female body), while others inhabit a zone "between" the sexes.

Transsexuals are individuals whose gender identity is at odds with their physical sex. Some transsexuals undergo gender reassignment surgery to make their anatomy coincide with their gender. Others use hormones to reshape their body. Not everyone who identifies as transsexual uses medical interventions to change their physical appearance. Transsexualism is classified under "Gender Identity Disorders" in the *Diagnostic and Statistical Manual.*

Intersexuals are individuals whose external sex or genitalia are indeterminate. These are people who appear to be males but are biologically females, people with female physical attributes who are biologically males, and people who have the external appearance of both sexes as well as the DNA chromosome karyotypes of both sexes.

Homophobia, biphobia, and **transphobia** describe an individual's and/or society's fear and hatred of gay men, lesbians, bisexuals, and transgendered persons.

The Rise of Community Activism

In the 1950s, before the rise of the new understandings described in the earlier sections of this chapter, the psychiatric profession officially labelled homosexuality as a mental disorder. The profession's response to such perceived deviance included administering drugs to people, performing lobotomies, and subjecting gay men and lesbians to electroshock treatment. Some lesbians endured hysterectomies and estrogen injections (Warner, 2002: 24). Early gay and lesbian community activists challenged medical authority, and homosexuality was removed from the *Diagnostic and Statistical Manual* of the American Psychiatric Association in 1973.

The emergence of gay communities in Canada can be traced back to at least World War II. During this time, the traditional patriarchal family structure was disrupted to some extent. There were increasing opportunities for people to socialize in predominantly same-sex groups, since men were in the army and at war, while many women were working together in large factories. Many people moved to cities, where anonymity and lack of parental supervision allowed more opportunities for sexual exploration. This freedom was circumscribed, however, by the hunt for "subversives" that characterized the Cold War in the 1950s. Any kind of deviance became suspect, because the logic of the day was that if you had anything to hide (and same-sex attraction was considered something to hide), then you were more likely to be blackmailed into working for a foreign government (Girard, 1987).

Thus, the 1950s were a terrible time for gay men and lesbians, especially in the Canadian civil service. The RCMP collected close to 9,000 names of people within the service who were suspected of being homosexual (Kinsman, 2003). Many of these people were subjected to police interrogation and surveillance. It was within this climate that in 1952, homosexuals were prohibited from entering Canada under the *Immigration Act*. While the next few decades brought an easing of anxieties over communism, it would not be until 1976, after significant activism, that the provision denying entrance to homosexuals was removed from the act.

Throughout the late 1950s and 1960s, a growing gay and lesbian political movement began to shape public discourse and scientific understandings about sexuality. This movement symbolically coalesced on June 27 and 28, 1969, when a series of riots erupted in response to a police raid on the Stonewall Inn, a New York City gay bar. The riots, which were later called the **Stonewall Rebellion**, marked the beginning of a more public, large-scale movement for gay and lesbian rights. A new national organization, the Gay Liberation Front (GLF), was formed with the mandate to create freedom for all oppressed people, not just members of LGBTQ+ communities. Prominent transgender activists at the time, such as Sylvia Rivera and Marsha P. Johnson, who subsequently co-founded Street Transvestite Action Revolutionaries (S.T.A.R.), were also involved in clashes with police during the Stonewall riots.

Gay and lesbian organizations worked systematically to challenge laws limiting the civil and social rights of members of LGBTQ+ communities. An important year for the recognition of the civil rights of gays, lesbians, and bisexual persons in Canada was 1969. With the passing of Bill C-150 and then-justice minister Pierre Trudeau's statement that "there is no place for the State in the bedrooms of the nation," gross indecency and buggery (the legal terms used to describe gay sex) were decriminalized as long as these acts were committed in private between two consenting adults over the age of 21. Since then, there have been a number of changes to the Criminal Code (see the feature on "Same-Sex Rights in Canada: A Timeline and Highlights").

Human Rights Laws

While same-sex sexual activity was decriminalized in Canada in 1969, it was not until decades later that it became illegal to discriminate against gay men, lesbians, and bisexual persons in the areas of immigration, employment, military service, housing, pensions and other benefits, marriage, and custody of children.

Even then, the removal of prohibitions against same-sex relations had little effect on the lives of transsexual people, whose human rights are still not explicitly protected through legislation in Canada.

Heteronormativity
The belief that people fall into distinct genders (male and female) with natural roles in life and that heterosexuality is the only sexual orientation

Cisnormativity
The mistaken assumption that all, or almost all, individuals are cisgender

Transmisogyny
The negative attitudes, expressed through cultural hate, individual and state violence, and discrimination, directed toward trans women and trans and gender non-conforming people on the feminine end of the gender spectrum

Queer Activism

A disparaging term once often directed at gay men and lesbians, "queer" has been reclaimed by LGBTQ+ communities to represent an inclusive celebration of all persons whose sexual and gender expressions differ from heterosexual norms. The founders of the first queer activist group, Queer Nation, belonged to ACT UP, a radical AIDS activist group that succeeded in getting pharmaceutical companies and governments to finally respond to the AIDS pandemic that swept through the United States and Canada in the 1980s.

As gay and lesbian activism became more prominent in the 1990s, **queer activism** popularized the term "queer" to be more inclusive of sexual minorities and other marginalized people. "By adopting 'queer' they reclaimed and politicized a derogatory term commonly used before gay and lesbian liberation. It represented the belief in an identity that is more ambiguous and more fluid than gay, lesbian, or homosexual" (Warner, 2002: 262).

Queer activists distanced themselves from gay and lesbian organizers by critiquing identity-based movements. Queer activists reject **heteronormativity**, **cisnormativity**, and **transmisogyny** and are skeptical of viewing identities as coherent, stable, and possessing clear boundaries. Instead, they suggest that such identities mask significant diversity among the members within various categories while also ignoring similarities between different categories.

PFLAG Canada is a national charitable organization founded by parents who wished to help themselves and their family members understand and accept their non-heterosexual children.

Same-Sex Rights in Canada
A timeline and highlights

Same-sex rights in Canada have come a long way since 1965

1965
Everett Klippert is the last person in Canada to be charged with and convicted of homosexuality. A Northwest Territories mechanic, Klippert acknowledges to police that he is gay, has had sex with men over a 24-year period, and is unlikely to change. In 1967, Klippert is sent to prison indefinitely as a "dangerous sex offender," a sentence that is supported by the Supreme Court of Canada that same year.

December 22, 1967
Justice Minister Pierre Trudeau proposes amendments to the Criminal Code that, among other things, would relax the laws against homosexuality.

1969
Trudeau's amendments pass into the Criminal Code, decriminalizing homesexuality in Canada.

1971
Everett Klippert is released.

1976
Toronto's first openly lesbian feminist organization—the Lesbian Organization of Toronto (LOOT)—is formed.

December 1977
Québec includes sexual orientation in its Human Rights Code, making it the first province in Canada to pass a gay civil rights law. By 2001, all provinces and territories take this step except Alberta, Prince Edward Island, and the Northwest Territories.

1978
Canada's new *Immigration Act* (1976) comes into effect, removing homosexuals from the list of inadmissible classes.

May 2, 1980
Bill C-242, an act to prohibit discrimination on grounds of sexual orientation, gets its first reading in the House of Commons by Member of Parliament Pat Carney. The bill, which would have inserted "sexual orientation" into the Canadian *Human Rights Act*, does not pass.

February 5, 1981
More than 300 men are arrested following police raids at four gay bath houses in Toronto, the largest mass arrest since the *War Measures Act* was invoked during the October Crisis. The next night, about 3,000 people march in Toronto to protest the arrests. This is considered to be Canada's "Stonewall."

1988
Svend Robinson goes public about being gay, becoming the first member of Parliament to do so.

November 1992
The Federal Court lifts the ban on homosexuals in the military, allowing gays and lesbians to serve in the armed forces.

May 1995
An Ontario Court judge finds that the *Child and Family Services Act* of Ontario infringes Section 15 of the *Canadian Charter of Rights and Freedoms* by not allowing same-sex couples to bring a joint application for adoption. He rules that four lesbians have the right to adopt their partners' children.

1996
The federal government passes Bill C-33, which adds "sexual orientation" to the Canadian *Human Rights Act*.

May 1999
The Supreme Court of Canada rules that same-sex couples should have the same benefits and obligations as opposite-sex common-law couples and equal access to benefits from social programs to which they contribute.

February 11, 2000
Prime Minister Jean Chrétien's Liberals introduce Bill C-23, the *Modernization of Benefits and Obligations Act*, in response to the Supreme Court's May 1999 ruling. The act would give same-sex couples who have lived together for more than a year the same benefits and obligations as common-law couples.

The bill passes on April 11, 2000, with the definition of "marriage" remaining as is ("the lawful union of one man and one woman to the exclusion of all others"), but the definition of "common-law relationship" expanded to include same-sex couples.

May 10, 2002
Ontario Superior Court Justice Robert McKinnnon rules that a gay student has the right to take his boyfriend to the prom after the Durham Catholic District School Board had said that he was not allowed to do so.

July 12, 2002

For the first time, a Canadian court rules in favour of recognizing same-sex marriages. The Ontario Superior Court of Justice rules that prohibiting gay couples from marrying is unconstitutional and violates the *Charter of Rights and Freedoms*.

June 2004

A lesbian couple files the first same-sex divorce petition in Canada. Lawyers for the couple ask the Ontario Superior Court of Justice to grant the divorce and declare the definition of "spouse" under the *Divorce Act* unconstitutional. A judge grants the divorce in September 2004.

December 9, 2004

The Supreme Court of Canada rules that the federal government can change the definition of "marriage" to include same-sex couples, but does not answer whether such a change is required by the *Charter*. It also reaffirms that religious leaders cannot be compelled to perform same-sex marriages.

July 2005

Bill C-38, the law giving same-sex couples the legal right to marry, receives royal assent and becomes law.

2008

The Canadian government increases the age of sexual consent from 14 to 16. The age of consent for anal sex remains at 18, despite court decisions that this difference is unconstitutional, leading to charges of discrimination against gay youth.

January 12, 2012

The federal government says it is considering how to make divorce possible for same-sex couples who had come to Canada to get married. Canada's laws do not allow people who have not lived here for at least a year to end their marriage.

2016

Prime Minister Justin Trudeau announces he will posthumously pardon Everett George Klippert, one of the last men convicted and imprisoned under Canada's anti-homosexuality laws in the 1960s. Klippert is largely credited for bringing about a change in Canada's laws on homosexuality.

The Liberal government tables legislation on May 17, 2016 (the International Day Against Homophobia, Transphobia and Biphobia) that adds "gender identity" for protection under the Canadian Human Rights Act and the Criminal Code, alongside race, religion, age, sex, and sexual orientation.

- *Source:* CBC News. (2012). Timeline: Same-sex rights in Canada. [For information up to and including 2012.] Canadian Broadcasting Corporation (January 12).

Recent Developments in LGBTQ+ Rights in Canada

In the past few decades, there has been a complete revamping of the legislative framework that excluded and punished homosexuality in Canada. Also, significant legislative changes have been made in order to actively include gay men and lesbians in mainstream society.

Until the early 1990s, gays, lesbians ,and bisexual persons were not allowed to serve in the Canadian military. In 1992, the federal courts lifted this ban, and with this ruling, the legislative barriers to LGBTQ+ persons joining the armed forces were removed. Nevertheless, LGBTQ+ persons have continued to raise concerns about the treatment they receive in the military. Changing the culture of the armed forces to become queer-positive has been a tremendous challenge that continues today.

In the late 1990s, a significant change occurred in the area of spousal benefits. In 1999, an act regulating survivor benefits, known as the *Public Service Superannuation Act*, was amended to extend such benefits to same-sex couples. The most comprehensive package of changes for people living in same-sex relationships came with Bill C-23, the *Modernization of Benefits and Obligations Act*. This bill amended 68 federal statutes to provide everyone in common-law relationships with nearly all the rights and responsibilities ascribed to heterosexual married couples.

In 1980, federal Member of Parliament Pat Carney first attempted to have sexual orientation included in the *Human Rights Act*, but the bill did not pass. While other attempts were made in the intervening years, it was not until 1996 that discrimination based on sexual orientation was officially added to the act.

During this period, major legal battles were also fought to challenge Canada's obscenity legislation, which allowed Canada Customs to confiscate gay literature, including safer sex material depicting anal sex. In December 2000, the Supreme Court of Canada confirmed that Canada Customs was discriminatory against lesbian, gay, bisexual, and transgendered materials, and placed the burden on the Crown to prove obscenity as opposed to requiring community bookstores or other importers to defend against the charge. Gay rights activists claimed a victory.

In February 2001, the *Immigration and Refugee Protection Act* was reformed so that same-sex partners can be recognized as members of the family class of immigrants. Now, a common-law partner is anyone who has been in a conjugal relationship for at least one year. Refugee processes also now recognize that people have legitimate refugee claims if they fear persecution in their country of origin due to their sexual orientation.

The battle over gay marriage in Canada was particularly intense, with some religious groups suggesting that the legalization of gay marriage would violate their religious freedom. However, in 2005, Canada enacted federal legislation providing for marriage for same-sex partners.

Transgendered and transsexual persons have also faced significant barriers to acknowledgement of their rights. Not every trans person wants gender-confirming surgeries, but for those who do, the surgeries are considered essential. After sustained battles, eight provinces (all but New Brunswick and Prince Edward Island) now fund some combination of gender-confirming surgeries (GCS). In a 2013 CBC radio documentary about the challenges faced by trans people waiting for GCS, freelance reporter Maggie Rahr stated that those on the lengthy surgical wait lists were "statistically at a higher risk of suicide than any other known population."

Jan Buterman is a transgendered teacher from the Edmonton area who was fired by the Roman Catholic school board in 2008 after being told his gender change from woman to man is not aligned with the teachings of the Catholic Church.

In October 2015, an Edmonton judge reserved his decision on whether Buterman can have his case heard in front of the Alberta Human Rights Tribunal. Buterman said the decision could take weeks or even months.

In 2011, Buterman was offered a $78,000 settlement, which he refused, largely due to a confidentiality clause prohibiting him from discussing the reason for his termination.

Buterman has been in legal proceedings for more than seven years.

In March 2013, the House of Commons passed Bill C-279 to include the rights of trans persons in the Canadian *Human Rights Code*. However, the bill has faced significant opposition in the Senate and remains in limbo at the time of the writing of this chapter.

Legislation that shows honour and respect for same-sex relationships has had little impact on the lives of transsexual people. Discrimination against transgendered and transsexual people is, even today, not explicitly illegal under the same human rights laws that formally recognize the human rights of gay, lesbian, and bisexual persons.

In the late 1990s, educational institutions began to face the problem of the bullying and subsequent suicides of LGBTQ+ youth in their schools and thus initiated sensitivity training for staff and students. Positive changes resulted from the activism of student-led, school-based gay-straight alliances (GSAs). This movement started in the United States, and the Canadian version (known as "Day of Pink") evolved when a teen was bullied with homophobic slurs for wearing a pink t-shirt. By the mid-2000s, GSAs had spread across Canada, and in 2006 the Canadian Teachers' Federation distributed a handbook on how to develop GSAs. While the courts and legislative changes have been proactive in ensuring that GSAs are allowed in every school, GSAs have been less successfully implemented in private and Catholic school settings.

The first transgender Miss Universe Canada contestant in 2012, Jenna Talackova.

Emerging Concepts of Sexual and Gender Diversity

As we learn more about the broad range of sexual behaviours, desires, and identities, it has become increasingly clear that social workers must be aware of and open to the complex and varied roles that sexual practices and communities play in our society. As societal understanding of sexual behaviour shifts, social workers must reflect on their own beliefs and values around sexuality and determine how they can work effectively with people whose experiences may be either quite different from, or very similar to, their own.

It is important to consider how to communicate acceptance when unexpected disclosures happen and how to create a sex-positive atmosphere in one's work so that clients can feel safe when discussing their sexuality or gender if it is relevant to the challenges they are facing.

Non-monogamy/Polyamoury

As the social work profession rethinks how it situates itself in relation to supporting healthy sexuality and healthy relationships, many workers have also had to grapple with our culture's deep investment in normative practices of heterosexual monogamy. Increasingly, non-monogamous and polyamorous communities and individuals are defending the moral and legal aspects of their relationships, viewed as contentious by many Canadians. Some observers view institutionalized non-monogamy in the form of polygamy as harmful to women, children, society, and the institution of marriage. At the same time, some female polygamists, female polyamourists, and female researchers question the ways in which we attribute harm to certain forms of non-monogamy such as polygamy, but not to others such as adultery (Rambukkana, 2015). While the impact of these debates on social work has been limited to this point, non-monogamous lifestyles are likely to continue to unsettle some of our ideas about sexual, romantic, and/or institutionalized relationships.

Asexuality

Another community that is challenging taken-for-granted norms related to sexuality is the one percent of our population who identify as asexual (Bogaert, 2004). This group challenges society to reflect on the fact that we define our most significant relationships as those that are romantic and sexual, and how by doing so, we can marginalize those people who are single and asexual (as either a life-long or a temporary identity). For social workers, especially those in the field of mental wellness, these are important considerations, as they question our notion that people must be romantically or sexually paired to be healthy and happy. Again, this emerging area of sexuality is one that social workers need to keep in mind when working with clients.

Kink

The kink community includes people who are interested in a wide range of kinky sex, including, but not limited to, bondage, sado-masochism, and leather, all of which involve manifestations of dominance and submission through consensual role-playing in a sexual context. While recent decades have seen social workers shift their perceptions of LGBTQ+ people and their sexual and gender practices, there has been less of a movement to understand and accept what are called "paraphilias" (Nichols, 2006). Kinky activities may be unusual, but they are generally safe and consensual. Kink communities have well-established codes of behaviour stating that all participants be fully informed, capable of consent, and free to avoid activities that incur medical or mental danger. There is no evidence that people who engage in kinky sex are any more or less healthy than people who do not. However, people who participate in kink communities sometimes struggle with internalized or external stigma.

Gender-Fluid Children

Our society has taught us that there are only two genders—male and female—but this is not the case. Not all people fit neatly into a male or female gender identity. This may be particularly confusing for children who best describe their reality as having the sense of being "both" or "neither." Some of these children may speak of being more male on some days and more female on other days; in other words, they see themselves as "gender fluid."

These are all normal variations in human gender and do not mean something is wrong with a child. A child's gender is not what others tell them, but who they know themselves to be. Parents of gender-fluid children can be supportive by accepting their children for who they are.

Sexual Trauma

A significant amount of social work is focused on working with people who are victims or perpetrators of sexual violence (or both). Rates of sexual trauma and sexual harm are high in this country, which means that social workers are likely to come into contact with people who have experienced and/or perpetrated sexual trauma. When working with such clients, whether they are gay, straight, or trans, it is crucial that social workers reflect on their own experiences of sexual trauma, if any have occurred, as well as their own feelings around such issues.

Family members commit half of all reported sexual abuse. This type of abuse is also the most harmful because it involves a significant violation of a trusting relationship. Friends, colleagues, and, less frequently, strangers can also perpetrate sexual violence.

Working with survivors of sexual abuse often involves helping people to cope with stigma and shame and to rebuild a sense of security and dignity. Some social workers support survivors by accompanying them through the medical system and/or the legal process of laying charges and going to court. This can be a particularly painful process for survivors. Most often, survivors of sexual trauma need an opportunity to speak openly about their feelings in order to deal with the effects of the trauma. Social workers play a vital role in ensuring that victims of sexual trauma have a say in decision-making processes and in what their healing will look like.

Intimate partner violence and sexual assault are also of concern in the LGBTQ+ community, partly because such incidents are often hidden and denied. In the practitioner profile for this chapter, for example, Ottawa social worker Dillon Black observes that intimate partner violence and gender-based violence have been occurring for many years within the queer community of which they are a member. It has been cloaked in silence and shame, however, and non-disclosure has made it difficult for social workers to reach out to help survivors of violence within the LGBTQ+ community. Dillon sees an urgent need to talk openly about this problem.

Sexual Offences

Social workers also work with people who commit sexual offences. Increasingly, the goal of this work is to encourage potential perpetrators to seek treatment before committing a crime. This requires that, as a society and as a profession, we communicate respect and value for people who have sexual fantasies that include harming others, while being clear that such acts are unacceptable. Preventative programs are becoming more prevalent across North America and Europe, and there are signs that early interventions, accompanied by ongoing support, can be very effective. While social work has taken a clear and important position that it is not possible or ethical to "fix" people's sexual desires, certain forensic programs have been quite successful in working with clients to increase their own understanding of their harmful sexual desires and to work effectively to reduce their risk of re-offending. These programs help people to see how sex with consent is better sex, and teach clients skills to increase the likelihood of having relationships in which they can enjoy consensual sex. The programs help clients to understand what triggers them to want non-consensual sex and how to avoid and/or manage these triggers.

Canada has been a pioneer in the establishment of Circles of Support and Accountability programs, in which citizen volunteers support convicted sexual offenders upon release from prison in order for them to avoid re-offending. Studies have found that without treatment, rates of recidivism for sexual offences are between 13 and 17 percent, but with treatment, this figure falls closer to 2 or 3 percent (Federoff and Moran, 1997).

Sexuality, Aging, and Disability

Until recently, society has imagined that people who are elderly or who have physical, psychiatric, or intellectual disabilities are non-sexual beings. In recent decades, these beliefs have been challenged. Increasingly, social workers are becoming more aware that many older people and people with disabilities are sexual beings and may be sexually active. Older people, as a group, enjoy the full spectrum of sexuality, sexual orientation, and gender identities. Social workers need to be well versed in how to support older people and people with disabilities in enjoying their sex lives. They can help prevent the spread of sexually transmitted infections (STIs) and also ensure that vulnerable persons who wish to be sexually active are protected from victimization.

Gender: No Longer an Immutable Quality
A positive but controversial movement

Gender, for many North American and European kids, is no longer seen as a fixed and immutable quality

Summer camp began last month for my oldest child with a sit-down during which the campers took turns declaring their pronouns. Most of the teenagers chose to be known by "he" or "she," generally but not always in ways that coincided with their physical appearance. There were a handful of "theys," and one "it."

This new camp ritual was not viewed by any of the teenagers I met there as controversial or weird; nor were the pronoun choices (though some of the more exotic ones, especially the plurals, fell by the wayside). Gender, for a good many middle-class North American and European kids, is no longer seen as a fixed and immutable quality.

This has taken many people by surprise. The movement to recognize people with changed or changing gender identities has been the fastest-emerging social movement of our age. Almost overnight, terms such as "cisgendered" (the name for those of us whose gender coincides with our physical sex) have leaped from the fringes of activism to mainstream vocabulary. The concept of "trans rights" is now part of government and corporate policy discussions.

In part, it is propelled by the very public gender changes of people such as Caitlyn (formerly Bruce) Jenner and Chelsea (formerly Bradley) Manning, or such public moves as the appointment of Raffi Freedman-Gurspan, a transgender woman, to the White House staff by U.S. President Barack Obama [in 2015]—but also by a dawning understanding that a number of people among us are more comfortable living under a different pronoun.

As successful as this movement has been, it has confused some otherwise liberal-minded people: Is this a movement to bring "trans" people out of the closet, to celebrate gender as a fluid matter of choice and will? Or is it to allow people to live within the "right" gender for them, not necessarily the one they were born with? Much of this confusion is rooted in two very different, and sometimes conflicting, ways of understanding gender.

For those who grew up admiring such well-known transgender figures as the synthesizer composer Wendy Carlos, once known as Walter Carlos; the travel writer Jan Morris, who until 1964 was James Morris; or the great economist Deirdre McCloskey, once known as Donald McCloskey, their former gender was a biographical curiosity and their current one an insignificant aspect of their personalities.

And for the vast majority, that invisibility is what is sought. "Put simply, our goal is to blend into the background and go about our lives unnoticed," the transgender activist Katie Glover wrote this week. "The less interesting we are, the better our lives become."

But another chain of thought has taken root. In 1993, the biologist Anne Fausto-Sterling created a stir with her essay "The Five Sexes," which argued that a large proportion of people—one in 25, she cited—were born without clearly male or female sexual characteristics, and were surgically or psychologically "adjusted" to fit a male or female pattern. That number was later revised far downward by its author and others, to four in 1,000 or fewer, but the essay became, and remains, influential—as does her initial argument that gender should be non-binary and provisional.

That combined with the argument, also gaining traction in the 1990s, that gender is a purely "performative" act, a societally determined costume play without biological basis. "One is not born a woman, one becomes one," Simone de Beauvoir famously wrote, and writers such as Judith Butler made that claim near-universal by arguing that gender was an artifice imposed from without; that nothing was innate.

That is certainly true at some level—much of what we call "femininity," for example, was a way of acting that only became popular during an era of female servility. But there is, most agree, a level at which gender—our understanding of our sexual role—does have at least some biological basis.

Our bodies and brains both start out female, in the womb; testosterone then sets off a masculization process in the genitals and brains of males, through different processes—but it doesn't always happen for everyone. It therefore is not uncommon, the neuroscientist Jaak Panksepp has shown, to have "female-type brains in male-type bodies...or male-type brains in female-type bodies."

Gender, then, is not necessarily a lifestyle choice: ambiguous or "wrong" gender can be as physical and real as anything in your body. We should support people in righting such wrongs, however they arose, so that their gender can go back to being, for everyone out of adolescence, part of our background noise.

- *Source:* Saunders, Doug. (2015). The battle to make gender boring again. *The Globe and Mail*, August 22.

Two Important Points for Discussion

In general, the trans community discourages references to trans persons' earlier identities, such as the several references made in Saunders's article. Some people wish to leave behind them a previous self that they feel was inauthentic.

Additionally, concerns are emerging about how social work is responding to trans children. There are two competing narratives: "gender fluidity" versus "right brain in wrong body." The latter is gaining dominance, and professionals are moving more quickly to transform children into their "right" gender. There is some justification for this, but the hormonal and surgical changes are irreversible and are based on the belief that the child's gender, once transformed, will be stable for decades to come—for which the evidence is not conclusive.

Some observers are raising concerns that in a decade or so, we may find that some children's gender identity was not as fluid as was assumed when their bodies were chemically and surgically altered. The number of trans students presenting themselves in the school system has so startlingly exceeded previous statistics on the rate of transgenderism that some experts are beginning to question the prevalence of the "right brain in wrong body" narrative. It is not clear at present which narrative will eventually prove stronger in terms of validity.

Combatting Oppression, Discrimination, and Stigma

In 1999, Carol-Anne O'Brien highlighted the ways in which social work may be implicated in the pathologization of gay, lesbian, and bisexual identities. She found that social workers can sometimes promote the belief that homosexuality is a phase that some people pass through. She concluded that the most common way in which social workers reinforce heteronormativity—the "normalcy" of heterosexuality—is through silence about non-heterosexual identities. This reinforcement of heteronormativity is exacerbated by the relatively few numbers of openly gay, lesbian, bisexual, transgendered, or transsexual role models in the profession.

There are two extremes in social work counselling involving lesbians, bisexuals, transgendered or transsexual persons, and gay men. The first occurs when social workers exaggerate the difficulties of living in a heterosexist society and obscure the fact that LGBTQ+ persons are often happy and healthy and enjoy positive relationships with family members, straight colleagues, and friends. The second occurs when social workers assume that sexual orientation and gender identity make no difference to a person's experience, attitudes, or behaviour. The challenge is to find a middle path between these two extremes in order to provide balanced support to members of queer communities (van Wormer et al., 2000).

Challenging Heterosexist Norms

There has been a long history of people in social work who have challenged the heterosexist norms of our society. Gay men, lesbians, bisexuals, and transgendered and transsexual persons have enriched society as a whole and our profession specifically. Their contributions have helped to develop queer-positive practices, HIV/AIDS services, responses to women's health needs, activism for social justice, and improved social work knowledge and practice.

The homophobia, transphobia, and heterosexism institutionalized within schools, the health-care system, and social services have led many gay, lesbian, bisexual, transgendered, and transsexual people to feel reluctant to ask for help. As a result, LGBTQ+ communities are developing queer-positive social services. These organizations are involved in policy change, community organizing, advocacy, and service provision. Most medium- and large-sized cities in Canada have social services specifically organized to meet the needs of LGBTQ+ persons.

The personal experience of heterosexism and oppression is felt through stigma, stress, guilt, and shame. It is often difficult to accept one's sexual and romantic attractions to people of the same sex because we live in a society that is generally hostile to such desires. It is equally difficult to accept one's sexual identity as different from what one is assigned at birth. Thus, many members of LGBTQ+ communities experience internalized homophobia. External cultural messages that suggest that lesbians, transgendered and transsexual people, and gay men are somehow failing to meet social standards become internalized as guilt, shame, and stress.

Often (although not necessarily) as a result of discrimination and devaluation by society, members of LGBTQ+ communities struggle with self-acceptance. On average, gay adolescents and young men are six to sixteen times more at risk for attempting suicide compared to their straight peers (Dorais, 2004). Studies have shown that it is not gay sexuality that causes suicide, but rather having a homosexual or bisexual orientation in a highly homophobic environment. Young gay men, lesbians, and transgendered youth are known to experience both ostracism and harassment in their everyday lives. They are sometimes rejected by their families and end up on the streets, where they are vulnerable to sexual and physical violence.

Social Workers as Advocates for LGBTQ+ Communities

The following are useful points to consider in this context:

- Just because someone presents outwardly as a particular gender does not mean that the person sees themselves as always, or even often, fitting within that gender norm.
- People make sense of gender discomfort in many ways. Attempting to be supportive of how people understand their gender, however complicated or counterintuitive, is important.
- There are no "cures" for transsexualism. In fact, the social work profession considers the conversion therapy practices that are sometimes used to "treat" homosexuality and gender identify issues to be largely discredited.
- Gender transitions can cause a great deal of anxiety and uncertainty in a family, so support for family members is also important. Couples and families do sometimes stay together during and after a gender transition.
- Employers/workplaces may need education and sensitivity training to respond respectfully to an employee's gender transition.

Social Work with Persons Who Are Homophobic and/or Transphobic

In their practice, social workers can encounter people hostile to LGBTQ+ persons. Generally, individual feelings of homophobia and transphobia are rooted in three different areas:

- **Religion.** In this situation, it can be helpful for the social worker to refer to religious teachings that promote acceptance and understanding. In addition, there is an increasing body of literature that argues that various religions do accept sexually and gender-diverse persons. See, for example, Daniel Helminiak's book *What the Bible Really Says about Homosexuality* (1994, 2000) and Samar Habib's *Islam and Homosexuality* (2010).
- **Insecurity in gender roles.** Sometimes homophobia and transphobia are rooted in insecurity about one's own gender identity. In this situation, exploring childhood messages about sexuality and gender and encouraging increased self-reflection can help to reframe the situation and make encounters with persons of diverse gender and sexual identities less threatening to the person concerned.
- **Negative past experience with someone who identifies as LGBTQ+.** In this situation, it can be helpful to increase someone's exposure to more positive experiences, first through films, books, or websites, and, when possible and safe for others, with people who are members of LGBTQ+ communities.

The challenge for social workers is to develop compassion for people who show little compassion for others and to see that such attitudes are often a survival skill for those who feel powerless and insecure. It can be important to help such people refocus their anger in a more appropriate and positive way that encourages healthy attitudes and healthy living.

Kael McKenzie, Canada's first transgender judge, credits his new position to lots of hard work and a determination to simply be himself.

Sexual and Gender Diversity
Communicating acceptance

Gay men, lesbians, bisexuals, and transgendered persons often seek social work support for issues similar to their non-queer counterparts. These problems may also be shaped by their experience of oppression. LGBTQ+ persons may also struggle with depression, suicidal ideation, alcoholism, and drug use, all of which can be prevalent among persons who live in a society that is hostile to their identities, desires, and relationships.

When working with a client to explore the problems that have brought them to counselling, it is important to see homophobia, heterosexism, transphobia, and cisgenderism as potential problems rather than perceiving the client's sexual or gender diversity as being the problem

For social workers who are not members of LGBTQ+ communities, the following are some guidelines for creating a space for diverse sexual and gender identities in their practice. Additionally, understanding the stages of coming out, the barriers faced by transsexual people, and the impacts of ethnicity, age, and ability are vital to effective practice in these communities.

- **Never assume people are heterosexual or cisgender.** Use words such as "partner" and other gender-inclusive language. When asking a person about their life, articulate the possibility that the person may be attracted to people of the same sex. For instance, you can ask if a person is dating a man, woman, or transgendered person—in other words, leave open the possibility of non-heterosexual relationships. You can also ask people to tell you their preferred pronoun.
- **Affirm and validate.** If someone discloses that they are transgendered, gay, lesbian, or bisexual, it is important for social workers to affirm and validate that identity. Queer-positive counsellors view same-sex desire and transgendered identities as normal human diversity. Similarly, they recognize same-sex relationships as having the same value as heterosexual partnerships.
- **Feelings about gender and sexual diversity.** You cannot expect to grow up in a culture that is hostile to gender and sexual diversity and not internalize some of those feelings and stereotypes. If you cannot provide affirming counselling or if someone would prefer to work with a counsellor who is a member of an LGBTQ+ community, then you are obliged, whenever possible, to make the appropriate referrals. Sometimes heterosexual counsellors avoid their own discomfort with same-sex desire by letting gay, lesbian, and bisexual clients talk only about their positive experiences of sexual diversity, but not about their struggles with feelings of shame or ambivalence.
- **Body language is important.** When working in areas of sexuality or gender that are uncomfortable, heterosexual counsellors may say supportive things, but their body language may convey discomfort. Body language can alienate clients with diverse sexual and gender identities.
- **Support your colleagues.** Support colleagues who are gay, lesbian, bisexual, or transgendered. Do not rely on them to teach you about sexual or gender diversity.
- **Increase your own self-awareness.** This begins by exploring the heterosexist attitudes that we have all developed as a result of living in a heterosexist and cissexist culture. In particular, it can be helpful to unpack our binary assumptions about gender and sexual orientation.

Many of us also need to move beyond positions of pity, tolerance, and acceptance to explore ways in which we can celebrate diversity and encourage others to do the same. It is important to see a client's decision to accept a transgendered, bisexual, gay, or lesbian identity as a positive outcome of counselling.

If you are heterosexual and/or cisgendered, it is important to challenge the ways in which you take your heterosexual privilege for granted. If you identify as LGBTQ+, it is important not to over-identify with clients who are queer-identified. Particularly in small, tight-knit queer communities, it is important to be careful about boundaries and dual relationships.

Supporting Clients in Coming Out

Revealing one's LGBTQ+ identity to family and friends (a process known as "coming out") can sometimes be a stressful and even frightening experience as the consequences can be perceived as unpredictable and perhaps risky. Katherine van Wormer and her colleagues (2000) identify a number of stages in the coming-out process; it is important that social workers understand and recognize these stages.

- The first stage occurs before a person comes out. People may feel discomfort, but do not consciously recognize being attracted to people of the same sex or not fitting within their assigned gender.
- The second stage takes place when people begin to become aware of same-sex attraction or gender discomfort.

- In the third stage, "exploration," people develop gay, lesbian, or transgender friendships and participate in the LGBTQ+ community.
- The final stage is marked by integration—people accept their identities and incorporate their identities into their lives.

Not everyone goes through all of these stages, however, or goes through them in this order. Also, people can be content without moving through all the stages.

Transitions for Transsexual People

For transsexual men and women, achieving alignment between their gender identity and their physical body often requires hormone therapy and sex reassignment surgeries. In order to access these treatments, most people must receive a diagnosis of a gender identity disorder (GID) from one of three recognized gender identity clinics in Canada (Toronto, Montréal, and Vancouver). The cost of transitioning varies significantly from province to province, depending on the provincial health plan. Even in a province where there is coverage, sex reassignment surgeries can include additional costs (such as travel) that make them prohibitively expensive.

For these reasons and others, some transsexual persons do not have complete sex reassignment surgery and instead use hormones to align their bodies to their gender identity to some degree.

Social workers can help by challenging how we designate washrooms or use language that excludes, marginalizes, and silences people who do not fit within the binaries of male and female or who seek transition from one to the other. For example, washrooms can be uncomfortable or even dangerous spaces for someone who does not fit within gender binaries. Transgendered people who cannot pass as the "appropriate" gender often face verbal harassment or even physical violence.

Acknowledging Diverse Communities and Sexuality

People's experiences of sexual or gender diversity are different depending upon their ethnicity, age, and abilities.

- **Ethnicity.** Members of LGBTQ+ communities are ethnically diverse. As one of countless examples, Manitoba trans judge Kael McKenzie is of Aboriginal descent.
- **Age.** In North America, sex is largely seen as the terrain of the young. Older people who identify as gay, bisexual, or lesbian often face discrimination.
- **Disability.** People with disabilities are typically perceived as asexual (devoid of or without sexuality). Stereotypes make it difficult for people with disabilities to feel confident enough to seek out a partner. In addition, systems and institutions often work to prevent people with disabilities (especially intellectual disabilities) from having sexual relations.

LGBTQ+ people also differ in terms of religion, education, socio-economic status, and other characteristics. Acknowledging this diversity prevents overly broad generalizations about LGBTQ+ people, and recognizes that they face multiple oppressions and have access to different levels of power.

Social Workers as Role Models

Social work practice and counselling LGBTQ+ clients

Coming out can be a difficult and even terrifying process for LGBTQ+ persons, as families and friends do not always react positively to this revelation. But many people report feeling relieved once they have come out and no longer have to hide their feelings and identities. People who live their lives "out of the closet" tend to have fewer experiences of isolation and depression.

Some people are out only to themselves and their partners. Others are out to family and friends, but remain closeted at work. If people are not ready to come out, or assess the risks of doing so to be too high, it is important to trust that they are the experts on their own experience and to support them in their decision. Most people in our society are not completely open to others' sexual desires, practices, feelings, or even gender. There is no reason to expect LGBTQ+ people to be any different. To help a person who is grappling with decisions about whether, when, and how to come out, social workers must attune themselves to that person's particular needs, feelings, and experiences by listening carefully and responding with appropriate support, as Mike's story illustrates.

Issues Confronting LGBTQ+ Social Workers

For social workers who are LGBTQ+, there are a number of important issues to take into account when working with clients and colleagues:

- Social workers who are LGBTQ+ can be excellent role models for people who are attempting to deal with their own same-sex desires or transgendered identity. Hiding one's sexual orientation can send a message that gay, lesbian, or bisexual persons should feel ashamed. Hiding one's gender identity or personal history can send a similarly negative message about transgendered, intersex, and transsexual people. However, LGBTQ+ social workers must also assess any potential risks that might accompany coming out in their workplaces, particularly as clients are not bound to confidentiality.
- It may be challenging for LGBTQ+ social workers to deal with clients who are hostile to LGBTQ+ communities. It may be appropriate to refer such clients to another counsellor, particularly if the social worker feels threatened on any level.
- As members of a marginalized community, LGBTQ+ social workers may worry that the risks of making mistakes are higher, as these mistakes might be attributed to their identity or community. This may add pressure to their workload if they are not practising in a queer-positive workplace. It is important to try to find allies and colleagues who can offer support.
- Gay, lesbian, transgendered, and bisexual service providers can themselves be uncomfortable with other forms of sexual and gender diversity. All social workers should think through and be aware of their own beliefs and preconceptions when working with members of LGBTQ+ communities.

Practising in a small community can present particular challenges, because social workers are more likely to meet clients outside of the counsellor–client relationship. It is important to be aware of the possibility of overlapping roles and to get support from colleagues to help maintain professional boundaries.

Reflecting on Mike's Story

1. In this story, how did the social worker respond to some stereotypes about gay men that the client appeared to believe?
2. What challenges do you think might arise in providing anonymous social work support?
3. If the social worker who had answered Mike's call had been LGBTQ+, how appropriate would it have been to disclose that fact to Mike? And at what point in their relationship?

Mike's Story...
Supporting the coming-out process

Social workers can help support people through the coming-out process, but they must always be mindful of their clients' apprehensions and possible ambivalence.

Kim, a social worker at a non-profit organization that supports youth, receives a call from a young man who is enrolled at the local university. Sounding distressed, the young man begins the conversation by asking for reassurance about confidentiality. He doesn't want to give his real name, so Kim agrees to call him "Mike" throughout the conversation. She assures him that the organization does not keep track of people's phone numbers and that she can work with him anonymously unless she becomes concerned that he might hurt himself or others. Mike agrees to this condition.

Mike tells Kim that he is scared and anxious because he has noticed himself becoming aroused in the university change room when showering with other men. He has never thought of himself as gay, and he had a few girlfriends in high school to whom he felt attracted. He is confused by his arousal and what it means. He tells Kim that he has fairly negative feelings about gay men, and he states that he doesn't want to be gay. However, he does admit that he has never felt the intensity of desire that he is now feeling when observing other men at the gym and in the showers. He is deeply conflicted, as he is experiencing feelings of fear and disgust, but also excitement and anticipation. He feels nervous that he will be "caught" if he acts on his desires, but at the same time he feels overwhelmed by his yearning for sexual intimacy with another man, and he tells Kim he can't stop thinking about it.

Kim spends some time talking with Mike to help him process his situation. Mike asks Kim whether she thinks he is gay, and she replies that whether he is gay or not depends on how he defines himself. She suggests that perhaps the definition isn't as important as taking some time to explore his new feelings and deciding whether he wants to act on them, and if so, how he can do so in a way that is safe. Kim points out that how an individual defines their sexual orientation is a personal choice and that Mike need not feel pressured into making that choice before he feels truly ready to do so.

Mike speaks about how sad he will be if he discovers that he is gay. He talks about disliking gay men and feeling a sense of loss because he won't be able to have a family and kids. He says that loss will be hard for him and his parents. Kim spends some time discussing Mike's perceptions and stereotypes about gay men. It is clear that he has not known any out gay men and that his images of gay sexuality derive mainly from popular culture. Kim suggests a few videos that Mike might watch to challenge his stereotypes. They discuss how a person's expression of gender is not just about sexual orientation and how some gay men are conservative and masculine in their gender expression, while others are more playful. Kim also points out that having a family and children is a possibility for gay men today. Kim also talks about safe places where Mike might go to meet other men.

Mike calls Kim several times over the next few weeks to talk more about his feelings of internalized homophobia and about how he could gain more social support. As Mike discusses his plans to try to meet some gay men for sexual encounters, Kim points out how important it is to practise safe sex by using condoms. They engage in explicit conversations about the risks of HIV and other sexually transmitted infections.

After a month, Mike calls Kim again and sounds much calmer. He has been to a gay bar a few times and has had good experiences. His fears are being replaced slowly with the realization that being gay might mean that he could meet other gay men, fall in love, and enjoy a loving relationship with another man.

Mike has also disclosed his feelings to a friend who has been supportive as Mike realigns his identity. Mike has not disclosed his transforming identity to family members, but he does not think that doing so will present any major threats to his relationships with them. He is certain that his mother will be understanding, and he thinks that eventually his father will come to terms with the situation as well.

Mike now tells Kim his real name and thanks her for all the support that she has given him over the past few months. He says that he is still not exactly sure how things will turn out, but he states that he is feeling less afraid and even excited about some of the possibilities that lie ahead for him.

Social workers must sometimes help clients who are coming out to address their own internalized homophobia.

Offering Unconditional Support

Social work with intersex, transgendered, and transsexual individuals

Despite the wide range of sexual and gender diversity, many people assume that everyone is heterosexual and cissexual. For example, how many heterosexuals and cissexuals have to think twice before deciding which washroom to use or whether they should display a photograph of their partner in their office? Without thinking through the ways in which heterosexuals and cissexuals move through the world, without an awareness of or support for gender and sexual diversity, heterosexual and cissexual social workers may consciously and unconsciously maintain heterosexual and cissexual privilege.

Supporting Intersex People and Their Families

The broad category of intersex includes people with a variety of chromosomal variations, those whose bodies have difficulty using androgens (male sex hormones), and people whose genitals are ambiguous at birth. The challenge is that while intersex people may have bodies that cross boundaries of sex, living in this manner is not a widely recognized option in our society; there is a great deal of pressure for children to adhere to the binary gender system.

Parents of intersex children need information, and sometimes advocacy, so that they can negotiate with doctors regarding what medical interventions they want taken or whether they would rather wait until their child reaches puberty to make any decisions. The Intersex Society of North America argues that intersexuality is mainly a problem of stigma and trauma, not gender, and that children with external sex characteristics or genitalia that are indeterminate should not undergo surgery, but rather should be assigned a gender based on their genetic and hormonal test results.

Supporting Sexual and Gender Diversity

While people who are intersex, transgendered, or transsexual deal with the same life issues as people who are not negotiating their gender identity, some counselling issues are specific to members of these communities. For example, many such persons experience harassment, physical violence, and estrangement from family and friends.

For transsexual men and women, achieving alignment of their gender identity and physical body often requires hormone therapy and sex reassignment surgeries. Barriers to transitioning are significant and can include expensive procedures and long prescribed wait times during which an individual must live as the gendered person they intend to become before receiving drugs or surgery. The social and regulatory issues that surround sex reassignment are highly specialized areas of practice. In most large cities, there are social work practitioners who specialize in gender counselling. It is important, when possible, to provide support and to refer people to counsellors with expertise in this area.

It is also important for social workers to be aware that transsexual people are homosexual, bisexual, asexual, and heterosexual in about the same proportions as cissexual people. And many transsexual people choose not to be part of LGBTQ+ communities, but to live ordinary lives in their affirmed sex and gender.

Reflecting on Jade's Story

1. Does your university, college, or workplace have gender-neutral washrooms? Where? What are the policies regarding use of preferred names?
2. Social workers can help clients navigate systems that marginalize people by not creating space for diverse experiences and identities. How can social workers balance system navigation with striving for institutional change?

Jade's Story...
A non-conforming gender identity

In a society struggling with long-held misconceptions that sex is a binary category that has only two possibilities, male or female, social workers can play a key role.

Zahide works for a counselling service located on a university campus. One day, Jade comes in for an appointment to discuss a troubling issue. Jade is in the process of transitioning from being a female to a gender-queer or non-binary person and thus prefers the pronoun "they." Jade is uncomfortable in several classes where their legal name is read out instead of their preferred name and is often uncomfortable having to speak with faculty in advance of these classes to ensure that this does not continue to happen. Jade also feels upset when in the company of peers who seem uncomfortable speaking with or even sitting next to a gender-queer person.

Sometimes professors and teaching assistants seem supportive of Jade's request to be referred to in the plural, but at other times they seem confused or irritated. Others do not respect the request at all, ignoring it entirely and refusing to engage in a conversation about gender diversity.

Jade becomes quite anxious at the beginning of each term, not knowing whether or how their request will be heard. When their request goes unheeded, Jade drops a course, or, in the case of a required course, is compelled to endure a very uncomfortable experience. This discomfort is adversely affecting their concentration and ability to learn. Jade is in a state of constant hypervigilance, feeling unsure whether seemingly critical comments made by an instructor are related to their learning, or whether the comments reflect the educator's discomfort with a gender-queer identity.

None of the educators has been explicitly hateful toward Jade, but they have expressed annoyance or impatience at times. Such responses are not grounds for a complaint, but they can create an environment in which Jade never feels certain that they are fully accepted in a particular classroom. This uncertainty is proving to be emotionally draining for Jade.

Jade describes other stressful experiences on campus; for example, when negotiating washroom use, showing their student card in order to gain access to the recreation centre or library, or paying for a coffee at a campus site. The photo on Jade's campus ID card was taken 18 months previously, when Jade's appearance was more gender conforming. As a result, university staff are sometimes confused and skeptical when they see the differences between the photo and Jade's current appearance.

While there are some gender-neutral washrooms on campus, they are situated relatively far apart from each other and are not always located in buildings where Jade is taking classes. Thus, Jade is sometimes forced to use a washroom in which their gender might be questioned, creating an unsafe situation. These daily experiences of having to justify a non-conforming gender identity are beginning to take a toll on Jade's mental health.

Zahide spends much of the first few sessions listening to Jade's story and validating their feelings. Zahide ensures that she reflects back Jade's preferred use of the plural pronoun. Zahide then does some research and finds out that the university has a "preferred name" policy that is in development. This should help Jade deal with some of the institutional challenges they are facing, as students will have the option to identify a preferred name that will appear on class lists and class websites. Zahide finds out what institutional pathways Jade should follow to have their photo ID changed and to have their preferred name entered into the system.

Zahide and Jade also discuss some trans-positive spaces on campus that Jade could access in order to develop more supports in navigating the cisnormative university environment. In this way, Zahide helps Jade develop a network to support them through a difficult transition. Zahide also knows some activists on campus who have been working to increase the number of gender-neutral washrooms, and she asks Jade if they might be interested in joining that group.

Alongside these concrete interventions, Zahide validates that it is challenging to be a non-binary person at this university and offers to provide Jade with ongoing support and counselling as necessary to help them cope with their situation.

Daily life can be especially challenging for individuals who have adopted a non-binary gender identity.

Harm-Reduction Strategies

Social work practice with sex-trade workers

The exchange of sex for money has taken on a peculiar shape in modern societies. It not only continues to be widespread, but also, with the freer movement of people around the world, it has become globalized, like many other things.

In 2013, the Supreme Court of Canada found that laws prohibiting brothels, public communication for the purpose of prostitution, and living on the profits of prostitution were unconstitutional and gave Parliament 12 months to rewrite the laws. In December 2014, the Harper government introduced new legislation that made it illegal to purchase sexual services, but legal to sell them. With this move, the government argued that it was recognizing prostitution as a form of sexual exploitation that negatively and disproportionately affects women and girls. The new legislation is contentious, with some applauding the changes and others worrying that it violates the Constitution and may be very difficult to implement.

Understanding the Challenges Faced by Sex-Trade Workers

Given the sub-legal nature of the sex-trade industry, it might be easy for some people to overlook the fact that individuals who work in the sex trade are human beings with their own private lives and private troubles. Many have families, children, and partners. For many of these workers, leaving the sex trade may seem impossible. Without sufficient education or job experience, it may be the only way to make money to support their families and pay the rent.

Sex-trade workers are a diverse group. Many, but not all, are poor. Some women and men work as expensive escorts and earn substantial money for their services. At the other end of the spectrum, however, are people who walk the streets and receive money to help pay the rent, buy food, or finance their substance use disorder. Some people choose to enter the profession voluntarily. There are also teenagers (many of whom are gay, lesbian, bisexual, or transgendered) who work in the sex trade so they can leave dangerous home situations and earn enough money to live. Many of these teenagers have fled or been kicked out of their homes and must earn money somehow in order to survive. Prostitution is often called "survival sex" for this very reason—it is the only means by which some people can support themselves.

Every person's situation is complex and unique, requiring individualized attention. For social workers, a clear understanding of the highly risky nature of this industry, both for those involved in it and for those working with persons involved in it, is of prime importance. After that, concern for the safety of those exploited by the industry is paramount.

Social workers often help sex-trade workers who are in trouble with the law or who are dealing with the challenges of poverty. A key early step in working with a sex-trade worker is to assess whether that person wants to remain in the sex industry and enjoys the work, whether they are involved against their will, or whether they are in the trade because they face limited alternatives. Once a social worker understands a sex-trade worker's experience, they can work respectfully with that client, as Cindy's story demonstrates. It is important for social workers to reflect on how they feel about sex work, and to ensure that, in taking on a case involving a sex-trade worker, they respond to their client's experience of sex work rather than to their own beliefs and values related to such work.

Reflecting on Cindy's Story

1. What are your views about sex work? What would you have to think through to work effectively with a client such as Cindy?
2. How does Michel manage the many challenges he faces, both with Cindy herself and with her situation?
3. What legislation or policy changes might help Michel and Cindy achieve their goals?

Cindy's Story...
Surviving as a sex-trade worker

Sometimes it is not the work itself that presents challenges to sex-trade workers, but rather other issues in their lives, such as substance use, poverty, and the threat of violence.

Michel, a social worker at a community health centre, is working with Cindy to help her find affordable housing. Cindy is struggling with poverty. At the moment, she is homeless and has been staying at a shelter or sleeping at friends' houses. Both arrangements are problematic: friends eventually get tired of her presence, but she fears for her safety at the shelter, where she also finds it difficult to follow the rules.

Cindy has been supporting herself in the sex trade for a long time, but over the last five or six years, she has struggled with a substance use disorder and a lessening of income as her overall health has declined. She has tried to get off drugs, but has found it impossible to stay clean. With her descent into extreme poverty, her work has become more dangerous. She often finds herself trying to negotiate with clients during drug deals and is often mistreated because people take advantage of the intensity of her substance use disorder. She sometimes ends up being abused and is unable on many occasions to demand that sexual partners wear condoms.

Cindy is in a vicious cycle: because she finds it so difficult to cope with poverty, she uses substances as a way to escape her anxieties, but this only makes things worse.

In trying to find housing for Cindy, Michel faces a number of obstacles. The first is to find accommodation that is safe and affordable. Second, there is some concern about whether Cindy will be able to maintain a home because she has been evicted a number of times as a result of noise and behaviour complaints, or failure to pay the rent.

Cindy is 37 years old and has very little education. She can read a little, but has trouble with comprehension. She has no other job training. For Cindy, working in the sex trade was one of the few options she saw available to her and, until recently, this work had allowed her to earn a decent living. She liked many of her clients and the other women with whom she worked, who helped to keep her safe. However, age, substance use, and health problems are now compromising Cindy's capacity to earn a living in the sex trade. Her work can no longer provide enough income and security for her to live with dignity. Cindy is proud that she has survived on her own for this long, but she is very worried about what the future holds for her.

Michel adopts a harm-reduction approach in his work with Cindy. This means that he is always looking for opportunities to reduce the risks that Cindy faces, whether that means trying to ensure that she practises safer drug use or safer sex, or attempting to help her gain some measure of stability in terms of her housing or health care. Michel focuses on small steps as being key to Cindy's survival. He tries to use these small steps as markers to help build Cindy's hope for a better future.

Michel and Cindy have worked together for many years, and Cindy now trusts Michel because he doesn't judge her on the basis of her substance use or the nature of her work. For Michel, this trust is crucial to his effectiveness as a social worker, but the work is daunting at times. He has been able to find Cindy housing and has set up supports for her on many occasions, but it has been hard for her to sustain these supports, and she often ends up back on the street, where she experiences significant risk of violence and abuse. Cindy has undergone treatment in the past but has always returned to using intravenous drugs. Cindy wants to continue doing sex work as it is the only form of job security she has known.

Michel knows that safe, supportive housing is vital for Cindy's survival, and he works with her to find a place that she can afford. They locate a rooming house, but it is a risky environment for Cindy because the other tenants are mostly men and, in all likelihood, many of them are struggling with substance use disorders as well. Michel puts Cindy's name on several wait lists for non-profit housing, but he knows that they are very long.

Ultimately, most of Michel's work with Cindy centres on maintaining the connection between them so that Cindy knows she always has someone to turn to if she is in crisis or needs immediate assistance.

Social work with sex-trade workers benefits from a non-judgemental approach that focuses on harm reduction.

A Complex Public-Health Issue

Social work practice with persons with HIV/AIDS

The human immunodeficiency virus (HIV) is a sexually transmitted blood-borne retrovirus that undermines a person's immune system. Acquired immune deficiency syndrome (AIDS) is the stage of HIV infection in which the immune system is destroyed. HIV/AIDS is a worldwide pandemic. In 2013, UNAIDS (a United Nations AIDS program) estimated that 35 million people were living with the disease. Of these, 3.2 million were children. The majority of these people live in the developing world. While the situation is serious, efforts by the UN and many national governments have significantly reduced the severity of the crisis. In 2005, AIDS-related deaths began to reverse, falling by 41 percent globally by 2014. Between 2000 and 2014, new HIV infections dropped from 3.1 million to 2 million worldwide, a reduction of 35 percent.

The Public Health Agency of Canada estimated that by 2012, there were 76,275 people living with HIV in Canada. In that year, 2,062 new HIV cases were reported, with 23.1 percent of them involving females. The most common modes of transmission for women were intravenous drug use (56.5 percent) and heterosexual sex (39 percent). For men, the most common transmission modes were heterosexual sex (39 percent), homosexual sex (31.6 percent), and intravenous drug use (23.7 percent).

Challenges Faced by Individuals and Communities Impacted by HIV/AIDS

People who have been exposed to HIV/AIDS are anxious about whether they have contracted the disease. If they test positive for HIV, they then confront stigma, the difficulties of managing a chronic disease, and sexual health issues. People who live with HIV must grapple with health-care coverage, disclosure, and maintaining employment while coping with fluctuations in levels of wellness. With the criminalization of HIV non-disclosure, people who are already vulnerable must negotiate very difficult disclosures of their HIV status.

The services that social workers can provide for people with HIV/AIDS include prevention initiatives, primary care, hospital care, home care, hospice care, support groups, family support, and advocacy. Social workers can also provide information and public education, make referrals to community resources, and prepare discharge plans. Social workers, like the one in James's story, often play a pivotal role as part of a larger health-care team.

In the community at large, social workers advocate on behalf of those living with HIV/AIDS through community organization and policy initiatives in relation to HIV/AIDS prevention, public education, and health promotion.

Social workers in community agencies can also facilitate support groups and provide counselling when necessary. The challenges of living with HIV vary significantly depending on a person's past experiences and social location. People who are recent immigrants to Canada or who belong to communities where HIV carries significant stigma often struggle with isolation. People who live in remote communities may find it difficult to access supports and services. In addition, for people who are already dealing with mental health challenges, addictions, or poverty, an HIV diagnosis is particularly difficult to manage. Whatever the situation, social workers play a vital role in terms of advocacy and support for people living with HIV/AIDS.

Reflecting on James's Story

1. Pre- and post-HIV test counselling involves talking about HIV in a way that recognizes the seriousness of the disease, but that also offers hope. What strategies did Anthony use to achieve this balance?
2. What issues might arise in long-term counselling with people who are HIV positive? How might these issues affect the type of social work support provided?

James's Story...
Adjusting to a diagnosis of HIV/AIDS

In many hospital cases, the social worker is the only team member who deals with a patient's non-medical or non-physical needs. They also work with family and friends to provide information and support after a patient leaves the hospital.

James comes into a health centre to receive an HIV/AIDS test. As the social worker on the team, Anthony provides pre-test counselling for James. The first topic that Anthony addresses is the limits of confidentiality, particularly in the context of HIV testing. In Ontario, the public health agency is notified of all positive HIV test results, and efforts are made to contact past partners without disclosing the patient's name so that these partners can take care of their own health. Another key point that Anthony discusses in the pre-test counselling session is the "window period" for infection. It can take up to three months from the moment of exposure to the virus for a person to test positive for HIV. If someone tests negative for HIV, it does not mean that they have not been exposed, and they might indeed test positive at a later date.

Anthony ensures that James understands the implications of an HIV test, the implications of a positive result, and ways to reduce one's risk of contracting HIV. Anthony spends some time discussing the pros and cons of an HIV test. Throughout the counselling session, he discusses how James might reduce his risk of exposure to HIV through safer sex and safer drug use practices. James doesn't use intravenous drugs. He practises safe sex with his long-time partner, and usually does so when they have a threesome or when he engages with another sex partner. However, in a recent sexual encounter that he and his partner had with another man, they had all agreed that since no one was HIV positive, they would engage in risky sexual play.

A while later, James returns to the health centre for his test results. Anthony discloses that James has tested positive for HIV. In this session, Anthony takes time to discuss James's reaction to the diagnosis and to assess ways in which James can keep himself and others healthy. The diagnosis stirs up a lot of turbulent emotions and concerns for James. He feels ashamed that he did not use a condom 100 percent of the time. He has worked in the area of AIDS prevention and is quite knowledgeable about how people can protect themselves from the virus.

Anthony supports James in developing self-compassion and in acknowledging that we are all human and do the best we can, yet sometimes we make risky decisions and sometimes we get hurt. James is worried about disclosing his HIV status to friends and family, who would have expected him to always practise safer sex to avoid infection. He is not sure whether to disclose his health status to his teenaged son. He is concerned about what the diagnosis will mean for his relationship with his current partner, including its effect on their sex life. James is also worried about his future health, the side effects of the HIV drugs he will be taking, and the challenges he could face in finding a drug cocktail that will help manage his disease.

Throughout the counselling session, Anthony makes sure that James has an opportunity to talk openly about his feelings and to have those feelings validated. He also works with James to try to decrease his shame and to strengthen his capacity to discuss his diagnosis with his partner. Together, Anthony and James weigh the pros and cons of James disclosing his diagnosis to others in his life. For James, this brings up a lot of old negative feelings associated with deciding whether and when to come out as a gay man. Those decisions were emotionally exhausting, and James feels frustrated that he may now have to live in "another closet."

At the end of the counselling session, James agrees to come back to see Anthony after he has had a few days to absorb the news of his diagnosis. Before James leaves, Anthony makes sure that James has someone he can talk to and that he feels supported. Anthony knows that James is at risk for depression as a result of his diagnosis. Anthony offers James the name of a counsellor working in the field of HIV who could provide ongoing support should he need it.

Apart from these counselling sessions, most of James's health-related questions are directed to his doctor, who outlines current changes in managing HIV and engages in a hopeful yet accurate discussion with James about his prognosis.

A diagnosis of HIV/AIDS raises personal and interpersonal dilemmas that social workers can help address.

Dillon Black

"I think it's important to look at how systems like sexism, misogyny, and rape culture affect our bodies and identities in different ways."

Dillon Black has worked with the Ottawa Coalition to End Violence Against Women for the past several years.

The work I am most passionate about is queering anti-violence and intimate partner violence. Few services and supports exist for queer and trans survivors of violence. LGBTQ+ intimate partner violence forces us as a sector to examine some of the differences between the experiences of LGBTQ+ survivors and those of other survivors, to see how patterns of power and control are established, and to analyze how heteronormativity, homophobia, and transmisogyny affect the lives of queer and trans folks.

I came to anti-violence work as a method of both healing and belonging. As a queer non-binary person who is also a survivor of violence, it's always been hard to see myself reflected in anything, so for me, a part of this work is striving to find and model who I am. My first exposure to this work was through grassroots social justice and feminist activism, finding and building community. I have worked with survivors and perpetrators, facilitated therapy groups, and done crisis counselling, prevention work, and case management. One thing that's clear to me is the importance of talking things through and situating gender-based violence within a larger context of tiny moments and choices between intent and affect. Queer and trans communities are full of strong and resilient people who have survived many barriers to simply being in the world, combined with so many other experiences of isolation and oppression.

For as long as I can remember, I have seen intimate partner violence and gender-based violence all around me. In the queer community, we don't talk about violence—a huge silence exists. The more I became involved in anti-violence and feminist work, the more people would approach me and disclose their experiences to me. I knew things had to change. I had to bring a queer and trans lens to this work and demand a rethinking of gender.

My work and praxis are grounded in queerness, social justice, anti-oppression, and resiliency frameworks. In the anti-violence movement, we often focus so much on eradicating violence that we don't always think about what is to be put in place of that violence. I am invested in creating a world in which our communities are equipped with the skills and knowledge to support everyone and in which there is no longer a need for crisis centres and hotlines. This work for me is about breaking through the shame induced by rape culture and bringing people together to build an alternative society.

I love that my gender and my body politicize any space I walk in and that I get to push those boundaries. It's crucial for me, and others like me, to be present in these spaces and to help this field rethink and deconstruct gender and its implications for anti-violence work. I love that I have this wonderful community of bad-ass feminists and advocates who stand in solidarity and embrace difference, while at the same time, I can challenge and push for change within those circles. I love the intergenerational community that I engage with and all of the teaching and knowledge translation that happens. I feel humbled that I am here to do support work but happy also that I can do prevention work; it helps me to understand transformative possibilities that help to build capacity for hope. While doing work with survivors of rape and sexual violence can be emotionally taxing, it's also incredibly healing for me to share and connect with folks who have survived, who have made choices, who have agency, and who keep pushing back. I think my favourite part of my role is engaging with young people who inspire me and help me to learn and unlearn, while I get to share my own stories and knowledge with them as well.

The Challenges of Doing Anti-Violence Work

Doing anti-violence or other community work is challenging because it's almost always reactionary and we often don't get to see change in our lifetime. Personally, one of the biggest challenges is my own gender and identity and where these fit in this work. As a gender non-conforming person who works to end violence against women, it can be incredibly invalidating to not ever see yourself represented or to feel that your experience is somehow being left out. For me, one of the biggest challenges is having my whole heart in this work and not letting it consume me. I don't think you have to cut off your emotions or your capacity for empathy, but I do know that it is incredibly important to keep ourselves grounded in this work and to make sure we are taking care of ourselves.

Chapter 12 Review

Review Questions

1. What are the main theories that are helpful in understanding sexuality? Briefly explain each one.
2. What is "internalized homophobia"? Why is it important for social workers (and others) to understand this concept?
3. What is the social work profession's perspective on gender and sexual diversity, and how has it changed in the last few decades?
4. What is "coming out," and what are some related factors of which social workers should be aware?
5. What are some key practice and policy issues that might help to ensure equality for trans persons?
6. Do you think that children born with indeterminate sex characteristics or genitalia should be assigned a gender based on their genetic and hormonal test results, as opposed to undergoing surgery? Why or why not?
7. How might social work practitioners ensure that their workplaces are supportive of people who do not fit within heterosexist gender binaries?
8. Give some examples of how some social and material relations privilege some genders and sexualities while marginalizing others.

Exploring Social Work

1. The Trans Ally Quiz helps the general public and service providers understand how to support members of trans communities. Download the quiz at www.trans-academics.org/TransAllyQuiz.doc and test your understanding of trans-positive service.
2. Some social workers consider their sexual orientation and gender identity to be private, but it can be important for clients exploring their sexuality to know the sexual orientation of their social worker. In small groups, discuss whether you think social workers should be obligated to disclose their sexual or gender orientation to LGBTQ+ clients.
3. Watch a film that has a gender or sexual diversity theme. While you are watching the film, pay attention to your own emotional reactions. After the film, reflect on what your reactions might indicate concerning your feelings about gender and sexual diversity.

Websites

Equality for Gays and Lesbians Everywhere (EGALE)
www.egale.ca
This national organization is committed to advancing, at the federal level, equality and justice for lesbians, gays, bisexuals, and trans-identified people. The website has a vast collection of news items, articles, and other resources. Included is a summary of lesbian and gay rights in each jurisdiction in Canada.

Gender Education and Advocacy (GEA)
www.gender.org
Gender Education and Advocacy (GEA) is a national organization focused on the needs, issues, and concerns of gender-variant people. It seeks to educate and to advocate for all persons who experience gender-based oppression in all of its many forms.

Parents and Friends of Lesbians and Gays (PFLAG) Canada
www.pflag.ca
This website includes information and resources for gay men, lesbians, and bisexuals, and for their families and friends. Most chapters have scheduled meetings that provide support and information.

International Gay and Lesbian Human Rights Commission (IGLHRC)
www.iglhrc.org
IGLHRC's mission is to protect and advance the human rights of all people and communities subject to discrimination or abuse on the basis of sexual orientation, gender identity, or HIV status. Its website contains excellent resources, news items, and urgent action items.

Asexuality Visibility and Education Network (AVEN)
www.asexuality.org
AVEN is not only home to a large number of resources about asexuality, but also hosts the world's largest online community for asexual persons.

Social Work and Persons with Disabilities

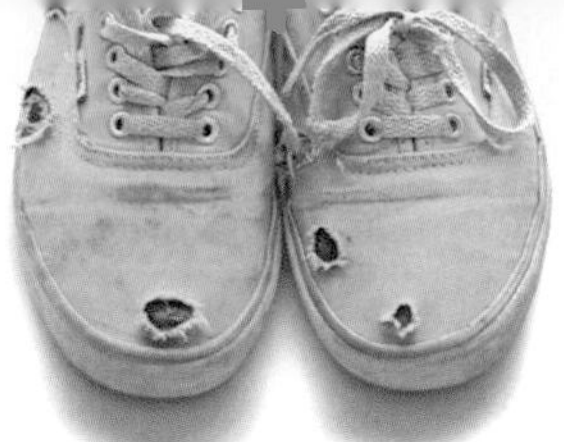

Roy Hanes

From Individual Support to Social Change

13

"Canadians with disabilities today seek equality, not charity."

Laurie Beachell, national coordinator, Council of Canadians with Disabilities

The disabled community is the world's largest minority group.

About 15 percent of the world's population, or an estimated one billion people, live with disabilities. They are the world's largest minority (United Nations, 2016). In Canada, it is estimated that 3.8 million people over the age of 15 have a disability, representing approximately 14 percent of the total Canadian population.

In this country, most people with disabilities live with family members or on their own, with close ties to family members. As a result, 53 percent of the Canadian population is directly affected by disability. Considering this fact, it is highly likely that most, if not all, social workers will at some point in their careers have a client with a disability or deal with a family member who is faced with the onset of a disability in a loved one.

In this chapter, you will learn how to...

- summarize the history of services for people with disabilities in Canada
- identify populations with a higher prevalence of disability, according to various national surveys
- differentiate between the medical and the political rights approaches to disability
- explain "ableism" and the reasons for the stigmatization of persons with disabilities
- discuss various types of impairment using respectful and person-centred language
- discuss the pros and cons of a Canadians with Disabilities Act
- describe the Independent Living Movement
- identify various income security programs for Canadians with disabilities

Key Concepts

- Persons with disabilities
- Multidisciplinary rehabilitation team
- Participation and Activity Limitation Survey (PALS)
- Canadian Survey on Disability 2012 (CSD)
- Medical model
- Political rights model
- Ableism
- Independent Living Movement (ILM)
- Disability rights movement
- Publicly-funded disability programs
- Privately-funded disability programs

Focusing Question

What specific skills do social workers need in order to provide effective support to people with disabilities and their families?

The History of Services for People with Disabilities in Canada

The distinction between persons with disabilities and those without dates back to the English Poor Law of 1601, which divided those seeking charitable support into the "deserving" poor and the "non-deserving" poor. Determining who was part of the deserving poor was based on the inability to work, or to serve one's master or landowner. The deserving poor were entitled to charitable support, such as permission to beg or to receive charity from religious institutions. These forms of charitable relief, known as "outdoor relief," were eventually brought from the old world to the new, including Canada. Other forms of outdoor relief included being lodged with a family or individual, in which case the homeowner would be given a small stipend.

By the mid-nineteenth century, outdoor relief had come to be seen as a mechanism that created rather than relieved dependency. Outdoor or community-based relief was gradually replaced with institutional care—asylums, work houses, poor houses, special schools, chronic care facilities, and later, hospitals (Splane, 1965). This new form of relief became known as "indoor relief." By the end of the nineteenth century, most of the charitable relief for individuals with disabilities in Canada had shifted to institution-based programs.

Each province developed its own relief programs for persons with disabilities, as well as special schools and institutions. As a result, no national support programs were established. Indeed, no significant national support care programs for persons with disabilities exist in Canada to the present day (Hanes and Moscovitch, 2002).

The Institutionalization of People with Disabilities

The replacement of outdoor relief with indoor relief represented a significant shift in the philosophy regarding charitable help. **Persons with disabilities**, who had previously been considered part of the social order, were now viewed as a nuisance population to be removed from society, isolated, and placed in segregated institutions. Disability was considered a source of shame, and many persons with disabilities who were not sent to institutions were hidden away in their homes by their family members. There are numerous examples of people with various forms of disabilities being hidden or kept at home in Canada, the U.S., and the U.K. throughout the nineteenth and twentieth centuries (Hanes, 1995). The public disdain toward individuals with disabilities became so severe that some municipalities, such as York (now known as Toronto), developed bylaws that banned people with disabilities from public streets.

As time progressed, more and more institutions for housing various disabled populations were constructed, and by the early twentieth century, tens of thousands of individuals had been placed in these institutions. Many of these facilities remained in operation until the mid-1990s and early 2000s. By the mid-twentieth century, many provinces had "special" residential schools for children and adolescents who were blind and/or deaf. Provincial institutions had been also established for people with psychiatric disabilities, and many provinces had institutions for people with developmental disabilities. Specialized hospitals were established for many disabled populations, including tuberculosis hospitals, orthopaedic hospitals, and rehabilitation hospitals.

The institutionalization of people with disabilities became so widespread that it was commonly believed to be the natural order of things, and that people with disabilities had always been separated from their communities (Bowe, 1978).

What Is Disability?

In recent years, the definition of "disability" has shifted from "something that is wrong" with an individual to reflect a more inclusive view that links an individual with impairments to broader social, political, cultural, and environmental characteristics.

According to the United Nations, "Disability results from the interaction between persons with impairments, conditions, or illnesses and the environmental and attitudinal barriers they face. Such impairments, conditions, or illnesses may be permanent, temporary, intermittent, or imputed, and include those that are physical, sensory, psychosocial, neurological, medical, or intellectual."

The Post-War Period and Beyond

Following World War II, Canada witnessed the gradual expansion of the "welfare state," and many new social security programs, such as pensions and disability benefits, were put in place. There emerged the notion of the **multidisciplinary rehabilitation team**, which included physicians, nurses, occupational therapists, physiotherapists, and later, social workers, psychologists, and vocational counsellors. The field itself eventually fell under the domain of the medical profession, which became responsible for determining whether there was a need for specialized care, income supports, pensions, educational supports, transportation supports, home care supports, and other benefits.

Medical and social services for people with disabilities have significantly expanded since this period. They include special schools, training programs, sheltered workshops, summer camps, recreational programs, special hospitals, and after-care facilities, as well as special trades and industries. Rehabilitation services of this type are still a primary area of social work with persons with disabilities. Social workers are also employed by provincial and federal governments and by charitable organizations, both in the provision of services and in the development of policies.

Since the 1970s, there has been a shift away from a strict, medical approach to a more "progressive" model in which persons with disabilities are accepted fully as equal citizens. The Independent Living Movement (ILM) has been been at the forefront of this new approach. The ILM philosophy promotes self-direction, self-determination, and full participation in the life of one's community and has single-handedly begun a new era for persons with disabilities.

Persons with disabilities
According to the World Health Organization, persons with disabilties include those with "impairments, activity limitations, and participation restrictions. An impairment is a problem in body function or structure; an activity limitation is a difficulty in executing a task or action; while a participation restriction is a problem in involvement in life situations."

Multidisciplinary rehabilitation team
A group of professionals from a variety of disciplines who work with an individual to maximize his or her physical, psychological, and/or social participation in work, education, and civic life

This photo shows the Huronia Regional Centre in Orillia, one of the first Ontario institutions to treat people with developmental disabilities. Attitudes have changed since the facility opened in 1861, when resident patients were viewed as "idiots," "imbeciles," and "feeble-minded."

The Prevalence of Disability in Canada

Until 2010, Statistics Canada used census data to carry out detailed research into disability. The **Participation and Activity Limitation Survey (PALS)** population consisted of all persons who answered "yes" to either of the census questions on activity limitations. The federal government discontinued the long-form census in 2010, however, and PALS was discontinued.

The most recent data on disability come from the **Canadian Survey on Disability 2012 (CSD)**, although many believe that this survey was not as comprehensive as PALS. The CSD examined only individuals with disabilities who were of working age (15 and older) living in private dwellings. As a result, there is limited information about the needs of children or of people residing in chronic-care facilities or nursing homes. There are also minimal data pertaining to First Nations, as the research did not apply to First Nations persons living on reserves.

Notwithstanding these limitations, the CSD reports that in 2012, an estimated 3.8 million adults were limited in their daily activities due to a disability (13.7 percent of the total Canadian population). The three most prevalent disability types are pain, mobility, or flexibility (see Figure 13.1). Of those Canadians who reported at least one of these types of disability, more than 40 percent experienced all three at the same time.

In 2012, 26 percent of persons with disabilities had impairments that were classified as very severe; 23 percent had severe disabilities; 20 percent had moderate disabilities; and 32 percent had mild disabilities. Additionally, 81.3 percent reported using some kind of assistive device—for example, to facilitate movement (e.g., wheelchairs, hand and arm supports) or to help them hear, see, or learn (e.g., hearing aids, magnifiers, specialized computers).

The Prevalence of Disabilities by Type

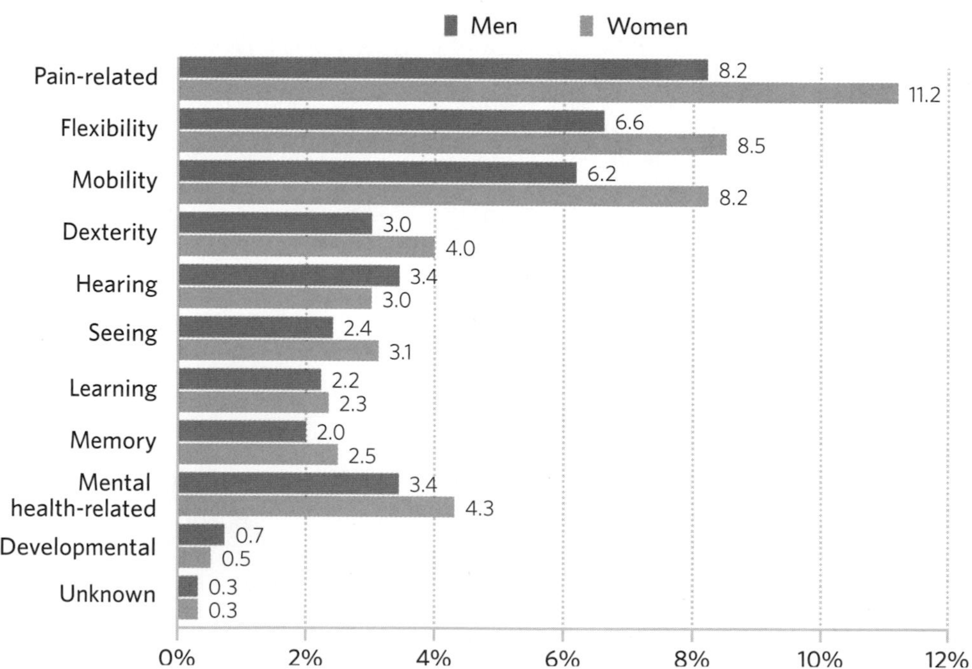

Figure 13.1 Disabilities related to pain, flexibility, and mobility are the most common. About 12 percent of Canadians aged 15 years or older (just over 3 million) reported having at least one of these disabilities, and many people reported more than one.

Source: Statistics Canada. (2012). *Canadian Survey on Disability, 2012* (89-654-X). Ottawa: Statistics Canada.

Disability and the Age of Canadians

Not surprisingly, the prevalence of disability among Canadians increases with age. In 2012, 2.3 million working-age Canadians (aged 15 to 64), or 10.1 percent of the total population, reported having a disability. Among Canadians 65 or older, however, 33.2 percent reported a disability. Of the working-age population, 4.4 percent reporting a disability were aged 15 to 24, 6.5 percent were 25 to 44, and 16.1 percent were 45 to 64. The proportion who reported a disability rose to 26.3 percent for those aged 65 to 74, and 42.5 percent for those 75 and older.

The most prevalent *types* of disability also vary according to age. In the youngest age group (15 to 24), the most commonly reported types of disability were mental or psychological (2.2 percent); learning related (2.0 percent); and pain (1.9 percent). Among those aged 45 to 64, the most common impairments were pain (12.7 percent), flexibility (9.8 percent), and mobility (8.6 percent). While these three types of disabilities were also the most commonly reported among seniors, the prevalence was much higher: 22.1 percent for pain, 20.5 percent for mobility, and 19.3 percent for flexibility. Perhaps not surprisingly, the prevalence of hearing-related disabilities was also high among seniors (10.4 percent).

As shown in Figure 13.2, Canadian women have a higher prevalence of disability in almost all age groups. The proportion of those reporting a disability among adult women was 14.9 percent, and only 12.5 percent for men. Among the oldest Canadians (those aged 75 or above), 44.5 percent of women reported a disability, compared to 39.8 percent of men. In the 15-to-24 age group, the proportion of men an d women reporting a disability was similar in 2012: 4.5 percent for men and 4.3 percent for women.

Participation and Activity Limitation Survey (PALS)

Statistics Canada's Participation and Activity Limitation Surveys (PALS) of 2001 and 2006 built on the Health and Activity Limitation Surveys (HALS) of 1986 and 1991. These "flagship" surveys established a kind of international "gold standard" for gathering and reporting statistical data on disability. In 2011, however, the Minister of Human Resources and Skills Development Canada (HRSDC) decided that the PALS would be cancelled and that, in its place, a new data strategy on disability would be launched.

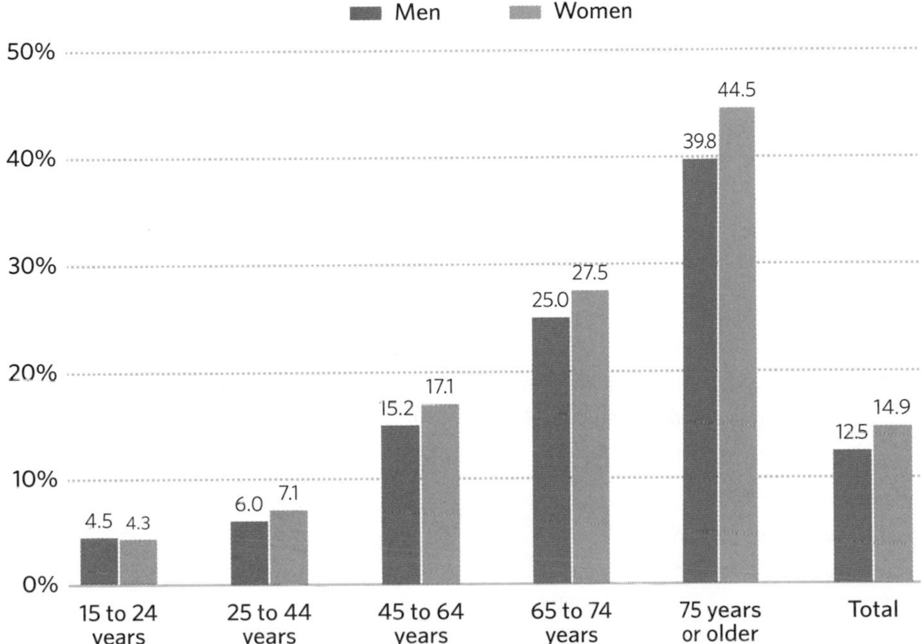

Figure 13.2 For both men and women reporting a disability, the prevalence of disability increases with age, with women having a higher prevalence in almost all age groups.

Source: Statistics Canada. (2012). *Canadian Survey on Disability, 2012* (89-654-X). Ottawa: Statistics Canada.

Theoretical Approaches to Understanding Disability

The American *Vocational Rehabilitation Act* of 1973 represented a pivotal point in the history of persons with disabilities in the United States, as well as in Canada. This legislation prohibited discrimination against people with disabilities, stating the following:

> No otherwise qualified handicapped individual in the United States as defined by Section 7 shall, solely by reason of his handicap, be excluded from participation in, be denied the benefits of, or be subject to discrimination under any program or activity receiving federal financial assistance (Zola, 1986: 1).

Spurred on by the successes of the U.S. movement, Canadians with disabilities began to advocate under their own national umbrella, the Coalition of Provincial Organizations of the Handicapped (which later became known as the Council of Canadians with Disabilities). Notable Canadian leaders such as Henry Enns, Allan Simpson, and Jim Doerksen united people around the Canadian Independent Living Movement. They were also at the forefront of the movement to have disability rights included in the *Canadian Charter of Rights and Freedoms*. With the passage of the *Charter* in 1982, Canada became one of the first countries in the world to have the rights of people with disabilities guaranteed under law.

Currently, two broad approaches characterize discussions of disability and social work involvement with persons with disabilities:

- **Medical model**. The medical model has its roots in rehabilitation medicine, where the focus of the intervention is on the individual. It views disability as an "impairment" and a "personal tragedy" and emphasizes the need of the individual to adapt or otherwise fit within mainstream society as much as possible.
- **Political rights model**. The political rights model, on the other hand, is concerned with the broader social and political context and with the need for society as a whole to adapt to the needs of persons who have disabilities.

The pre-eminent British disability advocate and theorist Michael Oliver coined the terms "personal tragedy theory" and "social oppression theory" to describe the differences between these two approaches to disability (Oliver, 1990).

The Medical Model

From the perspective of the medical model (or the "personal tragedy theory"), a disabling condition is an unfortunate life event calling for some form of professional and medical assistance (Oliver, 1990). Disability is seen primarily as a medical and rehabilitative problem. The various forms of professional rehabilitative and medical interventions are means of "curing" or "fixing" the individual. According to this theory, persons who become disabled, as well as their loved ones, must go through various stages of psychological and emotional adjustment before they can accept themselves or their loved one as a person with a disability.

Much of the literature pertaining to the impact of disability is based on this "stages of adjustment" approach (i.e., feeling anger, denial, and depression before accepting disability as part of one's life). However, this approach has been critiqued by many researchers on the grounds that, for most people, disability is *not* a tragedy, a "life sentence," or "a fate worse than death." Indeed, many disability activists and social workers contend that the day-to-day difficulties faced by people with disabilities are not the result of their limitations so much as the social and attitudinal barriers they encounter.

Immigration and Disabilities

Canada's immigration laws do not specifically state that people with disabilities are not welcome, but the "excessive demand" clause of the Immigration and Refugee Protection Act (Section 38(1) c) makes it very difficult for them to immigrate to Canada.

The regulations define "excessive demand" as (a) a demand on health or social services for which the anticipated costs would likely exceed average Canadian per capita health and social services costs, or

(b) a demand on health or social services that would add to existing waiting lists and increase the rate of mortality and morbidity in Canada (Immigration and Refugee Protection Act, Regulations 1(1)).

The Political Rights Model

In contrast to the medical model of disability, the political rights model (also referred to as the "independent living model") holds that the problems faced by people with disabilities are not the result of physical impairments alone, but are also the result of the social and political inequalities that exist between people with disabilities and those without (Oliver, 1990). This alternative model challenges the widely prevalent view that disability is essentially a rehabilitation problem requiring individual treatment and individual solutions. It also calls for a different focus for interventions on behalf of persons with disabilities.

This approach views people with disabilities as members of a minority population. "Many persons with disabilities," Lex Frieden suggests, "consider themselves as members of a minority group related not by colour or nationality but by functional limitation and similar need" (Frieden, 1983: 55). Environmental factors—such as a lack of employment opportunities, lack of affordable housing, and lack of accessible transportation, as well as the presence of negative stereotypes and prejudicial attitudes—are a major source of the problem. Structural and attitudinal changes, both social and political, are required if these obstacles are to be overcome.

According to the political rights model of disability, medical interventions alone are not enough. This approach calls for the incorporation of a full human-rights focus. Medical interventions are important, to be sure, but social, political, and legislative changes are required at the national, provincial, and community levels if the needs and concerns of people with disabilities are to be properly addressed.

Medical model
This model sees disability as an "impairment" and a "personal tragedy" for the person concerned, and therefore focuses on the need of the individual to adapt or otherwise fit in as much as possible.

Political rights model
This view of disability is concerned with the broader social and political contexts and with the need for society as a whole to adapt to the needs of persons with disabilities, not the other way around.

Table 13.1
Theories of Disability: Contrasting Approaches

	Rehabilitation Paradigm (Medical Model)	**Independent Living Paradigm (Political Rights Model)**
Definition of Problem	Physical impairment/lack of employment skills	Dependent on professionals, relatives, etc.
Locus of Problem	In the individual	In the environment and rehabilitation process
Solution to Problem	Professional intervention by physician, therapist, occupational therapist, vocational rehabilitation counsellor	Peer counselling, advocacy, self-help, consumer control, removal of barriers
Social Role	Patient/client	Citizen/consumer
Who Controls	Professional	Citizen/consumer
Desired Outcome	Maximize activities and living skills	Independent living

- *Source:* DeJong, Gerben. (1979). Independent living: From social movement to analytic paradigm. *Archives of Physical Medicine and Rehabilitation, 60* (October): 435-446.

Destigmatizing Disability

Many students of social work are familiar the terms "racism," "sexism," "heterosexism," and "ageism," but they may be less familiar with the term "**ableism**." This term refers to the stigmatization of disability and the existence of prejudicial attitudes held by people without disabilities toward people with disabilities. Ableism is a belief in the superiority of people without disabilities over people with disabilities. It can take the form of ideas and assumptions, stereotypes, practices, physical barriers in the environment, and larger-scale (systemic) oppression.

There is nothing inherent in disability that should lead to the stigmatization of people with disabilities or lead to the development of belief systems wherein biological difference is linked to biological inferiority. Yet in most Western industrialized societies, there has been a growing cultural emphasis on the "body beautiful." Physical attractiveness, sexuality, and desirability have become a valued cultural norm. People with disabilities often do not meet cultural standards of physical attractiveness, and this contributes to the stigma attached to disability, according to which having a disability is to be undesirable and unlovable. For persons with disabilities, this attitude has implications for many aspects of life, such as developing friendships and intimate relationships, socializing, and being involved in recreational activities.

Disability Culture
Since the early 1980s, the terms "person with disabilities" and "people with disabilities" came to be accepted as the most appropriate terms to be used when referring to individuals who have disabilities. In more recent times, however, more and more people with disabilities, especially those who promote disability culture, are using the term "disabled person" to self-identify.

Stereotypes Abound

As with all forms of discrimination, stereotypes abound concerning people with disabilities. For example, there is a common belief that people with disabilities are in a continuous state of emotional distress and psychological suffering. This stems from the long-held belief that if there is damage to one aspect of the system (physical disability), then there would be damage to the emotional and mental aspects as well. Yet, this is clearly not the case: most persons with disabilities cope well and have no negative emotional or mental side effects.

Sometimes a person with a disability is seen as *deserving* of the disability. For example, a young person who becomes disabled as a result of driving while intoxicated may be viewed as having received what he or she deserved. As well, there is often very little sympathy for adults who have disabling conditions as a consequence of a particular lifestyle—for example, because of drug use, prostitution, or unprotected sex. Some people still believe, too, that a disability is the consequence of sinful activities on the part of an individual or parent. Congenital disorders, for example, are often attributed to the risky behaviours of mothers during pregnancy, even though there is no scientific support for such claims. There are many examples in folklore, literature, TV programs, and films that portray persons with disabilities as being evil. Disability may even remind people of their own mortality. Indeed, much of the literature pertaining to the psychological adjustment to the onset of disability comes from the study of death and dying. Such stereotypes and fears may lead to the avoidance of people with disabilities, further contributing to their social isolation.

Just as in the case of sexism or racism, stereotyping and stigmatization abound in the case of persons with disabilities, though such negative portrayals are seldom acknowledged, let alone discussed publicly. For example, terms such as "defective," "crippled," or "lame" are now generally considered to be derogatory and inappropriate, but they are still used in everyday conversation. (For more respectful and appropriate terminology for referring to persons with disabilities, see Table 13.2.) Much progress has been made, but persons with disabilities are often still not treated as equal to able-bodied persons.

Table 13.2
Appropriate Terminology for Describing Persons with Disabilities

Instead of...	Please use...
Birth defect, congenital defect, deformity	Person born with a disability/who has a congenital disability
Blind (the), visually impaired (the)	Person who is blind, person with a visual impairment
Confined/restricted to a wheelchair, wheelchair-bound	Person who uses a wheelchair, wheelchair user
Cripple, crippled, lame	Person with a disability/mobility impairment, etc.
Hard of hearing (the), hearing impaired (the)	Person who is hard of hearing
Deaf-mute, deaf and dumb	Person who is deaf, "the Deaf" (sign language users)
Disabled sport/disabled community	Sport for athletes with disabilities/disability community
Epileptic (the)	Person who has epilepsy
Fit, attack, spell	Seizure
Handicapped (the)	Person with a disability
Handicapped parking, handicapped bathrooms	Accessible parking, accessible bathrooms
Inarticulate, incoherent	Person who has a speech disorder/speech disability
Insane (of unsound mind), lunatic, maniac, mental patient, mentally diseased, mentally ill, neurotic, psychotic	Person with a mental health disability (Note: The term "insane" should only be used in a strictly legal sense.)
Invalid	Person with a disability
Learning disabled, learning disordered, dyslexic (the)	Person with a learning disability
Mentally retarded, defective, feeble-minded, idiot, imbecile, moron, retarded, simple, mongoloid	Person with an intellectual disability
Normal	Person without a disability
Person who has trouble...	Person who needs...
Physically challenged/handicapped/impaired	Person with a disability
Spastic	Person who has spasms
Suffers from, stricken with, afflicted by	Person with a disability
Victim of cerebral palsy, multiple sclerosis, etc.	Person who has cerebral palsy, multiple sclerosis, etc.

- *Source:* Human Resources and Social Development Canada. (2006). *A Way with Words and Images*. Ottawa: Human Resources and Social Development Canada.

A "Canadians with Disabilities" Act

Arguments for and against

Either way, there needs to be action.

The social work profession has a long history of advocating for the rights of people with disabilities, including citizenship rights. Partly as a result of this advocacy work, social workers have witnessed the implementation of legislation at the provincial/territorial and federal levels that guarantees the rights of people with disabilities. For the most part, this anti-discriminatory legislation is rooted in the human rights acts of the provincial/territorial and federal governments. Canada is one of the few countries in the world with a constitution guaranteeing the rights of people with disabilities.

Social Work and Rights for People with Disabilities

While people with disabilities benefit by having their individual rights and freedoms protected through human rights codes and legislation, whether it is at the provincial/territorial or federal level, such legislation is said to be more reactive than proactive.

For example, a disabled individual who feels that his or her rights have been or are being violated can take their case to the human rights commission of their province or territory. If the issue involves the federal government, then the individual can go to the Canada Human Rights Commission. These commissions will investigate the claim and make decisions that may or may not be in favour of the individual. This reactive process can take years to resolve.

As Prince (2010) points out, however, much of the discussion pertaining to a Canadians with Disabilities Act (CDA) favours a *proactive* approach. Proactive, disability-positive legislation could establish principles that allow for greater opportunities for people with disabilities.

At the heart of a proactive CDA would be opportunities for public awareness, greater potential for barrier removal, and greater access to such items as education, employment, and community supports. As well, a CDA would have to provide a framework for "timelines for implementation and compliance, and enforcement" (Prince, 2010: 200–202).

The government of Canada is consulting with disability rights organizations across the country, seeking advice with regard to the development of a comprehensive, progressive, and inclusive Canadians with Disabilities Act.

Although many disability rights activists have advocated for a Canadians with Disabilities Act, many are still not in favour of such legislation. The following provides an overview of both sides of this debate. The material comes from Lana Kerzner and David Baker's "A Canadians with Disabilities Act?" (May, 1999) and is provided by the Council of Canadians with Disabilities.

Arguments in Favour

1. At the present time, Canada does not have a nationwide Canadians with Disabilities Act, and it is now time for a comprehensive piece of legislation in this area.
2. A comprehensive Canadians with Disabilities Act would offer greater opportunities for public awareness regarding the needs and concerns of people with disabilities throughout Canada.
3. Existing human rights legislation does not adequately address ongoing discrimination, whereas a comprehensive Canadians with Disabilities Act would address deep-rooted discrimination.
4. Present-day human rights legislation is primarily based on complaints and reactive protocols, whereas a CDA would be proactive and would provide the opportunity for greater systemic change.
5. A CDA endorsed by people with disabilities, government officials, and politicians offers the opportunity for government accountability whereby governments would have to report on milestones for implementing and carrying out the mandates of the legislation.
6. Presently, the federal government funds a small but very active Office of Disability Issues, and the present federal Liberal government created a Ministry for Persons with Disabilities. Both the Office and the Ministry can change as government mandates change, but a CDA could potentially lead to a permanent federal department for people with disabilities.

Arguments Against

1. The rights of Canadians with disabilities are guaranteed under the *Canadian Charter of Rights and Freedoms*, the *Canadian Human Rights Act*, and provincial and territorial human rights codes, so no additional legislation is needed.
2. Some of the factors that have contributed to the ineffectiveness of the current laws would not be resolved with the enactment of a CDA. All that would result would be yet another piece of legislation with a lot of potential but that still produces insufficient results.
3. Specific legislation aimed at ensuring rights for people with disabilities may lead to other disenfranchised groups (such as LGBTQ+ persons, people of colour, First Nations persons, and others) demanding similar legislation. The concern is that there may be a backlash and that a proposed CDA might only get limited support from other groups.
4. Federal legislators might view the disability-specific legislation as being precedent-setting, which could potentially lead to other groups, such as those noted above, to demand similar legislation that would be specific to the group's needs. Such considerations and possibilities might influence legislators and government officials not to support a Canadians with Disabilities Act.
5. Over the years, various federal governments conducted investigations into the creation of legislation aimed at supporting the rights of people with disabilities, but in the end, very little change occurred. Many of the people with disabilities who were involved in the process "were disillusioned as a result of the extensive amount of work involved with little or no results. There is a concern about expending energy to repeat a failure. The resources could be better spent by improving the effectiveness of the current laws and systems" (Kerzner and Baker, 1999).

The Council of Canadians with Disabilities (CCD)

The Council of Canadians with Disabilities (CCD), formerly known as the Coalition of Provincial Organizations of the Handicapped (COPOH), was founded in 1976 by people with disabilities. The organization was formed because people with disabilities, facing discrimination and exclusion, wanted an accessible and inclusive society; that is, a Canada where people with disabilities have the opportunity to work, volunteer, go to school, have a family, and participate in recreational, sports-related, and cultural activities.

Over the last 30 years, there has been a shift in thinking about disability. Through the human rights work of organizations like CCD, it has been recognized that traditional medical approaches to disability have not significantly improved the social or economic position of people with disabilities. CCD has been encouraging Canada's decision makers to adopt a human rights approach to disability issues that focuses on barrier removal.

To this end, CCD's volunteers have worked for

- a Canadian Human Rights Act that protects people with disabilities from discrimination,
- the inclusion of people with disabilities in the Equality Rights section of the *Canadian Charter of Rights and Freedoms,*
- an accessible federal transportation system, through law reform and test case litigation (e.g., the VIA Rail case and the One Person/One Fare case),
- improved disability-related supports through increased federal investment,
- increased knowledge of disability issues by participating in research initiatives such as the VP-Net and Dis-IT projects and by developing and leading a research project focusing on poverty,
- increased public awareness about disability and support for access and inclusion through public education programs, such as End Exclusion,
- accessible banking by working with the Canadian Bankers Association to develop more accessible banking machines,
- better assistive technology by participating on Industry Canada's Assistive Devices Advisory Committee, and
- better access to pensions by participating on the Canada Pension Plan Disability Benefit Roundtable.

▪ *Source:* Council of Canadians with Disabilities. www.ccdonline.ca.

The Independent Living Movement

The Independent Living Movement (ILM) has been a key player in the struggle to achieve human rights legislation for people with disabilities. Originating in the United States in the early 1970s and introduced to Canada in 1979, the philosophy underlying the **Independent Living Movement (ILM)** is to encourage and assist persons with disabilities achieve self-direction over the personal and community services needed to attain their own independent living.

Origins and Philosophy of the ILM

The origins of the Independent Living Movement can be traced to the Cowell Residence Program at the University of California, Berkeley. In the early 1960s, students with severe disabilities were housed in Cowell Hospital on campus. A group of students with disabilities began to recognize that medical and rehabilitation professionals largely controlled their lives. Their efforts to take back control inspired the ILM and the **disability rights movement** of the 1970s and continue to do so today.

Three major events in 1981 were central to the full development of the ILM in Canada: (1) the United Nations' declaration of the International Year of Disabled Persons, (2) the Canadian government's release of *Obstacles,* its report concerning disability, and (3) the personal commitment of one of its founding members, Henry Enns, to the independent living (IL) philosophy. These helped provide legitimacy to the social oppression approach to disability and promoted the philosophy of IL to the various levels of government, academics, and other disability organizations.

By 1985, Independent Living Resource Centres (ILRCs) were operating in Waterloo, Winnipeg, Thunder Bay, Calgary, and Toronto. In 1986, the Canadian Association of Independent Living Centres (CAILC) was formed to act as a national coordinating body for the ILM. In 2008, CAILC changed their name to Independent Living Canada. In 2015, a total of 25 ILRCs were operating across Canada.

Empowering Persons with Disabilities

According to the IL philosophy, persons with disabilities are citizens with the right to participate in community life. It therefore advocates an alternative model of program delivery. The IL philosophy empowers consumers to make the choices that are necessary to control their community and personal resources. Consumer control means that ILRCs are governed and controlled by persons with disabilities. ILRCs are non-profit and responsive to persons with all types of disabilities, including mobility, sensory, cognitive, emotional, psychiatric, and so forth.

In 1997, the CAILC undertook a study of the effects of the ILRCs and found that they succeed, in large part, not simply because they provide an opportunity to learn skills, access information, and receive support, but because they do so in a way that is consistent with the independent living philosophy. The Association concluded that improvement in the quality of life for people with disabilities requires skill development as well as the removal of environmental, social, and economic barriers.

Individual empowerment was found to be a key benefit. It was particularly important in fostering competency in a variety of community living skills, as well as resulting in increased confidence and self-esteem. The Association found that individuals involved with some of the programs of the ILRC have knowledge of other IL programs as well, and highly value the programs with which they are directly involved.

The Independent Living Movement

The IL movement differs from traditional service-providing organizations by emphasizing peer support, self-direction, and community integration by and for people with disabilities themselves.

Independent Living is founded on the right of people with disabilities to

- live with dignity in their chosen community,
- participate in all aspects of their life, and
- control and make decisions about their own lives.

Types of Disabilities
Adults and children

The 2006 Participation and Activity Limitation Survey (PALS) allowed for the identification of the following types of disabilities or impairments.

ADULTS

- **Hearing.** Difficulty hearing what is being said in a conversation with one other person, in a conversation with three or more persons, or in a telephone conversation. (Note: Many Deaf people argue that the inability to hear and to speak orally as a means of communication is not a disability, and that listing deafness as a disability or an impairment is incorrect. Many Deaf people suggest that sign language is a legitimate language that contributes to Deaf culture.)
- **Seeing.** Difficulty seeing ordinary newsprint or clearly seeing the face of someone from 4 metres (12 feet).
- **Speech.** Difficulty speaking and/or being understood.
- **Mobility.** Difficulty walking half a kilometre or up and down stairs, about 12 steps without resting, moving from room to room, carrying an object of 5 kilograms (10 pounds) for 10 metres (30 feet), or standing for long periods.
- **Agility.** Difficulty bending, dressing, or undressing, getting into and out of bed, cutting toenails, using fingers to grasp or to handle objects, reaching in any direction (for example, above one's head), or cutting own food.
- **Pain.** Limitations in the amount or kind of activities that one can do because of a long-term pain that is constant or recurs from time to time (e.g., recurrent back pain).
- **Learning.** Difficulty learning because of a condition, such as attention problems, hyperactivity, or dyslexia, whether or not the condition was diagnosed by a teacher, doctor, or other health professional.
- **Memory.** Limitations in the amount or kind of activities one can do, due to frequent periods of confusion or difficulty remembering things. These difficulties may be associated with Alzheimer's, brain injuries, or other similar conditions.
- **Developmental.** Cognitive limitations due to the presence of a developmental disability or disorder, such as Down syndrome, autism, or mental impairment caused by a lack of oxygen at birth.
- **Psychological.** Limitations in the amount or kind of activities that one can do, due to the presence of an emotional, psychological, or psychiatric condition, such as phobias, depression, schizophrenia, or a substance use disorder.

CHILDREN UNDER 15

- **Hearing*.** Difficulty hearing.
- **Seeing*.** Difficulty seeing.
- **Speech**.** Difficulty speaking and/or being understood.
- **Mobility**.** Difficulty walking. This means walking on a flat firm surface, such as a sidewalk or floor.
- **Dexterity**.** Difficulty using hands or fingers to grasp or hold small objects, such as a pencil or scissors.
- **Learning**.** Difficulty learning due to the presence of a condition, such as attention problems, hyperactivity, or dyslexia, whether or not the condition was diagnosed by a teacher, doctor, or other health professional.
- **Developmental delay***.** Child has a delay in his/her development, which may be a physical, intellectual, or another type of delay.
- **Developmental disability or disorder**.** Cognitive limitations due to the presence of a developmental disability or disorder, such as Down syndrome, autism, or mental impairment caused by a lack of oxygen at birth.
- **Psychological**.** Limitations in the amount or kind of activities that one can do due to the presence of an emotional, psychological, or behavioural condition.
- **Chronic condition*.** Limitations in the amount or kind of activities that one can do, due to the presence of one or more chronic health conditions that have lasted or are expected to last six months or more and that have been diagnosed by a health professional. Examples of chronic conditions are asthma or severe allergies, heart condition or disease, kidney condition or disease, cancer, epilepsy, cerebral palsy, spina bifida, cystic fibrosis, muscular dystrophy, and fetal alcohol syndrome.

* Applicable to all children under 15.
** Applicable to children aged 5 to 14.
*** Applicable to children under 5.

- *Source:* Statistics Canada. (2007). *Participation and Activity Limitation Survey 2006: Analytical Report.* Ottawa: Statistics Canada.

Income Security Programs for Persons with Disabilities

Canada's disability income support system is based on a loose-knit set of programs. These programs have different eligibility criteria, guidelines, and procedures. Social and income security programs for people with disabilities are derived from private and public sources in the form of either contributory or non-contributory benefits.

- **Publicly-funded disability programs.** Publicly-funded disability programs are covered by federal, provincial, and municipal legislation. These programs include the Canada Pension Plan Disability Pension (a federal program), the Family Benefits plan (a provincial program), and the General Welfare Assistance plan (a municipal program in Ontario). These programs are funded through government taxation, and except for the Canada Pension Plan, do not require contributions from recipients.
- **Privately-funded disability programs.** Privately-funded disability programs include programs that are provided through private insurance plans or long-term disability plans as part of job benefits. These private income security programs are based on the amount of funding that the recipient has contributed directly to the plan, or funding that has been contributed to the plan on behalf of the recipient.

Provincial and Territorial Disparities

Canadians have a universal public health-care system, but the benefits do not extend to providing full support for all people with disabilities. The primary similarity across the provinces and territories is the range and types of supports and services provided. Provincial and territorial programs, whether in Newfoundland, British Columbia, or Yukon, will cover the cost of wheelchairs, canes, eyeglasses, walkers, attendant care services, home care, transportation, and so forth. The differences are in the eligibility requirements and the amount of funding for the various supports and services. Some provinces, such as Newfoundland and Labrador, Prince Edward Island, Saskatchewan, and New Brunswick, have a single-tier program wherein services are directly funded by the province to the individual. Others, such as Nova Scotia and Manitoba, have a two-tier system: basically, provincial funding is transferred to the local government, which, in turn, funds the individual. There are also provincial programs based on specific legislation. In Ontario, people with disabilities are covered under the Ontario Disability Support Program Act; in British Columbia, they are covered under the Disability Benefits Program Act; and in Alberta, they receive benefits through the Assured Income for the Severely Handicapped Persons program.

Although there are many differences in the income support programs across Canada, one important similarity remains, and it concerns eligibility. All individuals with disabilities and/or their family members who apply for support are assessed first for disability. That determination is made by a medical professional. This process is then followed by an assessment for benefits, since merely having a disability does not necessarily qualify the individual and/or family members for coverage. Every applicant from St. John's to Vancouver is assessed according to a "means test," which basically investigates bank accounts, saving bonds, household income, trust funds, and so on. Since provincial and territorial programs are "non-contributory" welfare programs, individual assets cannot be greater than the amount being applied for. For example, an individual might be eligible for $600.00 per month, but if their income is $250.00 per month, then this amount is deducted from the $600.00 and they will receive $350.00 as a monthly payment.

The Canada Pension Plan and Other Federal Programs

Canadians with disabilities may be eligible for federally-sponsored income support programs such as the Canada Pension Plan, which is based on the amount of money an individual and his or her employer pay into the program.

In recent years, the federal government has developed two additional programs that can provide financial support for Canadians with disabilities.

- **Disability Tax Credit.** Individuals and/or family members can claim expenses related to disability (including the cost of equipment, medical supplies, and home renovation) as part of their annual income tax claim.
- **Disability Registered Retirement Savings Program (DRRSP).** People with disabilities and/or family members can contribute a sum of money to a DRRSP on a yearly basis and can use the funds to supplement income in retirement or take out the funds when needed.

Determining Levels of Benefits for Persons with Disabilities

Once a person is deemed to have a disability, a rigourous Social Assistance review takes place to determine the exact level of benefits that are due. No stone seems to be left unturned in this assessment process.

As noted, first there is an investigation of assets. Only if one's assets are deemed to be within the parameters of program funding will they receive coverage under the provincial or territorial program. The next step in a Social Assistance review is a needs test, consisting of three additional steps:

- The applicant's basic requirements for living are identified (food, clothing, shelter, utilities, other household expenses, and personal allowances). Each requirement is designated with a maximum dollar allotment, and the requirements are then totalled to determine the funds needed to meet basic needs.
- The applicant's available financial resources are determined, that is, income from resources such as pensions, including public or private funds, savings, or money received through paid employment or training programs.
- The difference between total resources and total basic needs is then calculated. A negative remainder indicates a "budget defect." If this is the case, then the applicant is considered eligibile for assistance.

Improving the representation of people with disabilities in the labour market has been one of the most challenging projects undertaken by advocacy groups for people with disabilities.

The amount of assistance will then be determined according to a variety of factors, including size of family, degree of employability of the family's main decision maker, size and type of accommodation, and so on.

Disability and Labour Force Status

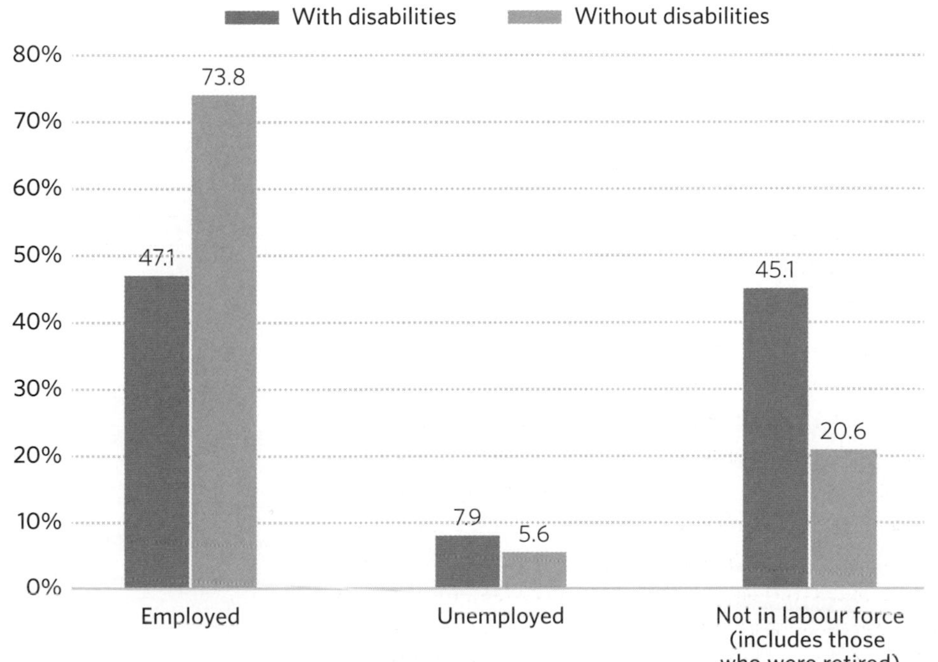

Source: Statistics Canada. (2012). *Canadian Survey on Disability, 2012* (89-654-X). Ottawa: Statistics Canada.

Figure 13.3 Persons with disabilities are more likely to be unemployed than persons without disabilities (7.9 percent versus 5.6 percent). They are also much more likely not to be in the labour force at all (45.1 percent versus 20.6 percent).

Social Work and Persons with Disabilities
Building on strengths, accessing resources

The onset of disability greatly affects the entire family unit

What skills should social workers have in order to work effectively with people with disabilities? Social workers should obviously have general practice skills, which include an understanding of individual and family counselling, as well as group work and community organization. In addition, they should have a knowledge of mediation and advocacy and be able to connect clients to available resources.

But to be effective, whether with persons with disabilities or with other groups, a social worker must be able to help an individual and family cope, while at the same time recognizing that many of their difficulties likely stem from the social and political contexts in which they find themselves. At times, the social worker may need to become a direct advocate for social and political change with, and on behalf of, his or her clients. This may involve petitioning for more or better services, organizing clients to protest a lack of accessible housing, or supporting boycotts against businesses that are not accessible to people with disabilities.

Disability and Social Work Practice

Following are some of the issues that social workers should consider as they support individuals and family members who are adjusting to the onset of disability.

- **Emotional coping and functioning skills.** The intensity and impact of disability on an individual or a family may be influenced by their experiences with previous life crises. People who have dealt effectively with previous crises may have acquired problem-solving and coping skills that can be used again to help them deal with the the onset of disability. If the social worker is aware of this, he or she can build on these strengths and help individuals and family members apply these skills in the new situation.
- **The family's post-trauma functioning.** It is important for the social worker to help individuals and family members recognize their strengths and to find, maintain, and develop resources and supports. These include "internal supports," such as strong, effective relationships between family members, spouses'/partners' stability, and strong parent–child bonds, as well as the effective decision-making and problem-solving skills of the family members. They also include "external supports," such as extended family members, friends, peer support, self-help groups, community resources, and supportive outside environments, such as the school or workplace.
- **The person's status within the family.** The impact of disability on a family is influenced by who has become disabled. For example, is the person a newborn, an infant, a spouse or partner, the primary wage earner, the primary decision maker, or the individual who provides most of the emotional support for other family members? Each circumstance will be different, and each will call for a particular type of response with respect to how family members may or may not cope with the onset of disability.
- **The person's stage in the life cycle.** The life cycle stage of the individual who has become disabled will influence how the family copes. For example, if the onset of chronic illness or impairment comes late in life, family members may have had an opportunity to plan. However, if the onset of disability comes earlier (as a consequence of birth impairment or injury, for example), the family may be affected quite differently. For example, a young couple may encounter financial difficulties resulting from a loss of income, and, depending on the type of disability, intimacy and sexuality may be affected. For other families, the birth of a child who has significant impairments may dramatically alter the hopes, plans, and dreams of the parents. Each situation is unique and will require its own solution.
- **The nature and extent of the disability.** The onset of disability can lead to many new relationships between family members and professionals (especially medical professionals). Uncertainty, use of medical jargon, and lack of information can create tension and frustration for family members. To be able to cope effectively, family members must be treated with dignity and respect, and they need to be involved in all aspects of treatment. In many situations, the social worker is a member of a multidisciplinary team, and part of his or her role is to advocate for the individual and the family in relation to the professional support services being provided.
- **Access to resources.** The impact of disability on a family unit is often influenced by the availability of community resources. Such services include support networks, daycare, schools, jobs, attendant care, retraining, respite care, hospice care, transportation, and recreational facilities. Other important factors include access to financial resources, including private pensions, insurance plans, or government-sponsored financial programs, such as the Canada Pension Plan and provincial financial assistance programs. Helping families access financial, community, social, recreational and/or medical resources is often central to the social work practitioner's role.

Support for Families

Until the 1970s, the medical care and treatment of both children and adults with disabilities was predominantly directed at the physical needs of the individual who was disabled. Less attention was paid to the emotional needs of the individual and the needs of his or her family.

During the past 25 years, however, there has been a greater recognition of the importance of the family and family members. This new focus was influenced by the introduction of family systems theory to social work. This theory argues that the family is an interrelated network and that an impact on one component of that network has significant consequences for all other components in the system. In other words, according to the family systems theory,

- all parts of the family unit are interrelated,
- each member affects and is affected by other members of the unit, and
- no single part of the family system can be understood in isolation from other parts.

Obviously, the onset of disability, whether at birth or later in life, will have a great effect the entire family unit. Family members (especially parents of a child with a disability) therefore have a critical role to play in the care, treatment, and emotional adjustment of the person who is disabled. Much of the work of the social work practitioner must therefore focus on the people on whom the person with the disability will increasingly depend.

Promoting Self-Sufficiency

Social work and young adults with developmental disabilities

In Tammy's story, a social worker encounters a young woman with developmental disabilities who wishes to move out of her parents' home and into her own apartment. Two issues of particular concern that need to be addressed are sexuality counselling and employability skills/job-readiness training.

A social worker's role in providing sexuality counselling requires a foundation of trust, care, and acceptance of the client's wishes. The goal is not to judge but to provide a service. It is important for social workers to remember that people with developmental disabilities have the same interest in sexuality as their non-disabled peers do. But due to the stigma attached to people with developmental disabilities, many clients do not receive appropriate information, support, and guidance. It has only been in the past two decades or so that social workers have provided sexuality counselling to people with developmental disabilities, as sexuality was once considered a taboo area. Indeed, historical accounts of people with developmental disabilities, especially women, reveal decades of forced sterilization of this population. Although the stigmatizing elements of sexuality and disability have been challenged in recent years, many people still view persons with disabilities as being asexual. This is not the reality, however. Persons with developmental disabilities are as drawn to sexual intimacy as are their non-disabled peers. Given this reality, effective social work practice must view a client's interest in exploring his or her sexuality as healthy and appropriate rather than problematic.

Once the social worker and the client commit to addressing issues related to sexuality, the social worker must be able to provide guidance, support, and information in a manner that the client can understand. Hence, the social worker should have training and expertise in this area. An important element of sexuality counselling is the provision of information about a wide range of issues, including socially appropriate private and public behaviours, safe sex, sexually transmitted diseases, wanted and unwanted advances, intercourse, contraception, pregnancy, parenting skills, self/other masturbation, and same-sex relationships. Literature regarding developmental disability and sexuality further suggests that the social worker may have to provide counselling about the mechanics of sex, coping with difficulties in relationships (including rejection and loss), and the facts about menstruation. Adults with developmental disabilities are often at risk of sexual abuse and exploitation. Therefore, sexuality counselling must also address the potential for harm and how clients can protect themselves.

Another area of focus for the social worker and the client is inquiry into subsidized housing options for people with disabilities. Canadians who can live independently and who are in receipt of a recognized disability pension, or who are considered disabled for income tax purposes, are eligible to apply for subsidized housing, which is rent geared to income. Social workers can help clients research the availability of social, non-profit, co-operative, or supportive housing; the eligibility criteria; and the application process. Because wait times for subsidized and supportive housing can be as long as ten years, it is often necessary to explore the availability of modest, non-subsidized housing that a client can afford.

Reflecting on Tammy's Story

1. What are some issues that may need to be resolved before Tammy can move out of her parents' home?
2. Tammy's interest in sexuality is one of her presenting concerns. What are the most important issues that Tammy and her social worker need to address in this area?
3. What social work services are provided to adults with developmental disabilities in your town or city?

Tammy's Story...
A quest for independence

Young adults with developmental disabilities experience the same "growing pains" as others do, as they strive to establish a separate identity from their parents, explore their sexuality, and seek a degree of independence from the family unit. Social workers can help these young adults and their families navigate some potentially complex situations.

Tammy, 25, has a mild to moderate developmental disability and has lived with her family for her entire life. For ten months now, Tammy has been enrolled in various social and recreational day programs provided through a local agency for adults who have disabilities.

Although Tammy has no job income, she receives a monthly cheque for $1,100 through the province's Disability Support Program. Her father, who oversees Tammy's financial affairs, gives her an allowance of $75 per week and deposits the remainder into a bank account for Tammy.

Over the past few months, Tammy and her parents have developed a good rapport with Britney, one of the young social workers at the agency. One aspect of Britney's job is to provide information, referrals, and supportive counselling to clients and their family members.

One day, Tammy visits Britney in her office and tells Britney that she would like to move out of her parents' home, possibly into her own apartment if she can obtain supported living resources. She is willing to learn more independent living skills, such as cooking and managing her own money. Tammy is also interested in broadening her social skills; eventually she would like to volunteer or work in the community.

Tammy tells Britney that her mother Ellen thinks Tammy will do well, as long as she has plenty of support and guidance. Tammy's father, however, is not as encouraging. Peter worries about Tammy being out on her own and wants her to continue to live at home.

In addition to her desire for financial and social independence, Tammy confides to Britney that she has developed a relationship with Josh, a young man with mild developmental disabilities who attends the same programs at the agency that Tammy does. Tammy discloses to Britney that she and Josh would like to date and possibly live together one day, but she acknowledges that this is a long-term plan and that they want to take time to get to know each other better before committing to a serious intimate relationship. Tammy indicates to Britney that for now, she would really like some information and counselling about healthy relationships and sexuality, as she has many questions and concerns about this area of adulthood.

Because of Tammy's mild to moderate cognitive impairment, Britney must keep in mind that Tammy will need to learn at her own pace. She may have some difficulties retaining information, and she may need help in terms of her literacy skills. Britney locates some books at an appropriate reading level and some online educational videos that she believes will help fill in some gaps in Tammy's understanding of human sexuality.

As part of a respectful counselling process, Britney must take care, as much as possible, to leave final decisions about sexuality and sexual activity up to Tammy. However, a concern for safety might arise if Tammy's relationship with Josh were to end and Tammy were to seek out new partners. Therefore, Britney talks openly with Tammy about the need for Tammy to learn how to be assertive with others and how to safeguard her physical and emotional safety in her dealings not only with Josh but also with possible future romantic partners. They determine together that Tammy will need to learn more about safe sex, contraception, and techniques for avoiding being pressured into having sex before she feels ready.

Tammy realizes that she will need to prove to her father that she is capable of living independently. She and Britney decide that another important part of Tammy's plan to establish self-sufficiency is to search for affordable housing that would suit a young person with developmental disabilities. They go online to find out for which subsidized housing programs Tammy might qualify. Together, Britney and Tammy learn how to submit an online application to non-profit and cooperative housing providers. They also search for nearby, inexpensive studio apartment vacancies. Tammy is excited that she is moving forward in her quest for adult decision-making power and autonomy.

With guidance and support, young adults with developmental disabilities can learn to live independently.

Complex Multiple Needs

Supporting parents of children with multiple special needs

The Shadbous' story pertains to a child with multiple disabilities. It reflects the interplay of systems at different levels of complexity that influences the family situation, while also acknowledging parental grief. Disability in a cross-cultural context also plays a role.

Research suggests that when a child with a disability is a member of a racial or cultural minority, the parents and child often have more difficulty accessing supports and services compared to non-racialized families. Zoebia et al. found that children of colour who have disabilities experienced being disabled quite differently compared to their white peers with disabilities because they experienced racism as well as ableism: "Many obstacles were rooted in institutional racism" (960). Studies regarding visible and ethnic minority children with disabilities indicate that this population faces significant obstacles in accessing health, social services, education, employment, and support services. In addition, the concerns of this population do not seem to be a priority for disability rights organizations or disability-related service agencies.

In some societies, the birth of a child with disabilities is considered a punishment from God, which makes the parents feel ashamed and reluctant to seek supports and services. Compounding these difficulties is the cultural belief that families are supposed to take care of their own, and thus seeking assistance from agencies is highly stigmatized, which inhibits many parents from seeking outside help. Many parents feel that they need to "save face" in their own extended families and cultural and religious communities, and thus do not apply for supports and services. Moreover, because of religious and cultural beliefs, parents may feel intimidated and misunderstood when applying for services. For example, observant Muslims may feel very uncomfortable with mixed-gender programs (Zoebia et al., 2006). Another reason why new immigrant parents, in particular, do not seek support for a child with disabilities is that they risk being deported if they do not have citizenship. As a matter of policy, Canada does not accept people with disabilities. Under section 19 of the *Immigration and Refugee Act*, people with disabilities can be denied permission to remain in Canada (Hanes, 2010). Fearing deportation, many new immigrant parents become very apprehensive when it comes to seeking out services for a child with a disability.

To work effectively with racialized or immigrant children who have disabilities, it is not only important that social workers develop an understanding of the impact of disability on family dynamics, but they must also develop practice skills based on cultural competence. This concept derives from the late 1980s, but being culturally competent is just as important today as it was 25 years ago. Cultural competence refers to "a program's ability to honour and respect those beliefs, interpersonal styles, attitudes, and behaviours of both families who are clients and the multicultural staff who are providing services. In so doing, it incorporates these values at the levels of policy, administration, and practice" (Roberts et al., 1990). Cross, Bazron, Dennis, and Isaacs (1989) identify five core principles of cultural competence that can be applied to social work practice with families whose children have disabilities: valuing diversity, conducting a cultural self-assessment, recognizing and understanding the dynamics of difference, acquiring cultural knowledge, and adapting to diversity.

Reflecting on the Shadbous' Story

1. How does the role of advocate differ from that of mediator? How might a social worker advocate for the Shadbous?
2. Why might joining a parent support group prove to be a positive step for the Shadbous?
3. Discuss some of the roles of the social worker in helping Omar and his parents deal with the various professionals involved in his care.

The Shadbous' Story...
Sharing an emotional journey

Parents who have recently learned that their child has a disability can benefit greatly from the professional support of a social worker. Not only do they need guidance navigating the medical system and information about the services available to their child, but their new reality calls for an empathetic ear and, often, individual and/or couples counselling.

Mr. and Ms. Shadbou first presented themselves to the Children's Treatment Centre when they moved back to Canada after having lived in the Middle East for a few years. Their son, Omar, aged six, has been diagnosed with severe cerebral palsy, as well as a developmental disability. His health was seriously compromised, and he was considered medically fragile. One of the Shadbous' primary concerns was that Omar did not yet have his Ontario Health Card—and he urgently required medical treatment and intervention.

As the social worker assigned to this case, my role was to communicate with the local children's hospital as well as with other community partners to help them understand the dire nature of Omar's medical status and to urge them to be ready to offer services as soon as possible once Omar's health card arrived. Omar's parents' priority was to have everything in place for a surgery that would allow Omar to be fed by means of a gastronomic tube, as he was at risk of failure to thrive. He also needed costly medication to help manage a seizure disorder.

My colleagues and I were able to advocate within our own organization to have the fees paid for by the Family Emergency Fund until Omar's family received his health card. The surgery was successful, and Omar has been gaining weight steadily.

Collaborating to Optimize a Child's Quality of Life

Mr. and Ms. Shadbou both have a university education. Ms. Shadbou stays at home full time caring for Omar and his two-year-old sister. Mr. Shadbou has not been able to secure employment in his field since returning to Canada and has been cleaning office buildings in the evenings to support the family. He has been taking courses in order to enhance his employability. The Shadbous attend many appointments with Omar, and they manage to cooperate effectively in assuming child-care responsibilities. Ms. Shadbou does not yet have her driver's license and often feels isolated and lonely when her husband is not home. Few extended family members have been supportive because they seem to feel uncomfortable and even embarrassed when the topic of Omar's disabilities arises. This alienation from their family is compounding the Shadbous' grief. Thus, the couple planned to join a network of parents who can relate to their unique situation. Mr. and Ms. Shadbou were keen to learn about the scope of services available to them, including respite offered by the local children's care home to help them regain some balance in their lives.

It is not easy for parents to accept that they need to seek help from such a facility. It is especially difficult for immigrants such as the Shadbous, who value self-sufficiency and self-determination and who do not wish to be perceived as a burden upon their adopted country. In a scenario such as this, parents need the help of professionals who are academically qualified, emotionally reassuring, and culturally competent. They need to know that their feelings will be respected, that their pain will be acknowledged, and that they will not be judged negatively.

I took care to ensure that Mr. and Ms. Shadbou were aware of the process whereby Omar could enter the education system, and I helped them make knowledgeable decisions about the most suitable classroom environment. Coordinating and communicating the details of Omar's care with education consultants and transportation representatives was crucial to the success of this transition.

One of the most complicated realities for families of children with complex physical needs is determining—together with physicians, a physiotherapist, and an occupational therapist—what type of equipment would be most beneficial, and at what point. Often, items such as wheelchairs, ceiling tracks, hospital beds, bath chairs, and standing frames must be procured. It is important for the team to work with the parents to review the various vendors who provide such equipment and to identify possible funding sources. Mr. and Ms. Shadbou have been active participants in collaborating with the numerous professionals involved in their lives to ensure that Omar is getting what he needs for an optimal quality of life.

Social work involving children with complex multiple needs requires collaboration with professionals in other fields.

Coping with the Onset of Disability

Social work practice with families of persons with disabilities

From the early 1950s until the early 1970s, the treatment of persons with disabilities focused on the individual only, and little or no attention was paid to the needs of family members. In fact, it was not too long ago that family members, including parents of children with disabilities, were considered a hindrance to treatment. As a result, people with disabilities were often removed from their families to be housed and treated in hospitals, rehabilitation centres, and institutions, which allowed only minimal contact with family, friends, and the outside world.

Indeed, during this period, very little attention was paid to the psychological and emotional effects of the disability on the individual or on family members. Rather, the focus of treatment tended to take only the "physical body" into account, ignoring the intellectual, psychological, emotional, and spiritual dimensions of a person with a disability.

Toward a Strengths-Based Practice

Since the late 1970s, health-care professionals have come to realize that the consequences of disability go far beyond the individual, and that, in reality, the disablement of one person has an effect on everyone connected to that person. There has been a shift in attitude wherein not only is an individual's emotional and pychological state deemed to be important, but family members are now viewed as essential elements of the rehabilitation and treatment process.

Over the years, a number of theories have attempted to explain the "stages of adjustment" through which families progress when coping with the onset of disability. Such theories have generally been found wanting insofar as they provide minimal reliability when it comes to positive adjustment to the onset of disability. Newer approaches have more validity. Power and Dell Orto (1980), for example, have outlined some effective guidelines in helping families adjust to disability. The key to effective social work in this area is to incorporate a strengths-based model of practice. Their approach includes the following:

- Respect and acceptance of each family's culture, ethnicity, structure, roles, values, belief systems, and ways of coping
- Recognition and acceptance of the strengths of families: family members, including the extended family kinship network, are most consistently involved in the provision of care, and so are able to provide valuable information and knowledge
- Close family-professional collaboration is essential so that both families and professionals can share information and learn skills to help in assessment and problem solving
- Inclusion of family members as part of the decision-making process with regard to all aspects of care, treatment, and follow-up

Whether they are parents, siblings, or grandparents, family members will often be affected in some way by the disablement of a loved one. With this in mind, social workers must remain aware that family members are struggling with various losses and so may be in need of professional support as well.

An approach that builds on the strengths, support networks, and resources available to family members can lead to positive outcomes for all those presented with the onset of a loved one's disability. The Rayners' story demonstrates such an approach on the part of a social worker.

Reflecting on the Rayners' Story

1. What might be the most common emotional responses of couples to their child being diagnosed with a disability?
2. Besides the provision of regular respite care, what other supports might the social worker have recommended for the Rayners?
3. What other strategies might the Rayners apply in order to improve communication in their marriage?

The Rayners' Story...
Building strength through adversity

Many parents who have children with disabilities prioritize everything except their own needs, and their relationship can suffer as a result. Parents need support in finding ways to boost their reserves of energy and strengthen their bond. This story demonstrates how a social worker can help couples adapt to their child's disability in positive ways. A strengths-based perspective assumes that most of the time, people can and do adapt to significant challenges in their lives in ways that provide them with renewed strength and increased energy.

I met Mr. and Mrs. Rayner following their appointment with the psychologist who had diagnosed both of their five-year-old twin boys with Autism Spectrum Disorder (ASD). Understandably, this diagnosis was very hard on the Rayners. My role was to help them work through the emotional difficulties associated with raising children with a disability, while also assisting them in accessing the various community resources for which they are eligible.

Mrs. Rayner is a stay-at-home mother, and Mr. Rayner is in the process of starting his own business, which has required a great deal of his time and energy for the past several months. According to both parents, they have been "just surviving" and are feeling overwhelmed and exhausted. They have very limited family support, and there are no family members with whom they feel comfortable leaving the twins.

Intervention

Like most parents of children with special needs, Mr. and Mrs. Rayner felt that their priority was to ensure that all applications to community programs had been completed before they addressed the impact of the situation upon themselves as a couple. They were eligible to apply for programs through the Ministry of Community and Social Services, which would extend financial assistance so that they could hire a worker to provide respite. They also wanted to ensure that they were connected to the community agency that offers Applied Behaviour Analysis (ABA) interventions, the empirically accepted treatment for persons with ASD. Mrs. Rayner had previously researched a number of alternative interventions—for example, a dietary change involving probiotics, which seemed to be benefitting both boys.

When addressing the impact of the diagnosis on the marital relationship, it was important to identify some of the losses experienced by both Mr. and Mrs. Rayner. Often, parents of children with a disability suffer a financial loss because one parent cannot work outside the home, and because the costs associated with the child's increased needs can be substantial. Grief also results from the loss of parents' initial hopes, dreams, and expectations for their child. For Mr. and Mrs. Rayner, one of the most significant losses was the lack of free time for each of them individually but also as a couple. Mr. Rayner was focused on the start-up of a new business, while Mrs. Rayner was responsible for all of the household and child-related tasks. There was little time left to relax.

I helped Mrs. Rayner feel more confident in expressing her feelings to her husband and revealing that she would like to find ways to connect with him on a more regular basis. She had feared that raising this topic would cause her husband to feel additional stress and that he might therefore reject her request. Mr. Rayner was, in fact, quite open to making a greater effort to sustain the health of the marriage. They discovered that they were both interested in exploring what they could do together that did not necessarily take up a lot of time but that would strengthen their relationship.

I shared some insights into the importance of effective communication for couples. Many parents who have children with a disability focus on everything except their own needs and their partner's needs. Relationships can start to buckle as communication weakens. If a couple overlooks these problems, they can become distanced from each other over time.

I worked with Mr. and Mrs. Rayner to devise a plan whereby they would arrange for respite care one evening a week so that they can visit friends, go out for a walk and a coffee, or browse through their favourite bookstore together. Enjoying unstructured time together as a couple will help replenish their energy levels and strengthen their sense of partnership as they confront the challenges that lie ahead.

Caring for children with a disability can strain a marriage; ensuring time together as a couple can fortify the bond.

Barb Juett

As a social worker with the Ottawa Children's Treatment Centre, Barb Juett helps families cope with the responsibilities of raising a child who has disabilities.

Barb Juett received her Bachelor of Social Work degree from Laurentian University in Sudbury, Ontario in 1987. While there, she benefitted from two excellent practicums, one at the John Howard Society and the other at the Elizabeth Fry Society. At the time, she was intrigued by the criminal justice system, but her career path took a different turn.

My education at Laurentian provided a solid foundation and an opportunity to develop my assessment and interviewing skills. After graduation, rather than pursuing work in the criminal justice field, I moved to Ottawa. Jobs were available there, and I managed to find employment at a group home for children with severe autism. This was one of a few specialized group homes operated by the Ottawa Children's Aid Society. After about a year, a social work position became available, and I was accepted as a member of a Child Protection Team. For the next ten years, I gained experience in child protection, as well as in intake services and adoption.

It would be fair to say that this was an eye-opening period in my life. Having been raised in a stable, middle-class family, I was at times unprepared for the level of poverty and the substandard home environments of some of the families we served. Education about family violence, substance use disorders, and oppression came not from a textbook but from exposure to the realities we were facing. I am still thankful for the support of my colleagues and supervisors, who shared their wisdom and knowledge with me during some emotionally challenging situations.

While I was working at the Ottawa Children's Aid Society, my supervisor encouraged me to pursue a Masters of Social Work degree. This was an opportunity that I could not pass up, as the organization was willing to cover the cost of my tuition. I was accepted at McGill University in Montréal, Québec, and moved away from my husband and friends for a year to live in a city where I didn't know anyone.

Over the years, my social work career has focused primarily on children and youth. Following ten years with the Children's Aid Society, I sought a new direction, which led to employment at the Ottawa Children's Treatment Centre (OCTC). I have been working at the OCTC since 1998.

A primary role of social workers at the OCTC is working with the families of children with disabilities, particularly parents, to ensure that the child receives appropriate services and to assist parents (as well as other family members) in coping with the day-to-day stresses and strains of raising a child who has one or more disabilities. Over the years, my social work practice has included the provision of supportive counselling as well as helping family members gain access to the many resources that children with disabilities need. Obtaining necessary resources sometimes included advocating for provincial government programs, working with school boards, and liaising with other professionals, such as doctors, physiotherapists, teachers, nurses, and occupational therapists. Throughout my career in working with children with disabilities, a core piece of my role as social worker has been communicating and interacting with professionals, agencies, and bureaucracies. Therefore, my role can be considered a multi-systemic one.

Presently, as the Professional Practice Leader for the Social Work Department at OCTC, one of my primary responsibilities is supervising social work services for the organization. While I have worked in a variety of capacities throughout my career, my areas of specialization now include grief counselling as well as addressing issues and concerns experienced by the siblings of children with disabilities.

In closing, I must add that like the social work role within many organizations, my social work activity goes beyond the bounds of the OCTC. I am involved with multi-service committees such as the Complex Care Advisory Committee for the Ottawa area. This is a multi-organization committee comprising agencies that serve families of children with multiple complex needs.

Last but not least, part of my professional life includes education. I teach an online course in the Autism and Behaviour Sciences Program offered by Algonguin College in Ottawa.

Chapter 13 Review

Review Questions

1. Give some of the basic statistics that capture the extent of disability within the Canadian population.
2. What are important highlights in the history of people with disabilities in Canada?
3. What are the differences between the medical model and the political rights model of disability?
4. Define and outline some causes of ableism in our society.
5. What are six important issues that a social worker should consider when working with the family of a person with a disability?
6. Briefly trace the origins of the Independent Living Movement and describe its main objectives.
7. Summarize the process for determining levels of benefits for persons who have disabilities.
8. Make a concept map showing the skills involved in effective social work practice with people who have disabilities.

Exploring Social Work

1. Persons with disabilities face many social barriers to becoming fully participating citizens. Spend a few days reflecting on how a particular disability might interfere with your daily life, independent of the disability itself. Write a brief report on your findings to share with your class.
2. Research and report on a destigmatization initiative in your community, province, or territory. Do you perceive it to be effective or ineffective in reducing the stigma associated with physical or mental disabilities? What evidence points to the effectiveness or ineffectiveness of the initiative?
3. Interview a spokesperson for an association that advocates for persons with disabilities to find out the major barriers faced by this population. What steps are being taken to overcome these barriers?
4. In the realm of championing the rights of persons with disabilities, who do you consider heroes or role models? Do some research and write a one-page profile that highlights how the qualities and accomplishments of one of these individuals are changing societal views on persons with disabilities for the better.

Websites

Human Resources and Social Development Canada
www.hrsdc.gc.ca
HRSDC offers information on federal programs for persons with disabilities. Select People with Disabilities from the A–Z Index.

Council of Canadians with Disabilities
www.ccdonline.ca
The Council of Canadians with Disabilities advocates at the federal level to improve the lives of men and women with disabilities in Canada by eliminating inequality and discrimination. Members include national, regional, and local advocacy organizations that are run by persons with disabilities.

DAWN-RAFH Canada
www.dawncanada.net
DAWN-RAFH Canada is an organization that works toward the advancement and inclusion of women and girls with disabilities and Deaf women in Canada. Its overarching strategic theme is one of leadership, partnership, and networking to engage all levels of government, the wider disability and women's sectors, and other stakeholders in addressing key issues such as poverty, isolation, discrimination, and violence.

Canadian Association for Community Living
www.cacl.ca
CACL is an organization that strives for the full inclusion of people with intellectual disabilities by providing leadership, promoting awareness, and using research and knowledge to inform efforts to advance rights and opportunities.

Canadian Centre for Disability Studies (CCDS)
www.disabilitystudies.ca
CCDS is a not-for-profit, national organization dedicated to research, education, and knowledge mobilization on issues facing people with disabilities. It promotes equal participation of people with disabilities in all aspects of society—locally, provincially/territorially, nationally, and internationally—and is guided by the philosophies of independent living and community living. It emphasizes human rights, self-determination, interdependence, equality, and full and meaningful participation of all citizens.

International Social Work Practice

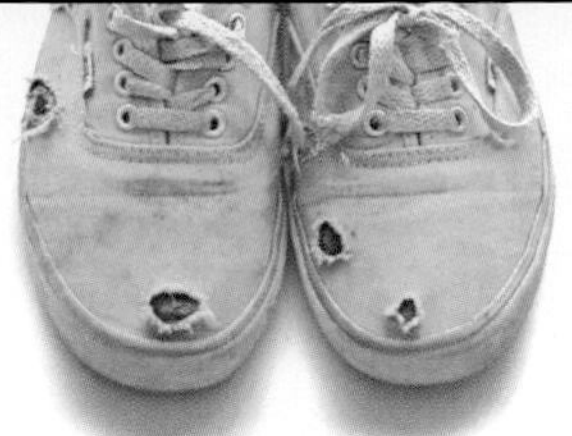

Social Work in an Era of Globalization

14

The history of international social work is a distinguished one.

Since the early days of Jane Addams (shown here), who was the profession's first Nobel Prize winner, social workers have been actively involved in various national and international forums. Social workers have also been and remain involved with the resettling of refugees and other persons displaced by war, operating emergency relief services for victims of natural and human-made disasters, advocating on behalf of disadvantaged and vulnerable populations, organizing groups of oppressed people into effective political entities, and otherwise extending various programs of assistance to populations in need. In all these areas, social workers play an indispensable and often unacknowledged role, sometimes working in extremely difficult and dangerous conditions.

In this chapter, you will learn how to...

- define the various purposes served by international social work practice
- identify the four domains of international social work
- explain some challenges posed for social workers by globalization
- explain some current and potential effects of climate change and global warming on international social work
- explain the applicability of the United Nations' Human Development Index (HDI) and Inequality-Adjusted HDI (IHDI) to international social work
- explain the concept of sustainable global development
- describe ways in which international social workers can protect and promote various types of human rights
- describe aspects of social work with intergovernmental, non-governmental, humanitarian, and community organizations
- analyze some issues related to Indigenous rights worldwide
- discuss four models or approaches to social work practice abroad

Key Concepts

- Developing countries
- Economic globalization
- Human Development Index (HDI)
- Inequality-Adjusted Human Development Index (IHDI)
- Sustainable development
- Sustainable Development Goals (SDGs)
- Human rights
- Intergovernmental organizations (IGOs)
- Non-Governmental organizations (NGOs)
- Cultural competence

Focusing Question

The phrase "Think global, act local" urges people to consider the health of the entire planet and to take action in their own communities and cities.

How does this idea apply in the context of international social work practice today?

What Is International Social Work?

The term "international social work" has a number of different meanings. It can refer to the examination and comparison of the social welfare systems in different countries (comparative social welfare). It can also denote work within international organizations, such as governmental or voluntary organizations that carry out social planning, social development, and welfare programs abroad, particularly in underdeveloped regions. Finally, it can simply refer to the day-to-day social work that social workers do with individuals, groups, and communities in a country other than their own.

The "Global South"

The countries of the Global South have 75 percent of the world's people, but only

- 15 percent of the world's energy consumption,
- 17 percent of the world's Gross National Product (GNP),
- 30 percent of the world's food grains,
- 18 percent of the world's export earnings,
- 11 percent of the world's education spending,
- 9 percent of the world's health expenditure,
- 5 percent of the world's science and technology, and
- 8 percent of the world's industry.

Protection of Human Rights and Ensuring Sustainable Development

Any discussion of international social work must begin by acknowledging the severe economic disadvantages faced by people in the so-called developing world. The globe can be divided, economically speaking, into the Northern and Southern hemispheres, with the industrialized countries of the North living in relative affluence and many of the **developing countries** in the "Global South" facing abject poverty. Nearly 11 million children under five die each year in these countries, mainly from preventable causes. Malnutrition contributes to 60 percent of all childhood deaths. Combined with preventable diseases, this is a "deadly duo." Poverty, of course, is one of the main causes of malnutrition and early death.

International social work is varied as well as challenging. It can range from involvement in an international cause in one's own country to working directly in another country to develop a program or policy. In each of these work situations, social workers require knowledge of international relations, other nations' social and political contexts, and an understanding of how international social work is practised throughout the world. For example:

- A social worker in a women's shelter in Guatemala helps bring in an undocumented immigrant whose life is endangered by an abusive husband.
- A social worker with Médecins Sans Frontières (MSF) helps a community in Sierra Leone deal with an Ebola outbreak.
- A group of social workers in a government social assistance department travel to Vietnam to help develop a similar program for its cities.
- Social workers with the Red Cross help with disaster relief in remote areas of Nepal.
- A social worker provides HIV/AIDS prevention workshops in Botswana.
- Social workers with War Child Canada provide trauma counselling to women and children affected by war in Sudan.
- Social workers from Canada and Bolivia work together to develop policies that protect children from abuse and neglect.

The opportunities for work are certainly endless. However, given the great inequalities around the world, and the lack of political stability in many countries, even the most dedicated social workers quickly realize that opportunities for bringing about lasting social change are limited. For this reason, social work activists are increasingly advocating an approach based on two complementary principles: (1) the promotion and protection of human rights, and (2) ensuring sustainable social and economic development.

The International Federation of Social Workers (IFSW) supports its 116 member countries by providing a global voice for the profession. It strives for social justice, human rights, and social development by promoting social work, best practice models, and international cooperation.

International Social Work Practice Today

International social work occurs at home and abroad and in many different contexts and forms. Broadly speaking, international social work occurs in four domains:

- **Domestic practice with international implications.** Social workers can contribute to international causes through work at home—for example, through refugee settlement and international adoption work. In the latter example, international adoption agencies hire social workers to link prospective parents with overseas agencies, guide them through the process, provide proper matching, and ensure that the child's rights are protected.
- **International practice.** Social workers can join international development agencies or agencies in other countries to contribute directly in communities around the world. Such workers need a commitment to cross-cultural communication and international development, as well as knowledge of the political and cultural contexts in which they work.
- **Professional exchange between nations.** Social workers often travel to participate in professional exchange opportunities (such as international conferences and trainings). These activities are a growing aspect of social work that help to improve practice and policy.
- **International policy work and advocacy.** As a worldwide movement, social work has contributed to research and advocacy for international causes, and has influenced governments and organizations on important issues. Cooperation between social workers from different countries is key for policy work that creates lasting positive change.

Developing countries
The underdeveloped countries of Central and South America, Africa, and Asia, also referred to as the "Global South" or, less commonly today, the "Third World"

Table 14.1
Levels of Development-Focused Practice in International Social Work

Practice Level	Major Focus Area
Individual and group empowerment	Individuals and groups learn—through self-help, mutual aid, and conscientization strategies— how to perceive and act on the contradictions that exist in the social, political, and economic structures intrinsic to all societies
Conflict resolution and peace building	Efforts directed at reducing (1) grievances between persons or groups, or (2) asymmetric power relationships between members of more powerful and less powerful groups
Institution building	Refers both to the process of "humanizing" existing social institutions and establishing new institutions that respond more effectively to new or emerging social needs
Community building	Through increased participation and social animation of the populace, the process through which communities realize the fullness of their social, political, and economic potential; the process through which communities respond more equitably to the social and material needs of their populations
Nation building	The process of working toward the integration of a nation's social, political, economic, and cultural institutions at all levels of political organization
Region building	The process of working toward the integration of a geopolitical region's social, political, economic, and cultural institutions at all levels of social organization
World building	The process of working toward the establishment of a new system of international relationships guided by the quest for world peace, increased social justice, the universal satisfaction of basic human needs, and the protection of the planet's fragile ecosystem

- *Source:* Estes, Richard J. (2009). *United States-Based Conceptualizataion of International Social Work Education.* Washington, DC: Council on Social Work Education: Commission on Global Social Work Education.

Globalization: The Context for International Practice Today

Canada does not exist in isolation from the rest of the world. This is especially true as the era of globalization increasingly takes hold. Whether we like it or not, we live in a highly integrated world economy.

Economic globalization is the growing integration of international markets for goods, services, and finance. It includes the expansion of free trade and investment, the geographical expansion and increase in power of transnational corporations (TNCs), and the use of agreements between nations and international bodies such as the World Trade Organization (WTO). There are differing understandings and perceptions as to the social impact of globalization. Some maintain that the present model of globalization has worsened problems of unemployment, inequality, and poverty, while others contend that globalization has helped to reduce them. For globalization to be politically and economically sustainable, it must meet the needs of all sectors of society, contribute to the reduction of inequality, and lead to a better life for all.

Economic globalization
The increasing economic integration and interdependence of national, regional, and local economies across the world, through an intensification of cross-border movement of goods, services, technologies, and capital

For poor countries themselves, the most pressing concern remains, of course, basic economic development. What has transpired to date under the banners of "globalization" and "development" has often led more to perpetual dependence on aid than to economic liberation. Indeed, many observers would argue that countries in the Third World are not so much "developing" as "underdeveloping." This type of situation contributes to cycles of inequality and socio-political instability.

Challenges for Canadian Social Workers in a Globalized World

How can social workers address instability, inequality, and injustice from a global perspective? All social work today is interwoven with global economic processes. Economic interdependence, war, politcal instability, and human migration all have implications for Canadian social work practice. The systems and processes that produce extreme disparities—in areas such as income, education, health care, and nutrition—are in constant flux. Canadian social workers need to stay informed about these systems and processes, and how they affect individuals and communities. They need to continually develop their knowledge and skills to deal with global-level problems and serve multicultural societies.

Are Western models of social work beneficial to other countries? Or do different cultural norms and social contexts require different models of social work? In any given situation, social workers need to challenge their assumptions, acknowledge their biases, and pay attention to local models of social work practice. Western social work should be influenced by non-Western social work, and vice versa.

Social work practice is more equitable and effective when in it incorporates ideas, perceptions, and methods from non-Western cultures. For example, John Graham, a professor at the University of Calgary, found that African perspectives on family and community can contribute to a holistic vision of social work practice—one that values shared experience and spiritual, family, and community engagement in resolving social and personal hardships.

There is a need to find ways to strengthen the status of social work in developing countries as well as in overpopulated countries such as India, China, and Japan. International partnerships that promote mutual respect for the exchange of knowledge between countries are key to achieving a universal social work, one that is based on openness to diverse cultures, accountability, responsiveness, and connectivity (Gray and Fook, 2004).

The Occupy Movement

The protester shown here was one of hundreds of people who marched through the streets of Toronto on October 17, 2011, to take a stand against corporate greed.

The march was part of the global Occupy movement, which calls for social, political, environmental, and economic justice. The movement started in New York in 2011 with Occupy Wall Street and grew into local chapters worldwide.

Participants use the slogan "We Are the 99%" to draw attention to the unequal distribution of wealth in most Western countries: it is estimated that one percent of the population in those countries controls more wealth (and therefore more power) than the other 99 percent.

Global Climate Change: The Role of International Social Workers

Climate change is one of the most significant challenges facing humanity today. The global climate is changing as a result of greenhouse gases caused by fossil fuel consumption, deforestation, and industrial processes. These gases trap infrared radiation and cause changes in air temperature, precipitation patterns, ocean acidity, sea levels, and the rate at which Earth's glaciers are melting.

Climate change is a global issue, but its consequences differ across communities, countries, and regions. Social workers are increasingly vocal on environmental issues and are active in climate change policy dialogues. For example, the journal *International Social Work* released a special issue on climate change in 2015, with articles addressing issues related to water, health, disaster prevention, and sustainability.

Social workers are increasingly working in areas such as post-disaster recovery, social support for victims of extreme weather events, crisis intervention, policy development, advocacy, program planning, and research. Dominelli (2011) explores how social work has an important role to play in helping people understand climate change, promoting sustainable energy production and consumption, mobilizing people to protect their futures through community social work, proposing solutions to greenhouse gas emissions, and fostering climate change endeavours that are equitable for all.

Climate change has and will have not only serious environmental, political, and economic repercussions for citizens around the world, but also moral and social justice repercussions because the degradation of the planet will harm future generations in countries both rich and poor.

The UN's Human Development Report

The Human Development Report (HDR) is an annual, independent report commissioned by the United Nations Development Programme (UNDP). It is the product of a team of leading scholars, practitioners, and members of the Human Development Report Office. The HDR was first launched in 1990 with the goal of putting *people* back at the centre of the development process in terms of economic debate, policy, and advocacy. The Human Development Report goes beyond measuring income as a means of assessing the level of people's long-term well-being, emphasizing that the goals of development are choice and freedom.

Human Development Index (HDI)
The HDI is a tool devised by the United Nations to measure and rank countries' levels of social and economic development based on four criteria: life expectancy at birth, mean years of schooling, expected years of schooling, and gross national income per capita.

The Human Development Index (HDI)

Since its first report in 1990, the HDR team has developed four composite indices: the Human Development Index (the principal index), the Gender-Related Development Index, the Gender Empowerment Measure, and the Human Poverty Index. In addition to releasing new data from the previous year, each HDR also focuses on a highly topical theme, providing path-breaking analysis and policy recommendations. The Human Development Report Office also issues global, national, and regional reports on topics of the day. The messages of these reports—as well as the tools to implement them—have been embraced by people around the world, evidenced by the publication of similar human development reports at the national level in more than 120 countries.

While the scope of human development is much broader than any single index can measure, the HDR's principal human development indicator, the **Human Development Index (HDI)**, offers a powerful alternative to using income alone as a measure of human well-being. The HDI focuses on three dimensions of development: (1) a long and healthy life, as measured by life expectancy at birth; (2) knowledge, as measured by the adult literacy rate and the combined gross enrolment ratio for primary, secondary, and tertiary schools; and (3) a decent standard of living, as measured by GDP per capita in purchasing power parity with U.S. dollars.

The HDI was created to emphasize that people and their capabilities should be the ultimate criteria for assessing the development of a country, not simply its economic growth. The Human Development Index itself does not claim to be comprehensive—for example, it does not include important aspects of human development, notably the ability to participate in political decisions. Likewise, it does not capture gender disparity and human deprivation, which are measured in other HDR indices (the Gender-Related Development Index and the Human Poverty Index). Nevertheless, the HDI is a powerful starting point for understanding and advocating for human development.

While advances in technology, education, and incomes hold ever-greater promise for longer, healthier, more secure lives, many of those who have escaped absolute poverty are highly vulnerable to setbacks. According to the UN, almost 800 million people worldwide are at risk of falling back into poverty. To capture this dimension, the 2014 Human Development Report introduced the concept of "human vulnerability" to describe the factors that threaten people's capabilities and choices. Human vulnerability is increasing because of human-made crises, financial instability, and mounting environmental pressures, such as climate change. All of these factors have the potential to undermine progress in human development.

Multidimensional Poverty

According to income-based measures of poverty, an estimated 1.2 billion people live on $1.25 USD or less per day. However, according to the UNDP Multidimensional Poverty Index, 1.5 billion people in 91 developing countries are living in poverty, with overlapping deprivations in health, education, and living standards.

The 2014 Human Development Report—Sustaining Human Progress: Reducing Vulnerabilities and Building Resilience—provides a fresh perspective on vulnerability and proposes ways to strengthen resilience.

Inequality and Human Development

More and more, development experts are realizing that inequality within a country and between countries is one of the great challenges of the modern world. Moreover, they are recognizing that inequality essentially breeds more inequality.

A country's HDI is an average measure of its human development and well-being. However, like all averages, this measure often masks inequalities in the *distribution* of human development within the country. In 2010, the UN introduced the new **Inequality-Adjusted HDI (IHDI)**, which takes into account inequalities in all three dimensions of the HDI. As inequality in a country increases, human development decreases.

Inequality-Adjusted HDI
The new IHDI takes into account how human development is distributed, measuring the sometimes vast disparities between different regions or groups within a country. Using the IHDI, countries with greater inequality see lower human development scores than countries with greater equality.

The map below presents a global picture of human development using the Inequality-Adjusted HDI. For example, Canada's HDI in 2014 was 0.913. However, when this value was discounted for inequality in the distribution of the HDI dimension indices, it fell to 0.832, a loss of 8.8 percent. In the same year, Australia and the United States showed losses due to inequality of 8.2 percent and 17.0 percent, respectively. The average loss due to inequality for countries with high HDI values was 12.1 percent. The average for the 34 countries that are members of the OECD was 13.3 percent.

Global Human Development Scores: Inequality-Adjusted HDIs

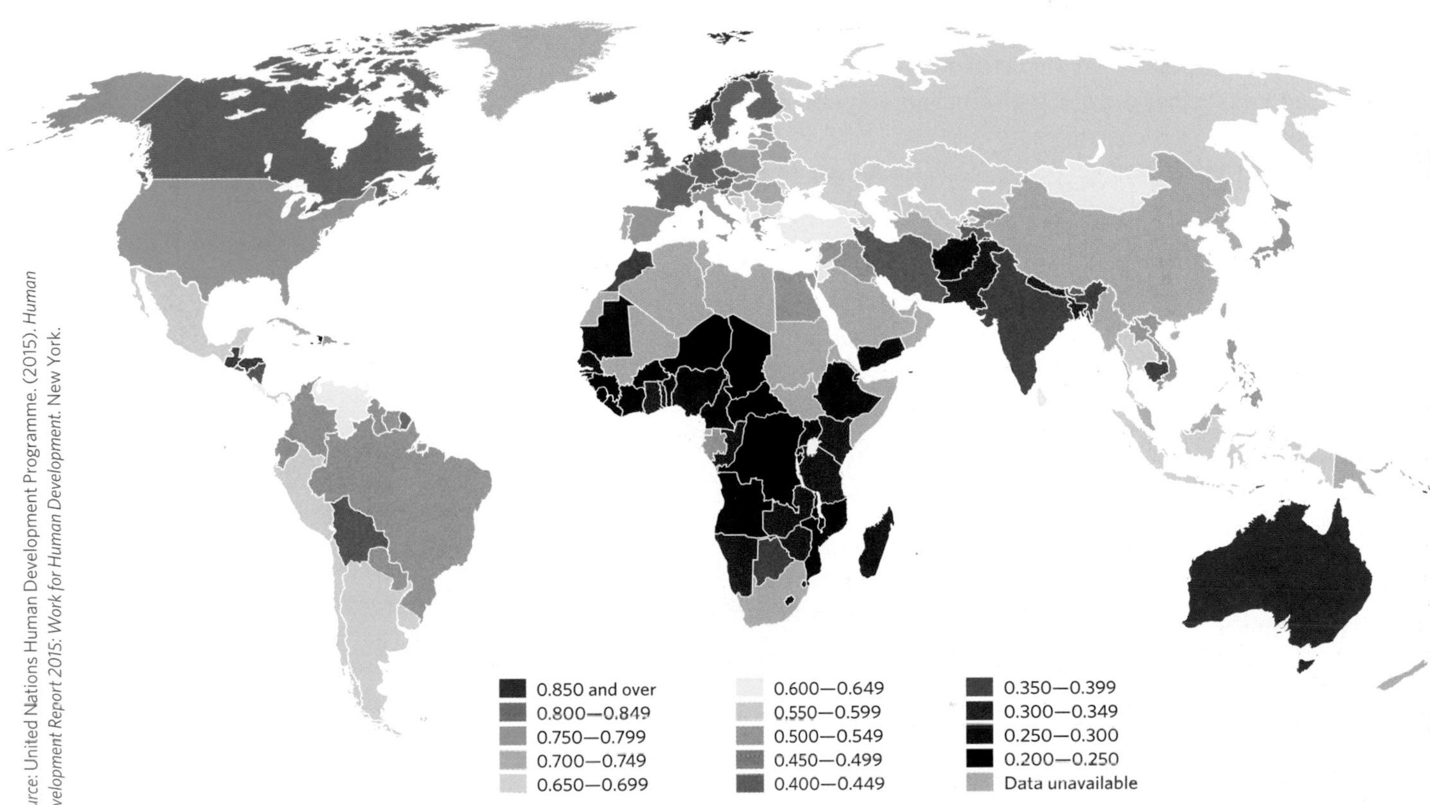

Source: United Nations Human Development Programme. (2015). *Human Development Report 2015: Work for Human Development.* New York.

Figure 14.1 A map of the world showing Inequality-Adjusted Human Development Index (IHDI) scores. The score for each country takes into account the negative effect of inequality within that country.

Sustainable Development

The concept of **sustainable development** is now becoming central to the programs of many governments, businesses, educational institutions, and non-government organizations around the world. There are many definitions of sustainable development, including the following landmark definition that appeared in *Our Common Future* (also known as the Brundtland Report) in 1987:

> "[Sustainable development is] development that meets the needs of the present without compromising the ability of future generations to meet their own needs."
> —World Commission on Environment and Development
> (the Brundtland Commission)

Sustainable development is about improving the standard of living by protecting human health, conserving the environment, using resources efficiently, and advancing long-term economic competitiveness. It requires the integration of environmental, economic, and social priorities into policies and programs, and requires action by citizens, industry, and governments.

Issues around the world such as inequality, poverty, pollution, and climate change negatively impact our planet and all who inhabit it. Recognizing the importance of these issues, the United Nations (UN) is calling on world leaders to come together to create change.

Sustainable Development Goals

The UN's Sustainable Development Goals offer major improvements on the Millennium Development Goals (MDGs). The SDG framework addresses key systemic barriers to sustainable development that the MDGs neglected, such as inequality, unsustainable consumption patterns, weak institutional capacity, and environmental degradation.

Millennium Development Goals (MDGs), 2000–2015

In September 2000, building on a decade of major United Nations conferences and summits, world leaders came together at the UN Headquarters in New York to adopt the United Nations Millennium Declaration. The Declaration committed nations to a new global partnership to reduce extreme poverty. It also set out eight time-bound targets addressing hunger, disease, gender inequality, and access to water and sanitation. These targets became known as the Millennium Development Goals (MDGs) and had a deadline of 2015.

The final MDG Report found that this 15-year effort produced the most successful anti-poverty movement in history:

- Since 1990, the number of people living in extreme poverty has declined by more than half.
- The proportion of undernourished people in developing regions has fallen by almost half.
- The primary school enrolment rate in developing regions has reached 91 percent, and many more girls are now in school compared to 15 years ago.
- Remarkable gains have been made in the fight against HIV/AIDS, malaria, and tuberculosis.
- The under-five mortality rate has declined by more than half, and maternal mortality is down 45 percent worldwide.
- The proportion of people who lack access to improved sources of water was cut in half.

These statistics show that the concerted efforts of national governments, the international community, civil society, and the private sector have helped expand hope and opportunity for people around the world. Yet the job remains unfinished for millions of people—we need to go the last mile toward ending hunger, achieving full gender equality, improving health services, and getting every child into school.

There is also an increasingly urgent need to take steps to mitigate both the short-term and long-term effects of climate change on resource distribution, migration patterns, food production, and food security. The mandate now is to shift the world onto a truly sustainable path.

Sustainable Development Goals, 2015–2030

At the United Nations Sustainable Development Summit on September 25, 2015, world leaders adopted the Agenda for Sustainable Development, which includes a set of 17 **Sustainable Development Goals (SDGs)** to end poverty, fight inequality and injustice, and tackle climate change by 2030 (see Figure 14.2).

The Sustainable Development Goals, otherwise known as the Global Goals, build on the Millennium Development Goals, the eight anti-poverty targets that the world committed to achieving by 2015. The new SDGs and the broader sustainability agenda go much further than the MDGs, however, in addressing the root causes of poverty and the universal need for development that works for all people.

Within the 17 SDGs are 169 targets. The targets under Goal 1, for example, include reducing the number of people living in poverty by at least half and eradicating extreme poverty (people living on less than $1.25 USD a day). Goals 2, 3, and 4 involve targets focused on ending hunger, ensuring good health and well-being, and providing quality education, respectively.

Under Goal 5, there is a target aimed at eliminating violence against women, while Goal 16 has a target to promote the rule of law and equal access to justice. UN member states will be expected to use the new goals, targets, and indicators to frame their agendas and political and social policies.

The SDGs will guide policy and funding for the next 15 years, beginning with the historic pledge taken on September 25, 2015, to end poverty. Everywhere. Permanently.

Sustainable development
Development that meets the needs of the present without compromising the ability of future generations to meet their own needs

Sustainable Development Goals (SDGs)
A set of 17 goals adopted by 193 countries at the United Nations Sustainable Development Summit in 2015. The SDGs aim to improve both human development and environmental sustainability.

Figure 14.2 The United Nations' 17 Sustainable Development Goals (SDGs) incoporate 169 targets. In 2015, 193 countries adopted these goals, aimed at ending poverty and mitigating climate change by 2030.

The Promotion and Protection of Human Rights

The Western idea of **human rights** is based on an acknowledgment that individuals possess certain inalienable political and civil rights. The concept has its origins in ancient religions and philosophies, and took flight in Europe during the Enlightenment in the eighteenth century. It was at the heart of the English, French, and Russion revolutions. In the upheavals of the twentieth century, it was the basis of the movement for universal suffrage, the civil rights movement, and feminist movements, among many others.

Universal Declaration of Human Rights

The recognition of universal human rights was finally consolidated in the *Universal Declaration of Human Rights* adopted by the General Assembly of the United Nations in 1948. All the major countries of the world are now signatories to this declaration. It consists of 30 articles that have been further elaborated in subsequent international treaties, regional human rights instruments, national constitutions, and other legislation. While the *Universal Declaration of Human Rights* is a non-binding document, it is a foundation document and is often invoked by national and other judiciaries around the world. The declaration has proved to be a powerful instrument in the advancement of individual rights around the world and has been widely used to apply political and moral pressure to governments that violate any of its principles.

The notion that there is a duty to protect the rights of all people has become a recognized part of our human heritage. Unfortunately, as everyone knows, individual and collective human rights are not always respected in practice, and the struggle to defend and advance human rights is not over by any means.

Three Types of Rights

When thinking about rights, it may be useful to distinguish between three types (or "generations") of human rights (see Table 14.2). This broad division was initially set out by the Czech legal scholar Karel Vasak in 1979. Vasak's divisions closely align with the famous watchwords of the French Revolution: Liberty, Equality, Fraternity.

- **Negative rights (Liberty).** The first type of rights represents civil and political rights as set forth in Articles 2 to 21 of the Universal Declaration of Human Rights. They pertain to liberty and political participation and ensure protection from torture, false imprisonment, or summary execution.
- **Positive rights (Equality).** The second type of rights represents economic, social, and cultural rights as detailed in Articles 22 to 27 of the Declaration. These rights are aimed at ensuring justice, freedom from want, and full participation in society. They would include employment rights, housing and health care rights, as well as the right to social security.
- **Collective rights (Fraternity).** The third type encompasses the collective rights contained in Article 28, which states that "everyone is entitled to a social and international order in which the rights and freedoms set forth in this Declaration can be fully realized." This category goes beyond formal civil and social rights usually enshrined in national and international law. It would include such things as self-determination, economic and social development, healthy environment, communication, cultural heritage, and sustainability.

International Human Rights Instruments

International human rights instruments can be classified into two categories:

- **Declarations** These are adopted by bodies such as the United Nations General Assembly, but are not legally binding.
- **Conventions** These are legally binding instruments that have been concluded under international law.

The *Universal Declaration of Human Rights* (1948), the *International Covenant on Civil and Political Rights*, and the *International Covenant on Economic, Social and Cultural Rights* are sometimes referred to as the International Bill of Human Rights.

Social Work and the Advancement of Human Rights

The concept of human rights gradually gained more prominence in social work in the nineteenth century. Following the two world wars and the great political upheavals and revolutions of the twentieth century, the protection of human rights took on a renewed importance within the profession.

The social work profession today is firmly at the forefront of promoting human rights around the world. For example, the *International Policy on Human Rights,* adopted by the International Federation of Social Work (IFSW), affirms that human rights are a common standard and guide for the work of all social workers. Its preamble states:

> The history of human rights is that of the struggle against exploitation of one person by another. It is based on the recognition of basic rights founded on the concept of the inherent dignity and worth of every individual.

The IFSW emphasizes that social workers not only respect human rights but also work to oppose all violations of human rights. Most practising social workers today see themselves as part of this human rights history and heritage.

Human Rights
Rights inherent to our nature and without which we cannot live as human beings, including individual political, civil, collective cultural, social, and economic rights

Table 14.2
The Three Generations of Human Rights

	First Generation	Second Generation	Third Generation
Type	Civil and political rights	Economic, social, and cultural rights	Collective rights
Origin	Liberalism	Socialism, social democracy	Collectivism, communitarianism
Examples	Right to vote Right to run for office Equality before the law Freedom of expression Freedom of assembly Right to a fair and prompt trial Freedom from torture and abuse Freedom from arbitrary arrest Freedom from discrimination Right to legal representation Freedom of association Freedom of movement Freedom from slavery	Right to education Right to housing Right to employment Right to health Right to earn an income Right to income security Freedom to spend money as one chooses Choice of partner Right to raise a family Right to safe working conditions Freedom of cultural expression Right to land Right to property Children's rights	Right to a healthy environment Right to clean air and water Right to enjoy nature Right to benefit from development Right to belong to a strong, cohesive society

Rights of Indigenous Peoples Worldwide

Canada officially adopts UN declaration

Questions remain about what the declaration means and how it will be implemented

There were cheers in the United Nations as Canada officially removed its objector status to the UN Declaration on the Rights of Indigenous Peoples Tuesday, almost a decade after it was adopted by the General Assembly.

"We are now a full supporter of the declaration, without qualification," [Canada's Indigenous Affairs Minister] Bennett said, as she addressed the Permanent Forum on Indigenous Issues at the United Nations in New York City on Tuesday.

"We intend nothing less than to adopt and implement the declaration in accordance with the Canadian Constitution."

The declaration recognizes Indigenous Peoples' basic human rights, as well as rights to self-determination, language, equality and land, among others.

Bennett — who received a standing ovation for her statement — is at the United Nations with Justice Minister Jody Wilson-Raybould.

"It was a very emotional moment for me," said Chief Wilton Littlechild, a Cree lawyer and former commissioner of the Truth and Reconciliation Commission of Canada who was at the UN on Tuesday. Littlechild has been involved with the UN for nearly 40 years and said he's rarely seen anyone receive a standing ovation.

Implementing the declaration

Littlechild said today's announcement marks a beginning to what could be a long process of "harmonizing" Canada's laws with the standards set in the declaration, and improving the country's relationship with Indigenous Peoples.

"The declaration is much like the treaties, it calls on us to work together," he said. "Today would not be too late to start the journey together."

Bennett told the UN that Canada is in a unique position to implement the declaration.

"Canada is now a full supporter of the [UN Declaration on the Rights of Indigenous Peoples] without qualification," Indigenous Affairs Minister Carolyn Bennett told the United Nations in New York on Tuesday.

"Through Section 35 of its Constitution, Canada has a robust framework for the protection of Indigenous rights," she said.

"By adopting and implementing the declaration, we are excited that we are breathing life into Section 35 and recognizing it as a full box of rights for Indigenous Peoples in Canada."

Bennett also said implementing the UN declaration in Canada will require the full co-operation of Indigenous Peoples and the support of all provinces and territories. Ontario Aboriginal Affairs Minister David Zimmer also attended the UN meeting.

"It can't be done unilaterally," said B.C. Grand Chief Edward John, who was also present for Tuesday's announcement.

John said that by adopting the UN declaration, more than ever Canada must now consult with Indigenous Peoples on any laws or administrative measures that affect them.

"Indigenous governments are not some inferior form of authority," John said. "They are the original form of authority over their lands, resources and territories."

Historic day

Shortly after the 2015 federal election, Bennett pledged that the new Liberal government would implement the UN declaration as part of its effort to rebuild its working relationships with First Nations, Métis and Inuit peoples.

Canada actually officially endorsed the declaration in 2010, but the Conservative government of the day called it an "aspirational document" and not legally binding.

Assembly of First Nations National Chief Perry Bellegarde — who will also be attending the Forum later this week — tweeted that it was a "historic day" as Canada moves toward reconciliation with Indigenous Peoples.

Source: CBC News. (2016) Canada supports UN Indigenous rights declaration: Now what? (May 11).

Chief Justice Murray Sinclair

As the starting point for true reconciliation, the Truth and Reconciliation Commission, under its Chair, Chief Justice Murray Sinclair (now Senator Sinclair), recommended that the Canadian government implement the United Nations Declaration on the Rights of Indigenous Peoples.

The UN's declaration outlines the minimum human rights standards for Indigenous peoples around the world and their rights to self-determination.

Canada did not sign the document when it was accepted by the UN in 2007. "They did adopt it as an aspirational document, and that's their words. And we agree with that," Justice Sinclair said. "It should be an aspirational document. So what we're saying to them is, 'Aspire to it.'"

On May 10, 2016, Indigenous Affairs Minister Carolyn Bennett received a standing ovation at the United Nations in New York when she announced that Canada was removing its "objector status" and would adopt the UN Declaration.

Social Work with Intergovernmental, Non-Governmental, Humanitarian, and Community Organizations

Social work, as a helping profession, is especially concerned with the problems and rights of the disadvantaged, not only at home but also abroad. International social workers can be found undertaking a wide range of activities in a variety of national, international, and humanitarian organizations. These organizations include the following:

- intergovernmental organizations,
- non-governmental organizations,
- religious groups and other humanitarian organizations, and
- community organizations.

Within these arenas, social workers participate as analysts and as direct practitioners in delivering and monitoring the assistance and protection provided by UN declarations and conventions. Social workers also frequently work in a front-line capacity, providing refugee settlement services, counselling children traumatized by war, distributing humanitarian assistance during disasters or war, and monitoring human rights abuses.

On the topic of working with the organization War Child in Kosova, social worker Steve Hick (shown here) comments, "I saw my job as listening to people, maximizing their power and participation, and applying my skills."

In Kosovo in the 1990s, for example, UNICEF provided life-saving assistance to children and women, and social workers were involved in distributing hygiene kits, blankets, water purification tablets, and basic medical supplies. They were also a part of trauma teams, along with medical professionals and psychologists, and participated in the long-term relief plans that emphasized support for educational systems and community organizations.

The United Nations, Religious Groups, and Other Humanitarian Organizations

Many social workers are active in various international **intergovernmental organizations (IGOs)**, of which the United Nations is the best known. Formed at the end of World War II, the UN seeks to develop a framework of international law that will be followed by all nation states around the world. Social workers are employed in a variety of roles in its 12 specialized agencies, which include the UN Development Programme, UNICEF, World Health Organization, International Labour Office, and the UN High Commissioner for Refugees.

Social workers also work for a multitude of **non-governmental organizations (NGOs)** around the world. NGOs are international organizations, but they are not directly linked to governments. This allows such organizations more freedom to take up important issues and bring about effective change.

NGOs tend to be small, dynamic groups that work on a variety of issues related to their particular political or philosophical stances. Social workers working with NGOs frequently find themselves participating in peace building and conflict resolution. For example, in the central Caucasus region—Georgia, Armenia, and Azerbaijan—social workers are using art therapy to help children heal from the trauma of war and to build peace between the various groups torn by inter-ethnic conflict since the late 1980s. The projects encourage the children to express their thoughts and feelings through coloured pictures and paintings. Children from all ethnic groups attend the projects, and it is hoped that links will be established between communities.

Religious groups and organizations have an extensive variety of overseas humanitarian programs, and they frequently employ the services of social workers. These groups tend to operate in the poorer countries of Africa, Asia, and Latin America.

Training Opportunities for International Social Workers

Many NGOs have entry-level positions for new social workers without extensive hands-on experience. It is a great training ground. Students of social work may find it helpful to do volunteer work for NGOs to build experience and make contacts for future work. Non-governmental organizations such as Canadian Crossroads International, Canada World Youth, and World University Service of Canada provide excellent opportunities for social workers to gain international experience.

Increasingly, Canadian NGOs are not deploying social workers or any other staff to work directly in their overseas projects. Instead, they hire local people to implement their programs, people who already live in the country and who are thus familiar with the culture. More and more, Canadian social workers are employed at headquarters in Canada, providing assistance for international causes by planning projects, creating budgets and financial reports, and reporting and communicating with funders and local fieldworkers. This trend is illustrated by the work of Samantha McGavin (profiled at the end of this chapter) at Inter Pares. NGOs mobilize financial resources, materials, and volunteers to implement localized programs in other countries. They hold fundraising events and apply to governments and foundations for grants or contracts to raise money for their projects. NGOs vary tremendously in their methods. Some act principally as lobbyists, while others primarily implement programs. For example, an NGO such as Oxfam, concerned with poverty alleviation, might provide people with the equipment and skills to cultivate food, whereas an NGO like Human Rights Watch helps through investigation and documentation of human rights violations.

It is no longer the norm for religious groups to use their international programs primarily as a way to acquire new members. Today, for example, the United Church provides excellent local training programs for social workers worldwide but does not send workers abroad unless requested by partner organizations.

In addition to churches and other religious organizations, there are large international grant foundations that employ social workers as consultants, field representatives, and national program directors for initiatives supported by the foundation. The Canadian government also maintains offices in many countries to provide services to visiting Canadians and local people. These services frequently involve social workers. Other federal government departments, such as the Department of Foreign Affairs, Trade and Development, and the International Development Research Centre (IDRC), hire social workers to help with their work.

Until March of 2013, the Canadian International Development Agency (CIDA) was an organization that administered foreign aid programs in developing countries, and operated in partnership with other Canadian and international organizations. CIDA was formed in 1968 by the Canadian government under Pierre Trudeau. In March of 2013, the Conservative government announced that CIDA would be folded into the Department of Foreign Affairs and would cease to exist as an independent entity.

Working directly for government agencies of other countries is another option for social workers seeking international experience. These agencies are not necessarily international in focus, but certainly can be considered as part of an international social work career. Generally, however, one must have extensive language skills and direct contacts within the country in order to obtain such a position.

Intergovernmental organizations (IGOs)
An intergovernmental organization or international governmental organization (IGO) is an organization, such as the United Nations, composed primarily of sovereign states (referred to as member states), or of other intergovernmental organizations.

Non-governmental organizations (NGOs)
Organizations that are neither part of a government nor conventional for-profit businesses. Usually set up by ordinary citizens, NGOs may be funded by governments, foundations, businesses, or private donors.

Cultural Competence—Respect for Cultural Diversity

Working in another country obviously involves fulfilling a role as a practitioner in another cultural context. How does one prepare for such work? How do social workers ensure that they are "culturally competent"?

In social work literature, the term **cultural competence** emphasizes the need for social workers to gain an understanding of the world views and cultural frames of reference of their clients. Thus, workers must make an effort to understand the history, language, religions, and values of the cultural groups with which they are working. At the same time, practitioners working abroad need to be careful to avoid attributing stereotypes to communities and members of any given culture. A sound understanding of cultural contexts will help international social workers to be more effective in bringing about positive change.

Culturally competent social work practice involves developing an understanding and respect for diverse cultural world views and forms of expression, including religious worship and beliefs.

For example, it would be inappropriate to work in China without considering the cultural differences among the various ethnic groups within the Chinese population. In addition, social workers must take their knowledge of the "other" culture and combine it with an analysis of how their own cultural outlook may influence their interventions. In other words, social workers need deep respect for the unique social conditions and cultural contexts within which they are working. Without such an appreciation of cultural differences, they will be less effective in assessing the problems at hand.

Culturally Competent Organizations

Cultural competence is clearly important for those social workers actively engaged in other countries. As Canada continues to evolve as a modern, ethnically diverse nation, cultural competence is an increasingly necessary skill set in our work, home, and community lives. Cherishing diversity is at the core of who we are as Canadians, and it is a value enshrined in our laws concerning multiculturalism. The Child Welfare League of America regards cultural competence as

> "the ability of individuals and systems to respond respectfully and effectively to people of all cultures, classes, races, ethnic backgrounds, sexual orientations, and faiths and religions, in a manner that recognizes, affirms, and values the worth of individuals, families and communities, and protects and preserves the dignity of each."

Social service organizations of all types have much to gain by providing services in ways that are respectful of those groups, as well as being accommodating to their diverse characteristics and needs. Being culturally competent enables service providers to offer equitable, person-centred care. It is the most effective way to ensure that clients' needs are being met and that clients are being provided with the best possible support.

Research has established that social and economic barriers—such as poverty, social exclusion, job insecurity, and lack of education—are equally or more important to a person's health than medical care or personal behaviours. These factors, known as social determinants of health, have a significant impact on one's well-being. Marginalized groups such as immigrants, Aboriginal people, and single-parent families experience a significant number of these barriers. Cultural competence—relating to people in these groups where they are and on their own terms—is an important part of the social work skill set and will allow social work practitioners to assist people in distress. Figure 14.3 shows six dimensions of cultural competence that play a role in international and cross-cultural social work practice.

Developing Global Capability Inside the Social Work Profession

In a world that is increasingly interdependent, the need for cross-border collaboration has required the introduction of new values and global capability in the social work profession. International social work practice is characterized by several guiding values and culturally sensitive practice assumptions:

- Social, political, and economic events in any region of the world have direct effects—often immediate, and sometimes lasting—on the quality of life and human rights in other regions.
- The human degradation and social injustice found in local communities often emanate from social, political, and economic forces that are international in character.
- International social forces contribute to and sustain social inequalities in particular locales (e.g., global poverty and discrimination on the basis of race, class, and gender).
- Only under conditions of peaceful coexistence can local, national, and international social development—and, in turn, human development—be accelerated.
- The need to restructure the national and international social orders is important in reducing the levels of misery, degradation, and violence in many countries and regions of the world.
- International social workers possess a unique body of knowledge and skills that can positively affect national and international causes, especially in helping to find sustainable solutions to recurrent social problems.
- Substantial numbers of international social work specialists, acting both individually and collectively, are continuing the national and international social movements begun by their predecessors, movements aimed at establishing a more peaceful and socially just world order (Estes, 2010).

Cultural competence
An understanding of the world view or frame of reference held by a client, including their history, language, culture, and background, while avoiding stereotypes and assumptions based on generalizations

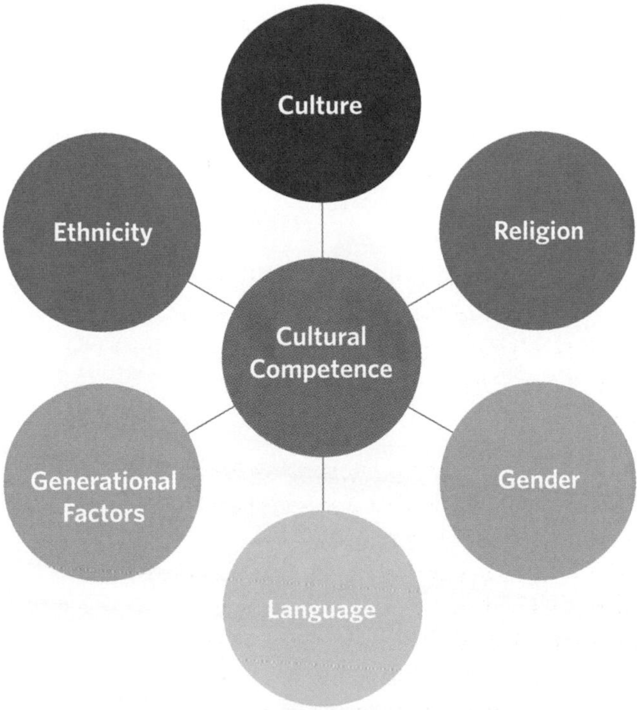

Figure 14.3 This graphic represents six important dimensions of cultural competence that social workers must take into account when working with clients or groups whose backgrounds differ from their own.

International Social Work Practice
Thinking beyond the here and now

Modelling effective international social work practice in the era of globalization

Within international social work, four broad approaches or models can be identified. They are, of course, "abstractions." They overlap and intesect and are not mutually exclusive.

The Social Welfare Model

The conventional model of international social work is largely based on the ideas of British economist John Maynard Keynes and, in particular, on American economist W.W. Rostow's "stages of industrialization" theory. Rostow (1960) postulates that all societies go through five stages on the road to becoming a developed country: (1) traditional society, (2) preconditions for growth, (3) short period of intensive growth ("take-off"), (4) drive to maturity, and (5) era of mass consumption.

Using this approach, the primary goal is to create the preconditions that will move a country through these stages of development. The immediate concern of social workers is with the satisfaction of basic social and material needs of people (e.g., standard of living and access to basic health care, education, and other essential social services). Once these are addressed, the society can move through the various stages toward full economic and social development.

The New World Order Model

The new world order model, by contrast, is more radical. It has its origins in the idea that the world order is not a democratic one at all, but rather is one controlled by a relatively small number of wealthy countries and powerful corporations.

Followers of this approach are concerned with bringing about sweeping changes in the institutional arrangements and relationships between and within nations, between the well-to-do and the less well-to-do. The focus is not only on inequality but on social participation, social justice, and the environment.

The new world order model focuses on

- the active participation of all relevant sectors in the transformation process,
- world peace and the prevention of war,
- the alleviation of human suffering,
- the creation of effective systems of social protection and social service provision,
- increased social and political justice, and
- the protection of the natural environment.

The Social Development Model

A third approach, known loosely as the social development model, falls somewhere between the first two approaches. The social development model has its roots in the community development field.

Less radical, perhaps, but no less committed, social workers who favour this approach focus on the immediate causes of human degradation, powerlessness, and social inequality, and seek to guide collective action toward the elimination of all forms of oppression, injustice, and violence. They are concerned with fostering social, political, and economic systems that are more humane, inclusive, and participatory.

An important corollary is that of "sustainable development"—that is, development that "meets the needs of the present without compromising the ability of future generations to meet their own needs" (World Commission on Environment and Development, the "Bruntland Commission," 1987).

The idea of development is not a new idea, of course—Indigenous cultures have emphasized the need for a holistic approach or harmony between the environment, society, and economy. What is new is the way in which the social development model is put forth as a systematic solution to problems related to international social and economic development.

The Sustainable Social Progress Model

Finally, there is an extension of the social development model—what the International Council on Social Welfare (ICSW) calls "sustainable social progress."

This approach to international social work goes beyond ecological and environmental concerns. Sustainable development (or sustainable social progress) involves three basic operating premises:

- **Equity and justice for all.** Upholding the rights of the poor and disadvantaged, and the rights of future generations.
- **A long-term view.** The view that claims on the Earth's resources have implications for future generations.
- **Structural understanding of the broader society.** Taking into account the many interconnections between individuals, communities, the economy, and the environment.

This approach challenges us to think beyond the here and now and to look at the wider implications of our actions.

In essence, this approach is a call to action—a call to do things differently and to realize that our actions have ripple effects throughout our increasingly interdependent world.

Community Development

Social work practice and international community development

International community work is a common type of social work activity in developing countries. Social workers partner with communities by assisting with problem solving and by planning effective social services. They use community work to organize people to bring about major social change between nations, within nations, and between groups of people. They work with communities to achieve the fullest participation of all members in transforming various aspects of their lives.

Social workers engaged in international community work need to be sensitive to local cultures and history. We may feel that the internationalization of social work is ultimately for the good of all, but in doing so we may fail to consider its relevance and transferability to local contexts. At worst, international social work may be viewed as a form of neo-colonialism, imposing an ethnocentric world view on many of the most vulnerable members of a society. For international social workers, spending time talking to key stakeholders to seek understanding of local perspectives is critically important.

Transforming Communities through Collaboration and Mutual Learning

As Kevin's story demonstrates, sensitive collaboration and mutual learning have the potential to transform communities, and ensure that the social work practices developed are responsive to specific cultural contexts. In this case study, Kevin Barnes-Ceeney describes his year-long employment as a social work advisor for the international development organization Voluntary Service Overseas. Kevin was based in a medical centre in Astana, the capital city of Kazakhstan. The notion of social work there had changed since the collapse of the Soviet Union in 1991, and Kevin's role was to develop and help advance the practice. As Kevin's story shows, the social work staff at the medical centre were struggling with the adoption of a completely new and different view of what a social worker does.

Community work is arguably more important today in the era of globalization. People living in localized communities are vulnerable to the large-scale social and political changes that occur within and between countries, changes over which they have little or no control. Social work practitioners can bring an understanding of the global context to those at the local level in order to mitigate potential disruption.

The ultimate goal of community work is the empowerment or fostering of the "sense in people that they have the ability and right to influence their environment" (Lee, 1999: 43). Empowering people means that they can take action on their own behalf to meet their physical, spiritual, and psychological needs and participate directly in the process of social change.

To be able to act on their own behalf, however, people must see themselves as agents, with the right and ability to express their opinions and to acquire resources. Reaching these objectives requires a genuine sense of community among participants (Lee, 1999). On the basis of community, new organizations can be built or improved upon, and change can be effected.

Reflecting on Kevin's Story

1. What factors are important to consider when working with interpreters?
2. What steps can social workers take to ensure that the knowledge they bring is responsive to local contexts?
3. How can a "foreign expert" role be leveraged to assist the development of social work practice?

Kevin's Story...
Training social workers in Kazakhstan

The social work staff at a medical centre in Astana, Kazakhstan, asked a social work advisor for help in making the transition from a concept of social work as "home help" to a profession that values social justice and empowerment.

My arrival in Kazakhstan was the beginning of a rapid learning curve for me. Securing safe and reasonably priced accommodation with a limited budget was challenging. Temperatures that dipped to –43° C exacerbated the day-to-day challenges of purchasing provisions with limited language skills. Finding an interpreter to work alongside me was difficult, as many of the applicants who responded to my advertisement had limited English language skills.

To understand the broader institutional landscape, I visited agencies across the city. Here, my identity as a foreigner helped me gain access to a variety of governmental and non-governmental organizations. I toured the Center for Social Adaptation (an agency that works with homeless people); visited orphanages, schools, and drug rehabilitation centres; met with a variety of NGO staff working on issues ranging from domestic violence to children with physical disabilities; spoke with professors at the Eurasian National University; and liaised with workers based at UNICEF. I asked the agencies to describe the key social problems affecting the residents of Astana. They discussed drug use, homelessness, corruption, inequality, HIV and STIs, and the need for activities and youth-friendly services, accessibility, and women's empowerment.

During my time in Kazakhstan, I witnessed a steady flow of international "experts" flying in with lectures and workshops on social work and rehabilitation issues. The implementation of such "cutting edge" Western interventions raised many concerns. For example, a large drug rehabilitation centre had set aside a room where detoxifying clients could relive the trauma of their passage through their mother's birth canal.

I observed some "imported" therapies that did prove successful. Equine therapy, which can help physically disabled children develop muscle tone, balance, and coordination, was popular, seemingly fitting within a deep cultural history of reverence for horses and horsemanship in Kazakhstan.

Mindful that I did not want to be yet another international actor importing disconnected advice and expertise, I devoted time to shadowing social work staff in the medical centre, and I observed the variety of social work-related activities that occurred. These included a weekly group for young people who had engaged in solvent and inhalant misuse, and a daily handicrafts group for women with physical disabilities. In addition, a handful of drug-using clients attended appointments with the resident psychologist.

I spent time building a rapport with the social work staff team, sharing cultural perspectives, discussing what social work meant to them, and listening to why they had chosen this particular field of work. They disclosed that their wages were often insecure, and at times some were not paid for many months. Many revealed fears of working with clients who might be violent, drug addicted, or homeless.

The staff members were keen for me to provide "trainings" for them and for youth volunteers from a local university. Seeking to work in a collaborative fashion, I pushed staff to identify potential training topics. They told me they wanted to know what social work is and what social workers do. So I developed a weekly skills-based training program that focused on communication skills, empathy building, assessment and case planning skills, and individual and group supervision. The training consisted of role plays, small-group discussions, and individual presentations, with overarching weekly themes (e.g., drug and alcohol use, homelessness, sexual abuse). At the team's request, we also explored harm reduction strategies and safer injection techniques, and together we developed a child protection protocol for staff in the medical centre.

Looking back at my year-long placement, I realize I should have spent more time focusing on the intra-organizational relationships between the social work staff/volunteers and the medical centre staff. Improved relationships would have helped to fashion a more integrated and sustainable role for the emerging social workers.

International social work advisors working overseas must demonstrate cultural sensitivity on many levels.

Human Rights Monitoring

Social work practice and safeguarding human rights

The situation of many of the world's people is perilous and precarious. For example, 6.3 million children under the age of five died in 2013 from preventable diseases, two-thirds of the world's illiterate people are women, and countless people continue to be killed or tortured by oppressive governments. Such statistics have been around for decades, and many experts believe they will worsen as poor countries are impacted by climate change.

Part of the hope for improvement lies in human rights instruments and their implementation, and in ever-growing international consciousness and solidarity. Social workers have a role in strengthening such solidarity and working to translate the principles enshrined in the human rights instruments into reality.

It is easy to apply a human rights critique to institutions "out there," particularly those in another part of the world. But to truly be human rights advocates, social workers should use the same critical eye to monitor the language they use and the work they undertake on a daily basis. It is essential that social workers operate in ways that observe human rights principles within their own practices as well.

Social Workers Can Help Make Human Rights Declarations a Reality

A key value toward this end is allowing people to maximize self-determination and control over the situations in which they find themselves. To truly reflect human rights principles, social work is practised in a manner that avoids stigmatizing, labelling, or controlling the lives of the people with whom we work. If social work practice truly encompasses the full range of values and ethics that inform the profession (which for the most part are identical to human rights principles), it is in a unique position to help make the vision espoused in various human rights declarations a reality.

Steve's story from the Philippines illustrates social work in action in protecting negative human rights, also known as first-generation rights. These are civil and political rights that ensure protection from torture, false imprisonment, or summary execution. As discussed previously in this chapter, social workers also address second-generation rights (economic, social, and cultural rights) and third-generation, or collective, rights. The profession's focus on human needs shapes its conviction that meeting these needs is not a matter of choice but an imperative of basic justice.

This transition from needs orientation to rights affirmation allows social workers to navigate different political systems to uphold and defend the rights of their clients and of society in general. As you may imagine, this can place social workers in a precarious role, as they are often employed by the state or agents of the state. Professional social workers are tasked with serving as reliable employees while at the same time serving clients as best they can. This often entails advocating for policy changes within the state agency that employs them. Viewing social work within a global human rights perspective provides a sense of unity and international solidarity without losing sight of the local context, conditions, and needs.

Reflecting on Steve's Story

1. What skills are needed to do international social work?
2. Vicarious trauma is a common concern in international social work. What are some techniques that can reduce this risk or mediate its effects?
3. What other kinds of short-term social work intervention might be helpful in such situations?

Steve's Story...in the Philippines
Documenting human rights violations

Human rights work isn't for everyone, but it is desperately needed. Combining direct practice, interviewing skills, and advocacy skills, social workers make invaluable contributions to human rights fact-finding teams.

I had worked briefly in Central America with World University Service Canada, and found the work to be rewarding and fast-paced. I applied to numerous organizations and was hired by the United Church of Canada (UCC) to work in the Philippines. The UCC was expanding its peace and justice work, and my interests fit perfectly. My spouse and I were both hired for a two-year term to assist Filipinos in documenting human rights violations.

Teams of 8 to 12 people, mostly comprised of Filipinos, trekked through the jungle to visit isolated communities that had experienced gross violations of human rights. We would collect affidavits documenting violations such as summary executions, mass killings, bombing, sexual assaults, and other atrocities. Our job was stated simply—to get the information and transfer it out of the community to the city.

Excellent social work interviewing skills were vital in this work. We would always begin with open-ended, inviting questions, and then listen carefully. People were sometimes hesitant to share their story for fear of reprisals. We were always careful to respect their rights and not try to push for a statement. I often used clarifying skills to probe for details about specific events. I would end the interview with a summary, in order to check the accuracy of my interpretation. I would also share information about how the statement would be used to let the world know what had happened in this community and how it might contribute to political change in the Philippines.

While my job was simply stated, it was not really that simple. When people share traumatic events with others, there is a kind of re-living of the trauma. It would have been unethical to request that someone share an event and not stay with that person to help them process their experience. Because our visits to the community were brief, long-term therapy was not an option. Instead, I offered brief interventions to help people work through the difficult thoughts and feelings they were experiencing. In particular, we identified negative thoughts that might lead to depression and looked at alternative ways of coping. CBT showed clients how to challenge their thoughts, and MBT taught them how to simply acknowledge their thoughts and view them with compassion. I also taught anxiety management techniques, such as relaxation and mindfulness meditation.

The work did not end with the collection of information on human rights violations. As you can imagine, the government security forces did not want this information to leave the community and be made public, and they would often stop us, harass us, arrest us, or worse. This work required a high level of resiliency. We had to be careful that we did not burn out or experience vicarious trauma (VT) (also called compassion fatigue). We used various strategies to protect ourselves, including mental preparation before potentially stressful situations and self-care methods such as mindfulness and yoga.

As a team, we met to debrief after each assignment. We would discuss the meaning of our work that day and look at its positive aspects. If we noticed signs that a colleague might be experiencing VT, then we would take action, referring the person to counselling and removing them from work for a while. Typical signs of VT include emotional numbing, a desire for social isolation, nightmares, feelings of despair and hopelessness, and a lack of energy.

Next, we entered our information into a database and ensured that it reached the appropriate organizations outside the country, such as Human Rights Watch and Amnesty International. I used my networking and advocacy skills to ensure that the information reached the proper people. I followed up with each organization to ensure that the information met their advocacy needs, discuss how we could make it more applicable and useful, and answer any questions. Working as a team and communicating with our partner organizations improved our interviewing skills greatly, which helped to ensure that our data were complete and reliable.

Well-honed interviewing skills and empathic listening are needed when gathering data about human rights violations.

Working in War Zones

Social work practice in countries torn apart by war

Conflicts in war zones can have dire effects on human rights. Fear of violence or persecution can spur inhabitants to flee, sometimes uprooting entire communities and leaving people traumatized and deprived of ways to meet their basic needs—food, water, shelter, and safety. The varied skill set that social workers develop equips them well for work in areas affected by war. This work often occurs in refugee camps or in areas to which large numbers of people have fled. Sometimes, the work occurs directly within areas of conflict and often involves providing help to women and children. As Steve's story from Kosovo shows, the work demands an array of activities and skills, including community organization; logistical support for the provision of water, food, sanitation, and health care; direct intervention to help people cope with trauma and sexual violence; advocacy; and peacemaking. Social workers often act as power brokers, using legal recourses and personal influence to secure resources and services that their clients cannot demand for themselves.

The Benefits of a Community-Based Approach

When social workers are engaged in war zones and refugee camps, they must try to maintain open lines of communication with the various factions involved in the conflict. They must refrain from taking sides. To do their job safely, social workers may need to find creative ways to win acceptance by members of the community they are trying to help. Establishing trust involves deep listening, networking, and mediation, as illustrated by Steve's story. It is important to listen to the people whose lives have been upended and to avoid making assumptions about how they feel or what they need.

A community-based approach is often effective. Refugee camps are filled with people who possess abundant skills, and tapping into these skills has a two-fold benefit: it can instill a sense of empowerment and usefulness in a situation where people often feel helpless and isolated, and it expedites the work that needs to be done.

For example, as of the writing of this text, the International Rescue Committee (IRC) is deploying social workers to provide support to Syrian refugees in Jordan, Lebanon, Iraq, Turkey, and Syria. Hundreds of thousands of people displaced by conflicts inside Syria and Iraq will receive winter emergency kits, medical and emergency supplies, clean water, sanitation, and education. Targeted emotional and educational support for women and children will include counselling for survivors of sexual violence and help for children who have crossed the border to reunite with their families. Job training, work placements, and access to legal assistance will be made available. Whenever possible, the IRC employs a community-based approach.

Peacemaking, conflict resolution, and nonviolent communication are other examples of social work skills that can benefit people affected by war. The goal is to de-escalate, prevent, or stop conflicts. Social workers engage in processes such as education, negotiation, mediation, conciliation, and arbitration, sometimes drawing upon international law. The objective is to move toward nonviolent dialogue, where differences can be settled without violent outcomes.

Reflecting on Steve's Story

1. In the end, what factors contributed to the success of the bakery?
2. Which aspects of this story do you think are relevant to international social work generally?
3. What key social work skills were required in the situation in this story?
4. Explain what the volunteer might have meant when he said, "Well, I think only a social worker could have made this happen."

Steve's Story...in Kosovo
Aiding displaced persons from Kosovo

Steve discovered that sustaining a collective effort in a war-torn region required a constant focus on the values of self-determination, empowerment, and social justice.

Having just co-founded a new organization tasked with helping children in war zones, I travelled to Kosovo after armed conflict began there in 1998. I ended up in Kukus, Albania, where approximately 150,000 Kosovars had fled to escape the war. Our organization's mission was to respond quickly to the immediate needs of these displaced people in a community-based manner that also emphasized self-determination and self-empowerment.

I arrived with no preconception of what such a response would look like. As I met with other social workers and relief workers, I learned that no one really knew what the people in the refugee camps needed or desired. Workers were basing their responses on their organization's specialized expertise. For example, organizations that specialized in trauma treatment proposed offering trauma treatment. However, responses that are informed by the people affected by traumatic events are more consistent with a community-based perspective, so I went to the camps to speak directly with different groups of people to determine their needs from their perspective.

Collective Efforts that Empower People

It quickly became clear that the primary need was adequate food. The camps were new, and relief supplies were slow to arrive and unsuited to the nutritional needs of the occupants. Over and over, people said that what they wanted most was a simple loaf of fresh bread—the staple food for Kosovars. Instead, they often ate fruit cups and canned herring. I can attest that this is not a tasty combination.

The lack of bread posed a huge challenge. First, getting fresh bread to a remote area of Albania to feed 150,000 people seemed impossible. The bakery in Kukus could only produce 100 loaves of bread a day—enough to feed the existing local population of 1000. Additionally, I knew nothing about baking bread and had no idea where to start. I recognized my limitations and began to seek help.

I began by talking to citizens, relief workers, and displaced people themselves. I connected with representatives of the World Food Programme, who said they would guarantee a supply of ingredients if I could build a bakery. I came across a British army officer who said, "We have an eight-oven field bakery used to supply bread to troops in the field that you can have; you just have to transport it yourself." More networking led me to a United States Air Force officer who agreed to supply the aircraft to pick up the field bakery and deliver it to Kukus. I was ecstatic.

Back at the camps, I asked for volunteers and immediately had a line-up 300 meters long. The president of the largest bakery in Pristina, the largest city in Kosovo, learned that many of his staff in the camps were eager to help. I found an engineering professor who volunteered to set up a generator and keep it running, and the head of Public Health volunteered to ensure that health concerns were addressed. After about four days, we had a fully staffed bakery—with perhaps the most qualified staff of any bakery in the world.

The bakery was operational within five days, producing upwards of 26,000 loaves of bread per day. Other relief agencies helped with distribution.

Not everything proceeded smoothly, however. Some groups of Kosovars rallied to question why they had been left out of the process. The answer was that it would have been impossible to involve all 150,000 people. So, an advisory committee was established to represent the various groups within the camps. Establishing, organizing, and facilitating this committee required sharp analytical and interpersonal skills, as well as political astuteness.

When a volunteer asked me how a social worker had managed to start up a bakery, I replied, "I saw my job as listening to people, maximizing their power and participation, and applying my skills in communication, community organizing, and networking." He smiled and responded, "Well, I think only a social worker could have made this happen."

Addressing primary needs in a community-based manner is the best approach to social work in war-ravaged regions.

Samantha McGavin

Samantha McGavin graduated from McGill University's social work program and is pursuing a lifelong vocation inspired by activism and social issues.

Samantha McGavin, a commmunications director with Inter Pares, an international social justice organization, believes that true social transformation begins with people working for change in their own communities and societies.

Had someone suggested social work to me as a career during my high-school or early undergraduate years, when I was interested in the helping professions, I would have become a clinical social worker. But my youthful interest in environmentalism led me first to a canvassing job with Greenpeace after high school, and then to the Québec Public Interest Research Group (QPIRG) at McGill University. Those two experiences were the start of a lifelong education and vocation inspired by activism and social issues.

After a year's involvement in mostly unpaid activism following the attainment of my B.A., I enrolled in McGill's post-graduate B.S.W. program in 1999. During this 16-month program, I immersed myself in learning about approaches to community development, Canadian social policy, and models of social change. My practicum with a local anti-poverty organization in an immigrant-rich, low-income neighbourhood familiarized me with social programs and community resources, and enhanced my previous experiences of working with others to raise awareness about injustice and avenues for change.

Inter Pares hired me in 2002 as a fundraiser—and I began an intense education in fundraising, communications, and event organizing, as well as consensus-building and non-profit management. I also gained more knowledge about social movements and the political histories of countries around the world. It took me a year or two to feel like I was truly familiar with our fundraising program, institutional structures, and management culture, and to fully participate in the political conversations about our programs. It took some time for me to be equally confident in my knowledge, opinions, and leadership.

Today, we work in nearly 20 countries in Africa, Asia, and Latin America, partnering with national-level organizations that are engaging in advocacy, social movement building, and support for grassroots community organizations. Our interests of common concern are broad—women's equality, peace and democracy, economic justice, food sovereignty, health, migrants' and refugees' rights, and control over resources such as minerals and water—but we are all joined by our values and belief in building change from the ground up.

Because we feel that it is important to serve as political actors in our own context, we also advocate for improved Canadian foreign policy, we support domestic social change efforts, and we play a bridging role in bringing together Canadian and international activists.

I have the opportunity to meet and build relationships with overseas colleagues when we bring them to Canada, by arranging radio and newspaper interviews and by organizing meetings with local activists who share similar concerns and struggles.

For instance, in 2012, we invited a Sudanese women's rights activist to speak at our annual public Speaker Series event, which I co-organized and moderated. Along with a colleague in our Africa program, I organized her visit and set up meetings for her with the local Sudanese diaspora, Muslim and youth activists, and community activists and legal experts in the area of violence against women. We discussed young people's leadership, mobilization in Islamic contexts, and working with women experiencing violence and oppressive laws.

My own role is focused on sharing stories of social change to help inspire and engage people to take action—whether through donating money, learning about issues, educating others about an issue, participating in a campaign, or creating change in their own lives and communities.

I make sure to complement my role with participation in community-building in my own city and neighbourhood. I now have two young children and am not as active outside of work as I was ten or fifteen years ago. However, I still feel that it is important for me to be politically engaged in my own name as well as Inter Pares' name. It is important for children to see their parents' involvement in social and political causes, so that as they grow and learn about social issues, they can also learn about avenues for social change.

Chapter 14 Review

Review Questions

1. What are some indicators of global economic and social inequality?
2. Define the two key principles that underlie international social work.
3. Define and distinguish the three generations of human rights. Why is it important for social workers to affirm and work toward all three generations?
4. What are four key approaches to international social work practice? Briefly describe each model.
5. Identify and describe the various types of agencies that employ social workers abroad.
6. How is the Internet changing the way that social workers advocate for human rights?
7. Describe the specific risks and challenges involved in social work practice in war-torn countries.

Exploring Social Work

1. Climate change affects people in all countries, but it seems that poorer countries are more vulnerable.What do you think that we in Canada might do to address this problem? Break into small groups and discuss this issue.
2. What role do you see for social workers in developing countries? Is it all one way (us helping them) or do you see it as more of a two-way sharing? What can we learn about community and family from other countries? Record your reflections in a two-page paper.
3. Re-read the feature in this chapter on "The Rights of Indigenous People Worldwide." In the *Globe and Mail* article, Professor Ken Coates describes the UN declaration as a powerful and emotional statement about the degree to which Indigenous peoples around the world have a similar history of mistreatment through colonialism and occupation. However, he also states that the document may not effectively respond to the needs and challenges of the twenty-first century. Do you agree or disagree with his statement? Explain your answer.

Websites

New Internationalist
www.newint.org
This monthly print magazine is available online. It provides a clearly written and concise overview of the important global issues of concern to social workers. It is an excellent resource to kick-start an essay on international issues.

United Nations Development Programme (UNDP)
www.undp.org
At the UN Millennium Summit, world leaders pledged to cut poverty in half by 2015. UNDP is charged with helping to make this happen. Their website contains comprehensive links, publications, and various UNDP speeches and reports. Their publications section has numerous complete books online, including their annual Overcoming Human Poverty Report.

Canadian Heritage Human Rights Program
www.pch.gc.ca
This Government of Canada website has basic information about human rights in Canada and internationally. It contains most of the official UN human rights covenants and an excellent overview of how the international human rights system works.

Appendices

CASW Code of Ethics, 2005
Canadian Association of Social Workers

[The Social Work Code of Ethics, adopted by the Board of Directors of the Canadian Association of Social Workers (CASW) is effective March 2005, and replaces the CASW Code of Ethics (1994). The Code is reprinted here with the permission of CASW. The copyright in the document has been registered with the Canadian Intellectual Property Office, registration No. 1030330.]

Acknowledgements

The Canadian Association of Social Workers (CASW) acknowledges with thanks the National Association of Social Workers (NASW) for permission to use sections of the copyrighted NASW 1999 *Code of Ethics* in the development of the CASW 2005 *Code of Ethics* and CASW 2005 *Guidelines for Ethical Practice.*

The CASW also acknowledges that other codes of ethics and resources were used in the development of this *Code* and the *Guidelines for Ethical Practice*, in particular the *Code of Ethics* of the Australian Association of Social Workers (AASW). These resources can be found in the Reference section of each document.

Purpose of the CASW Code of Ethics

Ethical behaviour lies at the core of every profession. The Canadian Association of Social Workers (CASW) *Code of Ethics* sets forth values and principles to guide social workers' professional conduct. A code of ethics cannot guarantee ethical behaviour. Ethical behaviour comes from a social worker's individual commitment to engage in ethical practice. Both the spirit and the letter of this *Code of Ethics* will guide social workers as they act in good faith and with a genuine desire to make sound judgements.

This *Code of Ethics* is consistent with the International Federation of Social Workers (IFSW) *International Declaration of Ethical Principles of Social Work* (1994, 2004), which requires members of the CASW to uphold the values and principles established by both the CASW and the IFSW. Other individuals, organizations and bodies (such as regulatory boards, professional liability insurance providers, courts of law, boards of directors of organizations employing social workers and government agencies) may also choose to adopt this *Code of Ethics* or use it as a basis for evaluating professional conduct. In Canada, each province and territory is responsible for regulating the professional conduct of social workers to ensure the protection of the public. Social workers are advised to contact the regulatory body in their province or territory to determine whether it has adopted this *Code of Ethics.*[1]

Recognition of Individual and Professional Diversity

The CASW *Code of Ethics* does not provide a set of rules that prescribe how social workers should act in all situations. Further, the *Code of Ethics* does not specify which values and principles are most important and which outweigh others in instances of conflict. Reasonable differences of opinion exist among social workers with respect to which values and principles should be given priority in a particular situation. Further, a social worker's personal values, culture, religious beliefs, practices and/or other important distinctions, such as age, ability, gender or sexual orientation can affect his/her ethical choices. Thus, social workers need to be aware of any conflicts between personal and professional values and deal with them responsibly.

Ethical Behaviour Requires Due Consideration of Issues and Judgement

Social work is a multifaceted profession. As professionals, social workers are educated to exercise judgement in the face of complex and competing interests and claims. Ethical decision-making in a given situation will involve the informed judgement of the individual social worker. Instances may arise when social workers' ethical obligations conflict with agency policies, or relevant laws or regulations. When such conflicts occur, social workers shall make a responsible effort to resolve the conflicts in a manner that is consistent with the values and principles expressed in this *Code of Ethics.* If a reasonable resolution of the conflict does not appear possible, social workers shall seek appropriate consultation before making a decision. This may involve consultation with an ethics committee, a regulatory body, a knowledgeable colleague, supervisor or legal counsel.

Preamble

The social work profession is dedicated to the welfare and self-realization of all people; the development and disciplined use of scientific and professional knowledge; the development of resources and skills to meet individual, group, national and international changing needs and aspirations; and the achievement of social justice for all. The profession has a particular interest in the needs and empowerment of people who are vulnerable, oppressed, and/or living in poverty. Social workers are committed to human rights as enshrined in Canadian law, as well as in international conventions on human rights created or supported by the United Nations.

As professionals in a country that upholds respect for diversity, and in keeping with democratic rights and freedoms, social workers respect the distinct systems of beliefs and lifestyles of individuals, families, groups, communities and nations without prejudice (United Nations Centre for Human Rights, 1992). Specifically, social workers do not tolerate discrimination[2] based on age, abilities, ethnic background, gender, language, marital status, national ancestry, political affiliation, race, religion, sexual orientation or socio-economic status.

Core Social Work Values and Principles

Social workers uphold the following core social work values:

- Value 1: Respect for Inherent Dignity and Worth of Persons
- Value 2: Pursuit of Social Justice
- Value 3: Service to Humanity
- Value 4: Integrity of Professional Practice
- Value 5: Confidentiality in Professional Practice
- Value 6: Competence in Professional Practice

The following section describes each of these values and discusses their underlying principles.

Value 1: Respect for the Inherent Dignity and Worth of Persons

Social work is founded on a long-standing commitment to respect the inherent dignity and individual worth of all persons. When required by law to override a client's wishes, social workers take care to use the minimum coercion required. Social workers recognize and respect the diversity of Canadian society, taking into account the breadth of differences that exist among individuals, families, groups and communities. Social workers uphold the human rights of individuals and groups as expressed in the *Canadian Charter of Rights and Freedoms* (1982) and the United Nations *Universal Declaration of Human Rights* (1948).

Principles:

- Social workers respect the unique worth and inherent dignity of all people and uphold human rights.
- Social workers uphold each person's right to self-determination, consistent with that person's capacity and with the rights of others.
- Social workers respect the diversity among individuals in Canadian society and the right of individuals to their unique beliefs consistent with the rights of others.
- Social workers respect the client's right to make choices based on voluntary, informed consent.
- Social workers who have children as clients determine the child's ability to consent and where appropriate, explain to the child and to the child's parents/guardians, the nature of the social worker's relationship to the child.
- Social workers uphold the right of society to impose limitations on the self-determination of individuals, when such limitations protect individuals from self-harm and from harming others.
- Social workers uphold the right of every person to be free from violence and threat of violence.

Value 2: Pursuit of Social Justice

Social workers believe in the obligation of people, individually and collectively, to provide resources, services and opportunities for the overall benefit of humanity and to afford them protection from harm. Social workers promote social fairness and the equitable distribution of resources, and act to reduce barriers and expand choice for all persons, with special regard for those who are marginalized, disadvantaged, vulnerable, and/or have exceptional needs. Social workers oppose prejudice and discrimination against any person or group of persons, on any grounds, and specifically challenge views and actions that stereotype particular persons or groups.

Principles:

- Social workers uphold the right of people to have access to resources to meet basic human needs.
- Social workers advocate for fair and equitable access to public services and benefits.
- Social workers advocate for equal treatment and protection under the law and challenge injustices, especially injustices that affect the vulnerable and disadvantaged.
- Social workers promote social development and environmental management in the interests of all people.

Value 3: Service to Humanity

The social work profession upholds service in the interests of others, consistent with social justice, as a core professional objective. In professional practice, social workers balance individual needs, and rights and freedoms with collective interests in the service of humanity. When acting in a professional capacity, social workers place professional service before personal goals or advantage, and use their power and authority in disciplined and responsible ways that serve society. The social work profession contributes to knowledge and skills that assist in the management of conflicts and the wide-ranging consequences of conflict.

Principles:

- Social workers place the needs of others above self-interest when acting in a professional capacity.
- Social workers strive to use the power and authority vested in them as professionals in responsible ways that serve the needs of clients and the promotion of social justice.
- Social workers promote individual development and pursuit of individual goals, as well as the development of a just society.
- Social workers use their knowledge and skills in bringing about fair resolutions to conflict and in assisting those affected by conflict.

Value 4: Integrity in Professional Practice

Social workers demonstrate respect for the profession's purpose, values and ethical principles relevant to their field of practice. Social workers maintain a high level of professional conduct by acting honestly and responsibly, and promoting the values of the profession. Social workers strive for impartiality in their professional practice, and refrain from imposing their personal values, views and preferences on clients. It is the responsibility of social workers to establish the tenor of their professional relationship with clients, and others to whom they have a professional duty, and to maintain professional boundaries. As individuals, social workers take care in their actions to not bring the reputation of the profession into disrepute. An essential element of integrity in professional practice is ethical accountability based on this *Code of Ethics*, the IFSW *International Declaration of Ethical Principles of*

Social Work, and other relevant provincial/territorial standards and guidelines. Where conflicts exist with respect to these sources of ethical guidance, social workers are encouraged to seek advice, including consultation with their regulatory body.

Principles:

- Social workers demonstrate and promote the qualities of honesty, reliability, impartiality and diligence in their professional practice.
- Social workers demonstrate adherence to the values and ethical principles of the profession and promote respect for the profession's values and principles in organizations where they work or with which they have a professional affiliation.
- Social workers establish appropriate boundaries in relationships with clients and ensure that the relationship serves the needs of clients.
- Social workers value openness and transparency in professional practice and avoid relationships where their integrity or impartiality may be compromised, ensuring that should a conflict of interest be unavoidable, the nature of the conflict is fully disclosed.

Value 5: Confidentiality in Professional Practice

A cornerstone of professional social work relationships is confidentiality with respect to all matters associated with professional services to clients. Social workers demonstrate respect for the trust and confidence placed in them by clients, communities and other professionals by protecting the privacy of client information and respecting the client's right to control when or whether this information will be shared with third parties. Social workers only disclose confidential information to other parties (including family members) with the informed consent of clients, clients' legally authorized representatives or when required by law or court order. The general expectation that social workers will keep information confidential does not apply when disclosure is necessary to prevent serious, foreseeable and imminent harm to a client or others. In all instances, social workers disclose the least amount of confidential information necessary to achieve the desired purpose.

Principles:

- Social workers respect the importance of the trust and confidence placed in the professional relationship by clients and members of the public.
- Social workers respect the client's right to confidentiality of information shared in a professional context.
- Social workers only disclose confidential information with the informed consent of the client or permission of client's legal representative.
- Social workers may break confidentiality and communicate client information without permission when required or permitted by relevant laws, court order or this *Code*.
- Social workers demonstrate transparency with respect to limits to confidentiality that apply to their professional practice by clearly communicating these limitations to clients early in their relationship.

Value 6: Competence in Professional Practice

Social workers respect a client's right to competent social worker services. Social workers analyze the nature of social needs and problems, and encourage innovative, effective strategies and techniques to meet both new and existing needs and, where possible, contribute to the knowledge base of the profession. Social workers have a responsibility to maintain professional proficiency, to continually strive to increase their professional knowledge and skills, and to apply new knowledge in practice commensurate with their level of professional education, skill and competency, seeking consultation and supervision as appropriate.

Principles:

- Social workers uphold the right of clients to be offered the highest quality service possible.
- Social workers strive to maintain and increase their professional knowledge and skill.
- Social workers demonstrate due care for client's interests and safety by limiting professional practice to areas of demonstrated competence.
- Social workers contribute to the ongoing development of the profession and its ability to serve humanity, where possible, by participating in the development of current and future social workers and the development of new professional knowledge.
- Social workers who engage in research minimize risks to participants, ensure informed consent, maintain confidentiality and accurately report the results of their studies.

Glossary

Capacity

The ability to understand information relevant to a decision and to appreciate the reasonably foreseeable consequences of choosing to act or not to act. Capacity is specific to each decision and thus a person may be capable of deciding about a place of residence, for example, but not capable with respect to deciding about a treatment. Capacity can change over time (Etchells, Sharpe, Elliot and Singer, 1996).

Recent references in law point to the concept of "a mature minor," which Rozovsky and Rozovsky (1990) define as "...one with capacity to understand the nature and consequences of medical treatment. Such a person has the power to consent to medical treatment and parental consent is not necessary" (p. 55). They quote the comments by The Honorable Justice Lambert in *Van Mol v. Ashmore*, which help clarify common law with respect to a minor's capacity to consent. He states:

> At common law, without reference to statute law, a young person, still a minor, may give, on his or her own behalf, a fully informed consent to medical treatment if he or she has sufficient maturity, intelligence and capacity of understanding what is involved in making informed choices about the proposed medical treatment.... Once the capacity to consent has been achieved by the young person reaching sufficient maturity, intelligence and capability of understanding, the

discussions about the nature of the treatment, its gravity, the material risks and any special and unusual risks, and the decisions about undergoing treatment, and about the form of the treatment, must all take place with and be made by the young person whose bodily integrity is to be invaded and whose life and health will be affected by the outcome.

Child

The *Convention on the Rights of the Child* passed by the United Nations in 1959 and ratified by Canada in 1990, define a child as a person under the age of 18 years unless national law recognizes an earlier age of majority (Alberta Law Reform Institute, 1991). The age of majority differs in provinces and territories in Canada. Under the *Criminal Code of Canada*, the age of consent is held to be over the age of 14 years; age in the context of the criminal code frequently refers to capacity to consent to sexual relations. All jurisdictions in Canada have legislation regarding child protection, which defines the age of a child for the purposes of protection. In Canada, in the absence of provincial or territorial legislation, courts are governed by common law. Social workers are encouraged to maintain current knowledge with respect to legislation on the age of a child, as well as capacity and consent in their jurisdiction.

Client

A person, family, group of persons, incorporated body, association or community on whose behalf a social worker provides or agrees to provide a service or to whom the social worker is legally obligated to provide a service. Examples of legal obligation to provide service include a legislated responsibility (such as in child welfare) or a valid court order. In the case of a valid court order, the judge/court is the client and the person(s) who is ordered by the court to participate in assessment is recognized as an involuntary client.

Conduct Unbecoming

Behaviour or conduct that does not meet social work standard of care requirements and is, therefore, subject to discipline. In reaching a decision in Matthews and Board of Directors of Physiotherapy (1986) 54 O.R. (2d) 375, Saunders J. makes three important statements regarding standards of practice, and by implication, professional codes of ethics:

1. Standards of practice are inherent characteristics of any profession.
2. Standards of practice may be written or unwritten.
3. Some conduct is clearly regarded as misconduct and need not be written down, whereas other conduct may be the subject of dispute within a profession.

(See "Standard of Practice.")

Confidentiality

A professional value that demands that professionally acquired information be kept private and not shared with third parties unless the client provides informed consent or a professional or legal obligation exists to share such information without client informed consent.

Discrimination

Treating people unfavourably or holding negative or prejudicial attitudes based on discernible differences or stereotypes (AASW, 1999).

Informed Consent

Voluntary agreement reached by a capable client based on information about foreseeable risks and benefits associated with the agreement (e.g., participation in counselling or agreement to disclose social work report to a third party).

Human Rights

The rights of an individual that are considered the basis for freedom and justice, and serve to protect people from discrimination and harassment. Social workers may refer to the *Canadian Charter of Rights and Freedoms* enacted as Schedule B to the *Canada Act* 1982 (U.K.) 1982, c. 11, which came into force on April 17, 1982, as well as the *Universal Declaration of Human Rights* (1948) proclaimed by the United Nations General Assembly December 10, 1948.

Malpractice and Negligence

Behaviour that is included in "conduct unbecoming" and relates to social work practice behaviour within the parameters of the professional relationship that falls below the standard of practice and results in, or aggravation of, injury to a client. It includes behaviour that results in assault, deceit, fraudulent misrepresentations, defamation of character, breach of contract, violation of human rights, malicious prosecution, false imprisonment or criminal conviction.

Self-Determination

A core social work value that refers to the right to self-direction and freedom of choice without interference from others. Self-determination is codified in practice through mechanisms of informed consent. Social workers may be obligated to limit self-determination when a client lacks capacity or in order to prevent harm (Regehr and Antle, 1997).

Social Worker

A person who is duly registered to practice social work in a province or territory; or where mandatory registration does not exist, a person with social work education from an institution recognized by the Canadian Association of Schools of Social Work (CASSW) or an institution from outside of Canada that has been approved by the CASW, who is practising social work and who voluntarily agrees to be subject to this *Code of Ethics*. **Note:** Social workers living in Quebec and British Columbia, whose social work education was obtained outside of Canada, follow a separate approval process within their respective provinces.

Standard of Practice

The standard of care ordinarily expected of a competent social worker. It means that the public is assured that a social worker has the training, the skill and the diligence to provide them with social work services. Social workers are urged to refer to standards of practice that have been set by their provincial or territorial regulatory body or relevant professional association (see "Conduct Unbecoming").

Voluntary

"In the context of consent, 'voluntariness' refers to a patient's right to make treatment decisions free of any undue influence, such as ability of others to exert control over a patient by force, coercion or manipulation. ...The requirement for voluntariness does not imply that clinicians should refrain from persuading patients to accept advice. Persuasion involves appealing to the patient's reason in an attempt to convince him or her of the merits of a recommendation. In attempting to persuade the patient to follow a particular course of action, the clinician still leaves the patient free to accept or reject this advice." (Etchells, Sharpe, Dykeman, Meslin and Singer, 1996, p. 1083).

Notes

[1] To find the IFSW declarations or information about your relevant regulatory body, visit the CASW web site: http://www.casw-acts.ca

[2] Throughout this document the term "discrimination" refers to treating people unfavourably or holding negative or prejudicial attitudes based on discernible differences or stereotypes. It does **not refer** to the positive intent behind programs, such as affirmative action, where one group may be given preferential treatment to address inequities created by discrimination.

References

AASW. (1999). *AASW code of ethics*. Kingston: Australian Association of Social Workers (AASW).

Alberta Law Reform Institute. (1991). *Status of the child: Revised report* (Report No. 60). Edmonton, Alberta: Law Reform Institute.

BASW. (2002). *BASW: A code of ethics for social workers*. British Association of Social Workers (BASW).

Canadian Charter of Rights and Freedoms. Enacted as Schedule B to the Canada Act 1982, c.11 (1982). [http://laws.justice.gc.ca/en/charter/]

CASW. (1994). *Social Work Code of Ethics*. Ottawa: Canadian Association of Social Workers (CASW).

Criminal Code, R.S., c. C-34, s.1. (1985). [http://laws.justice.gc.ca/en/C-46/40670.html]

Etchells, E.; G. Sharpe; C. Elliott and P. Singer. (1996). Bioethics for clinicians: 3: Capacity. *Canadian Medical Association Journal*, 155, 657-661.

Etchells, E.; G. Sharpe; M.J. Dykeman and P. Singer. (1996). Bioethics for clinicians: 4: Voluntariness. *Canadian Medical Association Journal*, 155,1083-1086.

IFSW. (1994). *The ethics of social work: Principles and standards*. Geneva, Switzerland: International Federation of Social Workers (IFSW).

____.(2004). *Ethics in social work: Statement of principles*. Geneva, Switzerland: International Federation of Social Workers (IFSW).

Lens, V. (2000). Protecting the confidentiality of the therapeutic relationship: Jaffe v. Redmond. *Social Work*, 45(3), 273-276.

Matthews and Board of Directors of Physiotherapy. (1986). 54 O.R. (2d) 375.

NASW. (1999). *Code of Ethics*. Washington: National Association of Social Workers (NASW).

Regehr, C. and B.J. Antle. (1997). Coercive influences: Informed consent and court-mandated social work practice. *Social Work*, 42(3), 300-306.

Rozovsky, L.E. and F.A. Rozovsky. (1990). *The Canadian law of consent to treatment*. Toronto: Butterworths.

United Nations. (1948). *Universal Declaration of Human Rights*. New York: United Nations. [http://www.unhchr.ch/udhr/]

United Nations Centre for Human Rights. (1992). Teaching and learning about human rights: A manual for schools of social work and the social work profession (Developed in co-operation with International Federation of Social Workers and International Association of Schools of Social Workers). New York: United Nations.

Canadian Association of Social Workers (CASW)
383 Parkdale Avenue, Suite 402, Ottawa, Ontario, Canada K1Y 4R4.
Telephone: (613) 729-6668 / Fax: (613) 729-9608

Email: casw@casw-acts.ca

Website: www.casw-acts.ca

The Truth and Reconciliation Commission Calls to Action

In order to redress the legacy of residential schools and advance the process of Canadian reconciliation, the Truth and Reconciliation Commission makes the following calls to action.

LEGACY

Child welfare

1) We call upon the federal, provincial, territorial, and Aboriginal governments to commit to reducing the number of Aboriginal children in care by:
   i. Monitoring and assessing neglect investigations.
   ii. Providing adequate resources to enable Aboriginal communities and child-welfare organizations to keep Aboriginal families together where it is safe to do so, and to keep children in culturally appropriate environments, regardless of where they reside.
   iii. Ensuring that social workers and others who conduct child-welfare investigations are properly educated and trained about the history and impacts of residential schools.
   iv. Ensuring that social workers and others who conduct child-welfare investigations are properly educated and trained about the potential for Aboriginal communities and families to provide more appropriate solutions to family healing.
   v. Requiring that all child-welfare decision makers consider the impact of the residential school experience on children and their caregivers.
2) We call upon the federal government, in collaboration with the provinces and territories, to prepare and publish annual reports on the number of Aboriginal children (First Nations, Inuit, and Métis) who are in care, compared with non-Aboriginal children, as well as the reasons for apprehension, the total spending on preventive and care services by child-welfare agencies, and the effectiveness of various interventions.
3) We call upon all levels of government to fully implement Jordan's Principle.
4) We call upon the federal government to enact Aboriginal child-welfare legislation that establishes national standards for Aboriginal child apprehension and custody cases and includes principles that:
   i. Affirm the right of Aboriginal governments to establish and maintain their own child-welfare agencies.
   ii. Require all child-welfare agencies and courts to take the residential school legacy into account in their decision making.
   iii. Establish, as an important priority, a requirement that placements of Aboriginal children into temporary and permanent care be culturally appropriate.
5) We call upon the federal, provincial, territorial, and Aboriginal governments to develop culturally appropriate parenting programs for Aboriginal families.

Education

6) We call upon the Government of Canada to repeal Section 43 of the Criminal Code of Canada.
7) We call upon the federal government to develop with Aboriginal groups a joint strategy to eliminate educational and employment gaps between Aboriginal and non-Aboriginal Canadians.
8) We call upon the federal government to eliminate the discrepancy in federal education funding for First Nations children being educated on reserves and those First Nations children being educated off reserves.
9) We call upon the federal government to prepare and publish annual reports comparing funding for the education of First Nations children on and off reserves, as well as educational and income attainments of Aboriginal peoples in Canada compared with non-Aboriginal people.
10) We call on the federal government to draft new Aboriginal education legislation with the full participation and informed consent of Aboriginal peoples. The new legislation would include a commitment to sufficient funding and would incorporate the following principles:
   i. Providing sufficient funding to close identified educational achievement gaps within one generation.
   ii. Improving education attainment levels and success rates.
   iii. Developing culturally appropriate curricula.
   iv. Protecting the right to Aboriginal languages, including the teaching of Aboriginal languages as credit courses.
   v. Enabling parental and community responsibility, control, and accountability, similar to what parents enjoy in public school systems.
   vi. Enabling parents to fully participate in the education of their children.
   vii. Respecting and honouring Treaty relationships.
11) We call upon the federal government to provide adequate funding to end the backlog of First Nations students seeking a post-secondary education.
12) We call upon the federal, provincial, territorial, and Aboriginal governments to develop culturally appropriate early childhood education programs for Aboriginal families.

Language and culture

13) We call upon the federal government to acknowledge that Aboriginal rights include Aboriginal language rights.

14) We call upon the federal government to enact an Aboriginal Languages Act that incorporates the following principles:
    i. Aboriginal languages are a fundamental and valued element of Canadian culture and society, and there is an urgency to preserve them.
    ii. Aboriginal language rights are reinforced by the Treaties.
    iii. The federal government has a responsibility to provide sufficient funds for Aboriginal-language revitalization and preservation.
    iv. The preservation, revitalization, and strengthening of Aboriginal languages and cultures are best managed by Aboriginal peoples and communities.
    v. Funding for Aboriginal language initiatives must reflect the diversity of Aboriginal languages.

15) We call upon the federal government to appoint, in consultation with Aboriginal groups, an Aboriginal Languages Commissioner. The commissioner should help promote Aboriginal languages and report on the adequacy of federal funding of Aboriginal-languages initiatives.

16) We call upon post-secondary institutions to create university and college degree and diploma programs in Aboriginal languages.

17) We call upon all levels of government to enable residential school Survivors and their families to reclaim names changed by the residential school system by waiving administrative costs for a period of five years for the name-change process and the revision of official identity documents, such as birth certificates, passports, driver's licenses, health cards, status cards, and social insurance numbers.

Health

18) We call upon the federal, provincial, territorial, and Aboriginal governments to acknowledge that the current state of Aboriginal health in Canada is a direct result of previous Canadian government policies, including residential schools, and to recognize and implement the health-care rights of Aboriginal peoples as identified in international law, constitutional law, and under the Treaties.

19) We call upon the federal government, in consultation with Aboriginal peoples, to establish measurable goals to identify and close the gaps in health outcomes between Aboriginal and non-Aboriginal communities, and to publish annual progress reports and assess long-term trends. Such efforts would focus on indicators such as: infant mortality, maternal health, suicide, mental health, addictions, life expectancy, birth rates, infant and child health issues, chronic diseases, illness and injury incidence, and the availability of appropriate health services.

20) In order to address the jurisdictional disputes concerning Aboriginal people who do not reside on reserves, we call upon the federal government to recognize, respect, and address the distinct health needs of the Métis, Inuit, and off-reserve Aboriginal peoples.

21) We call upon the federal government to provide sustainable funding for existing and new Aboriginal healing centres to address the physical, mental, emotional, and spiritual harms caused by residential schools, and to ensure that the funding of healing centres in Nunavut and the Northwest Territories is a priority.

22) We call upon those who can effect change within the Canadian health-care system to recognize the value of Aboriginal healing practices and use them in the treatment of Aboriginal patients in collaboration with Aboriginal healers and Elders where requested by Aboriginal patients.

23) We call upon all levels of government to:
    i. Increase the number of Aboriginal professionals working in the health-care field.
    ii. Ensure the retention of Aboriginal health-care providers in Aboriginal communities.
    iii. Provide cultural competency training for all health-care professionals.

24) We call upon medical and nursing schools in Canada to require all students to take a course dealing with Aboriginal health issues, including the history and legacy of residential schools, the United Nations Declaration on the Rights of Indigenous Peoples, Treaties and Aboriginal rights, and Indigenous teachings and practices. This will require skills-based training in intercultural competency, conflict resolution, human rights, and anti-racism.

Justice

25) We call upon the federal government to establish a written policy that reaffirms the independence of the Royal Canadian Mounted Police to investigate crimes in which the government has its own interest as a potential or real party in civil litigation.

26) We call upon the federal, provincial, and territorial governments to review and amend their respective statutes of limitations to ensure that they conform with the principle that governments and other entities cannot rely on limitation defences to defend legal actions of historical abuse brought by Aboriginal people.

27) We call upon the Federation of Law Societies of Canada to ensure that lawyers receive appropriate cultural competency training, which includes the history and legacy of residential schools, the United Nations Declaration on the Rights of Indigenous Peoples, Treaties and Aboriginal rights, Indigenous law, and Aboriginal–Crown relations. This will require skills-based training in intercultural competency, conflict resolution, human rights, and anti-racism.

28) We call upon law schools in Canada to require all law students to take a course in Aboriginal people and the law, which includes the history and legacy of residential schools, the United Nations Declaration on the Rights

of Indigenous Peoples, Treaties and Aboriginal rights, Indigenous law, and Aboriginal–Crown relations. This will require skills-based training in intercultural competency, conflict resolution, human rights, and anti-racism.

29) We call upon the parties and, in particular, the federal government, to work collaboratively with plaintiffs not included in the Indian Residential Schools Settlement Agreement to have disputed legal issues determined expeditiously on an agreed set of facts.

30) We call upon federal, provincial, and territorial governments to commit to eliminating the overrepresentation of Aboriginal people in custody over the next decade, and to issue detailed annual reports that monitor and evaluate progress in doing so.

31) We call upon the federal, provincial, and territorial governments to provide sufficient and stable funding to implement and evaluate community sanctions that will provide realistic alternatives to imprisonment for Aboriginal offenders and respond to the underlying causes of offending.

32) We call upon the federal government to amend the Criminal Code to allow trial judges, upon giving reasons, to depart from mandatory minimum sentences and restrictions on the use of conditional sentences.

33) We call upon the federal, provincial, and territorial governments to recognize as a high priority the need to address and prevent Fetal Alcohol Spectrum Disorder (FASD), and to develop, in collaboration with Aboriginal peoples, FASD preventive programs that can be delivered in a culturally appropriate manner.

34) We call upon the governments of Canada, the provinces, and territories to undertake reforms to the criminal justice system to better address the needs of offenders with Fetal Alcohol Spectrum Disorder (FASD), including:
    i. Providing increased community resources and powers for courts to ensure that FASD is properly diagnosed, and that appropriate community supports are in place for those with FASD.
    ii. Enacting statutory exemptions from mandatory minimum sentences of imprisonment for offenders affected by FASD.
    iii. Providing community, correctional, and parole resources to maximize the ability of people with FASD to live in the community.
    iv. Adopting appropriate evaluation mechanisms to measure the effectiveness of such programs and ensure community safety.

35) We call upon the federal government to eliminate barriers to the creation of additional Aboriginal healing lodges within the federal correctional system.

36) We call upon the federal, provincial, and territorial governments to work with Aboriginal communities to provide culturally relevant services to inmates on issues such as substance abuse, family and domestic violence, and overcoming the experience of having been sexually abused.

37) We call upon the federal government to provide more supports for Aboriginal programming in halfway houses and parole services.

38) We call upon the federal, provincial, territorial, and Aboriginal governments to commit to eliminating the overrepresentation of Aboriginal youth in custody over the next decade.

39) We call upon the federal government to develop a national plan to collect and publish data on the criminal victimization of Aboriginal peoples, including data related to homicide and family violence victimization.

40) We call on all levels of government, in collaboration with Aboriginal people, to create adequately funded and accessible Aboriginal-specific victim programs and services with appropriate evaluation mechanisms.

41) We call upon the federal government, in consultation with Aboriginal organizations, to appoint a public inquiry into the causes of, and remedies for, the disproportionate victimization of Aboriginal women and girls. The inquiry's mandate would include:
    i. Investigation into missing and murdered Aboriginal women and girls.
    ii. Links to the intergenerational legacy of residential schools.

42) We call upon the federal, provincial, and territorial governments to commit to the recognition and implementation of Aboriginal justice systems in a manner consistent with the Treaty and Aboriginal rights of Aboriginal peoples, the Constitution Act, 1982, and the United Nations Declaration on the Rights of Indigenous Peoples, endorsed by Canada in November 2012.

RECONCILIATION

Canadian Governments and the United Nations Declaration on the Rights of Indigenous Peoples

43) We call upon federal, provincial, territorial, and municipal governments to fully adopt and implement the United Nations Declaration on the Rights of Indigenous Peoples as the framework for reconciliation.

44) We call upon the Government of Canada to develop a national action plan, strategies, and other concrete measures to achieve the goals of the United Nations Declaration on the Rights of Indigenous Peoples.

Royal Proclamation and Covenant of Reconciliation

45) We call upon the Government of Canada, on behalf of all Canadians, to jointly develop with Aboriginal peoples a Royal Proclamation of Reconciliation to be issued by the Crown. The proclamation would build on the Royal Proclamation of 1763 and the Treaty of Niagara of 1764, and reaffirm the nation-to-nation relationship between Aboriginal peoples and the Crown. The proclamation would include, but not be limited to, the following commitments:

i. Repudiate concepts used to justify European sovereignty over Indigenous lands and peoples such as the Doctrine of Discovery and terra nullius.
ii. Adopt and implement the United Nations Declaration on the Rights of Indigenous Peoples as the framework for reconciliation.
iii. Renew or establish Treaty relationships based on principles of mutual recognition, mutual respect, and shared responsibility for maintaining those relationships into the future.
iv. Reconcile Aboriginal and Crown constitutional and legal orders to ensure that Aboriginal peoples are full partners in Confederation, including the recognition and integration of Indigenous laws and legal traditions in negotiation and implementation processes involving Treaties, land claims, and other constructive agreements.

46) We call upon the parties to the Indian Residential Schools Settlement Agreement to develop and sign a Covenant of Reconciliation that would identify principles for working collaboratively to advance reconciliation in Canadian society, and that would include, but not be limited to:
i. Reaffirmation of the parties' commitment to reconciliation.
ii. Repudiation of concepts used to justify European sovereignty over Indigenous lands and peoples, such as the Doctrine of Discovery and terra nullius, and the reformation of laws, governance structures, and policies within their respective institutions that continue to rely on such concepts.
iii. Full adoption and implementation of the United Nations Declaration on the Rights of Indigenous Peoples as the framework for reconciliation.
iv. Support for the renewal or establishment of Treaty relationships based on principles of mutual recognition, mutual respect, and shared responsibility for maintaining those relationships into the future.
v. Enabling those excluded from the Settlement Agreement to sign onto the Covenant of Reconciliation.
vi. Enabling additional parties to sign onto the Covenant of Reconciliation.

47) We call upon federal, provincial, territorial, and municipal governments to repudiate concepts used to justify European sovereignty over Indigenous peoples and lands, such as the Doctrine of Discovery and terra nullius, and to reform those laws, government policies, and litigation strategies that continue to rely on such concepts.

Settlement Agreement Parties and the United Nations Declaration on the Rights of Indigenous Peoples

48) We call upon the church parties to the Settlement Agreement, and all other faith groups and interfaith social justice groups in Canada who have not already done so, to formally adopt and comply with the principles, norms, and standards of the United Nations Declaration on the Rights of Indigenous Peoples as a framework for reconciliation. This would include, but not be limited to, the following commitments:
i. Ensuring that their institutions, policies, programs, and practices comply with the United Nations Declaration on the Rights of Indigenous Peoples.
ii. Respecting Indigenous peoples' right to self-determination in spiritual matters, including the right to practise, develop, and teach their own spiritual and religious traditions, customs, and ceremonies, consistent with Article 12:1 of the United Nations Declaration on the Rights of Indigenous Peoples.
iii. Engaging in ongoing public dialogue and actions to support the United Nations Declaration on the Rights of Indigenous Peoples.
iv. Issuing a statement no later than March 31, 2016, from all religious denominations and faith groups, as to how they will implement the United Nations Declaration on the Rights of Indigenous Peoples.

49) We call upon all religious denominations and faith groups who have not already done so to repudiate concepts used to justify European sovereignty over Indigenous lands and peoples, such as the Doctrine of Discovery and terra nullius.

Equity for Aboriginal Peoples in the Legal System

50) In keeping with the United Nations Declaration on the Rights of Indigenous Peoples, we call upon the federal government, in collaboration with Aboriginal organizations, to fund the establishment of Indigenous law institutes for the development, use, and understanding of Indigenous laws and access to justice in accordance with the unique cultures of Aboriginal peoples in Canada.

51) We call upon the Government of Canada, as an obligation of its fiduciary responsibility, to develop a policy of transparency by publishing legal opinions it develops and upon which it acts or intends to act, in regard to the scope and extent of Aboriginal and Treaty rights.

52) We call upon the Government of Canada, provincial and territorial governments, and the courts to adopt the following legal principles:
i. Aboriginal title claims are accepted once the Aboriginal claimant has established occupation over a particular territory at a particular point in time.
ii. Once Aboriginal title has been established, the burden of proving any limitation on any rights arising from the existence of that title shifts to the party asserting such a limitation.

National Council for Reconciliation

53) We call upon the Parliament of Canada, in consultation and collaboration with Aboriginal peoples, to enact legislation to establish a National Council for Reconciliation. The legislation would establish the council as an independent, national, oversight body with membership

jointly appointed by the Government of Canada and national Aboriginal organizations, and consisting of Aboriginal and non-Aboriginal members. Its mandate would include, but not be limited to, the following:

i. Monitor, evaluate, and report annually to Parliament and the people of Canada on the Government of Canada's post-apology progress on reconciliation to ensure that government accountability for reconciling the relationship between Aboriginal peoples and the Crown is maintained in the coming years.

ii. Monitor, evaluate, and report to Parliament and the people of Canada on reconciliation progress across all levels and sectors of Canadian society, including the implementation of the Truth and Reconciliation Commission of Canada's Calls to Action.

iii. Develop and implement a multi-year National Action Plan for Reconciliation, which includes research and policy development, public education programs, and resources.

iv. Promote public dialogue, public/private partnerships, and public initiatives for reconciliation.

54) We call upon the Government of Canada to provide multi-year funding for the National Council for Reconciliation to ensure that it has the financial, human, and technical resources required to conduct its work, including the endowment of a National Reconciliation Trust to advance the cause of reconciliation.

55) We call upon all levels of government to provide annual reports or any current data requested by the National Council for Reconciliation so that it can report on the progress towards reconciliation. The reports or data would include, but not be limited to:

i. The number of Aboriginal children—including Métis and Inuit children—in care, compared with non-Aboriginal children, the reasons for apprehension, and the total spending on preventive and care services by child-welfare agencies.

ii. Comparative funding for the education of First Nations children on and off reserves.

iii. The educational and income attainments of Aboriginal peoples in Canada compared with non-Aboriginal people.

iv. Progress on closing the gaps between Aboriginal and non-Aboriginal communities in a number of health indicators such as: infant mortality, maternal health, suicide, mental health, addictions, life expectancy, birth rates, infant and child health issues, chronic diseases, illness and injury incidence, and the availability of appropriate health services.

v. Progress on eliminating the overrepresentation of Aboriginal children in youth custody over the next decade.

vi. Progress on reducing the rate of criminal victimization of Aboriginal peoples, including data related to homicide and family violence victimization and other crimes.

vii. Progress on reducing the overrepresentation of Aboriginal peoples in the justice and correctional systems.

56) We call upon the prime minister of Canada to formally respond to the report of the National Council for Reconciliation by issuing an annual "State of Aboriginal Peoples" report, which would outline the government's plans for advancing the cause of reconciliation.

Professional Development and Training for Public Servants

57) We call upon federal, provincial, territorial, and municipal governments to provide education to public servants on the history of Aboriginal peoples, including the history and legacy of residential schools, the United Nations Declaration on the Rights of Indigenous Peoples, Treaties and Aboriginal rights, Indigenous law, and Aboriginal–Crown relations. This will require skills-based training in intercultural competency, conflict resolution, human rights, and anti-racism.

Church Apologies and Reconciliation

58) We call upon the Pope to issue an apology to Survivors, their families, and communities for the Roman Catholic Church's role in the spiritual, cultural, emotional, physical, and sexual abuse of First Nations, Inuit, and Métis children in Catholic-run residential schools. We call for that apology to be similar to the 2010 apology issued to Irish victims of abuse and to occur within one year of the issuing of this Report and to be delivered by the Pope in Canada.

59) We call upon church parties to the Settlement Agreement to develop ongoing education strategies to ensure that their respective congregations learn about their church's role in colonization, the history and legacy of residential schools, and why apologies to former residential school students, their families, and communities were necessary.

60) We call upon leaders of the church parties to the Settlement Agreement and all other faiths, in collaboration with Indigenous spiritual leaders, Survivors, schools of theology, seminaries, and other religious training centres, to develop and teach curriculum for all student clergy, and all clergy and staff who work in Aboriginal communities, on the need to respect Indigenous spirituality in its own right, the history and legacy of residential schools and the roles of the church parties in that system, the history and legacy of religious conflict in Aboriginal families and communities, and the responsibility that churches have to mitigate such conflicts and prevent spiritual violence.

61) We call upon church parties to the Settlement Agreement, in collaboration with Survivors and representatives of Aboriginal organizations, to establish permanent funding to Aboriginal people for:

i. Community-controlled healing and reconciliation projects.

ii. Community-controlled culture and language-revitalization projects.

iii. Community-controlled education and relationship-building projects.

iv. Regional dialogues for Indigenous spiritual leaders and youth to discuss Indigenous spirituality, self-determination, and reconciliation.

Education for reconciliation

62) We call upon the federal, provincial, and territorial governments, in consultation and collaboration with Survivors, Aboriginal peoples, and educators, to:

i. Make age-appropriate curriculum on residential schools, Treaties, and Aboriginal peoples' historical and contemporary contributions to Canada a mandatory education requirement for Kindergarten to Grade Twelve students.

ii. Provide the necessary funding to post-secondary institutions to educate teachers on how to integrate Indigenous knowledge and teaching methods into classrooms.

iii. Provide the necessary funding to Aboriginal schools to utilize Indigenous knowledge and teaching methods in classrooms.

iv. Establish senior-level positions in government at the assistant deputy minister level or higher dedicated to Aboriginal content in education.

63) We call upon the Council of Ministers of Education, Canada to maintain an annual commitment to Aboriginal education issues, including:

i. Developing and implementing Kindergarten to Grade Twelve curriculum and learning resources on Aboriginal peoples in Canadian history, and the history and legacy of residential schools.

ii. Sharing information and best practices on teaching curriculum related to residential schools and Aboriginal history.

iii. Building student capacity for intercultural understanding, empathy, and mutual respect.

iv. Identifying teacher-training needs relating to the above.

64) We call upon all levels of government that provide public funds to denominational schools to require such schools to provide an education on comparative religious studies, which must include a segment on Aboriginal spiritual beliefs and practices developed in collaboration with Aboriginal Elders.

65) We call upon the federal government, through the Social Sciences and Humanities Research Council, and in collaboration with Aboriginal peoples, post-secondary institutions and educators, and the National Centre for Truth and Reconciliation and its partner institutions, to establish a national research program with multi-year funding to advance understanding of reconciliation.

Youth Programs

66) We call upon the federal government to establish multi-year funding for community-based youth organizations to deliver programs on reconciliation, and establish a national network to share information and best practices.

Museums and Archives

67) We call upon the federal government to provide funding to the Canadian Museums Association to undertake, in collaboration with Aboriginal peoples, a national review of museum policies and best practices to determine the level of compliance with the United Nations Declaration on the Rights of Indigenous Peoples and to make recommendations.

68) We call upon the federal government, in collaboration with Aboriginal peoples, and the Canadian Museums Association to mark the 150th anniversary of Canadian Confederation in 2017 by establishing a dedicated national funding program for commemoration projects on the theme of reconciliation.

69) We call upon Library and Archives Canada to:

i. Fully adopt and implement the United Nations Declaration on the Rights of Indigenous Peoples and the United Nations Joinet-Orentlicher Principles, as related to Aboriginal peoples' inalienable right to know the truth about what happened and why, with regard to human rights violations committed against them in the residential schools.

ii. Ensure that its record holdings related to residential schools are accessible to the public.

iii. Commit more resources to its public education materials and programming on residential schools.

70) We call upon the federal government to provide funding to the Canadian Association of Archivists to undertake, in collaboration with Aboriginal peoples, a national review of archival policies and best practices to:

i. Determine the level of compliance with the United Nations Declaration on the Rights of Indigenous Peoples and the United Nations Joinet-Orentlicher Principles, as related to Aboriginal peoples' inalienable right to know the truth about what happened and why, with regard to human rights violations committed against them in the residential schools.

ii. Produce a report with recommendations for full implementation of these international mechanisms as a reconciliation framework for Canadian archives.

Missing Children and Burial Information

71) We call upon all chief coroners and provincial vital statistics agencies that have not provided to the Truth and Reconciliation Commission of Canada their records on the deaths of Aboriginal children in the care of residential school authorities to make these documents available to the National Centre for Truth and Reconciliation.

72) We call upon the federal government to allocate sufficient resources to the National Centre for Truth and Reconciliation to allow it to develop and maintain the National Residential School Student Death Register established by the Truth and Reconciliation Commission of Canada.

73) We call upon the federal government to work with churches, Aboriginal communities, and former residential school students to establish and maintain

an online registry of residential school cemeteries, including, where possible, plot maps showing the location of deceased residential school children.

74) We call upon the federal government to work with the churches and Aboriginal community leaders to inform the families of children who died at residential schools of the child's burial location, and to respond to families' wishes for appropriate commemoration ceremonies and markers, and reburial in home communities where requested.

75) We call upon the federal government to work with provincial, territorial, and municipal governments, churches, Aboriginal communities, former residential school students, and current landowners to develop and implement strategies and procedures for the ongoing identification, documentation, maintenance, commemoration, and protection of residential school cemeteries or other sites at which residential school children were buried. This is to include the provision of appropriate memorial ceremonies and commemorative markers to honour the deceased children.

76) We call upon the parties engaged in the work of documenting, maintaining, commemorating, and protecting residential school cemeteries to adopt strategies in accordance with the following principles:

   i. The Aboriginal community most affected shall lead the development of such strategies.
   ii. Information shall be sought from residential school Survivors and other Knowledge Keepers in the development of such strategies.
   iii. Aboriginal protocols shall be respected before any potentially invasive technical inspection and investigation of a cemetery site.

National Centre for Truth and Reconciliation

77) We call upon provincial, territorial, municipal, and community archives to work collaboratively with the National Centre for Truth and Reconciliation to identify and collect copies of all records relevant to the history and legacy of the residential school system, and to provide these to the National Centre for Truth and Reconciliation.

78) We call upon the Government of Canada to commit to making a funding contribution of $10 million over seven years to the National Centre for Truth and Reconciliation, plus an additional amount to assist communities to research and produce histories of their own residential school experience and their involvement in truth, healing, and reconciliation.

Commemoration

79) We call upon the federal government, in collaboration with Survivors, Aboriginal organizations, and the arts community, to develop a reconciliation framework for Canadian heritage and commemoration. This would include, but not be limited to:

   i. Amending the Historic Sites and Monuments Act to include First Nations, Inuit, and Métis representation on the Historic Sites and Monuments Board of Canada and its Secretariat.
   ii. Revising the policies, criteria, and practices of the National Program of Historical Commemoration to integrate Indigenous history, heritage values, and memory practices into Canada's national heritage and history.
   iii. Developing and implementing a national heritage plan and strategy for commemorating residential school sites, the history and legacy of residential schools, and the contributions of Aboriginal peoples to Canada's history.

80) We call upon the federal government, in collaboration with Aboriginal peoples, to establish, as a statutory holiday, a National Day for Truth and Reconciliation to honour Survivors, their families, and communities, and ensure that public commemoration of the history and legacy of residential schools remains a vital component of the reconciliation process.

81) We call upon the federal government, in collaboration with Survivors and their organizations, and other parties to the Settlement Agreement, to commission and install a publicly accessible, highly visible, Residential Schools National Monument in the city of Ottawa to honour Survivors and all the children who were lost to their families and communities.

82) We call upon provincial and territorial governments, in collaboration with Survivors and their organizations, and other parties to the Settlement Agreement, to commission and install a publicly accessible, highly visible, Residential Schools Monument in each capital city to honour Survivors and all the children who were lost to their families and communities.

83) We call upon the Canada Council for the Arts to establish, as a funding priority, a strategy for Indigenous and non-Indigenous artists to undertake collaborative projects and produce works that contribute to the reconciliation process.

Media and Reconciliation

84) We call upon the federal government to restore and increase funding to the CBC/Radio-Canada, to enable Canada's national public broadcaster to support reconciliation, and be properly reflective of the diverse cultures, languages, and perspectives of Aboriginal peoples, including, but not limited to:

   i. Increasing Aboriginal programming, including Aboriginal-language speakers.
   ii. Increasing equitable access for Aboriginal peoples to jobs, leadership positions, and professional development opportunities within the organization.
   iii. Continuing to provide dedicated news coverage and online public information resources on issues of concern to Aboriginal peoples and all Canadians, including the history and legacy of residential schools and the reconciliation process.

85) We call upon the Aboriginal Peoples Television Network, as an independent non-profit broadcaster with programming by, for, and about Aboriginal peoples, to support reconciliation, including but not limited to:

   i. Continuing to provide leadership in programming and organizational culture that reflects the diverse cultures, languages, and perspectives of Aboriginal peoples.

   ii. Continuing to develop media initiatives that inform and educate the Canadian public, and connect Aboriginal and non-Aboriginal Canadians.

86) We call upon Canadian journalism programs and media schools to require education for all students on the history of Aboriginal peoples, including the history and legacy of residential schools, the United Nations Declaration on the Rights of Indigenous Peoples, Treaties and Aboriginal rights, Indigenous law, and Aboriginal–Crown relations.

Sports and Reconciliation

87) We call upon all levels of government, in collaboration with Aboriginal peoples, sports halls of fame, and other relevant organizations, to provide public education that tells the national story of Aboriginal athletes in history.

88) We call upon all levels of government to take action to ensure long-term Aboriginal athlete development and growth, and continued support for the North American Indigenous Games, including funding to host the games and for provincial and territorial team preparation and travel.

89) We call upon the federal government to amend the Physical Activity and Sport Act to support reconciliation by ensuring that policies to promote physical activity as a fundamental element of health and well-being, reduce barriers to sports participation, increase the pursuit of excellence in sport, and build capacity in the Canadian sport system, are inclusive of Aboriginal peoples.

90) We call upon the federal government to ensure that national sports policies, programs, and initiatives are inclusive of Aboriginal peoples, including, but not limited to, establishing:

   i. In collaboration with provincial and territorial governments, stable funding for, and access to, community sports programs that reflect the diverse cultures and traditional sporting activities of Aboriginal peoples.

   ii. An elite athlete development program for Aboriginal athletes.

   iii. Programs for coaches, trainers, and sports officials that are culturally relevant for Aboriginal peoples.

   iv. Anti-racism awareness and training programs.

91) We call upon the officials and host countries of international sporting events such as the Olympics, Pan Am, and Commonwealth games to ensure that Indigenous peoples' territorial protocols are respected, and local Indigenous communities are engaged in all aspects of planning and participating in such events.

Business and Reconciliation

92) We call upon the corporate sector in Canada to adopt the United Nations Declaration on the Rights of Indigenous Peoples as a reconciliation framework and to apply its principles, norms, and standards to corporate policy and core operational activities involving Indigenous peoples and their lands and resources. This would include, but not be limited to, the following:

   i. Commit to meaningful consultation, building respectful relationships, and obtaining the free, prior, and informed consent of Indigenous peoples before proceeding with economic development projects.

   ii. Ensure that Aboriginal peoples have equitable access to jobs, training, and education opportunities in the corporate sector, and that Aboriginal communities gain long-term sustainable benefits from economic development projects.

   iii. Provide education for management and staff on the history of Aboriginal peoples, including the history and legacy of residential schools, the United Nations Declaration on the Rights of Indigenous Peoples, Treaties and Aboriginal rights, Indigenous law, and Aboriginal–Crown relations. This will require skills-based training in intercultural competency, conflict resolution, human rights, and anti-racism.

Newcomers to Canada

93) We call upon the federal government, in collaboration with the national Aboriginal organizations, to revise the information kit for newcomers to Canada and its citizenship test to reflect a more inclusive history of the diverse Aboriginal peoples of Canada, including information about the Treaties and the history of residential schools.

94) We call upon the Government of Canada to replace the Oath of Citizenship with the following:

> I swear (or affirm) that I will be faithful and bear true allegiance to Her Majesty Queen Elizabeth II, Queen of Canada, Her Heirs and Successors, and that I will faithfully observe the laws of Canada including Treaties with Indigenous Peoples, and fulfill my duties as a Canadian citizen.

Credits

2, Rob Marmion / Shutterstock
4, Courtesy of City of Vancouver Archives / Thomson, Stuart (Photographer)
7, Alexandre Zveiger / Shutterstock
8, Food Lodging & Youth Counselling; Canadian Social Safety Net Open, John Larter (Cartoonist), *Calgary Sun* (The SFU Library Editorial Cartoons Collection)
10, Karnaval2018 / Shutterstock
11, Toronto Housing Corporation / City of Toronto
12, Ocskay Bence / Shutterstock
13, CP Photo / Chuck Stoody
14, Photographee.eu / Shutterstock
15, Gary Blakeley
17, Adobe Stock / Alexsokolov
18, Nadino / Shutterstock
19, Catalin Petolea / Shutterstock
20, The Canadian Press / Cole Burston
23, Photo courtesy of Mercedes Sinclair
24, Nagel Photography / Shutterstock
25, Monkey Business Images / Shutterstock
26, Mekcar / Shutterstock
30, Fifth Floor Photography and the Family Association for Mental Health Everywhere (FAME)
32, Men eating bread and soup in a bread-line during the Great Depression / Wikimeia Commons
34, Dorothea Lange / Wikimedia Commons
37, Lewis W. Hine, 1909 (Library of Congress) / Wikimedia Commons
38, Pieter Bruegel the Elder / Wikimedia Commons
39, United Neighborhood Houses, New York (www.unhny.org)
40, Chicago Daily News / Wikimedia Commons
41, Needham, Geo C. (1884), "Street Arabs and Gutter Snipes" / Wikimedia Commons
43, A Canadian soldier in a trench in 1916 during WWI / Public domain image
44, Courtesy of Library and Archives Canada
45, Courtesy of Library and Archives Canada (C-029399)
47, The Sisters of Mercy, 1859 (oil on canvas) / Wikimedia Commons
48, Bibliothèque et Archives nationales du Québec / Wikimedia Commons
51, Courtesy of Library and Archives Canada (PA-133616)
53, Monkey Business Images / Shutterstock
55, The Canadian Press / Adrian Wyld; Inset photgraphs, courtesy of Cindy Blackstock
64, Dario Ayala / Montréal Gazette
66, Dr. Morley Read / Shutterstock
68, Markus Mainka / Shutterstock
70, Reproduced with permission from the BC Association of Social Workers
71, Photo courtesy of McGill University Archives
72, Photo courtesy of Louise Carignan
74, © iStockphoto / Robert Churchill
76, City of Toronto, Archive Series (1908); Fonds 427, Series 1908, File 559, Item 2
78, SW Productions, Photodisc / Getty Images
80, Monkey Business Images / Shutterstock
82, A Katz / Shutterstock
83, The Canadian Press / Graham Hughes
84, Lopolo / Shutterstock
86, Rawpixel.com / Shutterstock
87, Lisa F. Young / Shutterstock
90, Native Counselling Services of Alberta (NCSA) (www.ncsa.ca)
91, Courtesy of Dr. Patti LaBoucane-Benson
92, Monkey Business Images / Shutterstock
94, Photographee.eu / Shutterstock
96, Dallas Events Inc / Shutterstock
97, Robert Kneschke / Shutterstock
98, Adam Gregor / Shutterstock
100, Courtesy of Michael Mandiberg; © Michael Mandiberg
102, Fifth Floor Photography and the Family Association for Mental Health Everywhere
104, Rawpixel.com / Shutterstock
106, http://blogs.newschool.edu / http://goo.gl/Wrs7m5
108, Antonio Guillem / Shutterstock
110, Office of National Statistics
111, Photographee.eu / Shutterstock
112, ©iStockphoto.com / Zhang Bo
113, Image Copyright JustASC 2009 Used under license from Shutterstock, Inc.
115, rSnapshotPhotos / Shutterstock
116, Monkey Business Images / Shutterstock
118, Wavebreakmedia / Shutterstock
119, Monkey Business Images / Shutterstock
120, ©Harinder Kau / Wikimedia Commons
121, Rawpixel.com / Shutterstock
122, RyFlip / Shutterstock
123, SpeedKingz / Shutterstock
124, SimonP / Wikimedia Commons
125, Photo: International Association for Social Work with Groups (www.aswg.org)
126, (Bottom) Sergei Bachlakov / Shutterstock; (Top) Wikimedia Commons (Unknown Source)
128, Paulo Freire (1921–1997) / www.fotoseimagenes.net
130, Edward Lynch, World-Telegram staff photographer / Wikimedia Commons
133, Monkey Business Images / Shutterstock
134, Courtesy of Susan Macphail
136, Monkey Business Images / Shutterstock
138, Pixelmemoirs / Depositphotos (ID: 31268705)
140, Lisa F. Young / Shutterstock
143, CP Images / Julian Wein
145, Tomertu / Shutterstock
146, Alan Cleaver / Flickr (https://goo.gl/aUABbx)
148, Luxorphoto / Shutterstock
150, The Canadian Press / Adrian Wyld
152, CP Photo / John Woods
154, Facebook / *The Huffington Post* (http://goo.gl/HWBnlF)
156, The Canadian Press / Fred Chartrand
158, Zurijeta / Shutterstock
160, Alray.nelson / Flickr (https://goo.gl/833pRd)
161, Nicolas Raymond / Shutterstock
170, Photo courtesy of Marian Anderberg
172, Gary Blakeley
174, Photo: Hôpital Montfort (www.hopital-montfort.com)
176, Library and Archives Canada / Ted Grant Fonds (Item No. 61-1180, Fr. 25-30)
177, CP Photo / *Globe and Mail* / Boris Spremo
178, CP Photo / Jonathan Hayward
180, Volt Collection / Shutterstock
182, CP Photo / Darryl Dyck
186, Rmnoa357 / Shutterstock
187, Artwork titled "All Canadians Share a Page in Canada's History" courtesy of Izra Fitch, a winner of the 2010 Mathieu Da Costa Challenge
188, Flashon Studio / Shutterstock
189, Gary Blakeley
190, Photo courtesy of Conseil du patrimoine culturel du Québec
192, ©2009–2010, National Collaborating Centre for Aboriginal Health
193, First Nations Health Authority; digidreamgrafix / Shutterstock
195, ChameleonsEye / Shutterstock
202, Photo courtesy of Marg Hancock
204, Monkey Business Images / Shutterstock
206, Marjan Apostolovic / Shutterstock
208, Zurijeta / Shutterstock
210, Monkey Business Images / Shutterstock
214, Monkey Business Images / Shutterstock
216, The Mental Health Commission of Canada (www.mentalhealthcommission.ca)
218, Kamira / Shutterstock
219, Marcos Mesa Sam Wordley /

Shutterstock
221, © Simon Fraser University - University Communications / Wikimedia Commons
222, Vespa Photo / Shutterstock
223, Gary Blakeley
224, CP Images / Graham Hughes
225, Torstar News Service
229, Courtesy of The Jack Project
230, Courtesy of Jennifer Chouinard
231, Monkey Business Images / Shutterstock
233, Racorn / Shutterstock
240, Fifth Floor Photography and the Family Association for Mental Health Everywhere
242, Justin Tallis / AFP, Getty Images
244, Library of Congress, Washington, DC
246, © Helen Levine
247, CP Photo / Chuck Stoody
248, Ted Rhodes / Calgary Herald
250, Illustration credit: Amanda Colvin, Mellontree Studios
251, Monkey Business Images / Shutterstock
253, Courtesy of Winnie Ng
254, Wikimedia Commons (www.pexels.com)
256, Courtesy of the Vancouver Rape Relief and Women's Shelter
258, Sylv1rob1 / Shutterstock
259, Courtesy of the Women's Centre of Calgary
261, Photographee.eu / Shutterstock
263, Monkey Business Images / Shuttterstock
270, Courtesy of Diana Wark
272, Drpeterstockdale / Wikimedia Commons (Buffy Ste. Marie at Truth and Reconciliation Commission Concert, Ottawa)
274, Michal Onderco / Shutterstock
276, CP Photo / Robert Dall
279, Wikimedia Commons (Canadian_Pacific_2317.jpg)
281, Ken Gigliotti / *Winnipeg Free Press*
282, Edmund Metatawabin collection / Algoma University (www.residentialschool.ca)
284, Jaclyn Mcrae-Sadik (Captis Photos: http://captisnews.com)
286, UM News (University of Manitoba)
287, The Canadian Press / Sean Kilpatrick
288, First Nations Child and Family Caring Society of Canada
291, Canadian Light Source Inc. / Wikimedia Commons
292, Edmund Metatawabin collection at the University of Algoma / Wikimedia Commons (students from Fort Albany Residential School reading in class overseen by a nun c 1945)
293, John Lappa / *Sudbury Star* / Postmedia Network
294, CP Photo / Mario Beauregard
297, CP Images, Copyright ©2009
304, Courtesy of Adolphus Cameron
306, CP Photo / Patrick Doyle
308, Michaeljung / Shutterstock
311, Photo: *The Chronicle Herald*
312, CP Photo, Kevin Frayer
313, Wikimedia Commons/ DRheaume
314, Gary Blakeley
315, CP Photo / Fred Lum *(The Globe and Mail)*
316, Wikimedia Commons / Chensiyuan
318, Imanhakim / Shutterstock
320, DFID-UK Department for International Development
322, Photo: Actionplan.gc.ca.
324, James Gordon / Shutterstock (top); Markus Mainka / Shutterstock (bottom)
326, Nicolas Economou / Shutterstock
329, Lassedesignen / Shutterstock
336, Courtesy of Francis Boakye
338, Monkey Business Images / Shutterstock
340, Grafvision / Shutterstock
342, A and N photography / Shutterstock
345, Barking Water (2009) & Johnny Tootall (Canada, 2005)
346, Belushi / Shutterstock
347, CP Photo / Fred Chartrand
348, Davids' Adventures / Shutterstock
350, Monkey Business Images / Shutterstock
352, SpeedKingz / Shutterstock
353, AdobeStock / Photographee.eu
354, The Canadian Press / Frank Gunn
355, Ruslan Guzov / Shutterstock
356, Monkey Business Images / Shutterstock
357, Alexander Raths / Shutterstock
359, Fotoluminate LLC / Shutterstock
360, Tom Wang / Shutterstock
368, Courtesy of Lorna MacGregor
370, Gary Blakeley
372, Gary Blakeley
374, Lightwavemedia / Shutterstock
375, CP Photo / AP Photo, stf
377, Max Halberstadt / Wikimedia Commons
379, Creatista / Shutterstock
380, Stefan Holm / Shutterstock
381, Wikimedia Commons / English Wikipedia
383, Kseniia Perminova / Shutterstock
384, The Canadian Press / Ian Jackson
385, The Canadian Press / Victoria Ahearn
386, Lisa Charbonneau / Shutterstock
388, © Jglsongs / Wikimedia Commons
389, Arindambanerjee / Shutterstock
391, The Canadian Press / Jason Halstead
393, Sergei Bachlakov / Shutterstock
402, Courtesy of Dillon Black
404, CP Photo / Nathan Denette
406, Wavebreakmedia / Shutterstock
406, Wavebreakmedia / Shutterstock
408, Viktorija Reuta / Shutterstock
409, CP Photo / © Copyright *The Globe and Mail*, Barrie Davis
412, Wikimedia Commons / TheTruthAbout
414, Belushi / Shutterstock
415, CP Photo / Dean Bennett
415, Rmnoa357 / Shutterstock
417, Blend Images / Shutterstock
421, Mezzotint / Shutterstock
422, Jaren Jai Wicklund / Shutterstock
430, Courtesy of Barb Juett
432, CP Photo / AP Photo, © Muhammed Muheisen
434, Jane Addams / Wikimedia Commons (Bain News Service)
439, Arindam Banerjee / Shutterstock
440, Ryan Rodrick Beiler / Shutterstock
442, Wikimedia Commons / Paulrudd
443, United Nations Human Development Programme, 2015
444, Wikimedia Commons / Blog do Planalto
445, United Nations Sustainable Development Goals (www.un.org/sustainabledevelopment)
446, Human Rights Denmark (http://goo.gl/NcRZzf)
449, Darryl Dyck / The Canadian Press (Public Domain Image)
450, Courtesy of Steven Hick
452, Erik Albers / Wikimedia Commons
454, Istvan Csak / Shutterstock
455, © Julien Harneis
462, Courtesy of Samantha McGavin

References

Aboriginal Healing Foundation. (2006). *Final Report of the Aboriginal Healing Foundation Volume III: Promising Healing Practices in Aboriginal Communities.* Aboriginal Healing Foundation: Ottawa, ON.

Absolon, K. (Minogiizhigokwe) (2009). Navigating the landscape of practice: Dbaagmowin of a Helper. In Bruyere, G., Anthony Hart, M. & Sinclair, R. (Eds.), *Wicihitowin: Aboriginal Social Work in Canada*. Black Point, N.S.: Fernwood Publishing.

Adams, C., Boucher, J., Cartier, G., Chalmers, D., et al. (2015). The helping horse: How equine assisted learning contributes to the wellbeing of First Nations youth in treatment for volatile substance misuse. *Human-Animal Interaction Bulletin*, 1(1), 52-75.

Adamson, N., et al. (1988). *Feminist Organizing for Change.* Toronto, ON: Oxford University Press.

Addams, J. (1961). *Twenty Years at Hull House.* New York, NY: Signet Books.

Alberta College of Social Workers. (2013). *Standards of Practice*. www.acsw.ab.ca

Alinsky, S. (1971). *Rules for Radicals: A Pragmatic Primer for Realistic Radicals.* New York, NY: Vintage Books.

Allan, B., & Smylie, J. (2015). *First Peoples, Second Class Treatment: The Role of Racism in the Health and Well-Being of Indigenous Peoples in Canada.* Toronto, ON: The Wellesley Institute.

Allen, M. (2014). *Victim Services in Canada, 2011/2012. Juristat*. Ottawa, ON: Canadian Centre for Justice Statistics,.

Allen, M. (2015). *Police-Reported Hate Crime in Canada, 2013. Juristat.* Ottawa, ON: Canadian Centre for Justice Statistics.

Allen, R. (1971). *The Social Passion: Religion and Social Reform in Canada, 1914-1928.* Toronto: University of Toronto Press.

American Art Therapy Association (2013). *What Is Art Therapy?* Retrieved from http://www.arttherapy.org/upload/whatisarttherapy.pdf.

Anglin, J. (2011). Making group home care a positive alternative, not the last resort. In Kufeldt, K. & McKenzie, B. (Eds.), *Child Welfare: Connecting Research, Policy, and Practice*. Waterloo, ON: Wilfrid Laurier University Press.

Armitage, A. (1970). *The First University Degree in Social Work.* Ottawa, ON: Canadian Association for Education in Social Service.

Armitage, A. (1993). Family and child welfare in First Nation communities. In Wharf, B. (Ed.), *Rethinking Child Welfare in Canada*. Toronto, ON: McClelland & Stewart Ltd.

Armstrong, P., Armstrong, H., and Neysmith, S. (2015). *Homecare for the Future.* Toronto, ON: Care Watch.

Arthur, N., Chaves, A., Este, D., Frideres, J., & Hrycak, N. (2008). Perceived discrimination by children of immigrant parents: Responses and resiliency. *Canadian Diversity*, 6(2), 69-74.

Assembly of Seven Generations (A7G). https://a7g.dotrust.org.

Auditor General. (2008). *May 2008 Report of the Auditor General of Canada*. Ottawa, ON: Office of the Auditor General of Canada. www.oag-bvg.gc.ca.

Auger, D. (2001). The Northern Ojibwe and their family law. Doctoral dissertation submitted to Osgood Hall Law School, York University. North York, ON: York University.

Aydemir, A., Chen, W.H., & Corak, M. (2005). Intergenerational earnings mobility among the children of Canadian immigrants. Analytical Studies Branch Research Paper Series. Catalogue no. 11F0019MIE. No 267. Ottawa, ON: Statistics Canada.

Bachi, K., Terkel, J., & Teichman, M. (2012). Equine-facilitated psychotherapy for at-risk adolescents: The influence on self-image, self-control and trust. *Clinical Child Psychology and Psychiatry*. 17(2), 298-312.

Bala, N. (2011). Setting the context: Child welfare law in Canada. In Kufelt, K. & McKenzie, B. (Eds.), *Child Welfare: Connecting Research, Policy, and Practice*, Waterloo, ON: Wilfrid Laurier University Press.

Balfour, M. (2004). *A Brief History of Aboriginal Child Removal in Canada.* Retrieved 8 Jan 2004 at http://www.allmyrelations.ca/north/time/time.html.

Baskin, Cindy. (2010). *Strong Helpers' Teachings: The Value of Indigenous Knowledges in the Helping Professions*. Toronto, ON: Canadian Scholars' Press, Inc.

Bauman, Z. (1989). *Modernity and the Holocaust.* New York, NY: Cornell University Press.

Bazron, Barbara J., Dennis, Karl W., & Isaacs, Mareasa R. (1989). Toward a culturally competent system of care: A monograph on effective services for minority children who are severely emotionally disturbed. National Institute of Mental Health, Child and Adolescent Service System Program. http://www.mhsoac.ca.gov/meetings/docs/Meetings/2010/June/CLCC_Tab_4_Towards_Culturally_Competent_System.pdf. Retrieved February 16, 2015.

Beck Institute for Cognitive Behavior Therapy. (n.d.). *What Is CBT: Frequently Asked Questions*. Bala Cynwyd, PA: Beck Institute for Cognitive Behavior Therapy.

Belanger, E., & Malenfant, C. (2005). *Population Projections of Visible Minority Groups, Canada, Provinces, and Regions, 2001-2017*. Catalogue no. 91-541. Ottawa, ON: Statistics Canada.

Bell, Banakonda Kennedy-Kish, Carniol, Ben, Baines, Donna, & Sinclair, Raven. (Forthcoming). *Case Critical: Social Services and Social Justice in Canada* (7th edition). Toronto, ON: Between the Lines.

Bell Let's Talk. (2015). 5 simple ways to help end the stigma around mental illness: Talking is the first step towards meaningful change and building greater awareness, acceptance, and action. www.letstalk.bell.ca.

Bhandari, B., Horvath, S., & To, R. (2006). Choices and voices of immigrant men: Reflections on social integration. *Canadian Ethnic Studies,* 38(1), 140-148.

Biles, J., Drover, G., Henley, M., Ibrahim, H., Lundy, C., & Yan, M. (2010). Introduction. *Canadian Social Work*, 12(2), 5-15.

Birnbaum, L., & Birnbaum, A. (2008). Mindful social work: From theory to practice. *Journal of Religion and Spirituality in Social Work, 27*(1-2), 87-104.

Blackstock, C. (2003). Restoring peace and harmony in First Nations communities. In Kufeldt, Kathleen and McKenzie, Brad (Eds.), *Child Welfare: Connecting Research, Policy and Practice*. Waterloo, ON: Wilfred Laurier University Press.

Blackstock, C. (2009). Reconciliation means not saying sorry twice: Lessons from child welfare. In *From Truth to Reconciliation: Transforming the Legacy of Residential Schools*. Ottawa, ON: Aboriginal Healing Foundation.

Blackstock, C., Clarke, S., Cullen, J., D'Hondt, J., & Formsma, J. (2004). *Keeping the Promise: The Convention on the Rights of the Child and the Lived Experience of First Nations Children and Youth.* Ottawa, ON: First Nations Child and Family Caring Society of Canada.

Blackstock, C., Cross, T., Brown, J., George, J., & Formsma, J. (2006). *Reconciliation in Child Welfare: Touchstones of Hope for Indigenous Children, Youth and Families.* Ottawa, ON: First Nations Child and Family Caring Society of Canada.

Blackstock, C., Prakash, T., Loxley, J., & Wien, F. (2005). *Wen:de: We Are Coming to the Light of Day.* Ottawa, ON: First Nations Child and Family Caring Society of Canada.

Blackstock, C., & Trocmé, N. (2005). Community-based child welfare for Aboriginal children: Supporting resilience through structural change. In M. Unger (Ed.), *Pathways to Resilience: A Handbook of Theory, Methods and Interventions.* Thousand Oaks, CA: SAGE.

Blackstock, Cindy. (2015). A MMIW inquiry must examine the child-welfare system. *The Globe and Mail* (December 2).

Blyth, J.A. 1972. *The Canadian Social Inheritance.* Toronto, ON: Copp Clark Publishing Co.

BMO Financial Group. (2013). The clock is ticking—Canadian boomers are more than $400,000 short of their ideal retirement nest egg. *News Release* (August 28). Bank of Montreal.

Bogaert, A.F. (2004). Asexuality: Prevalence and associated factors in a national probability sample. *The Journal of Sex Research.* 41(3), 279-87.

Boldt, M. (1993). *Surviving as Indians: The Challenge of Self-Government.* Toronto, ON: University of Toronto Press.

Bowe, F. (1978). *Handicapping America: Barriers to Disabled People.* New York, NY: Harper & Row.

Bratton, S., & Ray, D. (2000). What the research shows about play therapy. *International Journal of Play Therapy*, 9(1), 47-88.

Bratton, S.C., Ray, D., Rhine, T., & Jones, L. (2005). The efficacy of play therapy with children: A meta-analytic review of treatment outcomes. *Professional Psychology: Research and Practice*, 36(4), 376-390.

Breshears, E.M., Yeh, S., & Young, N.K. (2009). *Understanding Substance Abuse and Facilitating Recovery: A Guide for Child Welfare Workers.* Rockville, MD: Substance Abuse and Mental Health Services Administration.

British Columbia Children's Commission (1998). *Children's Commission Annual Report—1996/1997.* Victoria, BC: The Children's Commission, 1988-v.

Brooks, M. (2008). Imagining Canada, negotiating belonging: Understanding the experiences of racism of second generation Canadians of colour. *Canadian Diversity,* 6(2), 75-78.

Burgess, J.E. (2006). Hearing ordinary voices: Cultural studies, vernacular creativity and digital storytelling. *Continuum: Journal of Media and Cultural Studies,* 20(2), 201-214.

Caldwell, G. (1967). *Indian Residential Schools: A Research Study of the Child Care Programs of Nine Residential Schools in Saskatchewan.* Ottawa, ON: The Canadian Welfare Council.

Callahan, M., & Swift, K. (2007). Great expectations and unintended consequences: Risk assessment in child welfare in British Columbia. In Foster, L., & Wharf, B. (Eds.), *People, Politics, and Child Welfare in British Columbia* (pp. 158-183). Vancouver, BC: University of British Columbia Press.

Cameron, M. (2014). This is common factors. *Clinical Social Work Journal*, 42, 151-160.

Canada. (1996). *Report of the Royal Commission on Aboriginal Peoples.* Retrieved at: http://www.lop.parl.gc.ca/content/lop/researchpublications/prb9924-e.html.

Canadian Association of Social Workers. (2014). *Social Media Use and Social Work Practice.* Ottawa, ON: Canadian Association of Social Workers.

Canadian Centre for Justice Statistics (2013). *Family Violence in Canada: A Statistical Profile. Juristat.* Ottawa, ON: Statistics Canada.

Canadian Council for Refugees. (2014). *Temporary Foreign Workers: The Broader Context.* Montréal, QC: Canadian Council for Refugees.

Canadian Council for Refugees. (2015). *We Need Express Entry Family Reunification.* www.ccrweb.ca.

Canadian Hospice Palliative Care Association. (2009). *Caring for Canadians at End of Life: A Strategic Plan for Hospice, Palliative and End-of-Life Care in Canada to 2015* (October). Ottawa, ON: CHPCA.

Canadian Institute for Health Information (CIHI). (2015). *National Health Expenditures Trends, 1975-2014.* Ottawa, ON: CIHI.

Canadian Mental Health Association Ontario. (2015). *Concurrent disorders.* Retrieved July 25, 2015 from www.cmha.ca.

Canadian Mental Health Association Ontario. (2015). *Recovery.* Retrieved July 20, 2015 from www.cmha.ca.

Canadian Women's Foundation. (2015). Only 1 in 3 Canadians know what sexual consent means. Press Release (May 15).

Carey, M. (2008). Everything Must Go? The Privatization of State Social Work. *British Journal of Social Work,* 38(5), 918-935.

Carignan, L., (2014). Le travail social au Québec : Quelle évolution? Dans M. Fourdrignier, Y. Molina, et F. Tschopp, *Dynamiques du travail social en pays francophones* (Chapitre 8), Genève : IES Éditions.

Carniol, B. (2010). *Case Critical: Challenging Social Services in Canada* (6th ed.). Toronto, ON: Between the Lines.

Castellano, Marlene Brant, Archibald, Linda, & DeGagné, Mike. (2008). *From Truth to Reconciliation: Transforming the Legacy of Residential Schools.* Ottawa, ON: Aboriginal Healing Foundation.

CASW. (2005). *Code of Ethics.* Ottawa, ON: Canadian Association of Social Workers. www.casw-acts.ca.

CASW. (2005). *Guidelines for Ethical Practice.* Ottawa, ON: Canadian Association of Social Workers. www.casw-acts.ca.

CASW. (2014). *Social Media Use and Social Work Practice.* Ottawa, ON: Canadian Association of Social Workers. www.casw-acts.ca.

Catalani, C., & Minkler, M. (2010). Photovoice: A review of the literature in health and public health. *Health Education and Behavior,* 37(3), 424-451.

CBC News. (2012). Timeline: Same-sex rights in Canada. [For information up to and including 2012.] Canadian Broadcasting Corporation (January 12) .

CBC News. (2015). *Jen Chouinard, Saskatoon social worker, starts PTSD support group.* (February 28).

Centre for Addiction and Mental Health. (2015). *Dual diagnosis.* Retrieved July 25, 2015 from www.camh.ca.

Centre for Addiction and Mental Health. (2010). *Post-traumatic stress disorder.* Retrieved July 17, 2015 from www.camh.ca.

Centre for Addiction and Mental Health. (2010). *Stigma.* Retrieved July 11, 2015 from www.camh.ca.

Centre for Addiction and Mental Health. (2010). *Suicide.* Retrieved July 11, 2015, from www.camh.ca.

Centre for Addiction and Mental Health. (2015). *What are concurrent disorders?* Retrieved July 25, 2015 from www.camh.ca.

Centre for Suicide Prevention. (2015). Retrieved July 24, 2015 from www.suicideinfo.ca.

Chambers, N., & Ganesan, S. (2005). Refugees in Canada. In Waxler-Morrison, N., Anderson, J., Richardson, E., & N. Chambers (Eds.), *Cross-Cultural Caring: A Handbook for Health Professionals* (pp. 289-322) Vancouver, BC: University of British Columbia Press.

Chandler, M., & Lalonde, C. (1998). Cultural continuity as a hedge against suicide in Canada's First Nations. *Transcultural Psychiatry,* 35(2), 191-219.

Chappell, Neena, McDonald, Lynn, & Stones, Michael. (2011). *Aging in Contemporary Canada.* Toronto, ON: Pearson Prentice Hall.

Choudry, A. (2001). Bringing it all back home: Anti-globalization activism cannot ignore colonial realities. Unpublished article. Retrieved December 2, 2009 from http://www. wewrite.org/Articles/Aziz.pdf.

Citizenship and Immigration Canada (2012). *Canada Facts and Figures: Immigration Overview of Permanent and Temporary Residents, 2012.* Ottawa, ON: Government of Canada, Minister of Public Works and Government Services Canada.

Citizenship and Immigration Canada (2013a). *Annual Report to Parliament on Immigration, 2013.* Ottawa, ON: Government of Canada, Minister of Citizenship and Immigration.

Citizenship and Immigration Canada (2013b). *Backgrounder—Action Plan for Faster Family Reunification: Phase II.* Ottawa, ON: Government of Canada, Minister of Citizenship and Immigration.

Citizenship and Immigration Canada (2015). *Annual Report to Parliament on Immigration.* Ottawa, ON: Government of Canada, Minister of Citizenship and Immigration.

Cobb, R. A., & Negash, S. (2010). Altered book making as a form of art therapy: A narrative approach. *Journal of Family Psychotherapy*, 21, 54–69.

Cole, D. (2014). The skin I'm in: I've been interrogated by police more than 50 times—all because I'm black. *Toronto Life.* (April 21).

Coll, B.D. (1973). *Perspectives in Public Welfare: A History*. Washington, DC: U.S. Government Printing Office.

Commission on Systemic Racism in the Ontario Criminal Justice System. (1995). *Report of the Commission on Systemic Racism in the Ontario Criminal Justice System.* Queen's Printer for Ontario.

Conference Board of Canada. (2011). Women still missing in action from senior management positions in Canadian organizations. News Release (August 31).

Cook, R. (1985). *The Regenerators: Social Criticism in Late Victorian English Canada.* Toronto, ON: University of Toronto Press.

Copp, T. 1974. *The Anatomy of Poverty: The Condition of the Working Class in Montreal, 1897–1929.* Toronto, ON: McClelland & Stewart Ltd.

Corak, M. (2008). Immigration in the long run: The education and earnings mobility of second-generation Canadians. *IRPP Choices,* 14(13), 1-30.

Corcoran, J., & Pillai, V. (2009). A review of the research on solution-focused therapy. *British Journal of Social Work*, 39(2), 234-242.

Cornell, S., & Kalt, J.P. (1992). Reloading the dice: Improving the chances for economic development on American Indian reservations. In Cornell, S., & Kalt, J.P. (Eds.), *What Can Tribes Do? Strategies and Institutions in American Indian Economic Development* (pp. 1-59). Los Angeles, CA: American Indian Studies Center.

Correctional Services Program. (2015). *Adult Correctional Statistics in Canada, 2013/2014.* Ottawa, ON: Statistics Canada.

Coulshed, V., & Orme, J. (2012). *Social Work Practice* (5th ed.). London, UK: Palgrave Macmillan.

Cross T., Bazron, B., Dennis, K., & Isaacs, M. (1989). *Towards a Culturally Competent System of Care, Volume I*. Washington, DC.: Georgetown University Child Development Center, CASSP Technical Assistance Center.

Csiernik, R. (2011). *Substance Use and Abuse: Everything Matters.* Toronto, ON: Canadian Scholars' Press.

Dahlgren, G., & Whitehead, M. (1991). *Policies and Strategies to Promote Social Equity in Health.* Stockholm: Institute for Future Studies.

Dauvergne, M. (2003). Family violence against seniors. *Canadian Social Trends.* Spring. Cat. no. 11-008. Ottawa, ON: Statistics Canada.

Davidson, S., Cappelli, M., & Vloet, M.A. (2011). *We've got growing up to do: Transitioning from child and adolescent mental health services to adult mental health services.* Ottawa, ON: Ontario Centre of Excellence for Child and Youth Mental Health.

Davidson-Arad, B., & Benbenishty, R. (2010). Contribution of child protection workers' attitudes to their risk assessments and intervention recommendations: A study in Israel. *Health & Social Care in the Community*, 18(1), 1-9.

Davis, A.F. (1967). *Spearheads for Reform: The Social Settlements and the Progressive Movement, 1890–1914.* New York, NY: Oxford University Press.

Davis, J. (2014). Towards a further understanding of what Indigenous people have always known: Storytelling as the basis of good pedagogy. *First Nations Perspective,* 6(1), 83-96.

Davis, Stephen Spencer. (2015). Toronto most expensive in Canada for daycare: Report. *The Toronto Star* (December 10).

DeJong, Gerben. (1979). Independent living: From social movement to analytic paradigm. *Archives of Physical Medicine and Rehabilitation*, 60 (October), 435-446.

Department of Indian and Northern Affairs Canada. (2003). *Backgrounder: The Residential School System*. Ottawa, ON: Indian and Northern Affairs Canada.

Dion, K., & Dion, K. (2004). Gender, immigrant generation, and ethno-cultural identity. *Sex Roles,* 50(5/6), 347-355.

Dominelli, L. (2004). *Social Work: Theory and Practice for a Changing Profession*. Cambridge, UK: Polity Press.

Dominelli, L. (2011). Climate change: Social workers' roles and contributions to policy debates and interventions. *International Journal of Social Welfare,* 20, 430–438.

Dorais, M. (2004). *Dead Boys Can't Dance: Sexual Orientation, Masculinity and Suicide*. Montréal, QC: McGill-Queens University Press.

Dorfman, R.A. (2013). Eclectic clinical social work. In Dorfman, R.A., *Clinical Social Work: Definition, Practice And Vision* (pp. 91-92). New York, NY: Routledge.

Drachman, D. (1992). A stage-of-migration for service to immigrant framework populations. *Social Work,* 37(1), 68-72.

Drisko, J. (2013). The common factors model: Its place in clinical practice and research. *Smith College Studies in Social Work*, 83(4), 398-413.

Dulwich Centre. (2009). *Commonly Asked Questions About Narrative Approaches to Therapy, Community Work and Psychosocial Support*. Adelaide, SA: Dulwich Centre Publications.

Elder, G.H., Jr., & Johnson, M.K. (2002). The Life Course and Aging Challenges: Lessons and New Directions. In Settersten, Richard A., Jr., Ed., *Invitation to the Life Course: Towards New Understandings of Later Life* (pp. 49–81). Amityville, NY: Baywood.

Environics institute. (2010). *Urban Aboriginal Peoples Study.* Retrieved April 4, 2016 from http://www.uaps.ca/

Esses, V., Dietz, J., Bennett-AbuAyyash, C., & Joshi, C. (2007). Prejudice in the workplace: The role of bias against visible minorities in the devaluation of immigrants' foreign-acquired credentials. *Canadian Issues,* Spring 2007, 114-118.

Este, David, and Hieu Van Ngo. (2011). A resilience framework to examine immigrant and refugee children and youth in Canada. In Moreno, Robert P., and Chuang, Susan S. (Eds.), *Immigrant Children: Change, Adaptation, and Cultural Transformation.* Lexington, MA: Lexington Books.

Estes, Richard J. (2009). *United States-Based Conceptualization of International Social Work Education.* Washington, DC: Council on Social Work Education, 8-9.

Evans, Robert. (2010). *Don't Panic: The Fiscal Sustainability of Medicare, Past and Future.* Centre for Health Services and Policy Research, Vancouver, BC: University of British Columbia (June 17).

Fallon, B., & Trocmé, N. (2011). Factors associated with the decision to provide ongoing services: Are worker characteristics and organizational location important? In Kufeldt, K., & McKenzie, B. (Eds.), *Child Welfare: Connecting Research, Policy, and Practice* (pp. 57-73). Waterloo, ON: Wilfrid Laurier University Press.

Fallon, B., Van Wert, M., Trocmé, N., MacLaurin, B., Sinha, V., Lefebvre, R., Allan, K., Black, T., Lee, B., Rha, W., Smith, C., & Goel, S. (2013). *Ontario Incidence Study of Reported Child Abuse and Neglect—2013 (OIS-2013).* Toronto, ON: Child Welfare Research Portal.

Fang, L., Mishna, F., Zhang, V., Van Wert, M., & Bogo, M. (2014). Social media and social work education: Understanding and dealing with the new digital world. *Social Work in Health Care*, 53(9), 800-814 (Oct.).

Fast, E. (2014). Exploring the role of culture among urban Indigenous youth. Montréal, QC: McGill University Press.

Fecteau, J.-M. (1989). *La pauvreté, le crime, l'État au Québec, de la fin du XVIIIe siècle à 1840.* Montréal, QC: VLB éditeur.

Fedoroff, J. Paul, & Moran, Beverley. (1997). Myths and misconceptions about sex offenders. *The Canadian Journal of Human Sexuality,* 6, 4 (Winter), 263.

Ferguson, S. (2004). Hard sell adoption. *Macleans Magazine,* July 26 (pp. 8-20). Toronto, ON: Rogers Media Inc.

Ferns, H., & B. Ostry. 1976. *The Age of Mackenzie King.* Toronto, ON: Lorimer.

Findholt, N.E., Michael, Y.L., Davis, M.M., & Brogoitti, V.W. (2011). Environmental influences on children's physical activity and diets in rural Oregon: Results of a youth photovoice project. *Online Journal of Rural Nursing and Health Care*, 10(2), 11-20.

First Nations Child and Family Caring Society of Canada. (2013). Information sheet: Structural interventions in child welfare. Retrieved from https://fncaringsociety.com.

Flette, E. (2005). Personal conversation with Elsie Flette, Chief Executive Officer of the Southern First Nations Authority of Manitoba.

Fook, J. (1993) *Radical Casework: A Theory for Practice*. St. Leonards, NSW, Australia: Allen & Unwin.

Fook, J., & Victoria, G. (2000). Linking theory, practice and research. *Critical Social Work*, 2(1).

Fredriksen-Goldsen, K.I., Kim, H.-J., Emlet, C.A., Muraco, A., Erosheva, E.A., Hoy-Ellis, C.P., & Petry, H. (2011). *The aging and health report: Disparities and resilience among lesbian, gay, bisexual, and transgender older adults*. Seattle, OR: Institute for Multigenerational Health.

Freire, P. (1971). *Pedagogy of the Oppressed.* New York, NY: Continuum.

Frideres, J. (2008). Aboriginal identity in the Canadian context. *The Canadian Journal of Native Studies*, 23(2), 313-342.

Frieden, L. (1983). Independent Living in the United States and Other Countries. *Handicaps Monthly*, 54-61.

Friendly, M., et al. (2007). *Early Childhood Education and Care in Canada.* (7th ed.). Toronto: Childcare and Resource Research Unit.

Gaikwad, A.D., Lalitha, K., & Seshadri, S.P. (2015). Play therapy: An approach to manage childhood problems. *International Journal of Pediatric Nursing*, 1(1), 22-28.

Gaumer, B., & Fleury, M.J. (2008). CLSCs in Québec: Thirty years of community action. *Social Work in Public Health*, 23(4), 89-106.

Gelfed, B. (1988). *The Creative Practitioner*. New York, NY: Haworth.

Gentle-Genitty, C., Chen, H., Karikari, I., & Barnett, C. (2014). Social work theory and application to practice: The students' perspectives. *Journal of Higher Education Theory and Practice,* 14(1), 36-47.

Germain, C., & Gitterman, A. (1996). *The Life Model of Social Work Practice: Advances in Theory and Practice.* New York, NY: Columbia University Press.

Gibbins R., & Ponting, J.R. (1986). Historical Overview and Background. In J. Rick Ponting (Ed.), *Arduous Journey: Canadian Indians and Decolonialization.* Toronto, ON: McClelland & Stewart Ltd.

Giguère, B., Lalonde, R., & Lou, E. (2010). Living at the crossroads of cultural worlds: The experience of normative conflicts by second generation immigrant youth. *Social and Personality Compass*, 4(1), 14-29.

Girard, P. (1987). From subversion to liberation: Homosexuals and the *Immigration Act* 1952-1977. *Canadian Journal of Law and Society,* 24(2), 1-27.

Gitterman, Alex, & Knight, Carolyn. (2013). Response to Thyer's "Evidence-Based Practice or Evidence-Guided Practice." *Families in Society: The Journal of Contemporary Social Services,* 94:2, 85-86.

Glasner-Edwards, S., & Rawson, R. (2010). Evidence-based practices in addiction treatment: Review and recommendations for public policy. *Health Policy,* 97(2-3), 93-104.

Goldstein, H. (1973). *Social Work Practice: A Unitary Approach*. Columbia, SC: University of South Carolina Press.

Gonzales-Prendez, A.A., & Brisebois, K. (2012). Cognitive-behavioral therapy and social work values: A critical analysis. *Journal of Social Work Values and Ethics*, 9(2), 21-33.

Graham, J., Swift, K., & Delaney, R. (2012). *Canadian Social Policy: An Introduction* (4th ed.). Toronto, ON: Pearson Canada Inc.

Grant, A.M., & O'Connor, S.A. (2010). The differential effects of solution-focused and problem-focused coaching questions: A pilot study with implications for practice. *Industrial and Commercial Training*, 42(2), 102-111.

Grant, Tavia. (2015). Indigenous people six times more likely to be murder victims: Statscan. *The Globe and Mail* (November 25).

Gray, Mel, & Fook, Jan. (2004). The quest for a universal social work: Some issues and implications. *Social Work Education: The International Journal*, 23(5).

Grebinski, Leisha. (2010). Horses offer hope to troubled Aboriginal youth. *Saskatchewan Sage,* 14(12). The Aboriginal Multi-Media Society (AMMSA).

Green, J. (2009). Decolonizing social work practice through Oolichan fishing. In Bruyere, G., Anthony Hart, M., & Sinclair, R. (Eds.), *Wicihitowin: Aboriginal Social Work in Canada.* Black Point, NS: Fernwood Publishing.

Greenwood, M., de Leeuw, S., Lindsay, N. M., & Reading, C. (Eds.). (2015). *Determinants of Indigenous Peoples' Health in Canada*. Toronto, ON: Canadian Scholars' Press.

Groulx, L.H. (1983). Le service social confessionnel au Canada français: ses énoncés et son rôle, *La Revue canadienne de service social*, vol. 1, 141-160.

Guest, Dennis (1997). *The Emergence of Social Security in Canada* (3rd ed.). Vancouver, BC: University of British Columbia Press.

Guo, Y. (2009). Difference, deficiency and devaluation: Tracing the roots of foreign credentials for immigrant professionals in Canada. *The Canadian Journal for the Study of Adult Education,* 22, 37-52.

Guss, W. (2004) Personal conversation with Elder Wilma Guss.

Habib, Samar (Ed.). (2010). *Islam and Homosexuality* (2 volumes). Santa Barbara, CA: Praeger.

Hanes, R., & Moscovitch, A. (2002). Disability supports and services for people with disabilities in the social union. In Puttee, Allen, *Federalism, Democracy and Disability Policy in Canada.* Institute of Intergovernmental Affairs, School of Policy Studies, Queen's University. Montréal, QC: McGill-Queen's University Press.

Hanes, R. (1995). Linking mental defect to physical disability: The case of crippled children in Ontario, 1890-1940. *Journal of Developmental Disability.* 4(1).

Hanes, Roy. (2010). None is still too many: An historical exploration of Canadian immigration and citizenship legislation as it pertains to people with disabilities. Ottawa, ON: Council of Canadians with Disabilities.

Haque, N., & Eng, B. (2011). Tackling inequity through a Photovoice project on the social determinants of health: Translating Photovoice evidence to community action. *Global Health Promotion*, 18(1), 16-19.

Health Council of Canada. (2015). *Seniors in Need, Caregivers in Distress: What Are the Home Care Priorities for Seniors in Canada?* Ottawa, ON: Health Council of Canada.

Heart and Stroke Foundation of Canada. (2013). *Reality Check: 2013 Report on the Health of Canadians.* Ottawa, ON: Heart and Stroke Foundation of Canada.

Helminiak, Daniel A. (1994, 2000). *What the Bible Really Says about Homosexuality.* Estancia, NM: Alamo Square Press.

Henry, F. (1994). *The Caribbean Diaspora in Toronto: Learning to Live with Racism.* Toronto, ON: University of Toronto Press.

Henry, F., & Tator, C. (2006). *The Colour of Democracy: Racism in Canadian Society* (3rd ed). Toronto: Nelson Canada.

Herberg, D. (1985). Social work with new immigrants. In Yelaja, S. (Ed.). *An Introduction to Social Work Practice in Canada* (pp. 234-251). Scarborough, ON: Prentice Hall.

Herwitz, D. (2003). *Race and Reconciliation.* Minneapolis, MN: University of Minnesota Press.

Hibel, J., & Polanco, M. (2010). Tuning the ear: Listening in narrative therapy. *Journal of Systemic Therapies*, 29, 51–66.

Hick, Steven, & Bien, Thomas (Eds.). (2008). *Mindfulness and the Therapeutic Relationship.* New York, NY: Guilford Press.

Hick, Steven F. (Ed.). (2009). Mindfulness and Social Work: Paying attention to Ourselves, Our Clients, and Society. In Steven F. Hick, *Mindfulness and Social Work.* Chicago, IL: Lyceum Books

Hoffman, L. (2002). *Family Therapy: An Intimate History.* New York, NY: Norton.

Hofmann, S.G., Asnaani, A., Vonk, I.J., Sawyer, A.T., & Fang, A. (2012). The efficacy of cognitive behavioral therapy: A review of meta-analyses. *Cognitive Therapy and Research*, 36(5), 427-440.

Hong Fook Mental Health Association. (2008). *Understanding, Support and Self-Care: A Resource Manual for Family Members and Caregivers.* Toronto, ON: Hong Fook Mental Health Association

Hope, A., & Timmel, S. (1984). *Training for Transformation: A Handbook for Community Workers.* Rugby, UK: ITDG Publishing.

Horkheimer, M. (1993). *Between Philosophy and Social Science: Selected Early Writings.* Cambridge, MA: The MIT Press.

Howard, H.A., & Proulx, C. (2011). Transformations and continuities: An introduction. In Howard, H.A., & Proulx, C. (Eds.), *Aboriginal People in Canadian Cities: Transformations and Continuities* (pp. 1-22). Waterloo, ON: Wilfred Laurier University Press.

Hughes, R., & Rycus, J. (2007). Issues in risk assessment in child protective services. *Journal of Public Child Welfare*, 1, 85-116.

Human Resources and Social Development Canada. (2006). A Way with Words and Images. Ottawa, ON: Human Resources and Social Development Canada.

Hurwitz, D. (2003) *Race and Reconciliation.* Minneapolis, MN: University of Minnesota Press.

Ighodaro, M. (2006). *Living the Experience: Migration, Exclusion, and Anti-Racist Practice.* Halifax, NS: Fernwood Publishing.

INAC & Tungavik. (1993). *Agreement Between the Inuit of the Nunavut Settlement Area and Her Majesty the Queen in Right of Canada.* Ottawa, ON: Indian and Northern Affairs Canada.

International Association for Suicide Prevention. (2015). *International Association for Suicide Prevention.* Retrieved July 24 from www.iasp.info.

Isajiw, W.W. (1999). *Understanding Diversity: Ethnicity and Race in the Canadian Context.* Toronto, ON: Thompson Educational Publishing.

Ives, N., Denov, M., & Sussman, T. (2015). *Introduction to Social work in Canada: Histories, Contexts, and Practices.* Don Mills, ON: Oxford University Press.

James, C., Este, D., Thomas Bernard, W., Benjamin, A., Lloyd, B., & Turner, T. (2010). *Race and Well-Being: The Lives, Hopes, and Activism of African Canadians.* Black Point, NS and Winnipeg, MB: Fernwood Publishing.

Jantzen, L. (2008). Who is the second generation? A description of their ethnic origins and visible minority composition by age. *Canadian Diversity*, 6(2), 7-12.

Jennissen, Therese, & Lundy, Colleen. (2006). *Keeping Sight of Social Justice: 80 Years of Building CASW.* Canadian Association of Social Workers (www.casw-acts.ca).

Jennissen, Therese, & Lundy, Colleen. (2011). *One Hundred Years of Social Work: A History of the Profession in English Canada, 1900–2000.* Waterloo, ON: Wilfrid Laurier University Press.

Johns, A. (2012). Social networking and electronic communication. *Connecting Voices*, 16(2), 18-19.

Johnson, P. (1983). *Native Children and the Child Welfare System.* Toronto, ON: Lorimer.

Katz, J.N. (1995). *The Invention of Heterosexuality.* New York, NY: Penguin Group.

Kendall, D., Nygaard, V.L., & Thompson, E.G. (2008). *Social Problems in a Diverse Society.* (2nd ed.) Toronto: Pearson Education Canada Inc.

Kerzner, Lana, & Baker, David. (1999). *A Canadians with Disabilities Act?* Ottawa, ON: Council of Canadians with Disabilities.

Kim, J., Smock, S., Trepper, T., McCollum, E., & Franklin, C. (2010). Is solution-focused brief therapy evidence-based? *Families in Society: The Journal of Contemporary Social Services*, 91(3), 300-306.

King, Thomas (Ed). (1990). *All My Relations: An Anthology of Contemporary Canadian Native Fiction.* Toronto, ON: McClelland & Stewart Inc.

Kirst-Ashman, K.K., & Hull, G.H. (2009). Introducing generalist practice: The generalist intervention model. In Kirst-Ashman, K.K., & Hull, G.H. *Understanding Generalist Practice* (5th ed.) (pp. 3-43). Stamford, CT: Cengage Learning.

Kobayashi, A. (2008). A research and policy agenda for second generation Canadians: Introduction. *Canadian Diversity*, 6(2), 3-6.

Krane, J., & Davies, L. (2000). Mothering and child protection practice: rethinking risk assessment. *Child and Family Social Work*, 5, 35-45.

Kufeldt, K. (2011). Foster care: An essential part of the continuum of care. In Kufeldt, K., & McKenzie, B. (Eds.), *Child Welfare: Connecting Research, Policy, and Practice*, Waterloo, ON: Wilfrid Laurier University Press.

Lacharité, Carl. (2014). Transforming a wild world: Helping children and families to address neglect in the province of Québec, Canada. *Child Abuse Review*, 23(4).

Lambert, L., & Regehr, C. (2005). *Stress, Trauma, and Support in Child Welfare Practice.* Research Institute for Evidence-Based Social Work. Toronto. ON: Children's Aid Society of Toronto. University of Toronto.

Lavallee, T. (2005). Honouring Jordan: Putting First Nations children first and funding fights second. *Paediatric Child Health*, (10), 527-529.

Lawrence, B. (2004). *"Real" Indians and Others: Mixed-Blood Urban Native Peoples and Indigenous Nationhood* (p. 303). Retrieved from http://muse.jhu.edu/books.

Lee, B. (1999). *Pragmatics of Community Organization.* Toronto, ON: CommonAct Press.

Lee, B. (2011). *Pragmatics of Community Organization* (4th ed.). Toronto, ON: CommonAct.

Lee, K. (1999). Measuring poverty among Canada's Aboriginal people. *Insight*, 23(2). Ottawa, ON: Canadian Council on Social Development.

Lee, M.Y. (2013). Solution-focused brief therapy. *Encyclopedia of Social Work.*

Leiby, J. (1978). *A History of Social Welfare and Social Work in the United States.* New York, NY: Columbia University Press.

Lenette, C., Cox, L., & Brough, M. (2015). Digital storytelling as a social work tool: Learning from ethnographic research with women from refugee backgrounds. *British Journal of Social Work*, 45(3), 988-1005.

Leonardo, Z. (2004). Critical social theory and transformative knowledge: The functions of criticism in quality education. *Educational Researcher,* 33(6), 11-18.

Linehan, M.M. (1993). *Cognitive-Behavioral Treatment of Borderline Personality Disorder.* New York, NY: Guilford Press.

Loxley, J., De Riviere, L., Prakash, T., Blackstock, C., Wien, F., & Thomas Prokop, S. (2005). *Wen:de: The Journey Continues.* Ottawa, ON: First Nations Child and Family Caring Society of Canada.

Lynn, R. (2010). Mindfulness in social work education. *Social Work Education*, 29(3), 289-304.

Macdonald, David, & Wilson, Daniel. (2013). *Poverty or Prosperity; Indigenous Children in Canada.* Ottawa, ON: Canadian Centre For Policy Alternatives and Save The Children Canada.

Macdonald, Noni, & Attaran, Amir. (2007). Jordan's Principle, governments' paralysis. *Canadian Medical Association Journal,* 177(4).

MacDonald, R-A. J., & Ladd, P. (2000). *First Nations Child and Family Services Joint National Policy Review: Final Report,* June 2000. Ottawa, ON: Assembly of First Nations

Mackrael, Kim. (2015). Federal government wary of UN Indigenous rights declaration. *The Globe and Mail* (June 5).

Mann-Feder, V. (2007). Issue editor's notes. In V. Mann-Feder (Ed.), Transition or eviction: Youth exiting care for independent living. Special issue of *New Directions for Youth Development*, 113, 1-8.

Mann-Feder, V. (2011). Aging out of care and the transition to adulthood: Implications for intervention. In Kufeldt, K., & McKenzie, B. (Eds.), *Child Welfare: Connecting Research, Policy, and Practice.* Waterloo, ON: Wilfrid Laurier University Press.

Martel, Brittany. (2013). *Information Sheet: Structural Interventions in Child Welfare.* Ottawa, ON: First Nations Child and Family Caring Society of Canada.

Martin, Karen L. (2003) Ways of Knowing, Ways of Being and Ways of Doing: A theoretical framework and methods for Indigenous research and Indigenist research. *Journal of Australian Studies*, 76, 203-214.

Mayer, R. (2002). *Évolution des pratiques en service social.* Boucherville, Québec: Gaëtan Morin Éditeur.

McDonald, L., & Collins, A. (2000). *Abuse and Neglect of Older Canadians: A Discussion Paper.* Ottawa, ON: Health Canada.

McGrath, S., Moffatt, K., George, U., & Lee, B. (1999). Community capacity: The Emperor's new cothes. *Canadian Review of Social Policy,* 44, 9–23.

McKenzie, B., & Shangreaux, C. (2011). From child protection to community caring in First Nations child and family services. In Kufeldt, K. & McKenzie, B. (Eds.), *Child Welfare: Connecting Research, Policy, and Practice*, Waterloo, ON: Wilfrid Laurier University Press.

McKnight, J., & Kretzmann, J. (1993). Introduction and asset-based community development: Mobilizing an entire community. In *Building Communities from the Inside Out.* Chicago, IL: ACTA Publications. 1–11, 345–354.

McLeod, J. (2006). Narrative Approaches to Therapy. In Feltham, C., & Horton, I., (Eds.), *The SAGE Handbook of Counseling and Psychotherapy* (2nd ed.). (pp. 289–292). Thousand Oaks, CA: Sage Publications.

McSheffrey, E. (2015). Trudeau promises full federal action on final TRC report. *National Observer* (December 15).

Mensah, J. (2010). *Black Canadians: History, Experience, Social Conditions.* (2nd ed.) Halifax, NS: Fernwood Publishing.

Mental Health Commission of Canada. (2011). *Mental Health First Aid Canada.* (2nd ed.). www.mentalhealthfirstaid.ca.

Mental Health Commission of Canada. (2012). *Together against stigma: changing how we see mental illness.* Retrieved July 24, 2015 from www.mentalhealthcommission.ca.

Mental Health Commission of Canada. (2015). *Executive Summary: Taking the next step forward: Building a responsive mental health and addictions system for emerging adults.* (February 23).

Mental Health Foundation. (2015). *Recovery*. Retrieved July 20, 2015 from www.mentalhealth.org.uk.

Mesbur, E. (2002). Social group work practice: The Canadian experience. In Turner, F.J. (Ed.), *Social Work Practice: A Canadian Perspective.* Toronto, ON: Pearson Education Canada.

Mignolo, Walter D. (2011). *The Darker Side of Western Modernity: Global Futures, Decolonial Options.* Durham and London: Duke University Press.

Mikkonen, J., & Raphael, D. (2010). *Social Determinants of Health: Canadian Facts.* Toronto, ON: York University School of Health Policy and Management.

Miladinovic, Zoran, & Mulligan, Leah. (2014). *Homicide in Canada, 2014. Juristat.* Canadian Centre for Justice Statistics.

Miley, Karla Krogsrud, O'Melia, Michael W., & DuBois, Brenda L. (2013). *Generalist Social Work Practice: An Empowering Approach* (7th ed.). New York, NY: Pearson Education.

Miller, J.R. (1989). *Skyscrapers Hide the Heavens: A History of Indian-White Relations in Canada.* (Rev. Ed.). Toronto: University of Toronto Press.

Miller, L. (2005). Drawing on cognitive behavioural therapy in social work practice. In *Counselling Skills for Social Work* (pp. 49-79). Thousand Oaks, CA: SAGE Publications Ltd.

Miller, S.E., & Tice, C.J. (2008). The generalist model: Where do the micro and macro converge? *Advances in Social Work*, 9(2), 79-90.

Milloy, J. (1999). *A National Crime: The Canadian Government and the Residential School System 1879-1986.* Winnipeg, MB: University of Manitoba Press.

Montgomery, H.M. (2003). Important considerations in the development of Nisga'a specific social programs for Nisga'a citizens who reside outside of the Naas communities. Victoria, BC.

Montreal Urban Aboriginal Health Committee (MUAHC). (2012). Montreal Urban Aboriginal Health Needs Assessment. Retrieved from http://reseaumtlnetwork.com/wp-content/uploads/2015/02/Final-Report-Health-Needs-Assessment.pdf.

Moran, G. (1992). *Little Rebellion.* Vancouver, BC: Arsenal Pulp Press.

Moreno, Robert P., & Chuang, Susan S. (Eds.). (2011). *Immigrant Children: Change, Adaptation, and Cultural Transformation.* Lexington, MA: Lexington Books.

Morgan, A. (2015). The suffocating experience of being Black in Canada. *The Toronto Star* (July 31).

Morrissette V., McKenzie, B., & Morrissette, L. (1993). Towards an Aboriginal model of social work practice: Cultural knowledge and traditional practices. *Canadian Social Work Review*, 10(1), 91–108.

Muckle, R. (1998). *The First Nations of British Columbia.* Vancouver, BC: University of British Columbia Press.

Mullaly, B. (2002). *Challenging Oppression.* Toronto, ON: Oxford University Press.

National Association of Social Workers. (2005). *Standards for Technology and Social Work Practice.* NASW and the Association of Social Work Boards.

National Council of Canadian Muslims. (2015). *2014 ODIHR Hate Crime Report.* Ottawa, ON: National Council of Canadian Muslims.

National Suicide Prevention Lifeline (2009). *Suicide Assessment Five-step Evaluation and Triage for Mental Health Professionals.* Retrieved July 24, 2015 from www.integration.samhsa.gov.

Neighbours of the Onondaga Nation. Two Row Wampum Renewal Campaign. Retrieved from http://honorthetworow.org/new-poster-how-to-be-an-ally-to-indigenous-peoples/.

Neiman, S. (2002). *Evil in Modern Thought.* Woodstock, UK: Princeton University Press.

Newhouse, D., & Peters, E.J. (Eds.) (2001). *Not Strangers in These Parts: Urban Aboriginal Peoples.* Policy Research Initiative, Government of Canada.

Ngo, H., & Este, D. (2006). Professional re-entry for foreign-trained immigrants. *Journal of International Migration and Integration*, 7(1), 27-50.

Ngwenyama, O.K. (1991). The Critical Social Theory Approach to Information Systems: Problems and Challenges. In *Traditions*, Nissen, H-E., Klein, H.K., Hirschheim, R.A. (Eds.) *Information Systems Research: Contemporary Approaches and Emergent* (pp. 267-280). Amsterdam: North Holland.

Nichols, M., (2006). Psychotherapeutic issues with "kinky" clients: Clinical problems, yours and theirs. *Journal of Homosexuality,* 50(2-3), 281-300.

Norcross, J.C. (2002). *Psychotherapy Relationships That Work: Therapist Contributions and Responsiveness to Clients.* New York, NY: Oxford University Press.

Norcross, J.C., Karpiak, C.P., & Lister, K.M. (2005). What's an integrationist? A study of self-identified integrative and (occasionally) eclectic psychologists. *Journal of Clinical Psychology*, 61(12), 1587-1594.

OEDC. (2013). *Pensions at a Glance (Canada).* OECD and G20 Indicators. Paris, France.

Office of the Auditor General of Canada. (2008). First Nations Child and Family Services Program—Indian and Northern Affairs Canada. Ottawa, ON: Office of the Auditor General of Canada.

Office of the Auditor General of Canada (2009). First Nations Child and Family Services Program—Indian and Northern Affairs Canada, Chapter 4. Report of the Auditor General of Canada. Retrieved May 27, 2009 from http://www.oag-bvg. gc.ca/internet/English/aud_ch_oag_200905_04_e_30700. html#hd3a.

Office of the Provincial Advocate for Children and Youth. (2014). *Feathers of Hope: A First Nations Action Plan.* Toronto, ON: Provincial Advocate for Children and Youth.

Oliver, M. (1990). Disability definitions: The politics of meaning. In *The Politics of Disablement.* London, UK: Macmillan.

Oliver, M. (1996). The social model of disability. In *Understanding Disability: From Theory to Practice.* London, UK: St. Martin's Press.

O'Neil, J.V. (2001, January). *Expertise in addictions said crucial.* NASW News, p. 10.

Ontario Human Rights Commission. (2003). *Paying the Price: The Human Cost of Racial Profiling.* Toronto, ON: Ontario Human Rights Commission.

Orbach, S. (1990). Gender and dependency in psychotherapy. *Journal of Social Work Practice,* 4(3-4), 1–15.

Parton, N. (2000). Some thoughts on the relationship between theory and practice in and for social work. *British Journal of Social Work*, 30(4), 449-463.

Payne, M. (2006). *Narrative Therapy* (2nd ed.). London, UK: Sage.

Perlman, C.M., Neufeld, E., Martin, L., Goy, M., & Hirdes, J.P. (2011). *Suicide Risk Assessment Guide: A Resource for Health Care Organizations.* Toronto, ON: Ontario Hospital Association and Canadian Patient Safety Institute.

Peters, E.J. (1996). Aboriginal people in urban areas. In Long, D., & Dickason, O.P. (Eds.), *Visions of the Heart: Canadian Aboriginal Issues* (pp. 305-334). Toronto, ON: Harcourt Brace.

Peters, E.J. (2011). Emerging themes in academic research in urban Aboriginal identities in Canada, 1996-2010. *Aboriginal Policy Studies,* 1(1), 78-105.

Peterson, D., & Boswell, J.N. (2015). Play therapy in a natural setting: A case example. *Journal of Creativity in Mental Health*, 10(1), 62-76.

Pew Research Center. (2011). *Global Digital Communication: Texting, Social Networking Popular Worldwide.* Washington, DC.

Philip, M. (2001). Children's Aid staff face burnout. *The Globe and Mail.* (February 20).

Phillips, Ruth, & Cree, Viviene E. (2014). What does the "Fourth Wave" mean for teaching feminism in twenty-first century social work? *Social Work Education: The International Journal,* 33(7).

Phipps, W.D., & Vorster, C. (2009). Narrative therapy: A return to the intra-psychic perspective? *South African Journal of Psychology*, 39, 32–45.

Picard, André. (2015). Canada needs coalition of the willing to improve health care. *The Globe and Mail* (November 18).

Pitsula, J. (1979). The emergence of social work in Toronto. *Journal of Canadian Studies*, 14(1).

Power, P.W., & Dell Orto, A.E. (Eds.) (1980). *Role of the Family in the Rehabilitation of the Physically Disabled.* Baltimore, MD: University Park Press.

Prince, Michael J. (2010). What about a Disability Rights Act for Canada? Practices and lessons from America, Australia, and the United Kingdom. *Canadian Public Policy*, 36(2), 199.

Proulx, C. (2003). *Reclaiming Aboriginal Justice, Identity and Community.* Saskatoon, SK: Purich Publishing.

Provincial Advocate for Children and Youth. (2012). *25 Is the New 21: The Costs and Benefits of Providing Extended Care and Maintenance to Ontario Youth in Care Until Age 25.* Office of the Provincial Advocate for Children and Youth Ontario.

Psychology Foundation of Canada and Desjardins Financial Security. (2007). *Managing to Manage Workplace Stress.* www.desjardinslifeinsurance.com.

Public Health Agency of Canada. (2006). *The Human Face of Mental Health and Mental Illness in Canada 2006.* Ottawa, ON: Public Health Agency of Canada.

Public Health Agency of Canada. (2010). *Canadian Incidence Study of Reported Child Abuse and Neglect—2008: Major Findings.* Ottawa, ON: Public Health Agency of Canada.

Public Health Agency of Canada. (2011). *Diabetes in Canada: Facts and Figures from a Public Health Perspective.* Ottawa, ON: Public Health Agency of Canada.

Public Health Agency of Canada. (2014). www.publichealth.ca.

Purich, D. (1988). *The Métis.* Toronto, ON: James Lorimer & Co.

Rambukkana, Nathan. (2015). *Fraught Intimacies: Non/Monogamy in the Public Sphere.* Vancouver, BC: University of British Columbia Press.

Reamer, F. (2013). Social work in a digital age: Ethical and risk management challenges. *Social Work*, 58(2), 163-172.

Regehr, C., Stern, S., & Shlonsky, A. (2007). Operationalizing evidence-based practice in the development of an institute for evidence-based social work. *Research on Social Work Practice*, 17(3), 408-416.

Reid, W. & Epstein, L. (1977). *Task-Centred Practice*. NY: Columbia University Press.

Reitz, J., & Banerjee, R. (2007). Racial inequality, social cohesion, and policy issues in Canada. In Banting, K., Courchene, T.J., & Seidle, F.L. (Eds.), *Belonging? Diversity, Recognition and Shared Citizenship in Canada* (pp. 489-545). Montreal, QC: Institute for Research on Public Policy.

Ricks, L., Kitchens, S., Goodrich, T., & Hancock, E. (2014). My story: The use of narrative therapy in individual and group counseling. *Journal of Creativity in Mental Health*, 9(1), 99-110.

Robbins, Susan P., Chatterjee, Pranab, & Canda, Edward R. (2012). *Contemporary Human Behavior Theory: A Critical Perspective for Social Work* (3rd ed.). New York, NY: Pearson Higher Education.

Roberts, R., et al. (1990). *Developing Culturally Competent Programs for Families of Children with Special Needs*. Washington, DC: Georgetown University Child Development Center.

Robin, B.R. (2008). Digital storytelling: A powerful technology tool for the 21st century classroom. *Theory Into Practice*, 47(3), 220-228.

Rogers, C. 1951. *Client-Centred Therapy*. Boston, MA: Houghton.

Romanow, R. (2002). *Building Values: The Future of Health Care in Canada*. Ottawa: Commission on the Future of Health Care in Canada.

Rondeau, G., et Commelin, D. (2005). La profession de travailleur social au Québec. In Deslauriers, J.-P. et Hurtubise, Y. (sous la direction de). *Le travail social international. Éléments de comparaison*. Québec : Les Presses de l'Université Laval.

Rooke, P., & Schnell, R.L. (1983). *Discarding the Asylum: From Child Welfare to the Welfare State in English Canada, 1800–1950*. Boston, MA: University Press of America.

Rostow, W.W. (1960). *The Stages of Economic Growth: A Non-Communist Manifesto*. Cambridge, UK: Cambridge University Press.

Royal Commission on Aboriginal Peoples. (1996). *Report of the Royal Commission on Aboriginal Peoples*. Ottawa, ON: Indian and Northern Affairs Canada.

Russinova, Z., Rogers, E.S., Gagne, C., Bloch, P., Drake, K.M., & Mueser, K.T. (2014). A randomized controlled trial of a peer-run antistigma photovoice intervention. *Psychiatric Services*, 65(2), 242-246.

Saleebey, Dennis. (2013). *The Strengths Perspective in Social Work Practice* (6th ed.). San Francisco, CA: Peachpit Press/Pearson.

Saunders, Doug. (2015). The battle to make gender boring again. *The Globe and Mail* (August 22).

Scheer, Jessica, & Groce, Nora. (1988). Impairment as a human constant: Cross-cultural and historical perspectives on variation. *Journal of Social Issues*, 44(1), 23-37.

Schwartz, L.R., Sable, M.R., Dannerbeck, A., & Campbell, J.D. (2007). Using Photovoice to improve family planning services for immigrant Hispanics. *Journal of Health Care for the Poor and Underserved*, 18(4), 757-766.

Scott, K.A. (1994). *Aboriginal Health and Social History: A Brief Canadian History*. Unpublished.

Sealander, J. (2003). *The Failed Century of the Child: Governing America's Young in the Twentieth Century*. Cambridge, UK: Cambridge University Press.

Segal, Zindel V., Teasdale, John D., Williams, J. Mark, & Gemar, Michael C. (2002). The mindfulness-based cognitive therapy adherence scale: Inter-rater reliability, adherence to protocol and treatment distinctiveness. *Clinical Psychology & Psychotherapy*, 9(2), 131–138.

Shah, C., & Moloughney, B.W. (2001). A Strategic Review of the Community Health Centre Program. http://www.health.gov.on.ca/en/common/ministry/publications/reports/chc_stratreview/chc_review.pdf.

Sharratt, Anna. (2015). Hidden health-care costs can be a shock for retirees. *The Globe and Mail* (November 18).

Sheldon, Mia. (2011). LGBT seniors afraid they will have to go back in the closet. *Global News* (November 26).

Sheppard, B. (1997). *Deemed Unsuitable*. Toronto, ON: Umbrella Press.

Shier, M.L., & Graham, J.R. (2011). Mindfulness, subjective well-being, and social work: Insight into their interconnection from social work practitioners. *Social Work Education*, 30(1), 29-44.

Shulman, L. (1992). *The Skills of Helping Individuals, Families and Groups*. (3rd ed.). Itasca, IL: Peacock Publishers.

Sidhu, J. (2008). Social workers and immigrant advocacy. In Chang-Muy, F., & Congress, E. (Eds.). *Social Work with Immigrants and Refugees: Legal Issues, Clinical Skills and Advocacy* (pp. 329-366). New York, NY: Springer.

Simpson, Jeffrey. (2012). *Chronic Condition: Why Canada's Health Care System Needs to be Dragged into the 21st Century*. Toronto, ON: Penguin Canada.

Sinclair, M., Bala, N., Lilles, H., & Blackstock, C. (2004). Aboriginal child welfare. In Bala, N., Kim Zapf, M., Williams, R. James, Vogl, R., & Hornick, Joseph P. (Eds.), *Canadian Child Welfare Law*, (2nd ed). Toronto: Thompson Educational Publishing.

Sinclair, R. (2004). Aboriginal social work education in Canada: Decolonizing pedagogy for the Seventh Generation. *First Peoples Child and Family Review*, 1(1), 49-61.

Sinha, Marie. (2013). *Portrait of Caregivers, 2012* (Catalogue no. 89-652-X—No. 001). Ottawa, ON: Statistics Canada.

Sinha, V., Ellenbogen, S., & Trocmé, N. (2013). Substantiating neglect of First Nations and non-Aboriginal children. *Children and Youth Services Review*, 35(12), 2080-2090.

Sinha, V., Trocmé, N., Blackstock, C., MacLaurin, B., & Fallon, B. (2011). Understanding the overrepresentation of First Nations children in Canada's child welfare system. In Kufeldt, K., & McKenzie, B. (Eds.), *Child Welfare: Connecting Research, Policy, and Practice* (pp. 307-322). Waterloo, ON: Wilfrid Laurier Press.

Sinha, V., Trocmé, N., Fallon, B., MacLaurin, B., Fast, E., Prokop, S., et al. (2011). *Kiskisik Awasisak: Remember the Children. Understanding the Overrepresentation of First Nations Children in the Child Welfare System*. Ottawa. ON: Assembly of First Nations.

Sitter, K.C. (2015, October). Connecting advocacy with social media (Panel Presentation: D.V. Mullings, moderator). Social work education for the global twenty-first century graduate. Atlantic Universities Teaching Showcase. St. John's, Newfoundland and Labrador, Canada.

Smith, D.G. (1993). The Emergence of Eskimo Status: An Examination of the Eskimo Disk List System and the Social Consequences, 1925–1970. In Dyck, Noel, & Waldram, James B. (Eds.), *Anthropology, Public Policy and Native Peoples in Canada*. Montréal, QC: McGill-Queen's University Press.

Soniat, Barbara A., and Micklos, Monica Melady. (2010). *Empowering Social Workers for Practice with Vulnerable Older Adults*. Washington, DC: NASW Press.

Splane, R. (1980). Review: The role of public welfare in a century of social welfare development (originally published in 1965). In Meilicke, Carl A., & Storch, Janet A. (Eds.), *Perspectives on Canadian Health and Social Services Policy: History and Emerging Trends* (pp. 38-49). Ann Arbour, MI: Health Administration Press.

Stall, S., & Stoecker, R. (1998). Community organizing or organizing community?: Gender and the crafts of empowerment. *Gender and Society*, 12(6), 729–756.

Stanké, A. (1987) *Encyclopédie du Canada*, Montréal, Québec: Éditions internationales, 2153.

Statistics Canada. (2003). Ethnic diversity survey: Portrait of a multicultural society. Catalogue No. 89-593-XIE. Ottawa, ON: Government of Canada.

Statistics Canada. (2005). Aboriginal people living in metropolitan areas. *The Daily*. June 23.

Statistics Canada. (2006). *Aboriginal Peoples in Canada in 2006: Inuit, Métis and First Nations, 2006 Census*. 2006 Census: Analysis Series.

Statistics Canada. (2007). *Participation and Activity Limitation Survey 2006: Analytical Report*. Ottawa, ON: Government of Canada.

Statistics Canada. (2011). *National Household Survey (NHS)*. Ottawa, ON: Government of Canada.

Statistics Canada. (2011.) *Living Arrangements of Seniors: Census in Brief* (Catalogue no. 98-312-X2011003). Ottawa, ON: Statistics Canada.

Statistics Canada. (2012). *Aboriginal Peoples Survey.* Retrieved from http://www.statscan.gc.ca/aps.

Statistics Canada. (2012). *Canadian Survey on Disability, 2012* (89-654-X). Ottawa, ON: Statistics Canada.

Statistics Canada. (2013). *Section B—anxiety disorders.* Retrieved July 17, 2015 from http://www.statcan.gc.ca/pub/82-619-m/2012004/sections/sectionb-eng.htm#a6.

Statistics Canada. (2013a). *Generation Status: Canadian-born Children of Immigrants.* Catalogue No. 99-010-X2011003. Ottawa, ON: Government of Canada.

Statistics Canada. (2013b). *Immigration and Ethno-cultural Diversity in Canada, National Household Survey, 2011.* Catalogue No. 99-010-X2011001. Ottawa, ON: Ministry of Industry.

Statistics Canada. (2014). *Population Projections: Canada, the Provinces and Territories, 2013 to 2063.* Ottawa, ON: Government of Canada.

Statistics Canada. (2015). *Canadian Transition Home Survey*. Ottawa, ON: Centre for Justice Statistics.

Statistics Canada. (2015). *Elder Abuse: It's Time to Face the Reality* (Cat. No. HS4-61/2009). Ottawa, ON: Government of Canada.

Status of Women Canada. (2002). *Assessing Violence Against Women: A Statistical Profile.* Ottawa, ON: Federal, Provincial, Territorial Ministers Responsible for the Status of Women.

Stevens, M., Sharp, E., Morarty, J., Manthorpe, J., Hussein, S., Orme, J., Mcyntyre, J., Cavanagh, K., Green-Lister, P., & Crist, B.R. (2012). Helping others or a rewarding career? Investigating student motivations to train as Social Workers in England. *Journal of Social Work*, 12(1), 16-36.

Stewart, A. (2014). *Visitor: My Life in Canada.* Black Point, NS and Winnipeg, MB: Fernwood Publishing.

Stobert, S., & Cranswick, K. (2003). Looking after seniors: Who does what for whom? *Canadian Social Trends*. Spring. Cat. no. 11-008. Ottawa, ON: Statistics Canada.

Struthers, J. (1991). How much is enough? Creating a social minimum in Ontario, 1930–44. *The Canadian Historical Review*, 72(1): 39.

Swift, K. (2011). Canadian child welfare: Child protection and the status quo. In Gilbert, N., Parton, N., & Skivenes, M. (Eds.), *Child Protection Systems: International Trends and Orientations* (pp. 36-59). New York, NY: Oxford University Press.

Taft, J. (1948). *Family Casework and Counseling: A Functional Approach*. Philadelphia, PA: University of Pennsylvania Publishing.

Tamburro, A. (2013). Including decolonization in social work education and practice. *Journal of Indigenous Social Development*, 2(1), 1-16.

Timpson, J.B. (1990). Indian and Native special status in Ontario's child welfare legislation: An overview of the social, legal and political context. *Canadian Social Work Review*, 7(1): 49-68.

Toope, Stephen. (2015). Reconciliation begins by closing the graduation gap. *The Globe and Mail* (August 31).

Toseland, R., & Rivas, R. (2005). *Introduction to Group Work Practice*, (5th ed.). Boston, MA: Allyn & Bacon.

Trainor, J., Pomeroy, E., & Pape, B. (2004). *A Framework for Support.* (3rd ed.) Toronto: Canadian Mental Health Association, National Office.

Trocmé, N., Fallon, B., MacLaurin, B., Sinha, V., Black, T., Fast, E., Felstiner, C., Hélie, S., Turcotte, D., Weightman, P., Douglas, J., & Holroyd, J. (2008). *Canadian Incidence Study of Reported Child Abuse and Neglect 2008 (CIS-2008): Major Findings.* Ottawa, ON: Public Health Agency of Canada.

Trocmé, N., Knoke, D., & Blackstock, C. (2004). Pathways to the over-representation of Aboriginal children in Canada's child welfare system. *Social Service Review*, 78(4), 577-601.

Trocmé, N., Kyte, A., Sinha, V., & Fallon, B. (2014). Urgent protection versus chronic need: Clarifying the dual mandate of child welfare services across Canada. *Social Sciences*, 3(3), 483-498.

Trocmé, N., MacLaurin, B., Fallon, B., Shlonsky, A., Mulcahy, M., & Esposito, T. (2009). *National Child Welfare Outcomes Indicator Matrix* (NOM). Montréal, Québec: Centre for Research on Children and Families, McGill University.

Truth and Reconciliation Commission (TRC). (2015). *Truth and Reconiliation Commission: Calls to Action*. Ottawa, ON.

Tuckman, B.W., & Jensen, M.A. (1977). Stages of small-group development revisited. *Group and Organization Studies*, 2(4): 419–427.

Tuckman, B.W. (1965). Developing sequence in small groups. *Psychological Bulletin*, 63(6), 384–399.

Turcotte, M., & Schellenberg, G. (2007). *A Portrait of Seniors in Canada. 2006.* Cat. no. 89-519-XIE. Ottawa, ON: Statistics Canada.

Turner, K. (2009). Mindfulness: The present moment in clinical social work. *Clinical Social Work Journal*, 37(2), 95-103.

Turner, Linda M. (1999). Creativity: An overview and framework for the social work practitioner. *Canadian Social Work*, 1(1), 91–97.

Tweddle, A. (2005). Youth leaving care—How do they fare? Briefing paper prepared for the modernizing income security for working age adults (MISWAA) project (Ontario). Retrieved from: http://www.stchrishouse.org/modules/ImageAV/lib/getImage.php?koId=15139.

Tyyskä, V. (2009). *Youth and Society: The Long and Winding Road.* (2nd ed.) Toronto. ON: Canadian Scholars' Press Inc.

Union of BC Indian Chiefs (2002). *Calling Forth Our Future: Options for the Exercise of Indigenous Peoples' Authority in Child Welfare*. Vancouver. BC: Union of BC Indian Chiefs.

United Nations. (1948). *Universal Declaration of Human Rights.* www.un.org/Overview/rights.html.

United Nations Development Programme (2014). *Human Development Report 2014: Sustaining Human Progress: Reducing Vulnerability and Building Resilience.* New York, NY: United Nations Development Programme.

United Nations Development Programme (2015). *Human Development Report 2015: Work for Human Development.* New York: United Nations Development Programme.

United Nations High Commissioner for Refugees (UNHCR). (2015). Worldwide displacement hits all-time high as war and persecution increase. *Global Trends 2014*. New York; NY: UNHCR.

United Nations Secretariat for the Convention on the Rights of Persons with Disabilities. (2016). Retrieved from: www.un.org/esa/socdev/enable/disabout.htm.

The United States Association for Play Therapy (2013). *Why Play Therapy?* Retrieved from http://www.a4pt.org.

United States Department of Health and Human Services. (2015). *Mental health and substance use disorders.* Retrieved July 25, 2015 from www.mentalhealth.gov.

Vaillancourt, Roxan. (2008). *Gender Differences in Police-reported Violent Crime in Canada, 2008.* Canadian Centre for Justice Statistics Profile Series. Ottawa, ON: Statistics Canada.

Vaillancourt, Y. (1988). *L'évolution des politiques sociales au Québec : 1940–1960.* Montréal, Québec: Presses de l'Université de Montréal.

van de Sande, A., Beauvolsk, M.A., & Renault, G. (2011). *Le travail social : Théories et pratiques.* 2éd. Boucherville, Québec: Gaëtan Morin Éditeur.

Vayda, E., & Deber, R.B. (1995). The Canadian health care system: A developmental overview. In Blake, R.B., and Keshen, J. (Eds.), *Social Welfare Policy in Canada: Historical Readings.* (pp. 311-325) Toronto, ON: Copp Clark Ltd.

Vick. R.M. (2003). A brief history of art therapy. In C.A. Malchiodi (Ed.), *Handbook of Art Therapy.* New York, NY: The Guilford Press.

Walker, J. (1995). African Canadians. In M. Magocsi (Ed.), *Encyclopedia of Canada's People* (pp. 139-176). Toronto, ON: University of Toronto Press.

Walker, J. (1997). *Race, Rights and the Law in the Supreme Court of Canada.* Waterloo, ON: Wilfred Laurier University Press.

Wallis, J., Burns, J., & Capdevila, R. (2011). What is narrative therapy and what is it not? The usefulness of Q methodology to explore accounts of White and Epston's (1990) approach to narrative therapy. *Clinical Psychology and Psychotherapy,* 18(6), 486-497.

Walsh, C.A., Shier, M.L., Sitter, K.C., & Sieppert, J.D. (2010). Applied methods of teaching about oppression and diversity to graduate social work students: A case example of digital stories. *The Canadian Journal for the Scholarship of Teaching and Learning,* 1(2), 1-15.

Walzer, M. (1983). *Spheres of Justice: A Defence of Pluralism and Equality.* New York, NY: Basic Books.

Wang, C.C. (1999). Photovoice: A participatory action research strategy applied to women's health. *Journal of Women's Health,* 8(2), 185-192.

Wang, C.C., & Burris, M. (1997). Photovoice: Concept, methodology, and use for participatory needs assessment. *Health Education and Behavior,* 24, 369-387.

Wang, C.C., Yi, W.K., Tao, Z. W., & Carovano, K. (1998). Photovoice as a participatory health promotion strategy. *Health Promotion International,* 13(1), 75-86.

Warner, T. (2002). *Never Going Back: A History of Queer Activism in Canada.* Toronto, ON: University of Toronto Press.

Wayland, S. (2006). *Unsettled: Legal and Policy Barriers For Newcomers in Canada.* Ottawa, ON: Community Foundations of Canada and Law Commission of Canada.

Weeks, Carly. (2015). Canada needs to find solution to serious regional health inequalities. *The Globe and Mail* (October 18).

Weeks, Carly. (2015). Some minorities more likely to see heart health deteriorate. *The Globe and Mail* (August 10).

Welfel, E.R., Danzinger, P.R., & Santoro, S. (2000). Mandated reporting of abuse/maltreatment of older adults: A primer for counselors. *Journal of Counseling and Development,* 78(3), 284–292.

Whitaker, T., Weismiller, T., & Clark, E. (2006). *Assuring the sufficiency of a frontline workforce: A national study of licensed social workers.* Special report: Social work services for children and families. Washington, DC: National Association of Social Workers.

White, M. & Epston, D. (1990). *Narrative Means to Therapeutic Ends.* New York, NY: W.W. Norton & Co.

Whitton, C. (1943). *The Dawn of Ampler Life.* Toronto, ON: Macmillan.

Wilson, J.P., & Keane, T.M. (Eds.) (2004). *Assessing Psychological Trauma and PTSD.* (2nd ed.). New York, NY: The Guildford Press.

Wilson, K., Sinclair, I., & Gibbs, I. (2000). The trouble with foster care: The impact of stressful "events" on foster carers. *British Journal of Social Work,* 30, 193-209.

Women's Centre of Calgary. (2016). Copyright © 2016. Reprinted with permission. Website: www.womenscentrecalgary.org.

Woodroofe, K. (1962). *From Charity to Social Work in England and the United States.* Toronto, ON: University of Toronto Press.

World Commission on Environment and Development. (1987). *Our Common Future.* New York, NY: Oxford University Press.

World Economic Forum. (2014). *The Global Gender Gap Report, 2014.* Geneva, Switzerland: World Economic Forum.

World Health Organization. (2015). *World Report on Ageing and Health.* Geneva, Switzerland: The World Health Organization.

Yan, M.C., & Chan, S. (2010). Are social workers ready to work with newcomers? *Canadian Social Work,* 12(1), 16-23.

Yang, J., Allen, K., & Dempsey, A. (2015). The growing impact of dementia—are we ready? *The Toronto Star* (November 21).

Yelaja, S. (1985). *An Introduction to Social Work Practice.* Scarborough, ON: Prentice-Hall Canada Inc.

YMCA Canada. (2009).*Life beyond Shelter: Toward Coordinated Public Policies for Women's Safety and Violence Prevention.* ywcacanada.ca.

Zoebia, Al, Fazil, Qulsom, Bywaters, Paul, Wallace, Louise, and Singh, Gurnam. (March 2006). Disability, ethnicity and childhood: A critical review of research. *Disability and Society.* 1(2), 949-967.

Zola, I.K. (1986). *The Independent Living Movement.* San Francisco, CA: Jossey-Bass Publishers.

Index

Social Work in Canada

Social workers seek to make a positive difference in people's lives. But what is it like to be a social worker? What exactly do social workers do to help individuals, families, and communities discover their own unique strengths and overcome difficult barriers?

This updated and expanded edition introduces the major concepts and contemporary issues in Canadian social work. It encourages students to consider social work as a career path and to join other professionals in helping people make positive changes in their lives and communities.

Features of this new edition

- Thoroughly updated by a nationwide team of Canadian authors and contributors
- Compelling stories from the field, providing a sense of what it's like to be a social worker today
- A new chapter on social work practice in the field of mental health
- Up-to-date coverage of developments in Indigenous social work theory and practice
- A survey of the unique history of social work practice in Québec
- Career profiles of social work activists and practitioners from coast to coast

About the authors

Steven Hick, an award-winning professor of social work at Carleton University (now retired), is also the author of a companion text, *Social Welfare in Canada: Understanding Income Security.* He has practised at home and abroad as a human rights worker, social services worker, and social policy analyst. He is the co-founder of War Child Canada.

Jackie Stokes has an M.S.W. from the University of Northern British Columbia and an Ed.D. from Simon Fraser University and is an assistant professor of social work at Thompson Rivers University. She has practised social work in northern British Columbia for more than twenty years, primarily in the areas of substance use and child protection.

ISBN 978-1-55077-256-2

www.thompsonbooks.com